MODERN JAPAN

MODERN JAPAN

A Historical Survey

FOURTH EDITION

MIKISO HANE
late of Knox College

LOUIS G. PEREZ
Illinois State University

Westview Press
A Member of the Perseus Books Group

Library of Congress Cataloging-in-Publication Data
Hane, Mikiso.
    Modern Japan : a historical survey / Mikiso Hane, Louis G. Perez. — 4th ed.
        p.   cm.
    Includes bibliographical references and index.
    ISBN 978-0-8133-4409-6 (alk. paper)
    1. Japan—History—19th century.   2. Japan—History—20th century.
I. Perez, Louis G. II. Title.
    DS881.H36 2009
    952.03—dc22
                                                                2008045539

10 9 8 7 6 5 4 3 2 1

Contents

Preface

The Gold Standard for Chutzpah used to be the no-doubt apocryphal story of Lizzie Borden, who at her trial for having chopped up her parents with an axe, begged the mercy of the court on account of being an orphan.

I now suggest that my revision of this book might similarly qualify as an act of chutzpah. When I first came to the Midwest in the mid-1980s, Mikiso Hane became a friend and something of a mentor. He was among the half-dozen scholars in attendance at my first professional presentation at the Midwest Conference on Asian Affairs in 1986. He came up afterward and introduced himself, then offered some valuable suggestions about my paper. He later read a version of that paper and wrote a letter on my behalf to the editor when I submitted it to a refereed scholarly journal.

Two years later his kindness to me continued. When approached to do some very lucrative consultation with a Midwestern company, he demurred because he was busy writing this very book. Instead he gave the company my name, and I very gratefully accepted the job. The consultant's fee I received went a long way in the Perez household that year.

But it was not out of a sense of obligation that I have assigned this book as required reading for my Modern Japanese History classes. I have done so because it was simply the best book available for my students. It was written for students who knew absolutely nothing about Japan. It probably gave them more information than they would ever use, but it was always as readable as it was erudite.

When approached by Karl Yambert, editor at Westview Press, about the possibility of my revising the book, I immediately declined the honor. How could I ever consider messing with Miki's timeless classic? Karl finally convinced me to do it after assuring me that the book would probably go out of print unless it was revised to include the latest scholarship.

So how does one go about editing the work of a deceased friend? Karl elicited the views of a handful of historians of Japan. Their anonymous comments were invaluable, and I thank them for their perspicacious suggestions. I also decided to go to the readers for advice. I subsequently asked over fifty of my students at Illinois State University to critique the book in the fall 2007 semester. What did they like? Dislike? What would they keep or jettison? Many said that the text contained too many names and far too many statistics. Like Miki, I believe that history is nothing without the people; so I kept the names. I decided that the statistics should remain also, but that they could be relegated to meaty endnotes. As chapter endnotes, the interested student could still find the information, but the average reader could read the narrative without being distracted with what they consider to be minutiae (they really just want to know "will it be on the exam?").

I removed little else from the text; a few inaccuracies (no doubt the fault of editors and typesetters) and a few infelicitous phrases. I believe that I could best contribute to the new revision by incorporating some recent scholarship into the narrative.

I updated the bibliography, of course. I also chose to reorganize it into some new categories such as "Cinema," "Fine Arts," and "Religion" and to split the long section on literature into Premodern and Modern. The new bibliography is nearly twice as long as Miki's original work. Not because I was less selective than he, but because I have long argued that the best scholarship on Japan has been done in the past two decades. I know this is nearly heresy for a historian to say. I still cherish the work of the Usual Suspects: Edwin Reischauer, Sir George Sansom, John Whitney Hall, et al. We troglodytes complain about the postmodern neologisms, but after the silly chaff of the Oh-So-Trendy has blown away, there is much to recommend. Can anyone rationally argue that we would not be bereft without some of the recent feminist and subaltern scholarship? We are reminded that Miki contributed much to those early genres in his seminal books *Reflections on the Way to the Gallows: Rebel Women in Prewar Japan,* and *Peasants, Rebels, and Outcastes: The Underside of Modern Japan.*

I have also updated the Appendices to include the latest prime ministers and the like. I have chosen to attenuate the chronology timeline somewhat. I have excised the entries of incidents that happened before about 1800—purely an artificial starting point for "Modern" Japan.

I have tried to do as little damage to Miki's text as possible. I dedicate this revision to Miki himself. The book is still his. The revision was accomplished with much assistance from editors at Westview Press. Karl Yambert, acquisitions editor, gave me excellent advice; Meredith Smith was the project editor and is to be thanked for her gentle prodding to keep me on track and on time; finally, Michelle S. Asakawa, copy editor, provided her expertise, including a number of excellent suggestions. I am tempted to blame the lot of them—Karl, Meredith, and Michelle—for any mistakes that I have made; after all, they should have caught my errors. But, alas, I remain alone responsible for any problems in the text.

Perhaps this would be a good place to tell the reader something about Miki. I quote extensively from the press release posted on the internet by his friend Peter Bailey at Knox College (http://www.knox.edu/x6196.xml) at the time of Miki's memorial on Valentine's Day, February 14, 2004:

"No scholar has done more than Mikiso Hane to enable Westerners to understand what Japan's modern history has really meant to the Japanese people," wrote historian John Dower of the Massachusetts Institute of Technology about Hane's books in 1992. Hane was born in 1922 in Hollister, California, to Japanese immigrant parents and lived there until the age of ten, when his parents sent him to Japan, where he lived with an uncle and attended school in Hiroshima.

Hane returned to the United States in 1940, and following the outbreak of war with Japan in 1941, he was interned by the United States government in a camp in Arizona from May 1942 until October 1943.

After 18 months in the internment camp, Hane applied for a position teaching Japanese at a program operated by the US Army at Yale University. Following the war he earned college degrees at Yale—a bachelor's degree in 1952, a master's degree in 1953, and a doctoral degree in 1957—paying his own way through college by teaching Japanese and setting type for an Asian studies journal.

Prior to coming to Knox in 1961, Hane taught at the University of Toledo and did post-doctoral research in Japan and Germany as a Fulbright Research Fellow.

Hane taught a wide range of history courses at Knox—including Japanese, Chinese, Indian and Russian history, as well as the traditional Western civilization sequence—from 1961 until his retirement in 1992. He also taught independent study courses in Japanese language at Knox and directed off-campus studies programs in Japan and Hong Kong. Hane continued researching and teaching at Knox until last month [January 2004].

Hane wrote numerous scholarly articles and 14 books, including four widely used college textbooks on Japanese history and two highly regarded studies—*Reflections on the Way to the Gallows: Rebel Women in Prewar Japan*, and *Peasants, Rebels and Outcastes: The Underside of Modern Japan*.

Hane's books on women and peasants—segments of Japanese society often overlooked in traditional histories—are credited with revolutionizing Japanese historical scholarship through extensive use of personal narratives. "The oral history tradition started in the United States with Studs Terkel's interviewing style," Hane told an interviewer in 1983. "I wanted to know what life meant for peasants, as individuals, in pre-war Japan; how women viewed life. I am interested in the personal experiences of individuals."

According to Dower, Hane went beyond "the elites and famous intellectuals . . . to those ground beneath the wheels of so-called progress, and he has revealed this to us in the most simple and eloquent way possible—by letting the Japanese speak in their own numerous and varied voices."

Dower said Hane's research has been "more than just a significant scholarly accomplishment. It is a great humanistic contribution as well."

Hane published a number of English translations of important Japanese works, including *Studies in the Intellectual History of Tokugawa Japan,* by the Japanese historian Masao Maruyama. He wrote four articles for the *Japan Encyclopedia,* including the article on Emperor Hirohito, and spoke and presented papers at scholarly conferences worldwide.

In 1991 Hane was nominated by President George H. Bush and confirmed by the United States Senate for membership on the National Council on the Humanities—the most prestigious appointment that a humanist can receive.

Hane also served on the committee on teaching of the American Historical Association, and as a grant consultant for the National Endowment for the Humanities. He was elected to the Northeast Asia Council and the board of directors of the Association for Asian Studies.

Following Hane's retirement in 1992, Knox College created the Mikiso Hane East Asian Studies Prize in his honor. And earlier this year [in 2004], the Midwest Conference of Asian Studies created the Mikiso Hane Undergraduate Research Prize in Asian Studies.

"Miki Hane's thoughtful teaching of generations of Knox students, his acclaimed scholarship and his life as a good humored and gentle member of the Knox Community defy hasty summarization," said Knox College President Roger Taylor. "Virtually all members of the campus community and his hundreds of students cherish fond memories of Miki's life. Those memories can serve as some solace in this time of loss to the Hane family and to the Knox Community."

Louis G. Perez
Normal (really!), Illinois
October 2008

1

Japan Before the Seventeenth Century

EARLY HISTORY OF THE JAPANESE PEOPLE

There is no definitive evidence concerning when and from whence the original inhabitants arrived in Japan, but it is assumed that they came from different areas of the Asian continent and the South Pacific region. The predominant strain is Mongoloid, including a considerable mixture of people of Malayan origin. The Japanese language appears to be related to both the Polynesian and the Altaic languages. Evidence suggests that as early as 200,000 years ago, paleolithic humans (who used chipped stones for tools) inhabited the islands. Also among the early inhabitants of Japan were the ancestors of the Ainu, a people of proto-Caucasian origin who live in Hokkaido today. Currently only about 50,000 Ainu remain. Their early history and their relationship with the neolithic people who inhabited the islands are not known.

Jōmon and Yayoi Periods (ca. 8000 BC to AD 250)

The early stage of the neolithic age in Japan is known as the Jōmon period. It is believed that Jōmon culture started as far back as 7000 or 8000 BC and survived until about 250 BC. The term Jōmon (meaning cord-marking) describes the type of decoration found on potteries of this age. The people of the period were hunters and food gatherers, and they lived in pit-dwellings.

The next stage in neolithic Japan was the Yayoi period, which extended roughly from 250 BC to AD 250. This culture is believed to have been the product of a new wave of immigrants of Mongoloid stock who came to the islands in the third century BC. Yayoi pots (named after the place in which they were first found in 1884) were wheel-made and less elaborately decorated than

1

Jōmon pots. They were fired at a higher temperature and are technically superior to Jōmon pieces. Around the second century BC bronze and iron tools filtered into Japan from the continent. The rice culture, which originated in South China or Southeast Asia, filtered in around 100 BC. This latter development revolutionized the entire Japanese way of life, for it established the basis for the economy until the industrial age.

The first written accounts about Japan are found in two historical records of ancient China: *The History of the Kingdom of Wei* (a kingdom in north China, AD 220–265), written in AD 297, and *History of the Later Han Dynasty,* compiled around AD 445. According to these histories, Japan underwent a period of civil strife in the second century AD, but the land was eventually unified under a queen named Pimiku (Himiko in Japanese). Pimiku, as *The History of the Kingdom of Wei* relates, was a shaman who "occupied herself with magic and sorcery, bewitching the people." Whether Pimiku was related to the clan that established hegemony over Japan is impossible to verify, but in the years after the Second World War a great deal of speculation has taken place about the origin of the early Japanese rulers, in particular their links to Korea.

Yamato Period (ca. 300–710)

The period in which regional forces began to emerge in the Yamato area to roughly the time when a fixed capital was established in Nara is known as the Yamato period (ca. 300 to 710). It is also referred to as the age of Tomb Culture because huge keyhole-shaped tombs were constructed to bury the chieftains of the time. Numerous artifacts such as ornaments, tools, and weapons, as well as clay figurines known as *haniwa,* were buried with the dead.

From the fifth century on, Japan was exposed steadily to Chinese and Korean culture as immigrants from these countries arrived in fairly large numbers. Refugees from advancing Han Chinese armies probably displaced Koreans down that rocky peninsula. Some of those displaced Koreans probably migrated across the narrow Tsushima Straits to Japan. The social, material, political, intellectual, and cultural life of the Japanese was profoundly influenced by these immigrants. Prince Shōtoku Taishi (574–622) is traditionally credited with having played a major role in adopting Chinese civilization, strengthening the imperial authority, and propagating Buddhism. He is also credited with promulgating the "Constitution of Seventeen Articles," a series of moral injunctions.[1] In 645 Nakatomi-no-Kamatari (614–669), the founder of the Fujiwara family, removed his rivals from the court and gained political supremacy. His descendants dominated the court down through the ages. Nakatomi and his followers are credited with having instituted the Taika Reforms, which involved the adoption of Chinese (Tang and Northern Wei) political institutions and policies as well as their land and tax policies.

Nara and Heian Periods (710–1185)

One of the practices adopted from China was the construction of a fixed capital city. In 710, Nara was made the seat of the imperial court, and it remained so until 784, when the capital was moved briefly to a community near Kyoto. In 794, the capital was moved again—this time to Kyoto, then known as Heiankyō. From then until 1868 the emperors resided in this city. The period from 794 to 1185 is known as the Heian period, or the era of the court aristocracy, because the court nobles led by the Fujiwara family dominated the political and cultural life of the society. Eventually cadet houses of the Fujiwara would dominate the imperial government during the feudal eras to follow. During the Nara and Heian periods Japan continued to adopt and assimilate Chinese culture and institutions as well as Buddhism. The Heian court aristocrats cultivated a highly refined taste in art and literature, and placed great emphasis on form, appearance, and decorum. Extravagant luxury, ostentatious display, and decadent sensuality prevailed at the court in its heyday.

Among the measures adopted from China during implementation of the aforementioned Taika Reforms was nationalization and equalization of land-holdings. But this policy was not fully implemented, and land soon came to be concentrated in the hands of the court aristocrats and Buddhist monasteries. Eventually privately controlled estates, or *shōen,* came into existence. The estates were not taxed; they were also free from the jurisdiction of government officials. Estate managers, district officials, and local estate owners began to emerge in the form of local magnates with private coteries of warriors. Eventually major military chieftains, with large circles of warriors, managed to control numerous estates and challenge the authority of the central government.

In the 1160s, one of the samurai chieftains, Taira-no-Kiyomori (1118–1181), gained control of the imperial court and had himself appointed chancellor. The Taira clan (also known as the Heike) soon found its supremacy challenged by the leader of a rival military clan known as the Genji (or Minamoto) family, led by Minamoto Yoritomo (1147–1199).

Kamakura Period (1185–1333)

After Minamoto defeated the Taira forces, he established his headquarters in Kamakura in 1185. Theoretically, he performed the role of supreme military commander (shōgun) in the service of the emperor, a post to which he was appointed in 1192. But his Bakufu (tent headquarters) became the *actual* locus of power. He controlled a large part of the land as his own *shōen* and acquired the right to appoint constables and land stewards (whose chief function was to collect taxes) throughout the land. Minamoto's assumption of the position of shōgun, then, marked the beginning of rule by the warrior, or samurai, class.

Thenceforth, except for brief periods, power was retained by the shōgun until 1867, while the emperor remained in Kyoto as the nominal ruler and high priest of the Shinto religion.

After Minamoto died in 1199, actual power of the Bakufu was taken over by his wife's family, the Hōjō clan. Until 1333, the head of the Hōjō family wielded power as regent to the shōgun. Following an abortive attempt by the imperial court to regain power in 1221, the Hōjō family consolidated its control over the land both by confiscating the shōen of those who had supported the imperial cause and by tightening its surveillance over the imperial court.

With the emergence of the warrior class in the last years of the Heian period and during the years of warrior rule in the Kamakura period, political, social, and economic institutions and practices similar to those associated with European feudalism began to evolve. In 1232, the Hōjō government issued the Jōei Code, which defined property rights, land tenure, inheritance, and other social economic rights and obligations, thus laying the basis for later feudal laws and practices.

In the Kamakura period, popular Buddhism emerged and the code of the warriors began to take form (see Chapter 2). It was also during this period that the Mongols attempted to invade Japan in 1274 and again in 1282. Both attempts failed because devastating typhoons (known as *kamikaze,* or divine winds) destroyed the Mongol fleet.

Between 1333 and 1336, the imperial court led by Emperor Godaigo managed to regain power briefly with the assistance of certain disaffected military chiefs. But in 1336, one of these chiefs, Ashikaga Takauji (a relative of the Hōjō; 1305–1358), decided to take power himself; it was then that he drove the emperor out of Kyoto and established his own Bakufu. Godaigo fled south to the mountains of Kii Peninsula, while Ashikaga placed another member of the imperial family on the throne. As a result, until 1392 there were two imperial courts—one in the north and one in the south. In 1392, the two courts merged with the understanding that the two branches would alternate in occupying the throne. But this agreement was not kept, and the Northern Court members hold the throne to this day.

The Muromachi Period and the Era of Warring States (1336–1590)

The Ashikaga shogunate, also referred to as the Muromachi Bakufu (after the district in Kyoto where the shōgun resided), remained in existence until 1573. In that year the last Ashikaga shōgun was driven out by Oda Nobunaga (1534–1582), a military chief who aspired to become shōgun himself. The Ashikaga family had failed to gain a firm grip on the land and was plagued by contentious lords. Eventually regional lords, known as *daimyō* (great lords), emerged. The country fell into a state of chaos as regional chiefs contended for power. This dog-eat-dog period, known as the era of the Warring States (Sengoku), lasted from the later years of the fifteenth century until the nation was unified under Toyotomi Hideyoshi in 1590. It was during this era that feudalism became firmly entrenched throughout the land. These feudal lords built castles to defend themselves from first the Ashikaga and eventually each other. Towns formed around these castles. The merchants and artisans who gathered there to provide for the samurai residents gave rise to urban professional classes that changed Japanese society.

During the same era, the economy expanded as a result of improvements in agriculture and increased trade with China. Money came to be used more widely, and commercial cities and market towns sprung up throughout the land. Some cities—notably, Sakai (near Osaka)—became autonomous political entities with their own military forces. In the middle of the sixteenth century, Portuguese traders arrived. They were soon followed by merchants from other European countries as well as by Christian missionaries led by the Jesuit Saint Francis Xavier (1506–1552).

Oda Nobunaga, a daimyō in central Japan, managed to extend his power by making effective use of the firearms introduced by the West. He appeared to be on the way to establishing his hegemony over the land. In 1568 he succeeded in gaining control of Kyoto and soon deposed the last Ashikaga shōgun. However, he was attacked by one of his generals, preferring to commit suicide rather than be captured. Then Toyotomi Hideyoshi (1536–1598), who rose from the peasantry, subdued the regional lords and completed the task of national unification. He subsequently decided to conquer Korea and China and launched an invasion of Korea in 1592. His grandiose plan was frustrated, however, when the Ming forces moved into Korea to stop his warriors.

Toyotomi came up from the peasantry himself. But in order to prevent the political order he had established from being disrupted by free-wheeling peasant-warriors, he launched a campaign to confiscate all weapons from the peasants. He also forbade them from moving off the land and instituted a nationwide cadastral survey for tax purposes, thereby establishing the social and economic policies that his successor, Tokugawa Ieyasu (1542–1616), eventually adopted to ensure social stability in his regime.

Tokugawa was one of Toyotomi's major rivals. Because of Tokugawa's formidable power base in the Kanto region, Toyotomi did not try to eliminate him by force but, instead, allowed him to retain his holdings in return for recognition of Toyotomi as the suzerain lord. Tokugawa, through patience, cunning, and good fortune, gained power after Toyotomi's death. Thereafter, he established a sociopolitical system that enabled his descendants to remain in power for two and a half centuries, thus ushering in the Tokugawa period (to be discussed in detail in Chapter 2).

TRADITIONAL CULTURE AND
INSTITUTIONS OF THE PRE-TOKUGAWA YEARS

The social systems, the culture and literature, the intellectual currents, and the political institutions that evolved in the pre-Tokugawa years not only persisted but also profoundly influenced the lives of the Japanese people throughout the ages.

Shinto

The indigenous religion of Japan is known as Shinto (the way of the gods). Starting as an animistic religion, which incorporated the shamanism that came in from Southeast Asia as well as from the northern Tungus, Shinto eventually became a part of the Japanese culture. The people go to Shinto shrines to pray, and during harvest festivals they join with other villagers to celebrate and give thanks to the gods for their bountiful harvest. The Japanese, like the Chinese, see no conflict in paying homage to different deities in numerous shrines and temples.

Before the imperial clan established its hegemony over the land, a number of clans (*uji*) contended for supremacy. Each clan worshipped its own patron god. The patron god of the imperial family was the Sun Goddess (Amaterasu Ōmikami), and the emperor or empress served as the high priest or priestess of the cult of the Sun Goddess. To this day the emperor undergoes the ritual of planting rice seedlings every spring and harvesting a few ears of rice in the fall. It was not until the Meiji period that this cult was elevated to the level of State Shinto, when the government designated most Shinto shrines as state institutions.

In short, the inhabitants of ancient Japan believed that gods and spirits were present in all aspects of the natural world. Some were cosmic forces; others resided in the woods, streams, and rocks and in animals such as foxes and snakes. The ancestral spirits were also respected and revered. Great military and political leaders were enshrined as *kami* (gods or superior beings). Even modern leaders like Emperor Meiji (1852–1912) and General Nogi Maresuke (1849–1912), who captured Port Arthur during the Russo-Japanese War of 1904–1905, were honored in this way. Soldiers who died in the service of their country have been similarly enshrined (i.e., as kami) in Yasukuni Shrine in Tokyo.

Shinto, in contrast to other major religions, is not founded on complex metaphysical and theological theories. Shinto has no body of divinely inspired written canon, no established ethical code, and until the late nineteenth century, not even a hierarchical priestly caste. A Western visitor once asked a Shinto priest about Shinto ideology, upon which the priest replied with a smile, "We do not have ideologies, we do not have theology. We dance."[2] Although his answer may be an oversimplification, Shinto is indeed based upon a sense of affinity with nature and the universe. As one scholar has explained it, "Where the Christian theologian explains Nature in the light of the numinous, the Japanese reach the numinous through their experience of nature."[3]

Shinto rituals are rather austere: the priest simply waves a sacred wand (made of *sakaki* branches) over the worshippers' heads to expel the evil spirits and thus to purify them spiritually. Purity and cleanliness are cardinal elements in Shinto thought; to this day, abhorrence of pollution by unclean things remains an important concern. This idea is reflected in the moral thought recorded through the ages. "To do good is to be pure; to commit evil is to be impure," asserts a thirteenth-century Shinto tract. A good person, then, is a person with a "clean" mind and heart.

This emphasis on purity, of course, posits the presence of the unclean. And, indeed, it is the function of the many shamans of the village shrines to exorcise the darker forces that possess the spirit. Charms and amulets are also utilized to ensure good fortune and stave off evil spirits. To prompt the gods to cure a family member's illness, a person might be advised to run around the compound of a shrine one hundred times each night; or, in the ground-breaking ceremony preceding construction of a new house, a Shinto priest will bless the site. (Such manifestations of "superstition" are not unique to Shinto, of course.)

Even after the members of the imperial clan gained political hegemony, they did not seek to compel others to worship their deity, the Sun Goddess; nor did they ban the worship of other gods. In fact, when Buddhism was introduced into the country, the struggle that occurred between the supporters of the new religion and their opponents had more to do with political control than with any effort to impose religious orthodoxy. The two religions coexisted down through the ages. Some effort was even made by the Shintoists to create a more philosophical religion by borrowing certain concepts from Buddhism. In this way, doctrinal Shinto came into existence. But common people continued to practice their traditional "folk" Shinto.

The Emperor System

The imperial family was closely linked to Shinto. The scholars of National Learning, who emerged in the Tokugawa period, made Shinto and the emperor system the core of their thinking. The emperors, after all, were the direct descendants of the Sun Goddess, who sent her grandson to Japan from heaven to rule over the land. Because of his "divine" descent, the emperor had a dual role to perform—a role both religious and political. In fact, these role functions were regarded as one and the same: political functions were called *matsuri*, a word that means worship of or service to the gods. Shinto festivals are also called matsuri. Moreover, the state of being possessed by the gods when receiving their words is called *noru*. The noun of the word, *nori*, means law. Shinto prayers are called *norito*. Thus the laws themselves were divine decrees.

According to the mythological account, the founding of the imperial dynasty occurred in 660 BC, when the first emperor, Jimmu, the great grandson of Ninigi who descended from heaven, established his rule. In addition, the Shinto nationalists insisted (until the end of the Second World War) that the imperial dynasty persisted, unbroken, from that date to the present. These accounts of the founding of Japan and the history of the imperial rulers were taught in the schools before the Second World War as factual truths.

But the imperial clan did not rely on ancient myths alone to buttress its authority. Upon the advent of Chinese culture in the fifth century, and from that time on, Confucian concepts about loyalty to the lord were utilized to indoctrinate the people. For example, the "Constitution of Seventeen Articles," ascribed to Prince Shōtoku, states, "When you receive the imperial commands, fail not scrupulously to obey them. The lord is Heaven, the vassal is Earth. Heaven overspreads, and Earth upbears." Then, too, "In a country there are not two lords: the people have not two masters. The sovereign is the master of the people of the whole country."[4] It was in the early seventh century that the term *tennō* (heavenly prince) was adopted from China and used to refer to the emperor.

Even though the court authorities formulated an ideology that was designed to strengthen the imperial institution, the practice of personal rule by the emperor did not come about. Only in rare instances did the emperor seek to exercise authority directly. During the Heian period the heads of the Fujiwara family wielded power as regents while the emperor merely sat on the throne. When Taira-no-Kiyomori took power, he married his daughter to the emperor and exercised power himself. Once the shogunate had emerged, the emperor in Kyoto remained merely a ceremonial head. That situation, except for a short interregnum in 1333–1336, prevailed until the end of the shogunate in 1867. However, although the shōgun became the real wielders of power, no shōgun ever tried to eradicate the emperor system. Even Ashikaga Takauji, who turned against Emperor Godaigo, did not attempt to eliminate the institution but, instead, established a rival court in Kyoto. The Tokugawa rulers also kept alive the fiction that they were ruling on behalf of the emperor.

Buddhism

Buddhism originated in northern India in the sixth century BC. The founder, referred to variously as Gautama, Shakyamuni, or Siddhartha Buddha, taught that the way to overcome suffering was to rid oneself of the sense of the "self." The self that we think of as being real, permanent, and absolute is merely an illusion. Rather, all things are in a constant state of flux; all things are ephemeral. Our suffering comes from the cravings of the self, to gratify the ego. To extinguish the ego one must follow the eightfold path as taught by the Buddha—that is, right views, right intentions, right speech, right conduct, right livelihood, right effort, right mindfulness, and right concentration. In this way we will become free of our illusion and thus able to achieve the state of bliss known as *Nirvana*.

Originally, the Buddha taught that enlightenment could be acquired only through self-effort. He did not speak of the existence of any gods or other superhuman beings. Later, however, there arose the Mahayana school—a school of Buddhism that posited the existence of many Buddhist deities. Gautama Buddha himself came to be looked upon as a divine being. Also assumed to exist were people who had achieved enlightenment but were postponing their entrance into the state of Nirvana in order to help others attain enlightenment. These compassionate beings are known as Bodhisattvas. The school is known as Mahayana Buddhism (the Greater Vehicle) because it opens the way to salvation for everybody. The tenets of this school spread into and flourished in Tibet, China, Korea, Vietnam, and Japan.

When Buddhism was introduced from Korea in the sixth century, the ruling class of Japan was impressed by the beautiful artifacts, rituals, and scriptures associated with it; hence the religion received strong support from the rulers. Initially it was the magical aspects of the religion that were emphasized by the several sects that entered from China. The religion not only influenced the moral outlook of the people; it also had a significant effect on the art and culture of the society.

Two sects became prominent during the Heian period. One was the Tendai sect, whose founder, Saichō (767–822), emphasized the significance of the Lotus Sutra, taught that salvation was possible for all living creatures, and upheld Mahayana Buddhism over the Hinayana school, which preached salvation through self-knowledge and self-effort. The other sect was the Shingon sect, whose founder, Kūkai (774–835), taught that all forms of the Buddha emanated from the Dainichi Nyorai (the Great Illuminator). Kūkai also stressed the importance of mystic formulas by which one could achieve salvation and also gain mundane benefits.

During the Kamakura period several new sects emerged and gained acceptance among the masses. Among the Buddhist deities that gained a wide following was Amida (Amitabha)—Buddha of infinite light—who, it was said, resided in the Western Paradise where all the faithful can enter. Among the preachers of Amidism was Hōnen (1133–1212), who started a sect known as the Pure Land sect. The Pure Land is where Bodhisattvas who are "pure in body, voice, and mind" reside. Hōnen taught that a person can enter the Pure Land by having complete faith in the Amida Buddha and by sincerely invoking his name.

For Hōnen's disciple, Shinran (1173–1262), salvation was even more easily attained than was taught by his teacher: if a person has complete faith in the Amida Buddha, one sincere invocation of his name would be sufficient to permit the entry of that person into the Pure Land. Rituals, knowledge of the scriptures, and ascetic behavior, Shinran insisted, were not essential for salvation; indeed, people could eat meat and imbibe alcoholic drinks, and monks and priests could marry—and still be saved.

Shinran taught that salvation was easily attainable because he wanted to help the suffering masses. Appalled by the hardships, misery, and poverty of the peasants he encountered during his exile in the provinces, he concluded that it was senseless to preach self-denial to people who were leading a beggarly existence. Because the good and bad alike are being put through the crucible of hardship, they all deserve salvation. The only thing they need is faith in the saving power of the "external" being, the Amida Buddha. Wicked persons know that they cannot gain salvation on their own merit so they are more likely to rely totally on the mercy of the Amida Buddha. Thus Shinran said, "If even a good man can be reborn in the Pure Land, how much more so a wicked man."[5] Because his followers claimed that his was the "true" path to the Pure Land, his sect came to be known as the True Pure Land sect. Now that salvation was made possible for the humblest and the most ignorant of the masses, the two Pure Land sects gained a strong following, particularly among the peasants.

The other major sect was started by a monk named Nichiren (1222–1282). Nichiren taught that salvation could be achieved through the repeated invocation of the Lotus Sutra, a scripture that emphasizes the importance of the three forms of the Buddha—that is, the Body of Universal Law, the Body of Bliss (Amida Buddha), and the Transformation Body (historical Buddha, Shakyamuni). The other sects were in error, Nichiren claimed, because they emphasized only one of these forms. He too stressed faith—faith in the Lotus Sutra—as the only path to salvation.

Nichiren's movement is unique among Buddhist sects specifically because of the extremely dogmatic, intolerant, and fervently nationalistic character of its originator. Nichiren not only proclaimed, "I will be the Pillar of Japan. I will be the Great Vessel of Japan";[6] he also believed that Japan was a unique and sacred land, the center of the true faith, his own sect. He too gained a wide following, and the Nichiren Sect remains a major movement today. Unlike other Buddhist sects, however, the Nichiren sect is aggressively proselytistic.

Zen Buddhism was another sect that won strong adherence, particularly among the samurai during the Kamakura period and after. This sect is distinguished by the fact that it emphasizes self-reliance and achievement of enlighten-ment *(satori)* through self-effort. Satori entails the gaining of insight into one's true or original nature and into the nature of reality, that "great void" underlying the surface manifestations. This insight is to be achieved through an intuitive grasp of reality, not by relying on the intellect or reasoned knowledge, nor by studying or performing rituals. Just as the hand that grasps cannot grasp itself, the reason that seeks to comprehend cannot comprehend itself. For "reality" is the Mind. As a Chinese Chan (Zen) master once said, "Buddha and sentient be-ings both grow out of One Mind. . . . This Mind is pure and like space has no specific form. As soon as you raise a thought and begin to form an idea of it, you ruin reality itself, because you then attach yourself to the form. Since the begin-ningless past, there is no Buddha who has ever had an attachment to form."[7]

A person who achieves satori cannot transmit it to others by words. Such is the message of Bodhidharma, who is said to have brought Chan Buddhism to China in the sixth century: "A special transmission outside the scriptures; No dependence upon words or letters; Direct pointing at the soul of man: Seeing into one's nature and the attainment of Buddhahood."[8] To achieve satori, then, one must meditate, contemplate, or work out enigmatic statements *(kōan)* designed to break one's habit of ratiocination (e.g., "What is the sound of one hand clapping?").

The state of enlightenment is acceptance of nothing else but this world as it actually is. When asked what enlightenment was, the Chinese Zen master Yong-jia replied, "It is the flute behind the dead tree; it is the eyes behind a skeleton." Another Chinese Zen master, Hui Neng, said, "Walking is Zen, sit-ting is Zen."[9]

Zen's demand for stern discipline, total concentration and meditation, and a decisive approach to life appealed to the samurai, who, while constantly fac-ing death on the battlefield, had to act resolutely and courageously. Zen also influenced Japanese art and culture in a profound way, as discussed later in the chapter.

Literary Tradition

The Japanese had no written history or literature until the Chinese writing sys-tem entered by way of Korea around the fourth or fifth century. The first ex-tant written works, the *Kojiki* and the *Nihongi*, were compiled in the 670s and completed early in the eighth century. These "histories," including the stories of the imperial ancestors' descent from heaven, have been treated as authentic accounts by nationalist historians, although they are based as much on oral tra-dition, Chinese and Korean tales, and myths and legends as on actual events. The compilers, it is believed, tampered with the facts to legitimate and glorify the imperial ruling house.

An important literary work of the eighth century is the *Man'yōshū*, a collection of over 4,000 poems that have been regarded as expressions of "pure" Japanese sentiment in the time before Confucian "moralism" influenced Japanese literature. Motoori Norinaga (1730–1801), the seminal mind among scholars of National Learning (see Chapter 2), asserted that the *Man'yōshū* embodied the quintessence of the Japanese spirit. Recent scholars have argued, however, that the influence of Korean poetry in the collection was much greater than traditional Japanese literary scholars have been willing to admit.[10] Be that as it may, its literary value is unquestioned, and the work itself is regarded as one of the world's great collections of poetry.

As the Chinese cultural influence permeated the circle of the court aristocracy, efforts to compose poetry in the Chinese style became popular, and Tang poets such as Li Bo (701–762), Du Fu (712–770), and Bo Chuyi (772–846) were emulated. At the same time *waka*, a Japanese style of poetry wherein each poem takes thirty-one syllables, grew in popularity. This development was facilitated by the formulation of a Japanese phonetic writing system *(kana)*. It was also partly the result of a movement to assert the indigenous tradition against the excessive dependence on Chinese culture. At the beginning of the tenth century, an anthology of *waka* called the *Kokinshū* (Collection of Ancient and Modern Poetry) was compiled. As its editor, Ki-no-Tsurayuki, noted: "The poetry of Japan has its roots in the human heart and flourishes in countless leaves of words."[11]

The most extraordinary literary creation of the Heian period was *The Tale of Genji,* written by Murasaki Shikibu (978–1016?), a lady-in-waiting to Empress Akiko. It is still recognized as one of the world's masterpieces. Lady Murasaki's story, set in the court life of her day, centers on the love life of Prince Genji and other members of his family circle. The author's graceful, poetic style has been admired and emulated by all literary aspirants of Japan ever since. Other distinguished works of prose, poetry, essays, and diaries were produced in the Heian period; many of these were authored by women, who together created the golden age of Japanese literature.

The romantic war stories written during the Kamakura period reflected the turbulence of the late Heian and Kamakura years. The greatest of these is *The Tale of the Heike,* which depicts in melancholy tones the fall of the Taira clan. The Buddhist belief that all things are ephemeral permeates much of the writing of this period. For instance, *The Tale of the Heike* starts, "In the sound of the bell of the Gion Temple echoes the impermanence of all things. . . . The proud ones do not last long, but vanish like a spring night's dream. And the mighty ones too will perish in the end, like dust before the wind."[12]

The distinguished literary creations of the Ashikaga period are the Nō plays of Kan'ami Kiyotsugu (1333–1384) and his son, Seami Motokiyo (1363–1443).

The latter was strongly influenced by Zen, and his work is permeated with a sense of *yūgen,* or mystery—that which lies beneath the surface.

The Fine Arts

The beautiful natural environment of Japan undoubtedly fostered a sense of closeness to nature as well as an appreciation of natural beauty. But the Japanese did not simply imitate nature in their art. They added and subtracted from things in nature to create or reproduce the essential principles perceived there. The art of placement and design (i.e., decorative art) is an important aspect of Japanese life, as revealed not only in the fine arts but in everyday life as well.

In their fine arts the Japanese have also accentuated such qualities as the color, texture, and shape of natural objects. For example, in an art object constructed from a piece of wood, the grain will likely be accentuated and the natural color brought out by polishing. Although colorful and vibrant creations do occur in Japanese art, restraint and understatement are perhaps the most important elements in Japanese aesthetic taste. Simple, neat lines and forms, as well as plain, unmixed colors, are common characteristics as well. (Even in culinary dishes, meticulous attention is paid to the arrangement of form and color to make them aesthetically appealing!)

Another noteworthy characteristic of Japanese art is the careful attention paid to details—and, indeed, the miniature arts such as *bonsai* (dwarf trees cultivated in pots) and *netsuke* (miniature carvings), as well as flower arrangements, ceramics, and so on, have flourished. These creations are designed not so much for public display as for private appreciation. Aesthetic appreciation as a private matter is also evidenced in the beautiful gardens of the temples and private homes, which are enclosed behind walls and thus hidden from public view.

The aesthetic sensibilities of the Japanese have been regarded by some observers as unique national characteristics. Rabindranath Tagore, the Indian poet, called aesthetics "the unique Dharma of Japan." And D. T. Suzuki (1870–1966) contended that "if Japan did not produce any philosophical system of her own, she was original enough to embody in her practical life all that could profitably be extracted from Confucianism, Taoism, and Buddhism and turn them into the material for her spiritual enhancement and artistic appreciation."[13]

In the Japanese mode of thinking, the world is not seen in dualistic terms as it is in the West. As one scholar has noted, "Westerners tend to look at life, at the world, as though sitting in a helicopter above it, while the Japanese swim in the actual flow of events. This gives them great sharpness of intuition and the power to build things, to make things with their hands."[14] It is this trait, perhaps, that accounts for the many superb artisans and crafts-people in Japan, whose work is elevated to the level of artistry and who, it might be said, are in total unity with—and completely immersed in—the material they are working with. In combination with the obvious concern for detail, craftsmanship, and quality, this trait may also account for the current Japanese economic success.

The origins of Japanese art can be traced back to the Jōmon and Yayoi pots, and to the *haniwa* (clay figurines) placed around the ancient burial mounds. In architecture the Shinto shrines, with their pure, clear lines and forms, their beauty of proportions, and their natural settings, remain distinctive features of the landscape. The arrival in Japan of Chinese and Buddhist cultures added new dimensions to the art and architecture of the country. The most visible consequence of the continental impact were the Buddhist temples and pagodas that were constructed first in the central region and then throughout the land. The most renowned of these is the Hōryūji, built in 607. Although the buildings were arranged in a relatively asymmetrical manner, they convey a sense of order, balance, and cohesion. Indeed, they were designed to blend harmoniously with the natural setting. The five-storied pagoda in particular has a stately dignity and grace.

Buddhist sculptures, paintings, scrolls, and images also became integral elements of Japanese life. The scroll paintings that originated in China, for instance, were modified through distinctive use of color, lines, forms, and concern for placement. These narrative picture scrolls, known as *Yamato-e*, depict events of the Heian era such as those related in the *Tale of Genji*. The art of calligraphy, too, came to be prized by the court aristocrats. Elegance in calligraphy was equated with good breeding and refinement of character.

In the Kamakura period, the influence from Song China (960–1279) and Zen Buddhism had a powerful impact on the culture. This dual impact is seen most strikingly in such art forms as black-and-white ink-painting *(sumi-e)*. The greatest of the Japanese sumi-e painters was Sesshū (1421–1506), who emerged during the Ashikaga period. Ernest Fenollosa (1853–1908), a Western authority on Japanese art, describes Sesshū as "the greatest master of straight line and angle in the whole range of the world's art."[15] The influence of Zen can also be seen in the art of flower arrangement, ceramics, landscape gardening, architecture, and Nō drama, and especially the tea ceremony. As Suzuki has noted, "What is common to Zen and the art of tea is the constant attempt both make at simplification." The aesthetic qualities that Zen masters prized were *wabi* and *sabi*. Sabi is associated with "age, desiccation, numbness, chilliness, obscurity." It is also the quality of mellowness and depth that comes from aging. Wabi is related to a sense of serenity, rusticity, solitude, and even melancholy. Both signify the "aesthetical appreciation of poverty."[16]

As noted, the art of gardening that flourished in the Ashikaga period is associated with aesthetic principles linked to Zen. Again, it is the art of placement that is critical in the gardens constructed in Zen temples. A striking example is found in the rock garden of Ryōanji in Kyoto, which reveals nothing but sand and fifteen natural stones arranged in groups of five.

In the sixteenth century the daimyō contending for power built massive castles that served not only as fortresses but also as edifices by which to display their power and glory. Hideyoshi, for instance, built two such castles—one in Osaka and another in Fushimi-Momoyama near Kyoto. The Osaka castle featured forty-eight large towers; the main tower stood on a stone base 75 feet high, above which it rose 102 feet. The interiors of these castles were decorated elaborately with painted walls, sliding doors, folding screens, and wood carvings by way of the art style developed by Kanō Eitoku (1543–1590), who was called upon by Nobunaga and Hideyoshi to embellish the interiors of their castles. Kanō, departing from the monochrome style of his predecessors in the Kanō school, used bright colors against luminous gold backgrounds, and bold, simplified forms.

Although no abrupt shift in cultural development occurred in the transition from the pre-Tokugawa to the Tokugawa era (indeed, the social, political, and economic institutions that had evolved in the previous centuries provided the basis for the policies and institutions adopted by the Tokugawa rulers), the hegemony established by Ieyasu marked the beginning of an order of things that would leave a lasting imprint on Japanese life. The peace and stability that characterized this period lasted for two and a half centuries. The Tokugawa rulers had set about deliberately to freeze the political and social order, and they achieved their objectives with remarkable success. Virtually cut off from the rest of the world, Japan emerged as a small "world state."

Notes

1. Some scholars have recently concluded that Shōtoku's role has been exaggerated and, indeed, that many of the reforms and policies attributed to him by the court historians may have actually been the work of the Soga family. See Kim Sok-hyong and Matsumoto Seichō, *Kodaishi no Naka no Chōsen to Nihon* (Korea and Japan in Ancient History), Chūō Kōron, December 1972, pp. 284–286. For the Korean influence on early Japan, see Gari Ledyard, "Galloping with the Horseriders," *Journal of Japanese Studies*, 1975, pp. 217ff.; Chong-sik Lee, "History and Politics of Japanese-Korean Relations," *Journal of Northeast Asian Studies*, October 1983, pp. 69ff.; Kim and Matsumoto, *Kodaishi no Naka no Chōsen to Nihon;* and Walter Edwards, "In Pursuit of Himiko: Postwar Archaeology and the Location of Yamatai," *Monumenta Nipponica*, vol. 51, no. 1, spring 1996, pp. 53–79.

2. Joseph Campbell, *Oriental Mythology* (New York: Viking Press, 1962), p. 476.

3. Fosco Maraini, in Ronald Bell, *The Japan Experience* (New York: Weatherhill, 1973), pp. 13–14.

4. Ryusaku Tsunoda et al., eds., *Sources of Japanese Tradition* (New York: Columbia University Press, 1958), pp. 50–52.

5. Ibid., p. 217.

6. Masaharu Anesaki, *History of Japanese Religion* (Tokyo and Rutland, Vt.: Tuttle, 1963), p. 198.

7. D. T. Suzuki, *Manual of Zen Buddhism* (New York: Grove Press, 1960), pp. 2, 112–113.

8. The quotation is attributed to Bodhidharma in *Zen Buddhism: Selected Writings of D. T. Suzuki,* ed. William Barrett (New York: Doubleday Anchor, 1956), p. 61.

9. Suzuki, *Manual of Zen Buddhism,* p. 94.

10. Some scholars believe that one of the three main poets of the *Man'yōshū,* Yamanoe Okura, was of Korean immigrant origin. See, for instance, Roy Andrew Miller, "Plus Ça Change," *Journal of Asian Studies,* August 1980, pp. 771ff.

11. Earl Miner, *An Introduction to Japanese Court Poetry* (Stanford: Stanford University Press, 1968), p. 18.

12. A. L. Sadler, trans., "Heike Monogatari" (The Tale of the Heike), in *Transactions of the Asiatic Society of Japan,* vol. 46, part 1, p. 207.

13. D. T. Suzuki, *Zen and Japanese Culture* (New York: Pantheon Books, 1959), p. 307.

14. Maraini, in Bell, *The Japan Experience,* pp. 16–17.

15. Ernest Fenollosa, *Epochs of Chinese and Japanese Art,* vol. 2 (New York: Grove Press, 1963), p. 81.

16. Suzuki, *Zen and Japanese Culture,* pp. 271, 284, 285.

2

Establishment of the Tokugawa Bakufu

THE SHŌGUN OF THE TOKUGAWA BAKUFU

In 1600, Tokugawa Ieyasu defeated his rivals and the supporters of the Toyotomi family in the Battle of Sekigahara. In 1603 the emperor designated him shōgun and made Edo (Tokyo) the seat of government. By 1615 he had eliminated the Toyotomi family, and he tightened his grip on the entire country by establishing a political and social order that brought all segments of the society under his firm control. He and the third shōgun, Iemitsu, adopted and implemented measures that would ensure the security of Tokugawa hegemony.

Ieyasu froze the social order, adapting Neo-Confucian China's four-class system—that is, scholar-officials (samurai), peasants, artisans, and merchants. In this Testament to his descendants, he stated: "The samurai are the master of the four classes. Agriculturists, artisans, and merchants may not behave in a rude manner towards samurai. . . . A samurai is not to be interfered with in cutting down a fellow who has behaved to him in a manner other than is expected."[1] In other words, the samurai were to be at the top of the social hierarchy, the peasants were to remain on the land, and the artisans and merchants were to keep their places and behave in a manner expected of humble people.

In order to control the feudal lords (daimyō), of whom there were 295 in the early seventeenth century and 276 at the end of the Tokugawa era, the Tokugawa rulers adopted the following measures. They classified the daimyō into three categories: members of the Tokugawa clan *(shimpan)*, lords who had been followers of the Tokugawa family before the Battle of Sekigahara *(fudai,* or hereditary lords), and those who submitted to or joined the Tokugawa family later *(tozama,* or outside lords). The fudai lords' domains *(han)* were placed

17

in strategic places, whereas the tozama lords were placed in outlying regions or between two fudai lords' domains. In 1635, Iemitsu issued the "Laws Governing the Military Households," which required that the feudal lords spend every other year in Edo and that their families remain in Edo (known as *sankin kōtai*); the feudal lords and their families were also forbidden to form marital ties with other daimyō families, or to build or repair castles without the Bakufu's permission.

Of the 30 million *koku* (1 koku = 4.96 bushels) in rice, or rice equivalents, produced nationwide, the Bakufu's own holdings yielded 7 million koku. It also retained control over foreign relations, controlled coinage, and regulated inter-han transportation. The local lords were allowed to manage their own internal affairs and to retain their own vassals, who, in most instances, received stipends in rice rather than land allotments as fiefs.

In foreign relations Shōgun Iemitsu decided to virtually seal off the country from the outside world in order to prevent Christian influences from seeping into the country. Restrictions against Christians had started under Toyotomi, who in 1587 ordered the missionaries to leave the country; but the edict was not stringently enforced until the last years of his life, when he crucified twenty-six missionaries and converts in 1597. Ieyasu initially pursued a policy of toleration, but in 1614 he issued an edict banning Christianity because he had come to believe that Christians were a threat to his plan to establish absolute control over the society. Thus commenced was a policy of ruthless persecution of Christians, who at that time numbered about 300,000. Iemitsu continued this policy with even less mercy than that shown by Ieyasu.[2] As the leadership was Christian, Iemitsu's distrust of Christians was reinforced. In 1639 he decided to virtually isolate Japan from the rest of the world. Only the Dutch and the Chinese were allowed to come to Nagasaki to trade in a limited fashion. The Koreans were permitted to trade through Iki Island off Honshu. In addition, books from the West were banned until 1720, when nonreligious works were allowed to enter Japan.

The shōgun was assisted in his administrative tasks by a group of councilors known as *rōjū* (senior councilors). To deal with extraordinary matters a great councilor *(tairō)* was appointed, but this action was taken only rarely. Usually four or five rōjū were chosen from the fudai domains. The three collateral houses of the Tokugawa clan (Mito near Edo, Owari around Nagoya, and Kii in Kii Peninsula) provided successors to the shōgun if he did not have an heir.

Once the foundations of the Bakufu were laid, the actions of succeeding shōgun did not seem to alter the course of events significantly. The difficulties that eventually confronted the Bakufu derived from objective and external developments such as the changing economic situation and the arrival of the Western powers in the nineteenth century.

TOKUGAWA DOMAINS, 1664

The fourth shōgun, Ietsuna (1641–1680), failed to play an active role in the affairs of the state and left the business of government to his uncle and other Bakufu officials. During his reign neo-Confucianism began to gain official sanction as the orthodox philosophy of the realm. During the reign of the fifth shōgun, Tsunayoshi (1646–1709), the culture of the townspeople flourished—a period known as the Genroku era. Tsunayoshi fostered learning and encouraged the study of Confucianism. But he was imprudent in managing the Bakufu's finances and left his successor with a huge deficit.

Ienobu (1666–1713), who followed Tsunayoshi, employed an erudite Confucian scholar, Arai Hakuseki (1657–1725), as his adviser. Arai hoped to solve the growing difficulties besetting the society by revitalizing Confucianism. He also adopted measures to strengthen the currency and check the outflow of gold and silver from the country. But he, too, failed to solve the growing economic difficulties of the Bakufu.

The eighth shōgun, Yoshimune (1684–1751), personally took charge of the affairs of the state and introduced a series of reform measures, known as the Kyōho Reforms (named for the Kyōho period, 1716–1736), to increase government revenues. He encouraged the reclamation of the new land and sought to prevent the peasants from illegally leaving the villages for the cities. He also issued sumptuary laws and censored literature in an effort to "uplift" the morality of the people. But his measures merely dealt with external symptoms, and the Bakufu's economic difficulties continued to mount.

TOKUGAWA INSTITUTIONS

Modern Japan cannot be comprehended without an understanding of the social, economic, political, intellectual, and cultural forces that emerged in the Tokugawa period. The hierarchical outlook and behavior, the emphasis on class order and social cohesion, the demand for obedience and submissiveness that the Tokugawa rulers insisted upon—all of these forces molded the values and attitudes of the people of the time and, in fact, have persisted to the present day. Specifically, it was during the Tokugawa period that the Confucian and samurai values and ideals became ingrained in the society.

Confucianism

With the advent of Chinese civilization, Chinese classics, history, and poetry entered Japan. Confucianism, however, did not affect the cultural and intellectual life of Japan as quickly as Buddhism had done. Nevertheless, because the Tokugawa rulers encouraged the study and propagation of Confucian values, Confucianism became the predominant intellectual force in this era—even though the early Tokugawa rulers had used Shinto and Buddhist concepts as well to legitimize their hegemony.[3]

Ieyasu wanted his vassals not only to be well trained in the martial arts but also, like the Chinese scholar-officials, to be steeped in Confucian learning. The Confucian school that received official backing was Confucianism as interpreted by the Song Confucian (Zhu Xi, 1130–1200). As the pursuit of Confucian studies continued for two-and-a-half centuries, the Japanese intellectual frame of reference came to be largely Confucian. Confucian values continued to be instilled in the society after the Meiji Restoration (1868) because they were incorporated in the school textbooks until the end of the Second World War.

Confucius and his followers were interested primarily in man's relationship with his fellow men and in maintaining social and political order, stability, and harmony. They believed there are five basic human relationships: those between lord and subject, father and son, husband and wife, elder brother and younger brother, and friend and friend. Of these, the relationship between father and son was the most important, and filial piety was considered the cardinal virtue.

Like their Chinese counterparts, the Japanese Confucians emphasized filial piety, but the Tokugawa rulers made loyalty to the lord equally or more important than filial piety. The two were linked together as *chū-kō* (loyalty and filial piety). Social order was to be maintained by means of a hierarchical order in which the relationship between superior and inferior persons was strictly preserved. The superior person was expected to be benevolent and to set a moral example to those below, while those below were to be respectful, deferential, and obedient toward the superior.

Zhu Xi designated a universal force, the Supreme Ultimate, as the basis of morality and the font of the principle of all things. The Japanese Zhu Xi scholars equated the Supreme Ultimate with heaven. In this system of thought, the ruler governed in accordance with the Principle of Heaven, so the people were duty-bound to obey him. Thus Zhu Xi philosophy provided the ruling class with a moral anchor with which to preserve the established order of things. The Zhu Xi scholars also stressed the importance of the concept of *taigi-meibun*. *Taigi* means the highest principle of justice, and *meibun* means name and place (i.e., knowing one's proper place). *Taigi-meibun* thus means doing one's duty in accordance with one's status in society. Of course, this concept necessitated the stifling of both individuality and individual interests. The emphasis was instead directed to the "group" or class to which one belonged—an emphasis that also characterized the other schools of Confucianism as well as the imperatives of Bushidō and of Buddhism, which stressed denial of the self.

A rival school of thought to Zhu Xi Confucianism was the Wang Yang-ming (pronounced "Ōyōmei" in Japanese) school. Wang Yang-ming of Ming China emphasized the subjective basis of moral principles. The Confucian concept of *Li* (Principle) is in the mind, he asserted. "Mind is Li. How can there be affairs and Li outside the mind?" he asked. "Since there is the mind of filial love, there is the Li of filial piety."[4] Wang Yang-ming also emphasized the importance of acting upon the truth as perceived by the individual. His teaching that truth is subjective and that the individual must act upon this truth appealed to many Tokugawa samurai. It became the creed of the militant activists of the late Tokugawa period who challenged the legitimacy of Tokugawa rule.

Another Confucian school that gained adherents among Tokugawa scholars was the school of Ancient Learning, which stressed a direct reference to the texts of the ancient philosophers rather than a reliance on the interpretations of later scholars. Among these scholars was Ogyū Sorai (1666–1728), who rejected the Zhu Xi concept that a natural basis exists for moral principles. Rather, Ogyū insisted, all rules, regulations, and institutions are man-made. This idea opened the way for later thinkers to challenge the idea of the existing order of things, which, after all, are man-made and not ordained by nature or heaven. The emphasis of this school on the importance of studying ancient texts also contributed to the rise of the school of National Learning (Kokugaku).

The Samurai and the Way of the Warriors

During the years of Tokugawa peace, warrior-philosophers began to formulate what they considered to be the ideal mode of conduct for the samurai. Of course, even before the Tokugawa era, righteous and unrighteous conduct had been defined, and samurai were expected to live by the principles of duty, loyalty, integrity, honor, justice, fidelity, and courage. In the Kamakura period, the life of the samurai was spoken of as *yumiya no michi,* the way of the bow and arrow. The lord-vassal relationship that constituted the basis of the feudal system rose out of familial relationships. A follower of the lord was called *go-kenin* (man of the house), or *ie-no-ko* (child of the house). Hence the relationship between lord and vassal was akin to that of father and son. Like the European medieval knight, the samurai pledged allegiance to his lord in a ritualistic ceremony. In return, the lord was expected to reward the vassal with land, stipends, or the right to collect taxes.

In relating tales of warriors who were engaged in the power struggles of the late Heian period and after, storytellers have often idealized the conduct of the warriors, who were depicted as being chivalrous, selfless, and heroic. But, in reality, some samurai were motivated not by noble ideals but by self-interest. In times of strife the principle that prevailed for such samurai was the law of the jungle. What really counted were physical strength and martial skill. Expediency and opportunism guided the actions of many warriors who were ready to shift with the changing tide of fortune. For this reason, the period between 1337 and 1392, when the northern and southern imperial courts were in conflict, is referred to as the "great age of turncoats." The same situation prevailed during the years of the Warring States (Sengoku) in the fifteenth and sixteenth centuries. The strong conquered the weak; the powerful destroyed the helpless. Given the opportunity, a vassal would likely turn against his master. Thus, in order to ensure his vassal's loyalty, the master had to reward him properly. The vassal then was obligated to him; he owed him *on*. Eventually the concept of *on* became a cardinal virtue in the Japanese value system. A person owed *on* to his feudal lord, parents, teachers, emperor, society, and so on.

The samurai's interests were closely bound to the interests of his family. If he died in battle he expected his family to be properly rewarded. But self-interest caused frequent conflicts among family members, conflicts in which sons turned against fathers and brothers fought brothers.

As noted earlier, Zen influenced the life of the samurai during the Ashikaga period, for it disciplined the warrior to concentrate, control his emotions, and overcome the fear of death. One sixteenth-century warlord exhorted his retainers to "devote yourselves to the study of Zen. Zen has no secrets other than seriously thinking about birth and death."[5] Unfortunately, this belief reinforced the samurai's rather cold-blooded attitude about killing people, despite the fact that, ideally, the samurai was expected to behave in a compassionate and magnanimous fashion.

Among the Tokugawa warrior-philosophers who reflected upon the proper mode of conduct for the samurai *(bushidō)* were Yamaga Sokō (1622–1685) and Yamamoto Tsunetomo (1659–1719). In his *Hagakure* (Hidden Among Leaves), the latter wrote, "As long as a person values his master, his parents will be happy and the Buddha and the gods will respond to his prayers. I have no other thought but to serve my master." He also remarked, "I have discovered that *bushidō* means to die." The implication is that by thinking constantly about death, a person will become free and manage to perform his duties more perfectly.[6]

The samurai's code of proper conduct persisted through the years to the modern age. As one modern Christian writer, Nitobe Inazō, wrote in his book entitled *Bushidō*:

Chivalry is a flower no less indigenous to the soil of Japan than its emblem, the cherry blossom. . . . It is still a living object of power and beauty among us; and if it assumes no tangible shape or form, it not the less scents the moral atmosphere, and makes us aware that we are still under its potent spell.[7]

Bushidō, if strictly adhered to, was a stringently demanding code of life. It required the samurai to fulfill his responsibilities and obligations scrupulously. If he failed to do so, or if he disgraced himself in any manner whatsoever, he was expected to assume full responsibility and take his own life by means of a highly ritualized mode of disembowelment with a sword *(hara-kiri,* or *seppuku).* This custom evidently first came into existence in the twelfth century, when the samurai chiefs were contending for power. The defeated warriors, rather than be taken captive, committed seppuku. The vassals often joined their masters in death. Even during the early years of the Tokugawa era, vassals often committed seppuku upon their lord's death, thus compelling the Bakufu to prohibit this practice.

In the Tokugawa period seppuku was used to punish warriors who committed serious offenses. But it was regarded as an honorable way of dying; indeed, samurai of their own free will often committed ritual suicide to uphold their honor, to prove their sincerity, or to protest the unjust actions of their superiors. The occasional practice of seppuku continued into the modern era. After the end of the Second World War, a number of army and navy officers committed seppuku, taking responsibility for Japan's defeat. The most recent instance of ritual suicide was that of the novelist Mishima Yukio, who in 1969 committed seppuku to protest the decline in traditional values and the absence of the spirit of patriotism among his young compatriots.

A possession of the samurai that distinguished them from the commoners was the sword—the samurai's symbol of superior status. (The common people were prohibited from bearing a sword.) The sword supposedly embodied the spirit of the samurai. It was the emblem of their power, honor, and status, but for the common people it was an instrument of terror because the samurai were given the right to cut down any commoner who offended them. Thus, it might be said that the courtesy, politeness, humility, and subservience of the common people were instilled in them at the edge of the sword.

National Learning

In the Tokugawa period, when the scholars of National Learning (Kokugaku) began to emphasize the unique nature of Japanese culture and religion, the nativist aspects of Shinto were also emphasized. The scholars were influenced by the Confucian school of Ancient Learning, which, as noted, stressed the importance of going back to the original teachings of Confucius. In addition, Shinto scholars began to stress the need to return to the roots of Japanese culture and religion, to the time before Japan had become overwhelmed by Chinese culture and thought. Thus, the "native" texts of Japan, the *Man'yōshū* (Collection of Ten Thousand Leaves) and the *Kojiki* (Records of Ancient Matters), were extolled as true embodiments of the Japanese spirit because, according to these scholars, they were free of foreign contamination.

Among the pioneers of the scholars of National Learning was Kamo Mabuchi (1697–1769). He rejected Confucianism for having made people "crafty," in contrast to the ancient Japanese who were simple, honest, sincere, and free from abstruse teachings. The scholar who came to be regarded as the sage of National Learning was Motoori Norinaga. Motoori devoted his life to the study of the *Man'yōshū* and the *Kojiki*. The latter, he asserted, embodied "The Way of the Gods," and what was recorded in it were absolute truths. One such truth concerned the founding of Japan by the Sun Goddess, who was the Sun itself. Hence Japan, as a land favored by the gods, was believed to occupy a unique place in the world. Motoori's followers then insisted that Japan was superior to the other nations of the world. This mode of thinking culminated in the movement in the 1930s to bring "the eight corners of the world under one roof," so that the world could benefit from the "benevolence" of the descendant of the Sun Goddess (namely, the emperor).

Motoori believed that, previous to the advent of Chinese civilization, the Japanese behaved in a natural and uninhibited fashion and that this natural way was distorted by Chinese thought and culture—especially Confucianism, with its artificial rules and regulations about decorum and propriety. It was important to allow one's true feelings to have free play, he insisted, for only in this way could one be fully sensitive to all facets of life.

Even though Motoori spoke of the sacred origin of Japan and the imperial dynasty, he did not call for the restoration of political authority to the imperial court. Instead, he accepted the existing political order. This he justified by asserting that "great shōgun have ruled the land ever since Azumaterunokami [Ieyasu] founded the government in accordance with the designs of the Sun Goddess Amaterasu, and by the authority vested in him by the imperial court. . . . The rules and laws of the founder and succeeding shōgun are all rules and laws of the Sun Goddess Amaterasu." Hence "to obey the laws of the day is to follow the true way of the Gods."[8] It was not until the later stages of the Tokugawa era that Shinto nationalists began to urge the restoration of authority to the emperor.

THE STRUCTURE OF TOKUGAWA SOCIETY

The Peasants

During the years of the Warring States the peasants were exploited ruthlessly by the local warlords, who taxed them heavily. They were also victimized by the marauding samurai, who came to their villages to loot, pillage, and kill. Often the peasants armed themselves to defend their villages against the brigands. They also united under the leadership of one of the popular Pure Land Buddhist sects *(ikko)* and waged war against the warlords. Some became foot soldiers and joined a warlord's troops; others joined the ranks of the samurai. The most striking example of a peasant rising to the top as a warrior was that of Hideyoshi. Thus, despite their poverty, privation, and victimization by the brigands, the peasants of this period retained considerable freedom and social mobility. With the centralization of power, however, they lost their freedom. Hideyoshi took away their weapons and bound them to the soil, and Ieyasu subsequently froze the social and political order and kept the peasants tied to the land.

In adopting the aforementioned four-class system of Confucian China, Ieyasu identified the samurai with the scholar-officials. Class divisions were to be maintained rigidly: a person's status was fixed by birth, class lines were not to be transgressed, and interclass marriages were forbidden. A decree of the Bakufu stated, "Each person must devote himself to his own business, without negligence; and in all respects keep within the limits proper to his social position."[9] It was Ieyasu who gave the samurai permission to cut down any commoner who behaved "in a manner other than expected."

Confucian scholars upheld the class system. One Tokugawa Confucian wrote, "The samurai use their minds, the peasants and those below use their muscles. Those who use their minds are superior; those who use their muscles are inferior."[10]

Like the other commoners, peasants were forbidden to use surnames, bear swords, or wear their hair in samurai style. They had to be subservient and humble, and to bow deeply or kneel on the ground when samurai came strutting by. Theoretically, the peasants, who constituted about 80 percent of the population, ranked above the urban artisans and merchants, but in reality they were worse off than the others. Their sole function was to work the land and provide for the economic needs of the ruling class. One official was reputed to have said, "Sesame seed and peasants are much alike. The more you squeeze them, the more you can get out of them." The idea, then, was to tax the peasants as much as possible.[11]

In addition to taxing the harvest, many other forms of taxes were imposed. One Bakufu official in the late eighteenth century observed that there was "a tax on the field, a tax on doors, a tax on windows, a tax on female children according to age, a tax on cloth, a tax on sake, a tax on hazel trees, a tax on beans, a tax on hemp. . . . If a peasant added a room to his hut a tax was levied on it."[12] In addition, peasants were required to provide corvée whenever the lords or officials needed the services of such labor.

Because the peasants were the primary source of revenue for the Bakufu and the daimyō, they were encouraged to be as frugal and thrifty as possible—so as to leave more for the ruling class. The rulers not only regulated the peasants' mode of farming and other work but also told them what to eat, drink, and wear and what kind of hut to live in. The ruling class was particularly anxious to keep the villagers from being "contaminated" by the "extravagant" ways of the townspeople. They also preferred to keep the peasants ignorant and ill-informed so that they would not be exposed to "subversive" ideas. "A good peasant," it was said, "is one who does not know the price of grain." The ruling class believed that the peasants should not receive any education beyond learning the virtues of obedience, docility, humility, loyalty, frugality, and hard work. Some insisted that both peasants and townspeople should be forbidden from studying. However, the village elders who served as local agents for the ruling class were educated enough to oversee village affairs.

The status and condition of the peasants varied to some degree, of course. In most villages there were two classes of peasants: those who farmed their own land (although, in theory, the land was not theirs because it belonged to the shōgun or the daimyō) and those who were tenant farmers. The former were regarded as "regular" farmers and had a voice in village affairs, whereas the latter did not. The average holding varied from place to place, but the norm was about 1 *chō* (2.45 acres). The peasants were forbidden to leave the villages; however, as commerce grew and jobs became available in the towns and cities, tenant farmers, hired workers, and younger sons (who had no place in the economic life of the village) left for the cities to seek work.

In the later years of the Tokugawa era, the peasants grew increasingly discontented with their plight, and peasant disturbances began to break out with increasing frequency and greater magnitude (see Chapter 3).

The Townspeople

The artisans and merchants were placed below the peasants in the social hierarchy because the peasants provided the economic wherewithal for the samurai class whereas the merchants were regarded as a parasitic class. The Tokugawa rulers adopted the Confucian thesis that money-making is a demeaning preoccupation. As a Japanese Confucian moralist, Kaibara Ekken (1630–1714), wrote, "The enlightened kings of the ancient period valued agriculture and curtailed industry and commerce. They respected the five grains and held money in disdain."[13]

The Tokugawa ruling class was not indifferent to profits. If any profits were to accrue from commerce and industry, the members of this class intended to be the beneficiaries. Thus, they regulated commerce and industry and maintained monopolistic control of enterprises that were profitable. In some ways the Tokugawa accepted the political reality of the time in that they recognized that they could not ignore the economic power of some two hundred castle-towns that had arisen in the previous century. At the start of the era, perhaps up to 5 percent of Japan's population was urban.

The merchant class (called collectively *chonin*) tried to make the best of the restrictive system that hedged them in and set out to acquire as much wealth as possible. As Ihara Saikaku (1652–1693), a writer who depicted the life of the townspeople, asserted, "Money is the townsman's pedigree, whatever his birth and lineage. No matter how splendid a man's ancestor, if he lacks money he is worse off than a monkey-showman."[14]

A philosophical school upholding the way of the merchants even came into existence. Its founder, Ishida Baigan (1685–1744), came out of the peasantry, was apprenticed in a merchant house, studied independently, and eventually became a teacher of the common people. His school of thought is known as *shingaku* (teachings of the heart) because, as he asserted, in reading books the "heart" of the writer must be understood. This school of thought also came to be known as *chōnin-gaku* (creed of the townspeople). Baigan argued that the merchants' pursuit of profits was part of the Principle of Heaven. After all, the townspeople, like other members of the society, were performing useful tasks and should not be denigrated; moreover, the principle of frugality that guided the merchants was beneficial to all classes, including the government.

The vigor and determination with which the merchants pursued profits enabled them to gain wealth and, indirectly, power. They began to cause serious difficulties to the ruling class later in the Tokugawa era, for despite the Bakufu's policy of keeping the economy basically agrarian, internal commerce began to flourish. Both the Bakufu's capital, Edo, and the daimyō's castletown became centers of large populations. The vassals of the shōgun and the daimyō resided in these cities, and merchants, artisans, and servants congregated there. The towns along the major roads traveled by the daimyō and their entourages during their regular trips back and forth to Edo flourished as rest stops.

Rice and other products from the villages had to be transported to the castletowns and major distribution centers. Despite their haughty attitude toward the merchants, the members of the ruling class had to rely on them to serve as wholesale dealers, brokers, and money-changers to market the products of their domains. As a result, some of the merchant houses became extremely wealthy. In some instances, the Bakufu confiscated the properties of merchant houses to whom the samurai class had fallen heavily in debt. But a number of merchant houses managed to prosper and survive and eventually emerged in the modern era as major business firms. Such was the case with the House of Mitsui.

The major cities of Tokugawa Japan were among the largest in the world during these centuries. In the early eighteenth century, the population of Edo was estimated at 1 million, Osaka at about 400,000, and Kyoto at 350,000. By contrast, London's population in 1700 was about 600,000, and Paris's was about 500,000.

The Outcastes

Beneath the four classes of Tokugawa society was another consisting of people treated as outcastes. The Bakufu classified people broadly into *ryōmin* (good people) and *semmin* (base people). At the end of the Tokugawa period, out of a population of 28 or 29 million people about 380,000 were classified as semmin—the antecedents of the people known today as *burakumin* (hamlet people). In the Tokugawa period they were designated as *eta* (unclean people) or *hinin* (nonhumans). In the years before the Tokugawa period the two groups were not sharply differentiated, but the Tokugawa rulers classed the former as outcastes by birth whereas the latter were defined as such because of the occupation they held or as the result of some social infraction they had committed. In some instances the latter were able to rejoin the ranks of the ryōmin in the early Tokugawa years, but their status eventually became hereditary as well. The reason for which certain people came to be labeled as *eta* is not entirely clear, but in many instances the designation may have been related to occupations viewed as unclean, such as butchering and leather work. However, other occupations that had no stigma of being unclean, such as those held by basket makers, bamboo workers, and footwear makers, also became associated with this class. The hinin were itinerant entertainers, beggars, scavengers, prostitutes, and castoff commoners. The Bakufu used the hinin to work in prisons and to execute and bury criminals.

The government did not recognize the outcastes as legal entities. They were ignored in official surveys, and entire outcaste communities were left out of some official maps. A host of discriminatory measures were imposed on them. They were restricted in the kind of work they could engage in, they were forbidden to intermarry with other classes, and they were segregated in ghettos. In many places they were forbidden to wear footwear, or to enter the grounds of shrines and temples. The commoners expected them to bow and scrape and to move aside when their paths crossed. The treatment that the burakumin experienced would be similar, then, to the abuse suffered by the outcastes of India. As one Tokugawa official observed when an outcaste member was killed for trying to enter the grounds of a shrine, "The life of an eta is worth about one-seventh the life of a townsman. Unless seven eta have been killed, we cannot punish a single townsman."[15]

The Women

The Tokugawa social system was based upon the segregation of "superior" and "inferior" persons, but there was also a hierarchy of sex and age. The attitude about male-female relationships differed between the samurai class and the townspeople, and the attitude of the ruling class tended to influence the thinking of the peasantry.

It appears that women were accorded better treatment in antiquity than during the Tokugawa period. After all, the "ancestor" of the emperors is the Sun Goddess, and the ruler mentioned in *The History of the Kingdom of Wei,* Pimiku, was a woman. The occasional occupation by women of the imperial throne persisted into the Tokugawa period (although only one woman took the throne within the era itself). Ancient Japan was a matrilineal, if not a matriarchal, society. Until the eleventh century or so, upon marriage the husband and wife lived apart, the husband visited the wife in her home, and the children stayed with the mother. In the twelfth century the husband and wife began living together, but, again, it was the husband who joined the wife's household. With the ascendancy of the samurai class, however, the patriarchal structure became stronger. By the fifteenth century the custom whereby the bride went to live with the husband's family became the norm. Among the peasant families of northeastern Japan, however, the eldest daughter carried on the family line—a custom that persisted into the Tokugawa period. Vestiges of this custom are seen today in the practice by which the daughter takes a husband to carry on the family line when the family has no male heir.

With the rise of the samurai, physical strength and martial prowess became essential. Then the status of women began to decline. The growing influence of Confucianism also fortified this trend toward masculine ascendancy, for Confucianism insisted upon the maintenance of a rigid hierarchy of sex and age. Generally speaking, Buddhism also placed women in a disadvantageous position insofar as it held that salvation was not possible for them. These concepts permeated the thinking of the Heian court circle. For example, as Prince Genji in *The Tale of Genji* mused at one point, "But what was the good of trying to please women? If they were not fundamentally evil, they would not have been born women at all."[16] Moreover, Heian men believed that women were incapable of mastering the complex Chinese writing system. Thus, they were expected to rely primarily on the phonetic *kana* system. And yet it was Heian women like Murasaki Shikibu and Sei Shonagon (966–1017) who produced the masterpieces of Japanese literature.

The worsening of the status of women as the samurai class gained ascendancy was revealed in the growing difference between male and female speech during the Kamakura period. Women were increasingly expected to show their humility and subservience by using honorific speech when addressing men and by referring to themselves in humble terms. The end result was the evolution of the Japanese language to include the most minutely differentiated styles of speech between men and women, and between "superior" and "inferior" persons, by means of intricate levels of distinctions between humble and honorific words, phrases, and speech patterns.

In the early stages of samurai ascendancy, the women of the samurai class were expected to be skilled in the martial arts. Hojo Masako (1156–1225), the widow of Minamoto, led her warriors against the foes of Kamakura. Called the "nun shōgun," she ruled Japan for two decades. The Jōei Code of 1232 provided for women's right to inherit property and serve as vassals. But their rights were increasingly curtailed as the rule of the swordsmen gained in strength. By the Tokugawa period the status of women, especially upper-class women, had reached its nadir.

Even before the Tokugawa era, in the period of the Warring States, the samurai men were treating women as semi-slaves. As a Portuguese trader observed in the mid-sixteenth century, "Her husband may kill [his wife] for being lazy or bad. For this reason women are much concerned with their husband's honor and are most diligent in their household duties."[17]

The Tokugawa rulers gave the male family head absolute authority over all family members. In sexual relations the husband could be as promiscuous as he pleased, but even the slightest hint of infidelity on the part of the wife could result in her being executed by her husband. Ieyasu's Testament states, "If a married woman of the agricultural, artisan, or commercial class shall secretly have illicit intercourse with another man, it is not necessary for the husband to enter a complaint against the persons thus confusing the great relations of mankind, but he may put them both to death."[18] In one of his plays, Chikamatsu Monzaemon (1653–1724), a Tokugawa playwright, has a samurai mother tell her daughter, "When you are alone with any other man—beside your husband—you are not so much as to lift your head and look at him."[19] Moreover, a samurai woman was expected to kill herself if her chastity was threatened.

Marriages were arranged by the parents, and daughters had no say in the decision. The husband could easily divorce the wife, but the wife had to endure with self-sacrificing stoicism all forms of injustice and abuse at the hands of her husband and his family. In the samurai family, when the husband committed ritual suicide, the perfect wife would join him in death. This practice continued into the modern period. For instance, Mrs. Nogi joined her husband in death when he committed suicide upon Emperor Meiji's death—and, indeed, she was lauded as a paragon of the loyal Japanese wife. At the end of the Second World War, when General Sugiyama Hajime committed suicide, his wife joined him in death too.

As Kaibara Ekken wrote in his *Onna Daigaku* (Great Learning for Women), "From her earliest youth, a girl should observe the line of demarcation separating women from men. . . . In her dealings with her husband both the expression of her countenance and the style of address should be courteous, humble, and conciliatory. . . . A woman should look upon her husband as if he were Heaven itself."[20]

The townspeople adhered to a much less rigid and moralistic position about male-female relations. As the writer Ihara remarked, "For the husband to love his wife, and the wife to be affectionate towards her husband and maintain a gentle and friendly relationship is the proper way." He also believed that widows should remarry. "We cannot label as immoral the longing of a woman for another man, or her desire to have another man after her husband's death." Some townspeople disagreed with the Confucian thesis that the cardinal human relationship was that of father and son. Rather, they contended, it was that of husband and wife. "The way of humanity originated with husband and wife. First there was man and woman, and then husband and wife. After that came the gods, Buddha and the sages. Thus husband and wife constitute the source of all things."[21] Whereas in the samurai class the practice of primogeniture was rigidly adhered to and women had no property rights, among the townspeople the parents could choose a younger son to carry on the family business or divide the family property among their sons and daughters.

Curiously, despite the Tokugawa Neo-Confucianist misogyny, married women who could find their way to at least two Buddhist temples (Mantokuji and Tokeiji) could initiate divorce proceedings against their husbands.[22]

The Tokugawa ruling class tried to instill in the peasants the same restrictive practice and attitude that it had imposed on samurai women. Peasant women were denied property rights, and the practice of primogeniture was enforced. In 1649 the Bakufu advised the peasants, "However good looking a wife may be, if she neglects her household duties by drinking tea or sight-seeing or rambling along the hillside, she must be divorced."[23]

The Tokugawa samurai's thinking on the male-female relationship persisted into the modern period. Even Nitobe Inazō (1862–1933), a Christian, remarked around the turn of the twentieth century that "[feudal] woman's surrender of herself to the good of her husband, home, and family was as willing and honorable as the man's self-surrender to the good of his lord and country. Self-renunciation . . . is the keynote of the loyalty of man as well as the domesticity of woman."[24]

THE CULTURE OF THE TOKUGAWA PERIOD

Literature

The literary creations of the pre-Tokugawa years were products largely of the upper classes, but during the Tokugawa period the creative energies of the common people gushed forth. This culture flourished against the wishes of the Tokugawa ruler. As one Japanese authority has indicated, "The austere and moralistic regime despised and discouraged social intercourse. . . . The Tokugawa regime stopped giving public support to all cultural activities, expelling them into a narrow, private world. . . . The leading arts, such as kabuki, ukiyo-e, the love novels, and most of the musical works, were exiled from public places and confined to the world of the pleasure quarters."[25]

The period during which the Tokugawa townspeople exhibited their creativity and vigor most dramatically was the Genroku era, which extended from the end of the seventeenth century to the beginning of the eighteenth century. During these years the townspeople not only displayed their wealth in an extravagant, ostentatious fashion but also expressed their creativity in such diverse fields as puppet theater, Kabuki, haiku, novels, woodblock printing, ceramics, and other areas of arts and crafts. What they depicted was life in the "floating world," or *ukiyo*—that is, the world of transient pleasures.

One of the most prolific writers of this period was Ihara Saikaku, who came from a merchant family. It is said that he once composed 23,500 haiku poems in twenty-four hours. Ihara wrote about the love life of the townspeople in a humorous fashion, satirizing their hedonistic life. The hero in his first novel begins his amorous exploits at the age of eight and, by the time he reaches the age of sixty, has loved 3,742 women; then he goes off in search of the fabulous Island of Women. Ihara was also a defender of the townspeople's pursuit of profits.

The townspeople were patrons of the theater; under their patronage, two forms of theater—the puppet theater *(jōruri)* and Kabuki—emerged and flourished. In Kabuki, music, dancing, acting, the story, and the visual arts are combined to entertain the audience with drama, color, and vibrancy. The colorful costumes, the elaborate stage designs, various devices such as trapdoors and revolving stages, and the exaggerated gestures and expressions of the actors in Kabuki theater made for a lively, exciting experience.

The most prominent playwright of the Tokugawa period was Chikamatsu Monzaemon, who was born into a samurai family but eventually joined the ranks of the townspeople. One of the central themes he pursued was the conflict between social imperatives *(giri)* and the demands of human feelings *(ninjō)*. The former concerns the demand that society makes upon the individual, whereas the latter pertains to the claims of the heart. An individual cannot sacrifice the interests of the society for his or her own happiness, but, at the same time, the interests of the society must be checked and humanized by ninjō. The difficulty of maintaining or reconciling the two is often resolved by suicide. In Chikamatsu's plays, lovers who are caught in this dilemma commit double suicide.

Another literary form that flourished in the Tokugawa period (and after) is the seventeen-syllable poem known as the *haiku*. Strictly speaking, the haiku was not a product of the townspeople inasmuch as it rose out of the contemplative and philosophical spirit fostered by Zen. Nevertheless, it flourished among the townspeople as they reflected upon the wonders of nature: the flowers, the moon, the birds, the insects, and so on. Explaining the brevity of haiku, Suzuki Daisetsu, a Zen philosopher, wrote, "At the supreme moment of life and death we just utter a cry or take to action, we never argue, we never give ourselves up to a lengthy talk. . . . Haiku does not express ideas but . . . it puts forward images reflecting intuition."[26]

The greatest haiku poet of this period was Matsuo Bashō (1644–1694), who, like Chikamatsu, was born into a samurai family but became a Buddhist priest and wandered about the countryside composing haiku. Whether a poem qualifies as haiku or not was demonstrated by Bashō for his disciple in the following manner. His student, seeing dragonflies in the field, composed a poem that read as follows:

Red dragonflies!
Take off their wings,
and they are pepper pods.

Bashō said, "No, that is not haiku," and composed the following:

Red pepper pods!
Add wings to them
and they are dragonflies.[27]

Issa (1763–1827), a poet who came out of the peasantry, possessed a strong sense of compassion for all living things. Seeing a fly about to be swatted, he cried out: "Oh, don't swat the fly! He wrings his hands! He wrings his feet."[28]

The Fine Arts

The concern for clarity, form, color, and placement seen in the artistic creations of Japan's earlier years continued to be shown in subsequent eras. The new element in the Tokugawa period was the creative work of the townspeople. Their noteworthy contribution to the fine arts was the woodblock print, known as *ukiyo-e,* or "painting[s] of the floating world." Ukiyo-e are not "realistic" in their depiction of scenes and people but, rather, are two-dimensional with no shading.

Among the many prominent artists in this genre was Harunobu (1725–1770), who is credited as having been the first artist to use a variety of colors in his prints. He is best known for his delicate, doll-like female figures, whose fragile nature is indicated by their abnormally small hands and feet. Utamaro (1754–1806), in contrast, is known for his sensuous, voluptuous female figures. This artist effectively used lines to create a sense of sleek, soft flesh. Finally, Sharaku (d. 1801?), who concentrated on portraying Kabuki actors, captured the exaggerated expressions and poses used by actors in climactic moments within the plays.

The two Japanese artists best known in the West are Hokusai (1760–1849) and Hiroshige (1797–1858). Hokusai, who devoted his entire life to art, successfully conveyed a sense of force and vigor in his prints by means of lines and color. When he was seventy-five, he expressed the hope that "perhaps at eighty my art may improve greatly; at ninety it may reach real depth, and at one hundred it may become divinely inspired. At one hundred and ten every dot and every stroke may be as if living."[29] He signed his works "the old man crazy about drawing."

Hiroshige is best known for his prints of the fifty-three station stops along the route from Edo to Kyoto. Most interested in the relationship between light and natural phenomena, he tried to capture the moods of nature and the atmospheric conditions of the different seasons and weather. In particular, he created beautiful snow scenes through sensitive use of blank space, and his rain scenes were made fresh and beautiful by effective use of lines.

It is interesting to note that the treatment by Hokusai and Hiroshige of light and atmosphere in their scenic color prints influenced the French impressionist painters of the nineteenth century.

The age of creativity that characterized the Genroku era and the few decades that followed also coincided with the period in which the Bakufu was beginning to feel the pressures of the growing economic crisis. We shall now turn to an investigation of this and other related problems that plagued the Bakufu for the last remaining century of its rule.

Notes

1. James Murdoch, *A History of Japan*, vol. 3 (Tokyo: Asiatic Society of Japan, 1910), p. 802.

2. In the years from 1614 to 1640, between 5,000 and 6,000 Christians were executed. In 1637–1638 a peasant rebellion against the local lord erupted in the Shimabara Peninsula and the Amakusa Islands.

3. See Herman Ooms, *Tokugawa Ideology: Early Constructs, 1570–1680* (Princeton: Princeton University Press, 1985).

4. Fung Yu-lan, *A Short History of Chinese Philosophy* (New York: Macmillan, 1953), p. 309.

5. D. T. Suzuki, *Zen and Japanese Culture* (New York: Pantheon Books, 1959), p. 78.

6. Yamamoto Tsunetomo, *Hagakure* (Hidden Among Leaves), vol. 1, ed. Shiroshima Masayoshi (Tokyo: Jimbutsu Ōraisha, 1968), pp. 27, 41.

7. Inazo Nitobe, *Bushidō* (Tokyo: Teibi Publishing, 1914), p. 1.

8. *Motoori Norinaga Zenshū* (The Complete Works of Motoori Norinaga), vol. 6 (Tokyo: Yoshikawa Hanshichi, 1900–1903), p. 219.

9. *Transactions of the Asiatic Society of Japan* 39, 1910, p. 320.

10. Masao Maruyama, *Studies in the Intellectual History of Tokugawa Japan* (Tokyo: University of Tokyo Press, 1974), p. 9.

11. The average rate of taxation was between 40 and 50 percent of the harvest, but as the economic needs of the daimyō grew, some lords took substantially more. The Bakufu, however, kept its share to 40 percent throughout its reign.

12. E. H. Norman, *Japan's Emergence as a Modern State* (New York: Institute of Pacific Relations, 1940), p. 23.

13. Ienaga Saburō, *Nihon Dōtokushisōshi* (History of Japanese Moral Thought) (Tokyo: Iwanami, 1951), p. 120.

14. Howard Hibbett, *The Floating World in Japanese Fiction* (New York: Grove Press, 1960), p. 37.

15. Mikiso Hane, *Peasants, Rebels, and Outcastes: The Underside of Modern Japan* (New York: Pantheon Books, 1982), p. 142.

16. Murasaki Shikibu, *The Tale of Genji,* trans. Arthur Waley (New York: Random House, 1960), p. 666.

17. Michael Cooper, S. J., ed., *They Came to Japan: An Anthology of European Reports on Japan, 1543–1640* (Berkeley: University of California Press, 1965), p. 62.

18. Murdoch, *A History of Japan,* vol. 3, p. 803.

19. Monzaemon Chikamatsu, *The Major Plays of Chikamatsu,* trans. Donald Keene (New York: Columbia University Press, 1961), p. 76.

20. Basil H. Chamberlain, *Things Japanese* (London: Routledge & Kegan Paul, 1939), pp. 503–505.

21. All three quotations are from Ienaga, *Nihon Dōtokushisōshi,* pp. 43–46.

22. Diana E. Wright, "Severing the Karmic Ties That Bind: The 'Divorce Temple' Mantokuji," *Monumenta Nipponica,* vol. 52, no. 3, Autumn 1997, pp. 357–380.

23. Sir George B. Sansom, *A History of Japan, 1615–1867* (Stanford: Stanford University Press, 1963), p. 99.

24. Nitobe, *Bushidō,* p. 135.

25. Masakazu Yamasaki, "Social Intercourse in Japanese Society," in *Japan Today,* ed. Kenneth A. Grossberg (Philadelphia: Institute for the Study of Human Issues, 1981), p. 66.

26. Suzuki, *Zen and Japanese Culture,* p. 240.

27. Harold G. Henderson, *An Introduction to Haiku* (Garden City, N.Y.: Doubleday, 1958), pp. 17–18.

28. Ibid., p. 133. I have substituted *swat* for *mistreat* in this translation.

29. Robert T. Paine and Alexander C. Soper, *The Art and Architecture of Japan* (Baltimore, Md.: Penguin, 1955), p. 153.

3

The Late Tokugawa Period

POLITICAL DEVELOPMENTS

In 1745, Shōgun Yoshimune turned over the shogunate to his son, Ieshige, but he remained the de facto ruler until his death in 1751. An invalid with a serious speech defect, Ieshige proved to be a rather ineffective shōgun. During the reign of the next shōgun, Ieharu, chamberlain Tanuma Okitsugu and his son became influential figures and wielded great power. In fact, during the last fourteen years of Ieharu's reign, Okitsugu, acting as senior councilor, held near dictatorial power. As a result, Ieharu's regime (1760–1786) is referred to as the Tanuma era.

Unlike Yoshimune, who sought to solve the Bakufu's economic difficulties by reducing expenses, encouraging frugality, and increasing agricultural production, Tanuma Okitsugu hoped to resolve the difficulties by debasing coinage, granting monopolistic rights to wholesale dealers in return for payment of fees, and taxing the merchant guilds. In order to reverse the unfavorable balance of trade and curb the outflow of bullion, he sought to increase exports. He also initiated various reclamation projects. There is little question that Tanuma sought to serve the public good, but there is also no doubt that he was more than casually interested in advancing his private interests in the hopes of accumulating a vast fortune. Consequently, standards of rectitude began to decline throughout the official hierarchy, and graft and bribery, though surely engaged in to some extent under previous administrations, became widespread practices. One observer noted, "Villagers rush about in agitation crying out that officials are coming to assess the tribute; for days on end shrines and temples are piled high with all kinds of rare presents for them."[1]

In spite of Tanuma's efforts to solve the Bakufu's financial difficulties, natural calamities aggravated the situation, and conditions failed to improve. A great famine broke out between 1783 and 1787, the prices of goods soared, and rice riots occurred frequently. Tanuma was blamed for most of the difficulties, and with the death of Ieharu, he was summarily removed from office.

Under Shōgun Ienari (1773–1841), Yoshimune's grandson, Matsudaira Sadanobu (1758–1829), emerged as the chief Bakufu official. Matsudaira had gained a reputation as an able and enlightened administrator when he was the head of a small han in northern Honshu. During the great famine of 1783, when hundreds of thousands of people starved in the neighboring han, he took measures to ensure that not a single person in his han died of hunger.

The treasury was nearly depleted when Matsudaira became the Bakufu's chief councilor in 1787, a year of great floods, inflation, food shortages, and rioting. To cope with the crisis, Matsudaira started what has been called the Kansei Reforms (the Kansei period, for which the reforms are named, was from 1789 to 1801). The policies that he adopted were conservative in nature and patterned after those of his grandfather, Yoshimune. He concentrated, for instance, on reducing expenditures and encouraging frugality. He also imposed price controls, but they proved to be ineffective. To be prepared to cope with future famines, he increased the Bakufu's rice reserves and required the daimyō to set aside 50 koku for every 10,000 koku of rice they collected. After reducing the expenditures of the city of Edo, he had 70 percent of the savings set aside as relief for the needy and as low-interest loans for the poor. He also established a vocational training program for the unemployed and the vagrants in Edo. In 1789, to relieve the Bakufu's vassals, he canceled all the debts to the rice brokers that they had incurred before 1784 and reduced the interest rates on those incurred after 1784.

In the hope of increasing agricultural production, Matsudaira encouraged the peasants in the cities to return to the countryside. To foster frugality he issued sumptuary laws prohibiting them from indulging in any wasteful or extravagant activities. He also attempted to impose standards of austerity on the townspeople; he even went so far as to attempt to tighten their moral values by curbing unlicensed prostitution, censoring books that he deemed prurient, and banning mixed bathing of persons over the age of six.

To cope with the rising tide of unorthodox philosophies, Matsudaira issued the Kansei ban on heterodoxy and prohibited the teaching of any philosophy other than the Zhu Xi version of Confucianism in the Bakufu's schools. He also adopted a policy of denying employment in the Bakufu to anyone who had been trained in unorthodox philosophies.

It was during this period that Russia began probing Japan's northern islands. Matsudaira was not at first concerned about this, and in fact he arrested an advocate of national defense, Hayashi Shihei, for criticizing the Bakufu for neglecting its defenses against external threats. Later he did come to recognize the need to fortify the northern coastal regions.

In spite of his strenuous efforts, Matsudaira failed to solve the basic problems of the Bakufu. He remained in office for only six years, but his puritanical asceticism managed to cramp the lifestyles of influential people in the shōgun's entourage, including the ladies in the inner palace.

Matsudaira's departure was followed by an era of laxity under the leadership of the hedonistic Ienari, who was shōgun for the more than fifty years—from 1786 to 1837. Even after his resignation, Ienari dominated the Bakufu until his death in 1841. Moral standards declined, and graft and bribery became rampant once again. Government expenditures rose along with the considerable personal expenses of the self-indulgent shōgun (he had forty wives and concubines to support). The price of rice remained low, but the cost of other commodities rose sharply. The only steps taken by the Bakufu to deal with its financial difficulties were to repeatedly debase the coinage and make requests of wealthy merchants for financial contributions. Between 1806 and 1813, the Bakufu called upon the merchants and villagers to contribute money three times, and over 1.4 million ryō was collected. The Bakufu's difficulties, however, continued to multiply as famines broke out frequently and, as we will see later, peasant uprisings increased in size and number. In addition to the internal difficulties, pressures from the outside world were becoming more serious.

After Ienari's death another attempt at reforms was made, this time by the chief councilor, Mizuno Tadakuni (1793–1851), in what is called the Tempō Reforms. Like Matsudaira, Mizuno also endeavored to tighten moral standards, reduce expenses, encourage frugality by issuing many sumptuary laws, and curtail extravagance in food and clothing. In addition, he restricted what he considered to be frivolous and wasteful activities, such as festivals, kabuki, Nō, and other forms of entertainment. He even sought to curtail the operation of pawnshops, public bathhouses, hairdressers, and the like.

Like Matsudaira, Mizuno encouraged the initiation of reclamation projects and hoped to increase agricultural production by compelling the peasants who had migrated to cities to return to their villages. In addition, he sought to curtail secondary work such as weaving because he believed that it reduced the time the peasants could spend tilling the soil.

Mizuno also sought to curb inflation by fixing wages and prices. Convinced that a free flow of goods would reduce high prices, he ended the monopolistic privileges that had been granted to the wholesalers and merchant guilds by the Tanuma administration. This, of course, resulted in the loss of the fees they had been paying the Bakufu, and to offset this reduction in revenues Mizuno found it necessary to compel the wealthy Osaka merchants to donate money to the Bakufu. As another means of increasing the Bakufu's income, he sought to bring under its direct control the land held by the bannermen and daimyō in the vicinity of Edo and Osaka. This measure, however, was so vigorously opposed by the parties concerned that he was forced to abandon it. This episode served to unite opposition against him and provided the catalyst that eventually brought about his dismissal. As was the case with Matsudaira, Mizuno's austerity program displeased many people, including the shōgun's consort. As a result, he was removed from office in 1843, only two years after he had initiated the Tempō Reforms. He made a brief comeback in 1844 but was dismissed again after a short term in office. Many of his reforms were rapidly undone soon after he fell from power.

When he was in office, Mizuno encouraged the daimyō to follow his example by urging them to institute similar reforms in their han. Many failed to respond, but some han, such as Chōshū, initiated their own reform programs. None of these attempts were very effective, but some han managed to reduce their expenses and tighten official control over the marketing of cash crops. During his tenure in office Mizuno was also very much aware of the trouble China was having with the British, and he sought to strengthen his nation's military defenses by training the warriors in Western gunnery.

All the reforms initiated by the various Bakufu officials were basically ineffective because, though they were honestly intended to solve the Bakufu's economic difficulties, they were aimed at achieving this by actually preventing changes—that is, by curbing the rising merchant class and money economy. Essentially, the reform programs pointed to a return to the predominantly agrarian, natural economy of early Tokugawa. The reformers persisted in adopting reactionary measures with the best of intentions. But sumptuary laws to enforce simple living and uplift the people's moral standards could not solve the Bakufu's financial problems, nor could these legal maneuvers prevent the disintegration of the closed society. The Bakufu thus approached the middle of the nineteenth century having failed to solve its basic economic difficulties. At this juncture it was confronted with a major external crisis that ultimately brought about its downfall—the arrival of Commodore Perry. Before I turn to this event, however, I will examine more closely the economic difficulties of Tokugawa society.

ECONOMIC PROBLEMS

The basic cause of Tokugawa society's problems lay in the fact that the economy was supported by an agrarian base that, though expanded, was not sufficiently broad to meet either the increasing needs of the ruling class, whose size and standard of living did not remain static, or the rising expectations of the common classes. From the end of the seventeenth century, in particular, commerce began to grow, thus creating an economy evermore incompatible with agrarianism.

Large urban centers emerged, and the demand not only for basic necessities but also for what the ruling authorities regarded as luxury goods steadily increased. To meet the needs of the cities, the production of nonessential agricultural and industrial goods had to increase, and consequently, the number and size of local business entrepreneurs, wholesale dealers, and shippers grew. The sankin kōtai system also served to stimulate economic growth by increasing commercial and industrial activities along the routes that the daimyō crossed in their travels to and from Edo. There were, necessarily, growing expenditures that the daimyō sought to meet by fostering the production of cash crops and industrial goods that could be marketed to other han. Now that a greater variety and better quality of fabrics, utensils, household goods, and art objects were available, the taste and standard of living of the samurai as well as the wealthier people in towns and villages rose substantially. Such improvements, however, also tended to raise the level of expectation of other segments of the society. An increased imbalance between income and expenditures resulted. Despite the fact that rice production grew at a rate greater than the increase in population, instead of enjoying an augmented sense of ease and satisfaction, the people became increasingly restless about an economic and financial situation they found uncomfortable and dissatisfying.

We now turn to an examination of the problems confronting the daimyō and the samurai. Ogyū Sorai observed in the 1720s that whereas thirty or forty years earlier lower-class samurai never wore formal ceremonial suits and were unable to furnish their houses with *tatami* (reed mats), they now not only had better household furnishings and fancy formal suits, but their hair smelled of perfume and their sword guards were decorated with gold and silver inlays.

To be sure, the daimyō were certainly enjoying much greater luxury if the samurai were living in better houses and wearing finer clothing. According to Sorai,

In the way in which they comport themselves throughout the day, in their garments, food and drink, household furnishings, dwellings, employment of servants, the conduct of their wives, the retinues that accompany them, the manner in which they travel, the ceremonies of coming of age, marriage and burial—in all these matters they naturally tend to be extravagant in accordance with the trend of the times.[2]

The samurai and the daimyō needed more money to maintain their more elaborate style of living, and their financial needs were made evermore acute by the recurrent periods of inflation that beset the land. The monetary problems of the daimyō were further intensified by the need to defray the cost of traveling back and forth to Edo and maintaining two residences, one in the home province and one in Edo.[3]

The Bakufu added to the financial burdens of the daimyō by requiring them, whenever it felt the need to do so, to participate in public works and other expensive tasks. Saga han, for example, devoted 4 percent of its expenditures to guarding Nagasaki. In 1754, Satsuma, already in debt for 800,000 ryō, was asked to assist in the construction of a water-control project along the Kiso River in central Honshu. Participation in the project made it necessary for Satsuma to raise more than 200,000 ryō. To obtain the money, the already overtaxed peasants had to be taxed even further. After the completion of the project, the Satsuma official in charge committed seppuku to atone for the hardships inflicted upon the people.

In addition to these expenses, the daimyō's financial difficulties were aggravated by such calamitous events as floods, droughts, famines, and fires. Consequently, many han were continuously plagued with budgetary deficits.

There were only a limited number of ways in which the daimyō could cope with the rising costs of their personal and public needs. One way was to borrow from wealthy merchants, and there were, in fact, some merchant houses that specialized in loaning money to the daimyō and samurai. An interesting example of this was Yodoya Tatsugorō, whose wealth was legendary. So many daimyō had fallen deeply in debt to him that the Bakufu finally confiscated his fortune in 1705. The ostensible reason given for this action was that he was living in an outrageously extravagant fashion, far beyond the limits suitable to a person of his social status.

The Kōnoike family records showed that in 1706 its loans to the daimyō totaled over 278,000 ryō, and by 1795 this amount had risen to more than 416,000 ryō. After the Tokugawa era, the descendants of one merchant family found three cases full of certificates of loans to daimyō amounting to 10 million ryō.

To extricate the daimyō and the samurai from their indebtedness, the Bakufu sought to compel the merchants to settle for less than full payment of outstanding loans. In some instances it called for the total cancellation of long-standing debts, inflicting great losses upon the merchants.[4] These measures naturally caused many merchant houses to become bankrupt and induced others to become extremely wary about loaning money to military men. This in turn forced the daimyō and the samurai to abandon their traditional attitude of superiority and appeal to the wealthy merchants for money with lowered heads. In order to cultivate the goodwill of the merchants, they gave them seasonal gifts, extended special commercial privileges, and accorded them the rights of the samurai, such as the rights to bear swords and receive stipends.

The subservience of the warrior class to wealthy merchants led one contemporary observer to remark, "When the great merchants of Osaka get angry, the feudal barons of the land quake with fear."[5] Another commentator wrote, "Both large and small daimyō . . . are constantly plagued by their creditors to pay their debts and have no peace of mind worrying about how to make excuses. They fear the sight of moneylenders as if they were demons. Forgetting that they are samurai, they bow and scrape to the townspeople."[6]

Another way in which the daimyō sought to increase their revenues was to tax peasants more heavily. There was a limit, however, to this approach. Peasants were known to rise up against their masters when tax burdens became "excessive" in their minds. A han could ill afford to have a peasant tax revolt because the Bakufu was wont to use such uprisings in order to punish the han administrators. Some han made occasional tax reassessments to take into account the increase in rice production, but there is some evidence to indicate that in many han this was not actually done because of the laborious tasks involved in making thoroughgoing surveys. To compound the issue, peasants grew to be very adept at hiding increased yields, especially of "cash crops." Surplus rice and soybeans could be converted into sake or soy sauce *(shoyu)*, which were easier to hide than grains. Upland and dry fields could be converted to small plots of mulberry (for silk production), cotton, or vegetables to be sold in nearby castletowns. Many daimyō followed the example of the Bakufu reformers and periodically attempted to reduce their expenses by implementing austerity programs, but these measures repeatedly failed to solve their financial problems. Some daimyō sought to cope with their difficulties by reducing the samurai's stipends, but naturally this only worsened the already serious plight of the samurai. Some other measures that were resorted to were the extraction of forced loans from the merchants and the issuance of currencies valid only in the han.

The daimyō did adopt some measures that yielded very positive results. Many han attempted to increase their revenues by expanding agricultural production. They reclaimed wastelands, initiated water-control projects, built irrigation systems, and introduced improved methods of farming and better strains of seed. The acreage under cultivation was substantially increased, and greater yield per unit of land was achieved. It appears, however, that even this increased agricultural yield failed to meet the growing expenditures of the Bakufu and the han.

Another positive measure that was adopted by the Bakufu and the han was to foster production of crops and handicraft goods that could be marketed to other han. As a result, many han came to be known for special products. Some han even concentrated on the production of high-quality rice with the intention of competing more effectively for the urban rice market. Many han were known for their textiles, pottery, timber, and fish, whereas other han managed to produce commodities not readily available elsewhere, such as salt, sugar, indigo, wax, tea, and paper. Villages near major cities like Edo concentrated on producing vegetables for the urban consumers. Some han exploited the mineral resources that had not been claimed by the Bakufu. A few han in the south and the west managed to increase their revenues by engaging in trade with Korea and the Ryukyu Islands.[7]

In marketing the commercial and industrial crops many han either established han monopolies or granted monopolistic rights to selected entrepreneurs. To compete effectively with other han and increase their own revenues, han authorities paid the producers of the cash crops minimum prices. This frequently became a source of conflict between peasants and authorities.

Virtually every han experimented with various types of fertilizer to increase crop production. Human feces had always been combined with "green" waste (chopped weeds, leaves, etc.) in the countryside, but by the mid-eighteenth century, a commercial "nightsoil" industry existed outside almost every castle-town. At first, peasants volunteered to cart nightsoil away from urban privies in order to use the offal as fertilizer on their own fields. After a time, some entrepreneurs began to offer small gifts (vegetables, straw handicrafts, etc.) to the urban landlords in order to establish a monopoly over these privies. Before long, there were a number of urban networks of nightsoil purveyors in large cities. Fishers along most of Japan's extensive coast produced dried fishmeal as commercial fertilizer as well.[8]

The Bakufu and the daimyō were feeling the pressures of rising expenditures, but the samurai felt the imbalance between income and outlay even more acutely. As noted earlier, the samurai had also become accustomed to a more elegant way of life. Their expenses were growing, and their economic woes were further intensified by the fact that they had a fixed income in rice, even though the price of rice tended to drop in time of abundant harvest. The price of other commodities, however, not only did not drop but in some instances rose.

Another economic development that hurt the samurai was the policy adopted by the Bakufu and some daimyō to withhold a certain amount of rice stipends from time to time. In Chōshū as early as 1646, the retainers were asked to "loan" one-fifth of their stipends to the han. Later the amount was raised to one-third and then to one-half of their stipends. These were meant to be only temporary measures, but such reductions often lasted for years.[9] This practice, which was also followed by other han, forced the samurai to fall deeper and deeper into debt and had the effect of weakening the samurai's sense of loyalty to their lords, who, they felt, were failing in their duty to provide them with adequate means of living. A critic at the end of the eighteenth century observed, "Some daimyō have now ceased to pay their retainers their basic stipends. These men have had half their property confiscated by the daimyō as well, and hate them so much that they find it impossible to contain their ever-accumulating resentment."[10]

Occasionally the samurai would be aided when the Bakufu and the daimyō ordered a cancellation of debts, but before long they were heavily in debt again because the basic situation remained unchanged. Consequently, the poorer samurai were reduced to selling their military equipment, and there are instances of a few who even sold their daughters. Some turned to banditry, but the most common solution open to a lower-class samurai was to engage in some sort of handicraft work such as repairing umbrellas, lanterns, wooden clogs, or household utensils. This kind of menial work was considered beneath their dignity, but they were compelled to do it to survive. It was not uncommon for some samurai to establish family ties with merchant houses as a means of escape from financial problems. A samurai might adopt a young man from a merchant family or permit his son to marry a merchant's daughter.

In addition, peacetime conditions had brought about a deterioration in the warriors' moral standards. Many samurai began to frequent places of entertainment—brothels and the theaters—that existed primarily for the pleasure of the townspeople. It was estimated that in the middle of the eighteenth century 70 percent of the patrons of Edo's brothels were samurai. One observer, bemoaning the moral decay of the samurai, surmised that seven or eight samurai out of ten were effete weaklings.

To some extent, the economic distresses and consequent changes in moral standards of the ruling class tended to blur the social distinctions between the samurai and the chonin classes. At the same time, the bonds between the lord and his followers were weakened. These changes, together with the penetration of commercial interests into the rural areas and the growing unrest of the peasantry, were beginning to strain the existing social and political order.

THE LOT OF THE PEASANTS

The peasantry was the segment of society that supported the national economy and endured hardships and miseries in silence. The expanding money economy was affecting them most adversely, and, after the Genroku era, as the Bakufu and the daimyō faced growing financial difficulties, the plight of the peasants appeared to worsen as they were taxed even more heavily.

The infiltration of money and commercial economy into the villages also meant the penetration of Genroku culture. This was true despite the attempts of the Bakufu to keep the villages insulated from the more extravagant ways of the cities. As might be expected, the desire for better living conditions grew among the peasants, and they began to purchase items that the authorities re-garded as luxury goods. They also needed money to buy fertilizers and agricul-tural implements. Their expenses were rising at the same time that the authorities in many han were increasing the rate of taxation in order to meet their growing expenses. This situation became even more serious when, in some instances, the peasants were compelled to pay taxes several years in ad-vance. As was noted previously, there were also numerous additional taxes be-sides those levied on the rice crop. The peasants were also subject to corvée, the most burdensome being the obligation to provide men and horses for the courier or horse station system.

There is some indication that the ruling class was not uniformly ruthless in its financial demands, but this is not to say that the taxation was not burden-some. Some daimyō, in fact, raised the tax rate to exceed 50 percent, and in a few extreme cases, peasants were forced to pay 70 percent of the harvest. It should be noted that although many daimyō revised the method of assessment to increase the tax yields, the han in the poorer sections of the north and in the mountainous areas were especially stringent in exacting taxes. In contrast, the Bakufu retained its taxation rate of 40 percent.[11]

Abuses occurred in all the han when ambitious officials sought to impress their lords by increasing the tax yields. At the same time, however, there were officials who sought to further and protect the interests of the people and gained renown as practitioners of "benevolent rule."

An important point to consider in assessing the tax burden on the peasants is the fact that no nationwide land survey was made after the Kambun and Empō eras (1661–1681). The area under cultivation, however, had been steadily expanded through reclamation, and the productivity per acre of land was increased substantially through the years by better plant varieties, greater use of fertilizers, and improved methods of farming.[12] In light of the fact that no nationwide land survey had been made since the latter half of the seven-teenth century, it is possible that the amount of rice and other crops left in the hands of the villagers may not have decreased, even though the tax rates rose. Moreover, in order to encourage the reclamation of wastelands the officials were usually willing to overlook the fact that taxes were not paid on reclaimed plots, or else they imposed only a nominal levy. One study of eleven widely scattered villages indicates that from around 1700 to 1850 the official assess-ment of productivity varied very little; that is, there was no substantial move-ment upward. The same was true of the tax rate—no significant changes had occurred in these villages. This, of course, was a period during which produc-tivity was still increasing.

It would appear, then, that in spite of the financial pressures facing them, the Bakufu and many daimyō did not tax the peasants as severely as they might have. The growing determination of the peasants to resist additional levies and arbitrary measures may have been partially responsible for this. Furthermore, the changing attitude of the villagers perhaps accounts for the increase in uprisings at a time when the standard of living of the peasants may have been higher than that of their ancestors who lived during the early stages of Tokugawa rule.

There are also strong indications that the larger amount of rice and other products that remained in the villages after taxation did not benefit all the villagers equally, but was in fact primarily directed to the advantage of wealthier members. The villagers who were likely to increase the yield per acre and to enlarge their holdings through land reclamation were the wealthier farmers. This was the case because of the additional expenses and labor needed for such undertakings. These wealthy and thus prominent villagers were the ones to hold the key village posts, and this enabled them to determine each producer's share of taxation. It appears that in many villages increased yields and greater holdings were not taken into account in allocating each producer's share of the tax burden.

The fact that the wealthier villagers benefited from the taxation system is reflected in the many complaints lodged by the poorer peasants that they were being taxed more heavily than the rich. The clash of interests can also be seen in the growing number of peasant disturbances that were directed against the headmen and other prominent villagers. This is in sharp contrast to the many earlier disturbances, which were led by the village leaders to protest the policies of the Bakufu or han officials.

The rising rate of tenancy also indicates that the gap between the rich and poor peasants was widening. It was illegal to buy or sell land, but this law was frequently circumvented; some merchants even purchased land in the villages. Most of the land that belonged to the poorer peasants, however, passed into the hands of the wealthy villagers who held mortgages on the fields of impoverished farmers. The percentage of tenancy varied greatly from place to place, but it is estimated that in areas where the commercial economy had penetrated deeply, that is, near the major cities and the main roads, it had risen to 50 percent by the nineteenth century. Accompanying the increase in tenant farmers was an increase in the number of hired workers on the larger farms and in the village handicraft industries. A further indication of the growing disparity of wealth in the villages can be seen in the changing pattern of landholding: the number of large and very small holdings increased, whereas medium-size holdings decreased.

The wealthier villagers, in addition to enhancing their wealth through greater productivity per acre and acquisition of more land, began to invest their money in the commercial and industrial enterprises that were developing in the rural areas. Many were already involved in traditional commercial activities such as lending money and selling daily necessities (e.g., sake, salt, soy sauce, oil) to the villagers. Now some began to participate in such "manufacturing" enterprises as spinning, weaving, pottery making, and other handicraft industries. Others ventured into the business of marketing the cash and industrial goods that were produced in their villages. At the same time, urban merchants came to the villages to market the crops and became members of the rural communities. The consequence was the development of a group of rural dwellers, known as *gōnōshō* (rich farmer/businessman), who came into existence in villages that were affected strongly by the commercial economy.

An early-nineteenth-century observer made the following remarks concerning the growing disparity between the rich and the poor villagers: "The wealthy farmers have forgotten their rank, have been given the right to have surnames, wear swords or even have yearly allowances. They are addicted to wearing beautiful clothes, practice military arts, study Chinese books and poetry, and even call courtesans from the prosperous centres to their homes."[13] Essentially, then, they were living like members of the samurai class. In sharp contrast, the poorer farmers, he noted, were falling deeper into debt and losing their land. In the less productive sections of the country, poorer peasants found it difficult to raise a family and resorted to infanticide and abortion. A social critic writing in the later stages of the Tokugawa era claimed that in the northern provinces the number of children killed annually exceeded 60,000 or 70,000.

The fact that the population remained stable and even decreased from time to time after the eighteenth century indicates that a large percentage of the peasantry led a marginal existence. In 1721 the population of the common classes was officially noted to be 26 million. It fluctuated between 25 million and 27 million from that date until the end of the Tokugawa era.[14] Figures prior to 1721 are not available, but if we accept an estimated figure of 18 million for the period 1573–1591, it is conceivable that the population increased by 10 million from the end of the sixteenth century to the beginning of the eighteenth. The population during the latter half of the Tokugawa era was held down by periodic famines and epidemics and by abortion and infanticide.[15]

Mass starvation resulted whenever there were serious crop failures, which were caused by droughts, excessive rainfall, floods, typhoons, cold weather, or locusts. There were in all thirty-five famines in the Edo period. In 1732, for example, swarms of locusts descended upon western Japan, practically ruining the entire rice crop of that region.[16] In 1755 cold weather destroyed the crops in the north, and as a result, in one han alone it was reported that one out of five persons died of starvation. In 1773 droughts preceded a plague that claimed the lives of 200,000 people. The death toll rose as the plague spread through the northern provinces, with Sendai han reporting the loss of 300,000 people. This was followed by the great Temmei famine that began in 1783 and lasted until 1787. It was caused by continuous bad weather: excessive rainfall, unseasonably cold weather, and drought. The year the famine started, Mount Asama in central Japan erupted, causing much death and destruction. The bad weather and persistent crop failures continued year after year, and the northern provinces, which were again affected most seriously, experienced such mass starvation that the people were finally reduced to practicing cannibalism. No accurate figure is available on the number of people who starved to death in the Temmei famine, but one contemporary observer wrote, "During the three years of bad crops and famine which occurred since 1783, over two million people in Ōu Province alone starved to death."[17] This is an overestimation, but it is believed that several hundred thousand persons did perish, and much of the northern region remained uninhabited and untilled for years.

In the Tempō era another major famine occurred that lasted from 1833 to 1836. Once again, the northern provinces were most severely affected. Tsugaru han, which was said to have lost 80,000 persons in a single year during the Temmei famine, lost an additional 45,000.

The effects of these famines and catastrophes are reflected in the decreases in the population that followed each major outbreak.[18]

PEASANT UPRISINGS

The peasants did not remain completely passive when confronted with the rigid control and exploitation by the ruling class, growing economic hardships, and periodic disasters. There was little they could do about natural calamities, but they could and did protest against abuses on the part of the officials and demand relief in times of famine and disaster.

Recent studies show that between 1590 and 1867 there were 2,809 peasant disturbances. During the early years of Tokugawa rule these disturbances tended to occur more frequently in the poorer regions. Later on, however, they began to break out increasingly often in the more advanced areas, thus indicating that the penetration of commercial economy was causing difficulties in the villages. The number of peasant uprisings rose significantly in the latter half of the Edo period.[19]

The protest movements took various forms. The peasants could, of course, submit petitions through regular channels, but such actions were ineffective since they could be blocked so readily at the lower levels. Illegal actions took the form of mass flights into another lord's domain, forceful demonstrations, violent uprisings, and submission of petitions that bypassed the lower authorities and went directly to the daimyō or Bakufu. With the passage of time, the protest movements tended to grow increasingly violent, and from about 1710 forceful demonstrations and violent uprisings constituted between 40 and 50 percent of all protests. The houses and warehouses of the rich farmers, merchants, and moneylenders were frequently the objects of attack.

In a study of 2,755 peasant outbursts, it was determined that taxation, having been named in 628 of the incidents, was the most prevalent cause of violent action.[20]

During the latter half of the Tokugawa era, the number of participants and the areas covered by the disturbances tended to grow in scope. In 1738, some 84,000 peasants in Iwaki province in the north participated in a demonstration against excessive taxation. In 1754, some 168,000 peasants were involved in an outburst against unfair taxation in Kurume han in Kyushu. Ten years later, 200,000 peasants in the Kantō region rioted to protest the burdens of corvée in the horse stations. Following the Temmei famine, violent uprisings that involved thousands of peasants broke out with increasing frequency. One major riot in the nineteenth century was the 1831 uprising in Chōshū, where 100,000 peasants rioted, demanding a reduction in taxes and protesting the han's monopolistic policy in marketing industrial crops.

It is interesting to speculate why peasant unrest grew in the latter half of the Tokugawa period when, compared with the first half, more food and other commodities were available. The population remained more or less stable after the eighteenth century, and rice production increased somewhat, so there must have been more food to go around.[21] A partial answer is found in the fact that this was the time when the three major famines of the Edo period occurred: the Kyōho famine of 1732–1733, the Temmei famine of 1783–1787, and the Tempō famine of 1833–1836. In the decade or so during and following these major famines, the number of peasant disturbances increased significantly.

This period of increasing unrest also coincided with the growing financial difficulties of the Bakufu and the han. The various measures they adopted to cope with the situation, such as the Kyōho, Kansei, and Tempō Reforms, caused the people inconvenience and hardship. The growth of commercial economy and its consequent effects in the villages also gave rise to unrest by causing dislocations in the countryside. The economic difficulties caused by opening the country to the West touched off a large number of peasant disturbances in the 1860s. We have already made note of the growing conflict between the wealthier villagers and poorer peasants, which also contributed to the increase in agrarian troubles.

Another possible contributing factor that should not be overlooked is that the peasants were getting bolder in challenging the ruling class because the latter had lost some of its militaristic qualities. The samurai were no longer hardy warriors; they were more like gentleman-scholars who had been softened by urban living. Very few samurai lived in the villages where the peasants lived, and when these outsiders did appear it was only to collect taxes. Finally, the greater productivity and the improved standard of living being enjoyed by the village leaders and the townspeople must have had the double effect of raising the expectations of the peasants while making them more militant.

In some instances the protestors did succeed in gaining concessions and in having their grievances redressed; but, in all cases of violent or illegal action, the leaders were arrested and punished because any sort of conspiracy or group action was strictly prohibited. In order to ferret out the instigators, the suspected leaders were tortured cruelly and forced to confess. They were then beheaded or crucified. Some were buried alive.

The peasant uprisings were not motivated by any desire to change the social or political order. They were simply protest actions calling for redress of specific grievances. The peasants remained politically unsophisticated partly because of the Bakufu's success in keeping them isolated and politically ignorant. The rulers followed the adage that "the peasants should not be informed but should be made to depend upon the ruling class." Peasant riots did break out, particularly in the Kantō and northern regions, when the Bakufu was being overthrown by the imperial forces. These were called *yonaoshi ikki,* uprisings to reform the society, but they were isolated actions directed primarily against the wealthy villagers. In addition, there were certain areas around Kyoto where large concentrations of Pureland Buddhists *(ikko)* were predisposed to self-government. These largely egalitarian (even allowing female leaders in some areas) peasants were more prone to revolt against their feudal leaders over issues not directly concerned with economic problems.

It was not only the peasants who were forced to resort to violence because of economic difficulties; the urban poor also began to stage violent demonstrations. Inflationary prices and food shortages were the primary causes for these urban riots, which were usually directed against the rice and sake merchants and the pawnbrokers.

Prior to the Kyōho (1716–1736) era, only eight urban disturbances had occurred, and only one of these involved any violence. After 1717, however, 332 instances of urban conflict were recorded, and most of them entailed rioting and violence. One of the most widespread urban rice riots occurred late in the spring of 1787 in the wake of the Temmei crop failures and famine, when 50 separate violent incidents broke out in cities throughout the country.

The Tempō famine also touched off rice riots in the cities, where shortages and inflated prices caused rampant hunger and starvation. This series of disturbances culminated in a major uprising in 1837 in Osaka, which was led by a former police officer and a Wang Yang-ming scholar, Ōshio Heihachirō

(1792–1837). Ōshio was outraged at the indifference of the Osaka city commissioners and the rich merchants, such as Mitsui and Kōnoike, to whom he had unsuccessfully appealed for help. Instead of taking any positive action to alleviate the unfair conditions, one of the city commissioners accused Ōshio of violating the ban on making direct appeals to higher officials. Ōshio, as a result, decided that the only course left to him was to lead the people in an uprising against the rich and the established authorities. He had only about three hundred followers, largely impoverished townspeople and peasants from nearby villages, but they managed to set fire to one-fifth of the city. The uprising was quickly crushed, and he was forced to take his own life.

Urban disturbances continued to break out. The crisis facing the Bakufu and established authorities became acute after the advent of Perry, and the number of urban riots increased. Seventy such outbursts were recorded between 1854 and the fall of the Bakufu.

AGRICULTURAL IMPROVEMENTS

Agricultural production, as noted earlier, did not remain static during the Tokugawa period. A variety of factors contributed to the increased yields in rice and other crops. The variety of plants increased considerably, and it is estimated that the number of rice varieties swelled from about 175 in the early seventeenth century to over 2,000 by the mid-nineteenth century. Irrigation systems were improved with wider use being made of water wheels and treadmills. In the northern and Kantō regions, sericulture (silk) became important as a supplementary source of rural income. As suggested previously, commercial fertilizers also contributed to increases in crop production.

The production of commercial and industrial crops began to increase throughout the country. Cotton, indigo, sugarcane, tobacco, silkworms, tea, wax tree, and so forth were produced by the peasants to supplement their income or at the behest of their lords. Despite the increasing production of cash crops and growing commercial activities, Tokugawa Japan was still predominantly an agricultural country, not a commercial one.[22]

The fishing industry remained an important part of the Tokugawa economy, as did mining, forestry, and the various handicraft industries. Somewhat larger production facilities, especially in textiles, were emerging at the end of the era. Commercial capital began to enter the process of production to some extent, and the more advanced areas of the economy were showing signs of industrial growth. Sake and *shoyu* (soy sauce) brewers brought commercial ventures into largely rural areas. They were wont to establish money-lending and commodity futures (buying crops even before they were planted to ensure supply at constant prices) schemes in these areas. In view of the overall picture, however, all these changes were not really significant enough to affect the fundamentally agrarian character of the economy.

Not many Tokugawa thinkers concerned themselves with the practical aspects of farming, but there were a few who did. Among the more notable of these were Ōhara Yūgaku (1797–1858) and Ninomiya Sontoku (1787–1856). Ōhara, although born into a samurai family, was disowned for having killed a man in a duel and spent years wandering around the country. He finally settled in a village in the Kantō region, just as the Tempō famine broke out. Deeply distressed at the suffering of the peasantry, he sought to devise ways in which to assist them. In 1838 he organized a cooperative credit union encompassing four villages. Each member was required to transfer to the cooperative a plot of land worth five ryō, and the profits from this land were then put into a fund that was to be used to assist the members in time of need. Ōhara also introduced better methods of farming and initiated a land improvement program. In addition, he sought to instill a wholesome outlook into the peasantry and taught that the nature of things and the Way were fixed by the unity of Heaven and Earth. The common people too were created by this unity, so they were obliged to follow the Way. This consisted in practicing filial piety, adhering to one's station in life, and respecting the samurai.

In spite of his positive contributions to agrarian life, and his essentially pro-establishment philosophy, Ōhara was accused by the authorities of disturbing the existing order in the village and of exceeding his proper station in life by daring to propagate his own philosophy. He was forced to dissolve the cooperative before being incarcerated. After his release he committed seppuku.

The other agrarian reformer, Ninomiya Sontoku, referred to as the "peasant sage of Japan," was born into a peasant family and remained a tiller of the soil and a spokesman for the peasantry all his life. His family was plunged into the depth of poverty by the Temmei famine and a destructive typhoon. Through hard work, Ninomiya more than restored the family fortune and became a minor landlord of four chō. Like Ōhara he also sought to help his fellow peasants improve their lot. He taught them the importance of long-range planning and advised them to make an annual budget in which they always planned to spend less than they expected to make. He also proposed the establishment of voluntary credit unions, a suggestion that was adopted by a fairly large number of villages in Sagami, where Ninomiya came from, as well as in the neighboring provinces. He was active in relief work during the Tempō famine, and as he gained renown as an agrarian expert he was sought out by many han to assist in revitalizing villages that had fallen into decay.

Ninomiya believed that the peasants must be instilled with a philosophy of life that would be fitting to them while enhancing their well-being. Each person, he taught, owes his existence and well-being to his ancestors and society and, therefore, has as his duty the following of the doctrine of Repayment of Virtue, which calls for hard work, thrift, and sharing what one can with others. Ninomiya's interpretations of the Way of Heaven and the Way of Man were pragmatic and utilitarian: the Way of Heaven is the way of nature as seen in the physical world; the Way of Man is fixed by man's necessity to survive in nature. Thus, the Way of Man tells us "rice is good and weeds are bad; to build a house is good, to destroy it is bad. . . . All that is convenient for man is good and all that is inconvenient is bad."[23]

Unlike other Tokugawa-era thinkers, Ōhara and Ninomiya concerned themselves with practical problems and not with theoretical or idealistic moral concepts. This propensity to direct one's attention to practical matters came to be manifested increasingly in the intellectual world of the late Edo period.

INTELLECTUAL CURRENTS: REFORMERS AND CRITICS

During the latter half of the Tokugawa regime, heterodox views came to be embraced by a growing number of thinkers, and Zhu Xi philosophy, the official ideology, no longer dominated the intellectual scene. The Kansei edict prohibiting heterodox studies was issued in 1790 by Matsudaira Sadanobu, and it was intended to combat the rising tide of unorthodox points of view. It could, however, neither curb opinions critical of official policies nor restrict the diffusion of non–Zhu Xi, or for that matter non-Confucian, philosophies.

There were several schools of thought among the heterodox thinkers. Of course these cannot all be neatly classified into fixed categories, but for the sake of convenience we can list the following: the school of thought that was influenced by Dutch or Western learning; the pragmatic, rationalistic critics of the existing order; the nationalists of the Mito school; and the nationalists of the school of National Learning.

The school of Dutch learning *(rangaku)* came into existence after 1720, when the Bakufu relaxed its ban against Western books and permitted works not containing Christian ideas to enter the country. This led a small circle of interested scholars to begin studying Dutch in order to become acquainted with Western science. Japanese-Dutch dictionaries were compiled, and these men started to pursue such subjects as astronomy, physics, electricity, plant studies, cartography, geography, and medicine. The pioneer students of this school included Aoki Konyō (1698–1769), who compiled a dictionary of the Dutch language that he completed in 1758, and Hiraga Gennai (1729–1779), a versatile man who was interested not only in Western science but also in playwriting and Western painting. In his scientific work he engaged in botanical studies, conducted experiments in electricity, produced asbestos, and made a thermometer. He also taught Western painting, and among his students was

Shiba Kōkan (1738–1818), who became the foremost exponent of the Western style of painting.

The Bakufu was interested in encouraging the study of astronomy and built an observatory in Edo in 1744. Surveying and cartography were also studied at this center, and it was through mastery of these fields that Inō Tadataka (1745–1818) managed to survey the entire Japanese coastline and produce an accurate map of the country. Among early advocates of the Copernican theory were Miura Baien (1723–1789) and Shiba Kōkan. Miura, though a Confucian scholar, developed a naturalistic philosophy that departed from the traditional theoretical explanation of the nature of things. He believed that the principles underlying the natural world could be understood only by studying things in the physical world and not by projecting assumptions about human nature onto the natural world. He emphasized the importance of developing a thoroughgoing spirit of inquiry and skepticism, but the comprehensive system of logic that he formulated was too complex to be easily understood by his contemporaries. It was not until very recently that his position in the history of Japanese thought as a unique and original thinker came to be appreciated.

The science that had the greatest influence on the fostering of Dutch studies was medicine. Among the pioneers in this field were Maeno Ryōtaku (1723–1803) and Sugita Gempaku (1733–1817). In 1771 they had an opportunity to watch a dissection being performed, and they were thus able, through direct observation, to compare the human anatomy with illustrations and descriptions in a Dutch book on anatomy. They were profoundly impressed by the accuracy of the Dutch work and so appalled at the erroneous notions they had formerly held that they set about translating the Dutch text, which they had published in 1774. This was the first openly circulated Dutch book that was translated into Japanese, and it did much to arouse the interest of fellow scholars.

Dutch studies were advanced significantly when Philipp Franz von Siebold, a young German doctor, arrived in 1823 to serve as a medical officer at the Dutch factory in Nagasaki. He was allowed to open a clinic and a medical school outside the city, and it was here that he taught fifty-seven Japanese medical students. In 1828, Siebold got into trouble with the authorities when it was discovered that he was planning to take a map of Japan with him on his projected trip back to Europe. He was expelled from the country as a suspected spy, but he was able to return in 1859 after Japan opened its doors to the West.

The Confucians began to attack Dutch studies as interest in them mounted. Ōtsuki Gentaku (1757–1827), an advocate of Dutch learning, responded as follows to the critics: "Dutch learning is not perfect, but if we choose the good points and follow them, what harm could come of that?

What is more ridiculous than to refuse to discuss its merits and cling to one's forte without changing."[24] The scholars of Dutch studies grew increasingly critical of the Bakufu's anachronistic policy of seclusion and began as a result to experience growing official hostility. These men were bringing about an expanded awareness of the outside world and had become a force that could not be ignored.

Russian movements in the north along with stories about European activities in the rest of Asia induced some Japanese thinkers to turn their attention to the problems of national defense. They also considered, though usually in private, the policies that they thought Japan should adopt in coping with foreign powers. Hayashi Shihei (1738–1793) was one of the first of these thinkers to call for the adoption of appropriate defense measures to meet the impending threat from abroad. He urged the use of Western military science and arms, especially cannons, to repel foreign naval vessels. The Bakufu, then under the direction of Matsudaira Sadanobu, arrested him for publishing a book dealing with the affairs of state, but he had already set a precedent for such discussions, which others were to follow. In the nineteenth century Takano Chōei (1804–1850), who had studied under Siebold, and Watanabe Kazan (1793–1841), who was a student of the Dutch language, an accomplished painter, and an experienced administrator, expressed their disagreement with the Bakufu's policy of driving away all foreign ships approaching Japanese shores. For this they were both persecuted and driven to suicide.

The practical and rational critics and analysts of Tokugawa society had acquired, in addition to what was noted earlier about Dutch learning, some knowledge about the West. One of these men, Honda Toshiaki (1744–1821), favored development of foreign trade and colonization in order to strengthen Japan's economy. He believed that the government was responsible for the economic miseries of the people, and he was convinced that the ruling class had to provide vigorous leadership to change Japan into a wealthy, industrial nation like some of the European countries.

Honda believed that in order to strengthen the economy, centralized control had to be established. He felt it was particularly important to bring shipping and trade under state control. "As long as there are no government-owned ships and the merchants have complete control over transport and trade," he wrote, "the economic conditions of the samurai and farmers grow steadily worse."[25] In foreign policy he favored an expansionist course of action and bemoaned the fact that Hokkaido, Sakhalin, and Kamchatka were not being colonized. "Since," he wrote, "it is a national obligation to attempt to increase the size of the country, even if this involves invading other countries, it makes me speechless with despair when I realize that we have permitted all of our possessions to be snatched away by another country."[26] His desire was to make Japan "the greatest nation in the world." Honda was highly critical of the Bakufu and favored drastic changes, but because he did not publicize his ideas, he did not encounter any difficulties from the authorities. Consequently, he also failed to exert much influence on the thinking of his age.

It is interesting to note that men like Honda and Satō Nobuhiro (1769–1850) already recognized key concepts about the necessity of adopting Western science and technology and the importance of developing the nation's economy for military purposes—an idea that was to have full sway in the early Meiji period. Satō had studied Dutch and was interested in a variety of practical subjects. He was also seriously concerned about the external threat and was deeply disturbed by China's defeat in the Opium War. Like Honda, he believed in strengthening the economy in order to strengthen the nation; that is, he believed in what came to be known as a policy of *fukoku kyōhei* (enrich and strengthen the nation). Satō served as an adviser to Senior Councilor Mizuno Tadakuni and to several daimyō, so his ideas received the attention of the ruling authorities. His proposal for drastic economic reorganization was not adopted, but when the Bakufu sought to regulate the economy more stringently after 1855, it is believed that Satō's ideas had something to do with it.

In order to revitalize Japan's economy, he advocated the establishment of a highly centralized totalitarian government that would have the authority to control the entire economic life of the society while fully utilizing and completely regulating all natural and human resources. He suggested that the country's industries be divided into eight divisions with every person being assigned to a given occupation and strictly forbidden from engaging in any other work. The existing political order and the class system were to be abolished, of course, and the ruler given autocratic powers that would allow him to "manage freely the entire nation of Japan as if it were his hands and feet."[27] Satō, under the influence of the Shinto nationalism of Hirata Atsutane, whose views are discussed later in this chapter, envisioned Japan extending its divine rule over the rest of the world. "In terms of world geography," he argued, "our Imperial Land would appear to be the axis of the other countries of the world, as indeed it is. Natural circumstances favor the launching of an expedition from our country to conquer others, whereas they are adverse to the conquest of our country by an expedition from abroad."[28] It appears that an awareness of the outside world quickly led to the rise of expansionistic nationalism.

There were a number of other rationalist critics of the existing order who contemplated various ways of strengthening the society. Kaiho Seiryō (1755–1817), for example, advocated that since commerce constituted the basis of the social order, industrial activities should be extended to all segments of the society. Shiba Kōkan recognized the superiority of Western science and favored establishing trade with Russia. He also expressed egalitarian ideas: "From the emperor, and shōgun above, to the samurai, peasants, merchants, artisans, pariahs, and beggars below[,] all are human beings."[29] Yamagata Bantō (1748–1821), a scholar who had emerged from the merchant class, also recognized the superiority of Western science and adopted a materialistic, atheistic point of view. He noted the prevalence of conflict between the ruler and the people in Japanese history and, like Shiba Kōkan, asserted that all men were equal.

The nationalists, both the Mito school and the school of National Learning, though not yet in favor of overthrowing the Bakufu, were beginning to put increasing emphasis on the importance of the imperial family. They believed in "revering the emperor and respecting the Bakufu," and they tended to be outspokenly anti-Western. The Bakufu officials were willing to tolerate expressions of respect for the imperial family as long as these were accompanied by similar declamations about the Bakufu, but they were not willing to condone proimperial expressions that at the same time implied a criticism of the Bakufu. Followers of Yamazaki Ansai (1618–1682), syncretist of Confucianism and Shinto, were punished by the Bakufu as exponents of proimperial, anti-Bakufu sentiments. Proroyalists in the early nineteenth century were careful not to step into the danger zone.

This was true of Aizawa Seishisai (1782–1863) of Mito, one of the earliest advocates of the policy of *sonnō jōi* (revere the emperor and repel the barbarians). He argued in traditional fashion that obedience to one's lord and adherence to the Bakufu's laws signified loyalty to the emperor. In 1825 he wrote a book called *New Proposals,* in which he set forth his nationalistic, proroyalist opinions. This book appeared at a time when Japan's peace was being threatened by the attempts of foreign vessels to enter its ports. In fact, it was in 1825 that the Bakufu issued an order to fire upon all foreign ships approaching Japanese shores. Aizawa's *New Proposals* had a significant impact on the thinking of his contemporaries, and the volume came to be regarded as something of a Bible for the nationalistic patriots of the period.

Aizawa embraced the Shinto concepts of the divine origin of Japan and the uniqueness of the imperial family, who were descendants of the Sun Goddess. He held Japan to be "at the vertex of the earth" and the nation that sets the standard for others to follow. He elaborated upon the concept of Japan's *kokutai* (national polity), a theory that combined elements from Shinto mythology, Confucian ethics, and Bushidō. It was this theory that emerged in the twentieth century as a key element in the ideology of the ultranationalists. Japan's kokutai was unique, Aizawa asserted, because the nation was founded by the Sun Goddess and because the imperial line, which stems directly from her, has survived inviolate through the ages. Concepts of loyalty to the sovereign and filial piety were thus handed down to the Japanese people by the Sun Goddess herself.

Aizawa possessed a narrow, xenophobic point of view, as the following statement of his vividly illustrates.

Today the alien barbarians of the West, lowly organs of the legs and feet of the world, are dashing about across the sea, trampling other countries underfoot, and daring, with their squinting eyes and limping feet, to override the noble nations. What manner of arrogance is this! . . . Everything exists in its natural bodily form, and our Divine Land is situated at the top of the earth. . . . It [America] occupies the hindmost region of the earth; thus, its people are stupid and simple, and are incapable of doing things.[30]

As might be expected, Aizawa was highly critical of the scholars of Dutch learning. He accused them of being taken in by Western theories and of seeking to transform the civilized Japanese way of life into that of the barbarians. He was also rabidly anti-Christian, contending that Christianity's aim was to devour the countries that it entered.

The nationalists of the Mito school, although they were sympathetic to certain Shinto concepts, were basically Confucians, and as such they sought to reconcile the concept of taigi-meibun with loyalty both to the shōgun and to the emperor. Consequently, they did not agree fully with the scholars of National Learning who were critical of Confucianism.

The central figure among the scholars of National Learning during this period was Hirata Atsutane (1776–1843), a zealous Shinto nationalist. In seeking to place National Learning above all other schools of thought, he contended that all learning, including Confucianism and Buddhism, was encompassed in Japanese learning, "just as the many rivers flow into the sea, where their waters are joined."[31] Hirata hoped to establish Shinto's supremacy over all other doctrines, and he was almost irrational in his criticisms of Confucianism and Buddhism. He had been exposed to Western knowledge and was influenced to some extent by Christian concepts, which were entering the country through Chinese publications. For example, he equated the early Shinto gods Izanagi and Izanami with Adam and Eve, and in one of his works he quoted the New Testament as if it were a Shinto text.

Hirata sought to provide Shinto with a clearly defined theology by presenting a monotheistic interpretation of the religion, and by emphasizing life after death. He may have borrowed these two concepts from Christianity. In contrast to Motoori Norinaga, who envisioned two creator gods—Takami-musubi and Kami-musubi—Hirata contended that Takami-musubi was the sole Creator God who made Heaven and Earth. He was, Hirata said, omnipotent, the holiest among the many gods, and ruler over the world from his abode in Heaven. In his concept about life after death, Hirata again departs from the earlier Shintoists, who held that after death, the soul went to the polluted land of *Yomi*. According to Hirata, the soul enters the land of spirits, where it joins the gods. This earthly life, then, is only a temporary abode for man. It is "the place where we are tested for good and evil. It is a temporary world where we are allowed to live for a short while. The invisible land is our real world."

Hirata's ethnocentric nationalism was manifested in his belief that Japan, because it was begotten by the gods and thus especially favored by them, ranks far above other countries. People all over the world, he claimed, refer to Japan as the land of the gods and call the Japanese people descendants of the gods. Even the humblest of the Japanese, being descendants of the gods, are superior to others. He held the Chinese in contempt as being unclean, and although he compared the Dutch to dogs, he did recognize their devotion to intellectual pursuits and their superiority in the sciences. Hirata was not one of the furious antiforeigners who insisted on "repelling the barbarians." He sympathized with the seclusionist policy of the Bakufu but favored adopting those elements of Western science and technology that would benefit the country. He did not advocate overthrowing the Bakufu even though he was a Shintoist, and he believed that there was no conflict between revering the emperor and upholding the Bakufu.

Hirata, however, was fanatical in his opposition to Buddhism. He criticized its ascetic rejection of the mundane world, and he attacked the major Buddhist sects as "enemies of the gods." He renounced the Buddhist concept of *satori* (enlightenment) and contended that true enlightenment was to be attained by following one's natural inclinations. True enlightenment, he said, "is understood as soon as it is explained to a person. It can be performed at once; it is not a difficult matter at all. It is what a person is born with; it is his nature." According to Hirata, an enlightened person feels affection for his parents, loves his wife and children, and allows his innate sentiments to have free and natural expression. "Shakyamuni Buddha and Bodhidharma," he argued, "behaved contrary to this way so they were neither enlightened nor followers of the true Way." Consequently, he advocated the abandonment of "all things that smell of Buddhism" and the cultivation of "the Yamato spirit."

Hirata's influence was widespread. His anti-Buddhist sentiments found considerable support and took concrete form in the anti-Buddhist outbursts that followed the Meiji Restoration. His Shinto nationalist concepts have had a great impact upon the nationalistic thinking of modern Japan.

Notes

1. E. H. Norman, "Andō Shōeki and the Anatomy of Japanese Feudalism," in *Transactions of the Asiatic Society of Japan,* series 3, vol. 2, pp. 57–58.

2. Maruyama Masao, *Nihon Seijishisōshi Kenkyū* (Studies in the History of Japanese Political Thought) (Tokyo: Tōkyō Daigaku Shuppankai, 1954), p. 120.

3. The extent to which this cut into the daimyō's budget is illustrated by the example of Saga han. In the mid-seventeenth century 20 percent of Saga's expenditures were applied to travel costs for the sankin kōtai, and 28 percent was used for its residence in Edo.

4. For instance, when Senior Councilor Matsudaira canceled debts in 1789, ninety-six financial agents lost a total of about 1.2 million ryō. Some daimyō, in arranging the terms of a loan, demanded that they be given anywhere from 150 to 200 years to repay the debt.

5. Sakata Yoshio, *Meiji Ishinshi* (A History of the Meiji Restoration) (Tokyo: Miraisha, 1960), p. 19.

6. Maruyama, *Nihon Seijishisōshi Kenkyū*, p. 125.

7. For instance, Tsushima han, which was officially valued at 20,000 koku, managed to raise its revenues to about 200,000 koku by trading with Korea.

8. Anne Walthall, "Village Networks: Sodai and the Sale of Edo Nightsoil," *Monumenta Nipponica*, vol. 43, no. 3, autumn 1988, pp. 279–303, and Louis G. Perez, *Everyday Life in Early Modern Japan* (Westport, Conn.: Greenwood Press, 2001), pp. 217–226.

9. Between 1742 and 1762, for example, the Chōshū retainers were asked to take reductions annually, and for seven years in a row they were required to accept 50 percent reductions.

10. Donald Keene, *The Japanese Discovery of Europe, 1720–1830* (Stanford: Stanford University Press, 1969), pp. 168–169.

11. During the latter half of its rule it usually managed to collect about 1.6 million koku from assessed holdings of something over 4 million koku. In 1744, by revising the method of assessment, it managed to raise its intake to 1.8 million koku. After 1766, however, tax revenues gradually declined.

12. The area under cultivation in 1598 was 1.5 million chō, whereas by the Kyōho era (1716–1736) it had risen to 2.97 million chō. Agricultural production in 1598 was estimated at 18.5 million koku, whereas by the Genroku era (1688–1703) it had risen to 25.78 million, and by 1834 it had reached 30.43 million koku.

13. Hugh Borton, "Peasant Uprisings in Japan of the Tokugawa Period," *Transactions of the Asiatic Society of Japan,* series 2, vol. 16, p. 10.

14. For the total population, 2 to 3 million must be added to account for the daimyō and samurai, and their servants, as well as the outcastes, who were excluded from the census. It should be noted that in some instances children were not included in the count either.

15. Demographers have suggested that the Japanese were perhaps unique in using these methods to control family size for the purposes of improving an economic standard of living. See Susan B. Hanley and Kozo Yamamura, *Economic and Demographic Change in Preindustrial Japan, 1600–1868* (Princeton: Princeton University Press, 1977).

16. This is known as the Kyōho famine, and contemporary estimates held that while it lasted, 969,900 people died of starvation. No doubt this figure is highly exaggerated, but it does, nevertheless, indicate the strong impression that large-scale starvation made upon observers.

17. Keene, *The Japanese Discovery of Europe,* p. 182.

18. As a result of the Kyōho famine of 1732–1733, the population of the common people dropped from 26.92 million in 1732 to 26.15 million in 1744, when the next census was taken. Just prior to the Temmei famine, the population was 26.01 million, but it declined to 25.08 million in 1786, and then dropped even further, to 24.89 million, in 1792.

19. This was also true of the Bakufu's own domain: from 1590 to 1750 the Bakufu was faced with 146 peasant disturbances in its demesne, whereas between 1751 and 1867 it was confronted with 401 incidents.

20. The other incidents involved the following immediate causes: 355 were directed against some aspect of the administrative system, 214 involved demands for relief and assistance, 158 were rice riots, 146 were directed against abusive Bakufu or han officials, and 134 were protests against arbitrary measures taken by the authorities. In the later stages of the Edo period there was an increase in protests against the village leaders and merchants who had monopolistic rights. The source for the figures on peasant disturbances is Aoki Kōji, *Hyakushō Ikki no Nenjiteki Kenkyū* (A Chronological Study of Peasant Uprisings) (Tokyo: Shinseisha, 1966), p. 13.

21. During the seventeenth century the rice production increased by about 40 percent while the population may have grown by about 50 percent. From the early eighteenth century, however, the population remained fairly stable until the end of the Tokugawa era while the rice production grew about 18 percent by 1834.

22. It is estimated that in the 1860s, only about 20 percent of the agricultural products reached the commercial market, whereas a century later the figure had grown to 60 percent.

23. Nagata Hiroshi, *Nihon Tetsugakushisōshi* (A History of Japanese Philosophical Thought) (Tokyo: Mikasa Shobō, 1938), p. 237.

24. Keene, *The Japanese Discovery of Europe*, p. 25.

25. Ibid., p. 176.

26. Ibid., p. 221.

27. Maruyama, *Nihon Seijishisōshi Kenkyū*, p. 346.

28. Nagata, *Nihon Tetsugakushisōshi*, pp. 250–251.

29. Ryusaku Tsunoda et al., eds., *Sources of Japanese Tradition* (New York: Columbia University Press, 1958), p. 596.

30. Ibid., p. 543.

31. The source for this and the quotations that follow is Nagata, *Nihon Tetsugakushisōshi*, pp. 254ff.

4

The Fall of the Tokugawa Bakufu

ARRIVAL OF COMMODORE PERRY

The coming of Perry in 1853 turned out to be an epoch-making event in Japanese history, but even before his arrival the Bakufu's seclusionist policy was already being challenged by the arrival of other foreign vessels. Russia was the first nation to start probing the shores of Japan. In 1771 a Russian adventurer, Baron von Benyowsky, who had been exiled to Kamchatka, seized control of a small vessel with the aid of some other convicts and sailed to Awa in Shikoku. Benyowsky pretended to be a Dutchman and told the Japanese that Russia was planning to attack Hokkaido the following year. This caused consternation among the Japanese officials and stirred the advocates of national defense, such as Hayashi Shihei, into action. In 1778 a Russian merchant ship came to Kunajiri Island off western Hokkaido and asked the local daimyō to enter into commercial relations. This offer to engage in trade was repeated in the fall of 1792 when a Russian ship, the *Ekaterina,* arrived at Nemuro in Hokkaido to return some castaway Japanese seamen. The authorities rejected the offer but told the Russians to sail to Nagasaki and present their request there. Adam Laxman, the commander of the ship, decided, however, to return to Russia without bothering to go on to Nagasaki. In 1804 the head of the Russian-American Company, a man by the name of Rezanov, arrived in Nagasaki and requested the establishment of commercial relations. He too failed to persuade the Bakufu to abandon its seclusionist position.

In the face of increasing Russian activities in the north, especially in Sakhalin and the Kuriles, the Bakufu began to concern itself with the defense of the northern regions, and in 1808 it sent a survey team there and across into eastern Siberia. Under the leadership of Mamiya Rinzō, the group verified that Sakhalin was in fact an island and not a peninsula attached to Siberia. Russian interest in the Far East abated during the Napoleonic Wars, and it was not until 1847, when Nicholas Muraviev was appointed governor-general of eastern Siberia, that it began to press upon Japanese shores again.

England and America were also beginning to display some interest in opening Japan's ports. In 1818 the British sent a vessel to Uraga, near Edo, and asked for the commencement of commercial relations, but they too were summarily turned away. Also arriving on Japanese shores were whaling ships looking for food and water. As a result, in 1825 the Bakufu issued an edict ordering forcible ejection of all foreign ships from Japanese coastal regions. Upon receiving word of the Chinese defeat in the Opium War, the Bakufu began to strengthen its military forces by manufacturing cannons and training men in gunnery. In 1842 the edict of 1825 was relaxed by Senior Councilor Mizuno Tadakuni, and it was ordered that ships drifting accidentally to Japanese shores were to be provided with food, water, and fuel. Fundamentally, however, the basic seclusionist policy remained unchanged. For example, in 1844, when William II of Holland sent a message to the Bakufu courteously explaining the world situation and urging that Japan open its doors, his advice went completely unheeded.

The nation that finally succeeded in persuading Japan to open its ports was the United States. It was becoming a significant Pacific power and consequently sought to develop commercial relations with Asian nations. In addition, the United States had whaling ships roaming the north Pacific that needed supply bases and shelter. Moreover it was felt that arrangements had to be negotiated for the protection and care of American seamen shipwrecked on Japanese shores, who were heretofore treated as unlawful intruders by the authorities.

In 1837 an American merchant ship, the *Morrison,* arrived with the aim of establishing contact with Japan, but it was promptly driven off. The leader of this mission then recommended to the United States government that a naval expedition be sent to open Japanese ports. In 1846 Commodore James Biddle was dispatched with two American warships, but he too failed to achieve his objective. Commodore Matthew Calbraith Perry was next given the assignment, and on July 8, 1853, he arrived off the coast of Uraga with four warships. Edo was plunged into a state of crisis when the "black ships" sailed into Edo Bay, ignoring the protesting Japanese on small boats. Perry was determined to accomplish his mission, so he refused to be shunted aside and gave the Bakufu three days to accept President Millard Fillmore's letter to the shōgun asking for humane treatment of shipwrecked seamen, permission for American ships to enter Japanese ports for coal and supplies, and, if possible, trade between the two nations. The Bakufu had no choice but to accede to Perry's demands and allowed him to land in Uraga. He delivered the letter and then departed, stating that he would return early the following year for an official reply.

Perry's arrival placed the Bakufu in its most difficult predicament since its founding. It had virtually ignored the outside world for more than 200 years and now found that it could no longer continue to do so. The Bakufu officials knew that Japan was incapable of withstanding any military assault by the Western powers, but the ruling class was severely divided on how to deal with the difficulties posed by Perry. The blind fanatics favored "repelling the barbarians," but men who were better informed realized that such action was pure folly. The gravity of the situation and the Bakufu's inability to deal with it resolutely made it necessary to include radically new elements in the deliberative and policy-making processes. The Bakufu's officials turned for advice to the imperial court and all the daimyō, including the tozama (outside) lords, as well as to the shōgun's liege vassals. This, of course, gave potential opponents of the Bakufu and the politically ambitious elements an opportunity to move into the center of the political arena. The Bakufu was forced, reluctantly, to abandon its seclusionist policy, and the opposition then used the issue of *jōi* (repelling the barbarians) as a means to badger and embarrass it. At the same time, the inclusion of the imperial court in the decision-making process made it a rallying point for critics of the Bakufu. Thus *sonnō* (revering or honoring the emperor) was tied in with jōi as a political weapon with which to assail the Bakufu.

In response to the Bakufu's call for advice concerning the American request, 700 memorials were submitted. No one, however, managed to formulate a brilliant solution. Some men suggested that the Bakufu accede to Perry's demands, but a majority of the replies advanced the desirable though unrealistic position that the policy of seclusion be retained while war be avoided at all costs. A few of the respondents did advocate going to war against the intruders. The most eminent proponent of this policy was the lord of Mito, Tokugawa Nariaki (1800–1860), who contended that "if we put our trust in war the whole country's morale will be increased and even if we sustain an initial defeat we will in the end expel the foreigner." He bemoaned the fact that "in these feeble days men tend to cling to peace; they are not fond of defending their country by war."[1]

There were many men who agreed that the only practical solution would be to stall the Americans as long as possible. This, however, was not a feasible plan simply because Perry did return early in 1854, just as he had promised, and this time he had eight "black ships" with him. The Bakufu's officials were overwhelmed by this show of force and, fearing an attack if Perry's requests were not met, agreed to open two ports—Hakodate in Hokkaido and Shimoda on the tip of Izu Peninsula—to American ships, to treat shipwrecked sailors properly, and to permit a consul to reside in Shimoda. The most-favored-nation clause was also included in the treaty even though the Bakufu did not actually agree to establish commercial relations. This agreement, the Treaty of Kanagawa, was signed on March 31, 1854. England, France, Russia, and the Netherlands soon concluded similar agreements and thus brought to a close Japan's long period of seclusion. In effect this signaled the beginning of the end for the Tokugawa Bakufu, for its opponents and critics could now begin to intensify their attacks against it, criticizing its inability to stand up against the Western powers.

In August 1856 the American government sent Townsend Harris to Shimoda to press for a commercial treaty. Some Bakufu officials, realizing that the Western powers were far in advance of Japan in military, economic, and technological affairs, concluded that Japan could no longer refuse to establish full diplomatic and commercial relations with foreign powers. Iwase Tadanari, the official who was given the task of negotiating with Harris, was convinced that Japan had to open its doors and persuaded the Bakufu's high officials to accept this fact. Several leading daimyō also became convinced of the wisdom of opening the country, but one of the most influential of them, Tokugawa Nariaki, remained adamant in his opposition and sought to win the support of the imperial court. Emperor Kōmei (1831–1866) was surrounded by advisers who were grossly ignorant of the world situation, and so it was not exceedingly difficult to persuade him that opening the country would be disastrous. He decided, therefore, to support the antiforeign faction.

In the meanwhile, Harris and the Bakufu's officials concluded their negotiations on a commercial treaty, and the senior councilor, Hotta Masayoshi (1810–1864), seeking to allay the very strong opposition led by Nariaki, asked for imperial approval of the treaty. Hotta expected immediate imperial consent, but the emperor remained firmly committed to the policy of jōi. It was at this point that Ii Naosuke (1815–1860), who had just been appointed tairō (great councilor), decided that the treaty would have to be signed without imperial sanction. The Bakufu's officials, intimidated by Harris's information that the British and French fleets, fresh from their triumph over the Chinese, were on their way to extract greater concessions from Japan, finally signed the commercial treaty on July 29, 1858. It provided for the immediate opening of three ports to trade and the addition of two more a few years later. Duties of a varied scale on imports and 5 percent on exports were agreed upon. Edo and Osaka were to be opened to foreign residents by 1862 and 1863. American citizens were granted extraterritorial rights and freedom of worship in Japan. Similar treaties were concluded with England, France, Russia, and the Netherlands.

THE IMMEDIATE CONSEQUENCES

The impact of these contacts with the West was felt immediately in the political realm, even though involvement with foreign nations remained essentially limited until the Meiji government came into existence. The effects of the new relationships also became discernible in the cultural and economic areas, and the treaty ports such as Yokohama with their Western residents began to grow into important centers of Western culture.

In 1860 a Japanese embassy was sent to the United States to exchange ratifications of the treaty, and in 1861 a mission was dispatched to Europe. These trips exposed a considerable number of influential Japanese to the Western world, and some of them, like Fukuzawa Yukichi, a leading Meiji educator, returned convinced of the need to adopt Western practices and institutions. The general mood of the country nevertheless remained strongly anti-Western, so these men were compelled to remain silent until the advent of the Meiji era. The Bakufu, however, did recognize the need to train some officials in Western languages, and in 1857 it opened the "Institute for the Investigation of Barbarian Books." Initially only Dutch was taught, but by 1860 other Western languages were added to the curriculum, and in 1863 the institute was officially turned into a government college for Western studies.

Various educational programs served to increase the exposure of many Japanese to Western culture. In 1862 the Bakufu sent a group of eight students to study in Holland, and this example was soon followed by several han. In 1863 Chōshū dispatched five students to England, and in 1864, Satsuma sent sixteen students there. A number of students also went abroad on their own initiative, and many young men in Japan began to study Western languages with Western missionaries and Japanese instructors who were qualified in this field.

Commerce with the West, although still limited, began to increase in the 1860s. Exports exceeded imports until 1866 when the trend was reversed, and the total combined figure, not including arms and ships, exceeded $32 million. The chief trading partner was England, with whom 80 percent of Japanese trade from 1859 to the downfall of the Bakufu was conducted. Raw silk was the main item of export; tea, copperware, marine products, and lacquerware were among the other major export commodities. Imported goods included cotton yarn, cotton cloth, woolen fabrics, ironware, and sugar.

The tremendous demand for such items as silk and tea resulted in increased production, but it was quite insufficient to meet the enormous requests for these commodities. The demand for raw silk in particular created serious domestic shortages and inflationary prices. In contrast, the importation of cotton yarn and cotton cloth had the most adverse effects on the domestic producers. Foreign trade did, nevertheless, have the vitally important consequence of stimulating the growth of some factories in which many workers were brought together under one roof to work using reeling machines or processing tea. These factories were, of course, still limited in number and size, and the dominant mode remained domestic handicraft production.

A feature of foreign trade that particularly disturbed the Bakufu was the inordinate outflow of gold. Gold coins were exchanged with silver at a ratio of about one to five in Japan while the world rate was about one to fifteen. This meant that foreigners could make an enormous profit by first exchanging silver for gold in Japan and then taking the gold to China, where it commanded its full value in the world market. Before the Bakufu corrected the situation by debasing its gold coins in 1860, about 500,000 ryō in gold coins had flowed out of the country.

From a political point of view, the agreement to enter into commercial and diplomatic relations with the Western nations proved to be disastrous for the Bakufu. The antiforeign faction began to grow increasingly disenchanted with the Bakufu, and it commenced openly to espouse the cause of the imperial court. Thus, the movement "to revere the Emperor and repel the barbarians" began to congeal into a formidable force as it gained the support of a growing number of activist warriors known as *shishi* (men of high purpose or spirit). Ii Naosuke came under severe criticism for having signed the treaty with the United States without imperial approval, and the opposition to him soon became intermeshed with the struggle over succession to the shogunate.

The struggle to pick his successor unfolded even before the weak and feebleminded shōgun Iesada (1824–1858) passed away. One faction, which included the daimyō of Echizen and Satsuma as well as some reform-minded Bakufu officials, favored Nariaki's son, Yoshinobu (1837–1913), also known as Keiki, who had a reputation as an individual of considerable ability and intelligence. The support of the antiforeign faction was guaranteed him simply by virtue of the fact that he was the son of an avowed anti-Westerner. Keiki was also favored by some proponents of the open-door policy who believed that the old guard among the top Bakufu officials had to be removed.

Ii Naosuke, representing the fudai daimyō who traditionally controlled the top Bakufu posts, led the faction opposed to Keiki. They feared that this succession to the shogunate would mean the control of the Bakufu by Nariaki, who was not only anti-Western but sympathetic to the imperial court as well. In order to block Keiki, Ii succeeded in making Iemochi, the shōgun's cousin and eight-year-old head of Kii han, shōgun. Ii then began persecuting those who had opposed his policies or had supported Keiki. He placed Nariaki under house arrest, forced Keiki to retire, contrived the dismissal of anti-Bakufu court advisers, and executed some active samurai opponents and critics of the Bakufu.

Among Ii's victims was Yoshida Shōin, a zealous patriot and the leader of the young extremist warriors of Chōshū (see page 69). Another victim was Hashimoto Sanai (1834–1859), a warrior of Echizen, who was condemned for having worked for supporting Keiki. Unlike the other critics of Ii, Hashimoto had favored opening the country. Ten warriors, including two who died in prison, were condemned to death, and many others were exiled to offshore islands. From Ii's point of view, he was merely upholding the authority of the Bakufu, for lower-level warriors were forbidden from interfering in state affairs. The zealots, however, were no longer bound by such considerations as "knowing their place." In order to avenge the death of their fellow warriors, in March 1860 a group of activists from Mito waylaid Ii as he was entering Edo castle and assassinated him. This deprived the Bakufu of its strong man and forced its officials to try to cope with the opposition by winning over the cooperation of the imperial court. Consequently, the center of political action began shifting to Kyoto.

THE MENTALITY OF SONNŌ JŌI

Many proponents of sonnō jōi, the movement "to revere the Emperor and repel the barbarians," were young warriors who came primarily from the lower rungs of the samurai hierarchy, although there were some well-to-do farmers' sons as well as priests and scholars to be found among their ranks. Mito, Chōshū, Satsuma, and Tosa produced the largest number of these men, but they were to be found in other han as well.

These samurai, usually referred to as *shishi*, were inclined to be fiery extremists as well as fanatical political activists. They were usually expert swordsmen who rigorously upheld such traditional samurai values as duty, courage, and honor. Some of the shishi outgrew their earlier limitations and managed to emerge as perspicacious statesmen; by and large, however, they were men who lacked the vision to discern a meaningful role and place for Japan in the context of the changing world scene. They were not inclined to be reasonable and tended instead to be ruled by their passions. Self-righteous, intolerant, and dogmatic to the extreme, they envisioned themselves as the saviors of Japan, men with a sacred mission. They were convinced that they were on the side of truth, justice, and right, and that they were the only true patriots while those who failed to agree with them were self-serving traitors. The shishi were, in effect, the forerunners of the ultranationalist extremists of prewar Japan.

The shishi constituted only a minority in their han, but the influence they wielded was very strongly felt because of the readiness with which they would use force against those who disagreed with them. There were frequent outbursts of violence as the shishi repeatedly tried to seize power. In Chōshū and Satsuma they eventually did capture the han leadership. Their uprising against the established leadership in Mito, however, was crushed. In Tosa, even though they assassinated a moderate han official they failed to intimidate the han leaders and were finally driven out. Later, however, as the daimyō moved closer to the sonnō position, some of the shishi were restored to their good graces. Their terrorist tactics made the extremists a force to contend with not only in their own han but in Kyoto and Edo as well.

The shishi were as a rule rabidly anti-Western, but they disagreed about the tactics to be used in achieving their ends. Some men favored driving the Westerners out and closing the country; others favored opening the country in order to enable Japan to adopt Western military methods and thus become powerful enough to cope with the Western threat.[2] Some of the Bakufu officials who went along with the open-door policy did so because they felt it was an ineluctable necessity, but at heart they favored the seclusionist policy and the preservation of the old feudal order.

Sonnō jōi sentiments are generally believed to have originated in Mito, with men such as Aizawa Seishisai (1782–1863) and the Fujitas (father Yūkoku and son Tōko) among the early advocates. Initially, the proponents of sonnō jōi did not advocate an anti-Bakufu policy, believing that loyalty to both the imperial court and the Bakufu was possible. After the arrival of Perry, however, and the conclusion of the commercial treaties, the sonnō jōi movement took a sharp anti-Bakufu turn.

The man who emerged as the leading spokesman of this movement was Yoshida Shōin (1830–1859), a brilliant shishi from Chōshū, who was the son of a low-ranking samurai. He studied Zhu Xi Confucianism and Yamaga Sokō's military science, read treatises on Wang Yang-ming philosophy, and was exposed to Western technology in Nagasaki. In 1851 he went to Edo and became a disciple of Sakuma Zōzan (1811–1864), a leading student of the Dutch language and Western science. He also traveled to Mito to see Aizawa Seishisai, whose works he had studied earlier. The arrival of Perry had a decisive effect on him, and believing that he should get to know his enemy, he sought to board an American ship to go abroad to study. He was arrested for violating the law of the land and was turned over to his han to be placed under house arrest. After his release, Yoshida started a private school to indoctrinate the young men of his han with his loyalist, nationalistic point of view. Among his students were the future leaders of Meiji Japan, Itō Hirobumi and Yamagata Aritomo, as well as one of the three architects of the Meiji Restoration, Kido Kōin, and the would-be leaders of the extremists in Chōshū, Takasugi Shinsaku and Kusaka Genzui—a truly impressive galaxy of disciples. Yoshida believed that the old leaders were completely incapable of solving the national crisis, and so he envisioned the establishment of a new order under the leadership of people like himself and his followers, the "grass-roots heroes." His followers in Chōshū did indeed play a major role in overthrowing the old order.

Yoshida was intensely antiforeign and a loyal adherent to the Shinto notion of the divine nature of Japan. "One must," he wrote, "worship and revere the gods. The country of Yamato is . . . the honorable country which was founded by the lordly Gods."[3] His anti-Western sentiments burst forth with the coming of Perry, and he exhorted the Japanese people to unite and drive away the "wily barbarians." He was convinced that new leadership and new ideas had to be injected into the government in order to cope with the national emergency. He did not advocate the Bakufu's overthrow until it signed the commercial treaty with Harris without first receiving imperial sanction. When it finally did so, he turned against it in wrathful indignation that epitomized the feelings of the advocates of sonnō jōi:

> It is clear that the Americans' intentions are harmful to the Land of the Gods. It has been proven that the words of the American envoy have caused the Land of the Gods to be dishonored. In view of this, the emperor, in extreme anger, decreed that relations be severed with the American envoy. This command the Bakufu was obliged to obey without delay but it failed to do so. It behaved with arrogance and independence, and made flattery of the Americans the highest policy of the land. It gave no thought to the national danger, did not reflect upon the national disgrace, and disobeyed the imperial decree. This is the Shōgun's crime. Heaven and earth will not tolerate it. The anger of the Gods and men have been aroused. Now it would be proper to destroy and kill in accordance with the fundamental principle of righteousness. No mercy should be shown.[4]

Yoshida used all his resources in opposing the Bakufu and frequently plotted to take direct action against its officials. Six months before his death, he wrote, "As long as the Tokugawa government exists, American, Russian, English, and French control over Japan will continue. The situation is indeed critical. How can any red-blooded person bear to see our great nation which has remained independent and unconquered for three thousand years become enslaved by other nations?"[5] When the commercial treaty was signed with the United States, Yoshida was so outraged that he conspired with his followers to assassinate one of the Bakufu councilors. He was arrested, turned over to the Bakufu, and later executed.

Sakuma Zōzan, Yoshida's master, was also highly nationalistic, but he responded differently to the advent of the West. Sakuma was a Zhu Xi Confucian, but he was also interested in Western learning and had studied the Dutch language. He was particularly fascinated by Western science and technology, and in recognition of Japan's need to adopt Western military and naval techniques he became an expert on Western gunnery. He had a wide following as a teacher and influenced many young men. Sakuma, unlike Yoshida, favored opening Japan's doors in order to adopt Western science and technology. His attitude toward Western knowledge is reflected in the following statement:

In teachings concerning morality, benevolence, and righteousness, filial piety
and brotherly love, loyalty and faithfulness, we must follow the examples and
precepts of the Chinese sages. In astronomy, geography, navigation, surveying,
the investigation of the principle of all things, the art of gunnery, commerce,
medicine, machinery and construction, we must rely mainly on the West. We
must gather the strong points of the five worlds and construct the great learning of our imperial nation.[6]

He became identified with the policy of opening the country and was assassinated by fanatical sonnō jōi advocates. His faith in Eastern morals and Western science was the very attitude that was to be embraced by many of the
leaders of Meiji Japan. Basically, the Japanese were interested in the external aspects of Western civilization while they sought to retain in their inner life
those elements that they regarded as being intrinsically Japanese.

THE RISE OF THE ANTI-BAKUFU FORCES

The assassination of Ii Naosuke brought about some readily observable
changes in the political picture. As we have already noted, the imperial court
loomed larger in the national political scene. At the same time the Tozama
han, particularly Satsuma, Chōshū, and Tosa, as well as the han related to the
Bakufu, Aizu, and Echizen, began to exert their influence on the national political arena. Furthermore, with Ii gone the Bakufu's leadership fell to more
moderate officials who sought to neutralize their zealous opponents while effecting an alliance between the imperial court and the Bakufu. Emperor
Kōmei agreed to this strategy of cooperation in the belief that the Bakufu
would in return adopt the policy of driving out the Westerners. The alliance,
known as kōbu-gattai (union of the court and military), was cemented by the
marriage of Shōgun Iemochi to the emperor's younger sister Princess
Kazunomiya in early 1862. This policy was supported by the daimyō of Satsuma, Echizen, and Aizu.

The shishi angrily opposed this policy and launched a campaign of terror,
assassinating those who had cooperated with Ii in suppressing the shishi as well
as those who had supported kōbu-gattai. Another target of the anti-Western
fanatics was naturally enough the foreign officials. Starting with the killing of
two Russian sailors in the summer of 1859, a number of Westerners were murdered, among them Henry Heuskin, Harris's Dutch language interpreter, who
was killed in January 1861.

The most active elements among the shishi emerged from Chōshū. The
lord of Satsuma was able to keep the extremists in his han under control, but
the shishi in Chōshū were allowed to operate in a rather freewheeling manner.

The lord of Chōshū was willing to leave the management of political affairs to his chief officials. Around 1860, when the Chōshū leaders adopted a policy of playing an active role in the national scene, the han leadership was in the hands of Nagai Uta, an official who favored a policy of moderation. He sought to play the role of a mediator between the court and the Bakufu when Ii's departure offered Chōshū an opportunity to move into the national political arena. Nagai also favored the policy of opening the country to the West. His ideas were vehemently opposed by the shishi, and his failure to reconcile the court and Bakufu offered his opponents, led by Kusaka, a perfect opportunity to discredit him. He was ultimately ordered to commit seppuku, and the Chōshū leadership passed into the hands of the proponents of sonnō jōi.

Contrary to the expectations of the advocates of kōbu-gattai, the terrorists managed to swing the court back to a rigidly anti-Western position. Emperor Kōmei dispatched a messenger to Edo calling for the immediate expulsion of the foreigners. In early 1863 the shōgun and Keiki, who had been appointed his guardian, traveled to Kyoto to confer with the imperial court regarding the command. Seeing that the imperial court was dominated by the jōi faction, the daimyō who were opposed to such a policy, including the lord of Satsuma, departed for their home provinces. As a result, the Bakufu officials were forced to agree to implement the policy of jōi and May 10, 1863, was set as the date the policy was to go into effect.

The deadline arrived with the extremists of Chōshū firing upon Western ships passing through Shimonoseki straits. As might be expected, the Western powers were swift to retaliate; three American and French men-of-war attacked the Shimonoseki shore batteries before landing and completely destroying the gun emplacements. The attacks, however, against the Western vessels passing through Shimonoseki straits nevertheless continued. During the following summer, England, France, the United States, and Holland sent seventeen warships against Chōshū, destroyed its forts, and routed its forces on land. This caused Chōshū to abandon its blind anti-Western stance and begin Westernizing its military forces. In a similar way, Satsuma also underwent a kind of baptism by fire in the summer of 1863, when British warships attacked Kagoshima in retaliation for the killing of an Englishman the previous fall. This encounter resulted in bringing the British and Satsuma officials closer together.

In the fall of 1863, with the support of Satsuma and Aizu, the Bakufu managed to expel the Chōshū warriors and other anti-Bakufu court advisers from Kyoto. Bakufu swordsmen retaliated against the violence-prone anti-Bakufu shishi, and the lord of Aizu, the constable of Kyoto, kept the city under tight control.

Once the Chōshū radicals and the anti-Bakufu court officials were out of the way, the relationship between the Bakufu and the court improved. In order to fulfill its promise to expel the foreigners, the Bakufu agreed to close the port

PROMINENT DAIMYŌ DOMAINS, 1867

of Yokohama. The court accepted this pledge as adequate proof of the Bakufu's willingness to reimpose the policy of seclusion.

Chōshū now became the base for all the anti-Western, anti-Bakufu extremists. Its warriors succeeded in persuading the han leaders to re-enter Kyoto by force, and in the summer of 1864 the men of Chōshū marched against the imperial seat. They were driven back by the Satsuma-Aizu forces, and in the course of the conflict some of the extremist leaders, including Kusaka Genzui, were killed. That fall the Bakufu sent a punitive expedition against Chōshū. Having just been rather severely chastised by the Western powers, Chōshū was in no condition to engage the expeditionary army in combat. Consequently, it acceded to the Bakufu's demands that those responsible for the attack against Kyoto be executed. Leadership in Chōshū was then taken over by the conservatives.

The extremists who called themselves the "righteous faction," under the leadership of Takasugi Shinsaku (1839–1867), rebelled against the conservative officials in 1865 and succeeded in reestablishing their political influence. Takasugi had the support of those auxiliary militia units who were trained in Western military techniques and equipped with Western arms. These units had been organized in 1863 by Takasugi, who was authorized to do so in order to defend the han against the Western powers. A fairly large percentage of each unit consisted of peasants because of the fact that non-samurai men were now allowed to join. The samurai, who composed 25 to 30 percent of the personnel, provided the leadership. Masterless samurai and townsmen were also among the militiamen. The establishment of militia units that were open to non-samurai became necessary because upper-class samurai disdained the use of rifles, convinced that it was a dishonor to abandon their swords. Membership in the auxiliary militia opened the way to political success for many lower-class samurai. Future leaders such as Kido Kōin (1833–1877), Itō Hirobumi (1841–1909), Yamagata Aritomo (1838–1922), and Inoue Kaoru (1835–1915) were active in these units.

Even before the crushing defeat by the Western powers, some sonnō jōi leaders in Chōshū were beginning to realize the necessity of adopting Western military techniques and arms. The naval assaults by the Western powers naturally enhanced this already growing awareness. In addition, Itō Hirobumi and Inoue Kaoru had traveled abroad and returned thoroughly convinced that Japan could not return to its former seclusionist position. They began to urge their fellow shishi to accept the policy of broadening contacts with the outside world for the purpose of strengthening the nation. Kido Kōin and Takasugi shared their views. These men ceased concerning themselves solely with the interests of their own han and began thinking of the well-being of the entire nation. They concluded that the establishment of a strong centralized authority was essential if Japan were to withstand the foreign menace.

In order to strengthen Japan, they believed that it was necessary to attend to Chōshū first. Consequently, after Takasugi's rebellion, the han leadership adopted the policy of fortifying Chōshū's military power. Ōmura Masujirō (1824–1869) was given the assignment of building the Chōshū army into a modern military force. Western vessels as well as thousands of Western rifles were purchased through an English arms merchant, Thomas Glover. The money to purchase these ships and weapons was taken out of a special reserve fund that Chōshū had established in 1762 and preserved even when the han budget was running a yearly deficit.

Chōshū was busy strengthening its military forces as a momentous turn of events was occurring on the national scene. The policy of uniting the court and Bakufu was beginning to disintegrate; at the same time, behind-the-scene machinations aimed at bringing together the two rival han, Satsuma and Chōshū, were beginning to meet with some success. A group of daimyō, including those of Satsuma, Tosa, and Aizu, and Bakufu officials headed by Keiki, worked together to maintain harmony between the court and Bakufu after the departure of Chōshū from Kyoto. Soon, however, dissension began to break out because, while the leaders of Satsuma wanted a government controlled by the major han, a faction in the Bakufu was seeking to revive its autocratic powers. The leader of this group was Finance Commissioner Oguri Tadamasa (1827–1868), who was a member of the embassy that had visited the United States in 1860. Oguri hoped to modernize the Bakufu's military forces, reduce the influence of Chōshū and Satsuma, and establish a strong national government under the Bakufu. In order to accomplish this, Oguri favored obtaining the support of a Western power and turned to Leon Roches, the French minister, for advice and assistance.

Shimazu Hisamitsu (1817–1887), who was regent to the daimyō of Satsuma, disapproved of the new trend in the Bakufu and began to entertain the thought of joining hands with his former foe, Chōshū. Prior to this, the radicals in Satsuma, headed by Saigō Takamori (1827–1877) and Ōkubo Toshimichi (1830–1878), had begun agitating for the adoption of an anti-Bakufu position, but Shimazu had restrained them. Now that he was changing his attitude toward the Bakufu, they came to the fore as key leaders of the anti-Bakufu faction.

The man who served as a mediator between Satsuma and Chōshū was Sakamoto Ryōma (1835–1867), a shishi from Tosa who had outgrown the narrowly anti-Western position he had originally embraced. He now favored opening the country and introducing reforms at the national level. He brought Saigō of Satsuma and Kido of Chōshū together, and in early 1866 the two men agreed upon an alliance.

In June of that year the Bakufu, now led by the centralists, decided to eliminate Chōshū as an obstructive element once and for all and sent a second expeditionary force against it. This time, however, many major daimyō refused to support the move. Satsuma, naturally, declined to go against its recently acquired ally. Chōshū instituted a policy of total mobilization to stop the Bakufu's forces. Its troops were better trained and better armed, and their morale was higher, so it is no surprise that they managed to rout the expeditionary army. This failure revealed the Bakufu's weakness and served to strengthen the determination of the opposition to overthrow it.

Satsuma was also taking steps to modernize its armed forces by purchasing Western arms. Like the Bakufu and other han, Satsuma also had financial difficulties, but the measures it had put into effect during the Tempō era placed it in a far stronger financial position. It repudiated its debts to the merchants, reduced the samurai's stipends, encouraged the production of cash crops, and fostered trade with the Ryukus. In particular, it successfully exploited the sugarcane production on its offshore islands by allowing no other crops to be produced and by keeping stringent controls over the peasants. Those, for example, who produced poor quality sugar were severely punished. The han authorities established a rigid monopoly on sugar, using harsh methods to ensure its control; for instance, anyone who engaged in the private sale of sugar was put to death. The use of such ruthless measures enabled Satsuma to increase its sugar production to the point where it came to supply more than one half of all the sugar sold in Osaka. Principally because of its sugar monopoly, it managed to accumulate reserve funds, which it was able to draw upon when it began to modernize its armed forces.

Satsuma was a particularly dangerous foe of the Bakufu for numerous reasons. First, it was the second largest han, with an official yield of 770,000 koku. Second, it was located in the most distant part of the country, and this made it difficult for the Bakufu to exert its authority. Third, Satsuma had a far larger percentage of samurai in its population than any of the other han. Here the ratio of samurai to commoners was one to three, whereas the national average was one to seventeen. Fourth, the civilizing influence of the urban centers was much diminished in Satsuma, and the warriors tended as a result to retain a hardier and more militaristic outlook than the samurai of other han.

In evaluating the potential threat against the Bakufu, it should be noted that Chōshū also had a larger ratio of samurai to commoners—one to ten—than the national average. The Bakufu, in sharp contrast to Chōshū and Satsuma, retained fewer samurai than even its own scale called for, based on the official assessment of agricultural productivity. This was also true of Owari and Aizu, both collateral houses of the shogunate. Traditional feudal values along with a deep sense of loyalty and dedication to the han were strongly embedded in the Chōshū samurai. In its productive capacity, moreover, Chōshū was among the top ten han with more than 700,000 koku, well over the official estimate. In view of all these factors, the combination of Satsuma and Chōshū can be seen as posing a very serious threat to the Bakufu.

The opposition han were aided by the fact that the Bakufu lacked strong and resolute leadership. The shōgun died during the course of the second expedition against Chōshū, and although everyone's choice for successor was Keiki, he lacked confidence in his own ability to cope with the situation and hesitated for several months before accepting the offer. He then moved to strengthen the Bakufu by following Oguri's line of thinking. He also turned to the French minister Roches for advice and initiated steps to modernize the army and navy as well as the administrative system.

These moves disturbed the opposition leaders because they feared that if the Bakufu succeeded in introducing reforms and in strengthening its military forces, it could possibly regain its former status as the paramount authority. Consequently, the opponents, led by Saigō, Ōkubo, and Kido, moved swiftly to overthrow the Bakufu. They joined hands with the anti-Bakufu court nobles led by Iwakura Tomomi (1825–1883), the most able of the court aristocrats, and began to make plans for the restoration of power to the imperial court.

THE MEIJI RESTORATION

Sakamoto managed to persuade his fellow clansman, Gotō Shōjirō (1838–1897), to work for a peaceful solution to the power struggle at the same time that the Satsuma-Chōshū faction was plotting to overthrow the Bakufu. Under the prompting direction of Sakamoto and Gotō, Yamanouchi Yōdō (1827–1872) urged Shōgun Keiki to restore the powers of government voluntarily to the young Emperor Meiji, who had just ascended the throne. Keiki agreed to the proposal, and in November 1867 he formally petitioned the emperor to accept the restoration of power.

In describing his reasons for making this momentous decision, Keiki later explained that he had concluded that the restoration of power to the court was absolutely essential to the resolution of the crisis facing the country. Several loci of power had developed, and he was searching for a political system that would incorporate the various factions in such a way as to allow the new government to function effectively. At this point, he wrote,

> Matsudaira Yōdō (Lord of Tosa) submitted his memorial calling for the establishment of upper and lower houses. I decided that this was indeed a good proposal. The upper house would consist of court aristocrats and the daimyō and the lower house would consist of selected han warriors. In this way all matters would be decided by public opinion, and the actual task of restoring

imperial rule would be accomplished. As a result I acquired the courage and the confidence to bring about the restoration of imperial rule.[7]

The daimyō of Tosa as well as Gotō wanted to avoid a civil war that might offer the Western powers a chance to intervene and thus compromise Japan's independence. They also envisioned the establishment of a government that would be run along parliamentary lines, with the shōgun serving as the prime minister. Evidently Keiki also expected to become the chief executive of this new government. He may have relinquished his authority as shōgun, but as the head of the Tokugawa domains he was still a major feudal lord. The Tokugawa clan was bound to be a significant force in the new order as long as this situation remained unchanged. The anti-Tokugawa faction, however, had no intention of permitting the Tokugawa family to dominate the new government. Its members were prepared to destroy the Tokugawa clan by force if necessary, and they had even obtained a secret imperial mandate to do so. In a conference of court aristocrats and leading daimyō and their retainers, Iwakura, with Ōkubo and Saigō's support, demanded that the Tokugawa family relinquish its entire holdings and that Keiki renounce all his authority.

Yamanouchi fought strenuously to preserve a place in the new order for Keiki and the Tokugawa clan, but his efforts were completely undermined by Saigō. Convinced that an armed conflict was necessary if the Tokugawa clan was to be completely liquidated, Saigō decided to incite the Tokugawa forces into attacking by hiring a large number of ruffians and hoodlums in Edo to provoke their retainers. The latter fell into the trap set by Saigō and raided the Satsuma residence in Edo. News of the conflict soon reached Keiki, and he and his advisers felt that they could no longer endure the humiliations being inflicted upon them by the Satsuma-Chōshū faction. They decided to take up arms against them even though this meant defying the imperial court, which was now in the grip of the Satsuma-Chōshū clique. Consequently, the Tokugawa forces were branded as rebels. Even Yōdō of Tosa was forced to join the Satsuma-Chōshū faction against Keiki.

In the ensuing battle, the Tokugawa forces were easily routed at Toba-Fushimi outside of Kyoto. Keiki fled to Edo and permitted his commander, Katsu Kaishū—who was convinced of the necessity of establishing a new order—to surrender Edo without a fight in April 1868. Keiki was placed under house arrest, and he subsequently retired to Shizuoka. Some loyal Bakufu warriors continued to resist the imperial forces in the vicinity of Edo, but they were soon subjugated. The overthrow of the Tokugawa Bakufu was thus achieved without the country undergoing a major civil war.

The end of more than 260 years of Tokugawa rule and the subsequent restoration of imperial rule was primarily a political event, although it has been interpreted by many Japanese historians as the product of the new social and economic forces that developed during the latter part of the Tokugawa era. It is unquestionably true that social and economic problems had begun to trouble the Bakufu, but these had not become serious enough to undermine its political authority. Elements of the ascending social and economic forces—the townsmen and the peasantry—were not the ones that challenged the existing order of things. The opposition faction emerged from the same political, social, and economic background as the Bakufu. Basically the struggle that resulted in the downfall of the Bakufu was an old-fashioned power struggle between traditional feudal power blocs. Specifically, it was a struggle between the Bakufu and, primarily, Chōshū and Satsuma. The failure of the former and the success of the latter was not directly related to the rise of the peasantry, the emergence of the merchant class, and the growth of commercial capitalism. The Meiji Restoration was certainly not a bourgeois revolution. Furthermore, peasant uprisings were not politically motivated or even directly involved in the actual overthrow of the Tokugawa government.

The outcome of the power struggle was the result of a variety of factors. For one thing, the Satsuma-Chōshū forces were militarily better prepared and possessed more able leaders. They did not gain their advantage over the Bakufu through a more significant growth in commercial capitalism or by virtue of a stronger consciousness among the merchants and the peasantry in their domains. Neither did these forces in the Bakufu's domains align themselves with the Satsuma-Chōshū faction to assist them against the Tokugawa clan. The two han were better prepared militarily because they were financially capable of purchasing modern weapons from the West. This was not the result of their having moved from an agrarian to a commercial economy. As we noted, Chōshū had a special reserve fund that was utilized to purchase weapons, and Satsuma maintained strict control over its economy and had a profitable sugar monopoly.

The crucial factor that made the difference in the rivalry between the Bakufu and the opposition han was leadership. A large number of zealous, highly capable shishi who were willing to take drastic actions to achieve their objectives were present in Satsuma and Chōshū. Many new leaders had also emerged from the lower rungs of the samurai class in these han. The Bakufu, in comparison, lacked strong leadership, and control remained largely in the hands of the more conservative, high-ranking members of the feudal hierarchy.

In the smaller political communities of the han it was easier for able men from the lower ranks of the samurai to gain recognition and be utilized in time of crisis. In the larger political world of the Bakufu, the upper levels of the hierarchy were crowded with unimaginative, conservative men, and the chances of a low-ranking samurai attracting the attention of the higher officials were extremely limited. After he became shōgun, Keiki claimed that he sought to utilize "men of talent," but by that time it was too late. Furthermore, it is entirely possible that if Keiki himself had been rigorously determined to retain political power at all costs, the outcome may have turned out differently. He was severely lacking in determination and willpower, so he hesitated and procrastinated. The inevitable consequence of this was that power slipped away from the Bakufu almost by default.

Probably the single most important factor, however, that contributed to the downfall of the Bakufu was the arrival of the Western powers. The Bakufu, as the authority directly responsible for foreign relations, was confronted with an impossible dilemma. Perry's arrival forced the Bakufu into opening a Pandora's box that brought the imperial court as well as the daimyō and its retainers into the decision-making process. This was followed by a series of crises that were set off by the signing of the commercial treaty with the United States without first securing imperial sanction. The Western powers were demanding still broader contacts, and the Bakufu's opponents were thus given additional opportunities to play upon antiforeign sentiments and to forge an emotionally charged movement—the sonnō jōi movement—that cut across han barriers.

The Bakufu was unable to adopt a definitive policy that it could pursue with firmness. It wavered between opening the country and succumbing to the pressures exerted by the exclusionists. The Bakufu staggered along without resolute leadership after Ii Naosuke, who was willing to use strong measures to curb the advocates of sonnō jōi, was eliminated. The lower-ranking samurai, who would not have been permitted to meddle in the affairs of state under normal circumstances, were able to use terrorist means to intimidate and sometimes eliminate their political foes.

The opposition leaders used every opportunity to harass the Bakufu in its management of foreign affairs. The Chōshū proponents of sonnō jōi fired upon Western vessels, and when they were directly confronted by the foreign powers they sought to shift the blame to the Bakufu by claiming that they were following its orders to expel the intruders. In 1867, as the deadline for the opening of the port of Hyōgo approached, the leaders of Satsuma insisted that the Bakufu renege on its agreement to open the port because, as they claimed, it was too close to Kyoto and would be offensive to the imperial court. At the same time, the leaders of Satsuma were in fact themselves dealing with the Western powers by purchasing ships and arms from them. In order to embarrass the Bakufu, the British, in collusion with the Satsuma-Chōshū faction, were pressing for the opening of the port, fully expecting the Bakufu's opponents to block it. In the ensuing crisis the opposition forces were expected to overthrow the Bakufu. Ernest Satow, the British minister's interpreter, recalled, "I hinted to Saigō that the chance of a revolution was not to be lost. If Hiogo was once opened, then good-bye to chances of the daimios."[8]

Clearly, the situation that most seriously contributed to the undermining of the Bakufu's authority and self-confidence was the arrival of the Western powers. Without the crisis engendered by this situation, the Bakufu would not have collapsed as soon as it did. The end of Tokugawa rule, needless to say, did not bring about a completely new age and a new society overnight. In the course of the Meiji era significant transformations took place, but the new was built upon the foundations of the old. The attitudes, values, practices, and institutions that molded the Japanese mode of thinking and behavior prior to and during the Tokugawa era continued to govern the thought and actions of the people during the Meiji era and for a long time afterwards. Added to the old, however, were many new elements. These involved not only science and technology but new political, social, and cultural ideas that were imported. All of these were to contribute to the very difficult period of transition that ensued. Our next task is to survey this aspect of Japanese history.

Notes

1. W. G. Beasley, trans. and ed., *Select Documents on Japanese Foreign Policy, 1853–1868* (London: Oxford University Press, 1955), pp. 103, 107.

2. This latter group would correspond to what Arnold Toynbee calls the "Herodians": "The 'Herodian' is the man who acts on the principle that the most effective way to guard against the danger of the unknown is to master its secret; and, when he finds himself in the predicament of being confronted by a more highly skilled and better armed opponent, he responds by discarding his traditional art of war and learning to fight his enemy with the enemy's own tactics and own weapons." In contrast, the "Zealot" reverts to "archaism evoked by foreign pressure" (*Civilization on Trial and the World and the West* [New York: World Publishing, 1958], pp. 167–173). Perry's arrival brought forth these two types in Japan, and it was the Herodians who ultimately won out.

3. David M. Earl, *Emperor and Nation in Japan* (Seattle: University of Washington Press, 1964), p. 183.

4. Maruyama Masao, *Nihon Seijishisōshi Kenkyū* (Studies in the History of Japanese Political Thought) (Tokyo: Tōkyō Daigaku Shuppankai, 1954), pp. 355–356.

5. Ibid., pp. 356–357.

6. Naramoto Tatsuya, ed., *Nihon no Shisōka* (The Thinkers of Japan) (Tokyo: Mainichi Shimbunsha, 1954), p. 237.

7. Sakata Yoshio, *Meiji Ishinshi* (A History of the Meiji Restoration) (Tokyo: Miraisha, 1960), p. 202.

8. Ernest M. Satow, *A Diplomat in Japan* (London: Seeley, 1921), p. 200.

5

The Meiji Restoration

The New Order

In the fall of 1868, the era named Meiji was proclaimed. Edo, renamed Tokyo (Eastern Capital), was designated as the new seat of government. In the following spring the emperor moved into the former Edo Castle. Thus commenced the Meiji era, which was to last until 1912.

The new government was a very young one. The emperor was a callow youth, no more than a figurehead, and although he is believed to have been an intelligent, able person he would remain by and large a symbol of authority for the forty-five years of his reign. The powers of government at the beginning of the Meiji period were in the hands of a small clique of court aristocrats, the most prominent of whom were Iwakura Tomomi and Sanjō Sanetomi (1837–1891), and members of those han that had played decisive roles in the overthrow of the Bakufu: from Satsuma, Saigō Takamori and Ōkubo Toshimichi; from Chōshū, Kido Kōin, Itō Hirobumi, Inoue Kaoru, and Yamagata Aritomo; from Hizen, Ōkuma Shigenobu (1838–1922); and from Tosa, Itagaki Taisuke (1836–1919) and Gotō Shōjirō. They were mostly men in their late thirties and early forties. There were also han chieftains who still regarded themselves as members of the power elite, the most influential being Satsuma's Shimazu Hisamitsu. In the beginning, however, power was concentrated in the hands of Iwakura, Sanjō, Ōkubo, Kido, and Saigō. Japan, it would seem, was endowed with a rather considerable number of very capable and far-sighted men who, despite their many faults, could certainly be labeled as statesmen. These men may have had to fight for their power, but essentially, they were patriotic individuals possessed of a strong sense of public responsibility, dedication, energy, and vision. Their leadership was collective, that is, no single person emerged as a strong man, and they ruled in accordance with

83

the time-honored Japanese tradition of collective leadership and consensus politics.

The task confronting the new Meiji leaders was stupendous. The immediate and overriding necessity was to strengthen and enrich the nation *(fukoku kyōhei)*. Japan was still in a precarious position even though there seemed to be no concrete evidence to indicate that the Western powers were interested in colonizing Japan as they had done with other Asian nations. There was, however, real fear in the minds of the Bakufu and the Satsuma-Chōshū factions that England or France might intervene if a serious civil war erupted. Both nations had already demonstrated in China their willingness to resort to force. Japan had been baptized by the gunfire of the British men-of-war at Satsuma and by the combined forces of the Western warships at Chōshū in the early 1860s. In the treaties it had concluded with the Western powers it had been compelled to accept unequal terms. Japan was deprived of the right to regulate tariffs, and Western residents in the treaty ports were granted the privilege of extraterritoriality. The treaties were unilateral and eternal. Japan had to grant the Western nations most-favored-nation treatment but was not given the same right in return.

Clearly, Japan was viewed as a backward nation by the Western powers. The Meiji leaders did in fact recognize that in terms of military strength and economic development, Japan was indeed far behind the Western nations. They even suspected that this was true in political, social, and cultural affairs. Consequently, they set as their primary task the development of military and economic power so as to protect Japan from becoming a victim to any external menace. They wanted to join the community of nations as an equal member and thus be eligible to participate in the game of international power politics.

To achieve the goal of increasing the national wealth and power it was necessary first of all to strengthen the foundations of the new government, which were still quite fragile. There were remnants of pro-Bakufu forces that were continuing their resistance against the Meiji government. These were mainly in the northern sections, the most prominent being Aizu Han. An expeditionary force had to be sent to subdue them as well as the bands of samurai who were conducting guerrilla-type warfare against the imperial government. The most famous band of warriors who resisted the Meiji government was the *Shōgitai,* whose members numbered 2,000 to 3,000. They continued to harass the imperial forces in Edo even after the Bakufu had officially surrendered the city. It took the military skill of Ōmura Masujirō, who was well-versed in Western military techniques, to subdue them. Resistance was also sustained in Hokkaido by the Bakufu's naval commissioner, Enomoto Takeaki, who fled there with the Bakufu's warships and established a so-called republican government. By the early summer of 1869, he too was subjugated.[1]

The most serious threat to the new government, however, was posed not by the overt opponents of the new ruling authorities but by the daimyō who were still entrenched in the local domains. The Bakufu's overthrow did not automatically end the daimyō's control over their han. Only the Tokugawa family and the northern han that forcefully resisted the new government were eliminated or had their holdings reduced. There were still about 270 han that retained their status as autonomous authorities.

One of the major tasks confronting the new government was the subordination of these local authorities to the central government and the construction of new administrative machinery for the entire nation. It also had to eliminate the caste-like organization of the society if it wished to modernize successfully the political system, the armed forces, and the economy. In the financial realm the Meiji government, faced with an almost completely empty treasury, had to regulate its sources of revenue, systematize the currency, and pay its debts. In order to enrich the nation, as fukoku kyōhei demanded, the economy had to be revolutionized; that is, Western-style industries had to be introduced, agriculture techniques improved, and foreign trade fostered. This meant not only the importation of the products of Western technology such as railroads, telegraphs, and steamships, and the establishment of Western-style factories, but also the training and education of the people so that they could be employed in the new enterprises.

In other words, to achieve the goal of fukoku kyōhei Japan had to be modernized, Westernized. The men who succeeded in overthrowing the Bakufu did so by riding the crest of the wave of anti-Westernism, but once they gained power, it became imperative that they abandon their anti-Western position and embrace in its stead a policy of establishing full cultural and commercial relations with the West. This, of course, angered the true believers of jōi, who assassinated men like Ōmura Masujirō and Yokoi Shōnan[2] because they were regarded as the chief exponents of Westernism.

The fact that Japan was to open its doors completely to the outside world even in the face of some internal opposition was signified by the proclamation in April 1868 of the *Charter Oath of Five Articles,* stating:

1. Deliberative assemblies shall be widely established and all state affairs decided by public opinion.
2. All classes, high and low, shall unite in actively carrying out the administration of affairs of state.
3. The common people, no less than the civil and military officials, shall be allowed to pursue whatever calling they choose so that public apathy may not beset the land.
4. The evil customs of the past shall be abandoned and everything based on the just laws of Heaven and Earth.

5. Knowledge shall be sought throughout the world so as to invigorate the foundations of imperial rule.

The Five Articles, originally drafted by two men who were sympathetic to constitutional, parliamentary government, were revised by Kido Kōin in order to make the references to the common people and parliamentary government somewhat less explicit.

The business at hand for the new leaders, then, was the establishment of a new order and the modernization of Japan. The Meiji leaders were at the same time faced with the problem of consolidating their grip on the machinery of power. They had to dislodge those who formerly held power while fending off the efforts of new opponents who were seeking to expel them in the name of "freedom and popular rights." By the middle of the 1880s, the Meiji leaders had not only launched Japan on its path to modernization but had also gained a firmer grip on the reins of power as they emerged in the form of a small group of tightly knit oligarchs who came to be known as the *genrō* (elder statesmen). They were Itō Hirobumi, Yamagata Aritomo, and Inoue Kaoru from Chōshū and Kuroda Kiyotaka (1840–1900), Matsukata Masayoshi, Saigō Tsugumichi (1843–1902), and Ōyama Iwao (1842–1916) from Satsuma. These government leaders were providing official direction in creating a new order of things. Nongovernment leaders from the intellectual and cultural realms, by fostering the cultural movement known as *bunmei kaika* (civilization and enlightenment) and the political movement known as *jiyū minken* (freedom and popular rights), were also working toward the modernization of the society.

POLITICAL CHANGES

Early in 1868, after the Tokugawa forces were routed at Toba-Fushimi, the imperial faction established a provisional government. In June it was replaced by new political machinery, and what is sometimes referred to as the Constitution of 1868 was proclaimed, establishing a Council of State *(Dajōkan)* with supreme political authority. The Council of State had a threefold division—legislative, executive, and judicial—and in theory the principle of separation of powers was to prevail. In reality, however, the men who held key positions did not operate under the restraints of this kind of government, and a few men exercised power that cut across administrative divisions.

Further changes in governmental structure were made in the summer of 1869, but the form of government that the Meiji leaders finally settled upon and retained (until the cabinet system was introduced in 1885) was the one adopted in the summer of 1871. On this occasion the Council of State was divided into three parts: the Central Board, the Right Board, and the Left Board. The Central

Board was the supreme organ of the government and made final decisions on all questions of policy. It was headed by the *dajō daijin* (chancellor) and included the *dainagon* (deputies), who were later replaced by ministers of the left and right, and a number of councilors. The Left Board, although it was originally designed to perform legislative functions, acted merely as an advisory body. The Right Board consisted of heads of departments and their deputies. The departments of foreign affairs, finance, war, public works, imperial household, education, Shinto, and justice were created at this time. The department of home affairs was added in 1873. In theory the Right Board was separated from the Central Board, but because influential councilors also served as heads of departments, policy-making and administrative duties tended to merge.

Power was drawn increasingly into the hands of the Satsuma-Chōshū leaders while the court nobles and former daimyō gradually faded into the background. The post of dajō daijin was occupied by Sanjō and that of minister of the right by Iwakura, but the real authority actually rested with the councilors, who were primarily men from Satsuma and Chōshū.

Tampering with the administrative system of the central government did little to strengthen its authority because of the continued existence of the anachronistic feudal domains. From the outset of the Meiji era, men like Kido were convinced that it was imperative to compel the daimyō to return their domains to the emperor just as the shōgun had done. Fortunately for the Meiji government, the leaders from Satsuma, Chōshū, Tosa, and Hizen managed to persuade their lords to take the initiative in adopting this policy, and in March 1869 the daimyō of the four han appealed to the emperor to accept the restoration of their domains. Apparently, they regarded this action as a mere formality in which the emperor would agree to their offer but then would reinvest them with authority over their former han, and perhaps even add more land as a reward for their loyal gesture. Other daimyō quickly followed suit, fearing that otherwise they might be considered less loyal to the new imperial government than the four daimyō that initiated the policy. The government formally accepted the restoration of the han lands in July and ordered the remaining daimyō to do so. The former daimyō were reappointed as hereditary han chieftains and paid one-tenth of the han income as salary. The samurai retainers of the ex-daimyō were given a fraction of their former stipends as income.

The process of returning han lands to the emperor was completed by early 1870. Some han chieftains, like Shimazu Hisamitsu, were disillusioned with the outcome of the transaction because they had been led to believe that they would have autonomous power in the han and be allowed to retain their own armies. Now that all the daimyō had relinquished their authority to the imperial government, however, the Meiji leaders proceeded to eliminate han government entirely by replacing the han with prefectures.

The smaller han were facing bankruptcy, and some han officials petitioned the government to abolish them by the end of 1869. The government complied with these requests and brought several small han under the authority of the prefectural governors. Some han leaders were vigorously introducing reforms, but others did nothing to meet the challenges of the new era. Internal unrest among the peasantry and the samurai was also a problem in many han, and in order to suppress the malcontents the central government had to acquire immediate jurisdiction over the han. The government, moreover, needed the revenues that could be collected from the han.[3]

In order to replace the han with prefectural governments under the direct control of the central government, the Meiji leaders needed the cooperation of the most troublesome han, Satsuma. An effort was made to persuade Hisamitsu to enter the government, and although he personally refused, he did agree to allow Saigō, who had returned to Satsuma soon after the Meiji government was established, to join the central government. In the summer of 1871, Saigō began to serve as one of the first councilors of the government. Evidently, he did so expecting to build a strong government around the *shizoku* (former samurai).

The final decision to abolish the han was made with Saigō's entry into the government. In order to cope with any resistance that it might encounter, the central government organized an imperial army consisting of warriors provided by Satsuma, Chōshū, and Tosa. In August 1871 a decree was issued formally abolishing the han and replacing them with prefectures headed by governors appointed by the center. A number of daimyō welcomed this decision because of han severe internal weaknesses and financial troubles. Even those who were not wholeheartedly in favor of this policy nevertheless accepted the change without opposition because the settlement was very favorable to the former ruling caste. These daimyō were allowed to retain an income that was equivalent to one-tenth the income of their former han, and of course now they had none of the expenses involved in managing the han. The central government assumed the debts that had been incurred by the han and undertook the responsibility for the paper currencies that had been issued by them. In effect, the central government had bailed the han out of their financial difficulties and thus provided the former daimyō with very little to complain about. The people who were placed in a difficult situation were the former retainers of the daimyō.

The reorganization of the government in accord with the system adopted in 1871 was effected with the successful abolishment of the han and their replacement by the prefectures. A centralized bureaucratic government was beginning to emerge, and the key leaders, aside from Sanjō and Iwakura, were coming primarily from the four han of Satsuma, Chōshū, Tosa, and Hizen, with men from Satsuma and Chōshū predominating. These leaders, however, were not in complete agreement about the kind of government that should be established. The faction led by Ōkubo and Kido tended to prefer a strong centralized bureaucracy, while the faction represented by Saigō favored making the shizoku the core of the government.

Now that the decision to replace the han with prefectures was made, the government decided to move forward by sending a special mission abroad to lay the groundwork for revising the treaties that the Tokugawa Bakufu had concluded with the Western nations. The Meiji leaders wanted to remove the unequal provisions of the treaties, which were renewable in 1872. It was believed that the mission would also prove to be an important educational experience for the new leaders since they would be given an opportunity to observe directly Western societies in action. They were to study with particular care those legal and political institutions and practices that might be necessary to adopt if the Western nations were to be persuaded to revise the unequal treaties. The mission, which was led by Iwakura and included among its members such top government officials as Ōkubo, Kido, Itō, and Inoue, departed for the United States and Europe toward the end of 1871.

A caretaker government was established while members of the Iwakura Mission were abroad, with the following men holding key positions: Saigō, Itagaki Taisuke, Etō Shimpei (1834–1874), Soejima Taneomi (1828–1905), and Ōkuma Shigenobu. It was agreed that no major changes were to be introduced, but this was a rather unrealistic restriction in light of the fact that the Iwakura Mission was to remain abroad for a year and a half or more at a time when there were many pressing problems, such as growing agrarian discontent, threatening the country. As it turned out, many significant reforms and innovations were in fact made in the courts, the schools, the land tax, the military, the postal system, and the calendar.

So far as the mission itself was concerned, it failed to achieve its primary goal of persuading the Western powers to revise the treaties on the basis of equality. The members of the group, however, did return impressed with what they saw of Western industries, technology, and certain aspects of political life, particularly in Bismarckian Germany.

LOCAL GOVERNMENT

In 1871 the government reorganized the registration systems that had existed in the Tokugawa period (in which separate registers were kept for each class, primarily to ferret out hidden Christians) and established a uniform system of family registration. The task of maintaining the records was turned over to the local administrative districts that were established by bringing together several villages under the authority of a "minor district." Several of these were then joined together to form a "major district." The administrative heads of these units were appointed from above, and in effect they became members of the new bureaucratic class.

In 1878 the artificial division of the country into districts was abolished, and the towns and villages were made the basic administrative units. In 1880, town and village assemblies were established, the members of which were elected, to deal with matters prescribed by national law.

The administrative authority immediately below the central government was the prefectural government. Initially the former han, regardless of size, were transformed into prefectures so that there were three *fu* (metropolitan prefectures) and 306 *ken* (prefectures). During the following years the smaller ones were consolidated and the larger ones broken up until 1888 when the final redistricting occurred, dividing the nation into three fu and forty-three ken, including Okinawa. The prefectural governors were appointed by the central government, and they became its administrative arms.

SOCIAL REFORMS

The class system perpetuated by the Tokugawa government was one of the feudal vestiges of the society that had to be eliminated. The removal of feudal class distinctions began in 1869, when the daimyō began relinquishing their control over the han. They and the court aristocrats were classified as *kazoku* (peers), the upper-class samurai as *shizoku,* and the lower-class samurai as *sotsu.* In 1870 the common people, classified as *heimin,* were permitted to adopt family names,[4] and in 1871, intermarriages between the upper and lower classes were allowed. The common people were now given the right to wear formal apparel and travel on horseback, previously the exclusive privileges of the samurai. Also in 1871 wearing of the distinctive hairstyle and the characteristic sword bearing (which was ultimately banned in 1876) were made optional for the kazoku and shizoku. The samurai's right to cut down disrespectful commoners with impunity was also abolished. Aside from government officials, kazoku and shizoku were now permitted to become farmers, merchants, or artisans.

In 1872 the government reclassified the populace into three categories: kazoku, shizoku, and heimin. The lower-class samurai, the sotsu, were now reclassified as heimin. The purpose for retaining these distinctions, the government held, was for genealogical identification.

Another class of people who in theory were uplifted from their place at the bottom of the society were the outcastes, who had heretofore been treated as unclean members of the society. This group totaled about 400,000 people, or slightly over 1 percent of the population. The Meiji government abolished legal bias, but in reality social and economic discrimination against the outcastes did not cease, and, in fact, it continues to the present.

JAPANESE PREFECTURES

Equality was to prevail among all classes, theoretically, but in practice, the kazoku and shizoku were still accorded privileged treatment by law. In the code of 1873, for instance, both these groups were allowed to pay fines rather than face imprisonment for minor crimes. For offenses that resulted in incarceration with hard labor for commoners, kazoku and shizoku were imprisoned without hard labor. Commoners who became government officials, however, were accorded the same treatment as members of the shizoku. The government officials in effect constituted the new privileged class.

In the fall of 1872, as a by-product of the *Maria Luz* affair, slavery and human traffic were made illegal. The Peruvian ship *Maria Luz,* which was engaged in coolie traffic, arrived in Yokohama for repairs in the summer of 1872. Some coolies escaped and asked for aid. The Japanese, in extending assistance to them, were then confronted by the Peruvian authorities with the fact that practices akin to slavery, such as girls being sold to brothels, were prevalent in Japan. This led the government to ban slavery, although "voluntary" servitude in houses of prostitution was permitted.[5]

PENSIONS FOR THE KAZOKU AND SHIZOKU

As noted above, the central government adopted the policy of paying the former daimyō and samurai a portion of their feudal incomes and stipends. This naturally created a considerable drain on the government's revenues. Approximately one-third of the tax revenues collected in the period from the abolishment of the han to Saigō's rebellion in 1877 (see page 116) had to be allocated for these payments. The government had assumed in addition to this all the debts of the han. Consequently, about half of the government's total income was expended to meet these old feudal obligations.

In order to ease its financial burdens the government decided to commute the pensions in 1876. The pensioners were paid off in government bonds that were issued with interest rates varying in accordance with the former stipends. The recipients of smaller stipends may have been granted higher interest rates, but the original stipends of the upper class were so much larger that the 476 kazoku received one-third of the sum allocated for the commutation bonds, thus forcing the 320,000 shizoku to share the remaining two-thirds. The income of the kazoku dropped to about 45 percent of what they formerly received, but compared to the shizoku they were still well off. Many invested their money in land, business, and banks.[6]

The abolition of the class system and the adoption of the pension plan meant that the former samurai were actually dispossessed. As a result, they were bitterly disappointed in the new order and fell into a dangerously rebellious mood. This in part accounts for the growing number of samurai uprisings that broke out in the 1870s. Only 10 percent of the former samurai managed to obtain government positions. Some went into teaching, the army, and the police force, but the vast majority found it necessary to enter occupations totally alien to their background and aptitude, such as agriculture, commerce, and handicraft work. Some became so impoverished that they were reduced to selling their daughters to the houses of prostitution.

REVISION OF THE LAND TAX AND THE PLIGHT OF THE FARMERS

In accordance with its policy of removing feudal restrictions, the Meiji government lifted the ban on the export of rice in the summer of 1871. In the fall of that year it also removed the restrictions on land utilization and gave the farmers the freedom to grow whatever they chose. Private ownership of land, established by the issuance of title deeds, was recognized, and in the spring of 1872 the right to buy and sell land was finally granted.

The levy on rice was collected in the traditional manner and in accordance with the rates that had been fixed by the former daimyō until 1873, when a tax reform was instituted. This required the holders of title deeds to pay taxes in money at 3 percent of the assessed value of the land, while at the same time local taxes were limited to one-third of the national tax. This new system of taxation, however, did not lessen the burden of the farmers because the amount due remained close to what was collected under the old order; that is to say, the 3 percent tax on the land came to about 33 percent of the total yield.[7]

During the Tokugawa period peasants were allowed to utilize the woods and meadows belonging to the lord of the han for firewood and fodder, but now these were no longer open to them. They were now, along with the woods and meadows belonging to the community, classified as state property. The farmers agitated for a reduction in the land tax, and they did manage in 1876 to have the rate lowered to 2.5 percent.[8] The farmers were not allowed to deduct the equivalent of their wages from the taxable land value even though the wages of the townsmen were not taxed. The only favorable aspect of the land tax revisions as far as the peasants were concerned was the elimination of community responsibility for taxes.

The government did little to discourage the diffusion of tenancy because its primary interest was in the collection of the land tax. The question of land ownership mattered little to the officials, and at this time about one-third of the arable land was held in tenancy.[9] Many of the landowning farmers actually possessed very little land—about 40 percent of the farm families owned 1.1 acre or less.

Agrarian poverty was intensified by a variety of factors in addition to the heavy burden of taxation. Fluctuations in the price of rice affected the farmers adversely, and the penetration of the money economy into the countryside greatly increased their expenses. Those farmers who supplemented their income by raising silkworms were at the mercy of the fluctuating price of silk. The rural household industries were very badly hurt by the importation of cheap foreign manufactured goods, and the growth of Western-type factory production in Japan threatened their continued existence altogether.

New measures introduced by the Meiji government, such as universal military conscription and compulsory education, also added to the burden of the agrarian families. The pressures that were brought to bear by the implementation of these programs led to an increasingly large number of farmers being dispossessed of their lands. As a result, peasant disturbances began to increase, and many village leaders, hoping to improve rural conditions by gaining a voice in the political arena, became active in the popular rights movement.

LEGAL REFORMS

The Tokugawa legal system was based on the notion of rule-by-status rather than on the concept, prevalent in the West, of rule-of-law. From the Western point of view, then, the legal practices in mid-nineteenth-century Japan certainly seemed arbitrary, offering no protection for individuals unfamiliar with Japanese ways. The attacks against the Westerners who unknowingly violated the customs of the land hardened their distrust of Japanese justice. Consequently, there was little likelihood that the unequal treaties would be revised unless Japan adopted Western legal institutions and practices.

The Meiji authorities were eager to develop a legal system that would be acceptable to the West; they turned to the French model because, unlike the unwieldy Anglo-American common law, it had the advantage of having been codified. French laws were also especially appealing because they were administered by a corps of professional judges.[10]

The legal system that emerged in the Meiji period is defined by some legal scholars as rule-*by*-law rather than rule-*of*-law because although there was a formal commitment to the concept of administration under law, there were no legal limitations set on policy formation or legislation.[11]

The court system that emerged under the Meiji Constitution consisted, from the lowest to the highest, of summary police courts, district courts, local courts, courts of appeal, and the Court of Cassation, which heard appeals on points of law from inferior courts.[12]

A penal code and a code of criminal procedure were prepared and adopted in 1880 and 1890 with the assistance of a French adviser, Gustave Boissonade (1825–1910). A commercial code was designed with the aid of a German legal authority, Hermann Roessler (1834–1894), but it was not put into effect until

1899. The drafting and adoption of the civil code, the final version of which was patterned largely after the German model, was delayed until 1898.

THE POLICE SYSTEM

Under Tokugawa rule a police system whose primary function was the protection of the people did not exist. The law enforcement officials during this period functioned primarily as instruments charged with the responsibility of keeping the people under control. Some Japanese observers who went abroad were impressed by the courteous and helpful behavior of Western policemen, and they brought back with them the concept that the primary functions of the police should be to maintain law and order and to protect the people. The repressive, authoritarian tendency of the law enforcement officers, however, could not easily be altered. Initially the police were placed under the jurisdiction of the local governments, but in 1874 they were brought under the control of the Ministry of Home Affairs in accordance with the recommendation of Kawaji Toshiyoshi, who is regarded as the founder of the modern Japanese police system. He envisioned the police as an instrument for strengthening the nation, and he outspokenly favored the establishment of a "police state" in which the police would play a key role in maintaining "the good health" of the nation by aggressively ferreting out undesirable elements.

The Meiji government gradually centralized police power. Under the cabinet system that was introduced in 1885, the minister of home affairs retained supervisory authority over the prefectural police. Prefectural police commissioners were appointed by the central government and were made responsible to the police commissioner in the Ministry of Home Affairs. The authority of the police was extended: it was given the power to censor the press and control political activities; it was granted the authority to regulate aspects of personal behavior by curtailing such things as nudity, heterosexual bathing, and so on. It became an institution to be feared rather than an organization to which the people could turn for help and protection.

THE ARMY AND THE NAVY

In order to establish a strong central government and also cope with external problems, the Meiji government found it necessary to raise its own army instead of relying upon those maintained by the han. The need for a national army was generally agreed upon, but there was dispute over the question of the kind of army that should be established. Kido and Ōmura Masujirō favored one based upon universal conscription whereas Ōkubo advocated establishing a national army made up of the former samurai of the major han, Satsuma, Chōshū, and Tosa. Kido feared the power of the shizoku and objected to this scheme; Ōkubo, in contrast, distrusted the commoners who might gain power if universal conscription were introduced.[13] In 1871, with Iwakura in support of Ōkubo's position, the government established an army consisting of 6,000 to 8,000 warriors of Satsuma, Chōshū, and Tosa.

Ōmura became the object of hatred by the shizoku because his military plan would have deprived them of their traditional function. He was assassinated by reactionary samurai, but the plan for universal conscription did not die with him despite continued opposition by conservative officials. Eventually, Yamagata Aritomo succeeded in creating a new army that was based on universal conscription, and in January 1873 the military conscription law was promulgated. All male subjects, with certain exceptions, became liable for military conscription at the age of twenty.

Not only was universal conscription unpopular with the shizoku, who resented being deprived of their traditional function, but the common people also objected to being drafted. The use of the term "blood tax" for the obligation to serve in the military led to the belief that blood would be taken from the conscripts. It was even rumored that they would be killed and then turned over to foreigners who would extract oil from their corpses to be used for food. As a result, uprisings protesting military conscription broke out in different parts of the country. The new army, however, despite these difficulties, became an established institution, and by 1883 all the men in the army were conscript soldiers. The shizoku eventually came to accept the new system and in fact played a significant role as officers in the new army, which was designed after the Prussian model. The generals were primarily men from Chōshū and Satsuma, with the men from Chōshū predominating.

The government was also faced with the task of building a modern navy, but plans for this did not materialize rapidly, and it was not until 1875 that the government ordered three ironclad warships from England. As late as 1889, Japan had only three ironclad vessels and three composite (iron and wood) ships. The navy, modeled after the British prototype, was dominated by Satsuma men.

The soldiers had no *esprit de corps,* no sense of identity with the national interest or concept of public service, and so the government sought to foster such attitudes by issuing an imperial rescript to the soldiers and sailors in 1882. It emphasized such virtues as loyalty, duty, service, obedience, and valor while urging the men to abstain from political activities. The rescript stressed in particular the special role they were to play as servants of the emperor.

ECONOMIC DEVELOPMENTS

It was necessary to revolutionize the basically agrarian economy and transform the nation into an industrial society if the policy to "enrich and strengthen the nation" was to be realized. Meiji Japan had to enter the stage of modern economic growth, and this necessitated: (1) the application of modern scientific thought and technology to industry, transportation, and agriculture; (2) continuous and rapid rise in real product per capita together with high rates of population growth; (3) rapid and efficient transformation of the industrial structure (e.g., shift from agriculture to manufacturing); and (4) international contacts.[14]

Tokugawa Japan was essentially an agrarian society characterized by the small peasant cultivator who lived just above the subsistence level. "Isolated islands of modernity existed and exist in most backward countries, and these should not be confused with the genuine beginnings of an industrial revolution. A few spinning mills and iron foundries cannot be said to change the industrial structure of a country with a population of some 30 million people."[15] The amount of foreign trade after the arrival of Perry continued to remain very small, although of the four criteria of modern economic growth this was the one most clearly in evidence. At best, the following can be said:

> The Japanese economy of the 1860s was reasonably, but not outstandingly productive for a traditional economy. It had a high potential for saving and was already showing signs of quickening economic growth. At the same time a number of other features made it more responsive than most traditional economies to economic stimuli. It was basically commercial with a well-developed system of national markets. The population was comparatively well educated and economically motivated. Because of efficient and productive taxation systems and its tradition of economic activity and control, government was well placed to play an important role in the process of economic modernization.[16]

Under these circumstances the government had to play an active role in removing many of the feudal barriers and in creating and stimulating the conditions necessary for modern economic growth. As noted earlier, it abolished the Tokugawa class system along with the privileges customarily accorded to the samurai. Internal checkpoints that obstructed travel and trade were removed, and freedom of occupation was granted. The government fostered better agricultural techniques, instituted a uniform system of land tax, and established a new financial base by creating a public budget system and a modern currency and banking system. It also actively propagated Western knowledge and introduced compulsory public education. More directly, it encouraged the development of new industries by, among other things, building and operating key enterprises, constructing model plants, and granting government subsidies to private entrepreneurs.

The government took the initiative in constructing modern transportation and communication systems, which were essential for the modernization of the economy. The first railroad line, the Tokyo-Yokohama Railway, was opened in 1872, and this was followed by the Tōkaidō line linking Tokyo and Kobe, which was completed in 1889. In 1869 the telegraph line between Tokyo and Yokohama was completed, and in 1871 a postal system linking Tokyo and Osaka was introduced. In shipping, the government gave its support to the Mitsubishi Company so as to enable it to compete with foreign companies.[17] Shipyards, arsenals, foundries, machine shops, and technical schools were established and operated with foreign technical advisers.

In the realm of industrial development, the government established the first modern silk filature in 1870. Cotton spinning mills were built or reequipped with modern imported machinery. Experimental factories were built for the production of cement, tile, sugar, beer, glass, chemicals, woolen fabrics, and so on. Using foreign technicians, the government also played a role in developing the mining industry, particularly copper, coal, and precious metals. In order to foster and stimulate interest in industrial development, it staged an industrial exposition in 1877, in the midst of Saigō's rebellion. Needless to say, it placed great stress on agricultural improvement and also sought to encourage animal husbandry by establishing experimental stations.

In this transitional period neither agricultural nor industrial growth was spectacular.[18] Modern-style factories were still limited in number and rather small in scale. In 1886, for example, the steam power used for industrial purposes totaled 4,094 horsepower distributed through 217 plants.

The government did play a very significant role in the industrialization of Meiji Japan, but it was not the only force that was to contribute to a transformation of the economy. Private entrepreneurs took advantage of the fresh opportunities and initiated new enterprises, and despite the low standard of living, private savings did accumulate. Rural leaders also played an active role by introducing new agricultural knowledge into the villages. The one area, however, in which the government's role was critical was in the fiscal realm. The Meiji government was in a precarious financial situation when it came to power in 1868. During the period from September 1868 to December 1872, total public expenditures amounted to 148.3 million yen while revenue came to only 50.4 million yen. The government sought to offset this imbalance by issuing nonconvertible paper notes and by borrowing from big merchant houses and foreign nations. In 1872 it authorized the establishment of national banks and retired nonconvertible notes; in 1873 it instituted the land tax. Its financial position, even with the implementation of these measures, was still strained because so much of its revenue had to be used to fulfill the feudal obligations that it had assumed.

In 1877 the government was involved in the fiscally damaging enterprise of crushing the major uprising led by Saigō, and this necessitated the issuance of an additional 27 million yen in notes. The government was also compelled to allow banks to issue notes, up to 80 percent of their capital, against bonds deposited with the treasury. This encouraged the kazoku and shizoku, who were paid off in bonds in the commutation of stipends, to invest in the national banks, which then issued additional bank notes.[19] This created a serious inflationary situation that saw the price of rice nearly double. The government's real income dropped drastically, and it was compelled to introduce new taxes on sake and tobacco, and reduce its expenditures in developing new industries.

Confronted with this critical situation, Matsukata Masayoshi (1835–1924), who became finance minister in 1881 and remained in charge of fiscal affairs for the next sixteen years, adopted a policy of reintroducing convertible currency, severe austerity, and deflation. He ended public operation of costly factories and mines, introduced new indirect taxes, and started redeeming public debts.[20] In 1885 Matsukata reformed the banking system by establishing the Bank of Japan, which replaced the national banks as the bank of issue. Matsukata thus restored the financial health of the government and gave the country a modern currency system and an effective budget structure. Japan was finally ready to enter the stage of modern economic growth.

Matsukata undoubtedly deserves great credit for his achievements, but it should be noted at the same time that his taxation and deflationary policies had serious adverse effects on the farmers and created severe hardships that ultimately led to agrarian riots. Increased taxes on sake and tobacco, in addition to indirect taxes, burdened the common man more than the rich. Deflation was especially painful for the farming population because, although money was dearer, the land tax rate remained the same.[21] Local taxes also increased as a result of the central government making the local authorities responsible for some of the services that it had formerly provided.

A noteworthy characteristic of the developing economic policy was the close cooperation that was established between the government and certain favored business interests, a policy that culminated with the emergence of gigantic business houses, the *zaibatsu*. Cooperation between the big merchant families and the new government began when houses such as Mitsui, Shimada, Ono, and Kōnoike supplied the imperial forces with funds, through donations or loans, during their conflict with the Bakufu. Even so, the big merchant houses also maintained close ties with the Bakufu and thus made certain they would be on the winning side regardless of the outcome of the struggle.

Special consideration was given to these houses when the imperial faction triumphed. For instance, the merchant houses were used as tax collectors by the government. This proved to be a particularly lucrative enterprise since the farmers were required to pay their taxes in money and thus had to convert their rice into currency.[22]

The government facilitated the entry of these houses into the banking business when a system of national banks was established in 1872, and it encouraged their expansion into the industrial realm by transferring many state-owned enterprises to them at very low prices. In 1880 a law enabling the government to transfer factories to private hands was enacted, and factories in nonstrategic industries such as cotton spinning, glass making, and cement were turned over to private firms.

Initially the government maintained control of mining, with the exception of the Sumitomo Company, which was allowed to keep the Besshi copper mine, the largest in the country. As time went on, private firms increasingly moved into this industry.[23]

The government supported and subsidized the Mitsubishi Company in the area of shipping. It gave thirteen ships that had been used as military transports during the Formosan expedition of 1874 to the founder of the company, Iwasaki Yatarō (1835–1885), and beginning in 1875 the government subsidized his shipping business by granting it an annual subsidy of 250,000 yen for fifteen years.[24] The Mitsubishi Company was provided even further assistance when, in 1887, the government sold it the Nagasaki Shipyards. State support of sea transport was extended because, for strategic and economic reasons, it was deemed necessary to have a strong merchant fleet that was capable of competing on equal terms with foreign shipping firms. Also, there were frequently close personal bonds between key members of the government and the major business houses.[25]

EDUCATION

At the time of the Meiji Restoration some traditional scholars hoped to make Confucianism or Shinto the basis of learning. This was the case because what had presumably taken place was the "restoration" of imperial authority and traditional values. In 1869 a traditionalist scholar who believed that the object of education should be the elucidation of the "imperial way" was made the head of the Bureau of Educational Studies. It was intended that Shinto be made the national religion and the foundation of education. The goal of education, as stated in an official proclamation issued in 1870, must be the inculcation of "respect for the enlightened way of the *kami* [gods], and the clarification of human relations. The multitudes must rectify their minds, perform their work diligently, and serve the imperial court."[26]

This essentially reactionary trend in educational thought was soon challenged, however, by those who represented the movement to "enlighten and

civilize" the country. They maintained that in order to modernize Japan, Western educational ideas and practices had to be adopted. The movement was led
by private educators such as Fukuzawa Yukichi (1835–1901), but the need to
adopt and adapt Western educational concepts and institutions was also recognized by the more progressive of the government leaders.

The importation of Western knowledge necessarily required that a high
level of literacy be achieved. The literacy rate of Tokugawa Japan was indeed
relatively high, as was noted earlier, but the Meiji leaders set out to eliminate
illiteracy completely. They issued the Education Ordinance of 1872, which
stated that there shall be "no community with an illiterate family, nor a family
with an illiterate person."[27] Universal education was instituted by this act, and
every child was, in theory, required to attend school for eight years. The philosophy underlying this system was utilitarian and pragmatic, as the preamble
to the Education Ordinance demonstrates:

> In order for each person to make his way in life, husband his wealth wisely, en-
> joy prosperity in his business, and attain the goal of his life he must develop
> his character, broaden his knowledge, and cultivate his talents. . . . [All this,
> however,] cannot be achieved without education. For this reason schools are
> established. . . . Learning is like an investment for success in life. How can
> anyone afford to neglect it?

The practical aspect of learning was emphasized by the observation that

> language, writing, and arithmetic used in daily affairs as well as the affairs of
> the shizoku, officials, farmers, merchants, and practitioners of all kinds of arts
> and crafts, and matters pertaining to law, politics, astronomy, medicine, etc.,
> that is, all things that man concerns himself with belong to the domain of
> learning.

The new approach to learning was contrasted with the old approach in
which

> earning was regarded as the business of the samurai and his superiors while the
> peasants, artisans, merchants, women and children paid no heed to it, having
> no notion of what it meant. Even the samurai and his superiors who pursued
> learning tended to claim that it was done for the good of the state and were
> unaware of the fact that it was the foundation for success in life.

This emphasis on the practical nature of learning reflected the thinking of
Fukuzawa Yukichi, who had a significant influence on early Meiji education.

He rejected the study of classical literature and poetry and argued that learning should be practical because it must be applied to real life and used to improve the livelihood of the people and enrich the nation.

The structure of the educational system of 1872 was patterned after France's system. The country was divided into eight university districts, each containing thirty-two middle school districts. Each of these was to include 210 elementary school districts. All of this, however, merely remained a plan on paper, and very few universities or middle schools were actually established in the early Meiji era. Not many elementary schools were built, either, and much of the instruction that did in fact go on took place in private homes and Buddhist temples.

Normal schools were established, with the assistance of an American educator, Marion M. Scott (1849–1936), in order to train teachers for the new schools. Scott was a follower of Johann Pestalozzi (1746–1827), the Swiss educational philosopher who emphasized the use of actual objects, models, and specimens in instruction.[28]

The curriculum of the elementary schools was influenced mainly by the American educational system. The textbooks, containing lessons about Western societies and civilization, were written by men like Fukuzawa or were translations of Western schoolbooks, especially American readers. Particular emphasis was placed on the introduction of scientific knowledge.

Traditionalists steeped in the Confucian classics scoffed at the effort to teach children about "peaches, chestnuts, and persimmons" while pupils failed to be stirred by accounts of Napoleon and other Western heroes. School attendance began to rise despite the financial burden on the masses and the seeming irrelevance of much of what was being taught.[29]

In order to accelerate the pace of student enrollment and gain greater public support for the schools, the minister of education, Tanaka Fujimaro (1845–1909), with the assistance of David Murray, a professor from Rutgers University, revised the educational system in 1879. Following the example of the American school system, Tanaka decentralized the Japanese schools, and a locally elected school board was introduced in each community to establish and maintain the schools. The period of compulsory education was fixed at four years, with each school year consisting of four months. All of these reforms, however, failed to strengthen the educational system, which may in fact have become even weaker because in some instances the local communities chose to close the schools or amalgamate them in order to reduce expenses.

In 1880 Tanaka was replaced and a new ordinance was issued that served to centralize the system again while giving the prefectural governors greater authority over the schools. The length of compulsory education was changed to three years, but because the school year was extended to thirty-two weeks, the period of school attendance was in reality made longer.[30]

During the 1880s a more conservative philosophy began to permeate the educational system. A conscious effort was made to replace the more libertarian, individualistic values that were taught in the schools with traditional virtues such as loyalty to the emperor, filial piety, and benevolence and righteousness. The teaching of "morals" was made compulsory, and many of the textbooks then in use, like Fukuzawa's works and the translations of Western texts on moral science, were replaced by books that were Confucian or Shinto in orientation. Japanese history came to be emphasized in an effort to acquaint students with the virtues of their own country.

All this was part of the rising tide of cultural nationalism (see page 135) that was becoming increasingly discernible around this time. There was a marked shift away from the concept that education was intended to serve the interests of the individual and toward the philosophy that it was primarily aimed at serving the ends of the state. The movement dictating tighter control over educational content continued, and in 1883 a policy of state textbook certification was adopted, with more stringent curbs being added in 1886.[31]

Significant steps in the direction of tighter control of the schools and indoctrination and training of the young to serve the interests of the state were taken in 1886 under the leadership of the minister of education, Mori Arinori (1847–1889). He issued a series of educational ordinances directed at introducing greater uniformity in the educational system while patterning it somewhat after the military. He introduced military drills in the schools, selected an army officer as the head of the first president of the higher normal school, and organized the students in the normal school dormitories as if they were soldiers in barracks. Textbooks were also brought under closer government scrutiny. The University of Tokyo, which was established as a successor to the Bakufu's colleges, was renamed the Imperial University of Tokyo and brought under the close supervision of the ministry of education.[32]

Mori paid special attention to the education of the teachers, the molders of the young. The object of their training and indoctrination, he contended, was the creation of decent human beings who possessed the virtues of "obedience, friendship, and dignity." The last virtue was to be manifested in issuing and obeying commands.

By the 1880s, in line with the rise of conservatism, the American influence in educational thinking began to give way, and Japanese educators began to look to the Germans for guidance. The educational philosopher to whom they turned was Johann Friedrich Herbart (1776–1841). He focused his attention on the development of a student's moral character and held that the object of education should be the development of an enlightened will that is capable of making distinctions between right and wrong. These were particularly appealing notions at this time because of the growing tide of reaction against the superficial imitation of Western ways and the desire on the part of the traditionalists to restore Confucian moralism to the educational sphere.

CIVILIZATION AND ENLIGHTENMENT

In the cultural and intellectual realms, the first decade or so of the Meiji era was characterized by frantic efforts to adopt Western concepts, practices, and products in order to become "civilized." Initially, both the government and private leaders agreed upon the necessity of "civilizing and enlightening" the nation, which meant, in essence, the adoption of the utilitarian, rational, scientific, and technological aspects of Western civilization.

Students were sent abroad, and Western scholars and specialists in all fields were invited to Japan to assist in the modernization of the country.[33] A massive educational effort was launched to "enlighten" the populace. A large number of books, pamphlets, and journals were published to spread knowledge about the West. Many of these were translations of Western works, while others were written by Japanese. There was, however, strong opposition to Western learning by the exponents of the sonnō jōi movement until the Meiji government came into existence. With its establishment, the policy of seeking "knowledge throughout the world" was officially adopted, thus ushering in the era of "civilization and enlightenment." The government encouraged the movement to "civilize" and Westernize the people because it realized that this was essential if Japan was to become as rich and powerful as the Western nations.

Fukuzawa Yukichi was one of the leading private proponents of "civilization and enlightenment." Through his enormous publications he contributed more than any other individual toward the education of the people about the West.[34] Fukuzawa began publishing his *Conditions in the West* just prior to the fall of the Tokugawa Bakufu, and it became the most widely read and most influential book of that era. It provided the Japanese public with some inkling of the Western way of life and institutions.

With the advent of the Meiji era, when it became permissible to criticize the traditional way of life and values, Fukuzawa became a vociferous advocate of Western liberalism, thus ceasing to be merely a purveyor of information about the West. The values he extolled were freedom, independence, self-respect, rationalism, the scientific spirit, pragmatism, and what might be called "bourgeois materialism."

The best known of Fukuzawa's works that were designed to transform the mode of thinking of the people were *Encouragement of Learning*, published between 1872 and 1876, and *Outline of Civilization*, published in 1875. In the earlier work he emphasized the importance of education, arguing that all men are equal at birth but distinctions develop because of differences in education.

He believed that what must be pursued was practical, scientific learning that was based upon the spirit of inquiry and skepticism. He also emphasized the necessity of strengthening the spirit of freedom and independence in the people in order to guarantee the independence of Japan. He rejected the paternalistic, hierarchic, repressive values of the past and called for the fostering of individualism. In his *Outline of Civilization,* Fukuzawa continued to emphasize the importance of freedom in strengthening the spirit of the people, upon whom the advancement of civilization depended.

Fukuzawa's significance as the chief exponent of "civilization and enlightenment" is enormous, but there were also other scholars and writers who contributed to the diffusion of Western knowledge and sought to "enlighten" the people. Many Western books, such as Samuel Smiles's *Self-Help* and John Stuart Mill's *On Liberty,* were translated and widely read. Educational societies such as the Meirokusha (Meiji Six Society), organized by Fukuzawa and his friends, spread Western ideas and knowledge through their journals. The following were among the founding members: Nakamura Masanao, who translated Mill's *On Liberty;* Nishi Amane, who introduced utilitarianism and positivism to Japan; Mori Arinori, who became minister of education in 1885; and Katō Hiroyuki, who later turned to Social Darwinism and German statism. Newspapers also came into existence and began to flourish, but they tended to focus on political issues. They became primarily instruments for the government or the opposition forces, and did not concentrate on the diffusion of knowledge about Western civilization.

The number of students going abroad to study increased substantially with the advent of the Meiji era.[35] Western language schools, particularly those for English, mushroomed and flourished. In 1874 there were ninety-one foreign language schools, with a total enrollment of 12,815 students.

The Meiji government also invited a large number of Western scholars and specialists to assist in the task of modernization. They were particularly prominent in the field of education: in 1874 there were 211 Western professors in the higher schools; in 1877, 27 of the 39 professors at Tokyo University were from the West.[36]

The Christian missionaries were another important source of information about the West and its values. They translated the Bible into Japanese, established mission schools and charitable institutions, and had as their students many prominent Meiji leaders. Guido Verbeck was among the more influential missionaries, and he served in various capacities in Japan from 1859 to 1898. In 1871, while he was a college professor, more than 1,000 students attended his lectures on the American Constitution and the New Testament.

There was a movement to adopt Western artifacts and customs at the same time that the government was adopting the policy of Westernization in order

to strengthen and enrich the nation, and Fukuzawa and his cohorts were in-
stilling and fostering the "spirit of civilization" in the people. This extended
from such things as interest in Western languages and Christianity, to Western
art, apparel, hair styles, and even the eating of beef. The technological products of the West, of course, were regarded with awe by the people.[37] Baseball
was introduced as early as 1872, and by the late 1880s it had become a part of
the sports programs in the higher schools.

The admiration for Western things and the concurrent contempt for things
Japanese led some men to suggest that the Roman alphabet be substituted for
the traditional writing system, and that the English language replace Japanese.
It was also suggested that intermarriage with Occidentals be fostered in order
to improve the Japanese racial stock. This low regard for things native resulted
in precious art objects being abused or allowed to leave the country freely for
Western museums. Woodblock prints by prominent artists were used to wrap
fish and vegetables, many Buddhist temples and treasures were destroyed, and
precious wooden structures were used as fuel. The attacks against Buddhist artifacts were, to be sure, primarily the result of anti-Buddhist sentiments, but
the lack of respect for traditional things is also reflected in these actions.

The segment of the society that found it most difficult to adjust to the new
ways was the peasantry. Consequently, government leaders encouraged the
publication of popular, easy to read works on "enlightenment and civilization"
and endeavored to persuade the masses by rational arguments to adapt themselves to "civilized" ways.

At the upper levels of the society the desire to emulate Western ways culminated in the efforts of the government leaders to imitate the social life of the
West by holding fancy costume balls at the Rokumeikan, a social hall built for
the aristocracy. This style of living flourished for half a decade during the
1880s, but a growing sense of disenchantment with Western ways coupled
with a revival of cultural nationalism resulted in strong criticisms of the undig-
nified behavior of some of the government leaders. The decline in this lavish
social life occurred just about the time when the era of indiscriminate imitation of the West was coming to a close.

RELIGION

At the outset of the Meiji era, an effort was made to establish Shinto as the
state religion in order to fortify the foundation of imperial rule. Initially the
government established the Jingikan (Department of Shinto) and placed it
above the Dajōkan. Steps were taken to end the syncretic tendencies that had
prevailed between Shinto and Buddhism in the past. The Shintoists initiated a
frenzied move to suppress Buddhism, and consequently many Buddhist build-

ings and artifacts were damaged or destroyed. The anti-Buddhist trend at the center was followed by many local authorities with the result that a large number of Buddhist temples were eliminated.[38] The government, however, soon abandoned its policy of actively suppressing Buddhism, partly to check the activities of the extreme anti-Buddhists but also because it realized that popular support of Buddhism could not be eradicated. It was also feared that the vacuum created by the weakening of Buddhism might be filled by Christianity.

Having lost the patronage and protection of the ruling class, and being confronted with challenges from Shinto and Christianity, some Buddhist leaders began to bestir themselves from centuries of relative inaction. They endeavored to revivify the religion that had lost its vitality during the halcyon days of Tokugawa rule, when every person was required to register with a Buddhist temple.

The government insisted on functioning as a religious and moral agent even after it had abandoned its plan to impose Shinto upon the people as the official religion. It established the Board of Religious Instruction in 1872 to propagate the Great Teaching, whose principles were based upon Shinto nationalism. Efforts at Shinto revival abated with the onrush of Westernism, but the religion did manage to stage a comeback by the late 1880s. Shinto and Confucian moralism gained a powerful outlet in the Imperial Rescript on Education of 1890.

Out of an ardent desire to be accepted by the West, the Meiji leaders adopted the principle of religious freedom in 1873, thus putting an end to the long proscription against Christianity. The Meiji government had, prior to this, retained the Bakufu's ban against Christianity and continued the persecution of Japanese Christians, particularly the many thousands who had surfaced around Nagasaki after the centuries of hiding that followed the religious persecution of the seventeenth century.

Missionaries had been permitted to work in the treaty ports to serve the Western residents who lived there. Through their educational and medical work they also managed to establish contacts with the Japanese. Some missionaries, like J. C. Hepburn (1815–1911), made enormous contributions to Japanese culture.[39] Many future leaders of Meiji Japan came under the influence of the missionaries. For example, toward the end of the Tokugawa era Guido Verbeck had among his students in Nagasaki, Saigō Takamori, Gotō Shōjirō, Ōkuma Shigenobu, Soejima Taneomi, and Etō Shimpei; L. L. Janes (1838–1909) in Kumamoto influenced a number of young men including Tokutomi Sohō (1863–1957), who became a leading exponent of liberalism and nationalism; W. S. Clark in Sapporo, Hokkaido, was the teacher of such men as Nitobe Inazō, a prominent educator, and Uchimura Kanzō (1861–1930), who became a leading Christian.

The percentage of Christian converts before the Second World War remained fairly low—there were 300,000 Christians in the 1930s out of a total

population of about 70 million—but many of them came from the upper
rungs of the society and were rather well-educated. They had developed a
strong political and social consciousness, and as a result they exerted a much
greater influence upon the society than the relatively small number might otherwise indicate.

Notes

1. It is some measure of the nature of Japanese society that many of these "rebels" (loyalists
to the Tokugawa) were later allowed to join the new Meiji Government. For example, the ex-
shōgun was rehabilitated enough to become designated a prince. Enomoto served as foreign
minister in the early 1890s.

2. Yokoi, a former adviser to the daimyō of Echizen, was an exponent of fukoku kyōhei.
He was accused by the jōi advocates of favoring republicanism and Christianity.

3. The agricultural production of the entire country at this time was estimated at 30 million koku, but the central government had only 8 million koku under its control.

4. Ironically, the single most popular family name chosen by peasants was "Tokugawa."

5. Japan and Peru appealed to the Russian Tsarist government for international arbitration,
which Japan ultimately won. This was widely trumpeted as Japan's first "international law case."

6. The upper- and middle-class shizoku saw their incomes decline by as much as 47 to 74
percent. The lower-class samurai, however, were the ones affected most adversely, for they experienced an 88 to 98 percent drop in income. Their average annual income came to about
twenty-nine yen, which was comparable to the pay of an ordinary soldier, who, however, also
received free room, board, and clothing.

7. This was two to seven times the rates prevailing in Europe at this time. In some instances, in fact, the farmers had to pay even heavier taxes than they did in the Tokugawa era
because collection under the Meiji government was much more stringently implemented.

8. The fact still remained, however, that the agrarian sector was paying for the cost of modernizing and industrializing the nation. During the period from 1875 to 1879, 80.5 percent
of the government's tax revenues were derived from the land tax.

9. The average tenant paid in excess of 60 percent of his crop to the landowner, who used
about half of this to pay the land tax while retaining the other half as his revenue. The tenant's
share, after payment of miscellaneous dues, came to about 32 percent of the crop. In the
Tokugawa period the tenants kept, on average, 39 percent of the yield.

10. This was in sharp contrast to the Anglo-American practice of dividing the functions
between judge and jury, in which the former determined matters of law and the latter matters
of fact, a distinction unknown to the Japanese. An option making it possible to receive jury
trials in criminal cases was provided for in 1923, but it was little used before being suspended
in 1943.

11. Rule-of-law, in which these limitations are fixed by the law in deference to a consideration of fundamental human rights and the electoral process, did not come into existence until
the postwar era. Dan F. Henderson, "Law and Political Modernization in Japan," in *Political
Development in Modern Japan,* ed. Robert E. Ward (Princeton: Princeton University Press,
1968), p. 415.

12. A separate court system (Court of Administrative Litigation) was set up to deal with
cases involving administrative authorities. This, of course, meant that administrative abuses
could not be brought under the scrutiny of the courts of law.

13. In Satsuma, where Ōkubo came from, about 20 percent of the population belonged to the shizoku class and thus constituted a force that had to be reckoned with.

14. Kazushi Ohkawa and Henry Rosovsky, "A Century of Japanese Economic Growth," in *The State and Economic Enterprise in Japan,* ed. William W. Lockwood (Princeton: Princeton University Press, 1965), pp. 52–53. The years 1868–1885 are seen by economists Ohkawa and Rosovsky as a transition period during which the groundwork was laid for the initial phase of Japan's modern economic growth, which began in 1886 and extended to 1905. The second phase ran from 1906 to 1952. This was followed by a period of postwar growth that commenced in 1953.

15. Government figures of 1874 indicate that at that time, in a way that was typical of premodern manufacturing patterns, textiles and food accounted for over 70 percent of the value of all manufacturing output. Ibid., p. 58.

16. E. Sydney Crawcour, "The Tokugawa Heritage," in Lockwood, *State and Economic Enterprise,* p. 44.

17. By 1893, Japan had 2,000 miles of railroad, 100,000 tons of steam vessels, and 4,000 miles of telegraph lines.

18. The estimate of percentage increase in paddy rice yield in a given area from 1873–1877 to 1883–1887 is believed to have been between 2.5 and 6.6 percent. One economist estimates that the annual growth rate of agriculture over the period 1873–1877 to 1918–1922 was 1 percent while others estimate it at 2.9 percent. Harry Oshima, "Meiji Fiscal Policy and Economic Growth," in Lockwood, *State and Economic Enterprise,* p. 355. Cf. James Nakamura, "Growth of Japanese Agriculture, 1880–1935," in Lockwood, *State and Economic Enterprise,* p. 305; Kazushi Ohkawa and Henry Rosovsky, "A Century of Japanese Economic Growth," in Lockwood, *State and Economic Enterprise,* pp. 69–70 note.

19. The total number of notes in circulation rose from 106.9 million yen in 1876 to 164.4 million yen in 1879.

20. Under his financial management the government saved an average of 28 percent of its current revenues. Half of this savings was used for capital formation, and the other half was retained as surplus. The quantity of money was reduced by about 20 percent, and commodity prices fell sharply. In 1884 the general price level dropped to 75 percent of what it had been in 1881, interest rates declined, and foreign payments shifted in Japan's favor.

21. The price of rice in Tokyo dropped 50 percent in the years between 1881 and 1884, and this meant that the peasants had to allot twice as much rice for tax payments. In 1881 the peasants utilized 16 percent of the total rice production in tax, whereas in 1884 they had to allocate 32.8 percent.

22. Functioning as rice dealers and tax collectors, merchant houses such as Mitsui made huge profits by buying and selling the rice turned in for tax payments when the market price was the most advantageous for them.

23. The Miike coal mine was obtained by the Mitsui Company, a few gold mines were acquired by the Furukawa Company, and a number of gold and silver mines went into the hands of the Mitsubishi Company in 1896.

24. Later, as the shipping company amalgamated with another firm and formed the Nippon Yūsen Kaisha (Japanese Mail Line), the government granted it a yearly subsidy of 880,000 yen.

25. Inoue Kaoru, for example, was so close to the House of Mitsui that he was sometimes derisively referred to as "that Mitsui store clerk." The main reason the company was able to acquire the Miike coal mine was that it had obtained information about its competitors' bids from the minister of finance, Matsukata. Ōkuma was Iwasaki Yatarō's close friend. The owner

of the Ashio copper mine, Furukawa Ichibei, adopted Foreign Minister Mutsu Munemitsu's first-born son, Junkichi.

26. The Bakufu's Confucian academy, the Shōheikō, was reactivated as the center of learning for Confucianism and Shinto.

27. This and the following passages are the author's translation from the original text.

28. The cost of education was borne by the taxpayers, that is, primarily by the farmers. A tuition of between 12.5 sen and 50 sen per student per month was also charged (there are 100 sen to the yen). This tuition, if paid in full, would have been prohibitive for most families since the average income per month for the common people was 1 yen 75 sen in 1878. Only a small percentage of the tuition was collected, however, and it covered only 10 percent of the educational costs.

29. There was only 28 percent attendance in 1872, but this figure rose to 40 percent by 1878. The number of girls in school, however, remained small, and even as late as 1887 the ratio of boys to girls in school was three to one. The traditional notion that girls were inferior and had no need for an education was partly responsible for this lag.

30. In 1900 the period of attendance was extended to four years, and the system of charging tuition was abolished.

31. At first, textbooks had to be compiled in accordance with guidelines delineated by the ministry of education, but in 1903 the government took direct charge of the actual compilation and publication of primary school textbooks.

32. In fact, it was turned into an actual component of the state in which professors and students were expected to pursue learning that would further the interests of the state. Its chief function was to produce properly indoctrinated and trained future bureaucrats and leaders of the state.

33. Hundreds of foreign specialists (*oyatoi*, or "honorable employees") were employed on lucrative three-year contracts to teach a cadre of young Japanese boys. The oyatoi were not allowed to own land and were discouraged from forming coteries by forcing the young Japanese to learn the language of the oyatoi during instruction.

34. It is estimated that between 1860 and 1893, some 3.5 million copies—if the several volumes of some of the titles were counted separately, this figure would climb to nearly 7.5 million copies—of his published works circulated among the reading public.

35. In 1873 there were 373 Japanese students studying in the West. Approximately 300 students came to the United States between 1865 and 1885. England was also a popular destination, and in the early 1870s there were more than 100 students in London alone.

36. The number of Western educators, technicians, and advisers in Japan hit a peak of 524 in 1874 and then began to decrease gradually.

37. In a popular children's song, the following ten most desirable objects were enumerated: gas lamps, steam engines, horse-drawn carriages, cameras, telegrams, lightning conductors, newspapers, schools, postal mail, and steamboats.

38. For example, in Toyama han in north central Honshu, 1,630 temples were abolished, leaving only 7 remaining to serve the entire han.

39. A Japanese-English dictionary was compiled by Hepburn and published in 1867. He also devised a system of romanizing Japanese words.

6

The Continuing
Meiji Revolution (I)
Political Developments

The revolutionary changes that were introduced by the Meiji leaders and the large-scale exposure to a totally new civilization profoundly affected all segments of the society. The reactions to this were varied: some sought to resist or challenge the alterations, whereas others reacted positively by adjusting to the new situation and contributing to the process of modernization. The government leaders continued to introduce changes in a persistent attempt to adapt Western institutions and practices to make them suitable for Japan. In the middle decades of the Meiji era they managed to reinforce and consolidate the changes they had introduced while moving toward the goal of "enriching and strengthening" the nation. In the next two chapters we shall first examine the reactions, responses, and consequences that followed the initial phase of the Meiji revolution, and then have a look at the continuing process of that revolution.

The group that was most adversely affected by the initial changes was the former privileged class, the samurai. Now, with the loss of their hereditary stipends and rights, they had to shift for themselves in a strange new world that was apparently bent on destroying the values and institutions that were familiar to them. Some managed to join the emergent establishment by becoming government officials, military officers, policemen, and teachers. Others entered the business world and became successful participants in the emerging commercial economy; many more were reduced to penury through unproductive attempts at what they considered to be degrading activities such as farming, shopkeeping, handicraft, or common labor. Those who resented being denied a share of political power turned to antigovernment activities and occasionally staged armed uprisings, but more often these individuals turned to political agitation for democracy and parliamentary government by participating in the freedom and popular rights *(jiyū minken)* movement. These disgruntled men also constituted the core of antiestablishment intellectuals who often turned to journalism as a vehicle for launching their attacks against the government.

The peasantry was another, and considerably larger, segment of the society that experienced serious alterations in their customary way of life. They were, to be sure, enjoying greater freedom, but at the same time they had to defray the cost of modernizing the country and shoulder new compulsory duties such as military service and the education of their children. The peasantry frequently resorted to violence as a means of resisting the exacting arms of the efficient new government.

Discontent was not limited to the samurai and the peasantry. In the intellectual and cultural realms too there were those who regarded with distaste the vogue for Westernism and the many superficial changes that were being imposed at the expense of traditional values. The old ways, it was felt, deserved protection against the mindless pursuit of the new. It is probably true that some of the men who believed this were pure reactionaries of Shinto and Confucian proclivities, but many were individuals of discriminating taste who had undergone the exposure to Western civilization and still maintained that there were many things worthy of preservation in the traditional culture and way of life. Thus a growing tide of cultural nationalism began to rise around the middle of the 1880s.

This movement, however, should not be seen as a wholly new force in Meiji Japan; from the outset the architects of the new order were motivated by the desire to defend Japan against the potential menace from the outside and to build a strong and rich nation. The driving force behind the Meiji leaders was nationalism, and they never lost sight of their ultimate objectives in spite of the turbulence that buffeted them from all sides.

The most fervid advocates of Westernism were also motivated by considerations of national interest. For example, Fukuzawa Yukichi wrote in his *Outline of Civilization,* "There is no other way to preserve our independence except through the adoption of [Western] civilization. We must advance toward civilization solely for the purpose of maintaining our national independence."[1] Nonetheless, the tone of the country became more obviously nationalistic in the 1880s, reflecting an ascendancy of cultural nationalism as well as a growing militancy in Japan's relations with its Asian neighbors.

The Meiji government managed by the 1890s to establish the new order on a firm footing in spite of the resistance and unfavorable reactions that its revolutionary measures produced. This does not mean, of course, that the Meiji leaders had resolved all the difficulties facing the nation or that the entire populace was satisfied with or benefiting from the new order. Modernization did not really improve the economic or physical condition of the masses very much. The uncertainties and the turbulence that faced the Japanese at the outset of the Meiji era, however, were more or less resolved, or at least muted, by the 1890s. The people had been given a sense of identity with the nation and the living god-figure, the emperor, along with a sense of mission in the expansionist struggles that were unfolding on the Asian continent. By and large the people retained this sense of identity and purposefulness until the fateful week when the cities of Hiroshima and Nagasaki vanished in the devastation of atomic holocaust.

POLITICAL REACTIONS

In order to evaluate the events that occurred in the political realm before the new order was stabilized, we must return to nearly the beginning of the era, to the time when the Iwakura Mission went abroad. A caretaker government was left in charge at home with the understanding that no significant innovations were to be initiated by them. This, of course, was impossible, and they did in fact introduce many new measures, such as the freedom to buy and sell land, the educational ordinance, military conscription, land tax revision, and judicial reforms.

Nothing upset the absent government leaders more, however, than the ill-conceived plan to provoke Korea into committing hostile actions against Japan in order to establish a pretext for launching an invasion of that country. This scheme became the pet project of the chauvinistic Saigō Takamori. He was motivated not only by zealous patriotism but also by the hope that the conquest of Korea would serve as a means of restoring the former samurai to a place in the sun.

Saigō was certainly one of the most enigmatic figures of the Restoration. In many ways he was a selfless participant in and supporter of causes in which he believed. He was also a cunning Machiavellian who arranged, for example, to provoke the Bakufu forces in Edo when it appeared as if a compromise solution might effectively resolve the differences between the imperial and Bakufu factions. Yet he was not personally ambitious for political power; in fact, he left the seat of the new government that he had helped to establish and returned to Satsuma to concentrate on han reforms. In this respect he was, perhaps, an anachronism in the new age, for he acted out of a stubborn adherence to an old-fashioned notion that it would have been improper to place himself above the lord of Satsuma as a high government official. Saigō also seemed to be wedded to the interests of the lower-class samurai, and he was most unsympathetic to both the feudal aristocracy and the peasantry. The garnering of special privileges by the new Meiji leaders disturbed him a great deal, as did the intrusion of mercantile interests into the government and the growing trend toward utilitarian materialism. What he seemed to favor was the establishment of a military dictatorship based upon the lower-class samurai. He may have believed that a successful invasion of Korea would strengthen his faction and thus facilitate the establishment of military rule.

The ostensible excuse offered by the chauvinists for launching an attack against Korea was the allegedly insulting public pronouncement made by the Korean government about Japanese merchants illegally engaging in trade in their country. Saigō's proposal to stage an invasion of Korea was supported by the other officials of the caretaker government, with the exception of a few men, including Ōkuma Shigenobu. Among those concurring were Itagaki Taisuke, Foreign Minister Soejima Taneomi, Minister of Justice Etō Shimpei, Mutsu Munemitsu (1844–1897), and Gotō Shōjirō. Itagaki did not share Saigō's proclivity for military rule, but he was very much in sympathy with the idea of giving the shizoku a greater role to play in the new society. It was this sentiment that led him some time later to agitate for popular rights, an effort aimed essentially at securing a share of political power for the shizoku. Itagaki also seemed to have envisioned the invasion of Korea as a means of strengthening the central government against the remnants of the old order. Etō emerged from the ranks of the poorer samurai and seemingly favored liberal measures, but once he gained power as a high government official he inclined toward a policy of authoritarianism.

The Iwakura Mission had not completed its itinerary when word reached its members about the decision to move against Korea. Kido and Ōkubo were sent back to Japan in the middle of 1873 for the specific purpose of seeing to it that Saigō's plan be blocked. They argued that internal reforms had to be effected before any foreign ventures could be undertaken. Nevertheless, the nominal head of the government, the dajō daijin, Sanjō, had decided to dispatch Saigō to Korea as a special envoy to gain redress for the alleged insults to Japan. A concerted effort was made when Iwakura returned from abroad to force Sanjō to reverse his decision. Tremendous pressures by the opposing factions finally caused him to resign, whereupon Iwakura became acting dajō daijin and cancelled the Saigō mission to Korea.

Outraged at this decision, Saigō and the other advocates of the Korean war, Itagaki, Gotō, Etō, and Soejima, resigned from the government. Kido also left at this time, but he did so for reasons of poor health. Mutsu resigned in solidarity with Kido. Ōkubo then took charge of the government, relying upon Itō and Ōkuma as his key assistants. Thus, from October 1873 until his assassination in May 1878, Ōkubo was the de facto head of the government.[2] He created the Ministry of Home Affairs and assumed the chief post himself. This gave him jurisdiction over the police system, which he used to keep political dissidents under control. His basic objective was to establish a strong central government while seeing to the rapid development of Japanese industries. The entrenchment of Ōkubo in power was a victory for the faction that advocated modernization; it was also the triumph of the new bureaucrats over the feudalistic elements of the government.

The Ōkubo government did little to mollify the discontented shizoku, but it did launch what proved to be an unsuccessful invasion of Formosa (Taiwan) in 1874, partly as a means of providing an outlet for the chauvinism of the advocates of the Korean war. The official justification for the invasion had to do with fifty-four shipwrecked sailors from Okinawa who were massacred by head-hunting Taiwanese aborigines. The Chinese government's refusal to assume responsibility for the incident provided Ōkubo with an excuse for dispatching an expeditionary force to the island. The move was opposed by the British, and the military campaign floundered miserably. The question was ultimately resolved through negotiations with the Chinese government.

The hope of the dispossessed samurai that they might regain their special status had by now completely vanished. Saigō had departed from the central government, and the only recourse left to them, it appeared to many, was armed opposition to the Ōkubo regime. There had been active samurai opposition to the new order prior to this time. Early in 1870, for instance, the samurai of Chōshū, who were demobilized with very little compensation, were led by anti-Westerners to stage an uprising in cooperation with peasants and townspeople who were infuriated over rising prices. Similar antigovernment disturbances led by reactionary samurai broke out in various parts of the country at around the same time. The Meiji government continued to diminish the privileges of the shizoku, and its rejection of the proposal to invade Korea coupled with Saigō's departure from the government gave these frustrated and increasingly bitter ex-samurai a cause to rally around.

The first major uprising to be staged by the advocates of the Korean war was the rebellion led by Etō in Saga prefecture in February 1874. Etō, with the support of reactionary anti-Western elements who wanted to restore the former lord to power and reinstitute the samurai's stipends, led about 2,500 men against the prefectural government. Ōkubo viewed this as a major threat that, if not crushed swiftly, could touch off an uprising enveloping all of Kyushu. Assuming supreme military and judicial power, he moved troops from three garrisons against the rebels. Etō had expected other discontented men, including Saigō, to come to his support, but when no one rallied to his flag, he was defeated and later hanged.

The suppression of the Saga Rebellion, however, failed to put an end to antigovernment uprisings. In October 1876 a band of 200 warriors in Kumamoto rose in rebellion. This incident was touched off by the government's ban on sword-bearing, but among the complaints mentioned by the rebels were the issue of Westernization, the diffusion of Christianity, and the termination of their stipends. The rebellion was easily suppressed. It was soon followed, however, by a similar uprising of 400 warriors in Fukuoka prefecture and an insurgency in the city of Hagi in Chōshū led by Maebara Issei (1834–1876), a former councilor in the Meiji government, who was a proponent of the Korean war. Maebara opposed military conscription and had also shown himself to be a friend of the common man when, as governor of Echigo, he cut taxes in order to aid the people suffering from floods. He was reprimanded for this and subsequently became disillusioned with the new government. He considered their harsh treatment of the former samurai to be particularly outrageous. Maebara's rebellion was crushed, and he was executed.

All these unsuccessful efforts by the discontented samurai were preludes to the ultimate showdown, the confrontation with Saigō, the man toward whom all disgruntled shizoku looked with great hope. Many newspapers and journals advocating popular rights were sympathetic to Saigō, and the more extreme of these incessantly called for the overthrow of the "oppressive and despotic" government. Copies of inflammatory articles were widely distributed in Kagoshima, and this served to fan the already smoldering antigovernment sentiments.

Upon his return to Kagoshima, Saigō started a private school with branches throughout the prefecture, and he concentrated on the military training and indoctrination of youths. The prefecture was controlled by Saigō's followers and was in reality an autonomous region, a state within a state. Not a penny of the taxes that were collected was handed over to the central government. Here, none of the Meiji reforms such as the termination of samurai stipends, land tax revision, adoption of the new calendar, or the ban on sword-bearing were enforced.

In order to bring Kagoshima under the control of the central government, Ōkubo sent police agents into the prefecture to examine the situation, and at the same time he ordered the removal of some arms from the arsenal in Kagoshima. The outraged Kagoshima men captured the police agents and forced them, under torture, to say that they were assigned the task of assassinating Saigō.

Saigō's followers then urged him to rise up against the government and, even though he realized that the Kagoshima forces could not hope to defeat the government's troops, he agreed to challenge them. Thus, in February 1877, Saigō announced that he had some questions to ask the government and that he planned to proceed to the capital with his followers. He began his move toward Kumamoto with 15,000 warriors, and as he continued on his way he was joined by thousands of additional men. At the peak of his campaign Saigō's supporters numbered about 42,000 men.

The central government appointed a royal prince as supreme commander and moved its new conscript army against the challengers. Saigō's men first attacked Kumamoto castle, fully anticipating to take it with ease because of the fact that it was being defended by "dirt farmers." Contrary to expectations the fortress withstood a fifty-day siege until it was relieved. The imperial forces that arrived in Kumamoto engaged Saigō's men in a fierce battle lasting twenty days; finally, however, the insurgents were forced to retreat to the south. The conflict dragged on until September, but the imperial forces had clearly gained the upper hand and Saigō, realizing that there was no hope left, committed seppuku. Thus ended the career of one of the chief architects of the Meiji Restoration and a heroic figure in the eyes of many Japanese, even those who opposed him.

This rebellion, known as the Seinan War, was unlike the other uprisings in that it constituted a major civil conflict. The government utilized more than 60,000 men, of whom 6,278 died in battle and 9,523 were wounded. Saigō's forces consisted of more than 40,000 men, 20,000 of whom were killed or wounded. At the end of the conflict, 2,764 men were executed. In a quixotic plot loosely tied to the Satsuma Rebellion, a number of Tosa-affiliated rebels sought to use the disturbance to assassinate some hated members of the oligarchy. Over a hundred of these rebels, among them Mutsu and Oe Taku (1847–1921), were tried and sentenced to long terms of imprisonment.

The government's victory was a triumph for the conscript army of "dirt farmers" and served to destroy the myth that only the shizoku were capable of fighting with discipline and valor. The conflict also brought to an end, once and for all, armed resistance to the new government by the shizoku. They now turned to the other alternative method of challenging the new oligarchy; that is, the popular rights movement that was emerging as a significant force under Itagaki's leadership.

Before we turn to this movement we shall examine the other segment of the society that reacted against the government policies: the peasantry.

AGRARIAN UNREST

The Meiji Restoration did not materially improve the lot of the peasantry in spite of the belief that the victory of the imperial faction would result in a better way of life for them. The peasants in many regions staged what is referred to as *yonaoshi ikki* (uprisings to reform the society) when the imperial and Bakufu forces were struggling with each other. Their attacks were often directed against the rich and the leading members of the villages, but in the Kantō region where the Bakufu lands existed, peasant uprisings took on a distinctly anti-Bakufu coloring. Pro-imperial forces deliberately sought to stir up the peasants against the Bakufu by promising them a 50 percent reduction in taxes. Initially Saigō sanctioned this move. The most prominent of the warriors who incited anti-Bakufu peasant uprisings was Sagara Sōzō (1839–1868), the organizer of the Sekihōtai, "the band committed to the repayment of the imperial debt with blood."[3] The movement began to spread, but as it did the anarchistic, antitaxation tendencies grew increasingly strong, with the result that the leaders of the imperial forces became disenchanted with these uprisings and began to condemn the men who had stirred up the peasants. The leaders, including Sagara, were arrested and executed. Consequently, as far as many peasants were concerned, the new government had come into power by deceiving them.

Peasant distrust of the new government persisted and agrarian disturbances continued to erupt throughout 1869. The peasants demanded cancellation of debts, termination of feudal dues, reduction in rent, and land reforms. In 1870 there was a large-scale uprising in Matsushiro han (in present Nagano prefecture) involving 70,000 people. The central government sent its troops into Matsushiro and then executed or imprisoned more than 300 of the leaders.

The peasant disturbances of the first few years of the Meiji era were directed against traditional grievances, but as the government began to introduce new actions or procedures that disturbed the way of life to which the peasants were accustomed, these measures became the objects of protest activities.[4]

At the end of 1876, large peasant uprisings occurred in central Japan, touched off by what the peasants regarded as unfair tax assessments. The government, deeply concerned at this time about a possible confrontation with Saigō, decided to appease the peasants and reduced the land tax from 3 percent to 2.5 percent of the land value. During the years between 1876 and 1880, the government increased its overtures toward the peasants and sought to foster in the people a closer sense of identity with the new order by having the emperor tour about the country.

The village leaders turned increasingly to the popular rights movement as a way of gaining concessions from the government that would alleviate agrarian poverty. With the deflationary policy adopted by Matsukata, the economic plight of the peasantry worsened drastically. The price of farm products dropped, and agrarian revenues were cut in half, but at the same time there were increased excise and local taxes. As a result, a growing number of peasants fell into debt to usurious moneylenders, and by 1884 the debts incurred by agrarian families reached the astronomical figure of 200 million yen. Many peasants, unable to repay their debts, lost their homes and land to the moneylenders and the banks.[5]

Matsukata's policy also severely hurt the peasants who depended on the silk industry for supplementary income. The price of raw silk dropped 50 percent, and the villagers in Kanagawa, Shizuoka, Saitama, Yamanashi, and Nagano prefectures, where the raising of silkworms was prevalent, felt the effects of this most acutely. The farmers organized protest groups known as the Debtors Party and the Hardship Party to fight for the reduction of debts.

Peasant uprisings continued throughout 1883 and 1884, with troubles finally culminating in the Chichibu Uprising of November 1884. Like other rural areas, Chichibu county residents (in the Kantō region) suffered from the 50 percent drop in the price of raw silk and fell heavily into debt. A Hardship Party was organized, calling for a ten-year moratorium on debts, extension of payments over a forty-year period, reduction in local expenses, and cancellation of schools for three years as a measure to reduce expenditures. These demands were not met, and the leaders decided to resort to force. Under the direction of a prominent village leader, Tashiro Eisuke, more than 1,000 people attacked the homes of moneylenders and local government offices, destroying certificates of debt. Then, joined by additional supporters, a group of 5,000 men marched toward what is now the city of Chichibu. The government, under the leadership of Minister of Home Affairs Yamagata Aritomo, became alarmed and moved the military police as well as the regular troops against the undisciplined rebels. They were scattered within ten days, and the government then executed the main leaders and imprisoned others.

Uprisings on a smaller scale were staged by the Hardship Party in other areas, but they too were readily suppressed. What followed in the villages was extreme scarcity of food, starvation, and infanticide. A prominent Japanese social historian recalled hearing a story of a father in the late 1880s who, unable to bear the agonies of his starving children, decapitated them to release them from their miseries. This same historian also observed that peasant families in Ibaraki prefecture during this period had only one boy and one girl; the others were killed at birth.[6] The suicide rate was extremely high around 1885–1886. A majority of the poor did not "break the law" and resort to violence—they starved to death in silence.

The number of tenants, as might be expected, increased sharply, with close to 370,000 farmers suffering forced sales for arrears in the payment of the land tax between 1883 and 1890. In the early years of the Meiji era 20 percent of the cultivated land was farmed by tenants; this figure rose to 40 percent in 1887 and then to 45 percent in 1910, a year in which 39 percent of the tillers of the soil owned no land at all.[7]

In the difficult years that followed the Chichibu Uprising, the government did nothing to assist the peasants and only advised them to work harder. The Liberal Party, organized by Itagaki, and the urban intellectual journalists whose political agitations had helped to arouse antigovernment sentiments in the countryside, did nothing to assist the agrarian insurgents. They denounced the Chichibu rebels as arsonists, gangsters, and hoodlums. The leaders of the Hardship Party movement, if they were able to avoid being jailed, joined the ranks of the dispossessed or went into hiding. One leader of the Chichibu Uprising remained in hiding for thirty-five years in the backwashes of Hokkaido.

THE MOVEMENT FOR POPULAR RIGHTS

The movement for popular rights *(minken)*, although related to some extent to the discontent and despair of the peasantry, was more a product of the dissatisfaction of the shizoku, who wanted a share of the power that had been gathered in the hands of the Satsuma-Chōshū oligarchy. Furthermore, most of the advocates of popular rights were influenced by Western political philosophies and thus were motivated by a certain degree of idealism.

The rural segment of the movement was represented by the *gōnō,* well-to-do farmers and prominent members of the villages, who were not only wealthier but also better educated than the ordinary peasant. Their ancestors had served as village leaders during the Tokugawa era. What the gōnō wanted was to persuade the wielders of power to recognize the problems facing the agrarian communities. They hoped to compel them to introduce reforms or offer concrete assistance. Many of the organizers of the Debtors Party and the Hardship Party were from the gōnō, and they also took part in the popular rights movement at the local level.

Initially it was the Tosa faction led by Itagaki that constituted the core of the minken movement. This was probably the case because of the "liberal, democratic" tradition that had been implanted in Tosa by such leaders as Sakamoto Ryōma. Itagaki and Gotō Shōjirō, who were attracted to the idea of parliamentary government even before the Tokugawa Bakufu fell, both came from Tosa. Itagaki became the chief spokesman for the movement after he split with the government over the Korean question. He returned to Tosa and organized a small political party.

In January 1874, Itagaki, Gotō, Etō, and Soejima together with four other men submitted a memorial to the government calling for the establishment of a national assembly. The petitioners based their arguments on the tenets of Western liberalism, frequently quoting John Stuart Mill. They complained of official despotism and contended that for the good of the country free public discussion had to be permitted. The establishment of a national assembly, they argued, would be the best way to achieve this. The presentation of the memorial, which marked the beginning of the minken movement, aroused public interest and touched off animated discussions among journalists and intellectuals concerning the question of whether or not the Japanese people were ready for parliamentary government.

The Meiji Restoration had a revolutionary impact on the entire society insofar as it loosened the bonds of traditional institutions and unleashed the heretofore restrained energies and ambitions of people throughout the social hierarchy. The enthusiasm for new ideas and institutions was not restricted to the upper classes and the urban dwellers; educated leaders of the rural communities played very significant roles in the political and educational realms by establishing political societies, opening village schools, and propagandizing for popular rights and "civilization and enlightenment."

Many women were also active in the sociopolitical reform movements of early Meiji. Among them was Fukuda Hideko (1865–1927), who devoted her life to the advancement of freedom and justice.

Many young men who had been educated in Tokyo or at least exposed to its politically stimulating atmosphere returned to the countryside to practice law or to set up newspapers, thus establishing centers of political action. Fiery lecturers were brought to the countryside to educate and arouse the rural residents. The popular rights movement consequently changed from being primarily a movement of the discontented shizoku to one that included well-to-do farmers and merchants.[8]

An important driving force in the popular rights movement was the group of intellectuals and journalists in Tokyo who published newspapers, journals, and tracts. These influential men went on lecture tours to stir up support for the movement and arouse opposition to the government. Among these were the followers of Fukuzawa Yukichi, who himself began to adopt an increasingly moderate position as the minken movement became more and more radical.

In order to cope with the intensifying attacks against the government, the officials introduced press control laws to curb the activities of the journalists. In 1875 a press law was enacted that severely restricted political criticisms and called for preliminary censorship by the Ministry of Home Affairs. Heavy fines, imprisonments, and suspensions confronted violators of the law. The code was made even more stringent in 1876, and by the end of that year forty-nine editors and reporters were fined or imprisoned.[9] The influence that the press exercised in molding public opinion was considerable, even though in the early years the circulation of even the major papers was no more than several thousand copies daily.

Faced with the growing criticisms by the press, the activities of Itagaki and the political societies, and the ominous presence of Saigō's state within the state in Kagoshima, Ōkubo and his cohorts decided that the government must be strengthened by bringing Kido back into the fold. Before he would accept the invitation to return to the government, Kido insisted upon the inclusion of Itagaki in order to check the power of the Satsuma faction. In January 1875 a conference was held in Osaka, and both men, after provisions to broaden the base of power were agreed upon, consented to enter the government as councilors. No meaningful political reforms were made, however, and consequently, Itagaki left the government in October, once again turning to the popular rights movement. Kido also resigned when he realized that the Osaka agreement was not being implemented. He died soon after, in May 1877.

The failure of Saigō's rebellion served to intensify the agitation for the establishment of a national assembly, and its advocates organized political societies throughout the country. Itagaki and his faction formed a political party, the Aikokusha (Patriotic Society); it became the rallying point of the popular rights movement, and local chapters were organized throughout the nation. In March 1880 the minken leaders organized the Kokkai Kisei Dōmeikai (Association for the Establishment of a National Assembly) and then submitted a formal petition asking for a national assembly, but the government refused to accept it.[10]

Political agitation grew more intense, and the government responded by striking back at the agitators with the issuance, in April 1880, of the Law of Public Meetings, severely restricting political gatherings and associations. This did not, however, dampen the ardor of the political activists. On the contrary, they sought to develop even greater strength for the movement by establishing a national political party, the Jiyūtō (Liberal Party). They declared their political objectives to be the extension of civil rights, national progress and prosperity, equality of rights, and constitutional government.

The motives of the leaders of the popular rights movement varied from an idealistic desire for reforms to, among other things, a tremendous thirst for power. In most of the men there was, to be sure, a fairly strong strain of nationalism. The frequent use of the term *aikoku* (patriotism) in their organizations is indicative of this characteristic. In their pronouncements they make constant reference to the need to establish a national assembly in order to strengthen the nation. For instance, the Memorial of 1874 stated: "We fear . . . that if a reform is not effected the state will be ruined. Unable to resist the promptings of our patriotic feelings, we have sought to devise a means of rescuing it from this danger, and we find it to consist in developing public discussions in the empire."[11] The popular rights leaders did not concentrate solely upon the establishment of a national assembly in the central government. They also focused their attention on the prefectures, where they sought to build strongholds in the councils. The central government, however, repeatedly intervened to prevent the establishment of a nationwide organization of the prefectural councilmen.

From the beginning there were elements in the government who favored the establishment of a constitutional government with some form of parliamentary body. Kido returned from his visit abroad with the Iwakura Mission convinced that a constitutional government was essential if Japan was to emerge from isolation as a strong nation. He did not, however, favor granting the people a real voice in the government; he preferred the establishment of a constitutional monarchy with much of the power being retained by the ruler. Nevertheless, he was not in sympathy with the trend in which power was being gathered into the hands of a small clique.

Ōkubo Toshimichi also believed that eventually a constitution would have to be adopted, and as early as 1873 he requested Itō Hirobumi to look into the possibility of drafting a constitution. Gotō Shōjirō, who was in and out of the government, was a supporter of constitutional government, as were Ōkuma, Itō, and Inoue Kaoru, although they did not have specific ideas about the form it might take.

The popular rights movement received an unexpected boost from the government when a cleavage developed between Itō and Ōkuma, the two men who emerged as leaders after Ōkubo's assassination in May 1878 at the hands of a Saigō sympathizer. As the pressure for the establishment of a national assembly increased, Iwakura advised the emperor in December 1879 to ask the councilors to submit written opinions on the advisability of drafting a constitution. With the notable exception of Ōkuma, all the councilors submitted their memorials without undue delay, and they generally favored the establishment of some sort of constitutional government while insisting upon a gradual approach. The only person who took a radical position was Ōkuma. He delayed for some time before presenting his recommendations in March 1881. He counseled that a parliamentary government modeled after that of England be established immediately.

Itō exploded in anger when Iwakura showed him Ōkuma's proposal three months later because he believed that Ōkuma had not been frank with him and Inoue when they had discussed the question earlier. Ōkuma had violated one of the cardinal principles of Japanese politics, that is, the need for each individual to work with the group to which he belongs without departing radically from the consensus. Any attempt by a man to outdo or rise markedly above the others could not be tolerated for it threatened to disrupt collective leadership, which was the very principle that governed the Meiji oligarchy.

Moreover, Itō could not agree with Ōkuma's proposal to establish a parliament immediately; nor could he accept the plan to model the Japanese government after the British example. It seemed to Itō that Ōkuma was taking a more radical position than other councilors in order to curry favor with the minken advocates and thus consolidate his own political position. In anger Itō threatened to resign, saying he could not serve in the government with

Ōkuma. Iwakura managed to arrange a temporary truce between the two men by postponing further discussion concerning the national assembly.

The truce was broken, however, over another issue. In the summer of 1881 the government decided to sell its holdings in the Hokkaido Colonization Commission for 380,000 yen. This was a project into which it had invested 14 million yen. The recipient of this largess was a Satsuma entrepreneur who was a friend of Kuroda, the official in charge of the Hokkaido project. News of this transaction became known, and the government's critics launched a vigorous major campaign against what they considered to be a scandalous giveaway plan. The attack was spear-headed by the followers of Fukuzawa, who used the press and public opinion to full advantage.

Itō and his fellow officials looked upon this fresh assault on the government as a conspiracy on the part of Ōkuma, Fukuzawa, and the Mitsubishi interests to use this issue as a lever to overthrow the government. The move to expel Ōkuma from the government was thereupon initiated. His dismissal on October 12, 1881, was accompanied by a purge of his followers and those of Fukuzawa. At the same time, in order to placate public opinion, the government publicly announced its intention to draft a constitution and establish a national assembly by 1890.

Ōkuma and Fukuzawa vehemently denied the existence of any conspiracy, but what they said at this point mattered little. The Satsuma-Chōshū faction had its way. The by-product of the Itō-Ōkuma rivalry was of major importance: the government was forced to make a decision to frame a constitution and to establish a national assembly earlier than it had expected.

This announcement by the government took the wind out of the frenzied attacks that were being launched against the oligarchy and compelled the advocates of popular rights and national assembly to start getting ready for the election and the convocation of the assembly. The followers of Itagaki had been preparing for the formation of a national political organization, so they were able to establish the Liberal Party immediately after the government made its announcement on the constitution. Itagaki was chosen as the party's president. Among the other leaders were the early fighters for minken and parliamentary government such as Gotō Shōjirō, Kōno Hironaka (1849–1923), and Baba Tatsui (1850–1888). That the party ideologists, Ueki Emori (1857–1892), and Nakae Chōmin (1847–1901), were deeply influenced by Rousseau's *Social Contract* is clearly evidenced by their statement of principles, which starts with the sentence: "Liberty is the natural state of man and the preservation of liberty is man's great duty." It goes on to declare: "We will spread the heavenly bestowed liberty and control man-made authorities; at the upper level, we will correct and improve politics, and at the lower level we will foster the spirit of self-government."[12] The Liberal Party leaders advocated popular sovereignty, but they also felt compelled to pay homage to the authority of the emperor. The problem of reconciling these two conflicting principles continued to plague many minken advocates.

The second party that emerged was the Constitutional Reform Party (Rikken Kaishintō), which was organized by the followers of Ōkuma and Fukuzawa.[13] This party was inclined to be more conservative than the Liberal Party and looked upon English parliamentary government as a suitable model. The two intellectual assistants to Ōkuma, Yano Fumio (1850–1913), and Ono Azusa (1852–1886), were both influenced by English liberalism. The latter in particular was attracted to Bentham's Utilitarianism, as was Mutsu, who translated some of Bentham's writings into Japanese while in prison.

Reform Party members believed that by following the English model the imperial institution and popular rights could be reconciled. The party eschewed violence and tended to appeal to the propertied, "respectable" members of the society, as these remarks from Ozaki Yukio (1858–1954), a lifelong fighter for parliamentary government, reveal: "We of the Reform party decided to follow a moderate course in contrast to the Liberal party, which was organized mainly by hot-blooded members of the shizoku who tended to rely on radical actions. Hence we looked for members among those who were well educated, owned property, and were respectable."[14] The party also had close ties with capitalistic interests, such as Mitsubishi, and continued to strengthen its association with business leaders. Unlike some segments of the Liberal Party, the Reform Party members did not get involved in the agrarian protest movements. Its essentially conservative character led Itagaki to scoff at it as a party designed "to please the old and the rich."

The two opposition parties expended more energy fighting each other than they did combating the government. Numerous factors account for the inability of the Liberal Party and the Reform Party to cooperate. The differences in ideology may not have been basic, but they certainly were provocative; in addition, there were dissimilarities in the bases of support, in the temperament and personality of the leaders, and in the regional, social, and economic ties. Another factor contributed to serious fission within the parties themselves. From their very inception, there was present in the political parties the same characteristic that governs the behavior of today's Japanese political parties—that is, the existence of numerous factions built around the party leaders. In a sense it might be regarded as "bossism," but it would not be wholly accurate to depict the situation in this manner because a great deal more than personal ties were involved; regional loyalties also played a part in keeping the factions together. This led not only to the formation of different parties, with the Tosa faction generally gathering around Itagaki and the Hizen faction around

Ōkuma, but also to the operation of numerous cliques within each party at any given time.[15]

The personal ties were patterned after the traditional master-follower or father-son relationship, so that the paternalistic, authoritarian, and hierarchical mode of behavior present in the family prevailed in the political parties as well. Each member had fixed rights and duties, and he behaved in the manner that was expected of him. This situation resulted in the absence of any strong sense of personal responsibility. Those men who possessed power thought of their actions as being dictated by their position and hence beyond the realm of personal responsibility, whereas the followers, having no right to make independent decisions or take independent actions, possessed no sense of individual responsibility. Consequently, irresponsible, erratic actions were taken from time to time by the leaders and rank-and-file members, thus seriously undermining the party movement at critical moments.

A third group, the Constitutional Imperial Party (Rikken Teiseitō), was organized as a progovernment party, but it failed to develop into a major force because the government leaders were unsympathetic to political parties in general and did not actively support it. This party was opposed to the popular rights movement and parliamentary government.

In order to build their bases of support the two opposition parties sent speakers on tours to rally the public to their cause. The Liberal Party was particularly successful in developing a fairly broad base of support in the countryside by attracting the provincial landowners and businessmen as well as the peasantry. The well-to-do rural leaders were especially active, and they frequently sponsored public lectures and workshops.

The government leaders became concerned about this extension of party influence into the countryside. Consequently, in June 1882 they issued a law on public assembly that gave the prefectural governors the authority to curb public lectures and other political activities. The law also prohibited any party from establishing local organizations or developing ties with other organizations for the purpose of sponsoring public political talks. As a result, many local political organizations were forced to disband, and this in turn caused the more radical party members, particularly from the Liberal Party, to support those who turned to direct action. Some became involved in the local agrarian uprisings, such as the Chichibu affair.

In April 1882, while Itagaki was on a lecture tour, he was attacked by an assassin in Gifu. Fortunately, he was not seriously hurt, but this incident shocked and aroused the indignation of the party members. In order to remove the symbolic head of the party movement from the political scene and in this way attempt to cool down the heated political atmosphere, the Meiji leaders suggested that Itagaki take a trip abroad with funds provided by Mitsui. To the chagrin of his more principled political allies, Itagaki accepted the offer and went abroad together with Gotō. This produced a serious split in the Liberal Party that resulted in the more radically inclined Baba and others quitting it. Itagaki's behavior not only divided his own party but also exacerbated the rivalry between the two opposition parties. The Reform Party leaders heaped scorn on Itagaki for accepting the financial backing of Mitsui, while the loyal followers of Itagaki struck back criticizing Ōkuma's ties with Mitsubishi.

At the local level the confrontation between the officials representing the central government and the opposition forces grew increasingly acrimonious. In 1883 an authoritarian official, Mishima Michitsune (1835–1888), was appointed governor of Fukushima prefecture. Mishima boasted that he would not allow a single arsonist, burglar, or member of the Liberal Party to exist in the area under his jurisdiction, and he repeatedly closed down public lectures that were sponsored by the Liberal Party chapter in Fukushima. Popular opposition against him intensified as he launched a road-building project that was to be implemented by forced labor and higher taxes. The peasantry, encouraged by the advocates of popular rights, began organizing to resist Mishima's policies. At this point the well-to-do agrarian leaders began to dissociate themselves from the peasantry, realizing that there was an inherent conflict of interests between the two groups. Mishima started to arrest the peasants and party leaders and thus touched off a peasant protest movement that had to be dispersed by sword-wielding policemen. This was followed by a mass arrest of Liberal Party members, including Kōno Hironaka. Officials of the central government, such as Iwakura and Yamagata, hoped to use this incident as an excuse to launch a general attack on the popular rights movement. They weakened the prefectural councils, curbed the right to make petitions, placed even greater restrictions on the press, and permitted the police to carry swords with a cutting edge.

Rural uprisings continued to break out in spite of these repressive actions by the government, and while many Liberal Party members, particularly those at the top level, began condemning the reliance on violence, others were driven to more extreme measures. For instance, in May 1884 some Liberal Party members led 3,000 peasants in Gumma prefecture against a local moneylender and the police. The leaders of the incident were arrested and punished; some died while being tortured. This, however, did not deter other radicals of the Liberal Party. In September 1884, in Kabayama in Tochigi prefecture, Kōno's nephew led an uprising with fifteen other men. They raised the flag of revolution and called for freedom and the overthrow of despotism. The rebels were easily suppressed, and seven of the insurgents were executed while others received life or long-term prison sentences. The authorities, led by Mishima, who was now governor of Tochigi, used this occasion to arrest the Tochigi Liberal Party members indiscriminately.

The Kabayama insurgents were condemned by political party members, journalists, and even the Liberal Party leaders. This incident had the effect of hastening the dissolution of a party that was already badly divided. Less than a year and one-half before the uprising, Itagaki, already quite disturbed by growing radicalism, had proposed dissolving the party. He contended that radical political movements were out of step with the times, but he was persuaded to withdraw his proposal by a protégé of Mutsu, Hoshi Tōru (1850–1901), a leader of the moderates who was emerging as a key figure in the party. The Kabayama incident, however, induced Itagaki to revive his proposal to dissolve the party. This time his suggestion was adopted, and the Liberal Party was disbanded in October 1884, despite the opposition of Hoshi, who was then incarcerated in Niigata.

The Reform Party did not fare much better than the Liberal Party in its efforts to build a viable political organization before the first Diet elections were held. Ōkuma began to favor the idea of dissolving the party, but he was opposed by a faction led by Numa Moriichi (1843–1890), one of the founders of the party. As a result, Ōkuma left the party in December 1884 with many of his followers. A remnant of the members, however, managed to keep the party alive even after a majority had resigned. It would appear that it was impossible to sustain interest in the party movement before the constitution came into existence. This was primarily due to the fact that until then the parties could not play a truly meaningful role in the power struggle.

The opponents of the government, however, remained ready at all times to grasp any opportunity to rally public opinion against it. In 1887 Hoshi and Gotō united the advocates of popular rights in an attack against the government for considering treaty revisions that they contended were a national disgrace. According to the provisions of the treaty being negotiated, the entire country was to be open to Western residents. Furthermore, legal cases involving Europeans were to be tried by Western judges. Perhaps most offensive of all was the provision that Western nations were to review the legal codes that were to be adopted by Japan. The French legal adviser, Boissonade, opposed the proposed revisions because he felt they infringed upon the sovereignty of Japan, but the government leaders nevertheless decided to proceed with the changes. Appealing to the nationalistic sentiments of the people, Gotō and other minken leaders organized the Union of Like Thinkers to protest the government's policy. They also added other issues, such as the abolition of the system of peers and the reduction of arms and taxes, to the protest movement. The government had to postpone its plan to revise the treaties, but it retaliated by issuing the Peace Preservation Ordinance and ejected from Tokyo 570 men whom it regarded as troublemakers.

FORTIFICATION OF THE CENTRAL GOVERNMENT

Itō went abroad to study European constitutions in order to prepare for the drafting of the Japanese document, and he remained there for more than a year and a half during 1882–1883. Ostensibly he went to Europe with an open mind, but it is generally agreed that he had already decided to use the Prussian constitution as a model. Inoue Kowashi, one of Itō's key assistants in drafting the constitution, had translated it into Japanese in 1875. Hermann Roessler, a German professor of jurisprudence, arrived in 1878 to serve as legal adviser to the government, and he lent support to the idea of adopting the basic features of the Prussian constitution.

In light of the fact that the Meiji leaders had already decided on the kind of constitution that should be adopted, Itō's prolonged study abroad may have been unnecessary, but he did gain the prestige and understanding of theoretical ideas necessary to refute the critics who would have preferred the English model. He wrote in a letter to Iwakura:

> Thanks to the famous German scholars Gneist and Stein, I have come to understand the essential features of the structure and operations of states. . . . The situation in our country is characterized by the erroneous belief that the words of English, American, and French liberals and radicals are eternal verities. . . . I have acquired arguments and principles to retrieve the situation.[16]

Itō established the Office for the Study of the Constitution immediately upon his return from abroad. Before he could turn his attention to the tasks of drafting the constitution, however, he found it necessary to introduce certain governmental changes as a way of preparing for the day when power would have to be shared to some extent with the political parties. Consequently, he did not begin serious work on the constitution until 1886. A number of significant measures were adopted to fortify the emperor system and the power of the oligarchy. First, in July 1884, Itō created a new system of peers who were to serve in the upper house of the projected parliament as a check on the popularly elected lower house. The new peerage was modeled after the German system with five ranks: prince, marquis, count, viscount, and baron. Approximately 500 persons were selected from the existing kazoku, high government officials, military and naval officers, and other prominent men to serve as peers. Itō himself became a count as did Yamagata and Inoue. In 1888 the Privy Council, consisting of key members of the oligarchy, was created for the specific purpose of examining the proposed constitution. Even after this task was completed, it remained in existence as a special advisory body to the emperor.

As an organ functioning outside the purview of the constitution, it served as a stronghold of the oligarchy.

Two posts, independent of the cabinet, were created as additional means to prevent the imperial institution from falling under the influence of the political parties in the event that they gained control of the government. The Ministry of Imperial Household and the office of the Lord Keeper of the Privy Seal were filled by members of the oligarchy, giving them direct access to the emperor. Another measure designed to strengthen the imperial family was the enlargement of its material holdings.[17]

In the area of administrative changes, the Dajōkan was replaced by a cabinet system in December 1885. There were ten ministers, including the prime minister, who was responsible to the emperor. Itō became the first prime minister, and the cabinet included all the top leaders of the oligarchy except Kuroda. A neat balance was maintained between Chōshū and Satsuma with four ministers each, and it transpired that until Ōkuma became prime minister in 1898 the office was rotated between Chōshū and Satsuma men. A civil service system was introduced, and government officials below the highest level were, with some exceptions, to be chosen by examination. This measure was designed to prevent a takeover of the bureaucracy by the political parties in case they gained control of the government. The bureaucracy quickly developed into a formidable bulwark of the oligarchy. This was a society in which respect for and fear of the government officials had a long tradition, and the people continued to be overawed by these men. The attitude referred to as "respect for officialdom, contempt for the people" became deeply embedded in modern Japan.

The Imperial University of Tokyo became the most prestigious of the institutions of higher learning. The path to success in life was the route that led through government-run middle and higher schools, the Imperial University of Tokyo, and up the ranks of the bureaucratic hierarchy. Government-operated schools and the bureaucracy were thus linked closely together in this status-conscious society to produce the new elitist governing class.

In 1888 local administrative reforms were made in order to establish a system of local self-rule that was designed to preserve the influence of the rich. The cities, towns, and villages were granted the right to manage their own affairs through local assemblies and mayors who were chosen by the assemblymen. These assemblymen, however, were elected by voters with property qualifications, but in 1890 only 1 percent held the franchise. An additional provision aimed at ensuring that the wealthy would possess greater power was the procedure giving these first-class voters the right to choose one-third of the assemblymen. A further measure was the rule that mayors were to serve without pay. The poor were thus rather effectively prevented from holding office.

Above the towns and villages in the hierarchy were the counties, with no real administrative function. Next came the prefectural governments, whose governors were appointed by the central government. The prefectural assemblymen were chosen from the ranks of the county, city, town, and village assemblymen who paid more than 10 yen in national taxes. This arrangement for choosing local assemblymen remained in effect until 1899.

THE CONSTITUTION

In the fall of 1886 serious work on drafting the constitution was started by Itō. In this task, he was assisted by Inoue Kowashi (1844–1895), Kaneko Kentarō (1853–1942), and Itō Miyoji (1857–1934), all bright, able men who occupied the second rung of the power structure in Meiji Japan. Inoue Kowashi was the real architect of many of the conservative policies of the Meiji government. In addition to working on the constitution, he helped to draft the Imperial Rescript on Education, served as minister of education, and was a member of the Privy Council. Kaneko Kentarō attended Harvard Law School during 1876–1878, served in two of the cabinets headed by Itō, and later joined the Privy Council. Itō Miyoji served in Itō's cabinet as secretary and minister and also became a member of the Privy Council. He continued to exert his influence from behind the scenes until as late as the 1930s.

In the summer of 1887 Itō and his three assistants prepared the final draft of the constitution, which was then checked by Roessler. Next it was examined by the Privy Council headed by Itō, who had resigned the premiership in order to chair the council. In the course of the discussions two contradictory positions were simultaneously upheld by Itō. First, when it was suggested that the Diet should be given the right to appeal to the throne regarding illegal actions by government officials, Itō objected, saying, "This constitution was drafted to strengthen the authority of the ruler and make it weightier." Second, when Mori Arinori suggested replacing the term "rights of the subject" with "status of the subject," Itō held that "the spirit behind the constitution is to limit the authority of the ruler and protect the subject's rights."[18] In view of this, it can be said that "the Meiji Constitution was essentially an attempt to unite two concepts which . . . were irreconcilable: Imperial absolutism and popular government."[19] Consequently, if the constitution was to function effectively, compromises had to be made, but the side that was destined to make the major concessions was the one representing the popular elements.

After more than six months of deliberations in the Privy Council, the constitution was promulgated on February 11, 1889, as a gift from the emperor to the people. It was, as Itō stated, designed to shore up imperial authority. Sovereignty was lodged in the emperor, who held supreme command over the armed forces and possessed broad executive authority. He had the power to declare war, make peace, and conclude treaties. He was to control the administrative system and appoint the officials. He also held supreme authority over the legislative body for he "convokes the Imperial Diet, opens, closes, and prorogues it, and dissolves the House of Representatives." Legislation had to pass the two houses of the Diet, but the emperor held a veto power and possessed the authority to issue imperial ordinances. Government officials, including cabinet ministers, were responsible to the emperor, not the Diet.

The Diet consisted of two houses, the House of Peers and the House of Representatives. Seats in the upper house were to be filled by members of the imperial family, peers, and individuals appointed by the emperor. The 300 members of the House of Representatives were to be elected by the people on the basis of a limited franchise.

The lower house, which represented the popular elements, had limited power since both the emperor and the House of Peers could veto its legislation. It had no authority over the government officials, and its control over the budget was restricted. Certain items in the budget could not be changed, and if the Diet failed to pass it the government was authorized to operate on the basis of the previous year's budget. The Diet, however, did have to approve tax bills. This is where the opposition was able to exercise a certain degree of control over the executive branch because, as the need for military and naval expenditures grew, the government was often compelled to ask for new taxes.

The popular elements were curbed not only by the written provisions of the document but also by virtue of the fact that they were hindered by institutions and practices not provided for in the constitution. We have already noted, for example, the special status of the Privy Council. The Satsuma-Chōshū oligarchs also constituted an informal group of genrō, or elder statesmen, that met whenever the need arose to decide upon policies of major importance. The fact that the constitution was subordinated to the throne gave the real power to this clique of genrō because they in fact controlled the emperor.

Another institution that lay outside the purview of the popular elements was the armed forces, which were controlled by the oligarchs. The mantle of army leadership, after Ōmura Masujirō's assassination in 1869 and Saigō's departure from the government, fell to Yamagata. The army virtually became Yamagata's private dominion. The military was designed to serve as the stronghold of the emperor system—that is, the oligarchy—and as noted above, the concepts of loyalty and service to the emperor were rigorously instilled in members of the army and navy.

Yamagata, at the advice of his protégé Katsura Tarō (1847–1913), who had just returned from serving as military attaché in Germany, established the general staff office in 1879 in order to keep the military independent of civilian control. The supreme command was then placed completely beyond the control of the popular forces and even the cabinet under an ordinance issued in 1889 and revised in 1907. On matters concerning military command and military secrets, the chief of the general staff was given the right to report directly to the emperor, thus by-passing the cabinet. The military, already freed from interference by civilian leaders, acquired the power to intervene in political matters when an imperial ordinance was issued in 1900 that stipulated that only active officers of the two top ranks in the army and navy could hold the posts of war and naval ministers. This in effect gave the army and navy the power to veto cabinets of which they disapproved.

In theory the people were guaranteed certain rights and liberties in the constitution, but these were restricted "within the limits" of the law. Official abuses, for example, could not be challenged in the regular courts because they had to be brought to the Court of Administrative Litigation, whose authority could not extend into areas left to official discretion, which was indeed extensive. Hence in reality the Japanese subjects were only given very limited rights and freedom.

Also in 1890 Article Five of the Police Security Regulations Act made all political activity by women illegal and punishable by fines and/or imprisonment. Women could not attend public political meetings and could not even discuss politics, including Article Five itself. Perhaps this was in some way an attempt to limit all political influence by women, who had shown considerable support for the Liberals during the Jiyū minken movement.

Notes

1. *Fukuzawa Zenshū, The Collected Works of Fukuzawa*, 10 vols. (Tokyo: Jiji Shimpōsha, 1925–1926), vol. 4, p. 256.

2. Sanjō resumed the post of dajō daijin, and Iwakura became minister of the right. Nominally they held positions superior to Ōkubo's, but the de facto head was Ōkubo.

3. James I. Nakamura, "Growth of Japanese Agriculture, 1875–1920," in *The State and Economic Enterprise in Japan,* ed. William W. Lockwood (Princeton: Princeton University Press, 1965), p. 299.

4. In 1873, thirty-seven peasant disturbances broke out; among the grievances mentioned were military conscription, compulsory education, high taxes, and the removal of the restrictions against the eta. Major riots broke out in Okayama and Fukuoka prefectures. In the latter, 300,000 people were involved in the destruction of 4,590 buildings and 181 telegraph poles.

5. For example, at a time when 1 koku of rice was worth about 5 yen, the debt per family in one county in Kanagawa prefecture came to 108 yen. This figure becomes rather staggering in view of these statistics: 1.6 koku of rice was produced per tan (0.245 acres) of rice paddy and the average holding was about 1 chō (10 tan); thus the average rice harvest per family came to about 10.6 koku, or about 53 yen. In 1885 more than 100,000 families went bankrupt.

6. Irokawa Daikichi, *Kindai Kokka no Shuppatsu* (The Beginning of the Modern State) (Tokyo: Chūō Kōronsha, 1966), pp. 320–323.

7. The rent the tenants had to pay ranged from 45 to 60 percent of the crop on rice fields, while in some extreme cases, 80 percent of the crop was collected as rent. Another indication of the growing impoverishment was the diminishing number of men who qualified to vote by paying 5 yen or more in tax. Taking the year 1881 as index 100, for 1886 it was 84, for 1891 it was 64, and for 1894 it was 59.

8. For example, Kōno Hironaka, who was born into a prominent village family, became one of the key leaders in organizing political societies among leading rural farmers and merchants.

9. More than two hundred writers were punished during the five-year period following enactment of the press law. These measures, however, did not prevent the newspapers from proliferating. The major ones were concentrated in Tokyo, but regional papers also began to increase in number. In 1883 there were 199 newspapers throughout the country, and in 1890 there were 716.

10. During 1880, more than 240,000 persons signed similar petitions calling for a national assembly.

11. W. W. McLaren, ed., "Japanese Government Documents," Transactions of the Asiatic Society of Japan, vol. 42, part 1, p. 428.

12. Robert A. Scalapino, *Democracy and the Party Movement in Prewar Japan* (Berkeley: University of California Press, 1953), p. 69.

13. The Kaishintō has sometimes been called the Progressive Party, but I shall label it the Reform Party here in order to distinguish it from its successor party, the Shimpotō, which has also been referred to as the Progressive Party.

14. Ozaki Yukio, *Gakudō Kaikoroku* (The Memoirs of Gakudō), 2 vols. (Tokyo: Yūkeisha, 1952), vol. 1, p. 77.

15. For example, when the first Diet was convened the Liberal Party was split into four main factions.

16. George Akita, *Foundations of Constitutional Government in Modern Japan, 1868–1900* (Cambridge, Mass.: Harvard University Press, 1967), p. 61.

17. Real property increased by nearly 6,000 times between 1881 and 1890 (from 634 chō to 3,654,000 chō). Its holdings in stocks and bonds were also increased substantially, and by 1887 they were worth nearly 8 million yen.

18. Irokawa Daikichi, *Kindai Kokka no Shuppatsu*, pp. 440–441.

19. Scalapino, *Democracy and the Party Movement*, p. 150.

7

The Continuing
Meiji Revolution (II)

Cultural, Economic, and Social Developments

CULTURAL NATIONALISM

Early Meiji was a period in which the vogue for Western things was widespread and the tide of "civilization and enlightenment" swept through all facets of Japanese life. From about the middle of the 1880s, however, the frantic pursuit of Western things began to abate and a more critical, discriminating look at Western culture and institutions came to be taken. This kind of swing of the pendulum was to be expected, for after fairly extensive exposure to Western civilization, the people were beginning to develop more discriminating tastes and faculties.

Excesses in imitating Western ways, such as the behavior of the high officials at the Rokumeikan parties, contributed to the fortification of reactionary sentiments among those who wanted to revive Shinto or Confucian concepts and values. The critics of the blind emulation of Western ways were not, however, simply reactionaries. Most of these "cultural nationalists" were rational men who wanted to adopt the best from the West without having the people lose either their appreciation of things Japanese or their sense of cultural or national identity.

The influence of Confucian traditionalists was evident in the realm of moral education. The Confucian moralists were unhappy about the wave of individualism and utilitarianism that swept into Japan in the early Meiji years. The leading foe of this trend and the key spokesman for Confucian virtues was

Motoda Eifu (1818–1891), who as tutor to the emperor had a great deal of in-fluence at the court. He regarded with distaste the pragmatic attitudes held by men like Itō and Inoue Kaoru, who were willing to condone the pursuit of self-interest and the spread of materialism for what they claimed was the sake of developing the nation's economy. Motoda, who was imbued with Confu-cian values, believed there was a basic and irreconcilable conflict between self-interest and the public good. He believed that the decline of morals brought about by Western ways had to be corrected by the inculcation of the virtues of benevolence, righteousness, loyalty, and filial piety. Motoda's position was akin to that of Sakuma Zōzan, who believed in Eastern morals and Western science. Eastern morals were based on a hierarchical social order in which benevolence from above was to be reciprocated by obedience from below.

Motoda had an ally in Nishimura Shigeki (1828–1902), who was familiar with Western concepts and was active as an "Enlightenment" thinker when he was a member of the Meirokusha (see page 105). Nishimura was convinced, however, that moral education had to be conducted by the government, and he wanted the imperial family to exert its influence in this area. Mori Arinori became minister of education in 1885, and he favored stressing moral educa-tion in the schools but did not believe that the Confucian moral philosophy should be the basis for this.

Criticism concerning the absence of guidance on the question of moral ed-ucation became more vocal, with the result that a plan to issue an imperial re-script on education gained favor, and by the time Yamagata became prime minister, such a plan was finally implemented. Inoue Kowashi and Motoda Eifu collaborated in drafting the rescript, which was issued on October 30, 1890. The document was based on the Confucian five human relationships; it called for loyal service to the state and the throne, filial piety, modesty, obser-vance of the law, and furtherance of the public good. According to the rescript, the moral precepts were "the teaching bequeathed by Our Imperial Ancestors . . . infallible for all ages and true in all places." The rescript appealed to na-tionalistic sentiments by making the foundation of morality uniquely Japanese and by binding the throne and the people together in a common moral pur-pose. It served as a valuable instrument in making the young people loyal sub-jects of the emperor, since it was recited by every school child every morning much in the manner in which American school children pledge allegiance to the flag.

The dilemma that some Christian leaders subsequently found themselves faced with demonstrates how closely the credo verged on being a state religion. In January 1891, for example, the rescript was received in the school where Uchimura Kanzō, a conscientious Christian, was teaching. He refused to bow reverently toward it because he believed that to do so would be tantamount to recognizing the emperor as a divinity. He was denounced as a traitor and summarily dismissed from the school. In 1893 a renowned philosopher at the Imperial University of Tokyo contended that Christianity was incompatible not only with the spirit of the rescript but also with the Japanese national polity *(kokutai)*. Buddhism, which earlier had suffered at the hands of intolerant Shintoists, had by now recovered, and many of its leaders joined the nationalistic attacks against Christianity.

Besides these kinds of purely reactionary elements in cultural nationalism, we also find a group espousing what might be called "enlightened nationalism." This movement was led by men like Shiga Shigetaka (1863–1927), Miyake Setsurei (1860–1945), and Kuga Katsunan (1857–1907), who were not fundamentally anti-Western. Essentially, they wanted to establish a firm cultural or national identity that would enable them to adopt the best from the West while preserving the best, or the "essence," of Japan. They feared that if the blind imitation and worship of things Western continued, the Japanese would lose their identity. One member of this circle lamented, "Our people are no longer Japanese. The country is no longer Japan."

In 1888 the leaders of the enlightened nationalist movement organized the Society for Political Education and issued a fortnightly journal entitled *Nihonjin* (Japanese). Their objective, Shiga wrote, was to preserve the national essence *(kokusui)*. Many people tended to equate the concept of kokusui with reactionary traditionalism. Consequently, the society issued a manifesto stating,

> We seek to overcome the current evils by admonishing the so-called Westernizers who see the superb beauty of another country and forget the excellence of their own. We differ from those who rashly believe that preservation of kokusui means merely preservation of old things inherited from our ancestors and who mistakenly believe that we want to resist Western things and close the road to innovation and progress.[1]

Miyake had studied under Fenollosa (see page 139), and perhaps he was influenced by his teacher's concern for the preservation of Japanese culture. The best from the West in the realms of "truth, virtue, and beauty" must be adopted, according to Miyake, in order to augment aspects of these qualities already possessed by the Japanese. He took a position similar to Mazzini's in propounding a philosophy of nationalism that held that "to work for the good of one's country is to work for the good of the world. The elevation of the special characteristics of one race contributes to the general advancement of the human race."[2] He was a liberal nationalist who was very much opposed to militarism. It was a great disappointment to him that the nationalism he had helped to foster turned to antiforeignism and to a form of conservatism that stubbornly resisted social and political reforms.

Kuga believed that national independence was not possible without national pride. This, however, was not to be confused with self-aggrandizement or with blind anti-Westernism. Kuga claimed that his concept of nationalism was in harmony with universal love. In 1889 he started a newspaper, *Nihon* (Japan), to uphold the principle of "Japanism."

Some of the early advocates of Westernism and internationalism also began to have second thoughts. Most of the exponents of Westernism, such as Fukuzawa Yukichi, were motivated by nationalistic impulses and believed that the best way to strengthen Japan and thus ensure its independence was through Westernization. These men, however, became increasingly critical of the indiscriminate worship of Western things that was unfolding in the early Meiji period. In his *Encouragement of Learning,* Fukuzawa stated that the spirit of skepticism must also be applied to the examination of Western civilization. A few years after this volume appeared, he remarked that progress in Japan depended upon a proper balance between Japanese and Western concepts. He criticized the Westernizers for imitating Western ways without possessing any knowledge about Japan.

Fukuzawa, however, did not abandon his faith in Western liberalism and individualism, and he consistently opposed the growing xenophobic, anti-Western sentiments. Some early Meiji Westernizers, however, did begin to stress the importance of traditional moral values and the Chinese classics while turning to German statism as a philosophy more compatible to Japan. At the same time, German idealism was replacing English utilitarianism as the dominant Western philosophy in the academic realm.

The most dramatic shift from liberal internationalism to militant nationalism was made by Tokutomi Sohō, who was influenced by Christian humanism and English liberalism. In 1886 he wrote a book entitled *The Future Japan,* in which he called for peace and attacked militarism and expansionism. The following year he started a journal, *The Nation's Friend,* with the avowed aim of leading the "new Japan" along the path of peace and democracy. The outbreak of the Sino-Japanese War saw Tokutomi, in a radical change of position, become an active supporter of the war effort. He completely abandoned his earlier idealistic beliefs when the Triple Intervention occurred (see page 167), forcing Japan to return the Liaodong Peninsula to China. He concluded that force alone counted in this world, and he became a vociferous advocate of imperialism and militarism. Tokutomi remained an influential spokesman for expansionism to the end of the Second World War.

The arts was another area in which a significant revival of interest in things Japanese took hold. Ironically enough this movement was started by a Westerner, Ernest F. Fenollosa, an American who had arrived in Japan in 1878 to teach philosophy at the Imperial University of Tokyo. He soon became interested in Japanese paintings and woodblock prints and developed into a serious student of Japanese art. His studies led him to the conclusion that "the Japanese were denying an artistic heritage which they should honor and which the West could no longer overlook." He urged the Japanese to "return to their nature and its old racial traditions, and then take, if there were any, the good points of Western painting."[3] He advised them to establish an art school, assist and subsidize artists, and educate the public about art as a means of reviving their traditional art. He uncovered many long-neglected works and prepared a list of national art treasures for the government. He succeeded in restoring the use of the brush in primary school art classes where, during the mania for Western things, it had been replaced by the pen. With a missionary zeal he launched a virtual one-man campaign to revive Japanese art—and he succeeded.

Among Fenollosa's students at the University of Tokyo was Okakura Kakuzō (1863–1919), who became his devoted disciple and a central figure in the revival of Japanese art. Fenollosa and Okakura were instrumental in founding the Tokyo School of Art, which concentrated on the teaching of traditional art.

Okakura, like his teacher, emphasized the importance of securing the foundations of the traditional culture before adopting from the West. He wrote, "We shall be ready more than ever to learn and assimilate what the West has to offer, but we must remember that our claim to respect lies in remaining faithful to our own ideals." He was not impressed by the West's pursuit of progress on the basis of mechanical civilization, and he questioned: "When material efficiency is complete, what end will have been accomplished?" He believed that for Japan, Asia served as "the true source of our inspiration," even though in some areas Japan had already risen above its Asian mentors. "The expenditure of thought involved in synthesizing the different elements of Asiatic culture has given to Japanese philosophy and art a freedom and virility unknown to India and China."[4]

In literature, expressions of cultural nationalism did not appear as distinctly as they did in the visual arts. During the early years of Meiji, translations of Western novels were read and political novels with Western themes were written. An example of the latter is Yano Fumio's *Keikoku Bidan* (A Noble Tale of Statesmanship), a historical romance based upon Plutarch's depiction of the life of Epaminondas.

The first real step toward the modernization of Japanese literature occurred when Tsubouchi Shōyō (1859–1935), a student of English literature, wrote *The Essence of the Novel* in 1885. Tsubouchi rejected the traditional view that

novels were essentially instruments of moralism in which virtue must be rewarded and evil punished. He condemned the writers of his era for modeling
their stories after the didactic novels of such Tokugawa writers as Takizawa
Bakin. The primary task of the novelist, Tsubouchi argued, was the realistic
depiction of life. The aspect of experience that must be of primary concern to
the novelist is human emotions, which must be described in a psychologically
accurate manner.

The novelist who wrote the first important realistic Japanese novel was
Futabatei Shimei (1864–1909). He was strongly influenced by Russian writers, such as Turgenev and Goncharov, and he was responsible for the translation of many Russian novels into Japanese. His first novel, *The Drifting Cloud,*
was written between 1886 and 1889, and it was done in a realistic and colloquial style, rather unlike the formal literary mode used by the novelists before
him. It depicts dispassionately and somewhat humorously the behavior and
thoughts of an ineffectual young man who, lacking willpower and decisive-
ness, mopes about the girl he loves but with whom he fails to take any positive
action. *The Drifting Cloud,* influenced strongly by Western realism, can be said
to have inaugurated the era of modern Japanese literature.

Even in the early stages of the development of modern Japanese literature,
some writers manifested a desire to cling to traditional ways. Two very prominent authors, for example, turned back to the Tokugawa writers of the Genroku era for their inspiration. Ozaki Kōyō (1867–1903), a popular writer of
the second half of the Meiji era, studied the works of Saikaku and modeled
his style of writing after him. Kōda Rohan (1867–1947) was also strongly influenced by Saikaku, and his major works, dealing with the pre-Meiji era,
show clear signs of Buddhist thought. Kōda held Takizawa Bakin in high regard as a writer who did more than simply reflect the conditions and mores of
his society by making acute and perceptive observations. He saw the virtue of
sincerity *(makoto)* being manifested in the great literary works of the Tokugawa era, while in the other arts he noted the virtue of tenacious perseverance
being depicted.

The interaction of Western and Japanese literary traditions produced an era
of great creativity that culminated in the period spanning 1905–1915, when
scores of talented writers produced an abundance of significant works. Mori
Ōgai (1862–1922) was among the prominent writers of this era. He had studied medicine in Germany, and while serving as a medical doctor in the army
he translated the works of Goethe, Schiller, Ibsen, and Hans Christian Ander-
sen, and wrote a few novels of his own. He rejected utilitarian values and condemned the imitation of Western naturalism that was practiced by his fellow
writers. Mori himself wrote romantic novels that focused on the fulfillment of
the self. He turned increasingly to traditional subject matters for his stories

and displayed a growing admiration for the samurai, who lived only for the sake of honor. Forms and conventions, he also believed, were very important. He wrote, "If tea ceremonies were empty forms, the august ceremonials of the state together with ancestor-worship rituals would be empty forms also."[5] Concerning the past he said, "Civilization rests on history. To realize a well-thought-out ideal is an impossibility. One should never forget that ethics and customs which have been verified over many centuries must have a good core; otherwise they would not have endured so long."[6]

The naturalist writers sought to emancipate the individual from the conventions of the society and dealt honestly and openly with matters that were traditionally shunned or glossed over. For instance, Tayama Katai (1871–1930), who is regarded as a leading naturalist writer, dealt with the lustful passions that bewitched his heroes. Another writer who is regarded as a pioneer among naturalists is Shimazaki Tōson (1872–1943), who won renown for his novel *Hakai* (The Broken Commandment), which depicts the inner torments of an eta who conceals his social background. Shimazaki produced semiautobiographical works that also embodied criticisms of traditional as well as contemporary attitudes and ways. He culminated his literary achievements with *Yoakemae* (Before the Dawn), in which he depicts the effects of the Meiji Restoration on a rural community.

The influence of the various Western literary trends and authors became more pronounced, and many writers were beset by the problem of resolving the conflict between traditional and Western impulses. There was an outburst of "Japanism" in the literary realm following the Sino-Japanese War. Takayama Chogyū (1871–1902), the chief spokesman of this movement, formulated the credo for "Japanism," which called for "reverence of the national ancestors, the embodiment of the will of the nation's founders, vigilance in military preparedness even in time of peace, and the attainment of greater unity among the people."[7] Once he fell under the influence of Nietzsche, however, he readily abandoned the belief that the individual should be subordinated to the state and concluded that the unique individual, the superman, must be emancipated from all restraints. He resolved his inner conflict between the principles of statism and the notion of the superman by turning finally to Nichiren Buddhism. He saw in Nichiren a superman who "pursued the truth through the state."

A writer who straddled the Meiji and Taishō (1912–1926) periods and who is still widely read is Natsume Sōseki (1867–1916). He studied in England and began his career as a teacher of English literature. Natsume disliked the intensity of the naturalists and sought to maintain a certain aloofness from life. He wrote in a detached, dispassionate fashion, taking his subject matter from the quiet routine of daily life. He was particularly interested in delving into human relations at the family level, examining the contradictions, frictions, egoism, loneliness, foolishness, and dullness that were disclosed there.

Initially his works revealed a sense of humor in his clever satirizing of human foibles, but as he probed deeper into the inner workings of the mind and dealt with life more philosophically, his tone grew increasingly somber. He was also deeply disturbed by the problems created by the influence of Western civilization, and he had little hope that Japan would succeed in resolving these. He believed that the nation had failed to cope with, or digest, Western civilization, and those who were not content with merely dealing with it in a superficial manner would surely end up suffering from nervous exhaustion. A character in one of his novels asks, "But wouldn't Japan develop more and more in the future?" and another answers, "It will perish."

In poetry, works of long stanzas, exceeding the traditional limit of thirty-one syllables, became an accepted form of expression. Further innovations were introduced when poems came to be written in the colloquial style, and subjects dealing with everyday life and familiar social problems came to be treated. One of the most prominent of the late Meiji poets who represented this new approach was Ishikawa Takuboku (1885–1912). He wrote,

> Our ideal can no longer be fantasies about goodness and beauty. We must rigorously reject all fantasies and concern ourselves with the only truth that remains—necessity! This indeed is all that we should demand of the future. We must now examine the present with the utmost precision, courage, and freedom, and there we must discover the necessity of tomorrow. Necessity is the most reliable ideal.[8]

A renaissance was effected in the realm of haiku by a poet who more properly belongs to the cultural nationalism of the *Nihonjin* school. This was Masaoka Shiki (1867–1902), who worked briefly for the magazine *Nihon* and started a school of haiku known as the "Nihon School." Out of a tremendous love for Japan, he wanted to preserve the best in the traditional culture and vigorously opposed the Westernizers.[9] In seeking to revivify haiku, he instructed his disciples to "be natural," "keep the words tight," eliminate adverbs, verbs, and articles as far as possible, and use real rather than imaginary pictures. He believed that since haiku was not logical, no process of reasoning should appear on the surface. Furthermore, he contended that because haiku is so concise, delicacy cannot be applied to human affairs, whereas it can be put to use with natural objects. Here are two examples of Masaoka Shiki's haiku:

Cold moon:
shadow of a tombstone
shadow of a pine.

Night,
I wait for you:
Again the cold wind turns to rain.

Western drama was introduced into the theater as European plays were translated and then staged. At the same time an effort was made to revitalize Kabuki. Modern drama, or at least a theatrical form closer to real life that dealt with Meiji problems, also came into existence. One of the things that the supporters of the theater managed to accomplish was the uplifting of the status of playwrights and actors, who were traditionally held in low regard by learned men. High government officials and scholars were invited to attend new and traditional plays. This effort had the active support of men like Inoue Kaoru, and as a result, the prestige of the theater world was gradually enhanced. In 1887 Inoue invited the emperor to his home for a Kabuki performance; this was the first time that a Kabuki play had ever been performed in the presence of an emperor.

INITIAL MODERN ECONOMIC GROWTH

During the period between 1886 and 1905, the machinery, factories, corporations, and so on that came to characterize the modern Japanese economy began to develop significantly. Nevertheless, the economy was, for the most part, still dependent upon agriculture for its growth.[10] This period thus was characterized by the coexistence of the traditional and the modern forms of the economy, plus a composite sector that combined aspects of both. This hybrid element took the form of small shops using modern techniques and nonwage family labor.

There was a considerable growth in the traditional phase of the economy after 1885. This was necessary for the eventual realization of a modern economy because it provided the capital, labor force, food for the workers, and exports (such as tea and silk) that would be required to offset the imports needed for industrialization. Furthermore, this development created a domestic market for the industrial goods that were produced. The traditional sector's potential to expand reached its limit around 1905, after which its growth rate began to decline, thus bringing an end to the initial phase of Japan's modern economic growth. In the next phase the modern segment was no longer as dependent upon the traditional component and relied more upon its own strength and exports to develop rapidly.[11] In the twenty-five years before World War I, the total production of food and industrial materials doubled. Rice production increased by 40 percent between 1885–1889 and 1910–1914.[12] This greater yield per acre was accomplished through the use of more and better fertilizers, better seeds, double cropping, and improved methods of farming.[13] The well-to-do villagers played an important role in the diffusion of new agricultural knowledge by publishing farm journals and by taking the initiative in adopting new techniques.

There may be some disagreement about the extent to which Japanese agricultural production increased, but there is no question about the fact that industrial growth was largely sustained by the traditional sector during this period. In the early 1870s the land tax constituted 90 percent of the state revenue; in 1882 it was more than 80 percent, and in 1893, 45 percent. In subsequent years the tax burden on the farmers continued to be higher in comparison to what the merchants and industrialists shouldered.[14] The labor force for the growing textile industries was supplied largely by young girls from the farming communities. Raw silk and tea provided the chief export commodities.[15]

The rapid growth in the modern or industrial phase occurred after the Russo-Japanese War (1904–1905), but there was considerable expansion during the second half of the Meiji era.[16] During this period a number of large-scale industries came into existence, and this trend was fostered and supported by the government for military and political reasons. Government initiative, subsidy, and protection were readily extended to those industries that were deemed essential to national interests. One area in which this was particularly apparent was in railroad construction. Nevertheless, serious financial difficulties kept the pace of construction rather slow.

As early as 1873, the government decided to rely primarily on private enterprise for railroad construction, but because of its strategic and economic significance, it kept close watch over the work and provided assistance whenever it was needed. In the 1880s private firms began building the trunk lines linking the major cities.

Railroad construction enjoyed a minor boom in the 1880s as a result of substantial government backing. Private companies owned 671 miles of railroad by 1889, compared to the 551 miles of tracks owned by the state.[17] Following the Sino-Japanese War the railroad business expanded even further, with seventeen new companies coming into existence.

The recession that followed the war brought considerable financial difficulties to the railroad companies, and as a result, the government decided to nationalize the industry. It began taking over the railroads in 1906.[18]

Railroad travel in its early stages was a luxury that only the very rich could afford.[19] The most common means of transportation was the *jinrikisha* (rickshaw), which was invented in Japan in 1870.[20]

The government also played an active role in the development of marine transportation. As noted earlier, the government turned over to Mitsubishi the transport ships it had purchased for the Formosan expedition as well as some additional vessels, and granted it subsidies so as to enable it to compete effectively with foreign shipping companies. Government assistance was extended to other shipping firms as well, and by the Sino-Japanese War merchant ships numbered 528 with a tonnage of 331,000.[21]

The government paid similar attention to the development of heavy industry and mining. Initially the state operated a number of enterprises in strategically important fields, such as metallurgy, machinery manufacture, and shipbuilding. Fairly early in the Meiji period the policy of turning plants operated by the state over to private businessmen was adopted, but the government did retain the major arsenals, dockyards, machine shops, and wool and clothing plants for the use of the armed forces, and tobacco factories. Overall, however, state-run enterprises occupied a relatively small portion of the economy. In 1914 government plants employed only 12 percent of the total number of factory workers.

The state initially sought to operate the major mines; after 1885, however, it began to turn these over to private enterprise. Improvements in equipment and technique were introduced, but by and large the method of extraction remained primitive and the miners had to work under hazardously difficult conditions. Nonetheless, there was a steady increase in mineral production.[22]

In the iron industry no significant growth occurred until the state-operated Yawata Iron Works began production in 1901.[23] The number of private steel companies increased after the Russo-Japanese War, and there was a significant rise in iron and steel production.[24]

The shipbuilding industry made very little headway in the Meiji period. The production of machinery also showed only modest advancement, and most of the equipment used in the various industries had to be imported. For example, almost all the machines used for cotton spinning came from England.

The industry that expanded most rapidly and remained the most important component of the economy until the Second World War was textile manufacturing.[25] Japan attained a dominant position in the silk industry by the First World War. Mechanization in silk filature occurred slowly at first, but the pace was accelerated after the Sino-Japanese War. Prior to the war, in 1892, half of the raw silk was produced by hand-reeling; by 1910, some 70 percent was produced by machine-reeling filature.[26]

It was in cotton textile production that Japan's industrial revolution first occurred, with the extensive use of machinery in large plants. The man primarily responsible for the rapid mechanization in this field was the industrial entrepreneur Shibusawa Eiichi (1840–1931). A few cotton-spinning plants were established in the first decade of the Meiji period, but they failed to increase production sufficiently, and a large sum of money had to be devoted to the importation of cotton yarn and cloth. During this time 36 percent of the money spent on imports was expended on cotton textile goods. In 1878 the government sought to correct this situation by establishing model plants and importing spinning machines that were turned over to private entrepreneurs with very favorable terms of payment. These measures were effective, but the really big step forward in this field was taken by Shibusawa. He received financial support from businessmen and aristocrats and established a huge plant in Osaka that began operating in 1883. Shibusawa used steam power, and he was able to run his 10,500 spindles day and night by bringing electric lights into his plant.[27] In 1896 the Spinners' Association led by Shibusawa managed to have the import duties on raw cotton and the export duties on cotton yarn abolished.

The tremendous expansion in productive capacity led to rapidly increased output in this field. In 1896, with the domestic demand now being met, producers began to turn to foreign markets, particularly China.[28] As a result, cotton textile producers began to turn to the manufacture of cotton fabrics. In general, however, weaving remained essentially a cottage industry during this period of initial modern economic growth.

Weaving machines were employed in the manufacture of glossy silk for export, but in the production of brocades for domestic consumption traditional hand weaving was retained. The export of silk fabrics, particularly to the United States, steadily increased from about 1.5 million yen in 1889 to 21 million yen in 1899.[29] Cotton and silk textile products constituted the most significant part of Japan's exports. In 1913 they amounted to nearly three-fifths of its total exports.

The large-scale use of machines in the textile industry was followed by similar developments in other areas. The first modern pulp factory was established in 1889, and by 1896 paper was being exported to China. Sugar-refining plants were founded in 1895, and sugar manufacturing took a great leap forward after the acquisition of Formosa. Substantial gains were made throughout the 1890s in the production of cement, chemical fertilizers, drugs, beer, matches, and glass.

The most significant growth in industrial production occurred in the next phase (1906–1930), but by the time of the Russo-Japanese War, Japan was already well on its way to becoming an industrial nation, even though most of the work was still carried on in small establishments or workshops. This condition prevailed through the pre–World War II period and even in the postwar era. In 1930 there were over 1 million tiny shops, each employing an average of three persons, in many cases family members.

In terms of the percentage of people employed in factories, Japan was not yet an industrial society. Around 1913, only one-seventh of the country's total labor force was employed in manufacturing industries. The nation was still predominantly agrarian.[30]

THE PLIGHT OF THE WORKERS

Industrialization created new jobs for the people, but it also imposed new hardships upon the working class. In traditional Japan the relationship between the employer and the employee was assumed to be one of benevolence and kindness from above and loyalty and obedience from below. The ideal may not have always been followed in practice, but the employer was nevertheless expected to take a lifelong interest in the well-being of his employees. His interest was not to be limited to the employees' activities in the shop, but, much as if he were their father, he was to take their personal affairs, such as health, marriage, and family problems, as his direct concern.

The new industrialism that came into existence in Meiji Japan changed this relationship into an impersonal contract, a strictly business transaction. Some wily employers might have rationalized their exploitation of the workers in terms of the traditional values of benevolence and loyalty, but as the factories grew in size, it became clear that personal contacts between the employer and employee could not possibly be maintained. In the joint stock companies naturally there was no way to establish the traditional father-son, master-follower *(oyabun-kobun)* relationship between employer and employee. As a result, what frequently came to prevail was unrestrained exploitation; there were no laws regulating age, hours, wages, or working conditions.

Conditions in the textile factories and the mines were particularly bad, and there was extensive exploitation of female labor. Nine out of ten workers in weaving sheds and silk filatures were women, and in the cotton-spinning mills around the turn of the century, 80 percent of the operatives were women. In 1897, 49 percent of the workers in these mills were girls less than twenty years of age; 13 percent were younger than fourteen, and some were even less than eleven. These girls were recruited from the countryside and were under contract to work in the factories for a fixed length of time in exchange for a sum of money that was advanced to them. They were then housed in company dormitories ostensibly to protect them, but in reality the purpose of the facilities was to prevent them from running away.

In 1893 a reporter visited what was then regarded as a model cotton-spinning plant where working conditions were reputedly excellent, and he discovered that most of the operatives were girls between the ages of thirteen and twenty-four. They worked in twelve-hour shifts in order to keep the factory running day and night and were given only one rest period of thirty to forty minutes in which to eat. The workers were kept at their task for as long as nineteen hours if the plant was busy. Their food was poor and the bedding inadequate.[31]

Working conditions were worse than this in the small weaving shops. One employer kept his workers locked in the plant and dormitory, forced them to work until they produced a fixed quota, fined them, punished them by reducing their food, and on occasion even stripped and beat them. Similar conditions prevailed in the silk filature plants, many in fact being small sweat shops. Even in the larger factories the wages were lower than in the cotton-spinning mills. The death rate of the female workers in textile mills was high, with many contracting tuberculosis and beriberi.[32]

Low wages were justified by the employers, who claimed that it was necessary so as to enable them to compete effectively with the industrially advanced Western nations. Fukuzawa, a vocal spokesman for the businessmen's cause, admitted in 1893 that the Japanese textile workers were paid one-tenth the wages of their British counterparts, but he agreed with the employers that the cheap labor was necessary. The profits that were extracted by the owners and stockholders, however, were not at all modest. For example, five years after it went into production, Shibusawa's spinning company was paying dividends of 30 percent.

Another area in which harsh abuses occurred was in mining. One of the reasons for this was the fact that prisoners were used in the mines. This practice, although common in many of the state enterprises in the early Meiji era, was being discontinued in most of the privately owned mines. The Miike coal mines, however, which were the main source of coal that was extracted for export, utilized forced labor from 1873 to 1931. To be sure, the percentage of prisoners that were used there steadily declined.[33] The low cost of labor accruing from this practice enabled Miike to compete on more favorable terms than other mining firms. This led the Mitsubishi-owned Takashima Coal Mining Company to agitate for the sale of the Miike coal mines to private business.

At the same time, in order to compete with the cheap labor of the Miike mines, Takashima exploited its workers even more stringently, housing them in barracks as virtual prisoners, and working them for twelve hours for 30 sen a day. Any suspected slackers were punished severely.[34] Oxygen was scarce so it was difficult to breathe, but the miners were not allowed to pause and rest. Guards went around clubbing those who slackened their pace of work, while troublesome workers were trussed up and whipped. Those who attempted to escape were beaten savagely. In 1884, when a cholera epidemic broke out, one half of the 3,000 miners died of the disease. The victims were taken out and burned one day after they contracted cholera, whether they were dead or not. These conditions frequently led the Takashima miners to riot out of sheer desperation.

Faced with the cry of unfair competition, the government decided to sell the Miike coal mines. Mitsui purchased them in 1888 and, with the government's consent, continued to use prison labor. Under ordinary circumstances mining was a hazardous occupation. Not only was it back-breaking work, but the foul air shortened the miner's life, and frequent cave-ins and explosions took a high toll.

The workers were not the only ones affected adversely by the mining industry. Serious problems of pollution began to develop. The first celebrated case involved the damages caused by the poisonous elements that flowed into rivers of the Kantō region from the Ashio copper mines. The noxious ingredients killed the fish, ruining the fishing industries along the river routes. Moreover, the mining industry had stripped the adjacent areas of timber, thus creating serious erosion problems. This then brought about floods that spread the poisonous elements into the farmlands, causing a great deal of damage. In 1891 the matter was called to the attention of the government by a Diet member, Tanaka Shōzō (1841–1913), but to no avail. The desolation of the countryside became more critical, and finally a major protest demonstration was staged in 1900, but it was readily quelled by the police. The leader, Tanaka, in desperation submitted a direct petition to the emperor as he was leaving the Diet. The government, however, was readily able to dispose of the matter by claiming that Tanaka was insane.

The pay for workers in the heavy industries was better in comparison to the situation in the textile industries. Here too, however, private entrepreneurs sought to cut costs by reducing wages and by decreasing the number of workers while requiring the remaining laborers to make up for cutbacks by putting in more hours per day.

Christian leaders and men who were influenced by Western social reform movements began to criticize these conditions in the factories and the mines. The businessmen and their spokesmen adamantly opposed any government intervention in the way of giving protection to the workers, claiming that they were adhering to the tradition of "benevolence and kindness." Moreover, they argued that any deviation from the principles of laissez-faire, which fostered the growth of Western industries, would surely hamper Japanese industrial development.

The government was slow to act on behalf of the workers, partly because many high officials had close business ties, but primarily because they were mainly interested in industrial growth. Thus, the state supported the business interests at the expense of the workers. The Civil Code of 1890 upheld the concept of "freedom of contract," and state authority was used to prevent the workers from staging strikes. The Police Regulation of 1900 made it virtually a crime to organize and lead workers out on strikes.

Faced with the opposition of the industrialists, who were backed by the state, the advocates of reform were severely restricted in their efforts to organize the workers, and by the turn of the century labor movements were still in their infancy. Workers did stage strikes out of desperation, but they were usually sporadic, unorganized affairs. The strikes that occurred before the Sino-Japanese War were especially ineffective. The first strike on record was staged in 1886 by 100 female workers in a cotton mill in Yamanashi prefecture. The number of strikes began to increase after the Sino-Japanese War, with the government recording thirty incidents of labor disputes within one four-month period in 1897. This increase in labor unrest was caused by inflation, which was not accompanied by any increase in wages.

In 1897 the first serious move was made to organize the workers when the Society for the Protection of Trade Unions was established under the leadership of Takano Fusatarō (1868–1904), who had spent some time in the United States and was an admirer of Samuel Gompers, the American labor leader, and of Katayama Sen (1859–1933), who had studied at Grinnell College and Yale Divinity School and was also influenced by the doctrines of Christian socialism. Out of this movement spearheaded by these men, three labor societies emerged: the Association of Ironworkers, the Society to Reform the Railroads, and the Printers' Association. The objectives of these groups were still limited, and they all emphasized mutual assistance by the workers, played down strikes, and made clear that they were for reforms, not revolutions. The members of the association for railroad workers were the most aggressive, and they staged a strike in the spring of 1898 in northern Japan, protesting the firing of "agitators" and demanding better treatment.

The government's efforts to curb the movement forced the labor leaders to try to organize more effectively and thus attempt to carry the struggle into the political arena. In 1901 Katayama Sen and five other men organized the Social Democratic Party (Shakai Minshutō). The party was immediately disbanded by the government, but the leaders intensified their activities and propaganda work on behalf of socialism.

After the turn of the century the government did enact some legislation aimed at regulating conditions in the mines and the factories. In 1905 a mine act, and in 1911 a factory act, were put into law, but because of opposition from the industrialists, they were not enforced until 1916. The provisions were very modest. All mines and factories employing more than fifteen workers were required to limit the workday for women, and children under fifteen, to twelve hours, including one hour of rest. The minimum age of employment was set at twelve, except for light work, in which case the limit was ten years of age. No action was taken on night work.

SOCIAL CONDITIONS

The impact of industrialism, of course, was not all negative, although the positive effects were not felt by the masses until the twentieth century. As late as 1913, one scholar concluded, "the mode of living—housing, food, clothing, and other factors of living—has not made note-worthy improvement. The mass of the people live in just the same way as they did during the feudal regime."[35]

In many small ways, however, changes for the better did occur even before the turn of the century. To what extent economic changes in the Meiji era improved the quantity and quality of Japan's food supply would be difficult to assess. Agricultural production did increase, but so did the population.[36] Conservatively estimating the extent to which agricultural production increased in the Meiji period, economists contend that the caloric consumption per capita per day may have been over 2,100 during 1878–1882 and did not change significantly through 1915–1925, rising perhaps to about 2,300.

There does not seem to have been much improvement in the quality of the food during the Meiji era. Rice and other cereals constituted the bulk of what was consumed.[37] The taste of some of the food was improved by greater use of sugar, although again the per capita consumption was not high—10.4 pounds per capita annually in 1896–1898. Nevertheless, this was enough to make the diet more interesting for peasants who in the past were condemned to a diet of rice, barley, sweet potatoes, vegetables, and occasionally, fish.

Housing remained poor, and clothing did not improve much for the masses, but even in the countryside machine-made cotton fabrics replaced hand-woven cloth, and some Western-style clothing began to appear. Matches, soap, and kerosene lamps made life more convenient. In the cities there were gaslights and rickshaws. Later, of course, there would be electricity and bicycles.

The effects of the new age were felt most forcefully in the towns and villages located near railroads or near new factories. The technological and industrial changes together with the other new institutions—schools, newspapers, and military conscription—brought the outside world into the villages, and a broader perspective and a new way of life began to develop. In recalling the changes brought about by the establishment of a cotton-spinning mill in his village in 1890, one observer noted that the easygoing tranquility of the town vanished forever as three times a day the factory whistle echoed throughout the village shaking violently the stagnant air of the community. The impact the factory had upon the village was greater than the arrival of Perry's warships off the coast of Uraga. Consequently, traditional attitudes about social status and family standing disappeared quickly and were replaced by standards of wealth and poverty.[38]

For the peasants who lived within commuting distance of the factories, a way to supplement their income now became available. Fathers and sons often found work in the factories, leaving mothers and younger children to till the soil. This alleviated the traditional problem of underemployment in the farm villages. The more ambitious young men, drawn by the job opportunities and the more exciting life of the cities, left their villages, causing the agrarian leaders to bemoan the fact that the seductive cities were draining the villages of energetic young men.

Insofar as the effect of modernization in the area of health and sanitation was concerned, there is little evidence that much improvement took place in the first half of the Meiji era. In fact, with factories operating under the hazardous, unhealthy conditions described earlier, the mortality rate remained high among women of child-bearing age and young men. Medical care remained inadequate, although in 1900 there were 0.75 doctors for every 1,000 persons.[39] Life expectancy around 1891–1898 was 42.8 years for men and 44.3 for women. It remained approximately the same in the pre–World War II years. In the 1920s and the 1930s the infant mortality rate was well over 100 for every 1,000 live births as compared to 4 for every 1,000 in 1995.[40]

Crowded conditions and inadequate sanitation resulted in frequent outbreaks of epidemics. Cholera epidemics began to occur in the late Tokugawa years; the bubonic plague first broke out in 1899. The diseases tended to get out of control almost immediately after striking, and then they spread very rapidly. In 1879 there was a cholera epidemic in which more than 105,700 persons died. In 1886 a similar epidemic took the lives of 108,400 victims, and in the same year more than 20,000 persons died of typhus and dysentery, and 18,000 of smallpox. In 1886, then, more than 146,000 persons died as a result of epidemics.[41] The manner in which the victims were cared for was inadequate, to say the least. In 1892 Erwin Baelz, a German doctor who was teaching at the University of Tokyo, visited a smallpox hospital and observed

a scandalous state of affairs. There are four hundred patients, often fifty new cases every day; eight doctors, some of whom have had very little experience; and twenty nurses. Wooden sheds with torn paper windows in wintertime.

That's the way Tokyo treats the sick. Cholera—typhoid—smallpox! Not one hospital for such epidemic cases where the poor wretches are as well cared for as a horse in a good stable![42]

Another area in which the new age failed to eliminate a traditional hazard was the frequent incidence of large-scale fires. These monstrously destructive fires continued to plague the cities just as they had in the Tokugawa period.[43]

Another unfortunate legacy of the Tokugawa era that modernization failed to have an ameliorating effect on was the houses of prostitution. As noted earlier, slavery had been banned but "voluntary servitude" was permitted. There were six sections in Tokyo where these establishments were located.[44] A Swiss official in Japan observed that the girls were "publicly exposed like animals on display, to be freely scrutinized by all comers. After first examining the goods, they are purchased and used by the first man who sets the price. The impression I got of these unfortunate creatures was one of utmost misery."[45] Similar establishments existed in all the cities throughout the country. Many of the girls were sold into bondage by impoverished peasant families, victims of economic necessity and a feudalistic sense of loyalty to the family.

Efforts to end this practice and free the girls were spearheaded by Christians as early as 1882, but to no avail. In 1899–1900, however, a movement led by a missionary, U. G. Murphy, forced the courts to recognize the right of the prostitutes to leave the brothels. The girls were still obliged, however, to repay the money that had been advanced to their families for their services. The movement to free the prostitutes was joined by the Salvation Army and Christian journalists, and for a short period their efforts were rewarded. Some houses of prostitution went out of business, but this was only a temporary victory. The system survived until the end of the Second World War.

Notes

1. Kenneth B. Pyle, *The New Generation in Meiji Japan: Problems of Cultural Identity, 1885–1895* (Stanford: Stanford University Press, 1969), p. 70.

2. Murakami Shunryō and Sakata Yoshio, *Meiji Bunka-shi: Kyōiku Dōtoku-hen* (Meiji Cultural History: Education and Morality) (Tokyo: Yōyōdō, 1955), pp. 555–556.

3. Lawrence W. Chisolm, *Fenollosa: The Far East and American Culture* (New Haven: Yale University Press, 1963), p. 51.

4. Kakuzo Okakura, *The Awakening of Japan* (New York: Appleton, 1905), pp. 6, 97, 186, 188, 220.

5. Mitsuo Nakamura, *Modern Japanese Fiction, 1868–1926* (Tokyo: Kokusai Bunka Shinkōkai, 1968), part 2, p. 19.

6. Tatsuo Arima, *The Failure of Freedom: A Portrait of Modern Japanese Intellectuals* (Cambridge, Mass.: Harvard University Press, 1969), p. 79.

7. Toki Yoshimaro, *Meiji Taishō-shi: Geijutsu-hen* (Meiji-Taishō History: The Arts) (Tokyo: Asahi Shimbunsha, 1931), p. 199.

8. Ibid., p. 315.

9. Shiki, like many other Japanese writers and artists, signed his works with his given name and is therefore better known by that name than by his surname.

10. In 1898, 82 percent of the people still lived in towns and villages of populations under 10,000.

11. Taking the period 1910–1914 as index 100, from 1885–1889 to 1905–1909 the index of food production rose from an estimated 57 to 85 and the production of raw material from 22 to 78.

12. This was achieved by means of a 25 percent increase in yield per acre along with an increase in cultivated land. A 7 percent increase in cultivated area in rice was achieved between 1878–1882 and 1888–1892, and about 25 percent in the fifty years after 1885–1889.

13. There is disagreement about whether or not these factors actually had as much impact as is generally assumed. See James I. Nakamura, "Growth of Japanese Agriculture," in *The State and Economic Enterprise in Japan,* ed. William W. Lockwood (Princeton: Princeton University Press, 1965), pp. 291–295.

14. In 1908, for example, 28 percent of a farmer's income was paid in taxes, whereas a merchant or industrialist paid only 14 percent.

15. In fact, during the period from 1868 to 1893, raw silk accounted for 42 percent of Japan's total exports.

16. Imports and exports doubled from 1889–1893 to 1899–1903, and they doubled again during the next decade. Coal consumption in industry and transportation rose from 2 million tons in 1893 to 15 million tons in 1913. Railroad mileage more than tripled, and freight tonmileage increased seventeen times.

17. The number of private railroad companies increased from twelve in 1889 to twenty-four by 1895.

18. At which point there were 37,283 miles of private tracks and 1,499 miles of railway owned by the state.

19. For example, the third-class fare between Shinagawa in Tokyo and Yokohama was 31.25 sen in 1872, but at this time the highest paid female worker in a textile plant was receiving only 7.8 sen a day.

20. By 1877 there were 136,761 registered rickshaws in Japan.

21. By 1906 the shipping tonnage came close to 700,000, and in 1913, half of the overseas trade was carried in Japanese bottoms, this as compared to less than 10 percent before the Sino-Japanese War.

22. In 1877, 3.4 million yen worth of minerals was produced; by 1887 the figure had climbed to 8.2 million yen. The building of the railroads facilitated coal mining; whereas 220,000 tons of coal were mined in 1874, some 5 million tons were produced in 1897.

23. In that year the output of pig iron jumped to 56,000 tons and steel to 7,500 tons, as compared to 26,800 tons and 1,000 tons, respectively, in 1897.

24. In 1913 pig iron production came to 243,000 tons, and steel output advanced to 255,000 tons.

25. In 1900, 70.7 percent of the factories in Japan were involved in textile production. They consumed 46 percent of the motor power used in all industries and employed 67 percent of the factory workers.

26. The size of the filature plants also began to grow. In 1909, of the 3,720 plants, 471 with more than 100 workers employed over 49 percent of the total number of workers in this field. The number of hand-reeling establishments in the countryside remained high, however, and in 1913 there were still about 285,000 shops of this kind. The output of raw silk increased from 7.5 million pounds annually in the period 1889–1893 to 27.9 million pounds during 1909–1913. In 1897, 24 percent of the world's raw silk came from Japan, 39 from China, and 27 from Italy. By 1904, these figures had changed to 31 percent from Japan, 24 from China, and 26 from Italy.

27. The year after he began operation, Shibusawa was able to pay a dividend of 18 percent to the investors. By 1888, some 1,100 workers were employed in his Osaka Spinning Mill plants. Other industrialists followed the methods employed by Shibusawa, and between 1886 and 1894, 33 new plants were established in the vicinity of Osaka.

28. In 1880, 81 percent of the workers were in agriculture, fishing, and mining. In 1900 this figure dropped to 69 percent; by 1920 it had fallen even lower, to 55.4 percent. In the fields of manufacturing and construction the percentages for the same years were 6.4, 13, and 19.4, and in commerce and transportation they were 6.4, 10.1, and 15.5. See William W. Lockwood, *The Economic Development of Japan* (Princeton: Princeton University Press, 1954), p. 462. Exports to that country rose until 1903, when they began to decline because of competition from foreign cotton textile producers as well as from the growing Chinese textile industry.

29. The figure continued to rise in the next two decades, reaching a peak of 160 million yen in 1919.

30. At the turn of the century, three out of five families were still engaged in farming; that is, in 1903, out of a total of 8.4 million families, 5.4 million of them were on the farm.

31. Only 2 girls out of 1,600 workers received 22 sen a day in wages; 200 or so earned 11 sen or more; most of them were paid 8 to 10 sen; some received as little as 4 sen. They were charged for their food, having to pay 2 sen a meal, or 1 yen 80 sen for the month.

32. The overall pay in the textile industry remained low, even lower than was the case in India. In 1891 the labor cost to produce 100 pounds of cotton yarn was 135.5 sen for Japan and 151.9 sen for India. Men received better pay than women, and workers in heavy industry received better wages than those in textile plants. For example, in 1898 the average pay for men, including the salaries of executive officials, in ten cotton-spinning plants was 24.5 sen a day, compared to 13.9 sen for women; in 1901 workers at the Nagasaki shipyard received an average pay of 54.4 sen a day.

33. In 1889 it was 13.3 percent, whereas in 1907 it was down to 5.5 percent.

34. In 1888, a reporter for the magazine *Nihonjin* noted that the temperature in the mines got as high as 120 to 130 degrees.

35. Quoted in ibid., p. 34.

36. Specifically, the population increased from 35.9 million (index 71) in 1875–1879 to 50.6 million (index 100) in 1910–1914, while food production rose from somewhere below index 57 and increased to index 100.

37. In 1889–1893, 0.9 pound per capita per year of meat was consumed; in 1900, some 29 pounds of fish were consumed per person annually.

38. Sumiya Mikio, *Dai-Nipponteikoku no Shiren* (The Crucible of Imperial Japan) (Tokyo: Chūō Kōronsha, 1966), p. 63.

39. This figure does not compare too unfavorably with 1.1 in 1966, when you consider the fact that modern medicine had to start from the very beginning in early Meiji.

40. The overall death rate in 1920 was 25 persons out of 1,000 as compared to 7 out of 1,000 in 1998.

41. These epidemics continued to break out; in the second and third decades of Meiji more than 800,000 people died of one kind or another of these rapidly spreading diseases.

42. Erwin O. E. Von Baelz, *Awakening Japan: The Diary of a German Doctor,* trans. Eden and Cedar Paul (New York: Viking, 1932), p. 98.

43. Between 1876 and 1892, over 60,000 houses went up in flames in the city of Tokyo. This amounted to about one out of four dwellings in that city.

44. Between 1883–1888 anywhere from 3,000 to 5,000 prostitutes were kept in bondage in these brothels.

45. Irokawa Daikichi, *Kindai Kokka no Suppatsu* (The Beginning of the Modern State) (Tokyo: Chū Kūronsha, 1966), p. 107.

8

Political Developments in Later Meiji

The decade or two following the promulgation of the constitution and the convocation of the Diet was a period of trial and error in Japanese politics. Both sides, the oligarchy and the opposition parties, endeavored to learn how to fit the Diet into the political framework of the country. The idea of government functioning under a written constitution with the participation of a Diet that was composed of elected representatives was certainly a revolutionary concept. Despite all the theoretical discussions that had taken place before these institutions were adopted, the actual incorporation of these elements into the political life of the society required patience, willingness to compromise, and common sense—qualities that seemed scarce enough on both sides of the political battle line.

The internal power struggle was closely related to Japan's foreign relations. The opposition parties frequently used national interest as an issue to arouse popular opinion and support against the government whereas the ruling clique, in contrast, used external crises to deflect assaults launched by the opposition. The fact that the opposition parties were just as chauvinistic, perhaps even more so, than some government officials did not augur well for the future of parliamentary government. Their willingness to support militarism and expansionism necessitated their subordination of internal political goals to these ends. In the 1880s, as Japan became increasingly involved in Korean affairs, Fukuzawa was speaking for many of the advocates of popular rights when he said, "The question of control of political power at home is insignificant compared to the question of national interests. Even if the government in form and name is autocratic, as long as it is capable of extending our national interests, I am satisfied."[1] In effect, Fukuzawa was nudging the movement toward its eventual demise half a century later.

Another trait that weakened the political parties was their lack of unity of purpose and cohesiveness, which was no doubt the result of the persistence of traditional behavior and values. Not only were there intense conflicts between the parties, there were also various incompatible factions within each party that based their loyalties upon sectional and personal ties. The existence of these cliques led to numerous intraparty squabbles.

Factionalism and personal rivalries could have been expected to divide the oligarchs too, but the Meiji leaders, faced with the threat that the political parties might usurp their power, managed to subordinate their personal and factional interests. By and large they acted as a cohesive group until the turn of the century, when Itō organized a political party. The Satsuma and Chōshū factions shared the powers of government, alternating the post of the prime minister and more or less dividing the armed forces, with Satsuma dominating the navy and Chōshū the army. Eventually a rivalry of a sort did develop between Itō and Yamagata, but in the main they managed to work together as parts of a group in which power was shared collectively by the members. No one individual stood out above the others, that is until Itō and Yamagata began to emerge as the two most prominent leaders. The concept of the *genrō* was developing, and with it came the expectation that each member be loyal to the group and behave in a manner appropriate to a genrō. This, in effect, meant that individuals were to refrain from establishing ties with a political party.

The collective exercise of power and the emergence of the Privy Council and the council made up of the genrō, which operated outside the confines of the constitution, as political bodies of primary importance tended to obscure the real locus of power. In addition, since all governmental actions were taken in the name of the emperor, the system itself tended to draw a veil over those who actually exercised power. The emperor could not personally be held responsible for any particular action because he was "sacred and inviolable." As a result, the notion of *kuromaku* (the puppeteer who pulls the strings from behind the black curtain) came to play an important part in Japanese political thinking. The decision-making process tended to obfuscate the location of responsibility because "go-betweens, informal meetings, and group discussions were consistently used to reach decisions for which no individual or group was ordinarily responsible."[2]

To be sure, the desire to maintain power strongly motivated the oligarchs, but it is also true that they were sincere men who honestly wished to serve the state and the public good. They were convinced that they were better qualified to do this than the opposition party members. In order to retain their grip on political power, they took advantage of institutions and forces not available to the opposition, such as the emperor system, the bureaucracy, the army and navy, the police, and the general public's willingness to follow those in power.

In addition, of course, they were able to play upon the weaknesses of the opposition by aggravating their internally divisive conflicts through support of one faction against another. Frequently, they were able to induce key leaders to leave the opposition altogether and join their camp by offering them government posts.

PARTISAN POLITICS: 1887–1894

As noted earlier, the opposition forces led by Gotō Shōjirō launched an offensive against the Itō cabinet in 1887 by opposing the negotiations for treaty revisions. Itō was forced to discontinue the negotiations, but he tried to split the opposition by bringing Ōkuma Shigenobu into the cabinet as foreign minister. This not only failed to weaken the Union of Like Thinkers, but it also served to annoy his fellow clansman, Yamagata, who disapproved of Ōkuma's entry into the government.

In the spring of 1888, Itō resigned his post in order to devote full attention to the drafting of the constitution, and Kuroda Kiyotaka became the new prime minister. His cabinet also encountered difficulties in connection with treaty revisions, with the result that the task was turned over entirely to Ōkuma, who had remained in the new cabinet as foreign minister. The opposition party leaders persisted in their objections because Ōkuma, like Itō before him, was also willing to open the entire nation to Western residents and to allow Western judges to sit in trials involving Westerners. The other members of the oligarchy also disapproved of these concessions, and when Ōkuma was injured in an assassination attempt, they used this occasion to remove him from his post. As a result of these difficulties, Kuroda resigned in October 1889 and was succeeded by Yamagata.

At the time the announcement was made that elections for the Diet were to be held on July 1, 1890, the opposition forces were in a state of disarray. However, in cooperation with other leaders, Itagaki managed to revive the Liberal Party.

The first Diet elections were held in July 1890 as scheduled. The franchise was limited to male subjects over twenty-five years of age who paid a national land or income tax of 15 yen or more. Priests, teachers of religion, active servicemen, and the insane were denied the right to vote.[3] The country was divided into 257 electoral districts with each one having one representative, except for those with more than 180,000 residents, in which case two seats were given. There were 214 districts with one representative and 43 with two. The voter was required to sign his name and place his seal on the ballot. In the first national elections, 93.9 percent of those eligible to vote cast their ballots.

There were 130 Liberal Party and 41 Reform Party members in the lower house when the first Diet convened. A progovernment party won sixty-seven seats and merged with other similar groups to form the Taiseikai (The Great Achievement Society) with 79 members.[4]

The government's avowed position was "to stand above parties," a policy that was proclaimed by Prime Minister Kuroda immediately after the constitution was promulgated. Itō, the man who framed the constitution, took a similar position, holding that the bringing of political parties into the government would be extremely undesirable since the government had to maintain its independence. Yamagata was even less willing than Kuroda and Itō to cooperate with political parties, and he persisted in his rigid opposition to granting these organizations a role in government.

The Diet convened on November 25, 1890, and immediately there was a clash with the government as the opposition factions attempted to cut the budget. Some of these cuts, though, involved items excluded, under Article 67 of the constitution, from the Diet's jurisdiction; consequently, Yamagata was inclined toward standing firm and, if necessary, even going so far as to dissolve the Diet. However, the desire not to mar the inauguration of constitutional government by such a drastic step prevailed, and a compromise was reached. Factionalism in the parties also played a significant role in this affair since the Tosa faction of the Liberal Party was persuaded by the cabinet to split with the opposition and vote to uphold Yamagata's position.[5]

In order to split the opposition, the Meiji leaders frequently resorted to more persuasive techniques, such as the employment of thugs to exert physical force against Diet members. A cleavage developed within the Liberal Party between those who were in the Diet and those who were not. The latter, led by Ōi Kentarō (1843–1922), sought to intimidate the weak-kneed Diet members, with the result that a group of Tosa men finally split with the party and formed a separate organization.

Just as the political parties could not maintain unity, there were signs that a cleavage was developing among the government leaders. Itō was dissatisfied with the way in which Yamagata dealt with the Diet; when this became known to the latter, he resigned his post. This was the beginning of the growing fission between the so-called civil faction of the genrō, represented by Itō and Inoue, and the "military" faction, which was headed by Yamagata and included the remaining genrō, namely, Kuroda, Matsukata, Saigō Tsugumichi, and Ōyama Iwao.

Upon Yamagata's resignation, Itō was again asked to form a cabinet, but he refused, passing the task on to Matsukata, who organized a new government in May 1891. Matsukata adopted an uncompromising stance toward the opposition at the encouragement of his minister of home affairs, Shinagawa Yajirō

(1843–1900), who was a follower of Yamagata and an inveterate foe of parliamentary government and political parties.

The opposition parties had by this time somewhat fortified their positions. The Liberal Party leaders had expelled the more radical faction led by Ōi and curtailed the power of the non-Diet members. In addition, cooperation between the Liberal Party and the Reform Party was agreed upon in a meeting between Itagaki and Ōkuma. Ōkuma was thereupon "purged" by the government again, losing his membership in the Privy Council.

The second Diet convened in November 1891, and the opposition parties, bent upon a confrontation with the government, began to slash the budget submitted by Matsukata. His response was swift and decisive—dissolution of the Diet. Matsukata, now fully determined to increase the number of progovernment representatives, decided to intervene in the election. Shinagawa implemented the plan by instructing prefectural and local government officials to employ whatever means were necessary to obstruct the opposition candidates. Not only did government agents intimidate the voters by conducting house-to-house visits telling them that a vote for opposition candidates was an act of disloyalty toward the emperor, but they also bribed the voters and even employed thugs, hoodlums, police, and military troops to attack the opposition forces physically. Violence was particularly severe in Kōchi and Saga prefectures, the home bases of Itagaki and Ōkuma. Elections had to be postponed in Saga because of the extensive government intervention.[6]

Despite the measures taken by the government, the opposition parties nevertheless managed to win the election by securing 163 seats; the progovernment faction got only 137. As soon as the third Diet was convened, the opposition parties sought to impeach the government by introducing a resolution memorializing the emperor to dismiss the cabinet. The motion failed by three votes because some members did not favor involving the emperor in the struggle. Thereupon a motion of no confidence was passed by a vote of 154 to 111. The House of Peers also passed a resolution reprimanding the government for its actions in the election, but it supported Matsukata against the lower house's efforts to reduce the budget.

Matsukata was forced to resign in July 1892, when the minister of war and the minister of the navy resigned as a protest action against the inclusion of Ōkuma's crony in the cabinet. Itō was also disturbed by the way in which Matsukata had managed the election, and he consequently forced Shinagawa's removal from the cabinet. He had already begun to weigh the possibility of establishing a government party to deal with the difficulties posed by the opposition in the Diet.

Upon Matsukata's resignation, Itō took over the premiership again with the understanding that the other genrō would join the cabinet to give it the strength necessary to cope with the opposition forces. As a result, Yamagata, Inoue, Ōyama, and Kuroda entered what was to be labeled the Cabinet of Elder Statesmen. Mutsu agreed to serve as foreign minister.

The fourth Diet convened, and once again the opposition trimmed the budget by disallowing monies needed for naval expansion and the bureaucracy. The government refused to accept the cuts since they fell under Article 67 of the constitution, which excluded these items from the Diet's jurisdiction. Itō, finding that the impasse could not be resolved, asked the emperor to issue a rescript forcing the Diet to accept his budget. The emperor pointed to the importance of national defense and pledged a certain sum of his own money, asked the civil and military officials to contribute part of their salaries, and requested the Diet to appropriate the remainder of the funds. The opposition parties had no choice but to acquiesce in the face of imperial intervention.

The fact that their opposition could be quashed so readily by imperial intervention had a demoralizing effect upon the party men. This caused many to become cynical, leading them to yield to compromises and accept bribes. To make matters worse, the cleavage between the opposition parties began to widen again at about this time. The behind-the-scene efforts to bring Itō and the Liberal Party together was in part responsible for this situation. Moreover, a growing divergence of opinion on foreign policy between the Liberal and the Reform parties began to develop, with the latter taking a harder line.

The fifth Diet met in November 1893, only to find the political parties in serious disarray with the de facto leader of the Liberal Party, Hoshi Tōru, under severe criticism by his own party members for maintaining covert ties with the government. He was also accused of accepting bribes,[7] and his foes ultimately succeeded in having him expelled from the Diet. The split in the opposition forces was offset, however, by the fact that conservative antiparty Diet members joined in the attack on the Itō cabinet for its vacillating and irresolute foreign policy, and in particular for its weak stand in regard to treaty revisions. Among the leading critics of Itō's foreign policy was Shinagawa, behind whom, it was believed, stood Yamagata.

Itō finally dissolved the Diet after repeatedly proroguing it. The next Diet, also consisting of a majority hostile to Itō, passed a motion of no-confidence, severely attacking his foreign policy. In June 1894 Itō again dissolved the Diet, this time after it had been in session for only half a month. Clearly, a serious internal crisis was in the making. Precisely at this point, however, the domestic exigency was suddenly resolved by the eruption of a crisis abroad. The Korean government had asked the Chinese government to send troops to help quash a rebellion that was led by a religious cult, the Tong Hak (Eastern Learning) Society. Overnight the opposition parties and the press diverted their attention away from the internal conflict to focus on the Korean situation, and they collectively rallied behind the government's policy of intervention. The seventh Diet as well as the eighth, both of which were convened during the Sino-Japanese War, gave enthusiastic support to the government's foreign policy and war efforts. Mutsu used the crisis to negotiate a break-through revision of the hated Unequal Treaties. His secret negotiations with Great Britain in July 1894 were accomplished while the opposition parties had their attentions focused on the coming war. Once the deadlock was broken with the British, the other foreign powers fell into line within two years.

THE KOREAN QUESTION AND THE SINO-JAPANESE WAR

Japan had from the outset of the Meiji era harbored imperialistic designs toward Korea. Saigō's plan to contrive an incident to enable Japan to go to war against it was noted in an earlier chapter. In August 1875, Japanese men-of-war ventured into Korean waters at Kanghwa Bay, where they were fired upon by coastal defense forces. Japan used this incident as an excuse to persuade Korea, under the threat of force, to agree to establish diplomatic and commercial relations. Six months later, in February 1876, Korea agreed to open three ports and accepted an unequal treaty, not unlike the ones the West had imposed on China and Japan. The treaty may have held Korea to be an independent nation, but China still regarded it as a tributary state.

In Korea, conflicts were taking place between the conservatives and the progressives, who, looking to Japan as a model, wanted to reform and modernize the nation. In 1882 an uprising broke out that was directed against the ruling family, which was dominated by the queen's relatives, the Min family. The movement took an anti-Japanese turn because of the government's practice of employing Japanese officers to reform the army. Furthermore, the shortage of rice and the inflation were blamed on Japanese merchants who, it was charged, had hoarded Korean rice. The rebels forced the king to flee and attacked the Japanese legation. The movement widened its antagonism toward outsiders and became decidedly antiforeign when the conservative regent, Taewongun (the Grand Prince; 1820–1898), who had been out of power since 1873, took over the leadership. At the request of Queen Min, the Chinese government thereupon intervened.

In Japan the war faction, led by Yamagata, favored intervening for the purpose of gaining territorial concessions. A force of 1,500 troops was landed at Inchon, but the rebellion was subdued by the Chinese forces, and Japan had to be content with receiving indemnities. This incident spurred on the Japanese militarists to expand the armed forces in anticipation of further difficulties in Korea and of a potential confrontation with China over that nation. In 1882 a ten-year plan to expand the army was formulated, and in 1885, it was put into

effect. The navy also launched a program of expansion, and its budget continuously increased from 1883.

The conservative nationalists, the progressives, and even the radicals were
united by a determination to protect Japanese interests in Korea. They also favored supporting the Korean reformers led by Kim Ok-kyun (1851–1894)
and Pak Yong-hyo (1861–1939). The opposition party members, however,
were behaving in an irresponsible fashion because, although they were generally jingoistic when it came to the question of Korea and China, they continuously sought to reduce the government's military and naval budget.

China's position in Korea, after the troubles of 1882, was much strengthened by the presence there of its own military force, headed by Yuan Shikai
(1859–1916). The Korean reformers, with the encouragement of some leading Japanese, such as Fukuzawa and Gotō, staged a coup against the Min faction in December 1884. Kim and Pak had the support of the Japanese legation
in Seoul, but the coup was crushed by the Chinese forces, and the Japanese
minister had to flee with the rebel leaders. Thereupon the Japanese government, ignoring the fact that its own officials were at fault, dispatched Foreign
Minister Inoue Kaoru and two battalions to Seoul, demanding an apology as
well as indemnities. Public opinion in Japan, led by the liberals, called for a
tough stand against Korea and China. Itagaki even organized and trained a
volunteer army in Kōchi, while Ōi Kentarō actually made plans to go to Korea
and assassinate the leaders of the Min faction. The plot was uncovered, and Ōi
was arrested by the Japanese authorities.

Realizing that Japan was not yet ready for war, the government leaders led
by Itō took a more responsible position and sought a peaceful settlement. Itō
went to Tianjin to negotiate with the Chinese leader, Li Hongzhang
(1823–1901), and concluded the Li-Itō Convention, which provided for the
withdrawal of Chinese and Japanese forces and military advisers from Korea.
Both nations also agreed to notify each other if and when they planned to send
troops into Korea in the future.

In Korea, Chinese influence was exerted on behalf of modernization by
Yuan Shikai. Meanwhile, Japanese commercial activities continued to increase
in Korea, and this, in the opinion of the Koreans, only added to their economic woes. Japanese merchants cornered the Korean rice supply and imported manufactured goods, such as cotton fabrics and sundry items for
household use. Unrest among the people continued and a series of popular disturbances broke out in the decade following the 1884 incident.

The discontent among the Korean people enabled a conservative religious
cult, the Tong Hak Society, to gain popular support. It was basically antiforeign
and anti-Japanese in character. The founder of the organization incorporated
religious ideas from native shamanism, Daoism, Buddhism, Confucianism, and

even Catholicism to start a movement that, he claimed, would save Korea from Western encroachments while enriching and benefiting the poor. In 1894 the Tong Hak staged uprisings in the southern provinces with the support of impoverished peasants. This movement provided the poor with a way of venting their anger against the officials who had been exacting heavy taxes from them. Unable to suppress the insurgents, the Korean government was forced to ask Yuan Shikai for assistance.

The Japanese government immediately decided to dispatch a brigade of troops when it received a wire from its Korean legation on June 2, claiming that the Korean government was planning to ask for Chinese military assistance to quell the rebellion. Three days later a decision was made to establish a supreme military command under the emperor and begin mobilization. It appears, then, that the Japanese government was actually ready to go to war even before there was any real cause to do so.

The main architects of the policy that led to war were vice chief of staff of the army, General Kawakami Sōroku, and Foreign Minister Mutsu. By the time the Chinese government notified the Japanese government on June 7 of its decision to send troops into Korea, the Japanese soldiers were already on their way to Korea. They landed at Inchon despite the report by the Japanese minister in Korea that everything was under control. In order to find an excuse to justify the continued presence of these forces in Korea, Mutsu conceived of a proposal that called for Sino-Japanese intervention in Korea for the purpose of bringing about reforms there. China rejected this proposal, whereupon the Japanese government went ahead and submitted its demands to the Korean government while at the same time ordering its own minister in Korea to find a pretext that would enable Japan to take direct action before some foreign power, namely Russia or England, had an opportunity to intervene.[8] In line with this policy, Japanese troops moved into the palace, placed Taewongun in power, and then compelled him to request the withdrawal of Chinese troops from Korean soil. On July 25, a naval clash occurred off the coast of Inchon between Japanese warships and Chinese vessels transporting reinforcements to Korea. The Japanese authorities then dispatched their troops against the Chinese forces on July 29 before finally declaring war on China three days later.

So far as the fighting itself was concerned, the Japanese army, better trained and better equipped, managed to drive the Chinese forces out of Korea without too much difficulty. The First Army, under General Yamagata, moved against Pyongyang and captured it in two days. The Chinese forces were then pursued to the north, and by the end of October Yamagata crossed the Yalu into Chinese territory. In addition, the Japanese navy gained supremacy of the seas by defeating the Chinese navy on the Yellow Sea on September 17. By controlling the seas, the Japanese were able to send the Second Army, under

Ōyama, to the Liaodong Peninsula. On November 22, Ōyama's men captured Port Arthur, which had been built as an impregnable fortress. The Second Army was then sent to Shandong Peninsula to attack the port of Weihaiwei from the land while the Japanese navy attacked, and by February ultimately destroyed, the Chinese fleet that was anchored there. The First Army marked time during the winter months and subsequently launched its offensive against the southern Manchurian cities in February of 1895. It was then poised to strike against Peking (now Beijing).

At home the Japanese public was intoxicated by the repeated victories, and under the leadership of such liberals as Fukuzawa Yukichi and Tokutomi Sohō, the people were calling for the continued prosecution of the war until Peking fell. The entire nation was united behind the war effort, and the Diet swiftly approved the military appropriations requested by the government. Even Christian leaders, like Uchimura Kanzō, regarded the military effort abroad as a just war that was being fought to assist Korea against Chinese oppression.

The government officials were, to be sure, pleased with the moralistic sentiments that united the people behind it, but they were also realistic enough to understand what Japan's limitations were; they were thus keenly aware of the danger that might result from a crushing defeat of China. Itō concluded that "if Peking is captured, the Qing [Ch'ing] government will collapse and riots will break out throughout the land. Then the major powers will move in their troops, using as a pretext the need to protect their nationals in China. Also Japan would have no one to negotiate with and would be faced with an impossible situation."[9] As a result, the government moved with caution in spite of the fact that the press was clamoring for the annexation of Formosa (Taiwan), Manchuria, and other Chinese provinces. The two major political parties were vying to outdo each other in their imperialistic greed.

By the end of 1894, China showed its willingness to negotiate a settlement, and in March 1895, Li Hongzhang arrived in Shimonoseki to work out a peace treaty. After a slight delay caused by a Japanese fanatic's attempt to assassinate Li, the two parties agreed to the Treaty of Shimonoseki. The terms provided for China to do the following: recognize the independence of Korea; cede the Liaodong Peninsula, Taiwan, and the Pescadores to Japan; pay an indemnity of 360 million yen; conclude a commercial treaty with Japan similar to those China had contracted with the Western powers; open four additional ports; permit Japanese vessels to navigate the Yangtze River; and allow Japanese subjects to engage in manufacturing in China.[10]

The Sino-Japanese War successfully launched Japan's career as an imperialistic power by giving it increased influence in Korea, an outpost in Taiwan, and a substantial toehold on the continent in the Liaodong Peninsula. The war also gave Japan an opportunity to display to the other powers that it was a serious rival and a threat to their own imperialistic designs. The country that was most upset by this development was Russia, which had its own designs on Korea and Manchuria and consequently persuaded France and Germany to join to protest the Japanese acquisition of the Liaodong Peninsula. Germany backed Russia because it wanted that nation to turn its focus east rather than get involved in European affairs. Furthermore, Germany, as seen in its acquisition of concessions in Shandong in 1898, also had ambitions in China. France gained certain privileges in southern China, while Russia extended its influence in Manchuria.

This liaison of Russia, France, and Germany provided a turn of events that was not wholly unexpected so far as Itō and Mutsu were concerned. Faced with the Triple Intervention, they saw no alternative but to accede to the demand to return the Liaodong Peninsula to China. In exchange, Japan received an additional indemnity from China.

This was a shocking blow to the Japanese public, and the public opinion makers exhorted the people not to forget the galling experience. The government reacted by immediately launching a program of vast military expansion. The number of army divisions, which totaled seven at the beginning of the Sino-Japanese War, was increased to thirteen by 1903.[11]

China had ceded Taiwan to Japan, but this did not mean that it could simply move in and take over. Neither the Chinese residents of the island nor the indigenous inhabitants were willing to accept Japanese rule, and in May 1895, Taiwan declared its independence. Japan landed its troops and managed to disperse the Chinese forces on the island. The native inhabitants, however, persistently refused to accept Japanese rule and continued to carry on guerrilla warfare. The military campaign of subjugation was continued until 1896, but the guerrillas were not fully vanquished.[12]

Pacification by force was clearly not succeeding. In 1898, General Kodama Gentarō was appointed governor-general of Taiwan. He was convinced that the repressive measures adopted by his predecessors only served to fortify native resistance. His plan was to follow a policy of promoting the welfare of the populace as a means of winning their good will. He appointed Gotō Shimpei (1857–1929), who had proven himself an able civil administrator. He introduced such measures as land tenure reforms, health and sanitation programs, railroads, a postal system, telegraph, and other public services. The production of rice and sugar was increased through the adoption of scientific and improved methods in farming and land utilization. The implementation of these measures led to the restoration of peace and order, and subsequently, to a flourishing economy. The colonization of Taiwan thus proved to be a fairly successful venture.

The other legacy of the Sino-Japanese War, the Korean situation, continued to plague the Japanese government. During the Sino-Japanese War it had tried to introduce reforms in Korea but failed to accomplish very much. Instead it got caught in the rivalry among Queen Min, Taewongun, and pro-Japanese reformist factions. In 1895, Inoue Kaoru was sent to Korea as the Japanese minister; he managed to place the pro-Japanese Pak Yong-hyo in charge of the government. Pak, however, was soon driven out by Queen Min's faction, which had Russian support. The queen began to cooperate more and more with Russia, and this forced the new Japanese minister in Korea, Miura Gorō (1847–1926), to bring Taewongun out of retirement again. In October 1895 they staged a coup against the queen, killing her and many of her lady attendants. These atrocities placed Japan in a most unfavorable light in the eyes of the Western powers; the Japanese government recalled Miura and his supporters and had them arrested. Anti-Japanese sentiments in Korea, however, did not abate. The king fled to the Russian legation and condemned the pro-Japanese faction, whose leaders were thereupon killed. Hence, it appeared as if Japan's influence was waning while that of Russia was ascending. The rivalry developing between Japan and Russia in Korea contributed to the eventual outbreak of hostilities between the two nations.

POSTWAR DOMESTIC POLITICAL DEVELOPMENTS

The domestic political scene after the Sino-Japanese War saw Itō and the Liberal Party coming to terms and agreeing to cooperate. The leaders of the Liberal Party wanted a share of the political power, and they were also anxious to beat the rival Reform Party to the seat of that power. They realized that the methods used in the Diet before the war were clearly not enabling them to achieve their objectives. Now that the government had the support of the Liberal Party, it had little trouble passing its bills, including a record budget. In April 1896 Itagaki entered the cabinet as minister of home affairs. Despite Itō's growing flexibility toward political parties, he insisted that Itagaki sever his ties with the Liberal Party before joining the government.

Japan's foreign relations, particularly with Russia, were growing precarious, so when Foreign Minister Mutsu resigned because of ill health, Itō planned to bring Matsukata and Ōkuma into the government in order to form a cabinet that would foster national unity. Itagaki, however, strenuously opposed letting Ōkuma join the government; Matsukata refused to join the cabinet without Ōkuma. Itō thereupon decided to resign, turning the government over to Matsukata.

One of the reasons why the Meiji cabinet heads gave up the premiership so readily was that as members of the oligarchy they really did not remove themselves from the seat of power. They were genrō, and thus they remained a permanent part of the power elite as long as the oligarchy retained its power. There were, of course, disagreements and some personality clashes, but no genrō ever sought to remove a fellow oligarch from the inner circle. Hence Itō, who had been burdened with the office of prime minister for four years, gave up his post over an issue that was not really insurmountable.

Matsukata, in forming his cabinet, appointed Ōkuma as foreign minister. Prior to this the Reform Party was reorganized, and it merged with other minor parties to form the Progressive Party (Shimpotō). This group gave its support to Matsukata, who was thus able to get his program through the Diet. As a reward, members of the Progressive Party obtained many high posts in the bureaucracy. This alliance of convenience soon dissolved, however, because Matsukata became disturbed by the party's many ambitious members who wanted still more cabinet posts and a voice in formulating general policies. The Progressive Party members decided that Matsukata would not meet their demands, and they broke with him, joining the Liberal Party in a call for a vote of no-confidence against him. In response, Matsukata dissolved the Diet and resigned. Once again Itō was asked to form a cabinet, which he did in January 1898.

Itō intended to try once more to establish a coalition government that would include the leaders of the two major parties. He approached Ōkuma and Itagaki but was unable to meet their demands for key cabinet posts. Consequently, he formed another "transcendental" cabinet, that is, a cabinet above the parties.

The election held in March saw the Liberal Party win ninety-eight seats, thus again emerging as the largest party; this time, however, the Progressive Party was close behind with ninety-one seats. Itō sought to bring Itagaki into the cabinet, but his friend and minister of finance, Inoue Kaoru, objected. Itō was forced to face the Diet without the support of the Liberal Party, and his proposal to increase the land tax suffered a crushing defeat; after this, he dissolved the Diet.

By now it was clear that the Satsuma-Chōshū faction could no longer govern effectively without the support of one of the major parties. The only reason the political parties failed to gain greater power was their inability to work together. The oligarchy had consistently managed to take advantage of the feuds between the parties to split and thus effectively weaken the opposition. Now, however, after numerous efforts to achieve a coalition with the oligarchs had failed, the two parties finally decided to give interparty cooperation a try. On June 21, 1898, the Liberal and Progressive parties voted to dissolve themselves, and on the following day they joined together to form a new organization, the Constitutional Party (Kenseitō).

Itō now faced a difficult situation because this union of the two parties meant that he could no longer play one group against the other. The way to meet the challenge, he believed, was to form his own political party. He conferred with his ally, Inoue Kaoru, and asked him to obtain the support of the business leaders. Inoue contacted the business tycoons and was able to win over men like Shibusawa. Nonetheless, Itō failed to gain as much backing as he had hoped to receive. Iwasaki Yanosuke of Mitsubishi refused to support the movement because of his ties with Ōkuma and the Progressive Party, and as a result of this, other business leaders began to hesitate also. The most adamant opposition to Itō's new political plans, however, was provided by his erstwhile political partner, Yamagata.

There had been no open break between the two men prior to this, but their relationship had become somewhat strained ever since constitutional government was initiated. Itō and Yamagata were certainly the outstanding statesmen among the Meiji leaders, and both were equally dedicated to serving the national interests. Neither can be faulted when it comes to public service, patriotism, and unselfish devotion to the state, but there were important differences between their temperaments and beliefs.

Compared to Yamagata, Itō was not only more flexible and more "civilian" in his outlook, he was also far more humanistic. He was most distressed about the killings that wars inevitably entailed and, in commenting on the Russo-Japanese War, he once lamented to Erwin Baelz (1849–1913), "The fight goes on. Massacre without end." He had a warm, open personality and tended to be rather fun-loving. Baelz, who knew him well, called him "a devotee of Bacchus and Venus." Itō was apparently a fair and just man; he was not at all vindictive, nor did he tenaciously seek to control people or power. Baelz made this observation after Itō's death:

> He was neither choleric nor swashbucklerish, being tranquil in manner and almost always with a friendly smile . . . lighting up his face. He was disinclined to use strong measures. . . . In personal relationships Prince Itō was the unassuming and persistently cheerful little man that he had been thirty years earlier when I became acquainted with him as plain Mr. Itō.[13]

Even his critics credit him with having a broad perspective, an ability to get able men to work with him, and a talent for harmonizing conflicting forces. He was a moderate—conservative in some respects, progressive in others. It is said that of all the Meiji leaders, Emperor Meiji trusted and liked Itō the most. His major weakness was his tendency to be indecisive, and this became a particularly serious flaw toward the end of his career.

The impression that history records of Yamagata is of a severe, formidable, and inflexible figure. He was more austere, more disciplined, and more rigid than Itō, whose warmth and openness he lacked. Yamagata was cautious and calculating, and as his follower Katsura Tarō remarked, he was also vengeful and unforgiving.

Politically, Yamagata was much more conservative and authoritarian than Itō. He was the personification of the stern militarist, something of a Machiavellian who was willing to use any means to keep the oligarchy in control of power. His critics say that he contributed to the decay of the political parties by using bribery as a means to undermine and weaken them. Some even regarded him as a petty schemer. He gathered around him able men who shared his conservative philosophy, and, like Shinagawa, they were inclined to rely on ruthless tactics to suppress the opposition. He managed to establish a tremendous power base in the army and the bureaucracy, but he seemed not to have won the affection of many men.

Yamagata objected vigorously when Itō concluded that the political dilemma facing the government could only be resolved by the formation of a progovernment party.[14] In a meeting of the genrō, Yamagata contended that if Itō organized a political party, he would essentially be paving the way to party government. "This would clash with our national polity, run counter to the spirit of the constitution granted by the emperor, and would degenerate into a democracy. I fail to understand why you seek to join the mice who form factions and take such an irresponsible action."[15] Yamagata went on to admonish that it was unbecoming for a genrō to engage in such activities. As a result of these rebukes, Itō threatened to renounce all official ranks and ties and carry on as a plain citizen. Arguing that he could not maintain his cabinet without a political party, he proposed to resign and turn the government over to the Constitutional Party. The other genrō were shocked at this proposal, but when Itō asked who among them would volunteer to form a new cabinet, none would come forward. Thereupon Itō resigned his post and recommended to the emperor that Ōkuma and Itagaki be asked to establish a new cabinet.

The first party cabinet was formed on June 30, 1898, and for the advocates of popular rights the long struggle seemed to have ended in final victory. Yamagata wrote to one of his friends, "The Meiji government has finally fallen. . . . There is no need for a defeated old general to speak of wars any longer. There is nothing left to do but retire."[16] Itō was more sanguine: "Both Ōkuma and Itagaki are Japanese like us. There is no danger at all that they will let quarrels among Japanese affect relations with the outside world and lead the state astray."[17]

It was premature of the parliamentary leaders to rejoice in their victory, for they were still unable to overcome the most formidable obstacle: their inability to work together. Moreover, despite what he might have said, Yamagata had no intention of retiring. Regardless of who headed the cabinet, he could still exert considerable influence through the minister of war, Katsura. The generals and admirals refused to cooperate with the new cabinet without Yamagata's consent, and this state of affairs ultimately forced Ōkuma and Itagaki to ask the emperor to intervene. As a result, the war and naval ministers in the Itō cabinet were asked by the emperor to continue to serve in the new cabinet. Katsura, who was Yamagata's loyal follower, remained as minister of war, and Saigō Tsugumichi continued as minister of the navy. Hence, it was from the very outset that Ōkuma and Itagaki had to contend with Yamagata's agents in the cabinet. Even before the cabinet was formed, Katsura pressed Ōkuma about armaments and made him agree not to reduce arms in spite of the fact that this had been the policy publicly declared by the Progressive Party.

Theoretically there was one united party, but, in fact, the old party divisions remained and partisan rivalry prevailed. To begin with, there was the thorny problem of dividing the cabinet posts between the two factions. The Progressive Party seemed to have gotten the lion's share in that Ōkuma held the posts of prime minister and foreign minister, and three other posts were filled by Progressive Party members. The Liberal Party, in comparison, held only three posts, with Itagaki serving as minister of home affairs. The fierce contest for other high government posts further aggravated the hostilities between the two factions, and when a general election was held in August, they vigorously competed with each other despite the fact that nominally they belonged to the same party.

The breakup of the Ōkuma-Itagaki cabinet came about quickly through a quarrel over a cabinet post. In criticizing the influence of big business in politics, the minister of education, Ozaki Yukio, had said that Mitsui and Mitsubishi would be presidential candidates if Japan were a republic. Ozaki made it quite clear that he was speaking of a hypothetical situation and strictly for the purpose of illustration, but the members of the oligarchy and the Liberal Party pounced on this speech to force his resignation. Ōkuma replaced him with another Progressive Party member, Inukai Tsuyoshi (1855–1932), despite Itagaki's demand that a member of the Liberal Party be given that post. Thereupon Hoshi, who had been rebuffed in his attempt to become foreign minister, proposed that the Constitutional Party be dissolved and that the Liberal Party members leave the cabinet. This was accomplished on October 29. The Liberal Party reestablished the Constitutional Party without the men from the Progressive Party, who thereupon set about forming the Kenseihontō (Main Constitutional Party).

Despite Ōkuma's willingness to carry on without the support of the old Liberal Party men, he was compelled to resign. The Ōkuma-Itagaki cabinet had survived only four months. The political parties proved incapable of working together; rather than see their rivals succeed, they were willing to betray them and sell out to the genrō clique.

Hoshi had promised Yamagata the support of the Constitutional Party in return for cooperation in overthrowing the Ōkuma cabinet. As a result, Yamagata returned to office in November 1898, at which time Katsura advised him to take a tough stand against the political parties. If necessary, he said, "the Diet must be dissolved repeatedly, and even if the constitution has to be suspended the irresponsible activities of the political parties must be stopped."[18] Yamagata, however, felt he needed the support of the Constitutional Party, and he managed to gain its backing without having to allocate any cabinet posts to it. The man who was instrumental in keeping the Constitutional Party linked to Yamagata was Hoshi, who used a considerable sum of money to keep the party members in line. In addition, during this period Yamagata had obtained 980,000 yen from the secret funds of the imperial household to buy votes in the Diet. By resorting to bribery, Yamagata persuaded enough Diet members to support his tax bill, which substantially increased land and residential taxes, so that he was able to pay for military expansion.

The change in the land tax, which was scheduled to remain in effect for five years, entailed an increase from 2.5 percent of land value to 3.3 percent. Among other bills passed by the Yamagata cabinet was the revision of the voting regulations pertaining to the Diet as well as the composition of that body.[19] Moreover, the secret ballot was adopted at this time. This bill was passed in 1900 and put into effect for the elections of 1902.

Yamagata was genuinely concerned that the spoils system would corrode the bureaucracy completely if the political parties had their way. Consequently he revised the civil service regulations by removing from the appointment list all the bureaucratic posts, with the exception of a few top positions, and bringing them under the examination system. In so doing, Yamagata made certain that the spoils system would not undermine the bureaucracy, while at the same time he ensured its semi-autonomous existence as a bulwark of conservatism. The bureaucrats defied not only the political parties and the Diet, but at times they even challenged Itō. Yamagata revised the army and navy regulations to stipulate that only active army and navy officers of the two top ranks would be eligible to serve as ministers of the war and navy. He also enacted the Police Regulation of 1900, which was designed to curb the organizers of labor unions.

The members of the Constitutional Party decided to terminate their collaboration with Yamagata when they realized that he was freezing the party politicians out of the bureaucracy as well as the cabinet. The Yamagata cabinet did stay in office for several months after the break with the party, however, because of the international crisis caused by the outbreak in China of the Boxer Rebellion of 1900–1901. The ever-ambitious Constitutional Party leaders, such as Hoshi, then turned to Itō in an attempt to gain access to the government.

Itō had been planning to organize his own political party, and he was touring the country calling for an organization that would not make party interests its chief concern but would make the weal of the state its primary objective. The Constitutional Party leaders invited him to join their group as its head, but he refused, insisting upon the necessity of a new party that would correct the defects inherent in the existing parties. The Kenseitō leaders then decided to dissolve their own party and join Itō's emerging organization.

As chief advisers in forming his party, Itō relied upon Hoshi and a newcomer to the political scene, Hara Takashi (1856–1921), a protégé of Mutsu in the foreign office who was then president of a major newspaper, the *Ōsaka Mainichi*. Itō's plan was to form a national party that would include representatives from all segments of the society, not only existing political party members but businessmen and bureaucrats as well. He was, however, opposed to the entry of "propertyless scoundrels." As it turned out, the core of his organization came from the Constitutional Party; that is, they were old Liberal Party members who had abandoned Itagaki and rushed to Itō's side because he offered them a much better chance of gaining power. The party was formally established in August 1900 as the Rikken Seiyūkai (Association of Friends of Constitutional Government).[20]

Yamagata had indicated his desire to resign in August in favor of Itō, but the task of organizing his party was not yet completed, and Itō refused. Yamagata resigned anyway in the following month, fully expecting, his critics said, that the Seiyūkai would be hopelessly disrupted if it had to come to power before the various factions within the party had managed to accommodate each other.

Itō was thereby forced to form his fourth cabinet in October 1900, well before he and his party were ready to assume power. He filled all the cabinet posts with Seiyūkai men, with the exception of the ministers of foreign affairs, war, and navy. The Seiyūkai held a majority in the Diet, so Itō did not encounter much opposition in the lower house, but he ran into serious difficulties in the House of Peers. Yamagata had managed over the years to turn the upper house into his power base by appointing his followers to it. Moreover, the upper house had been purposely designed by Itō himself to curb the popular elements, and the peers thus resented his alliance with party men because they felt such an affiliation could result in a substantial strengthening of the lower house. In order to embarrass the Itō government, anti-Itō peers criticized him for not pursuing a more aggressive policy in China, where it was clear the Western powers were extending their spheres of interest. They also launched an attack against Itō's minister of communications, Hoshi,[21] who was implicated in a graft scandal. Hoshi was forced to resign, and Hara was appointed to replace him. The peers then proceeded to reject Itō's tax bill, which had already passed the lower house. They repeatedly refused to heed his pleas and remained intransigent, whereupon Itō again turned to the emperor and succeeded in having him issue a rescript asking the peers to cooperate. They reversed themselves immediately and passed the tax bill intact.

The House of Peers nevertheless remained hostile toward Itō, resenting the fact that he had once again turned to the emperor to extricate himself from his difficulties. In the lower house the opposition party, the Kenseihontō, tried to have him censured, but the motion failed to carry. Many high-ranking bureaucrats also objected to Itō's political party ties; some officials of the Ministry of Justice even threatened to go on strike because the Diet had not approved an increase in their salaries. Internal divisions beset the cabinet when the minister of finance clashed with Seiyūkai cabinet members over the question of government spending on public enterprises. Itō procrastinated in resolving the internal conflict, and in May 1901 he resigned his post after remaining in office for only seven months.

Thus, Itō's experiment with party government, which had aroused the hopes of many, failed miserably. Itō weakened rather than strengthened his position by seeking to be a member of the genrō clique and at the same time head of a political party. He could no longer count on the wholehearted backing of the genrō and the other components of the oligarchy, such as the House of Peers and the bureaucracy; yet his support in the Diet was not substantial enough to enable him to function without those establishment forces.

It turned out that the fourth Itō cabinet was the last one to be headed by a genrō. These men tried to perpetuate their tradition of leadership when Itō resigned, and they gave Inoue Kaoru the task of heading the next government. He failed in his effort to form a cabinet, however, and the genrō were then compelled to turn to Katsura Tarō and Saionji Kimmochi (1849–1940), who were at that time in the second rung of the power structure. For the next twelve years the cabinet was to be headed alternately by these two men, although the genrō did continue to exercise power from behind the scenes. The man who turned out to be the most influential figure was Yamagata, not Itō, who went into semiretirement.

Katsura had risen to the top in the army as Yamagata's follower, and he became minister of war in January 1898, in the third Itō cabinet. He served in that capacity in the Ōkuma, the second Yamagata, and the fourth Itō cabinets. The cabinet that he formed in June 1901 contained several Yamagata men. He lacked support in the lower house but managed to get through the Diet session by appealing to Itō, who directed the Seiyūkai to support Katsura's budget. In 1902 Katsura enhanced his prestige by concluding the Anglo-Japanese alliance.

During the same year, the first general election for the Diet since the franchise had been enlarged took place.[22] This election resulted in a decline in the number of representatives from the agrarian landowning class and an increase in those from the legal profession. The business class was not heavily represented in the Diet, but their influence was fairly strong because of the fact that many agrarian representatives had invested their money in business and were consequently very sympathetic to those interests. The businessmen's influence in politics continued to grow as they broadened their ties with the major parties. The enhanced status of the merchant class, which was formerly scorned by the shizoku, was reflected in the growing numbers of businessmen who were accorded the status of peers.

Katsura had to deal with the combined opposition of the Seiyūkai and Kenseihontō when he faced the newly enlarged Diet. In order to expand the armed forces, Katsura sought to renew the land tax of 1898, but this was opposed by the party members. Failing to get Itō to intervene, Katsura was forced to dissolve the Diet. The new Diet, however, turned out to be equally hostile, but this time Katsura managed to work out a compromise.

Exasperated with Itō's dual role as genrō and party head, Katsura, in consultation with Yamagata, asked the emperor to request Itō to sever his ties with the Seiyūkai and become the head of the Privy Council. Itō, in effect, retired from active politics in July 1903, because he was unable to defy the imperial command.

Itō's place as head of the Seiyūkai was taken by Saionji, a court noble who in his youth was interested in Rousseau's political philosophy. The political parties continued to bicker with Katsura, but he was now faced with a far more serious problem than domestic political infighting. This was the growing crisis in Russo-Japanese relations.

Notes

1. Fukuzawa Zenshū, *The Collected Works of Fukuzawa*, 10 vols. (Tokyo: Jiji Shimpōsha, 1925–1926), vol. 8, pp. 23–24.

2. Robert A. Scalapino, *Democracy and the Party Movement in Prewar Japan* (Berkeley: University of California Press, 1953), p. 150.

3. Those who did qualify numbered 450,365 out of the total population of 39,383,300 (i.e., 1.14 percent of the population).

4. As for the social composition of the first Diet, 109 members were shizoku (including Mutsu, who, although elected, chose to join the cabinet instead), 191 members were commoners, and 88 members fell into the category of absentee landowners by virtue of the fact that they paid more than 90 yen in land tax.

5. This was accomplished in large part by a substantial bribe funneled through Mutsu, who had been rehabilitated by Itō after having spent almost four years in prison for his 1877 treason. He had served as minister to Washington for two years and was now in the Yamagata cabinet. He had good relations with a number of his Tosa friends, including Hoshi Tōru, Oe Taku, Gotō, and later Komura Jutarō and Hara Takashi, the latter two being protégés of his in the Foreign Ministry.

6. Nationally, 25 deaths and 388 injuries were officially reported.

7. Again, Mutsu and Gotō served as the conduits for bribes from the oligarchy to Hoshi's Tosa faction.

8. England had offered to mediate between China and Japan, but China flatly refused.

9. Hiratsuka Atsushi, *Itō Hirobumi Hiroku* (The Confidential Papers of Itō Hirobumi), 2 vols. (Tokyo: Shunjūsha, 1930), vol. 2, p. 105.

10. The human toll that Japan paid in the Sino-Japanese War came to more than 17,000 dead, a majority of whom had succumbed to the frigid Manchurian weather.

11. The naval tonnage, which had stood at 63,100 tons, was increased to 153,000 tons by 1902. The defense allocations increased annually, constituting 29.5 percent of the total budget in 1890 but 55.6 percent in 1897.

12. The Japanese losses as a direct result of combat were small and only amounted to 164, but 4,600 men died of malaria and other tropical diseases, and more than 20,000 had to be sent home because of illness.

13. Erwin O. E. von Baelz, *Awakening Japan: The Diary of a German Doctor,* trans. Eden and Cedar Paul (New York: Viking, 1932), p. 392.

14. It has also been suggested that Itō actually favored the idea of forming a political party in order to curb the influence of the militarists led by Yamagata.

15. Masumi Junnosuke, *Nihon Seitōshiron* (Discourses on the History of Japanese Political Parties), 4 vols. (Tokyo: Tōkyō Daigaku Shuppankai, 1965–1968), vol. 2, p. 295.

16. Ibid., p. 297.

17. Ibid.

18. Ibid., pp. 302–303.

19. The qualification for suffrage was dropped from 15 to 10 yen, and the representation for the cities was increased, with the result that the total number of representatives rose from 300 to 369.

20. It included at its inception 152 Diet members, 111 of whom were from the Constitutional Party. The emperor supported Itō's venture into party politics by contributing 100,000 yen.

21. He was often called the "Boss Tweed of Japan."

22. The Seiyūkai still maintained a slim majority, with 189 seats out of 376, while the Kenseihontō won 104 seats.

9

The Conclusion of
the Meiji Era

THE RUSSO-JAPANESE WAR

After the Sino-Japanese War a rivalry between Russia and Japan developed in Korea, where the Russians seemingly had gained the upper hand by emerging as the king's protector. In the middle of 1896, Japan and Russia signed an agreement providing for mutual financial assistance to Korea and limitations on troops that could be stationed there. Russia, however, tended to be more active in Korea than was warranted by the agreement, and another convention, the Nishi-Rosen Agreement, was signed in April 1898, reaffirming the provisions of the prior arrangement. Russia also agreed not to "hinder the development of commercial and industrial relations between Japan and Korea." Russia was more interested in extending its interests in Manchuria than in Korea, so a number of Japanese officials favored a policy of persuading Russia to recognize Japan's special interests in Korea in return for Japanese recognition of Russian interests in Manchuria. Russia, however, was unwilling to relinquish its influence in Korea.

Japan continued to expand economic activities in Korea, and by the turn of the century it accounted for more than three-quarters of that country's foreign trade. Japan exported cotton products to Korea and imported rice. It also constructed railroads in southern Korea from Inchon to Seoul and from Pusan to Seoul, and it then began to move into the Yalu River Valley to develop the timber industry in a move to counteract the Russians, who had also gained timber concessions there.

In search of an ice-free port in the East, Russia was entrenching itself in Manchuria. Russia had already put China in its debt by intervening to force

Japan to relinquish the Liaodong Peninsula and by, at the same time, loaning it the money necessary to pay Japan additional indemnities. In May 1896, when Li Hongzhang went to Moscow to attend the coronation of Nicholas II, China and Russia signed an alliance, the Li-Lobanov Treaty. Russia agreed to defend China against any Japanese attacks, and in the event that Japan attacked Russia, China was to open all its ports to Russian warships. The two nations also agreed to build a railroad across northern Manchuria, which was to be financed by a new Russo-Chinese bank. This line was to be called the Chinese Eastern Railroad, and it was to link the Russian Trans-Siberian Railroad with Vladivostok. The immediate territory through which the railroad passed was to be under the authority of the Russian Ministry of Finance.

The next Russian advances in Manchuria occurred after Germany acquired concessions in the Shandong Peninsula in 1898. Russia persuaded China to lease the Liaodong Peninsula and Port Arthur for a period of twenty-five years, and it also obtained the right to build the South Manchurian Railroad, linking Harbin with Port Arthur. Thus Russia acquired from China what it had forced Japan to relinquish three years before. Port Arthur, though an ice-free port, was cut off from Vladivostok by Korea. Consequently, the Russian expansionists believed that they could not allow Japan to control Korea. Russia moved its troops into Manchuria when the Chinese Boxer Rebellion broke out in 1900 and then asked for further concessions from China as a condition for withdrawal. China, with Japanese diplomatic support, resisted these demands and compelled Russia, in April 1902, to agree to a three-stage withdrawal of its troops from Manchuria.

The Russian activities in Manchuria and Russia's continued interest in Korea caused some Japanese officials, led by Katō Kōmei (1860–1926), who was foreign minister in the fourth Itō cabinet, to begin to advocate an alliance with Britain as a way to strengthen Japan's position in case war should break out. Katsura soon became prime minister, and he asked the Japanese ambassador to England to sound out the British on the idea of an Anglo-Japanese alliance. He received a favorable response.

England was now prepared to abandon its policy of splendid isolation because it had felt the adverse effects of this policy during the Boer War of 1899–1902. Also, because of the growing international tension in Europe, England felt it could not safely extend its forces to the Far East for the purpose of checking Russian ambitions there. An alliance with Japan, however, would ensure the protection of British interests in that part of the world.

In Japan there was disagreement between the faction led by Yamagata, which favored an alliance with Britain, and the faction led by Itō, which felt that war could best be averted by arriving at some sort of understanding with

Russia. Prime Minister Katsura and Foreign Minister Komura favored an alliance with Britain, whereas Inoue supported Itō's position. Talks with England were started when the British foreign secretary, Lansdowne (1845–1927), asked that serious consideration be given to the proposed alliance. As Anglo-Japanese talks were proceeding, Itō took advantage of an opportunity to go abroad (to receive an honorary degree at Yale University) and then proceeded to Russia to investigate the possibility of resolving the differences between the two nations. Itō's efforts not only produced negative reactions in Russia but actually spurred on the negotiations with the British; in January 1902, the Anglo-Japanese Alliance was concluded.

The two nations agreed to maintain the status quo and general peace in East Asia, and to respect the independence and territorial integrity of China and Korea. They also recognized their respective spheres of interest in China as well as Japan's special interests in Korea. The alliance provided that in the event one of the parties got involved in a war with another nation, the other party was to remain neutral unless the first party was attacked by more than one power.

The alliance, which was to run for five years, did not deter Russia from continuing to pursue its interests in Manchuria and Korea. Many high Russian officials wanted to avoid creating a situation that might lead to a war in the Far East, but one of the tsar's advisers persuaded him to take a more aggressive stance. As a result, the exploitation of the Yalu River Valley timber concessions was continued, and a vice royalty in the Far East was established at Port Arthur, which was being turned into a major naval base.

Russia completed the first stage of its withdrawal of troops from Manchuria by October 1902, as scheduled, but instead of making further moves when the second stage was supposed to start in February 1903, it made additional demands on China. The Japanese leaders held a special meeting and agreed to pursue negotiations with Russia on the basis of the following: guaranteeing the independence and territorial integrity of China and Korea, recognizing Japanese and Russian rights and interests in Korea and Manchuria, and acknowledging Japan's special relationship with Korea. In an effort to resolve the differences between the two nations, four formal discussions between the two countries were conducted. Russia nevertheless continued its efforts to extend privileges in Manchuria and in Korea, where it leased the port of Yongampo and began fortifications.

Negotiations between Russia and Japan were proving unfruitful, and disagreement about how to cope with this situation began to develop among the Japanese leaders. The older leaders were anxious to avoid an armed conflict with Russia; Itō in particular was convinced that Japan could not possibly emerge victorious in such a war. In contrast, the middle-ranking officers and officials took a chauvinistic position while at the same time public opinion was also becoming increasingly jingoistic. Katsura later recalled to Erwin Baelz, "He himself had for a long time been reviled [by the press] day after day as a traitor and a coward, simply because he had wanted to avoid war if at all possible."[1]

Japan submitted its final proposals to Russia on January 13, 1904, and they were taken by the Russians to constitute an ultimatum because in urging quick action the Japanese insisted that "further delay in the solution of the question will be extremely disadvantageous to the two countries." An agreement could not be reached, however, because Russia was unwilling to give Japan a completely free hand in Korea and Japan was unwilling to grant Russia a free hand in Manchuria. Neither side, of course, asked the Koreans or the Chinese how they felt about the situation.

Having failed to effect an agreement, the Japanese government decided on war on February 4. It notified the Russian government of its decision to break off negotiations and of its intention to take such independent action as it deemed necessary for the defense of its interests. On February 6, Japanese ships moved into Korean waters and headed toward Port Arthur for the purpose of destroying the Russian Pacific fleet. There was a naval skirmish off the coast of Inchon on February 8, and each side blamed the other for firing first. The main fleet, under Admiral Tōgō, proceeded to Port Arthur and attacked the Russians there on February 9, severely damaging several Russian warships. On February 10, Japan declared war. The initial Japanese moves in the Russo-Japanese War are often compared to its attack on Pearl Harbor, but in this case the Russians had ample warning of what was coming.

Despite Itō's pessimism about the chances for victory, Japan was in far better condition than Russia to fight the war. It was, first of all, much to Japan's advantage that the fighting was to take place close to its home base. Japan had a trained manpower of about 850,000 men, with 180,000 in the active forces, and a male population of about 4 million who were capable of bearing arms. The navy consisted of seven battleships, thirty-one cruisers, and additional smaller craft.

Russia, of course, had a much larger population from which to draw fighting men, but it had the considerable problem of transporting them more than 5,000 miles from Moscow to Port Arthur. The Trans-Siberian Railroad at Lake Baikal was not yet completed, so the troops had to be ferried across or marched over the ice in the winter.[2]

In the first few weeks of the war the Japanese fleet crippled the Russian vessels at Port Arthur and immediately gained supremacy of the seas. This enabled Japan to send its troops to Korea and Manchuria without any threat whatsoever from the Russian fleet. The First Army defeated the Russian forces that were defending the border between Korea and Manchuria and then crossed the Yalu River into Manchuria on May 1. The Second Army landed on the Liaodong Peninsula and closed in on Port Arthur. The Third Army and the Fourth Army were added to these forces, and Field Marshal Ōyama, one of the genrō, was made commander in chief and had as his chief of staff General Kodama, who was regarded as the most able strategist among the Japanese generals.

On May 26, the Second Army clashed with the Russian forces around Jinzhou and for the first time encountered assault from machine guns, a weapon that the Japanese would not have until the closing months of the war. In this encounter the Japanese suffered 3,500 casualties but managed to capture the port of Dalny (Dairen), thus enabling General Nogi, commander of the Third Army, to concentrate on the seizure of Port Arthur.

The Russian commander, General Kuropatkin (1848–1925), planned to fight a defensive war until the Russian forces could be sufficiently strengthened by reinforcements. The Japanese, hoping to deliver a crushing blow before the arrival of those fresh troops, moved the First, Second, and Fourth armies toward Liaoyang, where 140,000 Russian troops were concentrated. The Japanese were outnumbered, but Ōyama nevertheless launched an offensive, and after twelve days of fighting the Russians commenced an orderly withdrawal to the north.[3]

From May to the end of the year, the Japanese launched a series of attacks against the Russian troops that were besieged in the fortress of Port Arthur. Every major attack resulted in heavy casualties for the Japanese soldiers led by General Nogi, who came under growing criticism for the futile and reckless expenditure of human lives. The port had to be taken before the Baltic fleet, making its slow and tortuous trip to the Far East, arrived. Finally on December 5, after bloody losses, they captured the 203 Metre Hill, from which the Japanese managed to shell the fortress and the Russian warships that were in the harbor. In January 1905, after 240 days of fighting—including 156 days of direct siege—General Stessel (1848–1915) decided to surrender the fortress.[4] General Stessel was severely berated for his action because when the fortress was surrendered there were 24,369 officers and men and 2.5 million rounds of small arms ammunition still left. However, more than half of the Russian soldiers were incapacitated.

The fall of Port Arthur gave a tremendous boost in morale to the Japanese, while in Russia criticism against the tsar and the bureaucracy mounted. The revolutionaries were delighted. Lenin hailed the defeat, saying, "The capitulation of Port Arthur is the prologue to the capitulation of Tsarism."[5]

The biggest land battle of the war was fought in March 1905 at Mukden, where 300,000 Japanese forces faced 310,000 Russian troops. After a fierce ten-day battle the Japanese forces occupied the city as the Russian army retreated further north. The fall of Mukden was hailed as a major triumph although it did not constitute a decisive victory for the Japanese. The Russian army was still entrenched in the north awaiting further reinforcements and the arrival of the Baltic fleet, with which it hoped to wrest the command of the seas from the Japanese navy.[6]

The Baltic fleet, led by Admiral Rozhdestvensky (1848–1909), started its 18,000-mile trek in October 1904. After a long and arduous journey fraught with difficulties, the weary fleet finally arrived at the Tsushima Straits on May 27, 1905, where Admiral Tōgō Shigenori (1882–1950) was waiting for it. He had accurately concluded that the fleet would try to make its way to Vladivostok by sailing between Korea and Japan rather than taking the longer route to the north of Japan. The naval battle, lasting twenty-four hours, resulted in a smashing victory for the Japanese fleet, which outdid the Russian ships in tactics and in the accuracy of its guns. Twenty Russian ships were destroyed, five were captured, six were interned in neutral ports, and only four managed to reach Vladivostok.

The Japanese victory had a decisive effect on the peace moves that had been in the offing since the fall of Port Arthur. The initiative for peace had been taken by President Theodore Roosevelt (1858–1919), who feared that the balance of power in the Far East would be upset if Russia were driven completely out of that area. Despite the victories, the Japanese leaders were aware of Japan's limitations in manpower and material resources.[7] There are indications that even as early as July 1904, Japanese officials were seeking ways to settle the war, but the Russians were not ready to participate in peace talks until the Baltic fleet had a chance to engage the Japanese navy in combat. After the Battle of Tsushima, however, both combatants were willing to accept President Roosevelt's invitation to negotiate. Russia still had sufficient manpower and resources to carry on the war, but there was a growing restlessness among its people, and the country was rife with troublesome revolutionary activities.

During the war the Japanese public was overwhelmed by a tide of patriotism and national pride, and they supported the war effort with enthusiasm and selfless dedication. Not all thinking Japanese, however, succumbed to the impetuous call of nationalism. Some men, admittedly only a small number and primarily from among the Christians and the newly emerging socialist group, continued to express antiwar sentiments even after the actual outbreak of hostilities. This time the Christian leader, Uchimura Kanzō, did not support the war effort. He had been disillusioned with the results of the Sino-Japanese War, which not only failed to ensure the independence of Korea but, he believed, also brought about moral decay in Japan. He did not, however, take any overt action to oppose the war with Russia.

The leaders of the embryonic socialist movement, such as Kōtoku Shūsui (1871–1911) and Sakai Toshihiko (1870–1933), were aggressive in their opposition to the war. In 1903 they organized the Heiminsha (Commoners' Society) and started a newspaper called the *Heimin Shimbun* (The Commoner Newspaper). They proclaimed egalitarianism, socialism, and pacifism as their guiding principles. A number of women, among them Fukuda Hideko, Kanno Suga (1881–1911), and Itō Noe (1895–1923), were active in this circle as well as in the women's rights movement. As socialists, they viewed the war as a conflict not between the people but instead between the aristocrats, militarists, and capitalists of the two countries. They sent an open letter to the Russian Social Democrats when the war broke out pledging their friendship because "for socialists, there are no distinctions of race, region, or nationality. You and we are comrades, brothers and sisters. We have no reason to fight each other. Your enemy is not the Japanese people, but it is the so-called patriotism and militarism of today."[8] The letter was printed in the Social Democrats' newspaper, *Iskra*, with the editors expressing complete agreement with the Japanese socialists. Kōtoku and Sakai's continued opposition to the war resulted in their imprisonment and the suspension of the *Heimin Shimbun.* Antiwar sentiments were also expressed by some writers. Yosano Akiko (1878–1942), for example, wrote a poem calling upon her brother not to sacrifice his life or kill the Russians. She asks, "Whether the fortress of Port Arthur falls / or does not fall, / is it any concern of yours?"[9]

In early August the Japanese and Russian delegations met in Portsmouth, New Hampshire, to participate in peace talks. The Japanese delegation was headed by Foreign Minister Komura Jutarō (1855–1911), and the Russian party was led by the veteran statesman Count Witte (1849–1915). Komura was instructed by his government to: (1) gain a free hand for Japan in Korea; (2) obtain the Russian concessions in the Liaodong Peninsula and also the South Manchurian Railroad between Harbin and Port Arthur; and (3) if possible, persuade the Russians to pay an indemnity and cede Sakhalin Island to Japan.[10] Russia's position at Portsmouth was that it had not been defeated and if necessary it could and would continue to carry on the war. The tsar was determined not to pay any indemnity and not to cede any Russian territory.

The plenipotentiaries of the two countries met for about a month, from August 10 to September 5, but they were unable to agree on the Japanese demands for an indemnity and the cession of Sakhalin Island. A settlement was finally reached, with Japan withdrawing its demand for an indemnity and Russia agreeing to relinquish the southern half of Sakhalin Island. The terms of the Portsmouth Treaty provided for Russia to transfer to Japan, with the consent of China, the Liaodong Leasehold, the southern section of the South Manchurian Railway, and the coal mines that had been worked by the Russians. The two nations agreed to withdraw their forces from Manchuria, except for guards to protect their respective railroads. Russia recognized Japan's "paramount political, military, and economic interests" in Korea and ceded the southern half of Sakhalin Island.

The Japanese public, which had been so thoroughly intoxicated by the succession of military victories that they were completely unaware of the nation's inability to continue waging war any further, received the news of the peace treaty with incredulity, and they reacted with violent opposition to it. They had been led to expect far greater territorial gains, perhaps the cession of all the land east of Lake Baikal. Expansionist newspapers and opportunistic political leaders stirred up public anger with the government, focusing their wrathful expressions on Katsura and Komura, who were accused of betraying the country by accepting a humiliating treaty. Public meetings were held condemning the government and calling for the renunciation of the treaty and the continuation of the war. The movement was led by such ultranationalists as Tōyama Mitsuru (1855–1944), a leader of an ultra-right-wing group, the Genyōsha,[11] and by leaders of the opposition party, such as Kōno Hironaka. On September 5, protesters who had gathered to denounce the treaty soon turned into a violent mob that attacked public buildings, police stations, Christian churches, and a progovernment newspaper. The rioting continued the following day, throwing Tokyo into a state of anarchy, with the result that the government was compelled to impose martial law. It suppressed those newspapers that were publishing incendiary editorials and arrested 2,000 rioters.

The public might have been dissatisfied with the peace settlement, but there is no question that the Russo-Japanese War established Japan as a major military and political power. The goal set by the Meiji leaders in the middle of the nineteenth century of "enriching and strengthening" the nation was seemingly achieved at last. Japan's victory had a great psychological impact upon the other Asian nations who were suffering from Western imperialism in that it proved conclusively that an Asian nation could successfully challenge Western powers in the battlefield. Furthermore, the Japanese triumph gave great impetus to nationalistic movements throughout Asia—in China, Vietnam, Indonesia, Burma, and India. Japan's success also brought about a shift in the attitude of Western nations toward it. This was especially true of England and the United States, who had been sympathetic during the Russo-Japanese War. Now, however, that the Russian advances into Manchuria had been stopped, Japan was seen as a potential threat to the balance of power in the Far East and to the open-door policy in China. Henceforth, Japan and the United States would find themselves frequently at odds on international controversies.

Victory in the war was achieved at a heavy cost: 60,083 killed in battle and 21,879 victims of disease. The people had been willing to endure the suffering and sacrifice because they were convinced that a better life would follow the war. The amelioration of conditions did not, however, come about as anticipated, and the struggle for social and economic justice became more intense. The war, in fact, had strengthened both the emperor system and nationalism to a considerable extent, so the advocates of reforms were faced with even more formidable obstacles.

FOREIGN AFFAIRS AFTER THE WAR

In November 1905, Komura proceeded to Peking and obtained China's consent regarding the Portsmouth Treaty provisions on the Liaodong Leasehold and Manchuria. In addition, he gained additional railway and economic concessions in Manchuria. The Japanese government then established the South Manchurian Railway Company to manage its railroad and other interests in south Manchuria. In order to prevent the other powers from extending their influence into Manchuria, Japan signed a secret agreement with Russia in 1907, which in effect divided Manchuria into Japanese (south) and Russian (north) spheres of interest.[12]

Korea was another area into which Japan moved swiftly. Japan wanted to consolidate the advantages acquired by Russia's recognition of its paramount interests there. Japan, in extending its influence, received the sanction of the United States by means of the Taft-Katsura memorandum of July 1905. In this agreement the United States in effect consented to Japanese control of Korea in return for Japan's assurance that it would not extend its influence into the Philippines. In the following month, when the Anglo-Japanese Alliance was renewed, England also recognized Japan's paramount interests in Korea.

Having received the green light from the major powers, Japan then proceeded to turn Korea into a protectorate and, finally, a colony. In November 1905, Itō Hirobumi, who was sent to Korea as the Japanese envoy, established a resident general, whose primary task was the management of Korea's foreign affairs. This arrangement was put into effect in February 1906, and Itō became the first resident general. His primary intention was to introduce enlightened policies in Korea that would capture the loyalty of the Korean people. The Koreans, not unreasonably, bitterly resented the violation of their sovereignty and made no distinction between "good" and "bad" imperialists.

Itō did not restrict himself to controlling Korea's foreign affairs; he boldly interfered in its internal affairs as well. In July 1907 he forced the emperor to abdicate in favor of his son, who then agreed to give the resident general the right to introduce administrative and legal reforms along with the right to appoint high-ranking officials. The Korean army was soon dissolved, whereupon patriots withdrew to the hills to organize opposition to the Japanese. Itō responded by moving 20,000 Japanese troops against the rebels and burning down the villages where Korean nationalists were active.[13]

On October 26, 1909, as Itō arrived in the Harbin railroad station to confer with Kokovtsov (1853–1943), the Russian finance minister, he was assassinated by a Korean patriot, An Joong-gun (1879–1910), who had vowed with his comrades to murder Itō and the Korean collaborators. Thus, the most significant architect of Meiji Japan died at the age of sixty-eight in a railroad car in northern Manchuria.

Yamagata and Katsura had both favored the annexation of Korea, but Itō had hoped to delay this action as long as possible. With his death, the annexationists moved swiftly; in August 1910 Korea was absorbed by Japan, and "the hardest and most relentless form of Imperial administration"[14] was imposed upon Korea.

INTERNAL AFFAIRS AFTER THE WAR

After the loose ends remaining from the peace settlement, such as the negotiation with China, were disposed of, Katsura decided to resign. He took it upon himself to recommend to the emperor that the head of the Seiyūkai, Saionji, be his successor. In so doing, Katsura broke with precedent because usually the genrō conferred only among themselves to choose the prime minister. During the Russo-Japanese War, Katsura had promised to turn the government over to Saionji in return for the cooperation of the Seiyūkai. One of the conditions of that agreement was that Saionji was not to form a party government, and as a result, the government that came into existence on January 7, 1906, had only two Seiyūkai men in the cabinet, one of whom was Hara, who became minister of home affairs.

The Saionji government, having come into existence under Katsura's auspices, continued its predecessor's policies in regard to the budget, retention of the emergency taxes, and nationalization of the railroads. This last measure encountered some difficulty since the foreign minister, Katō Kōmei, who was representing Mitsubishi's interests, opposed nationalization. He resigned, however, and the measure was approved by the Diet.

Now that the ministry of home affairs was under the direction of Hara, Yamagata became concerned that the power base that he had built in the bureaucracy would be eroded. Consequently, he set out to undermine the Saionji government, beginning his attack by criticizing its laxness in controlling the socialists. Saionji had taken the position that "socialism too is one of the great movements of the world and should not be suppressed recklessly by police power. The more moderate socialists should be guided properly so that they too may contribute to the nation's progress."[15] Hence, when the socialists applied for official approval in early 1906 for a political party they had organized, the government readily granted it. Katayama Sen and men from the *Heimin Shimbun* were among the leaders of this new Socialist Party. The membership was split between those led by Katayama, who favored employing legitimate means and working through the Diet, and those led by Kōtoku Shūsui, who favored direct action. The activists tended to gain the upper hand when it came to organizing public protests.

In March 1906 a public meeting to protest a projected increase in streetcar fare resulted in mob action and violence and the subsequent arrest of many socialist agitators. The publication of the *Heimin Shimbun* was revived, but because of the provocative articles that filled its pages, it constantly came into conflict with the authorities. In February 1907 the radicals, led by Kōtoku, managed to persuade the Socialist Party to modify its policy from one of working for socialism "within the limits of the nation's laws" to one favoring a more aggressive position. This led the government to order its dissolution. In June 1908, at a meeting of the socialists, two red flags with the words "Anarchism" and "Anarchic Communism" were hoisted. This resulted in the mass arrest of the participants.

Yamagata had advised the emperor of the need for stricter control of the socialists just prior to the Incident of the Red Flag, and when this event took place he urged the minister of war, Terauchi, to quit the cabinet. Saionji was informed of this, whereupon he immediately resigned without offering a plausible explanation, befuddling and disappointing those who had high hopes for the cabinet as the opening wedge for party government. Those who worked with Saionji during this period agree that he lacked political ambition; he was described as being "intelligent, indolent, and indifferent."

In July 1908 the second Katsura cabinet came into existence. Katsura still retained the collaboration of the Seiyūkai through an understanding with Hara that he would pass the reins of government back to Saionji again. Despite some restiveness on the part of the more aggressive Seiyūkai members, Hara was able to keep the party in line. The Kenseihontō, in comparison, was still unable to break out of its doldrums, strictly adhering to its negative position of inflexible opposition. During the second Katsura cabinet, the party merged with some minor parties and organized the Rikken Kokumintō (Constitutional Nationalist Party).

Katsura dealt with two important problems during his second tenure. The first of these was an external issue having to do with the annexation of Korea. The second was a domestic issue involving a conspiracy to assassinate the emperor. The plot was hatched by those on the extremist fringe of the socialist movement, the leader of which was Miyashita Takichi (1875–1911), a factory worker whose social conscience was aroused by the *Heimin Shimbun*. He conceived the idea of assassinating the emperor after reading a book on anarchism. He tried, unsuccessfully, to gain the support of Katayama Sen, who at this time was convinced that reforms could be achieved through legitimate means and was working for universal suffrage. Miyashita then contacted Kōtoku Shūsui. After being released from jail for his antiwar activities during the Russo-Japanese War, Kōtoku had come to the United States and spent some time in San Francisco and Berkeley becoming acquainted with refugee anarchists from Russia. Upon his return to Japan he became the leader of the extremist socialists. By the time he was approached by Miyashita, however, Kōtoku had become a syndicalist and was convinced that the way to bring about a socialist society was through general strikes rather than individual acts of terrorism.

Miyashita was joined by three other followers of Kōtoku, including Kanno Suga, a woman activist. In May 1910, before the conspirators could put their plan to assassinate the emperor into effect, they were arrested together with a large number of other socialists, including Kōtoku. Twenty-four persons were charged with treason; twelve, including Miyashita, Kōtoku, and Kanno, were executed, and the rest were sentenced to life imprisonment. Some of those who were executed, were, like Kōtoku, innocent of the crime with which they were charged.

Out of a deep sense of anger and despair, one writer, Tokutomi Roka (Tokutomi Sohō's brother; 1868–1927), had the following to say in an address to students at the First Higher School:

Looking at it from the long-range interests of the nation, we have executed twelve anarchists now but planted the seeds which will produce innumerable anarchists in the future. The government officials who killed the twelve conspirators in the name of loyalty to the Throne are in fact the ones who are truly disloyal and unrighteous subjects. My friends, Kōtoku was killed as a rebel who conspired against the existing government. But we must not fear rebellions. We must not be afraid to become rebels ourselves. What is new is always revolutionary.[16]

The Katsura government was very much frightened by the conspiracy to assassinate the emperor, and it therefore set out to repress all socialists. Its aversion and consequent vindictiveness reached such extremes that a school principal who had ordered some magazines on socialism just to find out what it was all about was fired from his post and prevented from ever gaining other employment. A book entitled *Society of Insects* was banned because of the word "society." The government then rallied the conservatives in the House of Peers to block a bill providing for universal male suffrage that had already passed the lower house in March 1911. One opponent in the upper house said, "This [universal suffrage] is based upon the theory of natural rights . . . and is founded on extremely dangerous thinking." The government disbanded the Association for Universal Suffrage, which had been in existence for ten years, and arrested anyone advocating universal suffrage. The political parties were so intimidated by these measures that they prohibited their members from introducing any bill calling for universal suffrage.

THE DEATH OF EMPEROR MEIJI

In August 1911, Katsura again transferred the reins of government to Saionji. The major event during Saionji's second cabinet was the death of Emperor Meiji in July 1912. The death of an emperor need not necessarily mark the end of an era, but in this case it certainly did.[17] The mode of control that the genrō had utilized for years was becoming ineffective, and the transition from their domination to party government took the form of Katsura and Saionji alternating in the office of prime minister. This game *à deux* was to come to an end also, and soon no cabinet could survive without the cooperation of one of the major parties. This change in the style of government was foreshadowed in the last Katsura cabinet (December 1912–February 1913), which was to last only two months because of the combined opposition of the major parties. Clearly, the days in which the oligarchy could pretty much have its own way were over.

On the international front, Japan's victory in the Russo-Japanese War brought the realization of the nation's initial objective of gaining recognition as a major power in the Far East. It also pulled Korea, an area that had been tantalizing the expansionists from the outset of the Meiji era, under its direct rule, thus bringing to a close phase one of its imperialistic dream. Japan had joined the ranks of modern nations.

The economy, as noted earlier, progressed to the second phase of modern economic growth around 1906. The working class was getting more restless, and the socialists, though suppressed temporarily, were emerging as a force with whom the ruling class would very soon have to reckon. In 1906 more than 1,000 miners at the Ashio copper mines rioted in protest against low wages and abuses by company officials. This was followed by troubles first in the Besshi copper mines and then in a coal mine in Hokkaido. During 1905–1906, workers in several major shipyards and arsenals rioted for higher wages. The year in which the emperor died was beset with major strikes throughout the land. The January 1912 strike by Tokyo streetcar workers is regarded as the first well-planned strike in Japan.

Emperor Meiji appears to have been manipulated by the genrō, but there is no question that he was very well-informed. To be sure, Itō and Yamagata were able to exercise what power they did only by virtue of the fact that the emperor agreed with the policies they pursued. In the words of Tokutomi Sohō, "The general order in the nation was tied to the person of the Emperor."[18] He carried on his ceremonial functions with majesty and dignity. His presence is what gave Meiji Japan its special flavor.

The emperor symbolizes the form of political authority, and this makes his ceremonial functions so important, particularly in a country like Japan. Western observers have noted that

> The familiar Western contrast of form and content is almost without meaning in the Orient. In this contrast, as well as in the word "form" itself, disparaging connotations are implicit. We say disapprovingly that a man observes the forms rather than the promptings of his inner nature; that he thinks in superficial analogies, regarding certain purely external features as the essential characteristics. In Japan and China, however, the formal is possessed of a constitutive meaning.[19]

Baelz, who had served the imperial court as a physician, made the following observations about the emperor's personality and character. He had a retiring, "one might almost say a shy, disposition," and in fact he left the palace only when he had to perform public functions for he preferred to stay in a small suite of private rooms most of the time. "He had no taste for sumptuous festivals or decorative posturings before the world's eyes."[20] He was known to be frugal and displayed a concern for the well-being of the people as well as for particular individuals. For example, when Yamagata wanted to replace General Nogi for failing to capture Port Arthur swiftly, the emperor rejected the proposal because, as he said, "if he were relieved, Nogi would probably not remain alive."

The institution of the emperor constituted the main pillar of the Meiji political system. It was the single most effective instrument employed by the ruling elite to retain their authority. The transformation of the imperial court from an empty institution, virtually unknown to the masses during the Tokugawa era, into an institution that claimed unquestioned, absolute sovereignty was one of the key achievements of the Meiji leaders.[21]

The emperor was given a religious, a political, and a military function to perform in the society. He retained his historical function as the god-king, who acted in a religious capacity as the intermediary between the gods and the people. The ancient concept of the unity of religion and government still prevailed, and the emperor was thus considered to be the spiritual and moral leader of the people. Politically, he derived his authority from his ancestors as well as from the Meiji constitution, which legally invested in him the sovereign power of the nation. The military function he had was that of supreme commander of the army and navy; all members of the armed forces were to remain loyal to him above all, while serving him "as limbs serve the head."

The moral textbooks, the Imperial Rescript on Education, and the constitution all contributed to the development in the people of a sense of loyalty and attachment to the emperor. For example, the moral textbooks depicted the emperor as the father of the entire nation, and loyalty to him was equated with the virtue of filial piety. The Sino-Japanese War also had an important effect in strengthening the emperor system. Baelz observed that the victory was

> explained as the outcome of the wonderful peculiarities of the Japanese and, in this self-adulation, talk of the "immemorial dynasty" of the imperial house played a great part. The upshot was that the position of the imperial family was strengthened by the crisis. . . . His portrait hung on the walls of every office, every school, and on ceremonial occasions all those present solemnly bowed their heads before it. An edict was issued describing the Emperor as the father of his people, and this edict was made the foundation of moral education in Japan. Thus was there revived a quasi-religious worship of the Emperor as the symbolical representative of the nation.[22]

This kind of reverence for the imperial symbol brought tragic results also. One popular novelist recalled that his father, who was a principal of a primary school, was compelled to take the blame and commit seppuku when the emperor's photograph, which was "enshrined" at the school, accidentally burned in a fire.

Emperor Meiji had, by the latter period of his life, won the affection and loyalty of most of his subjects, and when news of his illness appeared, thousands of people gathered before the imperial palace to pray for his recovery. Concerning his death, the central figure in one of Natsume Sōseki's novels says, "At the height of the summer, Emperor Meiji passed away. I felt as though the spirit of the Meiji era had begun with the emperor and had ended with him. I was overcome with the feeling that I and the others, who had been brought up in that era, were now left behind to live as anachronisms."[23] On the day of the emperor's funeral, General Nogi and his wife committed suicide so as to join him in death.

MEIJI JAPAN: AN ASSESSMENT

Despite all the difficulties and problems that beset the people, the Meiji era can nevertheless be considered to have been a magnificent half-century for Japan, perhaps the most remarkable such period in all its history. Japan emerged, with a modern army and navy, from a secluded feudal nation into one of the world's major powers. Japan had industrialized sufficiently during this period to lay the groundwork for the next phase of growth, in which it was to rank economically among the major industrial nations. It had adopted Western political and legal institutions and was consequently accorded equal treatment by the Western powers, who relinquished the special privileges they had acquired from it in the mid-nineteenth century. Party government had not yet come into its own, but it was very definitely on the horizon. Constitutional government, though imperfect, had unquestionably become an established institution; and if rule-*of*-law had not yet become a reality, at least rule-*by*-law had come about.

Some critics have labeled the Meiji government "totalitarian," but there was certainly nothing like the kind of authoritarianism that had prevailed half a century earlier. There were still, of course, aristocrats and commoners, and the gap between the rich and the poor did continue to grow. However, there was legal equality and, theoretically, an open society with some degree of social mobility had come into existence.[24] Universal education had been introduced; in 1900, tuition fees were eliminated, and in 1907 compulsory education was extended to six years. Despite the two-year extension, school attendance was over 98 percent in 1908.

The extent to which Japan was modernized by the end of the Meiji era is a matter of controversy. Okakura Kakuzō remarked at the turn of the century, "Accustomed to accept the new without sacrificing the old, our adoption of Western methods has not so greatly affected the national life as is generally supposed. One who looks beneath the surface of things can see, in spite of her modern garb, that the heart of Old Japan is still beating strongly."[25] A later Western observer saw vestiges of old Japan in "the ideal of feudal loyalty, the patriarchal system, the attitude toward women, the exaltation of the martial virtues."[26]

Vestiges of traditional Japan were still strongly embedded in the social practices and the attitudes of the people. In the rural areas, in particular, the traditional ways and values still governed all phases of the people's lives. Western individualism certainly had not permeated the society, and it would appear that even later, in the Taishō era, when "democracy" was in ascendancy, the rugged individualism so characteristic of Western societies never really triumphed. This was also true in the highly competitive business world, where the contending parties typically organized themselves around groups. Family-centered business empires like the Mitsui, Mitsubishi (Iwasaki), Sumitomo, and Yasuda constituted cliques of financial and business interests. Lafcadio Hearn (1850–1904), writing at the turn of the century, observed that the Japanese continued "to think and to act by groups, even by groups of industrial companies." Hearn went on to point out that

> In theory the individual is free; in practice he is scarcely more free than were his forefathers. Old penalties for breach of custom have been abrogated; yet communal opinion is able to compel the ancient obedience. . . . No man is yet complete master of his activities, his time, or his means. . . . The individual of every class above the lowest must continue to be at once coercer and coerced. Like an atom within a solid body, he can vibrate; but the orbit of his vibration is fixed.[27]

The ruling class deliberately fostered and strengthened the familial characteristics of Japanese life in the new institutions that were emerging. We have already noted this in the concept of the state and the emperor.[28] In the industrial realm, factory owners were depicted as being fathers of the workers, and as such they were expected to manifest a paternalistic interest in their welfare by, for example, sponsoring mutual aid societies and training the girl workers in the domestic arts of sewing and flower arrangement. In return the workers, as children, were expected to be obedient and loyal to their employers, their fathers. Even the large business combines, the *zaibatsu,* were basically family-centered organizations. In the army also an effort was made, after the Russo-Japanese War, to equate the relationship between the company commander and the soldier with that of father and son. Paternalistic "benevolence" and "humaneness" failed, however, to humanize the army, which on the contrary became one of the most mercilessly disciplinarian and inhumane institutions in the world.

Bearing these qualifications in mind, one can still say that Japan at the end of the Meiji era was well on the way to becoming a modern industrial power.

The question is frequently raised about why Japan managed to modernize in fifty years or so while China, which was exposed to the West much earlier, fell so far behind. A complex webbing of intertwining reasons accounts for this, but first some of the obvious differences in the situations facing the two countries should be noted. For one thing, Japan was a much smaller, more compact nation in which there was a stable, fairly centralized political system in existence even during the Tokugawa period. In China the pull toward regionalism got stronger as the central government weakened, whereas in Japan, even though the regional forces managed to overthrow the central government, they replaced the Bakufu with a much stronger central government instead of establishing diverse regional ones. Throughout the country, as a result, it could effectively enforce its policy of "enriching and strengthening" the nation.

Another obvious difference in the situations facing the two countries is that the Western powers interfered much less in the internal affairs of Japan than they did in China, which was ultimately reduced to the status of a semi-colonial nation. Still another noteworthy difference has to do with the fact that Japan was ruled by a military class that by its very nature was much more practical than the Confucian scholar-officials of China. The challenge posed to Japan, and to China for that matter, was primarily military in essence. The Japanese warriors immediately recognized the need to adopt Western arms and military techniques if they were to modernize and thus cope effectively with the foreign threat. They further realized that any program of modernization would depend heavily upon the adoption of Western science, technology, and industrialization. They were even willing to adopt Western political and social systems if these were deemed necessary for national survival.

In striking contrast to this rather pragmatic approach on the part of the Japanese military class, the Chinese ruling class was immersed in a sense of cultural superiority and ethnocentrism. This, of course, is quite understandable when you consider that China had been the center of the Asian world—which to the Chinese was the entire world—for thousands of years. China had a civilization that could be traced back 3,000 years or more, and its institutions, values, and ways had served the needs of the society for more than 2,000 years. As far as the Chinese were concerned, the golden age was in the past, and if disorder or troubles came about, they occurred because the people had departed from the traditional values and ways. As a result, whenever the country was faced with difficulties—and this includes the crisis in the nineteenth century—the ruling class endeavored to reform the institutions and tighten the moral standards to approximate as nearly as possible those of the golden age of the past. It did not seek to resolve the problems by introducing innovations or by adopting alien institutions and values.

Japan, in contrast, had been historically receptive to outside influences. As observed earlier, for several hundred years after the fifth century it readily adopted and adapted Chinese civilization on a large scale. Subsequently, from time to time Japan continued to subject itself willingly to influences from Korea and China. In the sixteenth century Japan even welcomed the advent of Christian missionaries. The ultimate rejection of Christianity, as we saw, was not due to cultural intolerance; it was strictly the result of political considerations. This long inbred tendency to learn and borrow from other cultures led the Japanese, when they were exposed to Western civilization in the nineteenth century, to reject the counsel of the seclusionists and turn enthusiastically to the importation of things Western. There was no psychological barrier to hinder seriously an all-out effort at modernization.

Another key factor that contributed to the relatively rapid modernization of Japan was the attitude or character of the people. The masses had been trained to be obedient and work hard during the centuries of feudal rule. Lafcadio Hearn made this observation about their tradition of obedience: "The probable truth is that the strength of the government up to the present time has been chiefly due to the conservation of ancient methods, and to the survival of the ancient spirit of reverential submission." Hearn goes on to comment about the great sacrifices willingly made by the people and their unswerving obedience "as regards the imperial order to acquire Western knowledge, to learn Western languages, to imitate Western ways."[29]

Undeniably the Japanese have always been a well-disciplined, industrious, and energetic people; and unlike people living in extremely impoverished countries, hard work enabled them to survive. These qualities should not, however, be considered as having given the Japanese an edge over the Chinese because the latter were also extremely diligent and industrious. Nevertheless, it is true that the Chinese were probably less regimented than the Japanese because they were not ruled by a sword-bearing military class that was ready to cut down any commoner who stepped out of line. The virtues of hard work, thrift, self-discipline, obedience, and selfless service had been instilled in the Japanese people by the edge of the sword.

It is also possible that the Japanese in the nineteenth century possessed a much more dynamic outlook than their contemporaries in China. Like the Chinese, the Japanese were influenced by Confucianism, but, in addition, they were molded by Shinto and the outlook of the warrior. Also, Zen Buddhism flourished to a greater extent in Japan than in China. Shinto had the effect of accentuating national pride, the sense of being unique, and the desire to excel. The samurai outlook fostered activism, stressing spiritual discipline, physical superiority, and military excellence. Zen Buddhism, which influenced the samurai more than the other classes, made the ruling class vigorous, decisive, and highly disciplined.

Another noteworthy factor is that Japan was endowed with a large number of exceptionally able leaders during the critical years of Meiji. These men had the foresight and willpower to chart the course of Japan and channel the energy of the people into enterprises that contributed to "enriching and strengthening" the nation. The Meiji Restoration was brought about by four outstanding leaders, Saigō, Ōkubo, Kido, and the court noble Iwakura. They were succeeded as architects of the new Japan by statesmen like Itō, Yamagata, Inoue, Matsukata, and Ōkuma. At the center was an enlightened monarch who knew precisely who could be trusted and relied upon. At the nongovernmental level there were outstanding educators and *philosophes,* like Fukuzawa, who helped to create the necessary climate of opinion for the advancement toward "civilization and enlightenment."

In the business realm a significant number of enterprising leaders emerged from the samurai class to build the new industrial society. Iwasaki Yatarō would be an especially prominent example, and as one economist notes, "The role of the samurai families in founding Japan's business class can hardly be exaggerated."[30] There were even some business leaders who emerged from an agrarian background, like Shibusawa, although his would be an exceptional case. The traditional merchant houses, of course, provided their share of leaders even though they tended to adhere more closely to merchandizing and banking. They did not actually turn to industrial activities until new blood was injected into them from the former samurai class. In this respect, also, Fukuzawa played an extraordinary role in that his academy produced a large number of exceptionally able businessmen who became key executives in the major companies and thus played crucial roles in the industrialization of Japan.

Another factor to be noted is the relatively high rate of literacy that prevailed in Tokugawa Japan. This meant that not only was the samurai class literate but also the leaders among the villagers and some common peasants were able to read and thus could be exposed to ideas from the West through books, tracts, and journals dealing with "civilization and enlightenment," as well as scientific and technological matters. The Meiji leaders were consequently able to count upon a fairly large body of informed and intellectually sophisticated leaders at the middle and even lower levels of the society to assist in the task of propelling the nation toward modernization.

As noted earlier, economic developments in the later stages of the Tokugawa era were sufficiently favorable for a fairly rapid transformation to take place from a feudal economy to a modern economic system.

At the end of the Meiji era it would have been difficult to assess whether or not modernization would be beneficial to the nation and the people as a whole. In fact the answer is still not available today, but Japan, like other modern industrial nations, is now faced with the task of reevaluating the entire process of modernization and the consequent changes that science, technology, rationalism, and individualism have brought about. For the Japanese of the Meiji era, modernization was already a mixed blessing. The cost was borne primarily by the masses in terms of the following: the greater burdens imposed upon the peasantry, the dehumanizing practices that accompanied industrialism in the exploitation of factory and mine workers, and the brutalizing effects of modern militarism.

The Meiji leaders envisioned as the object of modernization not so much the well-being of the people as *fukoku kyōhei,* the enrichment and strengthening of the nation. In terms of the goals they had established, they were well on the way to achieving their objectives. In the process, however, the masses were treated merely as means to an end, as laborers and cannon fodder. Voices were, nevertheless, beginning to be heard speaking up for the rights and welfare of the masses. The reign of Emperor Taishō was to be characterized by the ascendancy of democratic forces.

Notes

1. Erwin O. E. von Baelz, *Awakening Japan: The Diary of a German Doctor,* trans. Eden and Cedar Paul (New York: Viking, 1932), p. 312.

2. Russia had 135,000 troops east of Lake Baikal when the war started. Under the most favorable of conditions before the war it was able to transport about 7,000 men a month from Russia to Manchuria. At the outset of the war, however, the rate was lower because of numerous technical difficulties. Its fleet in the Far East consisted of seven battleships, eleven cruisers, and some smaller craft.

3. The Japanese forces managed to drive Kuropatkin out of Liaoyang, but they suffered severe losses of 5,500 dead and 18,000 wounded. The total Russian dead and wounded came to 16,000.

4. The Japanese toll of dead and wounded reached 57,780 in this conflict, while the Russians suffered 28,200 dead and wounded.

5. Quoted in Bertram D. Wolfe, *Three Who Made a Revolution* (Boston: Beacon, 1955), p. 279.

6. The Japanese casualties at Mukden were estimated at 70,000 and the Russian losses at 90,000.

7. Its national debt, for example, had risen during the war from 600 million to 2.4 billion yen.

8. Sumiya Mikio, *Dainipponteikoku no Shiren* (The Crucible of Imperial Japan) (Tokyo: Chūō Kōronsha, 1966), p. 290.

9. Fukao Sumako, *Yosano Akiko* (Tokyo: Jimbutsu Ōraisha, 1968), pp. 85–86.

10. The way had already been laid for the acquisition of Sakhalin by the Japanese seizure of the island in July 1905. During early Meiji both Russia and Japan had claimed the territory, but in 1875 the two countries signed a treaty by virtue of which Japan agreed to recognize Russia's claim to Sakhalin Island in return for Russian recognition of Japanese rights to the Kurile Islands.

11. The organization was named after Genkainada, the straits between Kyushu and Korea.

12. This move was initiated partly in response to the activities of American railroad magnate E. H. Harriman, who was seeking to gain railroad rights in Manchuria.

13. The resistance was not a minor affair—it is estimated that in 1907 some 50,000 men were involved in combating the Japanese and that by 1908 the number had risen to 70,000. Between July 1907 and July 1908, some 11,962 Korean "rioters" were killed.

14. Francis Hilary Conroy, *The Japanese Seizure of Korea: 1886–1910* (Philadelphia: University of Pennsylvania Press, 1960), p. 381.

15. Shinobu Seizaburō, *Taishō Demokurashiishi* (A History of Taishō Democracy), 3 vols. (Tokyo: Nihon Hyōron Shinsha, 1954–1959), vol. 1, p. 89.

16. Sumiya Mikio, *Dainipponteikoku no Shiren,* p. 444.

17. The generation of leaders who had ruled in his behalf had also passed from the scene or were in virtual retirement; only four genrō, all in their seventies, were still living—Yamagata, Matsukata, Inoue, and Ōyama. The only one, however, who was powerful and ambitious enough to keep meddling in public affairs was Yamagata.

18. Tokutomi Iichirō, *Taishōseikyokushi-ron* (Discourses on the History of the Taishō Political Situation) (Tokyo: Minyūsha, 1916), p. 46.

19. Emil Lederer and Emy Lederer-Seidler, *Japan in Transition* (New Haven: Yale University Press, 1938), pp. 100–101.

20. Baelz, *Awakening Japan,* p. 395.

21. As late as 1880, Baelz lamented on the emperor's birthday, "It distresses me to see how little interest the populace take in their ruler. Only when the police insist on it are houses decorated with flags" (ibid., p. 62).

22. Ibid., pp. 115–116.

23. Natsume Sōseki, *Kokoro,* trans. Edwin McClellan (Chicago: Regnery, 1967), p. 245.

24. An indication, though minor, of developing social mobility can be seen in the increase in the percentage of commoners in government posts, both civil and military, from 1891 to 1899. In 1891 the percentage was 29; it rose to 35 by 1895 and to 42 by 1899.

25. Kakuzo Okakura, *The Awakening of Japan* (New York: Century, 1904), pp. 189–192.

26. E. H. Norman, *Japan's Emergence as a Modern State* (New York: Institute of Pacific Relations, 1940), p. 8.

27. Lafcadio Hearn, *Japan: An Attempt at Interpretation* (New York: Macmillan, 1913), pp. 420–427, 496.

28. The prewar Japanese family usually consisted of the stem family, that is, a man, his wife, his unmarried siblings and children, and his eldest son and his family. The family register that was kept at the local government office was based upon the stem family. The head of the household held legal ownership of the family property, had the right to determine the occupation of family members, determined the place of residence, and approved or disapproved of marriages and divorces. A son under thirty years of age and a daughter under twenty-five had to obtain the approval of their father and the household head in order to marry. In return for his rights, the family head was responsible for the well-being of the family members. The principle of primogeniture governed the succession to the position of family head.

29. Hearn, *Japan,* pp. 454–455.

30. Yasuzō Horie, "Modern Entrepreneurship in Meiji Japan," in *The State and Economic Enterprise in Japan,* ed. William W. Lockwood (Princeton: Princeton University Press, 1965), p. 195.

10

The Era of Parliamentary Ascendancy (I)

The Emperor Taishō (1879–1926), who succeeded Emperor Meiji, was in poor health and did not take as active an interest in the affairs of the state as his father did. His physical difficulties, moreover, made it necessary for his son to assume his duties in 1921 and act as regent. Hence, Emperor Taishō did not leave a strong personal imprint upon his reign in the way that Emperor Meiji did. The most serious consequence of the emperor's weakness was that it created a situation in which the imperial institution could be more easily manipulated by the genrō clique, who were trying at the time to shore up their diminishing authority against the ascendant political parties. Nonetheless, the genrō, for all their desperate and scheming tactics, were incapable of preserving the tradition of nonparty government. They were unable to turn or hold back the tide of history because each man that came to head the government was compelled at one time or another to find some link and base of support in the existing political parties. In September 1918, the first true party government came to power under Hara Takashi. This form of rule, except for a brief hiatus, was to hold sway in Japan until the assassination of Prime Minister Inukai on May 15, 1932.

The period covered in this and the following chapter is the era during which democratic forces reached their high point in prewar Japan. It coincides roughly with the first part of the second phase of modern economic development, when the so-called modern sector of the economy grew significantly. This development intensified the reformist activities of the labor and socialist leaders. In the meanwhile, Japan, regardless of who was in charge of the government—bureaucrats or party leaders—continued its policy of continental involvement, which kept the military forces actively involved in politics even in the halcyon days of party government.

INTERNAL POLITICAL AFFAIRS: 1912–1918

The chief political problem confronting the second Saionji government was the army's desire to increase its size. In 1906, while the genrō were all still relatively active, a decision had been made to expand the army from seventeen to twenty-five divisions. In the first phase of the expansion program four divisions were to be added, but only two of these had been added by 1911. Since it was Saionji's policy to reduce expenditures, he favored delaying the army's project further. At the same time, however, he agreed to increase naval expenditures. The minister of war, General Uehara, tendered his resignation to the emperor when he discovered that the Saionji cabinet did not favor creating the two additional divisions immediately. Lacking the positive support of either Yamagata or Katsura, Saionji again resigned.

The leaders of the government, after failing to find a suitable successor to Saionji, finally turned once again to Katsura, who had been placed in semiretirement as the Lord Keeper of the Privy Seal. He formed a cabinet consisting largely of bureaucrats because, having been disappointed in his past associations with the Seiyūkai, he was not about to make any efforts to reestablish ties with Hara and his followers.

Katsura was confronted with strong opposition from the very outset. The journalists and party politicians aroused public opinion against the army's demands for more divisions, while the business leaders, who favored reducing government expenditures, vehemently opposed increasing the defense budget. The party leaders with the support of business leaders, especially Mitsui, proceeded to organize the Association to Protect Constitutional Government (Kensei Yōgokai) in order to eradicate the "han oligarchs." The supporters of the association held rallies directed against the ruling clique.

Katsura concluded that he needed to establish his own power base in the Diet and, following the path taken by Itō in 1900, he set out to organize a new political party under his control. He turned to the faction in the Nationalist Party (the former Kenseihontō) that had previously indicated a desire to collaborate with him, and in so doing he produced a serious split in that group. Katsura also expected a fairly large number of Seiyūkai men to break with their party and join him, but his organizational campaign failed to draw even a single one of them. His new party, the Rikken Dōshikai (Constitutional Association of Friends), consequently attracted only eighty-three Diet members.

The Seiyūkai leaders now threw their support behind the Association to Protect Constitutional Government and then joined forces with the remnant of the Nationalist Party to push for a vote of no confidence against Katsura. Thereupon Katsura prorogued the Diet and got the emperor to issue a rescript to Saionji asking him to resolve the political crisis. Saionji felt obliged to comply with the emperor's wishes, but he explained to the party leaders that he understood that they were representatives of the people and as such they would naturally have to persist in representing their views. Saionji severed his ties with the Seiyūkai and as chief retainer of the nation joined the ranks of the genrō. The Seiyūkai, however, refused to withdraw the no-confidence bill and, in effect, defied the imperial command. Katsura had decided to dissolve the Diet, but faced with growing support for the opposition, he unexpectedly resigned instead. Thus, public opinion and the opponents in the Diet succeeded in overthrowing the Katsura cabinet. This event is referred to as the Taishō Political Crisis.

The genrō Yamagata and Matsukata, now joined by Saionji, selected Admiral Yamamoto Gonnohyōe (1852–1933) of Satsuma as Katsura's successor. Yamamoto agreed to form the new cabinet with the understanding that the Seiyūkai would support him. As a result, three Seiyūkai men, including Hara, joined the cabinet organized in February 1913. Once again the Seiyūkai leaders failed to adhere to their pledge to break the power of the ruling clique and abandoned the Association to Protect Constitutional Government.

The Yamamoto cabinet introduced several popular reforms. For one thing, it succeeded, even in the face of strong opposition from the army, in revising the regulation, which was originally proposed by Yamagata in 1900, requiring the ministers of war and navy to be active generals or admirals of the two top ranks. The regulation was revised to make those who had already retired from these two top ranks eligible for these posts. Under the prodding of Hara, Yamamoto revised the civil service regulation that proscribed political appointments of high-ranking bureaucrats, making the post of vice minister an appointive position. Yamagata tried to block this change in the Privy Council, but Yamamoto threatened to purge that organ of the government and pushed through the revision. He also reduced the size of the Privy Council from twenty-eight to twenty-four and cut the number of bureaucrats by more than 6,800. Together with other government personnel, a cut of 10,000 employees was effected, reducing the budget for the year 1913 by 11 percent. Yamamoto, however, was not bent on economy for the sake of economy; the savings were to be used for naval expansion.

Just when it appeared as if Yamamoto had devised a very strong and stable cabinet, a wholly unforeseen event wrecked it all. In January 1914 the news broke that Japanese naval officers had been bribed by the Siemens Munitions Firm of Germany to obtain contracts for munitions and wireless materials. In the course of the investigation other instances of bribery involving naval officers came to light, whereupon the opposition parties seized this opportunity to strike at Yamamoto and rouse public opinion against him. At a protest rally held in Tokyo, clashes between the police and the protesters occurred, intensifying public hostility toward the government. The Yamagata faction then decided to take advantage of the situation and overthrow the Yamamoto cabinet by vetoing the budget in the House of Peers and then refusing to reconsider its position.

Yamamoto was consequently forced to resign, and as he did so, he recommended that Hara be appointed his successor. However, Yamagata, who was not about to accept a party government, sought instead to have his follower Kiyoura Keigo (1850–1942) selected to form the next cabinet. This posed a difficult situation because the navy refused to cooperate when Kiyoura failed to agree to call a special session of the Diet for the purpose of restoring the navy's budget, which had been cut (with Kiyoura's support) by the House of Peers. Inoue then pushed Ōkuma's candidacy, and got Yamagata's reluctant agreement.

Ōkuma, who had been out of politics for fifteen years since his retirement as head of the Kenseihontō, had been devoting his attention to social work and to Waseda University, which he had founded earlier. He accepted the premiership and immediately set about gaining the cooperation of Katō Kōmei, who was then the head of the Dōshikai. Next Ōkuma turned to Inukai and Ozaki, his erstwhile supporters. Ozaki, who was with a splinter group of a minor party, decided to enter the cabinet. Inukai, who was with a truncated Nationalist Party, refused, however, because he would not work with the Dōshikai, which had been created by splintering the Nationalist Party. The bureaucratic, pro-Yamagata faction was heavily represented in the Ōkuma government, which was formed in April 1914. In effect, the old champion of party government had become something like an agent for the oligarchic clique.

One of the very serious problems that faced the Ōkuma government soon after its accession to power was the outbreak of the First World War. Foreign Minister Katō Kōmei wanted to seize the opportunity to take over the German concessions in China and also enhance Japan's status in the international arena by participating on the side of the Allied powers. The excuse for joining the war was provided by a British request for Japan's participation in accordance with the Anglo-Japanese Alliance. Soon thereafter, Britain had second thoughts about Japan's entry, but Katō had already pushed through the war plans without even conferring with the genrō—a step that certainly did not endear him to the latter. He was determined, however, to end genrō and military intervention in the realm of the formation of foreign policy.

The Japanese forces captured the German fortress at Qingdao on the Shandong Peninsula and the German island possessions in the Pacific. Other than this, Japan's active role in the battle was limited to the use of its warships to patrol the Mediterranean toward the latter part of the war.

The other major foreign-policy matter that faced the Ōkuma government was the presentation of the Twenty-one Demands to the Chinese government in January 1915 (see page 208). This was another decision that Katō made without first consulting the genrō, and the unfavorable international repercussions that ensued further hardened the genrō's opposition to him.

On the domestic front, Ōkuma pursued a policy of naval and military expansion. He sought to add the two army divisions that had been on the army's agenda since 1906, but the Seiyūkai and the Nationalist Party so adamantly opposed this measure that Ōkuma found it necessary to dissolve the Diet. In the general election that followed in March 1915, Ōkuma launched a major campaign to aid the Dōshikai. This was the first time that a prime minister campaigned personally in Diet elections. Not only did Ōkuma make whistle-stop campaign speeches throughout the country, but his minister of home affairs, Ōura, a follower of Yamagata and a member of the bureaucratic clique, made major changes in the prefectural governorships and then had the new appointees campaign for progovernment candidates. Considerable money was spent on buying votes. As a result of this all-out effort, the Dōshikai increased its Diet seats from 99 to 150, and the Seiyūkai representation fell from 185 to 104. With additional backing provided by the minor parties, Ōkuma now had majority support in the Diet, and this enabled him to pass the measure to add two army divisions.

The economy was flourishing because of the First World War, and so it appeared that Ōkuma would remain in power for some time. However, now that the Seiyūkai had been weakened and the army enlarged, the genrō and the bureaucratic clique felt that Ōkuma had served his purpose. He was no longer needed, so their agents in the House of Peers began to set the stage for his elimination by criticizing his inept handling of foreign affairs and by attacking his fiscal policies.

Obstruction by the House of Peers finally forced Ōkuma to give up the premiership in the fall of 1917. He sought to install Katō as his successor, but Yamagata, who was still opposed to a party man heading the government, found him to be particularly objectionable because as foreign minister Katō had bypassed him in formulating foreign policy. Yamagata managed to have General Terauchi Masatake (1852–1919), the resident general of Korea, appointed as prime minister.

Terauchi formed a cabinet that was supposedly "above parties," but he did seek and receive the cooperation of Hara and the Seiyūkai. The Kenseikai (Constitutional Association), which had been formed by the Dōshikai and two minor parties, called for a vote of no confidence against Terauchi, and he had to dissolve the Diet. In the ensuing election of April 1918, the Seiyūkai managed to increase its representatives by about fifty while reducing Kenseikai seats by eighty.

In the realm of foreign affairs, Terauchi had to cope with the unstable China situation as well as with the problems arising out of the fall of the tsarist government in Russia. The issue, however, that ultimately brought the Terauchi cabinet down was inflation.

The Japanese economy was undergoing a recession when the First World War broke out, and the situation worsened because the war initially reduced foreign trade. The price of rice and other grains continued to drop until mid-1916, when the trend was finally reversed. Japanese exports began to rise from the middle of 1915, as the belligerent nations were unable to supply goods to foreign markets. Japan sold war supplies as well as other necessities to the Allied nations while at the same time increasing its exports to Southeast Asia and North and South America. In 1915 Japan's exports reached an unprecedented 708 million yen, and they continued to increase, reaching 1.96 billion yen in 1918.[1] This resulted in tremendous economic expansion, increased circulation of currency, greater demand for goods, and inflationary prices. As is usually the case, the rapid increase in prices was not followed by higher wages. Consequently, real wages declined.[2] Strikes, even though they were illegal, steadily increased in number as a result of the tremendous economic pressures.

The most pressing problem that confronted the government was the increase in the price of rice, which doubled between January 1917 and July 1918. This situation produced virulent riots throughout the country in the summer of 1918. In July, the housewives of a small fishing village in north central Honshu demonstrated against the high price of rice, and when news of this action spread, riots erupted in other areas of the country. The price of rice nevertheless continued to rise. By the middle of August, massive rice riots hit all the major cities, with the protesters attacking retail stores and warehouses of rice merchants as well as other shops and homes belonging to the rich. These riots, which lasted for fifty days until the middle of September, involved hundreds of cities, towns, and villages.[3] The government officials, believing that the situation was being aggravated by the sensationalist and sympathetic approach taken by the newspapers, sought to impose severe curbs on the press. This, of course, only increased public hostility against the Terauchi government.

These riots, the largest and most widespread in Japanese history, had several significant effects. They not only forced out the Terauchi cabinet, but fear of the violent mobs they assembled brought rival political leaders of the establishment, such as Hara and Yamagata, closer together. They also created a sense of urgency about the need for immediate social reforms and extension of the franchise. Thus, the riots actually gave a boost to democracy and to the labor and socialist movements.

The political parties, however, were somewhat cautious about joining the critics of the government, for clearly the riots of the masses were also a threat to the party members. Yamagata wanted Saionji to head the government again after Terauchi resigned, but this new member of the genrō responded to the invitation by urging that a party government under Hara be permitted to try its hand instead.[4] Yamagata, who had fought and resisted party government throughout his political career, finally accepted the inevitable and agreed to Saionji's proposal. Unlike Katō, Hara had neither circumvented established practices nor neglected to pay proper deference to the elder statesmen.

In September 1918, the first real party government in Japan came into existence. Hara was not a member of the House of Peers so was hailed as "the commoner Prime Minister." The long struggle for party government led by the advocates of popular rights had finally achieved its desired goal, which, ironically enough, was realized by cooperating closely with genrō officialdom. Hara's accession to power was a landmark for parliamentary government, even though nonparty cabinets would follow for a few years.

FOREIGN AFFAIRS

The second decade of the twentieth century saw a growing Japanese concern over developments in China, where revolutionary forces under the leadership of Sun Yat-sen (1866–1925) together with traditional military chieftains like Yuan Shikai had succeeded in bringing an end to the Manchu dynasty. A republic was established under Yuan Shikai, but political stability did not follow. Instead, internal divisions persisted as Yuan sought to establish a new dynasty. The republicans continued to carry on their struggle at home and abroad, but when Yuan died in June 1916, China found itself lacking a strong central government, and an era of "warlordism" was ushered into existence. Sun Yat-sen nevertheless continued his campaign to unify the country under a program emphasizing nationality, democracy, and people's livelihood. As a result of this fragmentation of authority in China, Japan was confronted with tempting opportunities to extend its influence and interests in that country.

During the first decade of the twentieth century, a considerable number of Chinese students came to Japan to study because they were convinced that its approach to modernizing society provided a model that their own country should follow.[5] Sun Yat-sen used Japan from 1897 to 1903 as a base from which to carry on his revolutionary activities. He then spent a great deal of time in Europe and the United States before returning to Japan in 1905 in order to organize the Tong-Meng-Hui (United League), by which he hoped to give the revolutionary movement a cohesive structure. Many of the visiting students established close friendships with Japanese political leaders who were interested in assisting the Chinese in reforming their country.[6]

There was also a fairly large number of Japanese who went to China as what were called rōnin (masterless warriors) to play a hand at political intrigue and revolution. Some went out of a sense of altruism, some were motivated by the spirit of adventure, and some, of course, wanted to advance the cause of Japanese imperialism.[7] There were also those men who were primarily interested in establishing business enterprises in China for the purpose of engaging in a kind of economic imperialism. Among them was Mori Kaku (1882–1932), who was not only a businessman interested in the economic exploitation of China but also a political intriguer who envisioned his role in China as comparable to that of Britain's Clive in India.

Attention had been focused upon Manchuria and Mongolia before the Russo-Japanese War, and many adventurers moved into that region to prevent Russian expansion in the Far East. The Kokuryūkai (the Amur River, or Black Dragon, Society) was formed in 1901 by Uchida Ryōhei (1874–1937), who was interested in furthering Japanese interests in Manchuria and Mongolia. This organization sent intelligence agents into these areas and Siberia, with the ultimate aim of making the Amur River into one of Japan's boundaries. The desire to achieve this goal was fortified with the victory in the Russo-Japanese War. The man who emerged as the real leader of the Genyōsha as well as the Kokuryūkai was Tōyama Mitsuru, who was to remain the patriarch and the gray eminence of the ultranationalistic expansionists until the Second World War. All right-wing politicians looked to him for guidance and advice, and his charismatic personality further enhanced his enormous following by attracting young "patriots" who were willing to kill and die for him.

Growing Japanese interest in China was reflected in the increasing number of Japanese residents in Manchuria, the Yangtze River Valley, and other parts of China. In 1900 there were only about 3,800 Japanese in China, but this figure rose to well over 26,600 by 1910, and to 133,930 by 1920. Most of these inhabitants were concentrated in the big cities of Manchuria. During the First World War political intrigues in these areas were supported by the general staff of the army as well as many other high-ranking officials.

One of the most controversial actions taken by the Japanese government toward China during the Taishō era was the submission of the Twenty-one Demands to the Yuan Shikai government in January 1915. Ōkuma and his foreign minister, Katō, engineered this scheme and had the demands grouped under five headings. The first had to do with the transference of German rights in Shandong Province to Japan as well as granting the right to construct a railway line there. The second called for the recognition of Japan's special position in south Manchuria and eastern Inner Mongolia. The third group dealt with the establishment of a Sino-Japanese company that would be given a mining monopoly in certain areas of the Yangtze River Valley. Group four asked that no harbor, bay, or island along the coast of China be ceded or leased to any other power. Group five involved the most controversial set of demands. Among other things it asked the Chinese government to employ Japanese political, financial, and military advisers.[8]

These demands were presented at a time when the major powers were preoccupied with the world war and were thus unable to intervene. The only country that Yuan Shikai's government could count on for support was the United States, but it was not willing to exert much pressure on Japan. Secretary of State William Jennings Bryan (1860–1925) claimed that the United States frankly recognized that the territorial contiguity existing between Japan and Shandong, south Manchuria, and eastern Mongolia necessarily created special relations between the two countries involved. Bryan did, however, go on to say that his government objected to those demands that came under groups four and five.

Negotiations between the Chinese and Japanese governments continued for several months. Japan made threatening gestures by increasing the forces it had stationed in Manchuria, Shandong, and Hankow. Yuan stalled, unable to defy Chinese public opinion, which was enraged at the Japanese action, while at the same time hoping for third-power support.

In early May 1915, the Japanese government deleted most of the demands in group five and presented Yuan with an ultimatum. He had no choice but to accede, and on May 25, the two nations signed an agreement that in effect conceded to Japan all the demands in the first four groups.[9]

Japanese-American relations tended to become strained because Japanese activities in Manchuria and China conflicted with the American concept of the open door in China. At the same time, the issue of Japanese immigration into Hawaii and the United States was causing tremendous ill feelings. Japanese immigration into Hawaii began to increase in the last decade of the nineteenth century, and by 1900 there were 61,000 Japanese immigrants in Hawaii, constituting 40 percent of the island's population. There were also 24,000 Japanese immigrants in California. Agitation against this immigration intensified in the West Coast states, and the Japanese government consequently sought to curb the flow of its people out of the country. There was, however, nothing it could do to prevent the Japanese in Hawaii from moving to the mainland of the United States.[10]

President Roosevelt vetoed a piece of clearly discriminatory legislation that had been passed by Congress, but he could do nothing about prejudicial activities that were going on at the local level. In San Francisco, for example, the local press, with rousing headlines about the Yellow Peril, and the Asiatic Exclusion League managed to foment considerable animosity toward Japanese immigration. In 1906 the San Francisco school board issued a "separate school order" providing for the segregation of Oriental children in the public schools in order "to save White children from being affected by association with pupils of the Mongolian race." The order was clearly directed at Japanese pupils (Chinese children were already segregated), who were called vicious and immoral. It was further charged that these pupils were overcrowding the school system, although at that time there were only ninety-three Japanese youngsters en-rolled in the twenty-three San Francisco schools.[11]

Roosevelt succeeded in blocking the entry of Japanese immigrants from Hawaii, Canada, and Mexico, while persuading the Japanese government to conclude a "Gentlemen's Agreement" in 1908 to restrict the flow of its people to the United States. The agreement severely limited the inflow of Japanese immigrants, but it did nothing to reduce the agitation against these people that continued to mount in California. Anti-Japanese riots broke out in San Francisco in May 1907, and there was even considerable talk of war between the United States and Japan. In 1913, an Alien Land Act was passed prohibit-ing aliens from owning land or leasing land for more than three years. In 1920 the right of Japanese to lease lands was denied completely, and in 1922 the Su-preme Court of the United States held that the Japanese were ineligible for cit-izenship. In 1924, Congress passed an immigration act that annulled the Gentlemen's Agreement of 1908 and prohibited persons who were not eligible for citizenship from entering the country at all.

These measures aggravated Japanese-American relations, which were at this time already coming into conflict in the political arena of the Far East. Here, however, conflicting interests were resolved, if only temporarily, by political agreements. For instance, in 1908, when there was talk of a Chinese-German-American alliance, the Root-Takahira notes were exchanged wherein the United States and Japan pledged to respect each other's territorial possessions in East Asia and the Pacific, to uphold the status quo in these regions and maintain the open-door policy, and to respect China's independence and in-tegrity. The statement, however, was couched in such vague rhetoric that both sides later disagreed about what was specifically intended. Japan interpreted the agreement to mean that it was not to attack the Philippines in return for a free hand in Manchuria.

As observed earlier, an American railroad magnate, E. H. Harriman (1848–1909), was interested in acquiring railroad rights in Manchuria. The effort to extend American interests in that part of the world was carried on af-ter Harriman's death by Secretary of State Knox, who wanted to neutralize foreign-owned railroads in Manchuria. Moves along this line only succeeded in driving Japan and Russia toward a virtual alliance to defend their common interests there.

The entry of the United States into the First World War raised hopes that American support could be garnered for Japan's claims to the German conces-sions in both Shandong and the Pacific islands north of the equator. Japan also wanted the United States to recognize its "paramount interests" in China, but such a commitment was refused. The only product that was to emerge from the Japanese overtures was the Lansing-Ishii notes, which recognized Japan's special interests in China while reaffirming the principle of China's territorial integrity and the open-door policy.

The next issue that exacerbated its relations with the United States was Japan's desire to send troops into Siberia following the fall of the Russian Provisional Government. The subsequent emergence of the Bolshevik government in the fall of 1917 brought an extension of Soviet control eastward into Siberia. The Japanese government under Terauchi then considered the possibility of countering this movement by establishing an independent anti-Soviet state in eastern Siberia. Without American consent, the Japanese leaders, including Terauchi and Yamagata, were unwilling to take aggressive action in the Far East, however, and at this point the United States was not willing to see Japan move into Siberia, even if it was to combat communism. The army leaders, headed by the vice chief of staff, General Tanaka Giichi (1863–1929), continued to agitate for the dispatching of an expeditionary force into Siberia, and when the Cossack leader Semenov (1890–1946) started his anti-Bolshevik movement in northern Manchuria, the Japanese army supplied him with weapons. Soon thereafter, when some Japanese were killed as a result of a clash between Bolshevik and anti-Bolshevik forces, the Japanese navy landed its marines in Vladivostok.

The American position on the question of intervention shifted when Czechoslovakian troops, which were moving across Siberia to return to the Western front, clashed with Soviet forces. The United States finally responded to the English and French appeal for intervention in order to extricate the Czech forces. In July 1918, the United States and Japan agreed to send military units under separate command into Siberia to assist the Czech troops.[12]

The original intention was to confine military operations largely around Vladivostok, but the Japanese forces were sent as far as Irkutsk. This seriously disturbed the United States, which then withdrew its troops just as soon as arrangements were made to repatriate the Czech soldiers. All US soldiers were withdrawn by April 1920, whereas the Japanese, hoping to control at least the Chinese Eastern Railroad in northern Manchuria, if not the entire region east of Lake Baikal, remained in Siberia until the latter part of 1922. Japan, headed now by Katō Kōmei, ultimately withdrew its troops for two primary reasons: first, considerable international pressure, particularly from the United States, was being brought to bear upon it; and second, the Soviet government was finally succeeding in consolidating control over Russia. Nevertheless, Japan did keep its troops in northern Sakhalin until 1925. In January of that year, under the leadership of Foreign Minister Shidehara, diplomatic relations were officially established between Japan and Soviet Russia. Essentially, Japan's intervention in Siberia accomplished nothing positive, while it served both to reinforce the distrust of Soviet leaders toward foreign powers and to impair even further Japanese relations with the United States.

The world powers met in Versailles in January 1919 to work out a peace settlement after the First World War, and Japan participated as one of the major powers even though its role in the war had been limited. The Japanese delegation, headed by Saionji, had as one of its key objectives the legalization of Japanese control over the former German holdings in both Shandong and the Pacific islands north of the equator. Despite vigorous Chinese opposition and reluctance on the part of the United States, Japan got what it wanted.

Much was made in Japan about the Western powers denying Japan a clause on racial equality in the Covenant of the League of Nations. The idea had been one of Wilson's Fourteen Points, but the European powers understood the implied criticism of their colonial policies of such a statement. It is unlikely that Japan really wished to grant self-determination of government to its colonial subjects in Taiwan or Korea as a clause of racial equality seemed to indicate. Some historians suggest that Japan merely used a request as a gambit to insure it received what it really wanted: control of Liaoning, Shandong, and the German Pacific islands.

The decade following the conference at Versailles was a period of international cooperation for Japan, which, in part at least, was brought about by the relative decline in the influence of the militarists and the emergence of party government. The formulation of foreign policy fell into the hands of men such as Shidehara who believed in cooperating with other nations.

In order to settle the differences that remained unresolved by the Versailles Treaty and also to end the naval armament race that was breaking out among England, the United States, and Japan, an international conference was convened under the auspices of the United States. In August 1921, President Warren Harding (1865–1923) invited Great Britain, France, Italy, and Japan to Washington for the purpose of discussing the limitation of arms and related questions concerning the Pacific and the Far East. China, Belgium, the Netherlands, and Portugal were also invited to the meetings devoted to these last problems.

The economic boom enjoyed by Japan came to a close with the end of the First World War. Its imports began to exceed exports, and the need for economic retrenchment was acutely felt. Even the most ardent advocates of naval arms expansion came to recognize the urgent necessity to reduce expenditures. Consequently, the Japanese government, under the leadership of Hara, readily accepted the invitation to the Washington Conference. A number of agreements resulted from this gathering. Among the more important ones were the Four Power Pacific Treaty involving the United States, Great Britain, France, and Japan; the Five Power Naval Treaty (adding Italy); and the Nine Power Treaty, which all the participants at the conference signed, dealing with the principles and policies to be followed concerning China.

The signatories to the Four Power Pacific Treaty agreed to respect each other's "rights in relation to their insular possessions and insular dominions in the region of the Pacific Ocean." All controversies were to be settled by a conference of the four powers. The earlier Anglo-Japanese Alliance was to be terminated upon ratification of this new treaty.

US Secretary of State Charles Evans Hughes (1862–1948) took the initiative regarding the limitation of naval armament by making concrete proposals on the opening day of the conference. He suggested that the naval tonnage ratio of 5–5–3 be set for the war ships of the United States, Great Britain, and Japan, respectively. Japan preferred a ratio of 10–10–7, but its delegation, headed by Admiral Katō Tomosaburō (1861–1923), accepted the American proposal with the proviso that the status quo would be maintained in the fortifications and naval bases in the Pacific. The United States had ports that could serve as naval bases, but none had been adequately fortified in 1921. Not included in this agreement were those American naval bases and fortifications located adjacent to the coasts of the United States, Alaska, and the Panama Canal Zone. France and Italy accepted a ratio of 1.75 each to the 5–5–3 ratio for the other nations. The naval agreement did not cover auxiliary crafts or submarines. The signatories also agreed to abstain from using "asphyxiating, poisonous, or other gases and all analogous liquids . . . in war."

In the Nine Power Treaty the parties concerned pledged to respect "the sovereignty, the independence, and the territorial and administrative integrity of China." Furthermore, they affirmed the Open Door by agreeing to maintain equal commercial opportunities in China for all nations, with no country seeking special rights and privileges. The sentiments were noble, but no nation was actually willing to renounce the unequal treaties imposed on China during the nineteenth century, despite the fact that China had been a full-fledged ally in World War I. Moreover, no effective sanctions were instituted to enforce the Nine Power Treaty.

Japan and China settled their differences on Shandong at the Washington Conference. Japan agreed to return the province to China but retained control of the Jinan-Qingdao Railway and its properties for fifteen years. Even though the problem of Shandong was solved, Sino-Japanese relations remained severely strained. The Versailles settlement unleashed an outburst of nationalism in China that was led by students and intellectuals. They staged what is known as the May Fourth movement, a patriotic demonstration directed against Japanese imperialism, and they also initiated boycotts of Japanese goods in all the major cities.

The tense situation between the two countries was no doubt seriously aggravated by the Japanese militarists who continued their intrigues in Manchuria and North China, backing warlords who might serve their ends and intensifying the exploitation of iron and coal mines.

The following episode involving Zhang Zuolin (1873–1928) provides a good example of Japanese intervention in China's political affairs and the deteriorating effects of that interference. In July 1920, Zhang, in cooperation with other warlords, drove Duan Qilui (1864–1936), a warlord backed by Japan, out of Beijing and succeeded in holding the capital until 1922. At that time he was removed by a coalition of warlords headed by Wu Peifu (1874–1939), who, the Japanese believed, was supported by England and the United States. In 1925 the "Christian General" Feng Yuxiang (1882–1948) rebelled against Wu and gained temporary control of Beijing, but he in turn was driven out by the combined forces of Duan Qilui and Zhang Zuolin. Late in 1926, when one of Zhang's more progressive generals rebelled against him, Japanese militarists in Manchuria intervened on his behalf and thus enabled him to gain supremacy in Manchuria and North China. As a result of Japan's participation in this struggle, there was a further intensification of antagonistic sentiments toward it in China.

Earlier in 1925, anti-Japanese feelings were aroused when a textile workers' strike against Japanese plants in Shanghai had led to bloodshed as the British police sought to suppress the demonstrators. Thus, despite Foreign Minister Shidehara's efforts to establish friendly relations by restricting Japanese interference, Chinese public opinion continued to grow inflamed by Japanese actions.

Nationalistic opposition also confronted Japan in Korea, where after annexing the nation in 1910, Japan imposed military rule. All the governors-general were either admirals or generals; the military police controlled the police force; and civilian officials, even teachers, carried sabers with them. The Koreans were granted no political rights and were denied freedom of speech and assembly.

The Japanese rulers confiscated large areas of farmlands from the Korean peasants, using as an excuse their failure to register their land and establish legal ownership in a given period of time. The Korean peasants, most of whom were illiterate, had no understanding of what the legal technicalities were all about. The unregistered land was nationalized and then sold cheaply to Japanese land development companies and immigrants.[13] A large number of Korean peasants were consequently reduced to tenancy or vagrancy. The Korean market was dominated by Japanese goods because measures had been introduced restricting the development of indigenous Korean industry. This massive importation of Japanese manufactured goods also undermined the traditional Korean handicraft industries. The Japanese landowners, merchants, and moneylenders prospered under this program of domination and exploitation while the Koreans became increasingly impoverished.

At this time the Wilsonian concept of self-determination was gaining wide publicity, and those Koreans who were in exile intensified their efforts to gain freedom. Students and Christian leaders within the country also began agitating for independence.[14] On March 1, 1919, the day set for the funeral of the

Korean king, the people staged a nationwide peaceful demonstration calling for independence. The Japanese authorities labeled the participants as rioters and used the army to suppress the demonstrators ruthlessly. The Koreans used whatever means they had to strike back, but after two months the resistance was brought under control.[15] This, however, did not put an end to the movement for independence, which was continued by Korean nationalists abroad. Among them was Syngman Rhee (1875–1965), who used Hawaii as his base. Disillusioned by the lack of concern for their fate by the Western powers, many Korean nationalists turned to the Russians for support.

Admiral Saitō Makoto (1858–1936) was appointed governor-general by the Hara government after these disturbances. He proclaimed a policy of "cultural rule," but the changes that Saitō introduced were at best superficial, such as the replacement of the military police with regular police, and the termination of the practice of having officials and teachers wear uniforms and bear sabers.[16] Cooperative Koreans were given seats in advisory regional councils, but these administrative bodies had absolutely no authority. The economic exploitation of Korea continued, and as half of its rice crop was shipped to Japan, per capita consumption of rice dropped by 47 percent between 1912 and 1933.[17] The Koreans were compelled to augment their diet with millet imported from Manchuria.

ECONOMIC DEVELOPMENTS: 1906–1930

After the Russo-Japanese War the Japanese economy entered the second phase of modern economic growth. In the first period, 1906–1930, the growth in the modern sector of the economy was accelerated while the traditional sector failed to grow as rapidly. As a result the gap between the two segments slowly widened.[18] In the second period of this phase (1931–1952), the growth of the economy was stimulated by the political and military policies of the government and was affected by abnormal circumstances; that is, war, defeat, and occupation.

The rapid growth in the modern sector was stimulated by the Russo-Japanese War. There were greater government expenditures in armaments and in transportation resulting from the nationalization of the railroads, new markets were developing in the freshly acquired colonies, and a stronger home market was coming into being as a result of increased per capita income.

The decline in the traditional sector during this same period was caused in part by competition from both the modern sector of the economy and the colonies. The growth of this sector was also stunted as a consequence of these key factors: by 1905 the limits to which new arable land could be opened had been reached, and the maximum increase in yield per unit of land had been achieved.

The gap between the modern and traditional sectors created a noticeable difference in living standards, and the impoverished rural dwellers became

increasingly dissatisfied. Greater efficiency in productivity in the modern segment resulted in a reduced demand for labor. This placed at the disposal of the
industries a ready supply of cheap labor. At the same time low incomes, particularly in the traditional sector, limited the growth of the domestic market. By
the end of the 1920s the Japanese economy was confronted with a serious crisis.[19] Compared to the increased production in the industrial realm, production in the traditional sector showed relatively modest advances, and food
production managed to stay only slightly ahead of the population growth.[20]

In spite of the rather significant growth in the modern segment, Japan was
still not a predominantly industrial nation.[21] Also, the standard of living did
not improve significantly, although conditions for people in the modern urban
areas were somewhat better than in the traditional rural sections. Taking the
increase in food production and imports together, there was a 20 percent rise
in per capita food supply.[22] So far as the life expectancy figures were concerned, there was no improvement over the previous decades.[23] Japan's mortality rate during this period was much lower than other Asian countries and
comparable to France, Spain, and Eastern European countries.

The physical comfort and convenience of the people, however, continued
to improve with the greater use of electricity in homes, the development of bus
and railway transportation, and the widespread use of bicycles. By the end of
the 1930s, nine out of ten homes were wired for electric lighting, and all of the
11,500 towns and villages (with the exception of about 200 small and very re-
mote hamlets) had electricity.

The wages of the industrial workers did increase during this period. This
nevertheless still meant a very austere existence of minimal subsistence for the
working man.[24] This relatively slow rise in the standard of living at a time
when the modern sector of the economy was growing at such a substantial
pace is the result of numerous factors, such as considerable growth in population, a high rate of savings and investment, unfavorable price ratio in imports
and exports, high expenditures in armaments and strategic industries, and
tremendous costs in the colonies.

Another very important factor that contributed to holding down the standard of living, even in the face of remarkable growth in the modern sector of
the economy, was the vastly unequal distribution of wealth. A great body of
the peasant and urban working families still had annual incomes of less than
800 yen by 1930.[25]

The concentration of wealth at the top reflects the concentration of industrial and commercial enterprises in the hands of a few large business combines,
the *zaibatsu*. Depending on the scope of the definition, there were from ten to
twenty big business houses classified as zaibatsu in prewar Japan, and there
were four indisputably gigantic ones: Mitsui, Mitsubishi, Sumitomo, and Ya-

suda. These huge business houses owned powerful banks and extended their activities into all areas of industry and commerce. As immense as these businesses were, they all remained essentially family owned and run. Sumitomo enterprises were almost all controlled by one family, while the Mitsubishi combine was held and run by two Iwasaki families. The Mitsui interests were controlled by eleven branches of the Mitsui family that acted as a unit in accordance with formal household rules—policy was decided by a family council and 90 percent of the wealth was held collectively.

The machinery used to manage the vast holdings of these gigantic enterprises involved the domination of each combine by a holding company where the bulk of the house fortune was usually concentrated. From this point, company control was extended through "a network of subsidiaries and affiliates by inter-corporate stockholdings, interlocking directorates, management agreements, and loans from the combine bank."[26]

The House of Mitsui was the largest and most powerful of these combines. In early Meiji it was active in commerce and banking before moving into mining and lumbering. Subsequently it branched out into textiles, shipping, warehousing, sugar, metals and machinery, and many other industries. By 1937 it owned properties valued at 1.635 billion yen, while its control extended over a business empire that was worth a great deal more.

Yasuda remained by and large a banking combine, and in 1944 it controlled assets in excess of 40 billion yen in banking and 2 billion yen in other enterprises. Sumitomo was engaged in mining, but in 1945 it also had investments in 123 companies spread over thirty industries. The Mitsubishi combine in 1944 controlled 25 percent of the nation's shipping and shipbuilding.[27]

Curiously enough, despite the fact that giant combines dominated the economy, no single one of them had an outright monopoly in any industry, though there are a few isolated examples of companies that came very near to this. For instance, the Ōji Paper Company controlled 75 percent of the output of Western-style paper; and in the steel industry, Nippon Seitetsu (Japan Ironworks), which was formed by a merger of the government-operated Yawata Ironworks and six private companies, produced nearly all of the pig iron and 52 percent of the raw steel in Japan and Korea in 1934. In the main, however, several major firms collectively dominated most critical industrial areas.

The growth of the major combines was fostered by the government since it believed that large concerns were vital to the development of the nation's heavy industries, foreign trade, and colonial enterprise. There were also close links between government officials and the families of these huge businesses. An increasing number of top executives from the zaibatsu circle began occupying high government posts. The zaibatsu also developed close associations with the major political parties by providing them with considerable financial support.

Consequently, neither the government nor the political parties showed any inclination to curb the growth of large business combines through legislation. In 1927 the Japanese government reported that "Japan has no particular legislation forbidding or establishing control over trusts and cartels. The judicature has not concerned itself with this question."[28]

The lack of government restraints made it quite simple for the bigger firms to eliminate or absorb smaller competitors. Not only were the zaibatsu able to increase efficiency, cut costs, and hire more able men, but because they dominated the field of bank credit, they were able to maintain control over customers, suppliers, and even those competitors that they did not actually take over.

Unquestionably, the zaibatsu played a significant role in the rapid development of the Japanese economy by investing their profits in new enterprises, developing export markets, building strategic industries, innovating, and taking considerable risks. There is a negative side to this picture, however, and that is that they also contributed to the growing disparity between the rich few and the poor masses. Through the concentration of economic power at the top, they stifled the growth of a strong middle class while curbing the rise of a vigorous trade-union movement. The agricultural realm of the economy was also characterized by a concentration of wealth in the hands of a few.[29]

SOCIAL REFORM MOVEMENTS: LABOR

The labor problems created by industrialism also grew in magnitude as the modern sector of the economy expanded. The number of factory workers continued to increase, but their rights and welfare remained inadequately protected. The demand for export goods intensified during World War I, and even the minimal factory law of 1911 was violated. For instance, match factories used children under eight years of age to meet the demand created by the inability of the Swedish producers to export matches to Southeast Asia.

The workers were essentially at the mercy of a fluctuating economy that went into a state of boom and inflation during World War I. This, as we observed, brought about the violent rice riots of 1918. The boom was followed in 1920 by a depression in which exports dropped 25 percent and the price of manufactured goods and textiles dropped 50 to 60 percent. This resulted in a serious decline in production and the elimination of many companies that had emerged during the wartime boom. This depression also hit the countryside as the price of cocoons and rice dropped by 50 percent or more. The economy managed to pull out of the tailspin somewhat by 1922, but in 1927 it underwent an even more severe crisis. In between, extreme hardship befell the people as a consequence of the Great Earthquake of 1923.

Socialist leaders had remained somewhat inactive in the labor movement since the trial and execution of Kōtoku and his followers. Consequently, labor leadership had to come from a different direction. In 1912 Suzuki Bunji (1885–1946), a Christian social worker, organized the Yūaikai (Fraternal Association) and emphasized the need for harmony between labor and capital. This focus on cooperation secured for the organization the support of prominent business leaders such as Shibusawa.[30] After observing the labor movement in the United States in 1915, Suzuki changed his focus to some extent and began supporting the right of workers to organize and strike. Thus, the Yūaikai started to develop into a labor union, whereupon the political authorities and the employers began to harass its members. This change in the organization gained it additional supporters, however, from the ranks of college graduates. Among them was Nozaka Sanzō (1892–1993), who became a prominent leader of the Communist Party in the post–World War II period.

The socialists, led by Sakai Toshihiko, and anarchists like Ōsugi Sakae (1885–1923) and Arahata Kanson (1887–1981) began to move cautiously into the labor field again. Initially, the socialist movement was led by intellectuals and theorists who had little connection with the working class, so they failed to establish rapport with the workers.

An increasingly large number of strikes began to be staged, even though they were illegal.[31] There was a slight decline in strike activities during the early 1920s, but they began to increase again in the mid-1920s, with a growing number of workers joining unions.[32]

In 1919 the Yūaikai began to broaden its base as a labor organization and changed its name to Dainihon Rōdō Sōdōmei Yūaikai (The Yūaikai of the All Japan Federation of Labor). Its declaration of principles proclaimed, "Man is by nature free. The working man is a human being. He is not to be bought and sold in the wage market." Among its objectives were the freedom to organize labor unions, the elimination of child labor, and the establishment of minimum wages. It also called for universal suffrage, revision of the Police Regulation Law, and democratization of the educational system.

A major triumph for the labor movement was achieved in 1919 by the workers of the Kawasaki shipyards in Kobe. They won an agreement for an eight-hour workday by engaging in "sabotage," which involved slowing down the pace of work. Following this, the eight-hour workday was obtained by workers in other heavy industrial plants. Female workers in textile plants, however, still labored for eleven or twelve hours a day.

In 1920 the first May Day demonstration was staged in Tokyo and the participants called for a minimum-wage law, an eight-hour workday, a solution to the unemployment problem, and repeal of the Police Regulation Law. The Yūaikai held its national meeting in the same year, and the tone of the organization showed a significant change, with the more radical leaders speaking in terms of overthrowing the capitalists and capturing the means of production for the workers. There were still some who believed in working within the existing system, such as Kagawa Toyohiko, a Christian social worker (see page 228), and they became increasingly disenchanted by the growing militancy of the advocates of direct action.

In the 1920s the struggle for leadership between the radicals and moderates continued. The syndicalists, led by Arahata, resorted to direct militant action whenever the opportunity presented itself, while the moderates continued through peaceful means to struggle for collective bargaining, protection against unemployment, and retirement payments. In 1921 a major labor dispute broke out at the Kawasaki and Mitsubishi shipyards in Kobe. The companies used the lockout, and then the governor of Hyōgo prefecture moved army troops against the strikers, arresting more than three hundred leaders and thus effectively breaking the strike. This diminished the influence of the moderates such as Kagawa, and greatly enhanced the following of the syndicalists and the Marxists in the unions.

After the Great Earthquake of 1923, strikes again began to increase along with a swelling in the membership of unions. However, leadership struggles and cleavages continued to undermine and weaken the movement. In 1925 the Communist-led unions broke from the All Japan Federation of Labor and organized the Labor Council (Rōdō Hyōgikai).

In the meanwhile, the political authorities were becoming somewhat more flexible. In 1925, for example, the Police Regulation Law was revised to eliminate the restrictions imposed on labor activities. At the same time, however, laws were adopted providing for compulsory arbitration in public enterprises and defense industries, and control of violence in labor disputes.

A depression preceding the worldwide Great Depression struck Japan early in 1927 and dealt the labor movement a severe setback. Labor, in fact, never recovered from this as Japan then moved on to militarism, and the government tightened its control over all aspects of the society, including labor movements.

AGRARIAN REFORM MOVEMENTS

The efforts in the cities to organize factory workers were mirrored in the rural areas by like attempts to organize tenant farmers. As noted previously, agrarian poverty resulted in a steady rise in tenancy. In 1917, 51.7 percent of the cultivated land was under tenancy with the tenants paying an average of 51 to 55 percent of the harvest as rent. Compared to a factory worker, a tenant's income was beggarly.[33]

Disputes over rental rates began to increase after the recession of 1920, and the urban intellectuals and social workers moved into the countryside to organize the tenant farmers. In 1922 the All Japan Farmers Union (Nihon Nōmin Kumiai) was organized by Kagawa and other Christian leaders. Reflecting Kagawa's idealism, the union called for mutual aid, love and friendship, rejection of violence, and the uplifting of the peasants' lives. By 1926 there were more than 150,000 members in the union.[34] The number of tenant disputes ran from 1,500 to 2,000 per year from 1921 to 1925, and hit a high of over 2,700 in 1926. In many cases the altercations were settled by compromise, but in some instances the landlords got court orders to prevent the farmers from entering the fields held in tenancy. The landlords had the law on their side, thus creating a situation in which it was almost impossible for the tenant unions to make much headway. Nevertheless, they did succeed in getting rents reduced to some extent. After the Manchurian Incident of 1931 and the upsurge of right-wing nationalism, the tenant movement collapsed.

THE OUTCASTES AND THE SUIHEISHA

Despite the fact that legal discrimination against the burakumin had been abolished in 1871, social discrimination against these so-called outcastes continued. They still lived in separate communities, suffered discrimination in jobs, and were restricted to endogamous marriages.

Another aspect of the general reform movement that was emerging in the Taishō era was the effort launched by the outcaste leaders in 1922 to organize the Suiheisha (Levelers Society) for the purpose of pursuing their struggle for equality. The government extended financial aid to the burakumin communities after the rice riots, in which a large number of eta were involved. The eta leaders, however, rejected this paternalistic approach and contended that true freedom could only be achieved through their own efforts. They urged their fellow burakumin to take pride in their heritage and fight for their dignity as well as economic and occupational freedom.

Initially, the Suiheisha leaders encouraged their members to denounce and extract public apologies from anyone who in any way insulted or expressed contempt for the burakumin. They hoped to eradicate social discrimination by taking aggressive actions against individual wrongdoers, but not surprisingly, this approach tended to harden and internalize the resentment and disdain that the other classes felt toward them. Consequently, the leaders decided that the social system itself had to be transformed, and they began to link their movement with the Marxist, proletarian class struggle.

MOVEMENT FOR WOMEN'S RIGHTS

Meiji Japan may have legally abolished the Tokugawa social class system, but it did nothing to change the status of women. They were still considered to be inferior beings subject to the control of the patriarchal head of the family. Legally, daughters could marry without the consent of the parents at the age of twenty-five, but this seldom, if ever, happened. Marriages were almost invariably arranged by the parents. "Marriage for the Japanese girl meant losing individual freedom," wrote one feminist leader. "The relationship between man and wife in a Japanese home is not that of two supplementary personalities, but that of master and servant. It is the relation between the absolute possessor and the property."[35]

The wife was treated as a minor by law. She could not enter into any contract without her husband's consent; her property was placed at the disposal of her husband; she could be divorced easily without her husband being required to provide for her livelihood; and in the event of divorce, the children were kept by the husband. Family property was inherited by the eldest son, with daughters seldom being given a share.

Except for factory work, few women were employed in the business or professional fields. The employment of married women in particular was very uncommon, and even those who worked in factories were released upon marriage. Politically, women were not only denied the franchise, but the 1890 Police Regulation Law prohibited them from joining political parties and even forbade them from sponsoring or attending public political discussions.

Female literary figures initiated the movement aimed at gaining recognition of rights for women. Among the leaders was Hiratsuka Raichō (1886–1971), who started a women's literary organization called the Seitō (Blue Stocking) Society in 1911.[36] The main purpose of this group was to discover and develop the hidden talent, particularly literary capability, in women. It may not have sought the liberation of all women, but it did, nonetheless, constitute a pioneer effort in combating the ingrained customs that fettered Japanese women. The feminist leaders were willing to defy public opinion and challenge the conventional mores.

As might be expected, members of the Seitō Society were subjected to hostile criticisms, and their journal, advocating equal rights for women, was suppressed by the authorities. These actions, however, only served to inflame the members, who then went on to defy the established mores all the more vehemently. Hiratsuka rejected the existing marital system and practiced community living with a younger male artist. Another feminist, Itō Noe, refused to accept the marital arrangement made for her by her parents and turned for intellectual inspiration to the anarchist Emma Goldman (1869–1940). Itō became increasingly conscious of the social injustices around her, and she grew steadily more radical. Eventually she became the companion of Ōsugi Sakae, the leading Taishō anarchist. She once wrote,

> When I was in girls' school all our teachers taught us that in order to attain happiness we must learn to be satisfied with our lot. They taught us to eliminate all the impulses that emanated from within our hearts. Why do they not teach us to destroy the environment and customs for the sake of the impulses that stir up from within?[37]

Hiratsuka began to work for equal political rights for women around 1919. She had the assistance of Ichikawa Fusae (1893–1981), who was active in the Yūaikai, and others in circulating a petition calling for the revision of the Police Regulation Law, which prohibited women from engaging in political activities. They also asked for measures that would prevent men afflicted with venereal diseases from getting married.

In 1920 the feminists organized the New Women's Association (Shin Fujinkyōkai) and asked not only for equal opportunities for women but also for the protection of the rights of mothers and children. They sponsored numerous lecture series on a variety of subjects for the purpose of uplifting the political, social, and cultural awareness of women; published a journal; and agitated for universal suffrage. Their efforts did not produce much in the way of immediate results. In 1922, however, women were granted the right to sponsor and listen to political speeches, even though they were still prohibited from joining or organizing a political party.

In 1924 the League for the Attainment of Women's Political Rights (Fujin Sanseiken Kakutoku Kiseidōmei) was organized, mainly by middle-class women. At the same time, a socialist women's organization, the Sekiran (Red Waves) Society, was started by those who believed that discrimination against women was a by-product of the capitalistic system. A number of women remained active in socialist and Communist circles and endured persecution and imprisonment. Among other organizations involved in "Women's Issues" were the Young Women's Christian Association (YWCA) and the Women's Christian Temperance Union, both affiliated with their American counterpart organizations.

Higher education for women was still limited even in the 1920s. The first women's college was established in 1911, and by 1928 there were only 37 college-level institutions for women, as compared to 222 for men. There were 161,430 men in colleges or universities and only 14,127 women.

An increasingly large number of girls were beginning to be employed in white-collar jobs as typists, telephone operators, and clerks, but they were paid anywhere from one-half to two-thirds of the pay that men received for the same work. The society still looked upon these business women with considerable disdain.

The status of women was measurably enhanced by the emergence of a number of prominent females in the entertainment world. Miura Tamaki became a world renowned opera singer, gaining fame for her renditions in *Madame Butterfly.* Matsui Sumako became the first Japanese female stage star, appearing as Nora in Ibsen's *A Doll's House.* She uplifted the acting profession, which was held in low esteem, to the level of respectability. Her personal life outside the theater was publicly known, and, like her career, it too clashed with existing conventions. For years she carried on a love affair with her teacher, who was a married man with children. The movies and the female stars who emerged from them also became a vehicle for advancing the status of women. Such stars as Kurishima Sumiko (1902–1987) frequently outclassed their male counterparts in popularity.

DEMOCRATIC AND SOCIALISTIC POLITICAL MOVEMENTS

The Taishō era was a period in which democratic concepts gained considerable support and influence. The chief spokesman for the theoretical underpinnings of this movement was Yoshino Sakuzō (1878–1933), a Christian humanist and a professor at the Imperial University of Tokyo. He did not advocate the establishment of a democracy in which sovereignty would reside with the people *(minshu-shugi).* What he propounded was a democracy in which the government would be rooted in the people and have as its main goal their general well-being *(mimpon-shugi).* Public opinion would be the deciding force in politics, but it was not to be simply an assessment of what the masses thought about a particular subject. The ideas that constitute public opinion would be originally formulated by a group of thinkers who would then have to win popular support for them. These ideas would have no moral value or political validity unless they received popular support. In the political system, public opinion would have to be represented by universal suffrage and party government. Yoshino's moderate political philosophy certainly did not appeal to the growing circle of socialists, but his ideas did find a receptive audience in liberal intellectuals, and his advocacy of universal (manhood) suffrage gave a strong boost to that movement.

Radical political thinking was represented by a wide range of socialist thinkers extending from democratic socialists, Bolsheviks, syndicalists, to anarchists. In December 1920 a rather motley group set about organizing the Socialist League (Shakaishugi Dōmei). Among the more prominent leaders were Sakai Toshihiko, the veteran socialist agitator, Yamakawa Hitoshi (1880–1958), who had turned from Christianity to socialism, and Arahata Kanson, an anarcho-syndicalist. Probably the most interesting of the lot was Ōsugi Sakae, an anarchist agitator who was something of a charismatic leader. He was the son of a military officer, but his political awareness was initially aroused by an antimilitary article written by Kōtoku. Ōsugi, like many other socialists, was also influenced by Christianity. He was baptized by a fiery evangelist, Ebina Danjō (1856–1937), who ironically enough was a right-wing nationalist.

Ōsugi was, to be sure, a dedicated anarchist and a defiant individualist, but perhaps above all he was a romantic. He said:

> I like that which is spiritual. But I dislike theorizing about it. . . . For this reason I really abhor scholars of law and government who talk about mimpon [see above] and humanity. . . . I have a strong aversion for socialism also. At times I even feel a distaste for anarchism. What I like above all is the blind actions of men, the natural explosion of the spirit. There must be freedom of thought, freedom of action, and freedom of impulses.[38]

The Socialist League was disbanded by the government just six months after its inception, but it nevertheless played a critical role in bringing together the labor leaders and the socialists. This was vitally important because until this point, the labor leaders never fully trusted these intellectuals and theorists who had never worked in factories. As a result of this cooperative venture, the influence of the anarchists and syndicalists came to be felt strongly in the labor movement. In fact, the cleavage they created between the radicals and the moderates rather effectively disrupted the Yūaikai.

The Socialist League itself was torn by internal dissension—there was constant feuding between the anarchists led by Ōsugi and the Marxists led by Sakai and Yamakawa. Ōsugi believed that the centralization of authority in Soviet Russia had destroyed the revolution; the Bolsheviks had been too eager to restore order. He maintained that if they had allowed anarchic conditions to prevail a bit longer, something approximating Kropotkin's ideal society would surely have come about. The socialists were divided further by the split between the revisionists, who took the name "Social Democrats," and the orthodox Marxists, who then used the term "Communists."

In July 1922, Yamakawa, Sakai, Arahata, and Tokuda Kyūichi (1894–1953), who became the leader of the Communist Party in the postwar period, secretly organized the Japanese Communist Party (Nihon Kyōsantō), with Sakai as the chairman of the central committee. The party then received the official recognition of the fourth Congress of the Comintern.

Yamakawa and the other Communists held a negative attitude toward universal suffrage and were disinclined to support the bourgeois parliamentary system because it contributed to the fortification of capitalistic control. How-ever, the Comintern under Bukharin directed the party leaders to support the bourgeois liberals in their fight against the semifeudalistic forces that were still in control of Japan. The Bukharin Theses held that the Communists must be-gin work for the overthrow of the emperor and the monarchic form of govern-ment by initiating a democratic revolution. Hence, it was clear that they had to work for universal suffrage if they hoped to realize their goals.

In 1923, the government arrested the Communist leaders after obtaining the party membership list through an informer. In order to curb Socialist and Communist activities, the government established the Higher Police Bureau in a number of prefectures. The task of this department was to combat advocates of "dangerous thought," an ever-growing category that began to encompass a larger and larger number of independent thinkers.

After their release, the Communist leaders voted to dissolve the party on the ground that the time was not yet ripe for the establishment of a Communist Party in Japan. The authorities, however, did not cease harassing the Commu-nists. In 1925 the government, headed by Katō Kōmei, drafted the Peace Preservation Law, which made it illegal to advocate either change in the na-tional polity or the abolition of private property.

Efforts were made to organize a broadly based Socialist party, but the cleav-age between the social democrats and the Communists kept the proletarian forces fragmented. By the end of 1926 there were several parties: the pro-Communist Rōdō Nōmintō (Labor-Farmer Party), headed by Ōyama Ikuo; the Socialist right-wing Shakai Minshūtō (Social Mass Party), led by Abe Isoo (1865–1949) and Yoshino Sakuzō; and the Ninhon Rōnōtō (Japan Labor-Farmer Party), led by Asō Hisashi (1891–1940), which stood midway between the first two parties. The Labor-Farmer Party was in effect an auxiliary of the Communist Party, while the Social Mass Party was closely affiliated with the Ni-hon Rōdō Sōdōmei (All Japan Federation of Labor). There was also the con-servative and nationalistic Nihon Nōmintō (Japan Farmer Party).

All of these various Socialist parties were to continue to split and unite in a chaotic fashion, while seriously diminishing their influence and effectiveness. Some began to swing to the right and organize nationalistic, Socialist parties; others aligned themselves with the militarists.

The Communists sought to revive their party under the leadership of younger men in late 1926, while some of the older leaders, such as Yamakawa and Arahata, fell out of favor with the Comintern and were consequently iso-lated from the movement. The new organization was first led by Fukumoto Kazuo (1894–1983), who sought to purge the party of fellow travelers and so-cial democrats because he held that it should consist exclusively of pure Marx-ist thinkers. In 1927 the Comintern condemned Fukumotism for its stress on the intelligentsia and ordered the party to get involved with the workers and peasants in order to achieve the socialist revolution.

The fragmentation in the socialistic political movement made it difficult for candidates from any of these parties to succeed in Diet elections. For example, in the 1928 election, the left-wing parties managed to win only eight seats (four of the victors were members of the Social Mass Party).

The government under General Tanaka Giichi, who became prime minister in April 1927, launched a vigorous campaign to ferret out and persecute the Communists. On March 15, 1928, midnight raids were staged throughout the country, and 1,600 persons were arrested. Torture was used freely during the interrogation of these men. The victims were beaten over their heads with bamboo poles, stabbed with thick needles, kicked, hung upside-down with their heads bounced on the floor, or repeatedly choked until they became unconscious. The proletarian writer Kobayashi Takiji (1903–1933), who wrote a novel exposing such brutalities, was himself arrested, and after several hours of "questioning" he died. Mass arrests of Communists and those suspected of being Communists continued into the 1930s, until the backbone of the movement was crushed. This relentless persecution of those who harbored "dangerous thought" resulted in many incarcerated Communists "converting" to the "imperial way" and renouncing their ideology.[39]

Marxism had a considerable number of supporters in the academic community with many professors and students participating in Marxist study groups. The Red hunt, however, also hit the universities, and a great many students were arrested while more than a few prominent scholars were dismissed from their positions.

In comparison to Marxism, Western liberalism, which entered Japan in early Meiji, constituted a much less serious threat to the traditional institutions, values, and way of life. To be sure, liberalism's stress on the worth and importance of the individual certainly challenged the traditional group-oriented values and lifestyle, but it did not seek to bring about changes through violence or revolution. It was essentially an optimistic philosophy holding that self-interest would serve the good of the whole society. Its emphasis on reason and science was in tune with the desire of the ruling elite to modernize and industrialize the country. The Meiji liberals accepted the emperor system, supported nationalism, and stopped just short of introducing self-interest into the family. They upheld social classes insofar as they believed that the propertied class, the middle class, should play a dominant role in society.

Marxism, in contrast, was primarily a revolutionary political movement. It rejected the emperor system and the propertied class and advocated class struggles, thus challenging the traditional emphasis on social harmony. It was rigid and doctrinaire, offering only an either/or choice of becoming a Marxist or a slave of capitalism. Hence, it conflicted with the traditional proclivity for compromise. It forsook nationalism while looking to a foreign authority for guidance.

Initially, however, the Japanese Socialists and Communists were not good Marxists; they were not at all well-versed in Marxian doctrines. In fact, the most potent influence on the early Socialists was Christian humanism, although many of them drifted away from it later in their lives. For instance, the founders of the Social Democratic Party, such as Katayama Sen and Abe Isoo, were Christians. Even Kōtoku, who denied that he was a Christian, was obsessed to the very end of his life with the problem of coping with Christianity.

The most influential of the Christian social reformers was Kagawa Toyohiko (1888–1960), who was born into a wealthy merchant family and devoted a major portion of his life to helping the industrial and agrarian poor. He was baptized at the age of sixteen and began working and preaching in the slums of Kobe at the age of twenty-one. He caught a variety of communicable diseases while living in the slums, including trachoma, which nearly blinded him. He nevertheless continued his evangelical work, pursued his own education, published a number of works based on his experiences in the slums, and participated in labor and agrarian reform movements. By 1920 he had become a prominent figure as both a Christian evangelist and a social reformer. His influence in the labor movement began to decline, however, as the anarchists, syndicalists, and Marxists extended their control, but he remained an active social reformer. Yamamuro Gumpei (1872–1940), the founder of the Salvation Army in Japan, compared Kagawa to St. Francis of Assisi, and he was often ranked with Albert Schweitzer by his American admirers.

Notes

1. Its balance of payments, which was unfavorable just prior to the war, shifted, so that by the end of the war it had accumulated a favorable balance of 2.8 billion yen.

2. From a wage index 100 in 1914, it dropped to 68 by 1918. Taking the year 1914 as index 100, in 1916 the price index rose to 144, and by 1918 it was up to 230.

3. A total of 700,000 people took part in the disturbances, and more than 1,000 of them were killed or injured. The government called out army troops and arrested 25,000 persons when the police failed to quell the rioters; more than 700 were prosecuted, and 71 were sentenced to prison for ten years or more.

4. The only surviving original genrō at this time were Yamagata and Matsukata; Inoue had died in 1915, and Ōyama in 1916. Saionji was the sole new addition to the clique of genrō.

5. One source estimates that whereas there were fewer than 100 Chinese students in Japan in 1900, by 1906 there were 13,000. In 1924, 50 percent of the executive-committee members of China's Nationalist Party had been educated in Japan. Between 1903 and 1921, 42.5 percent of all Chinese students studying abroad were in Japan.

6. The following list of sympathetic Japanese suggests the nature of the support that Sun and the Chinese revolutionaries attracted: Tōyama Mitsuru (ultranationalist), Inukai

Tsuyoshi (champion of parliamentary government), Kita Ikki (radical nationalist; 1883–1937), and Kōtoku Shūsui (radical socialist).

7. Tōyama and Inukai supported these continental rōnin, one of the more prominent of whom was Miyazaki Torazō, who became Sun Yat-sen's close friend and supporter.

8. It also asked to establish joint Chinese and Japanese police forces wherever necessary; to purchase 50 percent or more of China's arms from Japan, or else establish joint Sino-Japanese arsenals that would employ Japanese engineers and use Japanese materials; and to grant to Japan the right to construct railroads in south China.

9. The agreement, however, brought few actual benefits to Japan while it stirred up tremendous Chinese hostility. The governments that succeeded the Yuan regime never recognized the legitimacy of the concessions gained by the Japanese.

10. From 1902 to 1907, some 39,531 Japanese immigrants came directly to the mainland from Japan, and 32,855 arrived from Hawaii.

11. This despite the fact that Japanese private citizens contributed more money to that city's recovery from the 1906 earthquake there than the rest of the world combined.

12. The United States limited its expeditionary force to 7,000 men whereas Japan eventually dispatched 72,000 soldiers into Siberia.

13. By the end of 1918, one firm had acquired about 122,000 acres of rice paddy and 49,000 acres of dry land.

14. There were about 200,000 Christians in Korea out of a total population of 20 million.

15. Japanese officials reported 1,962 Korean casualties and close to 20,000 arrests.

16. As a matter of fact, the number of police actually increased tremendously, from about 1,400 to 16,900.

17. The per capita consumption of rice by Koreans was 78 *shō* (1 shō equals 3.81 pints) in 1912, and this figure dropped to 60 shō in 1918, and then down to 41 shō in 1933. Japanese rice consumption, in contrast, came to 115 shō.

18. The output per worker in the modern sector increased by about 6 percent annually, as compared to 2–3 percent in the traditional sector.

19. Taking the years 1910–1914 as index 100, by 1925–1929 manufacturing production had risen to 313, the volume of imports to 242, and exports to 217. As for specific industries, manufacturing production in the textile industry increased from index 100 in 1910–1914 to 270 in 1925–1929; metals and machinery increased to 355 in the same period; chemicals and ceramics to 453; electricity and gas to 653. The number of factories that were equipped with power machinery increased from 9,155 in 1909 to 48,555 in 1929. The number of factory workers increased from 1,012,000 in 1909 to 2,384,000 in 1929. At the same time, however, the number of small factories remained high. In 1934 there were a million workshops employing less than five workers. In 1909 the percentage of private factories employing between five and nine workers was 52.1, and in 1934 it was 56.5.

20. For instance, taking the year 1910–1914 as index 100, agricultural production rose to 129 by 1925–1929, fisheries to 299, and mining to 157. Food production rose to 135 while the population rose to 125 (that is, from 50.6 million to 61 million).

21. The percentage of workers engaged in the primary industries of agriculture, fishing, and mining declined from 81 in 1880 to 69 in 1900, and then to 55.4 in 1920, but it was still as high as 51.1 in 1930.

22. There was, however, a 40 percent increase in the use of all clothing fibers per person. During the decade after 1926, there was little change in the per capita intake of food, which remained at about 2,300 calories per day.

23. In fact, during 1921–1925, male life expectancy dropped somewhat to 42.06 years compared to 43.97 years in 1899–1903 and 44.25 years in 1909–1913.

24. Taking the year 1914 as index 100, wages rose to 317 by 1925–1929. This apparently dramatic increase was offset by the cost of living, which rose from 100 to 204. Thus, the increase in real wages came to 55 percent. The average urban worker earned an income of 3 yen (about seventy-five cents) a day in 1935–1936, and he had to spend at least a third of it to maintain even the simplest diet. His rural counterpart subsisted on a still smaller income. A comparison of real consumption per capita in Japan and the United States (in terms of 1955 dollars) reveals that in 1910, it was $156 for Japan and $723 for the United States; in 1925, it was $248 and $955; in 1940, it was $196 and $1,084. Alan H. Gleason, "Economic Growth and Consumption in Japan," in *The State and Economic Enterprise in Japan,* ed. William W. Lockwood (Princeton: Princeton University Press, 1965), pp. 439–440.

25. They constituted 10.6 million out of 12.6 million families, but they were the recipients of only half of the country's household income. At the top, about 24,000 families (a scant 0.0019 percent of the nation's total households), with incomes exceeding 10,000 yen, possessed over 10 percent of the aggregate family income. Above this group at the uppermost level, nineteen households had incomes over 1 million yen, and, at the very bottom, 2,232,000 families (18 percent of the nation's total households) received 200 yen or less, constituting a mere 3.8 percent of the national household income.

26. William W. Lockwood, *The Economic Development of Japan: Growth and Structural Change, 1863–1938* (Princeton: Princeton University Press, 1954), p. 215.

27. Also 15 percent of coal and metals, 16 percent of warehousing, 16 percent of the bank loans, 21 to 35 percent of electrical equipment, 50 percent of flour milling, 59 percent of sheet glass, 35 percent of sugar, and 15 percent of cotton textiles.

28. Lockwood, *The Economic Development of Japan,* p. 220.

29. After World War I there was a slight tendency toward dispersion of landownership, but in 1935, some 3,415 big landowners owned 4.7 percent of the nation's cultivated land, while 4,765,000 farm families, each with holdings of less than 7.35 acres, owned only 56 percent.

30. By 1916 the membership had swelled to 10,000.

31. In 1914 there were 50 strikes, involving only about 7,900 workers; but in 1919 there were 497 strikes, in which more than 63,000 workers participated.

32. In 1921 there were 103,400 union members, while in 1926 there were about 385,000. This, however, constituted only 6 to 7 percent of the industrial workers.

33. For example, around 1917–1920 in Aichi Prefecture, a factory worker earned from 1 yen 80 sen to 2 yen 50 sen a day whereas a tenant's income varied from 75 sen to 1 yen a day.

34. Subsequently, other tenant unions were organized, and by 1927, more than 365,000 men were in unions, encompassing 7 percent of all farm families.

35. Shidzue Ishimoto, *Facing Two Ways: The Story of My Life* (New York: Farrar & Rinehart, 1935), p. 349.

36. Named after the mid-nineteenth-century British women's reform society.

37. Itō Noe Zenshū, *The Complete Works of Itō Noe,* 2 vols. (Tokyo: Gakugei Shorin, 1970), vol. 2, p. 19.

38. Masumi Junnosuke, *Nihon Seitōshiron* (Discourses on the History of Japanese Political Parties), 4 vols. (Tokyo: Tōkyō Daigaku Shuppankai, 1965–1968), vol. 4, pp. 142–143.

39. The conversion of two prominent leaders in June 1933 was followed by 548 persons then under arrest or in jail disavowing communism. As a matter of fact, only a handful of leaders, including the postwar Communist leaders Tokuda Kyūichi and Shiga Yoshio (1901–1989), refused to recant.

11

The Era of Parliamentary Ascendancy (II)

CULTURE OF THE TAISHŌ ERA

The Taishō era was a period during which such concepts as individual rights, freedom, and democracy flourished in the intellectual and cultural realms. The Taishō intellectuals were not burdened with the task of "enriching and strengthening" the nation as were their predecessors in the Meiji era. These thinkers grew up in a relatively carefree atmosphere at a time when Japan had already joined the ranks of the world's major powers. The educational level of the people had been raised, and the intellectual and cultural sophistication of the better-educated members of the society had been heightened. Consequently, this was also a period during which a "cultural elite," who cherished "cultural refinement," flourished. The number of well-educated urban dwellers had steadily increased as the economy expanded and the society was modernized. There was a growing number of professional men, executives, engineers, technicians, and office workers as well as government employees, educators, writers, and entertainers. These people made up the core of those who enjoyed and participated in Taishō culture.

Taishō Japan was also characterized by a thriving popular culture. Popular novels, magazines, newspapers, and the new media of radio and motion pictures disseminated "culture" into the countryside and the lower levels of the cultural and intellectual spectrum.

In order to meet the demand for better-educated workers, the number of colleges, higher schools, and middle schools increased significantly. By 1925 there were thirty-four universities, twenty-nine higher schools, and eighty-four professional schools.[1]

A strong sense of individualism was manifested in the literary world through the White Birch *(Shirakaba)* School, whose journal was first published in 1910. The men who belonged to this school were usually young members of the upper class, most of whom had attended the aristocratic Peers School. The philosophy of the White Birch School was explained by Mushanokōji Saneatsu (1885–1976), who said the purpose of life was to be in harmony with the "will of mankind." This could be achieved by living in accordance with one's individual attributes or by letting one's individual personality have free play. The individual must place his trust in his own "spirit." "I do not believe that my spirit is only my own," wrote Mushanokōji. "It has something in common with the spirit of all mankind. . . . What I desire is what mankind desires."[2] Mushanokōji's philosophy was based upon the optimistic notion that "true happiness can be achieved by acting in accordance with the dictates of one's conscience. The value of man is found in the fact that the pursuit of one's authentic self-interest leads to the well-being of all of mankind."[3] This is not, however, to be confused with the prosaic concept of self-interest that was held by the nineteenth-century political economists. Mushanokōji's concept was that of an artist who believed in having "a heart that dances together with nature and mankind."[4]

In emphasizing the importance of individuality and the supremacy of subjectivity, Mushanokōji's circle made a deep impression on the Taishō youths. It induced some, who responded by limiting their attention to their own private lives, their immediate family members, friends, and nature, to become increasingly indifferent to the society in which they lived.

In turning inward to their private lives, the writers of the White Birch School produced a form of autobiographical fiction referred to as the "I" novel. The motivation for this kind of expression can be found in the remarks that Mushanokōji jotted down after being deeply impressed by the paintings of the French expressionists.

> A heart wants to embrace another heart. But man fears it for the sake of his own existence. He conceals where his heart is. He believes such an attitude is necessary to maintain his position in society. Thus every heart feels lonely. Recent art seems to be trying to satisfy this yearning. I feel that recent art is the exposing of one's heart boldly on paper, waiting for another heart to come to it to embrace it.[5]

The object of the "I" novel, then, was to bring the heart of the reader into contact with the heart of the writer.

The most influential author of autobiographical fiction was Shiga Naoya (1883–1971), whose great success with confessional stories induced many young writers to follow his example. "I" novels came to dominate the literary scene to such a considerable extent that Shiga earned the acclaim of having influenced contemporary Japanese literature more than any other modern writer. Philosophically, he held with the doctrine of the supremacy of subjectivity as espoused by the White Birch School, and this led him to make his likes and dislikes the yardstick for good and evil. In his writings he dealt mostly with his feelings about his family and about nature.

The other prominent writer of this school was Arishima Takeo (1878–1923). He had studied in the United States, where he attended Haverford and Harvard, and was deeply influenced by both Christian humanism and socialism. His desire to become a part of the social reform movement was so enthusiastic and sincere that he gave his 1,000-acre farm in Hokkaido to the tenants working the land. They were to operate the farm as a communal enterprise even though Arishima was convinced that communalism could not possibly succeed as long as the society remained capitalistic. However, as a member of the upper class he believed he had no right to meddle in the business of the proletariat. The working class, as far as Arishima was concerned, did not need the support of the intellectuals or scholars, not even of luminaries like Kropotkin or Marx. The struggle and eventual triumph of the working man will come out of his own proletarian experience. Arishima wanted desperately to participate in that struggle, but he could not do so because he was not a member of the working class. His growing sense of social impotence thrust him into a state of nihilistic despair, and seeking to find the ultimate meaning of life in love, he committed suicide with a female magazine reporter in 1923. The philosophical rationale for this final act can perhaps be found in his theory that if there are three stages to human life—habitual, intellectual, and instinctive—true freedom is found in the instinctive or impulsive phase.

A group of young writers who were influenced by Natsume Sōseki started a literary journal called *Shin Shichō* (New Thought). Among them, Kikuchi Kan (1888–1948) started his literary career by writing serious literature in which he sought to uncover the realities of life, but he soon abandoned the search for profound "truths" and shifted to writing for mass readership. His primary objective was no longer the creation of "pure" literature; he now sought to write entertaining stories by focusing upon a single aspect of human behavior, such as egoism, and treating it in a way that would appeal to the emotions of the reader. He may be accused of having succumbed to commercialism, but he did nevertheless contribute immensely to the popularization of literature.

The most brilliant member of the *Shin Shichō* circle was Akutagawa Ryūnosuke (1892–1927), whose work has been described as a manifestation of "pure intellect and refinement." Essentially, he had a pessimistic, almost cynical, attitude toward life, which he viewed as a wretched affair in which man is hopelessly entrapped in his egoism. Early in his work, Akutagawa was able to depict this with a sense of detachment, satirizing human foibles in a humorous vein. He also sought to find meaning in life through a philosophy that holds art to be transcendent above all else. "Life," he said, "is not worth one line of Baudelaire." Akutagawa could not, however, completely avoid ethical issues even though he believed that "morality was another name for convenience," and ultimately he lost confidence in the meaningfulness of art itself.

Akutagawa believed that unexpected events continuously prevent man from achieving happiness and the fulfillment of his desires. This view is reflected in the plot of "Jigokuhen" (The Hell Screen). In the story a court artist, who was commissioned by his lord to paint a screen depicting a scene in hell, asks that a woman be burned in a carriage so as to enable him to paint a realistic picture of a person burning in hell. The lord accedes to his request, but when the artist comes to paint the scene he finds that the victim, chained to the carriage, is his only daughter. He paints his masterpiece and then kills himself.

Akutagawa fell deeper and deeper into the abyss of pessimism, and his thoughts were drawn increasingly toward death. In one of his later works he wrote, "If by chance we are made to feel the attraction of death, it is very difficult to escape from it. And as if we are going around a concentric circle we are drawn gradually toward death." Finally, in 1927, he committed suicide, saying he felt "a vague sense of uneasiness about the future." To his children he left the words, "Do not forget that life is a battle that leads to death. If you are defeated in this battle of life commit suicide like your father."[6]

The writing career of Tanizaki Junichirō (1886–1965) extends from the Taishō to the postwar eras. He was influenced by such Western writers as Baudelaire, Poe, and Wilde, and in his early writings he revealed a strong interest in the sensuous as well as in sadomasochism. Tanizaki worshipped female pulchritude and considered men as being merely "manure" for the nurturing of feminine beauty, which often leads the men in his writings to commit abnormal acts of masochism and fetishism. Man's true happiness, in Tanizaki's opinion, consisted in being conquered by women.

Like many of his fellow writers who were opposed to naturalism, Tanizaki concentrated on evoking mood and atmosphere rather than defining things in concrete detail. His advice to aspiring writers was, "Do not try to be too clear, leave some gaps in the meaning. We Japanese scorn the bald fact, and we consider it good form to keep a thin sheet of paper between the fact and object, and the words that give expression to it."[7] He also believed that the Japanese prefer to see beauty left in the shadows rather than exposed to the harsh lights of critical scrutiny. "In the mansion called literature," he wrote, "I would have the eaves deep and the walls dark, I would push back into the shadows the things that come forward too clearly."[8]

Another writer whose literary career spanned more than half a century was Nagai Kafū (1879–1959), who started out as a naturalist writer but soon turned for his subject matter to traditional Japan, manifesting particular nostalgia for the city of Edo. This shift in focus was fostered by his visit to France, where he was struck by the strong and enriching influence that traditional culture had on that country. He developed an intense dislike of what he considered the "false civilization" that had emerged in Japan as a consequence of the impact of an alien, that is, Western, civilization. He came to manifest a reverence toward the past. "Let us be respectful of the past," he wrote. "The past is the mystical spring from which the future must always flow. It is the torch lighting the uncertain way of the present."[9]

To find remnants of the past, Nagai turned to the brothels of Tokyo, where the old ways of Japan were still preserved. He extolled feminine beauty, but this was not his primary interest. The life of the geisha fascinated him for its manifestation of the manners and mores of traditional Japan. Later in his career he turned his attention to the modern counterparts of the geisha, that is, the café girls, the street walkers, and the dance hall girls.

Proletarian literature was given impetus during this period by the increasing activities of the socialists and the Communists. The proletarian writers, in some ways similar to the naturalists, were unconcerned about literary style and concentrated on an almost scientifically precisioned treatment of reality. Unlike the naturalists, they focused exclusively on the life of the working classes. A few novels dealing with the plight of the impoverished had been written before the Taishō era. The most prominent of these, *Earth* by Nagatsuka Takashi (1879–1915), was published in 1910; it depicted the very difficult and bleak life of the peasants. In 1921 a journal devoted to proletarian literature, *The Sowers of Seeds,* came into existence.

A considerable number of proletarian novels were published, but because Marxist writers believed that art and literature should serve political ends, much of the work followed the pat formula of socialist realism or were rather blatantly dogmatic propaganda tracts. Few revealed any serious literary quality. One writer, indignant at the proletarian disregard for the conventions of style and form, exclaimed, "Who is it that's destroying the flower garden?" Kobayashi Takiji wrote one of the best-known proletarian novels. In his *Cannery Boat,* published in 1929, Kobayashi described realistically the terrible conditions under which the crews of fishing and canning boats had to work.

A group of young writers referred to as the neoperceptionists emerged as a reaction against the socialist realism of their proletarian counterparts. Their objective was to reaffirm the importance of literary values. Among them was Kawabata Yasunari (1899–1972), the winner of the Nobel Prize for Literature in 1968. The first of his works to be widely read was *The Izu Dancer,* written in

1926, and he continued writing until his death. He was not a prolific author, but all his works have been praised for their lyrical qualities. E. G. Seidensticker (1921–2007), Kawabata's translator, compares his style to that of the haiku masters. "Haiku seeks to convey a sudden awareness of beauty by a mating of opposite or incongruous terms. Thus the classical haiku characteristically fuses motion and stillness. Similarly Kawabata relies very heavily on a mingling of the senses." Seidensticker goes on to point out that his novels, like those of many other Japanese writers, are not built around the form of a carefully structured beginning, development, and dénouement. Instead, they "shift from one episode to another, each with rich lyricism, through a well-controlled flow of associations. . . . His expression is marked by extreme simplicity. He makes the most of all words and conveys to the reader meaning and atmosphere, not explicitly, but by a roundabout implicit style." After the Second World War, Kawabata said he would write only about "the grief and beauty of Japan. I will live with the mountains and rivers of Japan as my soul."[10]

Literacy became increasingly widespread with the consequence that newspaper circulations rose, popular magazines flourished, and novels designed to have mass appeal gained a large readership. There was frantic competition among the newspapers to capture the subscription market, and by the mid-1920s, those with nationwide distribution were claiming circulation figures of 1 million to 1.5 million. In order to attract readers, entertainment features were emphasized. One of the most appealing of these was the serialization of novels by well-known popular writers, such as Kikuchi Kan.

Magazines dealing with political, social, and literary matters began to increase in number and circulation, but they were still primarily directed at the more sophisticated urban reader. Noma Seiji (1878–1938), a genius when it came to popular journalism, was particularly inventive and successful in his pursuit of mass readership. He began publishing monthly magazines that contained stories of samurai heroics, sentimental romance, melodramatic events, and didactic tales. He brought together many of the talented popular story writers and put on a massive advertising campaign to draw attention to his publications. In 1925 he started publishing *Kingu* (King), which he vowed would become "the most entertaining, the most beneficial, the cheapest, and the best-selling magazine in Japan." The first issue appeared, and 740,000 copies were immediately sold out. Noma also published an extremely popular women's magazine as well as magazines for the young. He attributed his success to the fact that he included articles that "were always a step behind the times." In 1930 the total circulation of his nine magazines came to 6 million copies. It is conceivable that Noma, as the indisputable leader of the popular magazine field, exerted more influence in molding popular culture from the 1920s to the end of the Second World War than any other person in Japan.

Many writers turned to the newly opened outlets, such as newspapers, magazines, and pocketbook editions, for the publication of their work. One of the more unusual writers to do this was Nakazato Kaizan (1885–1944). He wrote what is reputed to be the world's longest novel, *The Mountain Pass of the Great Bodhisattva,* which is three times the length of Tolstoy's *War and Peace.* Nakazato's novel depicts the life of a nihilistic warrior who is destined by his karma to wander about as a blind swordsman. Nakazato commenced writing it in 1912 and was still working on it when he died in 1944. He was influenced by Christianity, Tolstoy, and socialism when he was a young man, but he eventually turned to nihilism, perhaps in despair as he saw the real world crushing his idealistic dreams.

Another very significant writer who wrote historical novels and tales of valorous swordsmen was Yoshikawa Eiji (1892–1962). He had received only an elementary education but became the most widely read of the popular writers. "History," Yoshikawa said, "has to do with the affairs of the present," and he wrote stories that were appropriate to the mood of the age. Hence, the novels he wrote in the 1930s manifested the militaristic temper of that era. The most renowned of his works is the historical novel *Miyamoto Musashi,* whose central character, Miyamoto, is a hero who uses the sword not only as a way to perfect himself but also as a means "to regulate the people and govern the land." Yoshikawa also wrote a popular version of the Heike story (see page 12).

The other forms of mass entertainment that began to capture a wide following were the phonograph, the radio (which was introduced in 1925), and the motion picture (which came to be mass-produced in the 1920s).

Some Japanese scientists and philosophers made noteworthy contributions during the Meiji and Taishō eras. The field of science posed particularly difficult problems because work had to start virtually from scratch after the Meiji Restoration. Japan was dependent largely on foreign scholars for the first few decades, but by the latter half of Meiji some Japanese scientists began formulating new theories and making new discoveries. The first internationally renowned scientist to come out of Japan was Kitazato Shibasaburō (1852–1931), who discovered the bacillus of bubonic plague in 1894. He also isolated the bacilli of dysentery and tetanus and prepared an antitoxin for diphtheria. Fukuzawa supported him in establishing an institute for the study of contagious diseases, and then Kitazato went on to develop it into one of the world's finest bacteriological-research institutes.

Other notable Japanese scientists soon began to emerge. Nagaoka Hantarō (1865–1950) pioneered in the theoretical construction of atomic models while also finding time to contribute to experimental research in atomic spectra. Kimura Hisashi (1870–1943) contributed to the verification of latitudinal changes. The renowned seismologist Ōmori Fusakichi (1868–1923) devised a formula for computing seismic tremors. Takamine Jōkichi (1854–1922), working in the field of pharmacology, discovered adrenaline and diastase. The internationally famous bacteriologist Noguchi Hideyo (1876–1928), who studied in the United States and did research for the Rockefeller Foundation, made discoveries concerning the cause and treatment of syphilis and yellow fever.

In the philosophical realm, the popularity during early Meiji of English utilitarianism and French positivism was followed by interest in Darwinism and the theory of evolution, which was fostered by E. S. Morse (1838–1925) and Fenollosa. In the 1890s, however, German idealism began to dominate philosophical studies in the academic world, and Kantian and Hegelian concepts continued to influence the Japanese thinkers until the postwar era. The fact that German philosophy combined deep moral and religious characteristics with strictly logical approaches to thought made it especially appealing to the Japanese.

As a result of this influence, attempts were made by Japanese thinkers to systematize their own thoughts by using the speculative and logical methods employed by the German philosophers. The first significant outcome of this approach came in 1911 with the publication of *A Study of Good* by Nishida Kitarō (1870–1945). Nishida continued to develop the basic concepts presented in this work for the next forty years and secured for himself the reputation of being the most important original thinker of modern Japan.

Nishida was influenced by many Western philosophers, such as Hegel, Bergson, William James, Husserl, and the Neo-Kantians. At the same time, he was also strongly influenced by Zen Buddhism; in fact, it was Zen intuition that constituted the very foundation of his thinking. He attempted, however, to develop his method of thinking logically in accordance with the Western philosophical tradition. He sought to construct a philosophy that included religious and mystical elements as well as rational science.

In his study, Nishida endeavored to define the nature of reality in terms of "pure" or "direct" experience—that is, a point before subject and object are separated. This pure experience is to be found in everyday life, but its most typical manifestations are "the dark consciousness of the infant, the creative process of artistic genius, and the consciousness of the religious man who has lost the distinction between himself and another."[11]

In his next work, *Intuition and Reflection in the Consciousness of the Self* (1917), Nishida extended the notion of pure experience into a concept of self-awareness in which "that which knows and that which is known are together identical as the self." He concluded from this that the ultimate character of self-awareness was "absolute free will." He sought to transcend the problem of the bifurcation of reality into subjective and objective realms by positing in their stead "the place of nothingness" wherein both subject and object exist and consciousness itself is established. In this domain of absolute nothingness, "the form of the formless is seen and the sound of the soundless is heard."

POLITICAL DEVELOPMENTS: 1918–1932

The political parties had changed somewhat in character by the Taishō era. They were now led by new men who came from the bureaucracy, journalism, and the business world. Those fighters for freedom and popular rights during the Meiji era were, by and large, gone except for a very few old-time stalwarts like Ozaki Yukio and Inukai Tsuyoshi. The leaders were not the "rabble rousers" of the past; now they were "respectable" members of the community. The parties were more closely tied to the officialdom and big business than ever before.

The extent of the influence and involvement of big business in the political parties is indicated not only by the number of party members who came from the business field but, perhaps more important, by the amount of financial backing provided to the political parties, which were finding it increasingly expensive to run election campaigns. Much of the money went to purchasing votes. The total number of bribery cases that were reported increased steadily after the Russo-Japanese War. The ties between Mitsui and Jiyūtō-Seiyūkai as well as those between Mitsubishi and the parties that stemmed from the Kaishintō were well known. These allegiances, however, were not rigidly fixed, and at times the companies would support the rival parties.

Party leaders solicited donations not only from the zaibatsu but from wealthy individuals as well. Those leaders who were independently wealthy, like Katō Kōmei, were expected to contribute from their own funds. The government usually gave money to progovernment and neutral party members. The ability to raise and dispense political funds to party members gave party leaders a great deal of power, thus making party discipline much tighter than in the earlier years. Hara's control over the Seiyūkai, for example, was based partly on his ability to raise funds. Graft and corruption were the unfortunate by-products of the tremendous need for political funding.

The number of businessmen entering political parties had been increasing, and Hara actively recruited them for the Seiyūkai. Among those he persuaded to enter politics was the president of the Bank of Japan, Takahashi Korekiyo (1854–1936), who eventually succeeded Hara as the head of the Seiyūkai and prime minister. In addition to Hara himself, a number of prominent leaders emerged from the bureaucracy, including Katō Kōmei, Hamaguchi Yūkō (1870–1931), and Wakatsuki Reijirō (1866–1949).

Hara took charge of the government in September 1918, and he was in a fairly strong position at the time. The Seiyūkai was the largest party in the

Diet, although it did not have majority control. Yamagata had reconciled himself to a party government headed by Hara, a man he saw as being an essentially responsible leader. Hara had strengthened the Seiyūkai's ties with the business world and officialdom, and he was able to maintain relatively tight control over the party. He was a popular choice and was viewed as the man best suited to heal the wounds left by the rice riots.

The problems, however, that confronted Hara were enormous. Japan's relations with China were becoming increasingly strained, Japanese troops were off in Siberia, there were pressing economic and social problems, the labor movement was growing stronger, and the demand for universal suffrage was gaining popular support. Hara was hardly the bold reformer that the times seemed to demand. He was basically a conservative whose primary objective was the replacement of the Satsuma-Chōshū clique in the government with the Seiyūkai. His policies seemed to be based on the old objectives of Meiji Japan—that is, "enriching and strengthening" the nation. The four major goals proclaimed by him were educational reforms, expansion of the means of transportation and communication, fortification of national defense, and industrial growth. These were certainly no different from the aims set by previous governments. As a result, the Seiyūkai under Hara's leadership remained relatively unresponsive to the demands for reform that were being voiced by the spokesmen for the awakening masses. The Kenseikai, on the other hand, as the party in opposition, became the exponent of reform.

The left-wing critics called the Hara cabinet a rich man's government. The cabinet posts, with the exception of the war, naval, and foreign ministers, were filled by party men, many of whom were former businessmen having close ties with the zaibatsu. Hara's policies showed that he was not sympathetic to the working-class movement or to the democratic forces advocating the adoption of universal suffrage. He was prepared to take a strong stand against strikers by using police and gendarmes to disperse them and arrest their leaders. He also turned a deaf ear to the plea by the labor leaders that the Police Regulation Law, which restricted union activities, be revised. To counteract their work and possible effectiveness, Hara allowed his minister of home affairs, Tokonami Takejirō (1867–1935)—a former bureaucrat—to set up an organization of labor contractors, their workmen, and ruffians to serve as strikebreakers. The organization was named the Dai Nippon Kokusuikai (Japan National Essence Society) and was supported by right-wing nationalists such as Tōyama Mitsuru. These "chivalrous patriots" insisted upon "the cooperation of capital and labor."

Hara pursued his repressive efforts by presenting an antisubversive activities bill to the Diet, but it was opposed by the lower house. He was responsible for the suppression of the Socialist League, and he openly supported the dismissal of Morito Tatsuo (1888–1984), a professor at the University of Tokyo, for publishing an article on Kropotkin's anarchism.

The movement for universal manhood suffrage was gaining popular support, particularly among the moderate labor leaders who believed that the only way that reform could be achieved was through a Diet elected by universal suffrage. Hara was opposed to this, but recognizing the need to broaden the franchise to accommodate public opinion, he proposed that tax qualifications necessary for the privilege to vote be lowered from 10 to 3 yen. The opposition parties (the Kenseikai and the Kokumintō) had favored a reduction to two yen, but Hara's proposal was approved by the Diet in 1919. The Diet also passed Hara's bill to reconstitute the electoral districts so as to replace the large electoral districts, from which anywhere from four to sixteen Diet members were chosen, with small, single-member election districts. Hara favored the small district because he believed that this would prevent men from the small splinter parties, especially socialists, from winning Diet seats.

The expanded franchise increased the number of voters from 2.6 percent of the population to approximately double that figure. That is, there was an increase from about 1.5 million voters to 3.3 million. This was still only a limited extension of the franchise, and it did not, of course, satisfy the advocates of universal suffrage. They continued their agitation, eventually winning over Katō's Kenseikai and Inukai's Kokumintō to their cause.

In February 1920 the Kenseikai and Kokumintō submitted a bill for universal suffrage to the Diet. Shimada Saburō (1852–1923) of the Kenseikai criticized the existing class system that was based on wealth and demanded that qualification for the franchise be changed from "things" to "human beings." Seizing upon this as an excuse, Hara promptly dissolved the Diet.

Hara had strengthened the Seiyūkai's power at the local level by bringing men with community influence and prestige into the party. He had also used the technique of "pork barrel" legislation to enhance the Seiyūkai's authority. The party had the strong support of big businessmen and landlords. The small election districts enabled the Seiyūkai to use these advantages effectively, and it won an overwhelming victory at the polls.[12]

This huge majority in the Diet made it possible for Hara to proceed with increases in the size of the navy, and expanded railroad, telephone, telegraph, and road construction. In the previous Diet, measures to increase the number of higher professional schools and colleges had been approved. Steps were taken to nationalize certain industries, so the economy continued to grow following the brief recession at the end of World War I. As a result, Hara was able to achieve the four objectives he had set for his government.

The economic boom that started in the middle of 1919 collapsed in early 1920. In order to save the faltering banks and business firms, the government extended financial aid. Charges of graft and corruption involving government officials and members of the Seiyūkai buffeted the Hara government. In addition, there was the troublesome controversy that arose when it became known that the crown prince's fiancée, whose mother came from the Shimazu family, might pass on the defect of color blindness to the imperial family. Yamagata pressed for the cancellation of the proposed marriage agreement, while the Satsuma faction, with the support of right-wing nationalists such as Tōyama Mitsuru, resisted this move and managed to have the engagement upheld. In 1921 the crown prince took a trip abroad, and upon his return he became regent for the feeble emperor.

In spite of all these problems, Hara managed to fend off his critics because he possessed so strong a majority in the Diet. He appeared to be at the height of his political career when he was struck down by a young assassin in November 1921. Thus he became the first, but not the last, of the incumbent prime ministers who were felled by fanatical assassins.

In order to preserve a continuity of policy in the Washington Conference to which Hara had just sent a delegation, the genrō asked Takahashi Korekiyo, Hara's minister of finance, to head the government. Takahashi was not the adroit politician that Hara was, and, in fact, he had rather little interest in party politics. Consequently, he was able to preserve neither cabinet nor party unity when rival factions in the Seiyūkai began squabbling over cabinet posts, and he resigned after only seven months in office.

Yamagata had died in the spring of 1922, so the task of selecting a successor to Takahashi was now the responsibility of Saionji and Matsukata. Ironically enough, Saionji, who had been regarded as a liberal and a supporter of parliamentary government, spent the next few years trying to thwart the efforts of Katō Kōmei and the Kenseikai to gain power. He too resorted to the practice of establishing nonparty cabinets, thus in effect following the practice that had been Yamagata's hallmark. The Kenseikai not only lacked a majority in the Diet, but Saionji had little confidence in Katō because of the manner in which he had managed the nation's dealings with foreign governments when he was foreign minister.

The Seiyūkai, in comparison, was torn asunder by dissension and a lack of strong leadership. As a result, Saionji turned to Katō Tomosaburō, minister of the navy since 1915, to form the next cabinet. Katō hesitated because he lacked support in the Diet, and so the Seiyūkai leaders, who were more than a little anxious to keep the Kenseikai out of power, pledged him their support. As a result, Katō agreed to become prime minister and formed a cabinet consisting largely of members of the House of Peers.

In carrying out the agreements made at the Washington Conference, Katō proceeded to withdraw Japanese troops from Siberia and reduce naval armaments. At the same time, a reduction of the army was also effected. Manpower in the two services was decreased by more than 100,000, and still further reductions were planned for the army. All this very clearly reflected a dramatic decline in the prestige of the military. No longer did bright young students aspire to join the army or navy; even officers began wearing civilian apparel when not on duty.

The Katō cabinet expired with the death of the prime minister in August 1923. Again Saionji bypassed the political parties in his choice of Yamamoto Gonnohyōe to succeed Katō. Yamamoto was expected to form a nonpartisan cabinet with the three major parties.[13] Both the Seiyūkai and Kenseikai refused to enter the government because to do so would necessarily have entailed cooperating with rival parties. As a result, Yamamoto formed his cabinet with only Inukai's Kakushin Kurabu supporting him in the Diet.

Yamamoto had not completed forming his cabinet when Tokyo was struck by a major disaster, suffering damages second only to those caused by the massive air raids of the Second World War. Just before noon on September 1, 1923, the entire Kantō region was hit by one of the biggest earthquakes in Japanese history. The quake was followed by a major conflagration that turned the city of Tokyo into a virtual inferno, with thousands of people seeking to flee the rampaging flames that raged on until the morning of September 3. Landslides and tidal waves added to the death and destruction.[14]

In addition to the havoc caused by the earthquake and fires, there were unfortunate by-products resulting from mass hysteria. In the chaotic situation created by the disaster, all sorts of wild rumors began to spread, the most pernicious of which was that the Koreans were responsible for the fires that broke out and that they were still setting fires, looting, stealing, and raping. The police believed these rumors and caused the people to panic by announcing that the Koreans were grouping together to attack the people of Tokyo. The newspapers helped to worsen the situation by reporting these rumors as facts. Stories also spread claiming that the socialists were taking advantage of the chaotic conditions to start riots. As a result, vigilante groups were organized, and many Koreans as well as a number of labor and socialist leaders were subjected to brutal abuses and atrocities.[15] In one area, the police arrested left-wing labor leaders and summarily executed them. Even the army, which was posted to guard the disaster areas, took part in the chaos by killing innocent Koreans. The number of Koreans who lost their lives in the Kantō region could not be determined precisely because of the confusion that prevailed.[16]

The police and army authorities denied committing atrocities against the Koreans. At the same time they justified whatever measures were in fact taken by blaming the socialists and Communists, who, they claimed, had incited the Koreans to riot. Consequently, they continued to arrest socialists and Communists even after the initial panic had subsided. One prominent victim of this

Red hunt was the anarchist Ōsugi Sakae, who on the evening of September 16 went out for a visit with his wife, Itō Noe, and his six-year-old nephew. They were apprehended by Captain Amakasu Masahiko (1891–1945), a gendarme, who then strangled the three and had their bodies thrown into a well. His object, Amakasu said, was to remove the poison that was destroying the state. The affair was hushed up until Ōsugi's friends, alarmed by his disappearance, began to press for an investigation. Amakasu was given a ten-year sentence, but after three years he was paroled and went to Manchuria, where he worked with the instigators of the Manchurian Incident.

The Yamamoto government was now faced with the tremendous job of reconstructing those areas that had been destroyed by the earthquake. The minister of home affairs, Gotō Shimpei, had hoped to rebuild the city of Tokyo by using the latest ideas in city planning and asked for a budget of 3 billion yen,[17] but conservative, short-sighted politicians and businessmen opposed the plan because of the high cost and the fact that property owners would have to relinquish their lands for new thoroughfares. Consequently, Gotō acquiesced to the demand that the city be rebuilt in accordance with the former layout.

The second Yamamoto cabinet remained in power for only several months because of an unexpected incident involving an assassination attempt on the regent's life. The murder of Ōsugi had angered his fellow anarchists, who vowed to avenge his death by acts of terror. However, before they managed to take any action, one of their number acted independently and took a shot at the regent while he was on his way to the Diet on December 27, 1923.

The would-be assassin was Namba Taisuke (1899–1924), the son of a member of the Diet. He was aroused by the social injustices around him and deeply influenced by radical writings, particularly those of the French syndicalist Georges Sorel (1847–1922) and the Russian anarchists. The atrocities committed against the Koreans, socialists, and labor leaders during the Great Earthquake fortified his decision to turn to terrorism. Using a pistol, which had been given to his grandfather by Itō Hirobumi, he fired at the regent but missed, only managing to injure slightly one of the attendants. Namba was arrested, tried, and executed. The judges sought to make him repent, but he refused to do so, claiming to the end: "I am not a criminal. I am a pioneer for social justice."

Yamamoto assumed the responsibility for allowing such an outrage as this assassination attempt to take place, and he resigned. Mortified, Namba's father relinquished his seat in the Diet and went into seclusion. Namba's former school teachers resigned their posts for fostering such a heinous criminal, and his entire village went into mourning.

A movement was started to sharpen the vigilance against "dangerous thought" and "to guide people's thinking in the proper direction." Hiranuma Kiichirō (1867–1952), who was Yamamoto's minister of justice, brought together like-minded leaders from all fields and organized the Kokuhonsha (National Foundation Society) to rectify and uplift the national spirit. The government sharpened its surveillance over Communists and other left-wing reformers, and this in turn encouraged right-wing nationalists, such as Ōkawa Shūmei and Kita Ikki, to begin intensifying their activities.

The departure of the Yamamoto government left the genrō with the task of finding a successor to form a cabinet. Once again Saionji and Matsukata turned to a nonparty leader, Kiyoura Keigo, who was then president of the Privy Council. Kiyoura formed his cabinet in January 1924, filling most of the posts with members of the House of Peers.

The two parties were left completely out of the government machinery, and this finally led them to reconsider their policy of placing the rivalry between them ahead of the principle of party government. A new effort was made to bring the parties together in a movement aimed at defending constitutional government. The Kenseikai and the Kakushin Kurabu were willing to join the coalition against the Kiyoura government, but the Seiyūkai was irreparably split down the middle, with Takahashi Korekiyo's supporters favoring the coalition and the more conservative elements headed by Tokonami opposing it. The Seiyūkai was splintered: 148 progovernment members left to form the Seiyūhontō (Main Seiyūkai Party) while the remainder of the members joined the other two parties. The movement to defend constitutional government then called for the establishment of a party government, but it failed to arouse a great deal of popular interest. Finally, when Kiyoura dissolved the Diet, the three parties managed to gain a majority in the ensuing election. Faced with this new and very hostile Diet, Kiyoura resigned. Now Saionji had no choice but to turn to Katō Kōmei and the Kenseikai. In June 1924, Katō at last came to power, thus inaugurating a form of government that was to persist until 1932, when Prime Minister Inukai was assassinated; that is, the practice of having the president of one of the two major parties head the government. The principle of party government then finally became a reality, although it was to survive for only eight years.

Katō brought members of the Seiyūkai and Kakushin Kurabu into the cabinet along with such able nonparty men as Shidehara (foreign minister) and General Ugaki Issei (minister of war; 1868–1956). He also selected men from his own party, such as Wakatsuki (minister of home affairs) and Hamaguchi Yūkō (minister of finance), both of whom later became prime ministers. Takahashi (minister of agriculture and commerce) and Inukai (minister of communications) also joined the cabinet. Katō succeeded in establishing a cabinet consisting of an aggregation of extremely capable men.

Katō possessed a patrician outlook even though he came from a lower-class samurai family, and he thus favored working with the upper classes rather than the masses. However, as the leader for so long of the party out of power, he was

compelled to favor universal suffrage. This, together with financial retrenchment and the rooting out of corruption from the government, became his key
objectives as prime minister.

Despite objections from those who would be affected adversely by budget
cuts, Katō managed to effect some economies. The army accepted a reduction
of four divisions, but only with the understanding that first, the savings would
be used to mechanize the military by establishing tank and aircraft units, and
second, military drills would be introduced in the schools at the middle-school
level and above. Reductions in the bureaucracy were also made, but Katō had
less success in decreasing "pork barrel" expenditures because of the considerable opposition of the Seiyūkai.

The major achievement of the Katō cabinet was the enactment of universal
manhood suffrage. The bill that was finally passed in March 1925 gave the
right to vote to all male subjects over the age of twenty-five who had lived in
their electoral districts for at least one year and were not indigent.[18]

Ten days before the bill for universal manhood suffrage passed the Diet, the
Peace Preservation Law was enacted. The purpose of this law, which had been
contemplated since Hara was at the head of the government, was to curb "dangerous thought" that was being spread, it was argued, by anarchists and Communists. The law was designed to punish those who either advocated
revolutionary changes in the national polity or rejected the system of private
property. The law was prepared separately from the bill on universal suffrage, but
its passage was clearly intended to mollify the conservatives, particularly those in
the House of Peers. These men had insisted that safeguards be established to
combat the spread of dangerous ideas that they were certain would follow in the
wake of universal suffrage. The law was also intended to guard against the further diffusion of communistic ideas, which would result, it was feared, from the
Japanese-Soviet Treaty that had just been concluded at the beginning of 1925.

The government also proposed a bill aimed at protecting the right of workers to organize unions and stage strikes, but this was effectively blocked by the
powerful business interests. However, Article 17 of the Police Regulation Law,
which had hindered labor union activities, was finally removed.

Members of the coalition parties also hoped to "reform" the House of Peers
so that it would merely have the right to check or restrain the lower house,
which would become the dominant legislative body. Katō, however, was unwilling to take such drastic actions; consequently, the only reform attempted
was some slight change in the composition of the House of Peers, reducing
somewhat the number of hereditary members.

Soon after the passage of the bill on universal suffrage, the coalition of the
three parties began to disintegrate. Takahashi resigned as head of the Seiyūkai,
and he was replaced by General Tanaka Giichi, a Chōshū militarist. Tanaka as-

sumed the presidency of the party, and almost immediately thereafter the Seiyūkai merged with the Kakushin Kurabu and another splinter party and began challenging the Katō cabinet. Confronted with the collapse of the coalition, Katō resigned. The big surprise came when the Seiyūkai members, who had hoped to form the next cabinet in cooperation with the Seiyūhontō, found themselves in the lurch because Saionji asked Katō to take up the reins of government once again.

Six months after he formed his second cabinet, Katō died and was succeeded by Wakatsuki Reijirō, his minister of home affairs. Wakatsuki, a weak leader, resigned after slightly more than a year in office when the Privy Council opposed his financial policy designed to deal with the bank crisis besetting the nation. Saionji then turned to the head of the Seiyūkai, General Tanaka, who formed a new cabinet in April 1927.

Tanaka came to power at a most critical moment when a financial crisis and a serious economic depression struck Japan. This was followed by severe agrarian hardship, urban unrest, an increase in ultra-right-wing activism, and expanded activities on the part of the military both at home, in the form of political assassinations, and abroad, in the form of aggression in China. Japan was about to enter the "valley of darkness," which was to involve it in wars on the continent and in the Pacific.

Tanaka saw two tasks before him: the solution of the economic crisis and the rectification of what he considered to be the soft policy that had been pursued by Shidehara during his tenure as foreign minister since June 1924. The economy had been in a precarious state ever since the end of the First World War because overextended capital investment and production had not been retrenched. Instead, Hara had increased government expenditures in the hope of keeping the economy from collapsing. Foreign trade declined at a time when other industrial powers were actively rebuilding their economies. As a result, Japan's balance of payment deficit began to grow.

The Great Earthquake strained the economy further, not only because of the losses incurred by the business interests but also because of the increase in government expenditures that were necessary to defray the tremendous cost of reconstruction. The yen weakened, and inflation set in as new bonds were issued and credit was extended to the banks and businesses that needed assistance. This, of course, further weakened Japan's foreign trade position. At the same time, unemployment and agrarian debt increased.

In March 1927 the minister of finance inadvertently released the information that a certain bank was on the verge of bankruptcy. This produced a panic, and the second-class banks of Tokyo were overwhelmed by terrified depositors trying to withdraw their money. As a result, these banks were forced to close their doors.

This panic was followed by the financial crisis of the Bank of Taiwan, which had over-extended credit to a company on the verge of bankruptcy. In an attempt to save the bank, the Wakatsuki government issued an emergency ordinance granting it funds, but this measure was quickly blocked by the Privy Council. Consequently, the Bank of Taiwan was forced to close its doors. This in turn caused another bank panic that led to the collapse of about twenty other banks. The run on the banks continued until the Tanaka government finally declared a three-week moratorium on bank payments and devised some measures aimed at saving the Bank of Taiwan. A temporary relief from the financial crisis was achieved, but the movement toward the elimination of middle- and small-sized banks was accelerated. The many depositors who felt safer with bigger banks certainly reinforced this trend, as did the government by its encouragement of mergers and consolidations.[19]

The financial panic was followed by a recession. The producers of silk and cotton textiles found it necessary to curtail production in the face of declining demand. A similar situation beset the producers of paper, cement, coal, and ceramics. The trend toward concentration of the means of production and the reduction of medium-sized businesses was accelerated by the economic crisis.[20]

In order to stimulate the economy, Tanaka increased military expenditures, exploited the colonies even more rigorously, accelerated the rebuilding projects of the Great Earthquake, and introduced agrarian aid programs. To finance these activities, the government issued bonds and was forced to dip into its reserve funds. These measures revived the inflationary trend and worsened the unfavorable balance of trade. They also led to a steady drop in the value of the yen in relation to the dollar.[21]

This unhealthy economic situation created social ills that intensified left- and right-wing agitations. At the same time Tanaka, acting as both prime minister and foreign minister, adopted a bellicose posture toward China and stimulated nationalistic sentiments among the military and right-wing extremists. He also sought to turn the people against the soft policies that Shidehara, the former foreign minister, had pursued. Sentiments hostile to the "decadent" liberals and "traitorous" Communists were also fostered by the government.

Tanaka was very aggressive in combating "dangerous thought," making full use of the Peace Preservation Law. In the election of February 1928 he used the power of the government in trying to prevent the election of communistic candidates. In spite of his efforts, however, eight socialists were elected to the Diet. Tanaka responded to this threat by arresting all persons suspected of being anarchists or Communists. The campaign to root out "dangerous thought" was extended to the academic world, and five professors, including Kawakami Hajime (1879–1946), a prominent Marxist economist, were dismissed from the imperial universities in 1928.

Tanaka also sought to add the death penalty to the Peace Preservation Law, and when this move was blocked by the Diet, he went ahead and issued an emergency ordinance putting this policy into effect. Hostility toward members of left-wing organizations was encouraged by the government, and this led to numerous incidents of violence. For example, in March 1929 a former policeman murdered Yamamoto Senji, a socialist leader. This was followed by another massive arrest of socialists and Communists. In April, the government banned the Rōdō Nōmintō, the Communist-led Labor Council, and Communist youth groups.

Tanaka adopted an aggressive stance toward China. About the time he assumed the premiership, Jiang Jieshi (Chiang K'ai-shek) (1887–1975) was securing his control of the Nationalist Party in China and taking decisive steps to unify the country under his authority. Shidehara's China policy was based upon the principle of nonintervention and cooperation, but this was rejected as being "weak and soft" by the military, the rightists, and the reactionary members of both the House of Peers and the Privy Council. Tanaka immediately dispatched additional troops into Shandong, ostensibly to protect the Japanese residents there, when Jiang began moving his troops toward Peking. In the summer of 1927, Tanaka held a conference with the top officials of the army and foreign office for the purpose of formulating a new China policy. During this conference the anti-interventionists in the foreign office managed to restrain the interventionists led by Mori Kaku, who was parliamentary vice minister of foreign affairs, and the officers of the Kwantung Army (Japanese forces in Manchuria).

The participants in the conference agreed to respect the political integrity of China, but at the same time they also agreed to take decisive actions if and when there was a threat either to Japan's interests and rights or to the life and property of the Japanese residents. They also agreed that since Manchuria and Mongolia were important to Japan's security and well-being, it was essential that all necessary steps be taken to prevent those areas from becoming embroiled in the internal conflicts that were unfolding in China. Japan launched rather aggressive actions in China, and, consequently, much was made of the "Tanaka Memorial," which was purported to be a blueprint for the conquest of China based on the formulations established at this conference.[22]

The conference developed a list of items that were to be negotiated in regard to Manchuria and Mongolia. The talks were to be conducted with Zhang Zuolin, warlord of Manchuria. Zhang could not possibly accede to all of the Japanese demands because of the strong anti-Japanese sentiment that was so prevalent among the Chinese in Manchuria.

In April 1928, as Jiang's army moved north, the Japanese commander in Shandong sent his troops into Jinan to block the Nationalist forces. A clash

resulted, and in order to overcome public opposition to dispatching reinforcements, the Japanese army claimed that more than three hundred Japanese residents had been massacred in Shandong. This was a gross exaggeration of an
incident in which thirteen Japanese, who had been accused of smuggling
opium into the region, had been killed. The Minseitō (Democratic Party),
which had been formed by the merger of the Kenseikai and the Seiyūhontō in
June 1927, opposed Tanaka's aggressive policies, but the newspapers stirred up
public opinion in favor of intervention. Tanaka sent an additional division
into Shandong, and the Japanese forces launched an attack against Jinan,
killing and injuring thousands of Chinese residents.

Zhang Zuolin withdrew his troops into Manchuria as Jiang's forces advanced
north. The possibility of the conflict spreading to Manchuria began to concern
the Tanaka government, and so it notified the Chinese leaders that Japan would
take "proper and effective measures to maintain peace and order" if the fighting
spread to Manchuria. Zhang was then persuaded by the Japanese authorities to
return to Mukden without engaging the Nationalist forces in combat so as not
to give Jiang the opportunity to extend the conflict into Manchuria.

The Kwantung Army officers hoped to disarm Zhang's army and then move
the Japanese troops beyond the areas they were entitled to remain in by treaty.
Tanaka, however, refused to approve their plan. In order to create a situation
that would provide the Kwantung Army with an excuse to control Manchuria,
Colonel Kōmoto Daisaku (1883–1955), staff officer of the Kwantung Army,
took it upon himself to insure Zhang's assassination. In June 1928, when
Zhang was returning from North China to Manchuria, Kōmoto had the train
in which he was traveling blown up.

Kōmoto expected local disturbances to break out after Zhang's death, thus
providing the Kwantung Army with an excuse to move its troops into key areas
of Manchuria "to restore peace and order." The anticipated skirmishes, however, never did materialize, and Tanaka continued to oppose the army's proposal to move its troops beyond the areas in which they were legally entitled to
be stationed. The role played by Kōmoto in the assassination of Zhang was
not revealed until the postwar years because the army and right-wing politicians opposed public disclosure of the facts.

In Manchuria, Zhang Zuolin's son, Zhang Xue-liang (1901–2001), took
charge and, much to the chagrin of the Kwantung Army officers, pledged his
allegiance to Jiang Jieshi. The Nationalist government was so successful in extending its authority over China that Tanaka finally decided to withdraw the
Japanese troops from Tsinan and recognize Jiang's government as the legitimate government of China.

Emperor Hirohito (1901–1989), who had succeeded Emperor Taishō upon
his death on December 25, 1926, and Saionji both pressed Tanaka to punish

the assassins of Zhang Zoulin. Tanaka was unable, however, to overcome the rigid opposition of the army leaders, and he decided to resign his post. Contrary to Saionji's high expectations, Tanaka turned out to be a weak leader who failed to control the army. He had seriously damaged Japan's international standing and vastly increased the hostility of the Chinese people through his aggressive policies. He also left an ominous legacy when he failed to take vigorous action against Kwantung Army officers like Kōmoto who acted arbitrarily and independently, ignoring the wishes of the government officials.

In July 1929 the president of the Minseitō, Hamaguchi Yūkō, succeeded Tanaka as prime minister. Hamaguchi adopted two basic policies: economic retrenchment and international cooperation. As his minister of finance he appointed Inoue Junnosuke, former head of the Bank of Japan, and as foreign minister he selected Shidehara, a man who was known to favor a peaceful policy toward China.

In order to solve the financial difficulties, the Hamaguchi government reduced the budget and also proposed a 10 percent reduction in pay for both civilian and military officials. Strong opposition by the officials, however, defeated implementation of the pay cuts. In the hope of buttressing the value of the yen and halting the trend toward inflation, Hamaguchi returned Japan to the gold standard and lifted the embargo on gold that had been in effect since 1917. A stable yen would, it was assumed, increase foreign trade, offsetting the outflow of gold. Unfortunately, this measure was adopted just at the time when the stock market crashed in the United States, and a prolonged world-wide depression followed. As a result, Japanese exports to the United States dropped sharply; raw silk in particular was seriously affected. The export of cotton textile goods and other sundry products that Japan normally sold to China and other Asian countries also decreased. Japanese exports dropped by 50 percent in the period from 1929 to 1931.[23]

It was assumed that the government would be forced to go off the gold standard again. This, of course, would cause the value of the yen to drop. In anticipation of this, the rich, led by the Mitsui interests, began frantically to buy up American dollars, thus accelerating the outflow of gold. This kind of selfish indifference to the public good coupled with the many instances of graft and corruption involving high government officials and businessmen gave credence, in the minds of the people, to the charges being directed against big business and party politicians. The right-wing critics accused them of being selfish, unpatriotic traitors who had "sabotaged the nation to enrich themselves."

In December 1931 the government, now headed by Inukai, finally took Japan off the gold standard and restored the embargo on gold. The damage, however, had already been done. The world depression, the drop in exports, and the outflow of gold all contributed to the onset of a severe economic depression in Japan.[24] The agrarian sector was hit especially hard. Four years of abundant harvest, increased imports from Korea and Taiwan, and the decline in the demand for rice in the cities because of the industrial depression caused a 55 percent drop in the price of rice. Rice and silkworm cocoons were the two major sources of income for the farmers; consequently, a simultaneous drop in prices of both these items proved disastrous for agrarian communities.[25]

As might be expected, the depression worked serious hardships on the masses, not only the workers and the farmers but also the shopkeepers and the small and middle-sized businessmen. The only business that prospered was the pawnshop. Complete and fully accurate statistics are not available, but there is no question that unemployment rose considerably as many workers were released from their jobs because of declining business.[26]

Actually, unemployment figures can be somewhat misleading in the story they tell because many unemployed persons returned to the villages to share with their rural relatives what little work and food there was.[27] The real problems, then, were hidden unemployment and the increased pressures on the rural communities, which were already suffering from the depression.

The factory workers who did not lose their jobs had to accept reductions in pay. As might be expected, the number of labor disputes increased sharply. The salaried workers were also underpaid, and in some cases they were not paid at all.[28]

The social scene was characterized by a growing number of children begging in the streets, infanticides, suicides of entire families, deaths by the roadside, prostitution, and robberies.[29]

Despite these deteriorating conditions and tremendous hardships, taxes in the rural areas remained high.[30] Many independent farmers lost their lands and became tenant farmers because they were unable to pay their debts. The enormous pressures of poverty intensified, and many farm families were forced to sell their daughters to houses of prostitution in the big cities.[31] To make matters worse, the northern communities were afflicted by a disastrous crop failure in 1934, and the people were reduced to eating grass and tree roots.

These were the circumstances that led morally indignant young men and army officers, many of whom came from the rural communities, to turn to right-wing extremism. They were convinced that the politicians and the rich were wallowing in luxury, corruption, and decadence, while in the countryside their friends and relatives were starving to death. One of the army officers involved in the assassination of Inukai in 1932 said at his trial:

> The impoverishment of the farming villages is a cause of grave concern to
> all the thoughtful people. It is the same with the fishing villages and the

small merchants and industrialists. . . . In utter disregard of the poverty-stricken farmers, the enormously rich zaibatsu pursue their private profit. Meanwhile the young children of the impoverished farmers of the north-eastern provinces attend school without breakfast, and their families subsist on rotten potatoes.[32]

The depression tightened its grip on the economy and the people, while the Hamaguchi government made some ineffectual attempts to alleviate the situation. Basically, the government failed to comprehend the enormity or the severity of the crisis, and so it persisted in its policy of retrenchment. The policymakers also had the notion that some degree of economic hardship would have to be endured in order to strengthen the economy. As a result, they concentrated on raising the efficiency of industrial production. This entailed increasing the productivity per worker, reducing the number of workers, and cutting wages. Thus, so far as the workers were concerned, greater efficiency meant aggravating the conditions created by the depression. This policy also resulted in a further concentration of financial power and the means of production into the hands of a few gigantic business combines, while at the same time more and more small and medium business enterprises disappeared.

Just as the Hamaguchi government's efforts to rectify the unhealthy economic situation resulted in a worsening of the crisis, in like manner, its efforts to establish harmonious relations with China and the other powers failed to produce positive results. Ever since Japan participated in the Washington Conference and adopted a policy of naval disarmament, each succeeding government adhered to the general policy of international cooperation. Even the Tanaka government participated in the Kellogg-Briand Pact of 1928, which outlawed war. Characteristically, the Privy Council objected to this peace pact because it contained the words "in the names of their respective peoples." The Minseitō joined the council in condemning this "insult" to imperial sovereignty.

In early 1930 the signatories of the Five Power Naval Treaty of Washington met in London to consider an extension of the earlier agreement and the reduction of other categories of warships besides battleships. The Japanese navy wanted to obtain a ratio of 10:10:7 in cruisers and other warships, while still maintaining a submarine tonnage of 78,000. Wakatsuki, the chief of the Japanese delegation, accepted a 10:10:6 ratio in heavy cruisers and succeeded in getting the United States and Great Britain to agree to a 10:10:7 ratio in destroyers. In submarines, Japan was allowed to maintain parity with the United States.

The leaders of the navy, directed by Admiral Katō Kanji, chief of the naval general staff, were unwilling to accept an agreement that provided for less than what they wanted. The Seiyūkai supported the discontented naval officers and launched an attack against the Hamaguchi government. Inukai and

Hatoyama Ichirō (a prime minister during the 1950s; 1883–1959) took up the cudgels for the navy and accused the government of violating the independence of the supreme command. In this way they gave support to the principle that the military was to use during the 1930s in order to undermine civilian control of the government. Hatoyama argued that the Hamaguchi government had no authority to overrule the naval general staff concerning matters of national defense.

Admiral Katō, exercising his right to have direct access to the throne, appealed to the emperor, expressing his opposition to the government's action, and then resigned his post. Members of the Privy Council, led by Itō Miyoji and Hiranuma Kiichirō, sought to castigate the government, but Hamaguchi, with the encouragement of Saionji and a Minseitō majority in the Diet, refused to succumb to these pressures, and pushed through the ratification of the agreement.

The willingness of members of the oligarchy and the political parties to play upon the discontent of the militarists for political gains did not augur well for the future of parliamentary government. Those who had played a role in upholding the naval agreement were marked for elimination by army and navy extremists and right-wing civilian radicals. Among those picked as future victims were Admiral Okada Keisuke (1868–1952), who worked for the acceptance of the naval agreement, and Admiral Suzuki Kantarō (1868–1948), who was then grand chamberlain. The first victim of the numerous assassination attempts that were made in the 1930s was Prime Minister Hamaguchi, who was shot and seriously injured by a right-wing extremist in November 1930. The assassin was sentenced to death, but his sentence was commuted and he was released in 1940, at which time he again became an active participant in ultra-right-wing movements.

Shidehara was appointed to act as prime minister while Hamaguchi was incapacitated. Factional strife, however, seriously weakened the Minseitō, and the Seiyūkai continued to attack the government, labeling Shidehara as a traitor for defending the London agreement. In April 1931, just a few months before his death, Hamaguchi resigned. He was succeeded by Wakatsuki, whose tenure was fraught with difficulties because of right-wing extremism as well as the arbitrary actions of army officers, particularly those of the Kwantung Army. Assassination plots were continuously hatched by right-wing nationalists and young officers in the army and navy. The Kwantung Army officers did not cease to contrive political intrigues in Manchuria, where they finally succeeded in starting an "incident" in September 1931, which resulted in the establishment of a puppet state there. At home, civilian and military extremists managed to put an end to party government when they assassinated Prime Minister Inukai on May 15, 1932. These events marked the end of an era of parliamentary and democratic ascendancy and the beginning of a grim era of assassinations and wars.

Notes

1. The growth in the number of middle schools was particularly impressive: those for boys increased from 218 in 1900 to 491 in 1924, and those for girls jumped from 52 to 576 during the same time period. The elementary school, which was compulsory, consisted of six years; middle school for boys was five years; middle school for girls was four years; higher school was three years; and college was three years.

2. Mushanokōji Saneatsu, *Atarashiki Mura no Seikatsu* (Life in a New Village) (Tokyo: Shinchōsha, 1969), p. 1.

3. Imai Seiichi, *Taishō Demokurashii* (Taishō Democracy) (Tokyo: Chūō Kōronsha, 1966), p. 119.

4. Mitsuo Nakamura, *Modern Japanese Fiction, 1868–1926* (Tokyo: Nihon Bunka Sinkokai, 1968), pt. 2, p. 36.

5. Ibid., pp. 32–33.

6. Kadokawa Genyoshi et al., eds., *Nihon Bungaku no Rekishi* (A History of Japanese Literature), 12 vols. (Tokyo: Kadokawa Shoten, 1967–1968), vol. 11, pp. 199–215.

7. Junichirō Tanizaki, *Some Prefer Nettles*, trans. Edward G. Seidensticker (New York: Knopf, 1955), p. xv.

8. Junichirō Tanizaki, "In Praise of Shadow," *Perspective of Japan*, supplement to *Atlantic Monthly*, 1954, pp. 47–48.

9. Edward G. Seidensticker, *Kafū the Scribbler* (Stanford: Stanford University Press, 1965), p. 49.

10. *Japan Report* (New York: Consulate General of Japan, 1968), vol. 14, nos. 20, 22.

11. The quotations on Nishida's concepts are from Toratarō Shimomura, "Nishida Kitarō and Some Aspects of His Philosophical Thought," in *A Study of Good*, by Kitaro Nishida, trans. V. H. Viglielmo (Tokyo: Japanese Government Printing Bureau, 1960), pp. 191ff.

12. It captured 117 additional seats to occupy 279 seats in the new Diet, compared to 108 for the Kenseikai and 29 for the Kokumintō.

13. In October 1922, the Kokumintō was dissolved, and some of its members, along with stray Diet members, organized the Kakushin Kurabu (Reformist Club).

14. In all, more than 106,000 persons died or disappeared, 502,000 were injured, and 694,000 houses were destroyed. Property damages came to 10 billion yen.

15. Earlier, in July 1921, atrocities were committed against Korean workers employed in a construction project in the upper reaches of the Shinano River in central Japan. Efforts were made to unite the cause of the Koreans with that of the labor unions, but the movement failed to gain sufficient support.

16. The police estimated that 231 Koreans were killed; another source estimated that the victims numbered 2,613. The Chinese Embassy reported that between 160 and 170 Chinese were killed by hysterical people.

17. The government's budget for 1922 was slightly less than 1.5 billion yen.

18. This increased the number of voters from about 3.3 million to 12.5 million.

19. For example, at the end of 1926 there were 1,420 ordinary commercial banks, but by 1929, there were only 881.

20. In 1928, companies with assets of more than 10 million yen constituted only 0.9 percent of the firms in existence, but they held about 55 percent of the capital assets; firms with

assets of less than 50,000 yen constituted more than 55 percent of the companies, but they owned only about 1.5 percent of the capital assets.

21. In March 1927, the yen was worth $0.49 whereas by April 1929 it had dropped to $0.44.

22. It was generally agreed after the end of the Second World War that this was a bogus document.

23. At the same time, Japan's gold reserves diminished steadily after it returned to the gold standard. In 1929, it stood at 1.072 billion yen; by 1931 it had dropped to 470 million.

24. In 1931–1932, compared to 1926, the price index had dropped by 35 percent, and industrial and mineral production had decreased by 25 percent.

25. The price of raw silk dropped 67 percent from 1925 to 1931, while the price of cocoons dropped by more than two-thirds. The value of the net product of agriculture fell 58 percent during this same period while the farmer's cost of living declined by only 28 percent.

26. Incomplete figures indicate that in 1932, 6.9 percent of the working population was unemployed. For the day laborers the figure was 11.6 percent. Only one out of three persons seeking jobs was able to find employment. It is estimated that as many as 3 million people were unemployed in 1930.

27. A survey taken in 1931 showed that of the 660,000 factory workers who were released, 280,000 returned to the villages.

28. The real wages of workers dropped from index 100 in 1926 to 69.5 in 1931. In 1929 there were 1,420 disputes, and in 1931 there were 2,456. In April 1930, when the Kanebō Textile Company reduced wages by 40 percent, 35,000 workers went on strike. Of the 7,384 primary schools, 557 were unable to pay their teachers.

29. The crime rate doubled from 1926 (720,000 cases) to 1933 (1,550,000 cases).

30. A survey in 1933 showed that a fairly well-to-do independent farmer had an annual income of 723 yen and paid a direct tax of 96 yen, or 13 percent. Rural indebtedness continued to rise: the average debt per farm in 1932 was 837 yen as compared to 135 in 1914.

31. In one village in northern Japan, for example, 110, or 23 percent, of the 467 girls between the ages of fifteen and twenty-four were sold to the cities, primarily as prostitutes, some as factory workers.

32. Masao Maruyama, *Thought and Behaviour in Modern Japanese Politics,* ed. Ivan Morris (London: Oxford University Press, 1963), p. 45.

12

The Ascendancy of Militarism

RADICAL NATIONALISTS AND MILITARISTS

The Kwantung Army officers' conspiracy, which touched off the Manchurian Incident, and the assassination of Prime Minister Inukai heralded the end of party government in Japan and the advent of military domination of the political scene. These key events mark the beginning of Japan's long road to war, conquest, and destruction. Questions naturally arise as to how and why Japan got on this path of war and conquest. The conspirators who planned the Manchurian Incident were not acting at the behest of the government. There were no clearly defined domestic or foreign policies advocating such aggression. Nevertheless, these conspirators and assassins did put Japan on the road to war by virtue of the enthusiastic support they gathered to their causes from the general public and from the political circles.

Japan won one "glorious victory" after another on the continent after the Manchurian Incident, and, in response, the public gave the military adventurers unrestrained support while condemning Shidehara's "cowardly" policies. The press, in fact, greeted his efforts to settle the Manchurian affair peacefully with charges of treason. The public also sanctioned the many acts of violence committed by the so-called simple-hearted and patriotic young men who assassinated business and political leaders one after another. The trials following these treacherous assaults evoked wide public sympathy, not for the victims but for the assassins. This support was frequently manifested in the form of severed fingers sent to the courts to protest the trials of the "righteous patriots."

The ultimate responsibility for Japan's acts of aggression and its involvement in the China and Pacific wars cannot, of course, be ascribed to a handful of conspirators. It is true that army officers and ultranationalists schemed to effect the conquest of Manchuria and North China, but the really critical factor here was the considerable support these factions had from political leaders. They had the backing of members of the Privy Council led by Hiranuma and a significant number of political-party leaders. Their causes found champions even among the socialists; for example, the former left-wing activist Akamatsu Katsumaro committed the Shakai Minshūtō to a policy of expansionism on the continent. Those among the party politicians who were especially active in supporting the military expansionists were Adachi Kenzō (Wakatsuki's minister of home affairs), and Suzuki Kisaburō and Mori Kaku of the Seiyūkai. For political purposes, the Seiyūkai as a whole supported the army and the navy, attacking the Wakatsuki government in general and Shidehara's foreign policy in particular.

The flames of nationalism, militarism, and imperialism were stoked by the economic and social frustrations felt by the masses as the depression brought them to the very brink of starvation. Their hardships were blamed on the selfish, decadent, and corrupt politicians and business leaders. The militarists and the ultranationalists spearheaded these attacks and offered the people the chance for a new order at home through a *Shōwa* (Enlightened Peace) Restoration and economic relief through expansion abroad.[1] The young officers were particularly disturbed about conditions in the agrarian villages because most of the army's recruits were from the rural communities. Many bright young boys from agrarian families who could not afford to go to college went to the military and naval academies. The sympathetic feelings expressed by the army officers toward the impoverished farmers were reciprocated by the farming communities displaying general admiration, respect, and support for the military.

The expansionist policies of the military were based on the belief that Japan's economic difficulties could be resolved by moving into Manchuria and other parts of China where supposedly unlimited reservoirs of wealth could be tapped. Kwantung Army officers Ishiwara Kanji (1886–1949) and Itagaki Seishirō (1885–1948) stressed the need to control Manchuria in order to improve the economic conditions of the Japanese people.

The economic depression that had beset Japan began to improve about the time it embarked on its path of conquest, but this recovery was not brought about by expansionism alone. Japan managed to pull itself out of the depression earlier than other major powers by abandoning the policy of retrenchment that had been pursued by Hamaguchi and Inoue, and by aggressively implementing a program to reflate the economy through greatly increased spending on arms and a substantial increase in exports. The appearance of the first signs that Japan was recovering from the depression coincided with the beginning of expansionistic activities on the continent, and thus the impression was created that imperialism was paying off.

The imperialists offered another excuse for expanding into the continent, and that was the need to acquire more space for Japan's surplus population. Colonel Hashimoto Kingorō (1890–1957), a leading jingoist, said after the Manchurian Incident, "We are like a great crowd of people packed into a small and narrow room." He argued that there were three ways to solve the problem: emigration, greater trade in the world market, and expansion of territory. The first two options, however, were blocked by other powers, so, according to Hashimoto, the only alternative left was expansion. He went on to point out that by developing the undeveloped resources, Japan would not simply be serving its own selfish ends but would be benefiting humankind.[2]

The army was growing increasingly concerned about the disarmament policies being pursued by the Minseitō government, which had participated in the London Naval Disarmament Conference. The Wakatsuki government was also determined to take part in the 1932 Geneva Conference on Armament Limitations. The military knew that the advent of an international crisis would put an immediate end to all talk of disarmament.

The desire to expand into the continent and the plan to introduce reforms at home were closely linked together. Both movements were led by middle-grade army officers and radical civilian nationalists. In the 1930s the army began more and more to interfere in political affairs. The factional rivalries in the army were intertwined with the desire to increase military influence in the government, and this served to complicate the political situation considerably. One issue that created a very serious cleavage in the army was the rivalry between the Chōshū and anti-Chōshū factions. Some of the more ambitious officers resented the long domination of the army by the Chōshū clique, even though the power of that controlling group had been declining since Yamagata's death, and they began to establish an informal anti-Chōshū faction. This was led by two influential generals, Mazaki Jinzaburō (1876–1956) and Araki Sadao (1877–1966).

The Chōshū faction had been led by Tanaka Giichi after Yamagata's death, but following Tanaka's demise it lacked a strong leader. General Ugaki Issei was Tanaka's protégé, and although he was an influential general in the 1920s he failed to develop a power base in the army, not only because he incurred the resentment of the anti-Chōshū faction, but also because his military plans upset the traditionalists. Ugaki, who maintained that the army should be modernized with the greatest emphasis placed on tanks and airplanes, agreed to accept a reduction in the size of the army. Those who still believed in the primacy of the infantry criticized him for ignoring the "spiritual power" present in the Japanese soldiers.

Those army officers who agreed with Ugaki included Nagata Tetsuzan (1884–1935), Tōjō Hideki (1884–1948), and Yamashita Tomoyuki (1885–1946). This faction, led by Nagata, believed that future wars would require the total mobilization of the nation's resources, both natural and human. Consequently, they favored a comprehensive scheme coordinating military, political, and economic planning. The opposing faction, led by Araki, believed that future wars would still be won swiftly and decisively by superior Japanese troops imbued with the spirit of Yamato. The split in the army did not rigidly follow any particular lines, but by and large the Nagata faction tended to consist of officers serving in the Ministry of War whereas the Araki faction drew most of its adherents from the general staff. The disagreement about whether to stress machines or the Yamato spirit contributed in part to the cleavage that divided the Control Faction *(Tōsei-ha)* and Imperial Way Faction *(Kōdō-ha)*, a problem that will be discussed later.

As might be expected, the military officers were, in the main, opposed to the ascendancy of democracy and party government. Through the mechanism of the "independence of the supreme command," the army and navy maintained a degree of autonomy from the government. They had direct access to the emperor, and the officers actually considered themselves to be the emperor's immediate retainers.

The military officers did not see any conflict of interest between themselves and the government while Yamagata and the genrō were in control because it was their own patrons who were in power. The passing of the old patriarchs and the ascendancy of the political parties, however, radically altered the situation, with the consequence that the military officers became very wary of any government programs that affected either the army or the navy. They especially resented the disarmament policies fostered by the party government. The sentiments of the more radical of these military men were expressed in the statement of purpose drafted by an organization of politically minded army officers, the Cherry Blossom Society (Sakurakai). It said:

[The political leaders] have forgotten basic principles, lack the courage to carry out state policies, and completely neglect the spiritual values that are essential for the ascendancy of the Yamato people. They are wholly preoccupied with their selfish pursuit of political power and material wealth. Above, they veil the sacred light, and below, they deceive the people. The torrent of political corruption has reached its crest. . . . Now, the poisonous sword of the thoroughly degenerate party politicians is being pointed at the military. This was clearly demonstrated in the controversy over the London treaties. . . . It is obvious that the party politicians' sword, which was used against the navy, will soon be used to reduce the size of the army. Hence, we who constitute the mainstay of the army must . . . arouse ourselves and wash out the bowels of the completely decadent politicians.[3]

As we already observed, the army officers were critical of what they considered to be the gross indifference on the part of politicians and capitalists to agrarian impoverishment. In order to rectify these conditions, the concerned middle-grade officers favored introducing radical political reforms; that is, they proposed effecting another restoration, the Shōwa Restoration. The proponents of this change tended to be members of the anti-Chōshū faction because it was the Chōshū faction that had been a key component of the established order from the beginning of the Meiji era.

Military officers advocating reform began getting together to discuss political issues, and a number of societies were organized by them. One of these, the Issekikai (One Evening Society), was organized in 1929 and included among its members Kōmoto Daisaku (who had murdered Zhang Zuolin), Nagata Tetsuzan, Tōjō Hideki, Yamashita Tomoyuki, Doihara Kenji (1883–1948), Itagaki Seishirō, and Ishiwara Kanji. All of these officers were to play critical political roles in the next decade or two.

In 1930 another military society, the Sakurakai, was organized by Hashimoto Kingorō. The membership at first included about twenty-five officers, later growing to about a hundred. The Sakurakai favored the overthrow of the existing government and the establishment of a military regime in its stead. The group, with the support of Major General Tatekawa, the officer in charge of military operations in the army general staff, planned to pursue the conquest of Manchuria once this military government was established.

Many of the military officers who favored internal changes and expansion abroad had established links with right-wing civilian nationalists. The latter also favored revolutionizing the existing political, social, and economic systems for the purpose of transforming Japan into a totalitarian state. Among such civilian radicals were Ōkawa, Shūmei, Kita Ikki, and Inoue Nisshō (1886–1967).

Radical nationalist thinkers—civilian and military—may have disagreed about the best means to bring about the new order and about some minor details in analyzing the ills of Japan, but, by and large, they all shared mystical notions about the superiority of the Japanese national character, the national polity *(kokutai)*, and the sacredness of the imperial institution, which was the source of all values. Another idea they held in common was the necessity of stressing spiritual rather than material values. Ōkawa Shūmei (1886–1957), for example, was opposed to capitalism and socialism primarily because they both pursued materialistic ends. The ultranationalists generally favored expansion into the Asian continent, development of a powerful military force, and the creation of a totalitarian state that inclined toward national socialism.

Consequently, they opposed liberal, individualistic values as well as the democratic parliamentary concepts that had entered the country in the mid-nineteenth century. In concert with these attitudes, they rejected the basically Western, urban culture in favor of the traditional, agrarian way of life and values. The family system, with its emphasis on the whole group rather than the individual, was envisioned as the appropriate basis for the structure of the state. The imperial household was to have the status of the main family, while all other families were to function as branch families.

In a sense, the conflict between the militarists and the radical nationalists on the one hand, and the bourgeoisie and the liberal intellectuals on the other, was a clash between the rural and the urban, the provincial and Tokyo, the traditional and the Western-oriented cultures of Japan. The triumph of the militarists and radical nationalists in the 1930s was, at the same time, the triumph of traditionalism or "Japanism" over Western liberalism. This victory, then, was the denouement of the conflict between traditionalism and Westernism that had its inception in early Meiji.

The radical nationalists[4] believed that the use of force was necessary for two primary purposes: first, to return Japan to its true character and values, which had been eroded by the artificial ideas imported from the West and by the evil advisers to the emperor; and second, to extend the influence of the imperial way throughout the world. Aside from this kind of mystical notion about the special mission of Japan, there was a tendency to see the nation as the champion of Asia against the Western world. Ōkawa Shūmei, who became intimately involved with the young military conspirators, contended that in order to realize a new world order, one nation representing the East had to fight one nation representing the West. "It is my belief," he said, "that Heaven has chosen Japan as the champion of the East."[5]

The most important thinker among the radical nationalists was Kita Ikki. Kita started out as a socialist and struggled to remain one, if not through party affiliation then at least ideologically, by attempting to reconcile socialism and the Japanese national polity (kokutai). He thus defined kokutai in a radically different way from the conventional interpretation by equating it with "socialism because sovereignty resides in the state, and [with] democracy because power rests with the people."[6] His view of the imperial institution resembled Minobe Tatsukichi's Organ Theory (see page 274). "The Emperor of Japan," Kita asserted, "is an organ who began and continues to exist for the purposes of the survival and evolution of the state."[7] His views on kokutai and the emperor caused the authorities to look upon him with suspicion. Even so, he did not share the political opinions of the left-wing thinkers either. He disagreed with the socialists because they did not favor a strong state, and he complied with Martin Luther's opinion that "the state is an ethical institution." He also favored imperialism because he considered it the natural precursor to internationalism.

Kita, however, was genuinely sympathetic to the fate of China, the victim of Western imperialism. Like many of his fellow Japanese, he favored extending a helping hand to China so as to enable it to break its shackles and move along the path of progress. He spent some time working with the Chinese revolutionaries, but as Sino-Japanese interests began to clash, Kita concluded that the relationship between the two countries could only be adjusted after an internal reorganization of Japan was effected. Consequently, he turned his attention back to the Japanese situation and published *A Plan for the Reorganization of Japan* in 1923. This essay established his reputation as the spokesman for Japanese radical nationalists in the eyes of his admirers as well as his critics.

In his *Plan,* Kita called for a radical reorganization of the political, social, and economic institutions as well as a commitment to an expansionist foreign policy. Domestically, he proposed the removal of the privileged cliques so that a true union between the emperor and the people could be achieved. The displacement of the ruling elite was to be brought about by a coup d'état. He advocated the abolition of the peerage and the House of Peers, the introduction of universal manhood suffrage, and the replacement of privy councilors, governors, and other officials. In the economic realm, Kita favored what was, in effect, national socialism—personal property and private landownership were to be limited and major enterprises nationalized. In the social sphere he envisioned the establishment of a welfare state in which the rights of the workers were protected with profit sharing and worker participation in management. Orphans, the aged, and the disabled were to be cared for by the state. In foreign affairs, Kita proposed that Australia and eastern Siberia be acquired by Japan as part of the proletarian nation's class struggle against wealthy capitalist nations.

CONSPIRACIES AND ASSASSINATIONS

The right-wing radicals among the civilians and the military began to hatch plots either to assassinate key officials as a prelude to the revolution or to stage a more elaborate coup. The first serious plot, devised by the members of the Sakurakai as well as other military officers, failed to materialize. This was the March Incident, which was planned by Hashimoto Kingorō and his cohorts, involving several generals as well as Ōkawa Shūmei. Among those who were consulted, or were at least aware of the plot, were generals Koiso Kuniaki (1880–1950), chief of the military affairs bureau, Tatekawa Yoshitsugu (1880–1945) of the general staff, and Sugiyama Gen (1880–1945), vice minister of war. The conspirators planned to stage a coup in March 1931 and place General Ugaki, then the minister of war, at the head of the new government.

The plot fell through, however, when Ugaki, who had initially showed some interest, refused to cooperate. This action by Ugaki turned the militants against him, and they began to look to generals Araki and Mazaki for leadership.

Had vigorous action been taken at this time against the plotters, the possibility of future conspiracies breaking out might have been lessened, but wanting to avoid trouble with the army, the military and civilian leaders behaved cautiously. One historian has observed,

> This caution was the tragedy of all temperate and liberal opinion in Japan. Give us time, said army "moderates" to civilian ministers and Court officials, and we shall have extremists under control. Give us time, said Japanese diplomats to foreign governments, and the pendulum will swing back from militant nationalism to common sense and moderation. It was a recurring theme, from 1931 almost to the eve of Pearl Harbor.[8]

With increasing audacity, the young officers continued to defy their superiors and civilian officials, thus posing a sharp contrast to the Meiji military men, who were strictly disciplined and accustomed to leaving political matters in the hands of their leaders. The Sakurakai conspirators were also intimately involved in the 1931 Manchurian Incident. The efforts of Foreign Minister Shidehara to settle the episode peacefully through diplomatic negotiations angered the militant army officers and the radical civilian nationalists, who devised another plot to overthrow the government. The same men who planned the March Incident, Hashimoto and Ōkawa among others, were involved in this affair, labeled the October Incident. Their plan was to assassinate Prime Minister Wakatsuki and other high officials and place General Araki, then inspector general of military education, at the head of the revolutionary government.

General Araki Sadao was a zealous advocate of "Japanism" and the Imperial Way (kōdō). He was critical of "frivolous foreign ideology," "egotistical foreign ideas," capitalism, Marxism, and materialism. Each Japanese, he said, must be clearly conscious of the thought, "I am a Japanese." He believed in the philosophy that mind has the capacity to conquer matter, and he contended that "if we have thirty million bamboo spears we can stand up to any major power."[9]

In planning the October Incident, the young officers did not inform their senior officers of the plot this time, but nevertheless, word of the conspiracy leaked out, and the plan was squashed by Araki himself. Once again, however, the conspirators went unpunished, although the officers who were involved in the plot did get scattered to different posts.

The military plotters were blocked temporarily, but their conspiratorial offensive was soon taken up by a group of civilian extremists who were also concerned about the impoverishment of the peasantry and favored the establishment of a new order. They had organized a group called the Blood Brother-hood League (Ketsumeidan), whose goal was the destruction of the existing order by means of terror rather than through a military coup. Some of the league members were nevertheless still in touch with the Sakurakai as well as some naval officers. The Ketsumeidan also had the indirect support of older ultranationalists, such as Uchida Ryōhei of the Amur River Society, and Tōyama Mitsuru. The members pledged themselves in blood to eliminate those public figures who had enriched themselves at the expense of agrarian families and who had betrayed the country internationally. Their leader was a Buddhist monk, Inoue Nisshō.

The Ketsumeidan compiled a list of thirteen prominent men who were to be assassinated; among them were Inukai (who had become prime minister in December 1931), Wakatsuki, Saionji, Inoue Junnosuke (1869–1932), and Dan Takuma (director of Mitsui; 1858–1932). In early 1932 the terrorists had managed to assassinate only Inoue Junnosuke and Dan Takuma. Inoue Nis-shō's connection with the killings was uncovered during the investigation, and he was sentenced to prison for fifteen years. This, however, failed to put an end to the activities of the Ketsumeidan. The remaining members conspired ever-more vigorously with navy officers who were in sympathy with their aims to assassinate Inukai.

Inukai, the champion of parliamentary government, had become prime minister after the fall of the Wakatsuki cabinet, which had been buffeted from all sides because of its efforts to resolve the Manchurian crisis peacefully. Ironi-cally enough, it was Inukai himself who had in fact led the Seiyūkai in attack-ing Shidehara's so-called soft policies. Inukai was advised not to accept the premiership by his friend Tōyama Mitsuru, who knew that right-wing extrem-ists were determined to put an end to party government. Unquestionably, as prime minister, Inukai would become the prime target of the assassins. He nevertheless accepted the assignment and, in accordance with the emperor's wishes, set out to curb army actions in Manchuria.

As soon as Inukai's policy regarding Manchuria was revealed, the extremists, led chiefly by Koga Kiyoshi, a naval lieutenant, and Tachibana Kōsaburō, a radical agrarian reformer who had worked with Inoue Nisshō, began plotting his assassination. Tachibana and his followers were influenced by a champion of agrarian radicalism, Gondō Seikyō (1868–1938), who was opposed to the highly centralized capitalistic state then in existence and favored a return to au-tonomous agrarian village communities united under the emperor. Gondō was extremely critical of privileged groups, that is, the zaibatsu, bureaucrats, the military, and the political parties.

On May 15, 1932, the plotters—naval officers and army cadets led by Koga—put into effect their plot to assassinate both Inukai and Makino, the lord keeper of the privy seal. The plan also involved attacks on the Seiyūkai headquarters, the Mitsubishi Bank, the police headquarters, and various electrical power plants. They succeeded only in killing Inukai. The officers broke into the prime minister's home with drawn pistols, whereupon Inukai urged a discussion of their grievances. The assassins, however, recognized no need for talk and fired their pistols.

Inukai's assassination effectively put an end to party government and presaged the domination of the political scene by the military. The removal of Inukai meant that the Kwantung Army could continue its arbitrary and aggressive actions without any serious restraints being placed upon it. In the future, few men would dare to oppose openly the wishes of the military.

Again the assassins were let off with light punishments. The heaviest penalty, life imprisonment, was meted out to the civilian participant Tachibana, who did not even take part directly in the murder of Inukai. The other plotters were sentenced to four to fifteen years in prison, but their sentences were soon commuted. For example, Ōkawa Shūmei, who had supported the conspiracy, was sentenced to fifteen years imprisonment, but he was released after serving only five years of his term.

THE MANCHURIAN INCIDENT

The desire on the part of the army to extend Japanese control over Manchuria and Inner Mongolia can be traced back to the time of the Russo-Japanese War. However, the sense of urgency about accomplishing these aims was heightened in the 1920s as the Nationalist Party began to unify China and as the possibility that Manchuria might be brought under the control of a strong central government became increasingly evident. The concern was intensified as Zhang Xueliang pledged his allegiance to Jiang and the Nanjing government.

The men who masterminded the Manchurian plot and thus set Japan on its road to conquest in 1931 were two Kwantung Army officers, Ishiwara Kanji and Itagaki Seishirō. Ishiwara's solution to the Manchurian-Mongolian question was to have the Kwantung Army overthrow Zhang Xueliang and then proceed to conquer Manchuria.

Ishiwara and Itagaki wanted Manchuria not only for economic reasons but also because they believed that it was strategically essential in guarding against Soviet ambitions. They also argued that the Manchurian people would benefit from Japanese rule, which would see to the maintenance of public security and the development of the economy. Ishiwara and Itagaki intended to contrive an incident that would provide the Kwantung Army with an excuse for extending control over all of Manchuria. Their desire was, of course, shared by other officers, such as Araki Sadao and Hata Shunroku (1879–1962) of the army general staff. Support for the ambitions of the Kwantung Army was also found among officers of the war ministry, such as Nagata Tetsuzan, who believed in the concept of total war and who wanted to acquire the vast resources of Manchuria.

A number of minor incidents served to keep the Manchurian situation rather tense. In the late spring of 1931, a clash over water rights between Koreans and Chinese in Wanpaoshan, northwest of Zhangjun, resulted in the intervention of the Japanese police. In retaliation for the maltreatment of Koreans in Manchuria, Chinese inhabitants in Korea were attacked, and 109 persons were killed. In June of that same year, two Japanese agents were caught in a restricted area in Manchuria, and they were summarily shot to death by the Chinese troops. This incident heightened anti-Chinese sentiments in Japan and intensified public criticism of Shidehara's policy of resolving Sino-Japanese problems peacefully.

Ishiwara and Itagaki decided that the time had arrived for their plan, and they got the approval of key officers in the general staff and the war ministry. The tension continued to mount, and rumors of impending action by the Kwantung Army began spreading, until finally the emperor expressed his concern to the military leaders. As a result, Minister of War Minami dispatched General Tatekawa, who was actually a supporter of the plotters, to restrain the Kwantung Army officers, asking them to wait one more year. One historian has remarked that "to have sent Tatekawa to Mukden at the critical time was like telling a pyromaniac to forestall an attempt at arson."[10] The object of his mission was communicated to the Kwantung Army officers by Hashimoto, who advised them to act before Tatekawa's arrival.

On the night of September 18, 1931, a small group of Kwantung Army men blew up a section of the South Manchurian Railroad in Mukden. The explosion was followed by a clash between the Japanese railroad guards and Chinese troops. Itagaki then sent reinforcements from the battalion headquarters in Mukden and turned the skirmish into a major offensive. By the next morning, the Kwantung Army had gained complete control of Mukden. It then claimed that the Chinese troops had blown up the South Manchurian Railroad and attacked the Japanese guards.

The Wakatsuki cabinet met as soon as the incident broke out, and at the insistence of Foreign Minister Shidehara and Minister of Finance Inoue, it decided to localize and settle the matter promptly. However, the army general staff contended that the cabinet decision did not bind the military forces because of the "independence of the supreme command" and that the staff of field armies possessed complete freedom in the area of operational planning. The Kwantung Army rapidly moved ahead and occupied all of southern Manchuria without delay. Moreover, to extend the scope of the conflict, the Kwantung Army asked the commander of the Korean Army, General Hayashi

Senjūrō (1876–1943), to send his troops into southern Manchuria. This Hayashi did, violating the principle that prohibited field commanders from sending their troops outside their command jurisdictions without first obtaining imperial sanction. Shidehara's insistence that Hayashi be censured was not approved, but the army promised to restrict further actions in Manchuria. The government in turn acceded to the army's demand that a new treaty be negotiated with the Chinese Nationalist government to guarantee Japanese rights and interests in Manchuria. The Kwantung Army nevertheless persisted with its aggressive operations by exercising the right of self-defense to carry out attacks against "bandits."

Zhang Xueliang was unwilling to risk his army in a major confrontation with the Japanese forces, so the Nationalist government, which was not prepared to engage the Japanese because it was already involved in a civil war against the Communists, appealed to the League of Nations to stop the Japanese aggression. The Japanese government wanted to keep the League of Nations out of the affair and sought to negotiate directly with the Nationalist government. Following the lead of the British, council members of the League were initially inclined to accept the Japanese government's word that it intended to "prevent the aggravation of the situation." As a result, the council adjourned on September 30 without taking any action. The Kwantung Army continued its activities, however, and so the council had to meet again in late October, at which time it passed a resolution calling for the withdrawal of Japanese troops by November 16.

In Japan, the army received the public's enthusiastic support for its bold actions, and criticism of Shidehara's efforts to achieve a peaceful settlement mounted even higher. Militaristic sentiments were buttressed throughout the country by the millions of members of the Zaigō Gunjinkai (Military Reservists Association). Not only did members of the Seiyūkai join Shidehara's critics, but even a member of Wakatsuki's own cabinet, Minister of Home Affairs Adachi, started to boycott cabinet meetings to protest the government policies advocating a peaceful settlement. Shidehara found himself in an impossible predicament because the Japanese army had absolutely no intention of withdrawing by November 16, and the Chinese government refused to participate in any negotiations before such a withdrawal. Shidehara now had virtually no support, and even Saionji, who had backed him up until this point, concluded that he had to reconsider his position "from the point of view of living diplomacy when the entire national opinion called it mistaken and wrong." Shidehara finally gave up the struggle, and on December 12, the Wakatsuki cabinet fell.

Wakatsuki was succeeded by the seventy-five-year-old Inukai of the Seiyūkai. Inukai served as his own foreign minister, but he appointed General

Araki as the minister of war and chose Mori Kaku, who favored establishing a dictatorship based on an alliance between the army and the Seiyūkai, as cabinet secretary. In spite of his attacks on Shidehara's policies, Inukai was deeply concerned about the army's arbitrary actions. Immediately upon his appointment, Inukai was informed of the emperor's desire that the army be restrained from meddling in domestic and foreign affairs. He promised to abide by the emperor's wishes and endeavor to curb the army.

Inukai hoped to devise a plan that would persuade the Kwantung Army to withdraw its troops to the South Manchurian Railroad zone in order to open the way for negotiations with the Chinese government. He even contemplated having the emperor issue a rescript ordering the army to cease further operations in Manchuria. This step was never taken, however, possibly because it was feared that if the rescript were issued and the army defied the emperor's command it would have a disastrous effect on the prestige of the throne. It was this very fear, in fact, that accounts for the civilian leaders' timidity in utilizing the imperial authority to curb the army throughout the 1930s.

Now that Shidehara was out of the way, the Kwantung Army proceeded to capture Jinzhow and Harbin. It also moved north into Amur Province, overcoming the initial concern that this action might draw Russia into the conflict. In January 1932, the Sino-Japanese conflict spread to Shanghai. In retaliation for the aggressive actions in Manchuria, the Chinese staged a boycott of Japanese goods, and some Japanese residents in Shanghai were molested by angry mobs.[11] For the protection of its own residents, the Japanese landed marines in Shanghai. This was followed, in the latter part of January, by a clash between the Japanese troops and the Chinese Nineteenth Route Army. Thereupon, the Japanese admiral in command ordered an aerial bombardment of a densely populated section of Shanghai. This atrocity aroused world opinion against the Japanese and hardened Chinese determination to resist them. It is believed that it was this action rather than the Mukden Incident that turned American public opinion against Japan.

The Inukai cabinet, with great reluctance, acceded to Araki's proposal to send two army divisions into Shanghai, and by early March, the Nineteenth Route Army was driven out of the city. The commanding general, Shirakawa, refused to pursue the fleeing Chinese forces and concluded an armistice in early May.

The Shanghai Incident further strengthened jingoistic sentiments in Japan. Consequently, Inukai found it increasingly difficult to continue his efforts to bring about a negotiated settlement with the Nanjing government concerning Manchuria. Hostility toward the League of Nations mounted considerably after its adoption of Secretary of State Henry Stimson's doctrine of nonrecognition.[12] The proponents of a peaceful conclusion to the hostilities with China found themselves being overwhelmed by public indignation and chauvinism. This kind of atmosphere naturally yielded tremendous support to the Kwantung Army officers, who proceeded to establish the state of Manchukuo. They brought together former officials of the Qing (Manchu) government who were willing to collaborate with them and organized the Northeastern Administrative Council. In February 1932 the council issued a declaration of independence and called a convention on the twenty-ninth of that month for the purpose of establishing a new state. The former emperor of China, Xuan Tong (Pu Yi) (1906–1967), was made the head of the state as regent on March 9, 1932.

The Inukai government had no choice but to accept the machinations of the Kwantung Army, although it did not extend formal recognition to the new state. Manchukuo was dubbed "a paradise where the way of the king prevails," but it was no more than a puppet state controlled by the Kwantung Army, Japanese officials, and the South Manchurian Railway. In September 1932 the Saitō government recognized the puppet state; in March 1934 it became a monarchy with Pu Yi on the throne. It did not succeed in gaining the recognition of other governments, with the exception of a few nations, such as Japan's Axis allies, Germany and Italy.

The Japanese government's failure to restrain the Kwantung Army compelled the council of the League of Nations to take a stronger position than its members initially desired. On December 10, 1931, the council appointed the Lytton Commission to look into the Manchurian situation. The five-member commission began its investigation in late February and pursued its inquiry for six months. In September 1932 a report was submitted to the League of Nations, which published it on October 2. The report held that the Japanese military actions of the night of September 18–19, 1931, could not be considered as legitimate measures of self-defense, and that the new state was not the product of a genuine and spontaneous independence movement. The report recommended the creation, under Chinese sovereignty, of an autonomous regime for the Manchurian provinces, and the withdrawal of all Chinese and Japanese forces. Japanese rights and interests were to be guaranteed by a Sino-Japanese treaty that would be designed to provide for the participation of Japan in the economic development of Manchuria.

The Lytton Commission's report was, as might be expected, wholly unacceptable to the Japanese army and the Saitō government. In February 1933 the assembly of the League adopted a committee report based in large part on the Lytton report, at which point the Japanese delegation, led by Matsuoka Yōsuke, angrily responded by walking out. On March 27, Japan formally withdrew from the League and embarked on a solitary path that, in the eyes of the world, made it an international outlaw.

The inability of the League of Nations to cope with Japanese aggression provided an unfortunate demonstration of the organization's fundamental impotence to future aggressors Benito Mussolini and Adolf Hitler. The post–World War I hopes for international cooperation and collective security were shattered, and it is in this sense that we can say that the road to the Second World War started in Mukden on September 18, 1931.

INTERNAL POLITICAL DEVELOPMENTS: THE TRIUMPH OF THE MILITARISTS

Party governments, as we noted earlier, went out of existence in Japan with Inukai's assassination, and they were not to return until after the Second World War. Eleven men were to head the government from May 1932 to August 1945. Four of these men were admirals, four were generals, and only three were civilians. The admirals tended to be moderate, the generals were inclined to chauvinism, and the civilians were all very conservative members of the establishment who were acceptable to the military.

In selecting Inukai's successor, the emperor told Saionji that the next prime minister had to be a man of integrity who was not sympathetic to the radical nationalists and who would uphold the constitution. Saionji believed that Admiral Saitō Makoto, the former governor-general of Korea, would fit the bill. Saitō was a moderate who was acceptable not only to the military but also to the inner circle of court advisers. As a result, Saitō was given the task of forming a "united, national" government.

The Saitō cabinet included representatives from the two major parties as well as from the bureaucracy, the business world, and the armed forces. Takahashi Korekiyo once again became minister of finance and sought to curb the army, which was represented in the cabinet by Araki.

Saitō was not an aggressive individual, and he consequently failed to provide the strong leadership that was vitally needed if the many difficulties facing the nation were to be resolved. His cabinet, known as the "slow-motion cabinet," did restore a degree of calm to the turbulent political scene, but fundamentally, its policy of "letting sleeping dogs lie" merely provided a temporary respite while militaristic, authoritarian forces were sinking their roots in deeper and more securely. The political parties were split into factions, with a large segment joining the ranks of the militant nationalists in the hope of riding the tide of imperialism to power. At the same time, Saitō diminished the influence of the party men in the cabinet by establishing the Five Ministers Conference—an inner cabinet consisting of the prime minister and the ministers of war, navy, finance, and foreign affairs—as the key policymaking body. This practice, which was retained by subsequent cabinets, diminished the influence of the other cabinet ministers while giving the army and navy a much stronger voice in the setting of foreign and domestic policy.

The Saitō cabinet succumbed to the army's insistence that Japan withdraw from the League of Nations, although Minister of Finance Takahashi vehemently opposed such a move. On the continent, the Kwantung Army continued to pursue its own objectives as if it were an autonomous organ, forcing the government to go along with its actions. In February 1933 it moved its troops against Jehol province in Inner Mongolia and advanced south of the Great Wall in pursuit of the Chinese forces. It also occupied Shanhaiguan Pass, but Minister of War Araki prevented the army from going further into Chinese territory. In May 1933 the Kwantung Army negotiated the Tangku Truce with the Chinese authorities, who were more concerned about suppressing Communists in China than curbing Japanese aggression. Under this agreement Manchuria was extended into Jehol province, the Kwantung Army gained control of the Shanhaiguan Pass, and a demilitarized zone was established north of Tianjin and Peking.

As a result of Japan's isolation from the international community and its successes in Manchuria, the tide of ultranationalism and militarism continued to sweep the country. One consequence of this was the campaign to rid the entire land of "dangerous thought." As we noted earlier, vigorous suppression of the Communists had been taking place since the time when Tanaka was prime minister. Now, as nationalistic sentiments began inundating the country, many of the incarcerated Communists recanted, pledged their loyalty to the Imperial Way, and embraced "Japanism." Many former left-wing socialists became staunch supporters of imperialism.

The initial effort to control thought may have been directed primarily at the Communists, but shortly the scope of what constituted "dangerous thought" was gradually enlarged until eventually socialism, liberalism, pacifism, and internationalism were all deemed threatening ideologies, and consequently, their adherents became objects of persecution. The first victim of this renewed effort to purge the intellectual world of "dangerous thought" was Takigawa Yukitoki (1891–1962), a law professor at Kyoto University. Prior to this, professors had been expelled from the universities for their espousal of communism. In Takigawa's case, his dismissal was ordered in 1933 by the minister of education, Hatoyama Ichirō, because the law books that he wrote were critical of the existing social and legal practices. This campaign to purge "Red professors" had the support of right-wing members of both houses in the Diet. Despite the protests of the president, faculty, and students of Kyoto University, Takigawa was dismissed and was prevented from publishing any of his works until the postwar period.

At the same time of this attack on "dangerous thought," the military won public sympathy for the "patriotic young men" who had assassinated Inukai.

More than 1 million signatures were gathered on petitions asking for clemency. In July 1933 another scheme to assassinate the prime minister and other leaders was uncovered. This plot, called the Shimpeitai Jiken (Divine Soldiers Affair), was led by a follower of Inoue Nisshō, and even Araki was among the projected targets.

The military became increasingly critical of the Saitō government as Minister of Finance Takahashi maintained tight control of the purse strings and as Hirota Kōki (1878–1948), who became foreign minister in September 1933, pursued a policy of adjusting Japan's relations with China. In international affairs, tensions were reduced in March 1935 after prolonged negotiations, when Russia sold the Chinese Eastern Railroad in northern Manchuria to Japan.

Right-wing nationalists grew impatient with Saitō's moderate policies and began to intensify their attacks against his government. For instance, the minister of commerce and industry was forced to resign after it was exposed that ten years earlier he had written an article that was favorable to Ashikaga Takauji, the founder of the Ashikaga Bakufu, who attacked the reigning emperor. Saitō resigned in July 1934 when it was charged that some government officials had taken bribes from a major rayon company.

In selecting Saitō's successor, Saionji introduced a new procedure. He called a conference of senior statesmen and conferred with all the former prime ministers as well as the lord keeper of the privy seal and the president of the Privy Council. Saitō recommended that Admiral Okada Keisuke be appointed as his successor; Saionji and the others concurred with the choice. Once again the advisers of the emperor had turned to a moderate admiral. The Okada cabinet was virtually an extension of the Saitō cabinet, but it lacked the cooperation of the Seiyūkai; in fact, the three Seiyūkai men who entered the cabinet were expelled from the party. This presaged trouble for the Okada government because it meant that the Seiyūkai would play the demagogic game of championing right-wing, ultranationalist causes by seeking to win the favor of the radical militarists.

The Okada cabinet may have enjoyed some success in adjusting Japanese relations with China, but by and large, it took a giant step backward in the realm of international cooperation. Going along with the wishes of the naval expansionists, led by the chief of the naval general staff, Admiral Suetsugu, the cabinet decided to abrogate the Washington and London naval agreements after the United States and Great Britain refused to agree to Japanese demands for parity. At the end of 1935 the departure of the Japanese delegation from the London conference catapulted the three powers into a naval arms race.

The Okada government was also influenced by Nagata Tetsuzan, who argued that all nations had to be prepared to wage total war. Nagata argued that there had to be an autonomous national defense program in which all phases of the system, particularly military and economic planning, were coordinated. To lay the groundwork for such a scheme, Okada established the Cabinet Research Bureau, whose task was the preparation of legislative proposals and position papers on important economic problems. Subsequently, this bureau became the agency responsible for formulating those laws that steadily diminished the rights and freedom of the people.

The Okada cabinet was confronted by an even stronger tide of right-wing nationalism than Saitō had faced. The attacks on the academic community were sustained by the ultranationalists, militarists, and political opportunists. A prominent authority on constitutional law, Minobe Tatsukichi (1873–1948), became a primary focus of their criticism. He supported the theory of the corporate state with a juristic personality and its corollary theory that the emperor was an organ of the state and is contained within the state rather than above or identical with it, as was argued by scholars who believed in a mystical notion of the national polity. Initially, arguments concerning Minobe's theory were confined largely to the scholarly world, and his interpretation was generally accepted by students of government and law. In the mid-1930s, however, as the forces of authoritarianism and ultranationalism gained strength, the theory that Minobe had first made public twenty-seven years earlier was turned into a major political issue by men who objected to all liberal and rational interpretations of the constitution.

The radical militarists objected to Minobe's Organ Theory because they favored an absolutist interpretation that would permit them to exercise power on behalf of the emperor, whom they claimed to represent directly under the provision of the "independence of the supreme command." Minobe had angered the army on many occasions by consistently espousing a narrow interpretation of this concept and by criticizing the army for advocating total planning for war. The army, therefore, was more than a little anxious to join the scheme to discredit Minobe.

Ultranationalist scholars and politicians initiated the attack on Minobe. In February 1935 a reactionary member of the House of Peers and director of the Kokuhonsha, Kikuchi Takeo (1854–1912), publicly condemned the Organ Theory as being contrary to the national polity and then denounced Minobe as a "traitor, rebel, and academic bandit." Right-wing nationalists led by Tōyama Mitsuru formed an organization to destroy the Organ Theory. The scope of the attack was widened when the army called upon the Military Reservists Association to rally public opinion against Minobe.

Perceiving this as an issue that could readily be exploited to overthrow the Okada government, the followers of Hiranuma and the members of the Seiyūkai joined the attack on Minobe. They criticized officials who were sympathetic to Minobe and excoriated the government for defending the "defiler of the national polity." Both houses of the Diet passed resolutions condemning his theory, and a member of the lower house brought charges against the scholar for lèse-majesté. Minobe was finally forced to resign his seat in the House of Peers and his teaching post at the University of Tokyo, and his books were banned. The following year a fanatical ultranationalist attempted, unsuccessfully, to murder him.

The assault on the Organ Theory had far greater significance than being merely an attack on the life and ideas of one man. In effect it presaged the end of freedom of thought in Japan. During the succeeding years, a strict surveillance was imposed over all political theories. No idea that ran contrary to the mystical and irrational concept of national polity could be propounded even within the narrow confines of the academic world. The army and the ultranationalists, who made it their sacred mission to "clarify the national polity," set out to eradicate all vestiges of the Organ Theory.

In March 1937 the Ministry of Education issued *Kokutai no Hongi* (Cardinal Principles of the National Entity of Japan), a booklet describing the unique characteristics of Japan. It stated, in part:

> Our country is established with the emperor, who is a descendant of Amaterasu Ohmikami, as her center, and our ancestors as well as we ourselves constantly have beheld in the emperor the fountainhead of her life and activities. For this reason, to serve the emperor and to receive the emperor's great august Will as one's own is the rationale of making our historical "life" live in the present; and on this is based the morality of the people.[13]

The booklet again identified the family system as the linchpin of the whole society: "Our country is a great family nation and the Imperial Household is the head family of the subjects and the nucleus of national life." The treatise went on to define and extol the virtues of loyalty, patriotism, filial piety, harmony, the martial spirit, and Bushidō. Western individualism was condemned as the root cause of democracy, socialism, communism, and anarchism, and it was blamed for "the ideological and social confusion and crisis" prevalent in Japan and in the West.[14] Thus, with the publication of this document, an official doctrine of "Japanism" was promulgated, and conformity to this ideology became virtually mandatory.

The Organ Theory not only gave rise to an official formulation of national polity but was also responsible for creating conflicting factions within the army. In the midst of the controversy, the most vehement army critic of Minobe's theory, General Mazaki, was transferred from his post as inspector general of military education. His radical followers blamed Minister of War Hayashi and Nagata Tetsuzan, chief of the military affairs bureau, for this demotion. Hayashi had contended some time earlier that the Organ Theory had not had an inimical effect on military education, and Mazaki, who favored military intervention in political affairs, openly contradicted this. The transferring of Mazaki was regarded as a plot on the part of the Tōsei-ha to diminish the influence in the army of the Kōdō-ha.

It has been customary to divide the army factions into these two groups, the Tōsei-ha and the Kōdō-ha, but the division was by no means rigidly fixed. There were no absolute and clearly defined disagreements about military and political matters between officers who supposedly belonged to these rival factions. Affiliation with one group or the other was informal, and the majority of the 6,000 army officers actually took no part whatsoever in the factional rivalry. The Kōdō-ha, gathering around generals Araki and Mazaki, had among its adherents a group of young officers at the company-commander level. The more loosely grouped Tōsei-ha consisted of officers who objected to the tactics and the personnel policies of the Araki-Mazaki faction.

In order to bring about the Shōwa Restoration, the Kōdō-ha officers believed that senior statesmen, members of the zaibatsu, and corrupt politicians had to be eliminated by direct action. This approach was vigorously opposed by Nagata and other key officers of his faction, such as Tōjō Hideki and Mutō Akira (1892–1948), who believed that isolated acts of violence would only upset the order of things and consequently impede the plan to prepare the nation for total war. These army officers, who came to be called the Tōsei-ha, believed that the necessary changes could be brought about without violence by using legitimate means under the leadership of the army central headquarters. They insisted that the realization of this end depended on the entire army being united and disciplined under the tight control of army leaders at the center.

The conflict between the two factions[15] came to the surface after Araki became minister of war late in 1931. He made personnel changes at the center by removing from key positions the followers of Ugaki, such as General Tatekawa, as well as some members of the Sakurakai. Among the latter was Hashimoto Kingorō, who had lost his enthusiasm for Araki when he disappointed the plotters of the October Incident. In their places Araki installed his friends and followers, including General Mazaki Jinzaburō, who was made the vice chief of the general staff. This policy of filling sensitive posts with his own followers caused those who were ousted to form a faction called the Seigun-ha (Purification Faction) under the leadership of Tatekawa and Hashimoto. They called for the purification of the army through the elimination of cliquism. The Seigun-ha tended to align itself with the Tōsei-ha.

In January 1934 Araki was replaced by General Hayashi Senjūrō as minister of war. The supreme war council, consisting of leading admirals and generals, had disapproved of Araki's personnel policies as well as of his repeated pronouncements that 1936 was going to be a year of crisis because a war with the Soviet Union was likely to break out at that time. Hayashi was thought to be sympathetic to the Araki faction, but upon assuming the post of minister of war, he made Nagata the chief of the military affairs bureau. Nagata, as we noted earlier, was opposed to isolated acts of violence and believed in maintaining discipline in the army. In November 1934 two Kōdō-ha officers, Muranaka Kōji and Isobe Senichi, contrived an assassination plot, which also involved the cadets of the Military Academy. Their aim was to murder the senior statesmen and establish a military government, but before any action could be taken the plot was uncovered by Nagata, who expelled the conspirators from the army. Nagata also removed Araki's men from the army's top positions, but he was unable to move immediately against Mazaki.

Now that Araki was out of office, the Kōdō-ha officers came to regard Mazaki as their main hope of regaining their influence. Their chances of ever succeeding in this regard were seriously threatened when, in the summer of 1935, Hayashi and Nagata finally made a move to place Mazaki on the inactive list. Mazaki was able to resist the plan to retire him, but he nevertheless lost his post as inspector general of military education. The Kōdō-ha officers were infuriated by his transfer, and they circulated statements in the army attacking the senior statesmen, members of the zaibatsu, and their servants in the army who, they asserted, had conspired against Mazaki and Araki. Nagata was singled out as most responsible for the injustices against the two generals. Aizawa Saburō (1889–1936), a fanatical Kōdō-ha officer, took matters into his own hands, and on August 12, 1935, he walked into Nagata's office and assassinated the man who was regarded as the most brilliant officer in the army. Hayashi, who all along was viewed as merely Nagata's puppet, shouldered the responsibility for this violent breach of army discipline and resigned. General Kawashima Yoshiyuki (1878–1945) was appointed as his replacement, but he turned out to be indecisive in dealing with radical army officers.

Aizawa's trial was held under the jurisdiction of the First Division, whose commanding general, Yanagawa Heisuke (1879–1945), was a follower of Araki. Consequently, the Kōdō-ha officers managed to turn the trial into a vehicle for denouncing the Tōsei-ha and for expounding their own political philosophy. The public, as a result, came to regard Aizawa as a sincere, selfless patriot whereas Nagata was seen as an unprincipled schemer.

The Kōdō-ha officers decided that a propitious moment to stage a coup d'état had arrived since public opinion had been aroused to their advantage by a number of important events; namely, the Aizawa trial, the controversy over the Organ Theory, and the campaign to clarify the national polity. The conspirators were led by Muranaka and Isobe, now civilians, and officers of the

First Division. Kita Ikki and his follower, Nishida Zei (1870–1945), another former army officer, were also informed of the projected coup d'état. The conspirators had the implicit support of generals Mazaki and Yanagawa, and they were given financial assistance from right-wing businessmen and politicians. It is also believed that General Yamashita Tomoyuki contributed to arousing the rebellious officers by talking of the need to cut down Prime Minister Okada. Minister of War Kawashima had a hand in supporting the conspiracy by hinting to the young officers that he would not intervene should they stage an incident. The insurgents decided that they would have to make their move in February 1936, before they were fully prepared. They were compelled to act prematurely because of the announcement in December that the First Division, to which most of the conspirators were attached, was to be dispatched to Manchuria.

The rebels struck on the morning of February 26 by moving more than 1,400 men of the First Division into the streets of Tokyo to occupy key government buildings and to murder a number of senior statesmen and high government officials. Among the intended victims were Prime Minister Okada; former prime minister Saitō; Minister of Finance Takahashi; General Watanabe, who had replaced Mazaki as inspector general of military education; the Grand Chamberlain, Suzuki Kantarō (1868–1948); and former Lord Keeper of the Privy Seal, Makino. Originally, Saionji was also on the list, but he was dropped when the rebels failed to agree on whether or not to liquidate him.

Three of the intended victims, Saitō, Takahashi, and Watanabe, were killed. An official announcement was made that Okada had also been murdered, but the assassins mistakenly shot his brother-in-law, and Okada escaped. Suzuki Kantarō received several bullet wounds, but he managed to survive and later served as prime minister during the last months of World War II. Makino succeeded in eluding the assassins.

The rebels occupied the heart of Tokyo after staging the bloodbath, and then issued a manifesto justifying their actions. They accused the genrō, senior statesmen, military cliques, bureaucrats, and party politicians of undermining the national polity and of creating a critical situation abroad. They explained that these reasons motivated them to eliminate the men responsible for the national crisis. They called upon Minister of War Kawashima to take charge of the situation and implement the Shōwa Restoration. They also demanded that General Araki be placed at the head of the Kwantung Army, while generals Ugaki, Minami, Koiso, and Tatekawa be placed under arrest.

The rebels had no concrete plans beyond assassinating the top government officials and court advisers, so the success of their coup actually depended upon whether or not the army leaders would support them. The generals, however, were unable to agree on the course of action to be followed. The central figure, Minister of War Kawashima, was basically irresolute, but he did tend to sympathize with the insurgents. Mazaki and Araki naturally opposed any move to suppress the rebellion by force. Mazaki, in fact, urged Kawashima to persuade the emperor to comply with the demands of the rebels. In sharp contrast, the officers of the general staff, Ishiwara Kanji in particular, insisted that the rebels be subdued, even by force if necessary. Ishiwara went so far as to advocate calling army divisions from the outlying districts into Tokyo.

The person most responsible for quashing the rebellion, however, was the emperor, who was adamant that the insurgents be subdued. The government, buttressed by the emperor's strong stand and headed by acting prime minister Gotō Fumio (1884–1980), proclaimed martial law in Tokyo on February 27. General Kashii, who was sympathetic to the rebels, was appointed the commanding general. The navy, also taking a strong position against the insurgents, brought its fleet into Tokyo Bay and moved the marines into the capital.

The rebels now pinned all their hopes on Mazaki and sought to have him appointed as prime minister. However, he began to waver after an imperial command was issued to the troops to return to their barracks. Considerable pressure from Ishiwara and the vice chief of staff, Sugiyama, finally forced General Kashii to move his forces against the rebels, and he surrounded them on February 28. The next day, a last appeal was issued to the mutineers to surrender. The leaders of the insurgents finally yielded, and the troops began moving back to the First Division compounds; by evening the insurrection was over. Two rebel officers committed suicide, but the others decided to stand trial and use the court as a rostrum from which to present their case to the public. They were, however, tried very swiftly and in secret. Nineteen men, including Muranaka, Isobe, Kita, and Nishida, were condemned to death and executed.

Kita's connection with the uprising was tenuous. He had no part in planning or executing the rebellion, and although he had been informed of the plot, the planners of the coup had not definitely decided to put his political concepts into effect once they secured control. Nonetheless, Kita was held responsible for the influence his *A Plan for the Reorganization of Japan* had on the rebel officers. Kita was a civilian but was tried by a military court-martial and, a year after his sentence was handed down, was executed. Mazaki's ties with the rebels were certainly stronger than Kita's, but he was absolved.

The attempted coup of February 26 was followed by a major purge in the army. The generals and officers who were linked to the Kōdō-ha as well as those officers who had caused strife in the army by participating in the activities of the Purification Faction were retired or removed from key posts. Araki and Mazaki were among those placed on the inactive list. In order to ensure that none of the generals who had been placed on the inactive list would return to power as minister of war, the military regulations were revised again to make only active generals and admirals eligible to serve as war and naval ministers. This change, however, also gave the army a veto power over cabinets of which it disapproved.

The purge was conducted by officers who have been categorized as members of the Tōsei-ha, but actually they were men who disapproved of factionalism and mindless acts of violence. The men directly responsible for the purge were the new minister of war, Terauchi Juichi, and his vice minister, Umezu Yoshijirō (1882–1949), who in effect masterminded the entire affair. Mutō Akira, Ishi-wara Kanji, and Umezu became the real wielders of power in the army.

The removal of the Kōdō-ha did not by any means put an end to the army's interference in political affairs. In fact, with internal strife eliminated, the army leaders became even more aggressive in meddling in politics. At the same time, civilians became very timid in dealing with the army, having had a taste of what a politically discontented military was capable of doing. The insurrection of February 26, therefore, greatly strengthened the army's hand and severely diminished the influence of the liberal senior statesmen and court advisers.

The army demonstrated the force of its newly won power immediately. Hi-rota Kōki, the new prime minister, set out to select his cabinet ministers, but Terauchi, who was chosen as minister of war, insisted on exercising a veto over all the liberal candidates who were recommended for cabinet posts. Hirota meekly succumbed to the army's demand, and as a result, Terauchi, with the assistance of Umezu and Ishiwara, rejected out of hand four of the men who were selected and shifted two others from the posts initially assigned to them. Yoshida Shigeru (1885–1967), who was serving as Hirota's chief adviser in se-lecting the cabinet members, was among those men rejected by the army. Yoshida was slated to become foreign minister, but the army objected because, not only was he the son-in-law of Makino, who was a target of the insurrection of February 26, but he was also known to be openly critical of the militarists.

Before turning to Hirota, Saionji had asked Prince Konoe, president of the House of Peers, to serve as prime minister, but he refused, claiming to be in poor health. Saionji then selected Hirota because, although he was known to have ties with the right-wing nationalists, as foreign minister he had insisted that the foreign office, rather than the military, be the organ of government charged with formulating foreign policy. He had also advocated a policy of harmony and cooperation with China.

The chief tasks facing the Hirota government were the formulation of a clearly defined national policy and the resolution of the North China problem. In August it adopted a policy statement entitled "The Fundamental Principles of National Policy," the basic points of which had been formulated by the offi-cers of the army and navy. According to this document, the primary objectives of Japan were held to be twofold: first, consolidate the position of the Japanese empire in East Asia, and second, advance into the region of the South Sea.

The navy had long been critical of the army's China policy, which it feared could lead to war with England and the United States at a time when Japan could not possibly match the combined fleets of those two countries. In order to gain access to the oil deposits in Southeast Asia, the navy wanted to adopt a policy of "defending in the north and advancing to the south." Consequently, a moderate policy in China had to be pursued, the navy argued, so as not to arouse British opposition there. This, in effect, was the very policy that was adopted by the Hirota government. At the same time, military defenses against Russia were to be strengthened. The move to the south was to be accomplished by peaceful means, but there was nevertheless to be a naval buildup to prepare for possible intervention by the United States.

Sweeping internal changes had to be made to achieve these goals. It deemed necessary the expansion of the military and naval forces; it was also decided that administrative reforms and new economic and fiscal policies were essential. A reorganization of the Japanese way of life, including "the wholesome development of the people's mode of thinking," was considered vital. In other words, what was contemplated was a comprehensive plan that would make effective use of all elements of the national life in order to achieve these strategic objectives: peace and stability in eastern Asia through the establishment of hegemony over China; naval supremacy in the western Pacific; and superiority over the Soviet army in the Far East.[16]

The outbreak of the China War in 1937, coupled with Japan's inability to extricate itself from the quagmire, effectively prevented the nation from realizing the strategic objectives that were outlined in "The Fundamental Principles of National Policy." Nevertheless, its goals were actively pursued by the government regardless of who headed it. Out of this policy, then, emerged the circumstances that ultimately led to the war in the Pacific. The International Military Tribunal, which tried and executed Hirota after the end of the Second World War, held "The Fundamental Principles of National Policy" to have been the blueprint for imperialism that actually led to the war in the Pacific.

The political parties had exercised very little influence ever since Inukai's assassination, but the army still regarded them as serious obstacles to its plan to place the nation on a wartime footing. It contemplated further restricting the role of the Diet in order to make the political parties wholly ineffective. Rumors of the army's plan aroused some of the party men, but a substantial number of them hoped to strengthen their positions by cooperating with the militarists.

In January 1937 a member of the Seiyūkai, Hamada Kunimatsu, criticized the army for its political activities and charged that the military was permeated with sentiments favoring dictatorship. Minister of War Terauchi was infuriated at Hamada and accused him of insulting the army. Hamada responded by saying that if in reviewing the transcript he discovered that he had in fact insulted the army, then he would commit seppuku. If he did not, however, then he believed Terauchi should do so. Incensed, Terauchi urged Hirota to dissolve the Diet. Hirota refused to comply, and Terauchi resigned, bringing down the entire cabinet with him.

The masterminds in the army, such as Ishiwara, wanted Hayashi appointed as Hirota's successor, but Saionji turned instead to Ugaki, believing that he would be able to keep the army radicals under control. Ugaki, however, was unacceptable to the army for at least three compelling reasons: first, he had been responsible for arms reduction while he was minister of war under Katō Kōmei; second, he had equivocated in the March Incident of 1931; and third, he was regarded as being too intimate with party politicians. The army officers led by Ishiwara sought to dissuade him from accepting the premiership, but when he insisted on going ahead anyway, the army refused to provide him with a minister of war. His numerous efforts to persuade at least several different generals to assume the post all failed. Reluctantly Ugaki abandoned his efforts to form a cabinet, and Saionji finally turned to the army's choice, General Hayashi.

Hayashi did not turn out to be the puppet that Ishiwara had expected him to be. For example, he refused to appoint Itagaki as minister of war, and for his minister of finance he would not accept Ishiwara's recommendation of Ikeda Seihin, a Mitsui executive who was known to be sympathetic to the militarists. Yūki Toyotarō (1877–1951), who was appointed minister of finance, did, however, favor cooperating with the military, and Ikeda was made the head of the Bank of Japan. Yūki reversed the Hirota government's policy of increasing government expenditures and reduced the budget by 10 percent, although he left the military budget untouched.

The Hayashi cabinet failed to include a single political party member, but the party men treated the new government gingerly and passed its budget and bills without offering much opposition. Nonetheless, Hayashi dissolved the Diet immediately after the session ended, claiming to be dissatisfied with the quality of the members. In what turned out to be the last prewar election contested by multiple parties, the Minseitō and Seiyūkai captured about the same number of seats. The especially notable result of this election was that thirty-six seats were captured by the Shakai Taishūtō, which doubled its membership in the Diet. This was the final, desperate resistance of the urban classes against the growing tide of militarism. Confronted by a hostile Diet, Hayashi resigned after staying in office for only four months.

The man who succeeded Hayashi was Konoe Fumimaro (1891–1945), who finally agreed to serve as prime minister. He belonged to the distinguished Fujiwara family of court aristocrats and was regarded favorably by all segments of the society. Not only was he well-educated and cultured but, it was believed, he was politically sophisticated. The military approved of him, and he also drew influential support from the political parties and from the business world. Saionji held him in high regard and in fact fully expected that eventually Konoe would take his place as the chief adviser to the emperor. He was only forty-six, a rather young age for a premier. His political views were not clearly known, so the newspapers wrote of "the attraction of the unknown quantity." Ironically enough the great hope of Shōwa Japan turned out to be a tragic failure—Konoe was hardly more than a tool of the military. During his tenure as prime minister the China War started and spread, and the circumstances that led to the war in the Pacific were allowed to get out of control.

The first Konoe cabinet, which came into existence in early June 1937, consisted primarily of his followers, who hoped to form a new political party under his leadership. It also included Hirota Kōki as foreign minister, General Sugiyama as minister of war, and Admiral Yonai as minister of the navy. Former vice minister of finance Kaya Okinori (1889–1977) accepted the post of minister of finance only after Konoe agreed to implement a program of economic controls that would effectively prepare the nation for total war.

A little over a month after Konoe took charge of the government the China Incident broke out and Japan was plunged into a situation that was eventually to draw it into a much larger war. The wartime footing of this period enabled the advocates of total planning and total mobilization to implement their programs, and the vestiges of liberal, democratic tendencies that had survived since Inukai's assassination were all but eradicated by the triumph of militarism and ultra-nationalism.

ECONOMIC DEVELOPMENTS

The military and the zaibatsu began to cooperate with each other from about the time that the Hirota cabinet came into existence. Prior to this, as was noted, the army radicals were hostile to the big capitalists, who were in return opposed to the army's plan to regulate the economy for its own strategic purposes. This animosity on the part of the army was demonstrated when Manchuria was brought under military control. The Kwantung Army leaders, led by Ishiwara, sought to keep the zaibatsu out of the new state. They planned to develop the Manchurian economy by relying upon small and middle-sized business firms or by turning to state capitalism. The Manchurian economy, however, could not be developed without the injection of capital from Japan.

Initially, much of the investment was channeled into Manchuria through the South Manchurian Railway Company, but eventually other firms began to participate in its economic growth. Special emphasis was placed on the development of heavy industries such as steel, coal mining, light metal, and automobile production. Soybean products had constituted 50 percent of Manchuria's industrial output before the Japanese takeover, but by 1940, nearly a third of the industrial output consisted of metals and machinery, and 15 percent was chemical products. The economy was dominated by Japanese interests, which held 84.1 percent of the capital investment. Some entrepreneurs managed to develop into "new zaibatsu" by using Manchuria as a base of operations and participating in defense production. All this was achieved by a ruthless exploitation of Chinese laborers in Manchuria, who were paid one-third the wages of Japanese workers.

The established zaibatsu also began to cooperate with the military in the building of defense industries as the military gained ascendancy and arms expenditures began to increase. In order to improve their image, the major zaibatsu families such as Mitsui and Mitsubishi began contributing to social welfare programs. They also removed family members from the top administrative posts and replaced them with managerial executives in the hope of masking the fact that these gigantic combines were controlled by family groups. At the same time, a nominal amount of stocks were sold to the public in order to refute the charge that they were tightly knit monopolistic combines.

The Japanese economy had recovered from the Great Depression sooner than the other industrial nations because of the tremendous increase in arms expenditures, which rose two-and-a-half times from 1931 to 1935. Recovery was also facilitated by the devaluation of the yen, which enabled Japan to compete more readily with other industrial powers.[17]

Japan's balance of trade steadily improved, and in 1935 its exports exceeded imports for the first time since World War I. The price of its imports had increased by 202 percent since 1931, but at the same time the price of its exports had increased by only 40 percent. This favorable export price was made possible by extremely low wages coupled with greatly advanced efficiency in production. Cotton textiles replaced raw silk as Japan's major export commodity.[18] The failure of raw silk to recover its status as a major export commodity affected the agrarian communities adversely since, as was noted previously, they relied heavily on the production of silkworm cocoons for supplementary income.

The influx of Japanese goods into foreign markets seriously disturbed its competitors, and in about 1932 they began to act to reverse the trend by raising tariffs and establishing quotas. These efforts to keep Japanese goods out of the Asian and African markets that were controlled by the Western powers aroused bitter sentiments in Japan and provided the militarists with additional excuses for seeking to establish a self-sufficient empire. It was essential for Japan to find markets for its manufactured goods because it had to import the bulk of its raw materials, and the imbalance in the export and import prices made it imperative to sell more than it bought.

The emphasis placed on arms production resulted in the expansion of heavy industries.[19] The established zaibatsu joined the new zaibatsu in developing strategic war industries. In shipbuilding, for example, Mitsubishi came to produce over 30 percent of the tonnage. It also moved into aircraft production, and by 1940 the company was testing the Zero, a highly effective fighter plane. It also entered the automobile and electrical industries.

In contrast to the gains made by the zaibatsu, the small and middle-sized enterprises suffered a decline, particularly those who were engaged in the production of nonessential goods. Most of these businessmen were unable to obtain raw materials, capital, or workers. Consequently, many small and medium-sized entrepreneurs went bankrupt or were absorbed by the bigger companies. Only those factories and shops that managed to get subcontracts for the production of war goods were able to prosper.

The firms engaged in defense production increased their profits substantially, but money wages for the workers remained more or less stable while real wages showed substantial declines.[20] Despite these serious declines, the president of a Japanese textile firm operating in China remarked that the capitalists in Japan were too timid in dealing with discontented workers. He went on to point out that in Shanghai they apprehended troublesome workers and summarily shot them. One Mitsui executive noted that the Manchurian workers were able to live on 10 sen a day while it cost the Japanese workers 50 sen a day. The Japanese workers, he concluded, should reduce their food costs by eating only rice and soybean cakes.

The period from 1931 to 1952 constitutes the second half of the second phase of modern economic growth in the twentieth century. The development in Japan during this period is attributed not only to such stimuli as the export of cheap goods but also to the "political solution," that is, military expansion.

The changeover to a wartime economy created hardship in the villages because the men were either drafted into the army or went to work in the factories, thus leaving only women, children, and the aged to do the farm work. The diversion of the nation's resources to war production resulted in shortages of chemical fertilizer and equipment needed on the farms. At the same time, the increased demand for rice in the cities and for the greatly expanded armed forces led the government to regulate prices and control sale and distribution. We shall now turn our attention to the political developments that caused these pressures on the economy to manifest themselves.

Notes

1. Shōwa is the era name for Emperor Hirohito's reign; Hirohito is known posthumously as Emperor Shōwa.

2. Ryusaku Tsunoda, W. T. de Bary, and Donald Keene, eds., *Sources of Japanese Tradition* (New York: Columbia University Press, 1958), pp. 796–798.

3. Ōuchi Tsutomu, *Fasshizumu e no Michi* (The Road to Fascism) (Tokyo: Chūō Kōron-sha, 1967), p. 297.

4. These men are often referred to as fascists, but because this term has become so fraught with associative significance, and in order to avoid the automatic equation of the Japanese version of aggressive nationalism with European fascism, the use of this term has been avoided except in the instances of material quoted from other sources. One factor that distinguishes the political situation in Japan during the 1930s from European fascism during the same period is that a totalitarian system under the strict control of one party did not emerge. Even during the height of military ascendancy, a kind of collective leadership still prevailed with the imperial court, the imperial advisers, the aristocrats, the senior statesmen, the bureaucrats, and the big business leaders retaining considerable influence. On this question of "fascism" see Masao Maruyama, *Thought and Behaviour in Modern Japanese Politics,* ed. Ivan Morris (London: Oxford University Press, 1963), pp. 25ff.; and George M. Wilson, *Radical Nationalist in Japan: Kita Ikki, 1883–1937* (Cambridge, Mass.: Harvard University Press, 1969), pp. 90ff.

5. Tsunoda et al., *Sources of Japanese Tradition,* p. 796.

6. Wilson, *Radical Nationalist,* p. 27.

7. Ibid., p. 28.

8. Richard Storry, *The Double Patriots: A Study of Japanese Nationalism* (Boston: Houghton Mifflin, 1957), p. 68.

9. Ōuchi, *Fasshizumu e no Michi,* p. 400.

10. Storry, *The Double Patriots,* p. 83.

11. It was revealed after the war that, just as the Chinese had charged, the attacks on the Japanese were actually masterminded by Itagaki, who bribed some Chinese to incite the mob to touch off an incident.

12. On January 7, 1931, Stimson declared that the United States "does not intend to recognize any situation, treaty, or agreement which may be brought about by means contrary to the covenants and obligations of the Peace of Paris of August 27, 1928."

13. Robert K. Hall, ed., *Kokutai no Hongi* (Cardinal Principles of the National Entity of Japan) (Cambridge, Mass.: Harvard University Press, 1949), p. 80.

14. Ibid., pp. 54, 89–90.

15. It was assumed until recently that the two factions were also divided over key issues of foreign policy. That is, it was claimed that the Kōdō-ha believed in engaging the Soviet Union in a conflict whereas the Tōsei-ha favored moving against China. The demise of the Kōdō-ha following the unsuccessful insurrection of February 26, 1936, was seen as having paved the way for the invasion of China. This interpretation has now been questioned. Factional strife in the army was not what determined the course of Japanese policies on the continent. The Araki faction was just as interested in extending Japanese influence into North China as was the Tōsei-ha. See James B. Crowley, *Japan's Quest for Autonomy: National Security and Foreign Policy, 1930–1938* (Princeton: Princeton University Press, 1966), pp. 247ff.

16. These moves in the direction of total planning are what lead many historians to speak of the rise of fascism in Japan during the 1930s. One authority speaks of the developments

under the Hirota government as an advance toward "a completed form of Fascism." See Maruyama, *Thought and Behaviour,* p. 71.

17. In 1931, 100 yen was worth 49.4 dollars, whereas in the following year it was worth only 20 dollars. The value of the yen rose somewhat after the United States went off the gold standard in 1933, but still 1 yen was worth only about 28 to 29 cents.

18. By 1936, Japan was the world's largest exporter of cotton piece goods. Textiles as a whole constituted 58 percent of its exports.

19. For instance, during the interval between the Manchurian Incident and the outbreak of the China Incident, the production of metals and machinery rose from 26 percent of the total industrial output to 34 percent. The textile industry, in contrast, dropped from 37 percent to 26 percent.

20. Taking November 1931 as index 100 we find that money wages stood at 93.5 in 1933, and 91.8 in June 1937, while real wages dropped to 87.8 in 1933, and then down to 75.7 in June 1937.

13

The Road to War

CHINA POLICY TO 1937

Following the Manchurian Incident, the Japanese government under Saitō proclaimed the "Asiatic Monroe Doctrine," the primary objective of which was the preservation of peace in Asia through "cooperative and friendly relations among China, Japan, and Manchukuo under the leadership of the Japanese empire." Hirota became foreign minister in September 1933, and he echoed the intentions of this doctrine by announcing a policy of "harmony and cooperation" and by expressing his desire to improve Sino-Japanese relations. The Nationalist government refused to recognize the establishment of the state of Manchukuo, but in July 1934 it did allow the passage of railroad traffic between China and Manchuria. This was soon followed by the establishment of customs offices and the resumption of postal services. In May 1935 Japan and China agreed to exchange ambassadors.

The Kwantung Army and the Japanese garrison in Tianjin, however, proceeded with plans to sever North China from the rest of the country. In late May 1935, using the outburst of demonstrations against them as an excuse, the Japanese, represented by General Umezu, commander of the Tianjin garrison, pressed the Peking Military Council to withdraw all Nationalist troops from Hebei province. The Chinese acceded to the Japanese demands, whereupon General Umezu and the representative of the Chinese Nationalist government, General Ho Yingchin (1893–1987), concluded the so-called Ho-Umezu Agreement in June. Not satisfied with this political victory, the Japanese army then proceeded to conclude a similar agreement concerning Chahar province. This was arranged by the head of military intelligence in Manchuria, General Doihara Kenji, who sealed an agreement with the general in charge of Chahar. All Nationalist officials and troops were then expelled from that province.

In October 1935 the Okada cabinet approved Hirota's Three Principles for presentation to China. They were: (1) the suppression of anti-Japanese activities and an end to the policy of dependence on Western powers; (2) the de facto recognition of Manchukuo and the resumption of economic and cultural relations between Manchuria and North China; and (3) the establishment of facilities to combat the menace of communism, which threatened China, Japan, and Manchuria from Outer Mongolia. The army officers in Manchuria and North China were not fully satisfied with these principles and wanted a fourth one adopted stating that the unification of China by the Nationalist Party was undesirable and unnecessary. This attitude reveals the basic reason for the eventual outbreak of the war with China.

The Japanese army officers on the continent, led by Doihara Kenji, proceeded to work for the establishment of autonomous regions in North China. In November, Doihara persuaded General Yin Jukeng (1885–1947), the Chinese administrator of the demilitarized zone, which had been established by the Tangku Truce, to proclaim the creation of the East Hebei Anti-Communist Autonomous Council. Doihara then sought to persuade the local warlord, General Song Cheyuan, to head an autonomous unit embracing Hebei and Chahar. These actions caused Chinese students and professors in Peking and Tianjin to demonstrate against the Japanese, who eagerly responded by gathering troops in Tianjin. In order to deprive the Japanese of an excuse to establish forcibly an autonomous state, Jiang's Nationalist government seized the initiative in December 1935 and created the Hebei-Chahar Political Council under General Song Cheyuan's direction. General Song was considered to be pro-Japanese, but the council, rather than being an autonomous political entity, was actually an agency of the Nationalist government. Nonetheless, the authority and prestige of the Nationalist government had been seriously compromised in North China. Further efforts to improve Sino-Japanese relations failed because Japan insisted on using Hirota's Three Principles as a basis for discussion while the Nanjing government was determined to bring North China under its authority.

As noted earlier, when Hirota took the reins of government his cabinet formulated "The Fundamental Principles of National Policy," which called for a moderate policy toward China and a stronger defensive posture toward Russia. In line with this policy, the Hirota cabinet concluded an Anti-Comintern Pact with Germany, which on an official level simply called for an exchange of information for the purpose of guarding against the subversive activities of the Communist International. However, by secret provisions in the pact, the two nations agreed that in case either of the contracting parties were attacked by the Soviet Union or were under the danger of being attacked without provocation, the other party would not take any action that would be helpful to the Soviet Union. The agreement was intended to restrain the Soviet Union in the

Far East while at the same time preventing Nationalist China from relying upon the Soviet Union for support against Japan. Contrary to expectations, the pact tended to harden Russia's position against Japan and also increase English and American distrust of Japan, who, as far as these Allies could surmise, seemed to be aligning itself with the European fascist powers. This impression was reinforced when Italy joined the Anti-Comintern Pact a year later.

The Hirota government sought to curb the activities of the field armies in North China and concentrate on economic penetration. It also endeavored to persuade the Nationalist government to join its camp by signing an anti-Communist military pact. Even so, it did nothing to restrain the Kwantung Army officers from plotting an invasion of Inner Mongolia. For example, in November 1936 a Japanese collaborator, Prince De, led his army into Inner Mongolia in the hopes of establishing an independent state there. This attempted invasion failed, and De's forces were defeated at Pailingmiao.

At this point, an important incident occurred that caused the Nationalist government to adopt a tougher position toward Japan. In December 1936, Jiang flew to Xian to oversee the launching of a new offensive against the Communists in Shensi Province. He was kidnapped by Zhang Xueliang, who hoped to persuade him to consent to a united front with the Communists in order to stop Japanese aggression. Evidently Jiang agreed to cooperate because, upon his release, he called an immediate halt to the campaign against the Communists.

When General Hayashi replaced Hirota as prime minister he pursued a policy of moderation toward China. He appointed as foreign minister Satō Naotake (1882–1971), who favored maintaining friendly relations with England and the United States. However, Hayashi was not in power long enough to effect a significant improvement in Sino-Japanese relations.

A month after Konoe succeeded Hayashi as prime minister, war with China broke out. The conflict was touched off by a minor incident that occurred during the night of July 7, 1937, between Japanese forces out on maneuvers and the Chinese troops of General Song Cheyuan at Marco Polo Bridge just outside of Peking. Initially, the authorities on the spot seemed to have the situation under control, and by July 11, a cease-fire had been concluded. It has never been verified as to which side was actually responsible for firing the first shot.

In Tokyo, the Konoe cabinet regarded the incident as a minor matter and adopted a policy of local settlement and "non-enlargement." The army was divided between those who wanted to seize this opportunity to strike a decisive blow against the Chinese forces and thus establish a separate state of North China, and those who opposed such drastic measures. The aggressive position was championed by Mutō Akira, a high-ranking general-staff officer, and Tanaka Shinichi (1893–1969), the chief of the military affairs department in the war ministry. Those who favored a policy of caution and restraint were led by Ishiwara, chief of the operations division of the general staff.

Ishiwara was convinced that Japan was neither militarily nor economically prepared to engage in a major war. Moreover, he felt that a full commitment to hostilities with China would surely result in a long, drawn out war of attrition. This of course would then make Japan vulnerable to the Soviet threat from the north. Vice chief of staff Lieutenant General Tada Shun (1882–1948) and Colonel Shibayama Kaneshirō of the war ministry (1889–1956) were also opposed to expanding the conflict. Of the officers in the field armies in China, it would be true to say that, by and large, the Kwantung Army officers favored an aggressive policy while the leaders of the army in North China favored a policy of localizing the conflict.

In the cabinet meeting that was held on July 9, Minister of War Sugiyama proposed sending three divisions from Japan and readying additional troops from Korea and Manchuria in case a greater military involvement became necessary. The proposal was shelved by the cabinet, but as local negotiators began to encounter new difficulties, Sugiyama, in attendance at the Five Ministers Conference on July 11, again asked that five divisions be mobilized for service in North China. Navy Minister Yonai Mitsumasa (1880–1948) voiced the only opposition to the plan, which was approved with the understanding that it would be cancelled if subsequent events made these troops unnecessary. This decision was made only a few hours before a cease-fire agreement was concluded in Peking.

On the same day, Konoe held a press conference in which he announced the mobilization plans and asked for public support. He also blamed the Chinese for the troubles in North China and demanded that they apologize, but he reiterated the government's intention of adhering to its policy of localizing the conflict. The Japanese officers in North China informed the government that it was now unnecessary to send reinforcements, but when word was received that the Nanjing government was taking steps to strengthen its military position in North China, the war ministry decided to dispatch one division from Korea and two brigades from Manchuria.

As might be expected, Chinese public opinion grew increasingly hostile toward Japan, particularly after Konoe's announcement concerning the mobilization of five divisions for possible service in North China. Japanese public opinion, in contrast, vigorously supported its government's tough posture.

The Japanese army officers in North China and foreign office officials remained confident that the affair could be settled amicably. However, on July 23, the Hebei-Chahar army ceased withdrawing toward the Baoding area as had been agreed by General Song and the Japanese army in North China; instead it began reentering Peking. It is believed that this reversal was ordered by Nanjing. On July 25 and July 26, skirmishes broke out between Chinese and

Japanese troops, whereupon General Katsuki, the newly appointed commander of the Japanese troops in North China, secured the approval of army authorities in Tokyo and proceeded to launch an attack against General Song's forces, driving them back toward Baoding.

The situation was further aggravated when during the night of July 28, the militia in Tongzhou, which was under the authority of the East Hebei Autonomous Council, attacked and killed 260 Japanese soldiers and civilians in retaliation for an accidental bombing of the Chinese barracks by a Kwantung Army plane. This incident was sensationalized to arouse anti-Chinese sentiments in Japan.

In order to prevent the situation from worsening still further, the Japanese government secretly dispatched an emissary to Nanjing to try to settle the dispute. Even before serious discussions could be started, however, the conflict spread to Shanghai. Growing anti-Japanese sentiment had compelled the navy to land additional marines in Qingdao and Shanghai so as to protect the Japanese residents there. On August 9 a Japanese marine officer and a seaman were killed by the Chinese security forces in Shanghai. Thereupon the navy, which had all along been insisting on moderation in North China, asked that three army divisions be sent to Shanghai because it considered central and southern China to be within its sphere of responsibility.

Minister of War Sugiyama was unenthusiastic about this proposal, but the cabinet went ahead and approved it on August 13. As a result the army, which had long favored an aggressive policy in North China while opposing an extension of the conflict to the south, sent two divisions to Shanghai. This affair brought the Sino-Japanese strife to a point of no return, and the emperor, who had insisted upon the localization of the hostilities in North China, resigned himself to the inevitable. Navy Minister Yonai remarked that "the policy of non-enlargement is dead. The North China Incident is now a Sino-Japanese Incident."

On August 13 the Sino-Japanese forces in Shanghai began exchanging fire, and by August 15 the Nanjing government deemed it necessary to order a general mobilization. On the same day, the Konoe government announced its plan to discipline the Chinese army for its atrocities and force the Nanjing government to reevaluate its position. The cabinet agreed on August 17 to abandon the policy of localizing the conflict and to turn its attention, instead, to preparing for a general war.

Thus the war in China commenced. Unlike the Manchurian Incident, it would appear that the Marco Polo Bridge confrontation was not staged by Japanese officers aiming to provoke a clash. Once the incident occurred, however, the expansionists managed to take advantage of every opportunity to get the Japanese army and government more and more deeply involved until the point of no return was reached. However, the responsibility for the war cannot be placed on the chauvinists alone because, regardless of the rhetoric used to conceal Japanese ambitions, the men responsible for the formulation of Japanese policy in China more or less agreed on the desirability of bringing North China under their control. None of the high officials seemed to feel any compunction about violating the political and territorial integrity of China.

THE CHINA INCIDENT

In the north, the Japanese army moved against the Nationalist forces in Chahar, and then General Tōjō Hideki led three brigades from there into Suiyuan Province in Inner Mongolia. Another contingent, led by General Itagaki, moved into Shansi province. By October the Kwantung Army had established autonomous governments in Chahar, Suiyuan, and northern Shansi. To coordinate this campaign, the North China Area Army was organized under the command of General Terauchi. Those who had favored the establishment of a separate state of North China wanted to occupy the line delineated by Suiyuan, Taiyuan, Shijiazhuang, Jinan, and Qingdao. General Terauchi also insisted that the Japanese forces must advance to the Yellow River. The general staff, under the leadership of the vice chief, General Tada, and with the support of Ishiwara, sought to limit the military campaign but failed to do so. By the end of the year the North China Area Army occupied Shijiazhuang, Taiyuan, and Jinan, thus achieving the initial objective to occupy most of North China.

On the other front, in Shanghai, the Chinese forces put up a much stiffer resistance than the Japanese military had anticipated. The city finally fell in early November, but only after additional reinforcements were sent. Thereupon the army commanders sought permission to pursue the Chinese and occupy the capital, Nanjing. General Tada was opposed to this plan, but Foreign Minister Hirota and the commanding general in central China, General Matsui, insisted that it was necessary to capture the capital in order to inflict a serious blow against the Nationalist government. Konoe agreed, and General Tada finally approved the plan.

The offensive against Nanjing began early in December and ended with the capture of the city on December 13. It was during this Nanjing campaign that the Japanese troops committed some of the most heinous atrocities in the history of warfare. They went through the streets of Nanjing indiscriminately killing Chinese men, women, and children without provocation. In the first two or three days after Nanjing was captured, at least 12,000 noncombatant Chinese were killed. During the first month about 20,000 cases of rape were reported and more than 20,000 Chinese males of military age were rounded up and shot. Similar atrocities were committed against residents living outside Nanjing; 57,000 refugees were captured, some of whom were starved, some tortured, and some machine-gunned and bayoneted to death. Even Chinese soldiers who surrendered were indiscriminately killed. In the first six weeks after the fall of Nanjing some estimates hold that more than 200,000 civilians and prisoners of war were killed in and around Nanjing.

One might speculate as to why the Japanese soldiers, who had behaved in a relatively exemplary fashion during the Russo-Japanese War, abandoned all sense of humanity in perpetrating "an orgy of murder, rape, and pillage which is almost beyond power of belief."[1] The answer no doubt is to be found in the complicated intermeshing of individual and group psychological forces that were at work. The Japanese people, with their long tradition of living under a hierarchic social order, had developed a dual tendency of submitting docilely to power and authority from above while domineering over the weak and the powerless below.[2] The old samurai concept that the commoners can be cut down with impunity is an illustration of the application of this attitude. The Japanese masses, once they donned the uniform of the imperial army or navy, became warriors with imperial sanction behind their every action. A strong feeling of national pride coupled with a sense of superiority over other races had been instilled in the youths of the nation, particularly after the Russo-Japanese War, when the officially prescribed textbooks emphasized the sacred nature of the Japanese nation.

The Japanese, who were essentially insular and parochial in their outlook, fell into an extreme state of hubris as a result of the indoctrination from early childhood about their unsurpassable excellence and uniqueness. The attitude of superiority toward fellow Asians grew more intense as Japan joined the ranks of the world powers by successfully adopting Western science and technology. Its neighbor, China, seemed to Japan to be mired in reactionary immobility. This contempt for the Chinese grew stronger after the Sino-Japanese War.

Intermeshed with the merciless attitude of the warrior who has no compunction about cutting down the helpless and the weak, there was probably a venting of all the frustrations and hostilities that had long been developing. The life of the average soldier had been inflexibly regimented by narrowly confined social rules and hard economic necessities. Moreover, the exceedingly harsh treatment that the young recruits were subjected to in the Japanese armed forces no doubt brutalized their spirit and inclined them to behave in a bestial manner when restraining forces were absent.

In general, people do tend to lose a sense of individual responsibility when acting with a mob. This is an especially pertinent fact when speaking about the Japanese soldier, in whom a sense of individual responsibility had not been fostered. The individual could behave in a totally reckless fashion toward people outside the group to which he belonged, although a strong sense of responsibility toward his own group was retained. The dissolution of this sense of personal accountability in the psychological core of the mob enabled the Japanese soldiers to behave in an utterly undisciplined fashion.

The officers charged with the obligation of preserving discipline among the soldiers disclaimed all responsibility. At the Tokyo War Crimes Trial, the commanding general of the Central China Area Army, General Matsui, had the following to say in response to the prosecuting attorney: "As Commander in Chief of the Central China Area Army I was given the power to command operations of the two subordinate armies under my command, but I did not have the authority directly to handle the discipline and morals within these respective armies."[3]

A commander of a brigade noted in his diary that angry soldiers, totally ignoring the officers' attempts to restrain them, massacred the Chinese troops who surrendered. However, the fact is that the officers actually condoned such behavior. This can be seen in his later remark that in light of the death of many of their fellow soldiers and the hardships of the ten days' campaign, one is compelled to join the soldiers in saying, "Get them all."

The army authorities did little to prevent further atrocities from being committed; in fact, as the officers and men began to boast of their exploits, the army central headquarters issued an order in February 1939 prohibiting the release of information concerning atrocities that were committed, but no orders were issued forbidding the commission of atrocities themselves.

Perhaps the real explanation and cause for atrocities is war itself, which not only condones but glorifies killing and thus brutalizes the human spirit. The revelation that atrocities have been committed by nations that presumably did not have the psychological problems that prevailed in prewar Japan (Serbia, Rwanda, Vietnam, Cambodia, etc.) would tend to confirm this thesis.

The brutal behavior of the Japanese soldiers in Nanjing did not break the Chinese will to resist the invaders. On the contrary, it reinforced the Chinese determination to resist and staunchly united the people around Jiang Jieshi.

Despite the fact that Japan had committed an open act of aggression against it, China found that it could not rely on other powers to assist in the struggle to repel the invaders. The Chinese government appealed to the League of Nations for support as soon as Japan commenced military operations, but the league responded with only a lukewarm condemnation of Japan. The Soviet Union was the only nation that was willing to offer tangible support to China by signing a treaty of nonaggression in August 1937 and by providing a certain amount of military equipment. A conference of the signatories of the Nine Power Treaty was called in Brussels, but because Japan boycotted the meeting, what little was produced had no significant effect. In the United States, President Franklin D. Roosevelt (1882–1945) made a speech in October 1937 proclaiming the need to quarantine aggression, but no concrete measures were taken to restrain the Japanese. The more jingoistic Japanese army officers sought to start a conflict with the Anglo-American nations by attacking their gunboats, the USS *Panay* and the HMS *Ladybird*, in the Yangtze River in

JAPANESE OCCUPATION OF CHINA. 1945.

Key to cities:				
1 Mukden	8 Paoting	16 Tsingtao	24 Shanghai	32 Taipei
2 Chinchow	9 Tatung	17 Yenan	25 Hangchow	33 Amoy
3 Shanhaikuan	10 Kalgan	18 Sian	26 Hankow	34 Hongkong
4 Dairen	11 Suiyuan	19 Loyang	27 Ichang	35 Canton
5 Port Arthur	12 Paotow	20 Kaifeng	28 Chungking	36 Kweilin
6 Tientsin	13 Taiyuan	21 Hsuchow	29 Chengtu	37 Nanning
7 Peking	14 Shihkiachwang	22 Taierchuang	30 Changsha	38 Kunming
	15 Tsinan	23 Nanking	31 Nanchang	

November. The matter, however, was resolved peacefully by prompt apologies and payment of reparations.

Germany was not enthusiastic about Japanese involvement in China because it felt this would prevent Japan from serving as an effective ally against the Soviet Union and the Western powers. This lack of ardor to have hostilities in China persist was shared by the Japanese general staff and cabinet, both of which still favored an early termination of the war. Consequently, when Germany offered to serve as mediator, the officials of the Japanese government accepted the offer and submitted their terms, which were then transmitted to the Nationalist government by the German ambassador in China. The terms were: creation of an autonomous Inner Mongolia, greatly expanded military zones in North China and Shanghai, an end to anti-Japanese activities, a pact against communism, and the reduction of tariffs on Japanese goods.

The Chinese officials believed that the terms were not particularly harsh, but they decided to wait before pursuing the matter further, at least until the results of the Brussels conference became known. As was noted, that conference proved ineffective, and Jiang immediately indicated his willingness to discuss the terms transmitted by the German ambassador, but by then Japan had captured Nanjing and the militant expansionists insisted upon adding more stringent conditions, which they were careful not to spell out too concretely. The Nanjing government asked for further clarification of the terms, whereupon the Japanese leaders, including Konoe, Hirota, and Sugiyama, insisted that the Nanjing government was not "sincere." They decided to terminate the negotiations despite the protestations of General Tada of the general staff. On January 16, 1938, Konoe issued a statement to the effect that the Japanese government would no longer have anything to do with the Nationalist government. The Konoe government now concentrated its efforts on the establishment of puppet governments in northern and central China with an eye toward the eventual creation of a puppet government for all of China.

Japan was now involved in a full-scale war with China, but the government did not officially declare war in the hope that the other powers would not cut off strategic goods from Japan in the name of neutrality. It was also believed that an "incident" would be easier to settle than a war.

The next stage in the military campaign was directed toward linking the battlefronts of northern and central China. After suffering a setback at the battle of Taierzhuang in April 1938, the North China Area Army began its drive toward Xuzhou, a vital railroad center that linked Nanjing and Jinan as well as the Yellow Sea and Xian. In early May the Central China Area Army drove from the south toward Xuzhou, which was captured on May 19. In late August an offensive was launched against the new capital, Hankow, and after encountering stubborn resistance, the Japanese forces were finally able to capture the a substantial diminution of the functions of the foreign office, was approved by the Five Ministers Conference in September. Ugaki was displeased with this arrangement and resigned, having failed to make any contribution toward the settlement of the war. He was succeeded by Arita Hachirō (1884–1965), a career diplomat.

In order to retract the January statement about not dealing with the Nationalist government and to lay the groundwork for the establishment of a government to be headed by Wang Jingwei (1883–1944), Konoe made a pronouncement on November 3 concerning his plan to establish a "New Order" in East Asia, which was to be based upon the cooperation of Japan, Manchukuo, and China. The defection of Wang Jingwei materialized in December when he fled Chongqing for Hanoi, calling upon his fellow countrymen to support his peace efforts. Wang had expected to establish a new government in the unoccupied regions of southwestern China, but failing to gain support from other Nationalist leaders, he was compelled to change his plans and become a puppet of the Japanese.

In another area of foreign relations, the Japanese suffered a serious setback at the hands of the Soviet Union. In July 1938 a border dispute broke out at the Changkufeng–Lake Khasan area where the borders of Siberia, Manchuria, and Korea meet. A number of army officers who were more concerned about the Soviet threat than the China war decided to eliminate the Soviet menace by taking advantage of the border dispute and using it as an excuse to engage the Soviet Union in a limited war. They expected to inflict a crushing blow upon the Russian forces in the region of Changkufeng, and on July 29, the commanding general of the Japanese forces in the disputed area started military action on his own initiative. Contrary to the expectations of the Japanese military leaders, the Russians possessed superiority in airpower, heavy artillery, and tanks, and they were thus able to deal a decisive blow. The Japanese troops were forced to withdraw, and the army was compelled to accept a negotiated settlement, although it remained adamant in its refusal to admit that it had suffered a defeat.

The self-delusion that the Japanese army so readily engaged in inhibited it from learning any lesson from the battle of Changkufeng, and so in the middle of 1939 it once again engaged Soviet forces in another "border incident." The scene of this conflict was Nomonhan at the border of Manchuria and Outer Mongolia. The incident started in early May, when a segment of the Kwantung Army clashed with Mongolian border guards. Fighting was limited to minor skirmishes during the first month, but as word was received that the Soviet Union was reinforcing its border forces, officials of the Kwantung Army began calling for a major offensive. This proposal was not well received by the army central headquarters because of its concern over the

city by the end of October. In the same month, a southern expeditionary fc
occupied the city of Guangzhou.

The Japanese had expected the fall of Hankow to lead to the capitulatior
the Nanjing government, but instead the capital was shifted to Chongqing ;
the battlefront was more or less stabilized, with Japan occupying the hea
populated and productive parts of China. The Japanese army now contro
the entire coast and the industrial centers. In the north it held the Peki
Tianjin area and the outlet to the Yellow River. In central China it contro
both banks of the Yangtze from the mouth to Hankow. In the south it o
pied Guangzhou and controlled the West River.

Early in the war, the Japanese confidence that a quick victory would su
follow a series of knockout blows was crushed by the indefatigable determ
tion of the Chinese to fight to the bitter end. However, now that the Japa
had control of the cities, railways, and rivers and could thus paralyze the (
nese economy, there was no question, the Japanese believed, that resista
would halt. Nevertheless, China did not capitulate, and the interminable
which men like Ishiwara had feared, became a reality. Japan got trapped
quagmire from which it could not extricate itself until seven years later w
it, rather than China, surrendered arms.

Konoe, however, did not abandon all hope of effecting a political se
ment, and he continued to make additional diplomatic efforts. In May
June of 1938 he reshuffled his cabinet, bringing Ugaki into the governmer
foreign minister, Araki as minister of education, and Itagaki as minister of
Konoe hoped that Ugaki's replacement of Hirota, who tended to follow
leadership of the army, would change the political situation regarding
China Incident. Konoe immediately informed his new foreign minister
the statement he had made earlier about not dealing with Jiang and the N
jing government was a mistake that he expected Ugaki to rectify.

Ugaki tried to conduct secret negotiations with H. H. Gung (1881–19(
the head of the executive branch of the Nanjing government, but before
tentative feelers could be extended further, the expansionists, insisting on
hering to the policy of ignoring Jiang's government, proceeded with their c
plans to create a puppet government. Konoe, contradicting what he had t
Ugaki, sanctioned these efforts to establish a rival to Jiang's government
Chongqing. A colonel in the war ministry was informed by his contacts w
Chinese officials that Wang Jingwei, the vice president of the Nationalist Pa
was ready to break with Jiang. As a result, negotiations were conducted w
Wang's friends to bring about his defection from Chongquing.

The army also sought to restrict the role of the foreign office in the set
ment of the China Incident and proposed the creation of a central organ t
would be responsible for managing Chinese affairs. This plan, which invol

many Japanese forces that were bogged down in China. Minister of War Itagaki nevertheless gave his approval, and the Kwantung Army launched a large-scale attack against the Soviet forces on June 27. As a result, a minor border clash was transformed into a major conflict. In August, the Soviet troops commanded by General Georgi Zukhov (1896–1974) launched a major counteroffensive using mechanized forces supported by airpower. The Japanese soldiers, completely lacking in this kind of strength, were reduced to confronting the Soviet tanks with Molotov cocktails. In view of their considerable advantage in mechanical power, it was not difficult for the Soviet forces to win a decisive victory.

The Kwantung Army asked for reinforcements in the hope of possibly recouping its losses, but the army authorities in Tokyo remained adamant in refusing to allow a further enlargement of the conflict. On September 1, Adolf Hitler launched his offensive against Poland and the world political situation became extremely precarious. The Japanese government was not prepared at a time like this to get involved in a major war with the Soviet Union over minor border disputes. Consequently, in mid-September, a cease-fire was arranged with the Soviets, who were also anxious to avoid a war in the Far East while Europe was in a state of turmoil.[4]

INTERNAL DEVELOPMENTS

The government moved to place the nation on an emergency footing immediately after the China Incident erupted. A Cabinet Planning Board was established to regulate production, foreign trade, finances, consumption, and labor. All unnecessary imports were curtailed, and the use of such items as cotton and iron in nonessential production was restricted. All factories engaged in arms production were brought under government supervision, and military officers were assigned to act as overseers in these plants.

The need for a more comprehensive mechanism of control was felt as it became increasingly evident that the China Incident was turning into a rather protracted affair. In February 1938, Konoe enacted a National Mobilization Act, which provided for the full control and utilization of all the nation's manpower and resources for the purposes of national defense.

The government did not restrict its activities to subjecting the economy to increasingly stringent controls for military purposes. The threats posed by border incidents with the Soviet Union, hostilities with China, and international insecurity caused the government to intensify its efforts to suppress "dangerous thought" by restricting the freedoms of speech, press, and assembly. In July 1936, and then again in the following February, there were mass arrests of Marxists as well as socialist professors who were engaged in academic disputations about the nature of the Meiji Restoration and where Japan stood in its stage of historical development.[5]

The next victims were the liberals. The Ministry of Justice proclaimed that "democracy and liberalism are hotbeds that breed communism." In the fall of 1937, Yanaibara Tadao (1893–1961), who became the president of Tokyo University after World War II, was dismissed from his teaching post at that institution because he denounced the war in China. In the following fall, Kawai Eijirō (1891–1944), a liberal and a foe of Marxism, was fired from his post at the same university and his publications were placed on the prohibited list.

A watchful eye was kept on publications that might reveal the Japanese military in a bad light. Censorship became increasingly stringent, and it was not at all uncommon to see the publication of articles and books in which one line after another was deleted. Newspapers and magazines that were in any way critical of the war effort were very effectively penalized by not being allotted their share of newsprint. Thus the authorities were able to weed out many undesirable papers and journals—by the end of 1939 more than five hundred publishers had gone out of business. As a result of this atmosphere of intimidation even the liberal newspapers headlined the news of the "glorious" victories of the "righteous" imperial army and condemned the "atrocious" Chinese "bandits." Military successes were exaggerated, defeats were never reported, and in this sense it can be said that the public was led blindly to the path of ultimate destruction and defeat while all along being firmly convinced that one magnificent victory after another was being won.

The government also began to place certain books, both Japanese and foreign works, on the "index of prohibited works," and the number of blacklisted titles increased year by year. In the early 1930s any work containing antiwar sentiments was rooted out and banned. Studies in economics were hit the hardest; not only Marxist writings but the works of classical economists were also prohibited. Any work with the word *capitalism* in the title was immediately rejected. The only acceptable theories in this field, as one economist later remarked, were the kind to be found in the *Kojiki* or *The Analects of Confucius*. The proletarian novelists were, of course, banned; but even those works of writers that had no political implications, such as Tanizaki's *Sasameyuki* (The Makioka Sisters), were proscribed because they were "useless literature of leisure." The censors did not restrict themselves to prohibiting contemporary literature or even the books of the Meiji period; instead, they reached all the way back into the past to blacklist the works of prominent writers whose ideas they found objectionable.

The government did not rely only on negative means to rectify the people's thinking; it sought actively to instill the right attitudes and beliefs in the people. It revised the textbooks that were used in the primary schools in 1933,

and again in 1941, in order to foster a more militaristic and nationalistic outlook among the children. Mythologies were presented as authentic history, and
students were taught not to question, but simply to memorize what they were
told they should learn. The teachers reinforced this approach by admonishing
the children to develop into courageous soldiers and by punishing those who
questioned the official truth. The indoctrination program in the schools
proved highly successful for it produced innumerable soldiers who willingly
gave their lives to the emperor and the country. During the war in the Pacific
many volunteered to become suicide pilots, no doubt sharing the conviction of
one of these young fliers, who said, "When I reflect upon the three-thousand-
year history of our imperial nation, I realize the truth that matters concerning
one puny individual or a single family are of no importance at all."[6]

In the realm of religion, periodic worship at Shinto shrines came to be almost a compulsory affair. At the same time, the persecution of Christians began to grow in intensity, and some Christian leaders were even forced to
choose between the Christian God and the Sun Goddess (or the emperor). By
and large, however, the Christians cooperated with the war effort. The Buddhist community, naturally, said nothing critical about the war or about the
growing trend toward totalitarianism.

The oppressive hand of the government was also extended to the labor
unions. In December 1937 the leftist Rōdō Hyōgikai was dissolved, and in
July 1940 the moderate Sōdōmei was compelled to disband. Agrarian unions
suffered the same fate, and in March 1941 the Nihon Nōmin Kumiai ceased
to exist.

The outbreak of the China Incident led the people onto the path of hardship, privation, sacrifice, and loss of freedom. Their lifestyle became more
sober and certainly more austere. These new times, when pervasive grimness
characterized their lives, were in sharp contrast to the early 1930s, when, despite the economic depression, the Manchurian Incident, and the growing ascendancy of militarism, there was a good deal of carefree gaiety. Movies,
musical revues, and light entertainment set the mood and the tone of the age.
Fashionable young men and women, known as "mobo" and "moga" (modern
boy and modern girl), went to dance halls, sang Western songs like "My Blue
Heaven," strolled the neon-lit streets of Ginza, and reveled in "ero-guro
[erotic, grotesque] nonsense." The more traditional-minded danced in the
streets in tune with the new folk songs, such as the "Sakura Chorus Song" and
the "Tokyo Chorus Song," chanting "yoi, yoi, yoi" ("It's good, good, good!").

Was all this carefree gaiety a form of escapism? In discussing possible answers to this question it becomes appropriate to note a rather lurid fad that
came into vogue with the young and sentimental. In May 1932 a young man
and his girlfriend committed suicide on a hillside because their parents would

not consent to their marriage. This incident was given extensive publicity, and twenty more couples committed suicide on the very same spot. The following year a couple of girls attempted to jump into the volcano of Mount Mihara on the island of Oshima off the coast of Izu Peninsula.[7]

Another avenue of escape was through the "new religions," which were essentially cults and offshoots of established religions. They began to emerge in the unsettled days of the late Tokugawa era, and they have continued to flourish to the present. The basic attraction of these new religions was that they were able to offer emotional solace to the downtrodden peasantry and townspeople who found little comfort in the established religions, which had become formalistic and stagnant. In the 1930s one such new religion, the Ōmotokyō (Great Fundamentals), gained wide support, even among the well-educated, and claimed to have a following of 8 million people. The leader, who was said to have direct access to the wishes of the Shinto gods, comported himself like an emperor. In 1935 the leaders of the movement were accused of lèse-majesté and violation of the Peace Preservation Law, and the cult was banned. In the following years other religious cults were also suppressed by the government.

The seemingly carefree attitude that prevailed among the people in the first half of the 1930s shifted, as was noted earlier, to a more austere, cheerless mood after the outbreak of the China Incident. The gloomy atmosphere was in part the product of the growing shortage of goods that resulted from the restrictions on imports and the diversion of raw materials to the production of war matériel instead of consumer goods. A variety of substitutes had to be used. Synthetic fibers were used instead of cotton, bamboo spoons took the place of metal ones, and charcoal-burning buses replaced gasoline-powered vehicles. Price control was introduced in 1939.[8]

The shift to a more somber, serious mood was caused also by the growing tide of nationalism and the attendant sense of national emergency. A rising current of anti-Westernism led to the condemnation of "frivolous, decadent" Western ways. These sentiments were so pervasive that even such things as permanent waves were frowned upon, not only because they wasted electricity but also simply because they were Western. Women were admonished not to wear rings and jewelry or to dress in a stylish fashion. Western-style apparel, which was common in the cities, was soon replaced by a khaki-colored "people's uniform" for men and pantaloons for women. Western movies became increasingly rare, and it was not unusual to find serious-minded women on street corners admonishing people to stay away from all movie theaters and coffee shops. By 1940 dance halls were banned, and sentimental love songs were supplanted by rousing war songs and military and naval marches. Dancing in the streets was replaced either by ceremonies to send friends and relatives off to war or by solemn rituals to receive little white boxes containing the ashes and bones of men killed in action.

FURTHER FOREIGN ENTANGLEMENTS

Frustrated by his inability to resolve the China conflict, Konoe had frequently expressed his desire to resign. He was finally able to use Wang Jingwei's defection from Chongqing as an excuse to call for a fresh start in Japan, and he resigned his post at the beginning of 1939. The ultranationalist Hiranuma was, as successor, handed the task of heading the government. He retained five men from the Konoe cabinet, including the minister of war, the minister of the navy, and the foreign minister. Konoe remained on as a minister without portfolio, and so the Hiranuma cabinet was virtually an extension of the Konoe cabinet.

One of the key tasks assumed by the new government was the plan to conclude a military alliance with the Axis powers. This project was championed by Lieutenant-General Ōshima Hiroshi (1886–1975), the ambassador to Germany. The negotiations floundered, however, because Germany, in anticipation of a possible conflict with England and France, wanted an alliance that would be directed against all potential enemies whereas the Japanese favored an agreement that would be restricted to deterring only the Soviet Union. The matter was debated back and forth and at great length between War Minister Itagaki, who pushed for an alliance, even a comprehensive one, and Navy Minister Yonai, who was against the alliance Germany was proposing for he feared it would draw Japan into a war with England as well as the United States, and he knew that the navy was not prepared to engage these two naval powers in battle simultaneously. Moreover, the naval leaders had always tended to be pro-British in their orientation. The army, in contrast, was willing to broaden the scope of the projected alliance because it had become increasingly anti-British in its outlook. It was proving unable to resolve the war in China, and its leaders began to ascribe China's stubborn resistance to the fact that it was receiving British assistance. Right-wing organizations, with army backing, began to stage anti-British rallies with increasing frequency.

The disagreement between the army and navy prevented the government from arriving at a final decision on the alliance, and then Germany turned around and stunned the pro-German militarists by concluding a nonaggression pact with Soviet Russia in August. This compelled Hiranuma to resign his post, and as he did so he remarked that European developments had produced a "strange and complex" situation. His successor was a retired general, Abe Nobuyuki (1875–1953), a relatively uncontroversial figure. The emperor took an unprecedented step when he made the appointment by insisting that either General Umezu or General Hata be chosen as minister of war. He believed that either man would attempt to make the army behave more in accordance with his wishes. Hata Shunroku was appointed as minister of war, and, as a matter of fact, during the four and one-half months that the Abe cabinet was in office, the army remained relatively subdued. This, of course, can be partially accounted for by the fact that the army was chastened somewhat by the reversal suffered by Hitler's rapprochement with Soviet Russia. Foreign Minister Nomura Kichisaburō (1877–1964), a retired admiral, sought to improve the US-Japanese relationship. One of the chief tasks confronting him was the need to negotiate a new commercial treaty with the United States, which had notified Japan of its intention to abrogate its 1911 treaty as of January 1940.

The Abe government fell, however, before it was able to accomplish anything of significance because of public discontent over the growing shortages of food and goods and the rapidly rising prices. Particularly troublesome was the rice shortage caused by the drought of the previous summer. The political parties, which had been wholly ineffective during the past several years, sought to pass a resolution of no-confidence. Lacking the support of even the army, Abe resigned in January 1940.

The policymakers of the army failed to persuade Konoe to return to power, so their next move was to get the premiership passed on to Sugiyama or Hata. Contrary to their desires, Admiral Yonai, their archrival, was chosen as the next prime minister thanks to the efforts of the Lord Keeper of the Privy Seal, Yuasa, who wanted to curb the arbitrary actions of the army. To prevent the army from blocking Yonai's appointment, the emperor personally requested the cooperation of General Hata. Thus, one of the most forceful exponents of peace and moderation was given an opportunity to reverse the direction in which Japan was headed. The Yonai cabinet, however, turned out to be a tremendous disappointment to those who wanted to see the military restrained. The militarists and the ultranationalists were firmly entrenched in the political arena, and the spectacular successes that Nazi Germany was enjoying against the Western powers unquestionably redounded to their favor.

The expectation that Wang Jingwei's defection would be followed by similar moves by other high-ranking Nationalist officials did not materialize; instead of setting a precedent for change, Wang was denounced as a traitor. Nonetheless, the Japanese government proceeded with the creation of a puppet regime headed by Wang even though it now realized that the conflict could not be settled unless direct contacts were established with Jiang. In March 1940 a government was established in Nanjing under Wang, who was bitterly disappointed because, contrary to what he had expected, he was given no real authority or power.

Hitler at this time was successfully overwhelming Europe with one victory after another, and this gave the pro-Axis elements in Japan an opportunity to begin to revive the plan to join Germany and Italy in a military alliance. This, the expansionists argued, would enable Japan to advance into Southeast Asia and bring all the European colonies under its control. The bellicose officers in the army insisted that Yonai, who favored cooperating with England and the United States rather than the Axis powers, be eliminated. In order to bring down the cabinet, Minister of War Hata resigned and then the army refused to recommend a replacement. Consequently, the Yonai cabinet fell in July.

Again the army's choice was Konoe; this time he was open to persuasion. Thus the stage was set for the implementation of the programs long sought by militarists, ultranationalists, and warmongers. Japan under Konoe joined the Axis powers, advanced to the south, and got ready for a decisive confrontation with England and the United States. Once again Konoe, to whom the moderates looked with great expectations, hoping he would restrain the expansionists, led the country directly down the path desired by the extremists.

The army chose Tōjō Hideki, a chauvinist who was reputed to possess a razor-sharp mind, to become its representative in the cabinet. To head the foreign office, Konoe chose the president of the South Manchurian Railway since 1935, Matsuoka Yōsuke (1880–1946), a flamboyant diplomat who was educated in the United States and who had led the Japanese delegation out of the League of Nations. He was considered to be "voluble and unconventional by nature" and guilty of the fault of "recklessly advancing in the wrong direction." He was an expansionist and thus favored concluding an alliance with the Axis powers.

On July 19, even before he filled all the cabinet posts, Konoe conferred with the men he had selected as war, navy, and foreign ministers and worked out the fundamental policies his government should follow. The basic ideas were embodied in a policy statement called "The Main Principles of Basic National Policy." On July 26, the cabinet approved the "Principles," which proclaimed Japan's intention to build a new order in East Asia, as the first step toward the achievement of world peace. It called for a military build-up, settlement of the China Incident, internal administrative reforms, educational reforms aimed at emphasizing the basic principles of the national polity while eliminating "selfish thoughts," and the creation of a strong new political structure. In addition, a planned economy was to be instituted at home with the goal of self-sufficiency being sought within the new order.

A conference was held on July 19 for the purpose of delineating the specific policies that were to be pursued in foreign affairs. The conferees agreed to strengthen Japan's ties with the Axis powers, conclude a nonaggression pact with Soviet Russia while at the same time strengthening defense measures against it, take active steps to bring the Asian colonies of the European powers into the new order in East Asia, and avoid unnecessary conflicts with the United States while at the same time preventing it from interfering with the construction of the new order in East Asia.

On July 27 a liaison conference of the cabinet and the supreme command was held to adopt officially the policies agreed to on July 19. The agenda was prepared by the middle-grade officers of the general staff and officers of the foreign service.[9] The policymakers in the liaison conference reaffirmed the basic points but spelled them out more concretely. A particularly significant decision was made regarding the use of force in advancing to the south. The participants agreed that whether or not the China Incident was settled, if domestic and foreign circumstances were favorable, Japan should move south at an opportune moment by resorting to arms. This, of course, would mean war with Great Britain and the United States, so military preparations were to be made with such a confrontation in mind. This decision to expand to the south even if it resulted in war constitutes a crucial turning point in Japan's road to the war in the Pacific.

The initial step taken to create what the Japanese hoped would be a strong new political structure was the voluntary liquidation of the existing political parties and the establishment of a single, all-embracing party. The idea for creating such an organization had been bandied about by Konoe's friends for several years. In June, just before he became premier again, Konoe made known his plan to resign from the presidency of the Privy Council in order to work for the establishment of a new political structure. The leaders of all segments of the society immediately expressed their approval of Konoe's plan and pledged their support. The military men, led by Mutō Akira, head of the military affairs bureau, favored the establishment of a promilitary Nazi-type party that would facilitate their plan to establish a "national defense state," that is, a military state. It is believed that Konoe's supporters, many of whom were "reformist" bureaucrats and scholars, hoped to establish a mass party that would enable them to curb the military and at the same time set up a "modern, rational" social order. The party leaders sought to regain their lost political leverage by attaching themselves to the new movement. There were many right-wing, promilitary leaders in the parties who took the initiative in liquidating their organizations in order to be first in line to join the new party. The Minseitō leaders were the most reluctant to join the movement, but because there could be no doubt that they would be squeezed out of the political scene if they did not join the parade, they dissolved their party by mid-August. Thus did the successors of Itagaki and Ōkuma abandon the cause of parliamentary government.

In October the Imperial Rule Assistance Association was established with Konoe as its head. This so-called party, however, turned out to be an ineffective agglomeration of diverse elements with irreconcilably different objectives. Some right-wing elements were critical of an organization whose leaders might eclipse the emperor the way the Tokugawa shōgun had. The big business leaders were suspicious of the economic philosophies of the "reformist" elements in the association, and they tended to look upon the party as a Communist Trojan horse. The emperor and the senior statesmen were also critical of the movement, and finally even Konoe lost his initial enthusiasm for the association.

A group of ultranationalists disapproved of the masses participating in politics, and what they wanted instead was for the association to function as an instrument to foster the "Japanese spirit" among the people. Konoe succumbed to their demands and turned the association into a nonpolitical organization that merely served as a vehicle that would transmit the government's wishes to the people and then rally them behind its policies.

The Imperial Rule Assistance Association stood at the top of the structure to guide the people, and "neighborhood associations," with each unit consisting of ten families, were organized at the local level. These were to serve as agencies that were specifically charged with the responsibility of dealing with the practical problems that arose as Japan was being transformed into a national defense state. Concerns such as rationing, air-raid practices, sending soldiers off to war, and public meetings were managed by the neighborhood associations. They also very closely checked and supervised all aspects of the people's lives, making it difficult for anyone to violate the many new rules and regulations that were being issued by the government.

As for the implementation of the basic policies in foreign affairs, the Konoe government proceeded to conclude a military pact with the Axis powers, Germany and Italy. The army found a spokesman for the pact in Foreign Minister Matsuoka, who argued forcefully in favor of the alliance. The naval leaders feared that the alliance might draw the nation into a conflict with the United States, but they gave no voice to their misgivings. Officially they accepted Matsuoka's argument that the alliance would, on the contrary, serve as a restraining force on the United States while Japan moved south. Matsuoka had insisted that only by taking a strong stand could a war with the United States be averted. The foreign minister also contended that the alliance would improve Soviet-Japanese relations because of the nonaggression pact linking Germany and Soviet Russia. He assured the more cautious officials that even though the pact provided for Japan's entry into the war on the side of Germany, should the United States join the European war against Germany, Japan would under no circumstances automatically enter the conflict. Prior to getting involved it would make an independent decision, taking all factors into consideration.

A decision was finally made after careful deliberation to proceed with the alliance; the pact was signed in September 1940. The agreement provided for Japan's recognition of the leadership of Germany and Italy in establishing a new order in Europe while those two nations in turn recognized Japan's leadership in establishing a new order in East Asia. Article III, the heart of the pact, held that if and when any of the signatories were attacked by any third power not then engaged in the European war or the China Incident, the other two would aid it with all political, economic, or military means. Article V stipulated that the alliance was not to affect the signatory nations' relations with Soviet Russia. It is rather clear, therefore, that the third power that the Axis nations had in mind was the United States. It was not at all difficult for the American officials to reach this conclusion also. Thus, rather than averting a conflict between the United States and Japan, the pact seemed to bring that eventuality one step closer. For the time being, however, the Japanese leaders felt that they could advance to the south with the assurance that they would not be standing alone.

The southern region that required Japan's immediate attention was French Indochina (Vietnam). The war with China continued to drag on endlessly, and the Japanese became increasingly critical of the French for allowing supplies to be sent from Indochina to China. The European conflict broke out in the fall of 1939, and Japan immediately took advantage of the French preoccupation with the European crisis and began bombing the Yunan Railroad in South China, which had been built with French capital. It also launched a vigorous campaign in Guangxhi province just north of the French colony. Just as soon as France fell before Hitler's armies, Japan began exerting greater pressure against it in Indochina. The Japanese government under Yonai asked Governor-General Catroux (1877–1969) to grant Japan the right to station a group of military observers in Hanoi and then to stop all shipment of war matériel into China. Being in no position to resist, Catroux acquiesced to the Japanese demands in June 1940.

Immediately upon assuming his post as foreign minister, Matsuoka demanded that the French give Japan the right to send troops through Indochina, to construct and use airfields, and to station troops to guard military installations. Once again the French lacked the means to resist, and so when the ultimatum was presented they were forced to yield. By September 23, Japan completed the occupation of northern French Indochina. The United States and England felt compelled to adopt retaliatory measures in the face of Japan's actions in Indochina. The United States placed all types of iron and steel scraps under embargo, while the British informed Japan that it would re-open the Burma Road into China, a supply route that the British had agreed to close that summer.

France's difficulties presented Thailand with an opportunity to regain territories it had lost half a century earlier. The ensuing dispute between the countries provided Japan with still further opportunities to extend its influence into Southeast Asia. It purported to act as a mediator between the two nations, but in fact it applied pressure against France on behalf of Thailand and thus laid the groundwork for an eventual alliance with Thailand. At the same time that the border dispute was settled, Japan obtained the assurances of both Thailand and French Indochina that neither would conclude with a third power any political or military agreements directed against Japan. This was designed primarily to prevent Thailand from aligning with England and the United States.

The region that Japan was most interested in because of its petroleum resources was the Dutch East Indies (Indonesia). The Japanese leaders hoped to gain access to the oil supplies without recourse to open hostilities since armed warfare would surely mean destruction of the oil wells and refineries. In September 1940 a Japanese mission was sent to Batavia to negotiate an agreement by which the Dutch East Indies would supply Japan with additional oil and other essential materials. The negotiations foundered, however, and the talks were discontinued in June 1941. Japan's failure to gain its economic objectives through diplomatic means only strengthened the argument of the militarists that it had to rely on military means in order to break through the ABCD encirclement, that is, the encirclement by America, Britain, China, and the Dutch.

During this time Matsuoka was pursuing the project that was to complement the Tripartite Pact—the improvement of Japan's relations with the Soviet Union. He wanted to bring Soviet Russia into that agreement. In March 1941 he left for Berlin, but when he arrived in Europe he found that Soviet-German relations had deteriorated so considerably that he was forced to abandon altogether his plan to effect a broader military alliance. The Germans did not, however, inform Matsuoka of their impending attack on Russia. Instead, they sought to discourage him from trying to bring about a Soviet-Japanese rapprochement, and they tried to persuade him that Japan should enter the war against England by attacking Singapore. Matsuoka expressed his personal agreement with the suggestion but indicated that other Japanese officials would not readily consent to such action.

Matsuoka next visited Moscow, whereupon he proposed that the Soviet Union sell northern Sakhalin to Japan and conclude a nonaggression pact with his country. Foreign Minister Molotov countered instead with a proposal for a neutrality pact. Matsuoka agreed to this, and on April 13, 1941, he and Molotov

signed a treaty that provided for the neutrality of the signatories in case one or
more powers attacked either party. Japan also pledged to respect the territorial
integrity of the Mongolian People's Republic while Russia pledged the same for
Manchuria. Joseph Stalin (1879–1953), in a jovial mood, saw Matsuoka off at
the station and, clasping him in a bear hug, said, "Now Japan can move south."
Matsuoka returned to Japan in a triumphant mood because he was convinced
that he had achieved a diplomatic coup. However, it was scarcely two months
later that Germany invaded Soviet Russia.

On June 25, following Germany's attack on Russia, a liaison conference of
the cabinet and the supreme command was called to determine the policies to
be pursued in light of the unexpected developments. Matsuoka, ignoring the
neutrality pact he had concluded with Russia and disregarding the strategic
problems involved, sought to persuade his colleagues that Japan should abandon its plan to move south and instead immediately join the war on Germany's side and attack Russia.

The conference rejected Matsuoka's pleas and decided to proceed with the
plan to advance southward. It agreed to seek air bases and access to harbors in
French Indochina as well as the right to station troops in the southern portion
of the French colony. If the Vichy government refused, the conferees agreed to
use the force of arms to attain their objectives. The military planners argued
that the occupation of southern Indochina would gain for Japan a foothold in
the strategic defense line running from southern China, Thailand, Burma, and
the Malay Peninsula.

On July 2, in a conference at which the emperor was present, the cabinet
and the supreme command adopted a policy statement that affirmed Japan's
determination to construct a Greater East Asia Co-prosperity Sphere, end the
China Incident, and advance to the south in order to establish the basis for
self-existence and self-defense. They also agreed not "to decline a war with England and the United States" if such a conflict were necessary for the realization of Japan's objectives in the south.

NEGOTIATIONS WITH THE UNITED STATES

In March 1941 the Japanese ambassador to the United States, Nomura Kichisaburō, opened discussions with Secretary of State Cordell Hull (1871–1955)
in an effort to resolve the difficulties between the two nations. The chief problems facing the negotiators were the January 26, 1940, expiration of their
commercial treaty; the China question; Japan's southward push; and Japan's alliance with Germany and Italy. In the lengthy discussions that took place between March and the end of November, the Chinese question turned out to be
the thorniest problem in that both sides remained intransigent. The United

States insisted on Japan's eventual withdrawal from that country while Japan intractably contended that complete withdrawal was not feasible.

Several private citizens from the two countries began exploring ways to resolve the difficulties confronting the powers at the same time that the official talks were being conducted. The initiative for these unofficial discussions was taken by two American Catholic priests, Bishop James E. Walsh (1891–1981) and Father James M. Drought (1896–1943), in cooperation with a Japanese businessman and acquaintance of Konoe's, Ikawa Tadao (1893–1947). In early April 1940, these men formulated a set of proposals that they thought could serve as a possible basis for official negotiation. The proposals called for the renunciation of force by Japan in the southwest Pacific, and its agreement to come to the support of Germany only if that nation were actually the victim of an attack by another power. In return, the United States was to restore normal trade with Japan, assist Japan in obtaining the raw materials it needed in the southwest Pacific, and ask Jiang to make peace with Japan in accordance with specified terms. If Jiang refused, the United States was to cease supporting his government.

Secretary of State Hull wanted to discuss the following four basic principles: (1) respect for the territorial integrity and sovereignty of each and all nations; (2) support of the principle of noninterference in the internal affairs of other countries; (3) support of the principle of equality, including equality of commercial opportunity; and (4) maintenance of the status quo in the Pacific, except as the status quo may be altered by peaceful means.

Matsuoka returned from his trip to Europe and seemed petulant about Nomura's talks with Hull. He responded negatively to the Walsh-Drought proposals, claiming that they were based on 70 percent ill will and only 30 percent goodwill. He also advised Nomura to continue negotiations but only to achieve a neutrality pact. The United States, however, was not interested in such an agreement because it meant that it would have to remain neutral in the event that an Anglo-Japanese conflict broke out during the course of Japan's push to the south.

On June 21, Hull presented the position of his government on the outstanding issues to Nomura and, in effect, asked Japan not to invoke the Tripartite Pact in case the United States entered the European war against Germany. He also called for the settlement of the China Incident on less favorable terms than Japan desired and without assuring it that normal commercial relations would be resumed after the settlement. These terms were wholly unacceptable to Japan, and Matsuoka, bellicose as ever, proposed breaking off the negotiations, which were now practically at a standstill.

The US leadership's distrust of Japan was reinforced by the information it gained as a result of having broken the code by which the Japanese government sent diplomatic messages from Tokyo to its representatives abroad. Consequently, American officials were well aware of Japan's plan to move south and of its preparations for war.

Konoe was determined to continue his efforts to effect a rapprochement with the United States, but Matsuoka's pugnacious stand was making negotiations difficult. Consequently, Konoe decided to remove Matsuoka from the cabinet. To do this diplomatically, he asked for the resignation of the entire cabinet in mid-July. The senior statesmen immediately asked Konoe to form another cabinet, which he did by reshuffling his old cabinet, replacing Matsuoka with Admiral Toyoda Teijirō (1885–1961), who favored maintaining friendly relations with the United States.

THE OCCUPATION OF SOUTHERN FRENCH INDOCHINA

The new Konoe cabinet pursued the same policies as the old one. Just as soon as it was formed the supreme command of the army and navy asked it to adhere to the decision to occupy southern Indochina and to uphold the spirit of the Tripartite Pact. The Konoe government decided to put the occupation plan into effect, but it thoroughly misjudged the reaction that this would evoke in the Western nations, particularly in the United States. In deciding to occupy southern Indochina it completely disregarded Nomura's warning that the United States would consider such a move to be the first step in Japan's plan to invade Singapore and the Dutch East Indies.

Toward the end of July, Japan presented an ultimatum to the French Vichy government compelling it to permit troops to move into southern Indochina. In retaliation, the United States government froze Japanese assets in the United States and followed through with a total embargo on exports to Japan, with the exception of cotton and food. As a result, Japan was cut off from its major source of oil. Great Britain and the Dutch East Indies followed suit by freezing the Japanese assets in their countries. Japan was thus confronted with the prospect of a total economic blockade.

Japan was heavily dependent on the United States for trade.[10] Of critical importance to Japan was the fact that most of the strategic materials that it desperately needed also came from these regions. Above all, Japan depended on the United States for oil, since domestically it produced less than 10 percent of the amount needed. The most serious consequence of the trade restrictions was the severance of Japan from all major sources of oil. The navy's oil reserves were expected to last two years, or a year and a half if Japan became involved in a full-scale war.[11]

This fact turned former moderates in the navy into advocates of immediate action. Their first objective was the oil fields of the Dutch East Indies. Aggression there would doubtless mean a general war in the south against England and the United States, since both Singapore and the Philippines would have to be occupied before the East Indies could be secured. Thus the navy officers who had previously wanted to avoid engaging both the United States and England in a war began talking of doing so even though they were not confident of winning. They were aware, however, that if the economic blockade continued and nothing were done, the navy would surely be immobilized without even firing a shot. The situation for Japan was like that of "a fish in a pond from which the water was gradually being drained away."[12]

The possibility of war, then, had become very real after August 1. Ambassador Joseph Grew (1880–1965) concluded that "the vicious circle of reprisals and counter-reprisals is on. . . . Unless radical surprises occur in the world, it is difficult to see how the momentum of the down-grade movement can be arrested, or how far it will go. The obvious conclusion is eventual war."[13] Konoe was aware of the desperate nature of the existing situation. A diplomatic breakthrough in the discussions with the United States had to be forthcoming or the military would unquestionably ask for positive action— that is, war. Time was running out for Japan, as each day another 12,000 tons of oil was being expended. Konoe decided to seek a conference with President Roosevelt in order to break the impasse. The navy supported the plan wholeheartedly, but the army insisted that Konoe be fully prepared to lead the nation to war if the United States refused to change its position. The summit conference must, the army contended, bring about the end of American aid to China, acceptance by the United States of the Tripartite Pact, and the resumption of normal economic relations between the two countries. Hence, it is quite obvious that even if Konoe had succeeded in persuading Roosevelt to meet with him, the chances of reaching an accord would have been very slight indeed.

On August 8, Konoe's desire to meet with Roosevelt was communicated by Nomura to Hull, who responded negatively, indicating that no purpose could be served by such a meeting unless Japan changed its policies. At this time Roosevelt was busy holding a summit conference with Winston Churchill on the Atlantic Ocean. In this meeting the two leaders agreed to issue a warning to Japan that "any further encroachment by Japan in the southwestern Pacific" might compel the US government to take countermeasures, even if these might lead to war. After returning from his conference with Churchill, Roosevelt procrastinated in deciding about Konoe's proposal, but both Hull and Secretary of War Stimson were skeptical of Japanese intentions. Stimson believed that it was "merely a blind to try to keep us from taking definite action."

On August 28, Konoe sent a personal message to Roosevelt reiterating his desire for a meeting. Nomura then met with Hull, who informed him that there had to be prior agreement on essential points before the meeting could be held. According to the secretary of state, Japan had to first indicate its intention to withdraw from the Axis Pact and abandon its plan to retain troops in North China and Inner Mongolia. Nomura asked if perhaps other questions could be settled, leaving the China question alone for the time being, and Hull replied that, in fact, the China question was "one of the pivotal ones." As it developed, it was "*the* pivotal one" that made the resolution of United States–Japanese difficulties impossible.

Roosevelt finally agreed with Hull's opinion, and on September 3 he told the Japanese that the disputed points must first be settled before a summit meeting could take place. A confrontation between the two nations now seemed inevitable because each side believed it had to stand firm to avoid war. The United States remained resolute in its conviction that it could not compromise its moral principles against aggression: it could not abandon China, and it could not allow Japan to join Germany in destroying Britain or Russia. Japan, in contrast, had been following an expansionistic policy ever since the Manchurian Incident, and with each step it became more deeply committed to the course of imperialism. It always seemed that just one additional step was necessary to consolidate the gains made with the previous step, until finally, after it had already stepped into southern Indochina, Japan was confronted with only two options: retreat or take the last fatal step forward.

THE DECISION FOR WAR

At the same time that Konoe was seeking a conference with Roosevelt, the supreme command of the armed forces began preparing for war in case diplomatic negotiations failed. If the differences between the United States and Japan were not settled at the conference table by early October, the decision as to whether or not to go to war was to be made at that time. Preparations for war were then to be completed by the end of October. The momentous decision was made, not as might be expected by the policymakers at the top, but by the staff officers, including the heads of the bureaus of military and naval affairs. The staff officers agreed upon the basic policies, and then the top officials of the government met to discuss these proposals in a liaison conference held on September 3. Some changes in the wording were made, but in the main the conference approved the basic policies formulated by the bureau chiefs of the army and navy. The representatives of the cabinet and the supreme command agreed to open hostilities against the United States, Great Britain, and the Netherlands if diplomatic negotiations failed to produce the desired results by the early part of October. The decision was presented to the imperial conference (that is, a meeting held in the presence of the emperor) on September 6, 1940.

The day before the conference, Konoe and the chiefs of the general staff met with the emperor, who had expressed concern over the fact that there seemed to be greater emphasis on war than on diplomacy. He pressed Konoe as well as the chiefs of staff, Sugiyama and Nagano, to affirm that efforts to achieve a diplomatic settlement would continue. The emperor also castigated Sugiyama when the latter said that the military operations in the south would take only a few months. He reminded him that he had said in 1937 that the China Incident would be over in one month but here it was four years later and the conflict was still unsettled.

In the imperial conference on September 6, the emperor reiterated his desire for peace and the need to give primacy to diplomatic negotiations. Even the military leaders, Tōjō, Sugiyama, and Mutō, were profoundly impressed by the emperor's sentiments. Nevertheless, the conference did adopt the policy statement ("Outline for the Execution of National Policy") formulated by the army and navy, which avowed a determination "not to be deterred by the possibility of being involved in a war with the America [and England and Holland]." The statement also called for the continuance of diplomatic efforts to get Japan's demands accepted by the United States and England, and the commencement of war preparations if by the early part of October diplomatic negotiations failed to produce "reasonable hope" that these demands would be accepted.

The minimum Japanese demands were to be: (1) The United States and Britain were not to interfere in the settlement of the China Incident by Japan. They were to close the Burma Road and abstain from giving aid of any sort to the Jiang Jieshi government. Meanwhile, Japan was to adhere rigidly to its plan of stationing troops in specified areas of China. (2) The United States and Britain were not to establish any military bases in Thailand, the Dutch East Indies, China, and far eastern Russia or increase their forces in the Far East. Japan was to retain its special relations with French Indochina as agreed upon with France. (3) The United States and Britain were to restore trade with Japan and, in particular, supply needed raw materials from their colonies in the southwestern Pacific area.

If these demands were met, Japan was to promise not to use French Indochina as a base for operations against any neighboring country, except China; to withdraw its troops from Indochina as soon as a just peace was established in the Far East; to guarantee the neutrality of the Philippines; and to observe the neutrality pact with the Soviet Union. In case the United States should enter the war in Europe, the Tripartite Pact would not be automatically invoked by Japan, who would instead make an independent decision at that time concerning the applicability of the pact.

Japan's course was fixed by the policy statement adopted by the imperial conference, but Konoe seemed not to have attached any great significance to

the statement. He believed that the one month or so still left for him to produce "reasonable hope" of having the Japanese demands accepted could be extended because of the ambiguity of the phrase "reasonable hope." During the
month of September, Konoe continued to press for a meeting with Roosevelt.
In fact, on the evening of September 6, after the imperial conference, he met
secretly with Ambassador Grew to continue his plea for a conference with
Roosevelt. However, Secretary of State Hull, now with Roosevelt's full concur-
rence, was intractable in his insistence that there be preliminary agreements on
basic issues before such a meeting could take place. The American leaders felt
that in light of his past record Konoe could not be fully relied upon to keep his
promises. Moreover, the United States officials believed that Konoe did not
have complete freedom and authority to negotiate and conclude binding
agreements. All along it was believed that the military would have the final say.

Ambassador Grew urged his government to respond positively to Konoe's
request instead of demanding clearly defined promises first. He insisted that to
do otherwise would surely bring about the fall of the Konoe cabinet and the
establishment of a military dictatorship. Evidently Konoe planned to have an
imperial rescript issued that would prevent the extremists from opposing any
settlement he might reach with Roosevelt, but even he himself was not confident that the diehard militarists could be held in check.

In the series of conferences that were held by the representatives of each of
the governments, both sides persisted in their intransigence, and consequently,
the differences remained as great as ever. "The terms offered by the Japanese
government would have permitted that country to emerge rewarded and
strong from its ten-year venture in arms and stratagem," wrote one scholar. In
contrast, "the terms offered by the American government would have meant
that Japan accept defeat; give up the gains of past effort, and the prospect of
future expansion. They would have meant, also, a triumphant China."[14]

On September 7, Tōjō told Prince Higashikuni (1887–1990):

> The essence of the United States' demands is the severance of Japanese ties with
> the Axis nations of Germany and Italy. If Japan were to move in this direction
> England and America would demolish Germany and Italy, and then turn to the
> destruction of Japan. The United States asks for the withdrawal of Japanese
> troops from French Indochina and all of China, a full peace settlement with
> [J]iang by the mediation of England and America, and the open door in China,
> but neither I, as war minister, nor the army can ever accept these conditions af-
> ter having sacrificed so many precious lives on the continent.[15]

On October 2, Hull wrote a note to the Japanese reiterating his position
that there could not be a meeting between Roosevelt and Konoe until there

was an agreement concerning the four principles he had submitted in the spring. This, in effect, ended Konoe's hopes for a summit conference. The early part of October had come, and the diplomatic situation seemed even worse now than it had been in March, when the talks first started.

If the United States seemed more rigid in October than in March it was probably due to the fact that it was in a much stronger position. American defense production was increasing rapidly, the situation in the Atlantic was improving, the British still had the Suez Canal, and it appeared as if Hitler would not be able to capture Moscow as swiftly as he had expected.

Hull's note arrived, and the army immediately asked Konoe to make the final decision to go to war with the United States. They cautioned that the longer Japan procrastinated the worse its economic and military situations would become. Tōjō told Konoe that a time comes in the life of every man when it becomes necessary to close his eyes and jump from the veranda of Kiyomizu Temple (in Kyoto) to the ravine below.[16] On the other hand, the naval officers, led by Minister of the Navy Oikawa, still wished to avoid a war with the United States but were unwilling to state their position officially because they were afraid of bearing the stigma of having turned away from a showdown with the United States. They equivocated instead by saying they were willing to leave the decision to the prime minister. Only Admiral Nagano, the chief of the naval general staff, agreed with the army and favored engaging the United States in a war. The army leaders repeatedly urged their counterparts in the navy to make their position clear. They suggested that if the navy would officially declare its opposition to war, the army leaders would then be able to keep their subordinates in line and even consent to further negotiations. The navy leaders, however, said that it was up to the prime minister to decide whether or not to go to war. They were placing their trust in a man who was less capable than they themselves were in making difficult decisions. Konoe favored continuing the talks with the United States, but he was unable to persuade the army to make concessions concerning China, which would make possible an agreement with the United States. In the face of this adamant position on the part of the army and the equivocal stand of the navy, he resigned his post on October 16.

Tōjō favored Prince Higashikuni, the emperor's uncle, as Konoe's successor. This appointment, he believed, would make possible a general review of the situation and the restoration of harmony between the army and navy. Kido Kōichi (1889–1977), the Lord Keeper of the Privy Seal, opposed the idea of having a member of the royal family head the next cabinet because it would mean that the imperial family would be directly responsible if war were to break out. He was convinced that in the event a decision were made to reverse the policy of September 6, the only person who could keep the chauvinistic

army officers under control was Tōjō. Konoe concurred, and despite opposition by some senior statesmen, Tōjō was selected as the next premier. He was
asked by the emperor to reexamine the existing situation without being bound
by the decision of the imperial conference of September 6; he was to start with
a clean slate.

The impression created by the selection of Tōjō as prime minister was that
Japan had decided upon war. Ambassador Grew, however, was somewhat encouraged when he learned that Tōjō planned to continue the negotiations,
and he admitted that perhaps it was still a bit early to brand the Tōjō government a military dictatorship. The chauvinists in the army were of course delighted with the choice of Tōjō, and they insisted that the new government
have a war cabinet.

In forming his cabinet, Tōjō retained his status as an active officer in the
army and occupied the post of minister of war; he also assumed the post of
minister of home affairs. Tōgō Shigenori, a career diplomat who was not at all
enthusiastic about the alliance with Germany, was chosen as foreign minister.
Admiral Shimada Shigetarō (1883–1976) became navy minister, Kaya Okinori finance minister, and Kishi Nobusuke (1896–1987) commerce and industry minister.

Tōjō held a liaison conference with the supreme command after the cabinet
was formed in order to reexamine the national policy. They deliberated from
October 23 to October 30, trying to evaluate how they would fare in a war
with the United States. Both the army and navy were confident of initial victories, but the navy expressed less confidence about the outcome of a lengthy
war. The foreign ministry argued in favor of delaying the start of the war until
March, but the general staffs of both branches of the military vigorously opposed the suggestion and insisted that it be set for November. Regarding negotiations with the United States, Foreign Minister Tōgō favored agreeing to the
withdrawal of Japanese troops from China and Indochina, but the army general staff insisted on the need to station troops in China in order to guard
against communism. Three options emerged after a week of discussions: (1)
avoid war at all cost and "swallow the bitter pill"; (2) decide immediately upon
war and direct all political and military planning to this end; and (3) decide on
war, and complete military preparations while at the same time continuing
diplomatic negotiations with the hope of peacefully resolving the problems.

The conferees met on November 1 to make a final decision on the momentous question. The army general staff, as might be expected, chose the second
alternative, calling for the commencement of hostilities by early December.
The general-staff officers went so far as to ask the army chief of staff to disrupt
the liaison conference if any of the other alternatives were chosen. The war
ministry decided, however, to adopt the third alternative because it believed

this would be the best way to lead the foreign ministry and the navy to the path of war. The navy favored the third alternative as did the minister of finance and the head of the cabinet planning board, Hoshino Naoki.

Foreign Minister Tōgō was strongly opposed to the second alternative, and, in the course of the discussion, he made it clear that if the third alternative were chosen the terms of negotiations would have to be made more flexible. In particular he wanted more time than the military leaders were willing to give him. The army general staff reluctantly agreed to continue negotiations but wanted the talks ended by November 13. It was, however, persuaded to accept December 1 as the deadline. Plans for war were to be abandoned if diplomatic negotiations proved successful by that date.

The conference next took up the question of the new proposals that were to be submitted to the United States. Two sets of proposals were presented by the foreign office. "Proposal A" included the following terms: Japan's willingness to uphold the principles of nondiscriminatory treatment in trade throughout the entire Pacific area and China if those principles were applied to the entire world; Japan's independent determination of the applicability of the Tripartite Act; Japan's withdrawal of its troops from China in two years with these exceptions: certain specified areas of North China and Inner Mongolia, and Hainan Island, where troops were to be stationed for twenty-five years after the conclusion of peace; and Japan's immediate withdrawal of troops from Indochina after the end of the China Incident.

A modus vivendi was to be arrived at if "Proposal A" was rejected by submitting "Proposal B," which called for the following: the United States and Japan were to refrain from advancing any troops into Southeast Asia (except French Indochina) and the South Pacific; the two countries were to cooperate in the acquisition of needed raw materials from the Dutch East Indies; the commercial relations that had prevailed before the freezing of the Japanese assets were to be resumed; the United States was to abstain from taking any actions that would be prejudicial to the restoration of peace between China and Japan; and Japan was, in return, to withdraw its troops from southern Indochina to the north.

The army officers objected to "Proposal B," which would have provided only a temporary respite, but Tōjō persuaded them to go along with it because he considered the likelihood of the United States accepting it to be very slight. As expected, Secretary of State Hull condemned it as a proposal that would condone Japan's past aggressions, assent to its future conquests, give it dominant control of the entire western Pacific, and pose a most serious threat to American national security.[17]

On November 5, the imperial conference formally approved a decision to go to war in early December if diplomatic negotiations failed to produce a

settlement by the first of that month. The army immediately began preparations for war in the south by appointing General Terauchi to command the
Southern Area Army. The navy also prepared for war, and by November 22 it
managed to bring together at Etorofu Island in the Kuriles the very task force
that was to attack Pearl Harbor.

The negotiations with the United States failed to produce any positive results. On November 7, Nomura submitted "Proposal A" to Hull. President
Roosevelt deliberated and then responded on November 10, suggesting that
Japan first prove its good intentions by starting to move troops out of China
and Indochina. Thus, "Proposal A," as was expected, failed to break the deadlock in the negotiations. At this point, Nomura was joined by Kurusu Saburō
(1886–1954), a professional diplomat who was supposed to assist him in the
talks. His arrival, however, did little to improve the situation, and in fact, his
presence had a negative effect because Hull distrusted him and suspected that
he was "deceitful."

Nomura believed that the presentation of "Proposal B" would only make
matters more difficult, but he was instructed to submit it. He did so on November 20, and once again Hull's reaction was negative. Hull did, however, entertain the thought of submitting America's own terms for a modus vivendi in
order to delay the military confrontation. Interestingly enough, the United
States and the Japanese military leaders were in agreement about the effects of
a delayed confrontation. The Japanese general staff opposed putting off the
commencement of the war beyond early December because it was believed
that any further delays would enable the United States to strengthen its defenses while Japan's economic situation grew ever more precarious. American
military leaders, however, wanted to delay the start of the war so as to gain
more time in which to prepare and strengthen their forces.

Secretary Hull considered the possibility of devising a modus vivendi to
keep Japan on a peaceful course for three months. The possible terms of the
arrangement were scribbled out by President Roosevelt. They were: "(1) US to
resume economic relations—some oil and rice now—more later; (2) Japan to
send no more troops to Indochina or Manchurian border or any place south;
(3) Japan to agree not to invoke Tripartite Pact if US gets in European war;
[and] (4) US to introduce Japs to Chinese to talk things over."[18]

The suggestion to work out a modus vivendi was opposed by England and
China, and consequently the idea was dropped. Instead, it was decided that
the Japanese envoys would be handed a basic proposal for a general peace settlement. This plan restated the essential principles Hull had been insisting
upon from the outset of the talks; it called for a nonaggression pact among all
nations who had interests in the Far East, and it proposed the withdrawal of all
Japanese forces from China and Indochina. In effect, the months of discussion

had led absolutely nowhere—the negotiators were as far apart as they had ever been. The Hull note was handed to the Japanese envoys on November 26, and Hull told Stimson the following day, "I have washed my hands of it, and it [the situation] is now in the hands of you and Knox, the Army and Navy."[19]

The officers of the Japanese army general staff looked with great enthusiasm upon the Hull note, for at last here was something that would enable them to end all talks of negotiation and start the war. The Tōjō government received the note as if it were an ultimatum and decided to go ahead with its war plans. In light of the previous decision to go to war if diplomatic talks failed to bring about a settlement by December 1, the Hull note left the opponents of the war without any ground to stand on.

The Japanese envoys, Nomura and Kurusu, appealed to their government not to decide on war. They asked Kido, the Lord Keeper of the Privy Seal, to have the emperor send a personal message to Roosevelt, but Kido rejected the suggestion because, as he claimed, any effort to negotiate a settlement on the basis of the Hull note would indubitably touch off a civil war. President Roosevelt sent a message to the emperor at the last minute on December 6, but it was not delivered to him until some time after the war had started.

The participants in the November 27 liaison conference agreed with Tōjō's interpretation of the Hull note as an ultimatum and had decided on war. On November 29, Tōjō set up a meeting with former prime ministers, in the presence of the emperor. Wakatsuki, Okada, and Yonai expressed their concern about the decision in favor of war, but no one was willing to take a strong stand against that decision. The plan to go to war was formally ratified by the imperial conference on December 1. Admiral Yamamoto Isoroku (1884–1943), commander of the combined Japanese fleet, ordered the task force, which had left Etorofu Island for Hawaii on November 26, to attack Pearl Harbor on the morning of December 8 (December 7 in the United States).

Ironically enough, Admiral Yamamoto had all along been opposed to engaging the United States in a war. Immediately after the Tripartite Pact was signed, he told Konoe that the Japanese navy could dominate the seas for a period of only six months to a year. He maintained that Japan's chances of victory would diminish tremendously if the war dragged on for two or three years. At the end of September he had informed Nagano, chief of the naval general staff, that all the fleet commanders agreed with him that a war with the United States would necessarily be a protracted one and that the Japanese fleet lacked the resources to win such a war.

The supreme command wanted the Japanese attack to be a surprise, but they acceded to the foreign ministry's insistence that a declaration of war be delivered prior to the commencement of battle. The officers of the supreme command asked that the note be delivered to the United States government at 1 PM on Sunday, December 7, but they did not inform the foreign minister of the exact time that they planned to commence military operations. The message was intercepted and deciphered by the United States government even before the Japanese embassy in Washington managed to do so. The envoys had made an appointment to see Hull at 1 PM, but because of technical difficulties there was a delay on their part in deciphering the message, and it was 2 PM by the time they arrived at the State Department. Finally at 2:20 PM they saw the secretary of state—an hour after the first bombs had fallen on Pearl Harbor.

The war crimes trials placed the responsibility for the war on the shoulders of a handful of leaders. This assumes that the course of history is determined by a small group of men and that the rest of the populace plays no role in molding the course of events. The Japanese public, however, with the exception of a small minority of thoughtful people, were completely behind the decision for war. By and large, the Diet members and the press were to all appearances more jingoistic than the government officials. In November, a veteran party politician in the Diet admonished the government "to stop grazing by the side of the road" and take action. A *New York Times* correspondent in Tokyo reported, "In so far as Diet members speak at all, they are so belligerent that the government appears moderate by comparison."

The ultranationalist extremists were naturally even more zealous in their desire to go to war with the United States. They constantly petitioned Tōjō to fight, and one ultranationalist openly accused him of "failing to heed the real voice of Japan." He called on Tōjō to listen to the voices in the streets and shops, which he said were clamoring for action. Any leading figure suspected of being an advocate of peace was in danger of being assassinated.[20] No doubt the danger of being murdered made the proponents of peace behave cautiously. It is nevertheless extremely unlikely that a small band advocating peace could have changed the course of events. Japanese public opinion had by this time been thoroughly conditioned to support the quest for a larger empire. That the Japanese people had come to support imperialism was not simply the result of the nationalistic, imperialistic propaganda that grew more intense after the Manchurian Incident.

Militaristic thinking originated in the ancient past and got stronger with the emergence of the samurai as the ruling class. The ethnocentrism of an island nation was transformed into a powerful force of nationalism in the nineteenth century as Japan encountered the West and felt compelled to revolutionize its institutions and way of life in order to survive in the international arena of power politics. The growth of Japan's strength soon transfigured the nationalistic sentiments into a hunger for more power and a desire to expand into the Asian continent.

Loyalty to the emperor and defense of the nation were the ideals that were inculcated into the Japanese as soon as they entered elementary school. Textbooks had taken on an increasingly militaristic coloring with each successive revision of the official editions. For instance, the first-grade reader issued in 1933 starts off with the words "Forward March, Forward March, Soldiers, Forward March." The outbreak of the Manchurian Incident caused the militaristic tone to grow increasingly pronounced in the schools, newspapers, journals, radio, and movies—in fact, in all media of communication and entertainment. The China Incident heightened the jingoistic, expansionistic sentiments of the people even more. Unquestionably, by the time Pearl Harbor was attacked, both the civilian population and military personnel were a war-minded people who believed in the justice of their cause. One historian writes, "The official brainwashing policy which had been directed at the Japanese people for more than a decade had by now taken full effect upon the leaders as well."[21] These leaders were no doubt right when they contended that the people would never have permitted them to accept a de facto defeat by agreeing to the terms that had been submitted by the United States. They had become the slaves of their own creation.[22]

The driving force in a nation's history would be the aggregate of the will and thought of the millions of people who constitute the "will" or the "mind" of that nation. The character and orientation of a nation cannot be changed except by a slow process of reeducation or by a truly soul-wrenching experience, such as the shocking defeat suffered by Japan in 1945. It is highly unlikely that any leader or group of leaders could have reversed the direction in which the "mind" of the people was moving during 1940–1941. Moreover, it would have taken leaders of much greater moral and intellectual caliber than those who led Japan along the road to war to even attempt to reverse the historical trend. Shōwa Japan lacked the leaders that Meiji Japan had; Konoe was certainly not Itō, Tōjō was not Yamagata, and Emperor Hirohito was not Emperor Meiji. Furthermore, for change to have been even remotely possible, a dramatic shift in the thinking of the military itself was needed. This, of course, was the last thing that one could expect to have occurred. The military leaders were governed by "a sort of a superpolitical autopropulsion."[23]

The events that led to the war in the Pacific can be traced back to the outbreak of the China Incident or even to the start of the Manchurian Incident in 1931. Each succeeding event drew Japan closer and closer to the larger confrontation until 1941, when it was clearly too late for Japan to turn back. The military leaders were perhaps correct in saying they could not withdraw from China after having sacrificed thousands of lives on the continent since 1937. Too much blood had been spilled, too many promises had been made, too many emotions had been stirred, too much poison had been spread, and too much fanaticism had been fostered.

The strong feelings that had been aroused were not confined to Japan alone. The enmity and hostility that Japan had incurred abroad—in China, the United States, England, and Russia—might have resulted in what Tōjō believed would be the fate of Japan. That is, even if Japan had not initiated the war, once the war in Europe was settled, it is possible that an isolated and weaker Japan would have been the next target of the victorious powers. Given this possibility, it was not wholly irrational for a samurai like Tōjō to conclude that "rather than await extinction it was better to face death by breaking through the encircling ring to find a way for existence."[24] There was a degree of inevitability after 1937 in the events that led to war. Japan probably could not have averted war in 1941; perhaps with the right leadership this could have been accomplished in 1937.

The final rupture in relations between the United States and Japan must be viewed from a broader historical perspective than from that of the immediate circumstances that led to the war. A complex web of political, economic, and psychological factors transformed what was a warm relationship following the Meiji Restoration into outright animosity. Until the Russo-Japanese War the United States had sympathetically looked upon Japan's emergence as a "modern" nation, but the interests of the two nations began to come into conflict with growing frequency and intensity as Japan began to assert itself as a major power in the Far East. The United States, as an exponent of the open-door policy, was committed to the preservation of the territorial integrity and independence of China. As a result, Japan's expansion into China became the central issue of contention between the two nations.

Economically, Japan had to trade with other nations in order to grow as a modern industrial state. When the Great Depression occurred it was faced with economic barriers established by nations that had marked out large sections of the world as their colonies and spheres of interest. Thus the pressure to stake out its own "co-prosperity sphere" grew in intensity.

Psychologically, a complicated ambivalence had developed in the Japanese attitude toward the United States. After the Meiji Restoration, the United States became the object of admiration and in many respects the model which the Japanese sought to emulate. Elementary school textbooks that were issued by the government and used until the eve of World War II contained numerous stories of such outstanding Americans as Washington, Lincoln, and Franklin, presenting them as models to follow. As Japan began to extend its power into the Asian continent, however, acrimonious feelings were aroused. This situation was aggravated by the difficulties over Japanese immigration into the United States. Whatever political, social, or economic reasons there were for the immigration policies adopted by the United States, the manner in which the opposition to Japanese immigration was expressed was unmistakably racist. This was a particularly galling pill to swallow for the Japanese, who thought of themselves as a unique race. The continuous talk of the Yellow Peril in the United States strengthened the position of the anti-American, radical nationalists in Japan. The central issue, however, was China, and by December 1941 public opinion on both sides had become so fierce that the outbreak of the war was greeted by many people with almost a sigh of relief.

Notes

1. Robert J. C. Butow, *Tojo and the Coming of the War* (Princeton: Princeton University Press, 1961), p. 100.

2. Maruyama Masao, an authority on Japanese political thought and behavior, speaks of the "transfer of oppression" in which "people preserve the total spiritual balance by progressively transferring downwards the pressure that they incur in their daily life from those above them." Masao Maruyama, *Thought and Behaviour in Modern Japanese Politics*, ed. Ivan Morris (London: Oxford University Press, 1963), p. 113.

3. Ibid., p. 117.

4. The Kwantung Army had committed 56,000 men in the Nomonhan conflict and suffered losses of 8,400 dead and 8,766 wounded, as compared to 9,000 dead and wounded for the Soviet and Mongolian forces. The Japanese losses were concealed from the public until the postwar era.

5. In December 1937 another mass arrest was conducted, this time involving more than 400 left-wing socialists.

6. Ienaga Saburō, *Taiheiyō Sensō* (The Pacific War) (Tokyo: Iwanami Shoten, 1968), p. 134.

7. This then became the favorite spot for suicides; in 1933, it was recorded that 804 men and 140 women jumped into the Mihara volcano, an average of three a day.

8. Rationing of matches and sugar followed in 1940, and then during the next year, rice and charcoal were added to the list of rationed items.

9. Regarding the usurpation of the decision-making power by the general staff officers, Robert Butow observes, "While lacking a basic understanding of political and diplomatic affairs, these virtually 'nameless ones' nevertheless possessed a confidence in their ability and in their program that was the more sublime because it was so misfounded. They proceeded, again and again, to draft policies to meet problems that were completely over their heads, and for which their narrow military approach was wholly inadequate." Butow, *Tojo*, p. 240.

10. For example, in 1939, 18.4 percent of its export trade and 38.7 percent of its import trade were carried on with the United States. In addition, 17.1 percent of its imports came from Asian lands under Anglo-American control, and 10.6 percent came from England and European nations aligned with it. In effect, 66.4 percent of Japan's imports came from the Anglo-American economic sphere.

11. In 1939, 85 percent of its oil came from the United States; in 1940 the figure was 80 percent.

12. Butow, *Tojo*, p. 245.

13. Herbert Feis, *The Road to Pearl Harbor* (Princeton: Princeton University Press, 1950), p. 248.

14. Ibid., p. 273.

15. Hayashi Shigeru, *Taiheiyō Sensō* (The Pacific War) (Tokyo: Chuō Kōronsha, 1967), pp. 240–241.

16. The Japanese idiomatic expression similar to "a leap of faith."

17. There is some indication that mistranslations of the intercepted messages by the US decoders tended to fortify Hull's distrust of the Japanese. Cf. John Toland, *The Rising Sun: The Decline and Fall of the Japanese Empire, 1936–1945* (New York: Random House, 1970), pp. 133–135.

18. Quoted in David J. Lu, *From the Marco Polo Bridge to Pearl Harbor: Japan's Entry into World War II* (Washington, D.C.: Public Affairs, 1961), p. 226.

19. Quoted in Feis, *The Road to Pearl Harbor,* p. 321.

20. Admiral Yamamoto was assigned to sea duty after mid-1939 so as to lessen the chances of his being assassinated. An ultranationalist tried to kill Hiranuma because he had not severed his ties with the cabinet after Matsuoka had been dropped by Konoe. Another group of fanatics also had him on a list of victims they planned to liquidate. There was, in addition, a plot to assassinate Konoe on September 18, 1941, but this was uncovered and quashed by the police.

21. Butow, *Tojo,* p. 327.

22. "People in an undemocratic society are . . . liable to become the slaves of fanatic xenophobia, the frustrations of their daily lives being effectively sublimated into jingoism. The rulers of such countries are only too ready to encourage these tendencies in order to counter the backwash of dissatisfaction below; yet in time of crisis they are themselves mastered by this irresponsible type of 'public opinion' and end by losing their autonomy of decision." Maruyama, *Thought and Behaviour,* p. 114.

23. Ibid., p. 115.

24. Feis, *The Road to Pearl Harbor,* p. 293.

14

War and Defeat

THE OFFENSIVE WAR

At 7:55 on Sunday morning, December 7, 1941, Japanese torpedo planes attacked Pearl Harbor, and the sanguinary struggle between the United States and Japan began.

The surprise attack on Pearl Harbor was conceived and planned by Admiral Yamamoto Isoroku, commander in chief of Japan's combined fleet, who believed that Japan could protect its expansion in Southeast Asia only by dealing a crippling blow to the American fleet in the Pacific at the outset of the war. The task force, commanded by Vice Admiral Nagumo Chūichi (1887–1944) and consisting of thirty-one ships, including six carriers, had left Tankan Bay on Etorofu Island in the Kuriles for Hawaii on November 26. The United States fleet at Pearl Harbor was caught completely off guard when the attack commenced. Every responsible official was aware that a war was imminent; but the American naval authorities were convinced that the Japanese navy could not mount more than one major naval or amphibious operation at a time, and all evidence pointed to a Japanese offensive to the south.[1]

Eighteen American ships had been sunk or seriously damaged by the time the Japanese planes ceased their attack at 10 AM. In addition to these serious losses to the United States fleet, 188 planes were destroyed and 159 were damaged.[2]

The raid was hailed as a great victory in Japan. A rather different evaluation of this event has been offered by the historian Samuel Eliot Morison:

> The surprise attack on Pearl Harbor . . . was a strategic imbecility. One can search military history in vain for an operation more fatal to the aggressor. On the tactical level, the Pearl Harbor attack was wrongly concentrated on ships

rather than permanent installations and oil tanks. On the strategic level it was idiotic. On the high political level it was disastrous.[3]

The Japanese attackers did not even destroy the American naval repair ships, which were able to restore to service the less severely damaged vessels at an amazingly fast pace. Nor did they attack the power plant or the oil tanks, whose loss would have weakened the United States navy in the Pacific far more than did the damage to the fleet.

Strategically, it is believed that had the Japanese not attacked Pearl Harbor, the United States would not have ventured to the southern or southwestern Pacific to contest Japanese expansion. The Japanese could have acquired the Philippines and Malaya without touching Pearl Harbor, since the strategy of the United States called for defending the Marshall and the Caroline Islands in the South Pacific, which, it was estimated, would take six to nine months. Politically, of course, the attack on Pearl Harbor united the American people behind their president more than any other event could have.

Coincident with the attack on Pearl Harbor, military operations were directed against Guam, Wake Island, the Philippines, Hong Kong, and Malaya. The Japanese aim was to wrest the resource-rich regions in the south from their European protectors and to ring their prize with an impregnable defense perimeter of fortified bases.

On the same December morning that Pearl Harbor was attacked, Japanese planes took off from Taiwan and bombed Clark Field and other American bases near Manila.[4] Within a week the Japanese controlled the skies over the Philippines and were thus able to launch amphibious operations on the key islands of Luzon and Mindanao. Lacking air or naval support, General Douglas MacArthur (1880–1964), commanding general of the United States forces in the Far East, ordered his troops to pull back to the Bataan Peninsula, declaring Manila an open city on December 26.

On January 2, 1942, Japanese forces occupied Manila, and as they moved on to Bataan the army commanded by General Homma Masaharu (1888–1946) met determined resistance. It was not until April 9 that Homma could claim Bataan, and even then the island fortress of Corregidor, long an American stronghold, still held out.[5] General MacArthur, on personal order from President Roosevelt, had slipped away from Corregidor in March and escaped to Australia, vowing to return. General Jonathan Wainwright (1883–1953), who was left in command, defended the island until May, when he was compelled to surrender. The Philippine campaign was over, although guerrilla activities were continued by the Filipinos. The beleaguered commanders of the American Pacific bases at Guam and Wake Island were also forced to submit to overwhelming odds. Guam fell on December 10; Wake Island was able to resist only until

December 23. On the China coast the British colony of Hong Kong was captured on December 25.

To the south, Singapore was the objective of the Malayan campaign. This great British port city had long dominated maritime trade in Southeast Asia. On December 8, Japan dispatched troops to southern Thailand; an alliance with the Thai government was secured on December 21. Concurrent with the troops dispatch to Thailand, Japanese troops deployed from northern Malaya and proceeded south toward Singapore. The British fleet guarding that city was virtually wiped out on December 10, when the battleship *Prince of Wales* and the cruiser *Repulse* were destroyed by torpedo and bomber plane attacks. On the Malay Peninsula the Japanese soldiers moved rapidly through the jungle and arrived at Singapore on February 8. One week later, General Arthur E. Percival (1887–1966) surrendered to General Yamashita Tomoyuki.

Elsewhere, the Japanese were equally successful. On January 23, 1942, the Australian airbase at Rabaul on New Britain Island in the Bismarck Archipelago was captured. The campaign in Burma resulted in the capture of Rangoon on March 8 and Mandalay on May 1. By the middle of May Burma was in Japanese hands.

The coveted prize of the entire southern campaign was the Dutch East Indies with their vast oil deposits and prodigious supplies of rubber, tin, rice, and bauxite. By the middle of December, Japanese soldiers were advancing on Borneo, the Celebes, Amboina, Timor, and Bali. In mid-February, Japanese parachute troops landed on Sumatra. The invasion of Java was launched at the end of the same month. On March 9, the Dutch defenders of Java surrendered unconditionally.

Prior to the invasion of Java, the first surface-to-surface naval battle of the war in the Pacific was fought off Surabaya on February 27, 1942, between Japanese and British, Dutch, and American warships. The Japanese fleet won the Battle of the Java Sea, sinking four Allied ships without losing a single vessel. On the following day, Japanese warships engaged American ships in a naval battle at Sunda Strait and sank three more cruisers. On March 1, Japanese warships sank three British vessels off the coast of Java. In April they attacked British warships in Ceylon, sinking several vessels including one carrier. Victory in these battles enabled the Japanese navy to gain control of the seas in the Southwest Pacific.

The initial campaigns by the Japanese armed forces had been far more successful than the military planners had anticipated. In less than six months the Japanese flag was flying from Burma to Wake Island. The Japanese had driven the Dutch, the British, and the Americans from Southeast Asia and the Southwest Pacific, and Japan gained control of the vital resources of these areas. Japanese strategists had expected the conquest of the Philippines, Malaya, and the

Dutch East Indies to take five months, and they had further calculated that an additional six months would be needed to get the oil fields operating again. However, the Dutch policy of destroying the oil fields failed, and Japan was consequently able to gain access to these in half the estimated time.

A liaison conference was held in March 1942, and it was decided that Japan must now consolidate its control over the newly won areas and strengthen its defense against an anticipated American counteroffensive. This was expected to begin sometime after 1943. By and large the leaders made an optimistic assessment of the overall situation even though a few saw protracted war as a distinct possibility. Actually, Foreign Minister Tōgō seemed to favor halting Japan's expansion, but, except for a few military and naval officers, no one shared his caution in the face of the spectacular successes of the war effort. The imperial advisers might have noted a portent of things to come when, on April 18, 1942, a squadron of B-25s led by Colonel James H. Doolittle (1896–1993) flew 668 miles from the carrier *Hornet* to drop incendiary bombs on Tokyo. The actual damage inflicted was slight, and the raid seemed merely to demonstrate that Admiral Yamamoto was correct in placing the destruction of American carriers at the top of his list of military objectives.

As a result of the initial successes, plans to extend the Japanese defense perimeter further into the Pacific were activated earlier than had been expected. A line of fortifications would be established at: (1) Tulagi on the Solomon Islands and Port Moresby in southeastern New Guinea; (2) Midway Atoll and western Aleutians; and (3) New Caledonia, Fiji, and Samoa (by which Australia would be cut off from the United States). The first objective resulted in the Battle of the Coral Sea, the second in the Battle of Midway; the third, however, was abandoned before any military engagement took place.

The Battle of the Coral Sea occurred on May 8, 1942—the first naval battle in history in which the fighting was done primarily by carrier-based planes. In this engagement the Japanese sank the American carrier *Lexington*, a fleet oiler, and a destroyer, and damaged the carrier *Yorktown*. The Japanese lost a light carrier, a destroyer, and three auxiliary vessels. Both sides claimed a victory. For Japan it was a tactical victory insofar as it exacted a heavier toll than did the United States, but it was a strategic defeat insofar as Japan was prevented from capturing Port Moresby.

The encounter that turned the tide in the Pacific was the Battle of Midway. The assault on the American naval base at Midway Island was conceived by Admiral Yamamoto, who believed that by extending the defense perimeter to the Aleutians and Midway the United States fleet would be drawn into a vulnerable position, thus providing the Japanese navy with an opportunity to destroy it.

In early June, the campaign to invade Midway Island and to engage the United States fleet commenced with a diversionary attack against the Aleutian Islands that was designed to lure the American fleet north. The carrier striking force with four carriers, led by Admiral Nagumo, and the Midway invasion force moved toward the island, while Admiral Yamamoto followed at a distance with the main force, waiting to ambush American warships as they sped to the defense of Midway. This time, however, Yamamoto was in for a surprise. Unknown to him, the Japanese military code had been deciphered by United States intelligence, and consequently the American navy knew of the Midway plan a month in advance and was prepared. Confident in the secrecy of their strategy, the Japanese admirals had not maintained strict aerial reconnaissance, and their search planes failed to detect the American warships steaming forward to intercept the Japanese striking force. Included in the American fleet were three carriers, the *Yorktown*, *Enterprise*, and *Hornet*.

On June 4, 1942, the fateful encounter began shortly after the initial Japanese air attack on Midway Island. Not anticipating a counterattack from the air, Nagumo's planes were armed with land bombs with which they intended to blast Midway Island a second time. Their plans were crushed when the American aircraft carrier *Yorktown*, which the Japanese thought they had sunk in the Coral Sea, came into view. Frantic efforts were made by the Japanese plane crews to replace the land bombs with torpedoes, but even before their aircraft could take off American bombers were overhead. The Japanese carriers dodged torpedo bombs, but they were quite helpless beneath the onslaught of the American dive bombers. The carriers *Akagi*, *Kaga*, and *Sōryū* were destroyed almost simultaneously. A fourth carrier, *Hiryū,* sent up planes against the *Yorktown* but was hit in turn by dive bombers from the *Enterprise*. Crippled, the *Hiryū* sank the next morning.

Confronted with the destruction of his carriers, Yamamoto abandoned the invasion of Midway and pulled back his remaining ships. He had lost four great aircraft carriers, one heavy cruiser, and 332 planes; a half-dozen other vessels were damaged. The United States lost one carrier, one destroyer, and 147 planes. Three hundred and seven Americans died during this encounter in contrast to about 3,500 Japanese. Among those were 100 of Japan's most experienced navy pilots. Thereafter the Japanese would be plagued with a shortage of able pilots. News of this disastrous defeat was kept from the Japanese public.

THE WAR AT HOME

Immediately after the outbreak of the war in the Pacific, the government, headed by Prime Minister Tōjō, enacted an emergency law to control speech, publication, assembly, and association. No war news could be released without

THE EXTENT OF JAPANESE EXPANSION IN WORLD WAR II

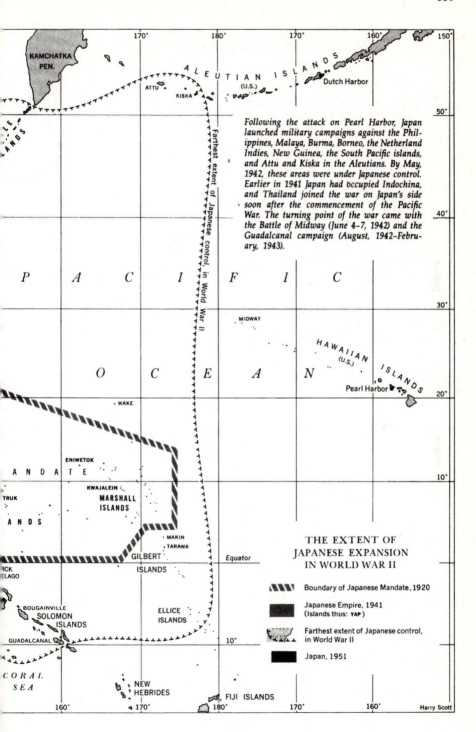

KAMCHATKA
PEN.

ALEUTIAN ISLANDS
(U.S.)
ATTU
KISKA
Dutch Harbor

Following the attack on Pearl Harbor, Japan launched military campaigns against the Philippines, Malaya, Burma, Borneo, the Netherland Indies, New Guinea, the South Pacific islands, and Attu and Kiska in the Aleutians. By May, 1942, these areas were under Japanese control. Earlier in 1941 Japan had occupied Indochina, and Thailand joined the war on Japan's side soon after the commencement of the Pacific War. The turning point of the war came with the Battle of Midway (June 4–7, 1942) and the Guadalcanal campaign (August, 1942–February, 1943).

P   A   C   I   F   I   C

O   C   E   A   N

MIDWAY

HAWAIIAN ISLANDS
(U.S.)
Pearl Harbor

Farthest extent of Japanese control, in World War II

WAKE

ENIWETOK

KWAJALEIN
MARSHALL
ISLANDS
TRUK

A N D A T E

A N D S

MAKIN
TARAWA
GILBERT
ISLANDS
Equator

BOUGAINVILLE
SOLOMON
ISLANDS
GUADALCANAL
ELLICE
ISLANDS

RCK
ELAGO

CORAL
SEA

NEW
HEBRIDES
FIJI ISLANDS

THE EXTENT OF
JAPANESE EXPANSION
IN WORLD WAR II

Boundary of Japanese Mandate, 1920

Japanese Empire, 1941
(Islands thus: YAP)

Farthest extent of Japanese control, in World War II

Japan, 1951

Harry Scott

the approval of the supreme command; hence, only favorable information concerning the battle was made available to the people. At the onset of the war, of course, the news was most favorable, and so in the first weeks after the attack on Pearl Harbor, victory after victory was reported. The exuberant joy of the Japanese people knew no bounds. Even sophisticated intellectuals reveled in the heady emotional outburst of national pride. One writer commented on the news of Pearl Harbor: "I did not believe that I would experience in my lifetime such a happy, exhilarating, joyous day. The oppressive, gloomy cloud that has been hanging over us for the past few years has suddenly been lifted."[6]

The news of Pearl Harbor was followed in eighteen days by the announcement of the capture of Hong Kong, and in seven more days of the occupation of Manila. A Victory Day was celebrated just seventy days after Pearl Harbor to triumphantly herald the conquest of Singapore. A second Victory Day followed the seizure of Rangoon and the Dutch East Indies. The government proclaimed its intention of establishing the Greater East Asia Co-prosperity Sphere once the liberation of Asian nations from their European overlords was achieved. The imperial forces seemed invincible, and it was said that the American soldiers, in the face of the advancing Japanese, were "trembling in their shoes." Some of the more astute leaders, including Prime Minister Tōjō, might have been a bit less sanguine, but even they believed that the "Japanese spirit" would triumph over American material strength. To be sure, the government leaders counted on Japan's European partners in the Tripartite Pact to aid in crushing the enemy. At the end of 1942, Tōjō saw clearly that the real war was just beginning, but he was not able to formulate a policy appropriate to this knowledge.

Tōjō is frequently depicted as having been a dictator as absolute and sinister as Hitler, but in fact, his powers were nothing like Hitler's. President Franklin D. Roosevelt probably had greater authority as a wartime leader than did Tōjō, who was subject to constraints by "establishment" leaders who exercised considerable influence as senior statesmen and advisers to Emperor Hirohito. Collective leadership characterized the Japanese political scene even in wartime.

Tōjō, as the head of state during wartime, had but limited influence over the army general staff, which insisted on the "independence of the supreme command." It was the supreme command that held ultimate power, not Tōjō, and he was not allowed to forget it. The story is told that once, when the army general staff was not allocated certain supplies that it had demanded, a staff officer confronted Tōjō and screamed at him, "You stupid fool!" Such an incident would have been unimaginable had Tōjō been a dictator like Hitler. Dealing with the military leaders was not a simple matter, however. There existed many petty rivalries between the army and the navy, and the progress of the war was consistently hampered because they refused to coordinate their efforts. The war situation worsened throughout 1943, and it was not until February 1944 that Tōjō at length received imperial sanction to assume the post of chief of the army general staff himself. He hoped this would put him in a better position to coordinate administrative and command policies. However, no amount of this kind of reform could roll back the tide of war, which by then was running strongly against Japan.

If Tōjō lacked sufficient power to shape events, the Diet lacked power even to question them. In the middle of the war, in April 1942, a Diet election was held. At this time the Diet was almost completely ineffective, but the government nonetheless endorsed a roster of 466 candidates—the exact number of seats in the lower house—to make quite certain that the new Diet would be compliant. More than 600 unendorsed candidates competed in the election, but not surprisingly, those who were officially favored won a huge majority. The Diet functioned as a rubber stamp until the end of the war.

In order to integrate the areas that had been brought under Japanese control into an overall framework, the government proceeded to establish what it called the Greater East Asia Co-prosperity Sphere. This plan, as a theoretical scheme, possessed considerable merit. In practice, however, the areas that were "liberated" actually remained under the jurisdiction of the military. Their harsh administrative policies alienated many potential allies, and the arrogant behavior of Japanese occupation soldiers, especially those in Singapore and Malaya where many atrocities were committed, aroused bitter hatred among the inhabitants of these areas toward the Japanese. To counteract this, in the middle of 1943, when the fortune of war was steadily growing more adverse, the Tōjō government decided to grant independence to the Philippines and Burma. In August 1943, Burma, led by Ba Maw (1893–1977), was granted independence; in October, an independent state headed by José Laurel (1891–1959) was established in the Philippines. Both these countries, however, remained under Japanese domination. Malaya, Sumatra, Java, Borneo, and the Celebes were annexed to the Japanese Empire though the policy was to allow the people limited participation in political affairs. Other areas were to continue under military control. The Japanese authorities supported the independence movement of the Indian nationalist Subhas Chandra Bose (1897–1945), but as Japan's plan to invade India was never implemented, Bose's dream of freeing India from the British with Japanese help failed to materialize.

In November 1943 a meeting of the Greater East Asian Nations—Japan, China, Manchuria, Thailand, the Philippines, and Burma—was held in Tokyo. The assembled leaders were, with almost no exception, Japanese puppets or collaborators, who were wholly dependent upon Japan for whatever power they had. Consequently the conference served little purpose, and when Japan's fortunes waned, anti-Japanese nationalist movements began to emerge throughout the Greater East Asian Co-prosperity Sphere.

THE DEFENSIVE WAR

The defeat suffered by the Japanese navy at the Battle of Midway was of such significant magnitude that its effects would entirely alter the course of the war. Thereafter the United States would slowly assume the initiative in the Pacific. American marines commenced the invasion of the Solomon Islands of Tulagi, Florida, and Guadalcanal in August 1942. On Guadalcanal a grisly war of attrition was fought for six months. A ground battle continued to rage on that island while a series of air and naval battles were fought elsewhere in the Solomons. Before dawn on August 9, a Japanese naval force at Ironbottom Sound off Savo Island sank four American cruisers and thus inflicted upon the United States navy "one of its worst defeats in history." In the several encounters that ensued, both sides lost twenty-four combat ships. The losses, however, proved more telling for the Japanese, and by the end of 1942 the United States had gained aerial and naval supremacy in the region of the Solomon Islands.

In February 1943 Japanese troops, decimated by combat, in need of reinforcements and equipment, and unable to reestablish their supply lines by air or sea, were forced to withdraw from Guadalcanal. In that half-year period of fighting, Japan lost 893 planes and 2,362 airmen. In the following year it would lose 6,203 planes and 4,824 aviators. These figures combined represent three times the number of planes Japan had had in the Pacific at the beginning of its expansion and a grievous proportion of its experienced aviators. It would have to use hastily trained pilots as time went on, and lacking the productive capacity of the United States, it would find itself increasingly incapable of replacing its aircraft. The United States's air and sea power, in comparison, would expand during the conflict. By the end of the war the United States would have 40,893 first-line planes and sixty aircraft carriers. There can be no doubt that after the Battle of Guadalcanal the United States definitely moved on to the offensive in the Pacific while the Japanese were forced to the defensive.

The Japanese supreme command stepped up defense measures in the South Pacific following the Battle of Guadalcanal. Reinforcements were ordered to Lae in eastern New Guinea. A convoy of sixteen ships left the huge Japanese bastion on Rabaul in New Britain at the end of February 1943. It was overtaken by American planes on March 3–4 in the Bismarck Sea, and all eight transports plus four destroyers were sunk. The Allies, realizing that their drive across the South Pacific would be constantly challenged by the Japanese at

Rabaul, now launched an offensive aimed ultimately at that seaport. It began with attacks on certain little islands in the upper and central Solomons group that stretched out between the American bases at Guadalcanal and Buna and the Japanese stronghold at Rabaul. Confronted with this very serious threat to their possessions in the Solomons the Japanese took prompt steps to protect their bases. In general there was a notorious lack of cooperation between the imperial army and the imperial navy in planning operations, but after the disaster in the Bismarck Sea the two services made some attempt to coordinate efforts in the campaign in the South Pacific. Admiral Yamamoto came to Rabaul to take charge of air strategy, and between April 7 and April 11 he dispatched a series of air raids against the new American airfields in the Solomons and against the warships protecting them. His planes returned with reports of splendid success. Believing that the operation had accomplished its purpose, Yamamoto terminated the raids. His aviators, however, had claimed more hits than they had in fact scored.

It was at about this time that American intelligence decoded details of a plan for Yamamoto to visit his troops in the Solomons to bolster morale. Knowing his exact flight schedule, American planes took off to intercept him in the air, and they shot him down over Bougainville Island. His death, according to one Japanese admiral, was "an almost unbearable blow to the morale of all the military forces."

Possession of the Solomon Islands was contested throughout 1943, with Bougainville the initial prize. Before long, however, the Allies adopted a policy of bypassing isolated enemy strongholds. Bougainville in the Solomons and Rabaul on New Britain were therefore left in Japanese hands to the end of the war. Cut off from reinforcements, they were in effect neutralized.

THE ALLIED STRATEGY: "ISLAND HOPPING"

In May 1943 the United States and Britain formulated a strategic plan for the defeat of Japan that encompassed three offensives. One offensive would recapture Japanese-held bases in the Aleutian Islands close by Alaska. A second offensive would drive through the South and Southwest Pacific. For this phase of the plan General MacArthur would lead the Allied armies up through New Guinea, the Celebes, the Sulu Seas, and Hong Kong. The third offensive would be largely naval and would strike through the Central Pacific islands. Admiral Chester Nimitz (1885–1966) was to be commander in chief of the assaults on the Gilberts, Marshalls, and Truk in the Carolinas. His fleet would join MacArthur's forces at the Sulu Seas. In the fall of 1943 this plan was changed to allow Admiral Nimitz to move on to the Marianas to establish airbases for the new B-29s on Saipan, Tinian, and Guam.

MacArthur vigorously opposed the third phase of the strategy, arguing that the essentially overland route through the islands of the Southwest Pacific was surer, and that the naval resources of the Pacific fleet could best be used in support of the invading army. However, strengthened by the first of the fast new carriers, the fleet was newly capable of conducting assaults over long stretches of ocean at high speed. By March of 1944 the Central Pacific phase of the overall plan was confirmed, and submarine activity was to be intensified in all areas.

The first part of the comprehensive plan was put into effect on May 11, 1943, when Allied soldiers landed on the Aleutian island of Attu, which, with the island of Kiska, had fallen to the Japanese during the previous summer. The small Japanese contingent on Attu, some 2,500 men, fought ferociously. More American troops were brought in, and by the end of May some 11,000 Allied soldiers had disembarked on the island. Almost all the Japanese defenders had fought to the death, and nearly 500 of the soldiers blew themselves up with grenades rather than face capture. Kiska was known to be more heavily fortified than Attu, and preparations for the attack there were carefully laid. Prior to the American landing in mid-August, however, Japanese naval vessels secretly evacuated their 5,600 men. Thirty-five thousand Allied soldiers came ashore and were met with a strange silence. They searched in the fog for the Japanese for five days but found only two or three mongrel dogs.

The second phase of the comprehensive strategy was put in the hands of General MacArthur. He was to lead the South-Southwest Pacific offensive through New Guinea, Mindanao, Luzon, and Taiwan. Later Mindanao and Taiwan were eliminated, and Okinawa became the target after Luzon. In June 1943 MacArthur's forces moved against Japanese bases in eastern New Guinea. The Japanese there had received neither reinforcements nor supplies since the destruction of their transports in the Battle of the Bismarck Sea. Those who survived the Allied advance would be left to struggle in the jungle for the rest of the war. This was also to be the fate of the Japanese troops in other sections of New Guinea.[7]

In November 1943 the third phase of the comprehensive strategy was activated when the Central Pacific naval forces, under the command of Admiral Nimitz, launched an attack on the atolls of Makin and Tarawa in the Gilbert Islands. The amphibious landing, followed by a four-day battle for Betio on Tarawa, began one of the bloodiest engagements of the war.[8]

By the end of the year, the Central Pacific offensive was making significant headway in "Island Hopping": conquering the key islands and constructing airfields from which huge land-based bombers could attack the Japanese home islands. In the Marshall Islands, the western edge of the Japanese defense perimeter, Admiral Nimitz bypassed many fortified atolls to focus on capturing the critical islands of Kwajalein and Eniwetok. Supported by the crushing efficiency of carrier-based bombers and preceded by naval gunfire, the marines landed on Kwajalein on February 1, 1944, and in three days of fighting they captured the island.[9]

After the fall of the Marshall Islands, the Japanese withdrew their forces to a new defense line stretching from the Marianas and Palaus to New Guinea. Accordingly, the Allies decided to bypass occupation of the heavily fortified island of Truk in the Carolines. Nevertheless, Truk, a major airbase in the old Japanese defense perimeter, was bombarded by massive naval and air attacks that smashed Japanese aircraft and transport ships. The 50,000 Japanese soldiers on Truk were cut off from aid and thus effectively neutralized.

Further to the south, MacArthur gained control of the Admiralty Islands in March 1944, capturing Seeadler Harbor, which became one of the largest naval bases in the Pacific, with elaborate repair facilities for all types of vessels. Moving swiftly, MacArthur attacked Hollandia in Dutch New Guinea in April. There the Japanese fought fanatically.[10]

In Burma during the spring of 1944, the Japanese suffered another costly reversal. Determined to sever the British-American supply route from India by which Allied air bases in western China were maintained, the Japanese mounted an offensive in March against Imphal in Assam. Ignoring severe problems of logistics, extreme difficulties of terrain, and the sheer fact of British air supremacy, they relied on brute determination and fighting spirit. Hindered by stiff resistance, the attackers were still in the field when an unexpectedly early monsoon struck. Having had their supply lines cut, the Japanese ran out of munitions and food. Nonetheless their commanders fanatically insisted that the campaign continue. By July, when withdrawal was finally ordered, many of the retreating troops starved to death before they could reach safety.[11]

During this same period, Allied forces under General Joseph Stilwell launched a counteroffensive in northern Burma and captured Myitkyina in the Mogaung Valley. Simultaneously, a Chinese army advanced from Yunan and captured Bhamo. Thus the Allies won firm control of the overland supply routes into China, linking the Ledo Road with the Burma Road. The Allied offensive continued into 1945, when in May, Rangoon was recaptured. From the autumn of 1944 to that time, the Japanese war dead mounted to 200,000 men.

By the spring of 1944 the Imperial High Command in Tokyo could anticipate the direction of MacArthur's stunning offensive in the South and Southwest Pacific, and it determined that the Allied forces must be engaged before they could move forward to the Philippines. Furthermore, MacArthur's advance threatened Japan's very lifeblood, for if its oil supplies were cut off, it could neither continue the war effort nor produce domestic necessities. Admiral Koga Mineichi (1885–1944), Yamamoto's successor, was charged with preventing the enemy from entering the Philippine Sea. Koga began to reorganize the fleet and draw up defense plans, but before he could act on these new strategies, he was killed in a plane crash in March, less than a year after Yamamoto's death. Admiral Toyoda Soemu (1885–1957) now took command and placed his best combat vessels into an assault force, designated the First Mobile Fleet, with aircraft carriers at the center of its strength. Vice Admiral Ozawa Jisaburō (1886–1966), a navy flier, was put in command. His unit included nine carriers, five battleships, 450 carrier planes, and 1,000 land-based planes that were stationed at various air bases in the islands. Toyoda believed that the Allies would advance unilaterally and he supposed that their protecting navy would come either from the northern coast of Australia toward the Philippines, or from the Caroline Islands toward Palau. The possibility existed that the advance might come past the Marianas, but those islands were fortified to the last degree and the nearest enemy approach base was Eniwetok Atoll, nearly 1,000 miles to the east. Toyoda was confident that the Allied offensive would come from the South or Southwest Pacific, and accordingly he held the main part of his fleet in readiness off the southwestern coast of the Philippines. He believed that one major naval encounter could decide the supremacy of the seas. With this in mind, he formulated a battle plan called Operation A.

On May 27, American assault troops landed on the tiny island of Biak just north of western New Guinea. The landing strip on this island would provide critical air mastery, and Operation A depended to a great extent on land-based air support. In view of its strategic importance, the Imperial High Command decreed that the island must be recaptured. Ozawa was dispatched with his First Mobile Fleet, and planes from Japanese bases in the Carolines and the Marianas were rushed into action. Large numbers of these sorely needed aircraft were shot down, carrying with them their irreplaceable pilots.

Early in June 1944 the electrifying news was radioed that the US Fifth Fleet was moving across the Pacific Ocean and shaping course for the Marianas. Admiral Toyoda immediately pulled his warships out of Biak and sent the combined fleet to the Marianas to put Operation A into effect.

The enormous Allied task force steaming toward the Mariana Islands consisted of 535 combat ships, auxiliaries, and transports carrying 127,571 men. Its destination was the Japanese strongholds of Saipan, Tinian, and Guam. As the task force neared the Marianas, planes from the carriers began a series of saturation bombings that lasted from June 11 to 13. Shortly before the first marines went ashore on June 15, naval bombardments pummeled the shores of Saipan in preparation for their landing. By June 17, a beachhead was secured.

The defending Japanese force had 32,000 men, but not all of them were fully armed. The lethal efficacy of American submarines had made it impossible to receive supplies. Nonetheless, the Japanese in Saipan were determined to hold out until Admiral Ozawa's First Mobile Fleet could counterattack under the strategy prescribed by Operation A. Ozawa's force was outnumbered in carriers and aircraft by about two to one, yet his ships were armed with newly designed planes that had longer range than the comparable American equipment. He hoped therefore to attack the American carriers before they could get within range of his fleet. He also banked on the support of land-based planes from nearby island airfields.

On June 19 Ozawa launched four major air attacks on the Allied task force. Intercepted by US fighter planes, they all failed to accomplish their mission. At the same time, American bombers attacked the Japanese airfield on Guam, destroying many of the land-based planes. American submarines then moved out against Ozawa's fleet, sinking his flagship *Taihō* and the carrier *Shōkaku*. The Japanese fleet finally withdrew northward, but the tracking Allied task force soon came within range and administered a crushing blow, sinking one carrier and damaging four more.[12]

Meanwhile, fighting on Saipan was ferociously intense, with the Japanese troops desperately holding until the "invincible fleet" could come to their rescue. The Americans consolidated their beachheads and moved inland while the Japanese retreated to the hills with the civilian residents and fought fiercely to the end, conducting *banzai* (suicidal) charges. On July 9, when the Allies announced the subjugation of Saipan, only 1,000 of the 32,000 Japanese troops remained. Identified among the dead was Admiral Nagumo, commander of the fleet that attacked Pearl Harbor, who had committed seppuku. Ten thousand civilian residents had also perished, many committing suicide with the soldiers who exhorted them against surrendering. "Men, women and children cut each others' throats, deliberately drowned, embraced death by any means they could. Parents dashed babies' brains out on the cliffs and then jumped over themselves; children tossed hand grenades to each other."[13]

The Allied assault forces moved on to Tinian, three and a half miles away. It was during the encounter over this island that the United States first used napalm, dropping tanks containing gasoline and this highly incendiary substance from fighter planes onto the defenders, who were dug in below. The island fell on August 2. Japanese losses were thirteen to one compared to Allied casualties. The campaign for Guam had started on July 21, and organized resistance by the Japanese ended by August 10, 1944. The Marianas invasion was over.

The defense of these islands cost Japan the terrible human toll of 50,000 men lost. In addition, it suffered a strategically devastating blow. Saipan had been "the naval and military heart and brain of Japanese defense strategy." On

Saipan now, and on Tinian, the United States engineers would construct the airfields from which deadly B-29 superbombers would fly over Tokyo and other cities. The first of these raids took off from Saipan on November 24, 1944. In August 1945, two B-29 bombers would leave Tinian for the fateful flights to Hiroshima and Nagasaki. On Guam the Allies would establish the naval base that serviced a third of the Pacific fleet, enabling it to penetrate deep into the Japanese defense perimeter and cut the vital supply lines to the south.

THE TRANSFERENCE OF LEADERSHIP FROM TŌJŌ TO KOISO

The fall of Saipan touched off a political crisis in Tokyo that led eventually to the fall of the Tōjō government. Senior statesmen Okada, Konoe, Hiranuma, and Wakatsuki, as well as other political leaders, were deeply dismayed by the course of the war as early as March 1944. Quietly they explored the possibility of removing Tōjō to pave the way for a negotiated peace. Anti-Tōjō feeling ran high among naval officers, many of whom were angered by the government's allocation of precious war matériel. They felt that Admiral Shimada, minister of the navy and naval chief of staff, was merely Tōjō's pawn and consequently functioned much to the detriment of the navy's interests. Okada proposed that Shimada be replaced by Admiral Yonai. Opponents of Tōjō readily endorsed this demand because they viewed Shimada's ouster as the opening move to tumbling the Tōjō government. Konoe also favored overthrowing the prime minister, but at the same time he observed that if the war should end unfavorably for Japan, it would be useful to have Tōjō (who was as much detested by the world as Hitler) around as prime minister to assume full responsibility, thus eliminating the possibility that the emperor might be held liable.

Tōjō was, of course, aware of the critical nature of the situation, and soon after he assumed the post of chief of the army general staff, he told a member of the staff to investigate ways in which the war might be ended. Then when Saipan fell, he expressed to Prince Higashikuni a desire to resign but was told that since he had started the war, it was his responsibility to remain at his post until he found a satisfactory way to conclude it. There was, of course, only one way that would be considered satisfactory, and that was through victory. No one dared even speak of defeat.

The senior statesmen continued to press for Shimada's resignation until Tōjō finally decided to accede to their demands. At the same time he proposed that former premiers Yonai and Abe be added to the cabinet as ministers without portfolio, and that Minister of Commerce and Industry Kishi resign so as to make room for them. Tōjō believed that the presence of Yonai and Abe in the cabinet would neutralize the efforts of the senior statesmen to overthrow his government. Yonai, however, declined to join the cabinet. The Lord Keeper of the Privy Seal Kido, whose influence was considerable, now began to lean in favor of the anti-Tōjō faction. At this point Kishi challenged Tōjō by refusing to resign and calling for a dissolution of the entire cabinet. Faced with opposition from his own cabinet members, Tōjō relinquished his authority and resigned on July 18, 1944.

As Tōjō's successor the senior statesmen selected Koiso Kuniaki, governor-general of Korea. In order to lend support to their choice the statesmen persuaded Yonai to serve as his deputy. Koiso failed to win the complete support of the army and was prevented from combining the post of prime minister with that of minister of war as Tōjō had done. General Sugiyama became minister of war, and many of Tōjō's followers continued to hold key posts in the war ministry.

Koiso immediately set about the task of implementing certain practical reforms. To coordinate the policies of the cabinet and the supreme command more effectively, he replaced the liaison conference with the Supreme Council for the Direction of the War, consisting of the prime minister, the ministers of war, navy, and foreign affairs, and the chiefs of the army and naval general staffs. The Supreme Council, however, soon proved as vulnerable to schism and rivalry as the liaison conference.

One of Koiso's chief concerns was to try to establish closer ties with Soviet Russia in order to prevent it from joining the Allied powers in the war against Japan. To this end, he attempted to mediate between Germany and the Soviet Union, but the Soviet government would not agree to having a special emissary sent to Moscow, and Germany indicated it would not negotiate with the Soviets. On November 7, 1944, Stalin denounced Japan as an aggressor. In February 1945, at the Allied summit meeting in Yalta, Stalin formally promised to enter the war against Japan after Germany's defeat. This pledge was not made in public at that time, but when in April the Soviet government announced that it would not renew the neutrality pact with Japan, the apprehension of the Japanese leaders was intensified.

Meanwhile, Koiso was seeking to settle the war with China, and he conferred with Miao Bin (1902–1946), an official of the puppet government in Nanjing. Miao Bin claimed to have contacts in Chongqing and volunteered to serve as a go-between. His reliability was questioned by Foreign Minister Shigemitsu, who, together with the army leaders, argued against working with him. Kido persuaded the emperor to express opposition to the Miao Bin venture, thus placing Koiso in an awkward position. This, and the deteriorating war situation, contributed to the fall of his government.

THE BEGINNING OF THE END

No longer could the government hide the fact that the war had turned against Japan. On November 24, 1944, the first massive raid of B-29 bombers left Saipan for Tokyo, where a major aircraft factory was all but destroyed. Raids against aircraft plants in other cities followed. Then, in March 1945, the dreaded planes sought out not factories but people; they concentrated on fire-bombings of congested, inflammable cities in order to coerce Japan into surrendering. On March 9, a sizable force of bombers—334 in all—from the Marianas flew over Tokyo and dropped 2,000 tons of incendiary bombs. This was the most destructive air attack in history up to that time.[14] Similar fire-bombings hit Nagoya, Osaka, and Kobe. The attacks continued for the remainder of the war and accounted for a large part of the devastation that Japan was to suffer. Before the end of the war, sixty-six major Japanese cities would be bombed and fire-bombed from the air or shelled by warships.[15]

Almost 1 million Japanese soldiers were garrisoned in China during the war in the Pacific. On the whole they constituted an occupying rather than a fighting force, although on the northern provinces Chinese Communist guerrillas created continuous harassment. In the spring of 1944 the Imperial High Command perceived that the supply routes between the north and the south were threatened by the presence in western China of Allied air bases. Fearing that even the home islands might be subject to attacks from that quarter, they accordingly broadened the front in China. The campaign accomplished little since most air attacks against Japan originated from Pacific island bases. Furthermore, broadening the front in China made guerrilla activities all the more difficult to contain.

By the summer of 1944, Japan's last fortifications stood in jeopardy. General MacArthur's Southwest Pacific forces were preparing to link with Nimitz's Central Pacific force, now under the immediate command of Admiral William F. Halsey (1882–1959). A massive offensive against the Philippines was the next objective. Japan's installations on these islands represented its last-ditch defenses for the precious cargo ships and tankers bringing oil and raw materials from the East Indies. In September and October 1944, the remains of its outer defense perimeter crumbled as the Allied air, naval, and amphibious forces attacked Peleliu and Angaur in the Palau Islands and converted the bases into landing fields for American bombers. Japanese airfields on Mindanao and in the East Indies were repeatedly struck by bombers. Close to home, air and shipping installations on Taiwan and the China coast were blown up by bombers from carriers and from the Allied bases in western China. Hundreds of Japanese planes were destroyed on the ground. American submarines stalked the sea lanes in search of ships bringing goods to Japan.

During one attack on Taiwan, the Japanese naval and air forces succeeded in downing seventy-eight planes and damaging two cruisers, a negligible victory compared to the mountainous evidence of imminent defeat. The jubilant Japanese pilots, however, were convinced they had scored far more spectacularly and sent home highly exaggerated accounts of victory. As a result, the Imperial High Command abandoned its plan to await the Allied invasion at Luzon and resolved to confront MacArthur at Leyte instead. To defend the home islands and to secure the bases on the Philippines, Taiwan, and the Ryukyus, the strategists devised a master plan, Operation Shō (Victory).

THE BATTLE FOR LEYTE GULF

In mid-October 1944, the combined Allied invasion forces, with some 700 vessels, had gathered for the momentous assault on the Philippines. Before dawn of October 20 the entire invasion force had converged on Leyte Gulf, and throughout the early hours of the day, the surrounding beaches were strafed, bombed, and shelled in an implacable barrage. At 10 AM the first ground forces were ferried to the shore, and by sundown more than 60,000 Allied soldiers were on the beaches with 100,000 tons of supplies.

Without land-based planes and unable, through lack of fuel, to maneuver at sea, Japanese forces were powerless to prevent the Allied invasion at Leyte. Nevertheless, they were determined to contain it and save Japan from blockade. On October 18, 1944, the First Striking Force, commanded by Admiral Kurita Takeo (1889–1977), left its base at Lingga Roads near Singapore and moved to Brunei Bay on Borneo to refuel. On October 22 it set forth across the Sibuyan Sea and headed for the Leyte Gulf. Among the warships under Kurita's command were the gigantic battleships *Musashi* and *Yamato*. At dawn on October 23 two American submarines guarding approaches to the Philippines sighted the fleet and loosed their torpedoes with incredible accuracy. Two heavy cruisers went down, including the flagship, and a third was disabled. Kurita escaped to a destroyer and thence to the *Yamato*. The next day, American carrier-based planes attacked and sank the reputedly unsinkable *Musashi*.

At the same time that Kurita was heading toward Leyte, a decoy unit of Admiral Ozawa's Mobile Fleet moved out of Japan's Inland Sea, luring Halsey's Third Fleet away from guard service at the north side of Leyte. Operation Shō called for Kurita's force to move to this side of the island and enter the gulf through San Bernardino Strait, now left unprotected by Halsey's departure. Simultaneously, Vice Admiral Nishimura Shōji, backed up by Admiral Shima Kiyohide (1878–1973), was to come up from the south across the Sulu Sea and enter Leyte Gulf through Surigao Strait. These naval forces were to meet in Leyte Gulf—one from the north, two from the south—and together, in a great pincer movement, they were to destroy the invasion support ships. The battle evolved quite differently from the plan, however, as Nishimura's advance unit of the southern force was virtually destroyed at Surigao Strait. The US Seventh Fleet, commanded by Admiral Thomas C. Kinkaid (1888–1972), had been apprised of the approaching Japanese force and lay in wait for the enemy to emerge from the narrow passage of Surigao Strait. Thereupon two battleships and three destroyers were blown out of the water and a heavy cruiser and a destroyer were severely damaged. Admiral Shima, following Nishimura by a few miles, observed the disaster from afar and retired his element of the force from the fray. American ships and planes pursued the remainder of Nishimura's fleet, sinking the crippled cruiser, and then went after Shima's retreating forces and sank another cruiser and a destroyer.

Meanwhile, Admiral Kurita with a reduced force proceeded to the north side of Leyte. Radio contact was erratic among elements of Operation Shō, and Kurita was not aware that Halsey, with the powerful Third Fleet, had been successfully decoyed to the north. He had, however, received word that Nishimura was under deadly attack in Surigao Strait. Therefore, he proceeded with extreme caution through San Bernardino Strait. Near Samar Island he sighted from afar the outlines of ships that he guessed to be part of the Third Fleet. Halsey at that moment was in fact some 300 miles away, and Kurita, with his powerful though depleted warships, was within range of Leyte Gulf. The ships he espied actually were a small task force on patrol, and they were scarcely prepared for combat with so formidable a force. Kurita, however, far from recognizing his great advantage and conscious that he could not count on help either from his southern units or from the gutted airfields within range, maneuvered badly. Consequently, the smaller American force was able to send three Japanese heavy cruisers to the bottom while crippling a fourth. Kurita managed to sink one carrier and four destroyers. He then withdrew, leaving the vulnerable cargo vessels in Leyte Gulf unmolested.

Halsey, whom Kurita thought he had encountered, had pursued Ozawa's decoy unit northward and had sunk four carriers and a destroyer. He was about to close in on the main unit of Ozawa's force, with every expectation of overwhelming it, when he was informed of Kurita's presence in Leyte Gulf. He immediately turned south to engage him, but by the time he arrived, Kurita had already departed. In the course of four days of combat, the Japanese lost three battleships, four carriers, six heavy cruisers, three light cruisers, eight destroyers, and six submarines. Thereafter the Japanese navy was virtually nonexistent as an effective fighting force.

THE END OF THE FIGHTING: THE KAMIKAZE

It was at this juncture that the Japanese sent the first of their suicide planes into battle. The idea of establishing units trained for this kind of combat was conceived by Vice Admiral Ōnishi Takijirō (1891–1945), commander of the First Air Fleet in Manila, and inspired by the fierce code of military honor. The pilots, known as *kamikaze* (divine wind), were trained to crash-dive into enemy ships with planes loaded with high explosives.

The same spirit of self-sacrifice that motivated the suicide pilots now seized all combat forces with new fervor. The Japanese defending their home islands were expected to fight to the death, and many thousands of them did.[16]

In January 1945 the troops of the US Sixth Army landed at Lingayen Gulf and fought their way to Manila. They claimed the island on March 4, and thus MacArthur fulfilled his vow to return. The contest for the Philippines did not cease with Manila, however. On Luzon some 170,000 Japanese troops were entrenched under the command of General Yamashita, who had just been re-called from semi-exile in Manchuria to lead the final defense of the Philippines. By the end of June the US Sixth Army had moved into all key points on Luzon, but Yamashita fought on. Many of his soldiers starved to death in their isolated strongholds.[17]

At the same time that MacArthur's forces battled through the Philippines, a segment of the Central Pacific force laid siege to the rock citadel of Iwo Jima. Bases on the Volcano Islands and the Bonin Islands were of great strategic importance to Japan's defense chain since they lay midway between the American B-29 base on Saipan and the Japanese home islands. From these bases Japanese planes could both intercept bomber missions before they reached Japan and conduct harassing raids over the Marianas. If the Americans were to capture an island in this region they would then have a base from which medium-range bombers and fighter escorts could operate over Japan. It would further provide a refuge for damaged bombers returning from Japan to Saipan.

On February 19, 1945, after six weeks of sustained preliminary bombing, American marines stepped ashore on the lava beaches of Iwo Jima. The Japanese defenders fanatically resisted, and bitter fighting lasted a month. On March 16 the United States finally declared Iwo Jima secured, though pockets of Japanese soldiers concealed in labyrinthine tunnels remained to be dealt with one by one. Virtually the entire Japanese garrison died in battle.[18] Just two weeks later American fighter planes were already lifting off the airstrip at Iwo Jima on the first of countless missions of escort, accompanying B-29s to Japan.

The last bastion of Japanese defense was Okinawa, largest of the Ryukyu Islands. Long before the liberation of the Philippines was complete and even before the fighting ended on Iwo Jima, final plans had already been completed for the capture of Okinawa. Amphibious, naval, and air elements of the Central Pacific force massed for the offensive. The beaches that were designated for invasion were readily accessible for attack from Kyushu, southernmost of the Japanese home islands and only 350 miles north of Okinawa. Therefore, preparation for the invasion required intensive bombardment of the airfields on Kyushu and of the remaining Japanese navy in the Inland Sea. Retaliating Japanese aircraft bombed four American carriers, damaging the *Yorktown*, *Enterprise*, and *Wasp*, and wholly disabling the *Franklin*.[19]

On April 1, 1945, a vast landing force stood off the shore of Okinawa, and the first companies of marines were ferried to the beach. They met little challenge. Deep in the rugged interior, however, some 100,000 defenders, entrenched in pillboxes, blockhouses, tunnels, and caves, awaited their advance. No longer capable of meeting the invaders on the beach, the Japanese were instructed to conserve ammunition until the enemy came close. They were pledged to prolong the defense as long as possible.

American troops swarmed across the fifteen miles of beachhead, while at the same time in Kyushu the last vestiges of the Japanese army and navy charted a final desperate counterattack. On April 6, a force of 341 bombers and 355 suicide planes took to the skies to seek out and destroy invasion supply ships and the warships guarding them. About 200 kamikaze pilots reached Okinawa, where 135 of them were downed by fighter planes and antiaircraft guns. Those that reached targets sank six vessels, including two destroyers, and damaged eighteen others.

Simultaneous with the air attack, the battleship *Yamato* (with a total displacement of 73,000 tons), escorted by eight destroyers and a cruiser, sailed out of the Inland Sea fueled with just enough oil for a one-way passage to Okinawa. There it would fire its guns into the beachholds until its ammunition was spent. En route, however, it was spotted and set upon by carrier planes. *Yamato* withstood bombardment for two hours, but at noon on April 7, the colossal warship went to the bottom, its admiral lashed to the bridge. The *Yamato* alone lost about 2,500 men and officers, and the other warships over 1,100. Only four destroyers of the entire task force survived to limp back to port. Japan no longer had any surface fleet.

The vicious land battle for Okinawa raged into June. By then some 190,000 American soldiers had been debarked to oppose 77,000 Japanese and 25,000 Okinawan militiamen. The Japanese would not be subdued, and day by day the bloody attrition assumed more horrifying proportions. At the end of two months of combat, American soldiers had killed 62,500 Japanese. On June 22, 1945, the commanding general of Okinawa, General Ushijima Mitsuru (1887–1945), committed seppuku, and official resistance ended.[20]

THE ECONOMICS OF WARFARE

The key factor that ultimately halted the progress of the war was not the number of Japanese dead, staggering though that figure was. Even after the carnage of Okinawa there were still Japanese soldiers to fill up regiments. The major single element in Japan's military defeat was the collapse of its economy. At the onset of the war Japan had stockpiles sufficient for a limited military engagement, during which time it was to appropriate the resources of Southeast Asia, especially Borneo and the Dutch East Indies. In comparing the raw materials necessary for waging warfare, it is estimated that in 1941 the United States had seventy-eight times the available resources that Japan had. Furthermore, most of Japan's supply of raw materials had to be obtained elsewhere. The Japanese planners knew that to prosecute a war for longer than two years they had to control the economic resources of Southeast Asia. Equally necessary, they had to be able to transport the raw materials back to Japan. For this, it was essential to control the sea lanes and to maintain adequate shipping tonnage. Early in the war the head of the cabinet planning board, Lieutenant General Suzuki Teiichi (1889–1989), estimated that 3 million tons of nonmilitary shipping would be needed to maintain adequate war production.[21]

In 1944 nonmilitary shipping had fallen to 2.56 million tons, and by the end of the war it was down to 1.56 million tons. The drop in tonnage, of course, represented a steady dwindling of vital raw materials. Japan's stockpile of scrap iron and steel dropped from 4.468 million metric tons in 1941 to 449,000 in 1944. More critical than these declines was the lack of crude and refined oil. This fuel oil shortage virtually immobilized the Japanese navy by the end of the war. In April 1945, of the five battleships still afloat, only the *Yamato* could be fueled for the battle of Okinawa.[22]

The Japanese economy was doomed once the raw materials essential for industrial production were depleted and replenishment made impossible by the ever-tightening Allied blockade. Obviously, the manufacture of the tools of warfare halted; but even before access to essential materials was cut off, the Japanese economy failed to expand rapidly enough to match the vastly expanded wartime production that was going on in the United States. From 1940 to the peak war year of 1944, total output in Japan increased by only one-fourth whereas in the United States it increased by two-thirds. In the early years of the war, when one might expect a great surge in output, the Japanese gross national product increased only slightly.[23]

In aircraft production, Japan increased its output from an index of 100 in 1940 to a peak of 339 in September 1944; by July 1945, however, the production fell 59 percent from the peak period. In the construction of naval vessels a 133 percent increase over December 1941 was reached in September 1943, but by the end of the war it had dropped 53 percent from the peak month. In the construction of merchant ships a 347 percent increase over December 1941 was attained in September 1944, but it dropped 81 percent from the peak month by July 1945.[24]

Just as raw materials diminished and production slowed, so also did industrial manpower decrease during the last year and a half of the war. At the onset of the war 2.4 million men were in the Japanese armed forces.[25] There was no overall plan to exempt skilled workers from the draft, so the quality of the labor force was continuously lowered. Women, students, and Korean laborers were mobilized to work in the factories to replace the men who were drafted, and consequently, per capita production lagged.[26]

Farming communities also suffered from serious shortages of help as farm workers left the villages for the factories. Coupled with the conscription of the male farmers, this left the work of cultivating the land largely in the hands of women, children, and old men. Actually, the rice yield did not diminish during 1941–1944, but rice imports from the colonies and Southeast Asia did fall as a consequence both of the shipping lanes being severed by the Allied sea and air forces, and of the severe crop failures in Korea.[27] Sugar became acutely scarce after shipping from the mandated islands and Taiwan was slowed by American submarines and planes. Per capita consumption of sugar before the war averaged thirty pounds per year, but by 1945 it was down to three pounds. The supply of fish, an important item in the Japanese diet, reflected the attrition of both fishermen and fishing boats as well as of the areas where they could safely venture. By 1945 the total supply of fish dropped 65 percent from the 1939 norm.[28]

Textile production was drastically curtailed because wherever possible textile plants were converted to war production. In consequence, clothing of all sorts was scarce. All daily necessities, such as rice, milk, meat, and charcoal, were rationed as well as cigarettes, matches, soap, paper goods, and footwear. This critical economic situation was aggravated by the intensive bombings that began to devastate the major industrial cities at the end of 1944.

THE FINALE

Immediately after the American troops landed on Okinawa, Prime Minister Koiso resigned. The senior statesmen and Kido chose as his successor a retired admiral and head of the Privy Council, Suzuki Kantarō, who had narrowly escaped assassination during the uprising of February 26, 1936. In the Suzuki cabinet, General Anami Korechika (1887–1945) became minister of war, Yonai remained as minister of the navy, and Tōgō, who was foreign minister at the time of Pearl Harbor, reassumed that post. The Suzuki cabinet may have been seen as a "peace cabinet" by some observers, but outwardly there were no changes in policy. In fact, the critics of the war continued to be harassed by the police.

The Japanese nation lost all hope of support from other governments as defeat followed defeat. On April 5, 1945, Molotov informed the Japanese ambassador in Moscow that the Soviet-Japanese neutrality pact would not be renewed and would expire in a year. On May 7, Germany surrendered; henceforth the Allied might would concentrate upon the defeat of Japan. In mid-May, the Supreme Council for the Direction of the War soberly considered how it might prevent the Soviet Union from entering the war, cultivate its friendship, and seek a negotiated peace through Soviet mediation. The minister of war strenuously objected to the last item, but the Supreme Council agreed to pursue the first two possibilities.

Despite all evidence of its dire plight the army was still determined to fight a decisive battle on the Japanese homeland and, if necessary, to continue the struggle until the last Japanese fell. It claimed 2.25 million soldiers in uniform who, with the navy's 1.3 million men, stood ready to fight for the home islands. About 10,000 airplanes, mostly converted training planes, were prepared for use in suicide attacks. On June 8 the imperial conference adopted the army's policy of defending the homeland to the bitter end, and for this purpose a national militia was to be organized. The conference also agreed to negotiate with the Soviet Union to prevent it from entering the war against Japan.

Many senior statesmen realized that the war was lost, and privately they even discussed the need to declare an end to the fighting, but no one attempted to start a peace movement. Kido, who had previously worked hand-in-glove with the militarists, at last concluded that the time had come to terminate the war before the army's policy of defending the homeland to the last Japanese became a reality. He was concerned above all about the preservation of the imperial court and the protection of the national polity. He proposed a plan by which the emperor would call for a solution of the "current difficulties" by requesting the Soviet Union to act as a mediator. On June 22 the emperor summoned the members of the Supreme Council and asked for approval of Kido's plan. Confronted with the imperial command, the army reluctantly agreed.

Soon after the mid-May decisions of the Supreme Council, Hirota, who was assigned the task of negotiating with the Soviet Union, had expressed to the Russian ambassador, Jacob Malik (1906–1980), Japan's desire to improve Soviet-Japanese relations. Once again, after the Supreme Council meeting of June 22, Hirota met with Malik, and this time he offered concessions in return for a nonaggression pact. Malik agreed to transmit the proposals to Moscow and suggested that further discussion be postponed until he received a reply from his government. More than once thereafter Hirota sought to make an appointment, but Malik repeatedly claimed to be ill and refused to see him.

Foreign Minister Tōgō then decided to send a special envoy to Moscow, and, with the approval of the Supreme Council, he asked Prince Konoe to undertake the assignment. Konoe, although convinced that it was too late to talk of "peace with honor" or "a negotiated peace," nevertheless agreed to go. He was prepared to end the war on any terms so long as the imperial household and the national polity were preserved.

The Japanese ambassador to Moscow, Satō Naotake, was instructed to inform Molotov of Japan's desire to send Konoe as a special envoy. Molotov was busy preparing for an impending visit to Berlin, so Satō saw the vice foreign commissar, Solomon Lozovsky (1878–1952), and transmitted his government's message on July 13. On July 18, Lozovsky responded by saying that the message was too general, and the purpose of Konoe's visit was not sufficiently apparent. Tōgō then instructed Satō to make clear that the object of Konoe's visit was to ask the Soviet Union to extend its good offices to end the war short of unconditional surrender.[29] Satō saw Lozovsky on July 25, and he asked him to transmit Tōgō's message to Molotov in Berlin. Stalin, however, was not interested in acting as a mediator to end the war. At Yalta in February, he had secretly agreed to enter the war against Japan after the surrender of Germany in return for certain concessions.[30] Now, while the Japanese foreign office was desperately trying to persuade the Soviet Union to act as a mediator to end the war, Soviet officials were making arrangements at Potsdam to enter the war against Japan.

The United States had deciphered the Japanese code and so was aware of the efforts to persuade the Soviet Union to proffer its good offices. Indeed, Stalin had informed President Harry Truman (1884–1972) about this but held that the Japanese proposal was a maneuver to prolong the war.

On July 26 the United States, Great Britain, and China issued the Potsdam Declaration calling upon Japan to end the war or face "prompt and utter destruction." The terms set forth were: (1) the elimination of the authority and influence of those who led the Japanese people into the path of world conquest; (2) the occupation of Japan until its war-making powers were destroyed, and a new order of peace, security, and justice was established; (3) the implementation of the terms of the Cairo Declaration,[31] and limitation of Japanese sovereignty to Honshu, Hokkaido, Kyushu, Shikoku, and such minor islands as decided upon by the three powers; (4) the complete disarming of the Japanese military forces; (5) the punishment of war criminals, the removal of all obstacles to the development of democratic tendencies among the Japanese people, and the establishment of freedom of speech, religion, and thought, as well as respect for fundamental human rights; and (6) the restriction of Japanese industries to those activities that would enable it to sustain its economy and still permit the extraction of just reparations in kind, but that would not allow it to rearm. The declaration also stated that the occupying forces would be withdrawn as soon as these objectives had been accomplished and a peacefully inclined, responsible government had been established. It concluded by asking the Japanese government to proclaim the unconditional surrender of all Japanese armed forces.

On July 27, the Supreme Council for the Direction of the War and the cabinet were convened to discuss the Potsdam Declaration. Foreign Minister Tōgō opposed an outright rejection of the declaration, but did not openly advocate its acceptance. The chiefs of the general staff and the minister of war favored its unequivocal rejection, but Tōgō persuaded the Supreme Council and the cabinet to postpone a response to the Allied proclamation until the Soviet Union replied to Japan's request for mediation. They agreed to inform the public of the Potsdam Declaration without any official comment. When the press broke the news on July 28, however, it reported that the government considered the declaration to be of no significance and that it planned to ignore it. That afternoon Prime Minister Suzuki held a press conference at the insistence of the military leaders, who argued that an unequivocal denunciation of the declaration was needed to sustain the morale of the troops. At the press conference Suzuki stated: "I consider the joint proclamation of the three powers to be a rehash of the Cairo Declaration. The government does not regard it as a thing of any great value; the government will ignore it. We will press forward resolutely to carry the war to a successful conclusion."[32]

The Allied powers interpreted this as an outright rejection of the Potsdam Declaration. The *New York Times* headlined the story, "Japan Officially Turns Down Allied Surrender Ultimatum." At this moment the United States government came to the grave decision to use the atomic bomb, which had just been perfected.

From the start, scientists and military advisers concerned with its development were sharply divided about its use. Weighing the possibility of a protracted war mile-by-mile over the Japanese home islands, President Truman, who had succeeded Roosevelt in April, agreed to permit the use of the atomic weapon. On the morning of August 6, at 8:15, the bomber *Enola Gay* flew over the city of Hiroshima. The single bomb it carried was dropped on the central section of the city and exploded with a force equivalent to 20,000 tons of TNT. A white flash of blinding intensity and a searing heat wave emanated from the point of explosion. The huge mushroom cloud spread overhead, while the city below was turned into a living inferno. One eyewitness recollected, "It was a horrible sight. Hundreds of injured people who were trying to escape to the hills passed our house. . . . Their faces and hands were burnt and swollen; and great sheets of skin had peeled away from their tissues to hang down like rags on a scarecrow."[33] Another witness observed, "The sight of soldiers . . . was more dreadful than the dead people floating down the river. I came onto I don't know how many, burned from the hips up; and where the skin had peeled, their flesh was wet and mushy. . . . And they had no faces! Their eyes, noses and mouths had been burned away, and it looked like their ears had melted off."[34] One survivor trying to help the afflicted reached down and "took a woman by the hands but her skin slipped off in huge, glove-like pieces. . . . He remembered uneasily what the great burns he had seen during the day had been like: yellow at first, then red and swollen, with the skin sloughed off, and finally, in the evening, suppurated and smelly."[35] And yet the injured bore their suffering with stoic dignity. Father Kleinsorge (1902–1969), a Catholic priest in Hiroshima, observed, "The hurt ones were quiet; no one wept, much less screamed in pain; no one complained; none of the many who died did so noisily." And when he "gave water to some whose faces had been almost blotted out by flash burns, they took their share and then raised themselves a little and bowed to him, in thanks."[36]

The victims numbered some 140,000 dead and tens of thousands injured. Radiation sickness afflicted a large number who had seemingly escaped without injury. "Many people," recalled a doctor who was injured in Hiroshima, "who appeared to be healthy . . . were beginning to die with symptoms of vaginal bleeding, nose bleed, bloody sputum, bloody vomitus, and hemorrhages beneath the skin and in the tissues."[37] The city of Hiroshima itself was turned into a wasteland; over 80 percent of the buildings were destroyed.

Even this horrendous disaster failed to shake the determination of the militarists to continue the war and fight the foe on Japanese soil. Civilian leaders such as Tōgō, however, realized that the war must be ended at once. But before the leaders could assess the true significance of the atomic raid on Hiroshima, the Soviet Union declared war on Japan on August 8, 1945, fulfilling Stalin's Yalta pledge and complying with Truman's request. On August 9, Soviet troops entered Manchuria, once the stronghold of the Kwantung Army but now weakened by the withdrawal of the bulk of the troops to the homeland.

On the morning of August 9 the Supreme Council met to discuss and reevaluate the Potsdam terms now that Soviet Russia had entered the war. Suzuki, Tōgō, and Yonai favored accepting the terms with only the one proviso: that the national polity, that is, the imperial household, was to be preserved. Minister of War Anami, along with Umezu, the army chief of staff, and Toyoda Soemu, the naval chief of staff, insisted that in addition to the preservation of the national polity the following considerations be set forth: (1) Japan proper was not to be occupied; (2) the Japanese forces abroad were to be withdrawn and disarmed by the Japanese themselves; and (3) war criminals would be tried by the Japanese themselves. In the midst of this meeting, news arrived that the city of Nagasaki had suffered atomic attack and was even then ablaze with the same infernal fire that had swept Hiroshima. Later it would be ascertained that about 70,000 people had been killed, 60,000 injured, and 5,000 lost without trace. It was also announced at the meeting that on that same morning a Soviet army had invaded Manchuria. The military leaders refused, even in the face of all this overwhelming news, to modify their demands, and the meeting ended in a deadlock.

Later in the day the cabinet convened to discuss the terms of the Potsdam Declaration. Here, too, the army refused to retreat from its position. Suzuki decided to call upon the emperor to make the final decision. An imperial conference was called around midnight, and after both sides presented their views the emperor expressed his agreement with the advocates of peace and called for the acceptance of the Allied terms and the termination of the war.

The decision to accept the Potsdam Declaration with the proviso that "the said declaration does not comprise any demand that prejudices the prerogatives of His Majesty as a Sovereign Ruler" was sent to the Allied nations through the Swiss and Swedish governments. The Allied response, in effect the American response, to the Japanese statement regarding the prerogatives of the emperor was: "From the moment of surrender the authority of the emperor and the Japanese government to rule the state shall be subject to the Supreme Commander of the Allied powers." It also stated that "the ultimate form of government of Japan shall, in accordance with the Potsdam Declaration, be established by the freely expressed will of the Japanese people."[38]

The statement was drafted by Secretary of State James F. Byrnes (1879–1972), who believed that the United States, not Japan, should set the terms of surrender. At the same time, he also wanted to make it possible for the Japanese to accept them. Hence, the imperial institution was to be allowed to remain, but it was to be subject to the authority of the supreme commander.

The reply placed the Japanese peace advocates in a difficult position because it failed explicitly to uphold the prerogatives of the emperor, and it was feared that this could provide the militarists with an excuse to reject the Potsdam Declaration. However, Matsumoto Shunichi, the vice minister of foreign affairs, and Sakomizu Hisatsune (1902–1977), the chief cabinet secretary, convinced Suzuki and Tōgō that the American response, that is, the Byrnes rider, was satisfactory, and that it in no way conflicted with the national polity.

The military leaders objected vehemently. The two chiefs of the armed forces appealed directly to the emperor to reject the Allied terms. Moreover, War Minister Anami and Privy Council President Hiranuma nearly convinced

Suzuki that the response of the United States violated the national polity. Tōgō managed to enlist the support of Lord Keeper of the Privy Seal Kido, who persuaded Suzuki to accept the foreign offices' interpretation of the Byrnes rider.

The Supreme Council met on August 13, and the old division remained, with the minister of war and the two chiefs of the armed forces contending that the term "subject to" meant "subordinate to" not "restricted by," and the foreign office arguing that such subordination was not intended. The military leaders also maintained that allowing the freely expressed will of the people to determine the form of government would conflict with the national polity. Again an impasse ensued. The issue was once again passed on to the cabinet, which, as on the previous occasion, failed to resolve the disagreement. Suzuki now petitioned Emperor Hirohito to make the final decision. On August 14 an imperial conference was held, and the issues were argued again. After listening to the military leaders' arguments against accepting the Byrnes note, the emperor finally spoke, saying that he could no longer allow his people to suffer death and destruction. He asked his officials to endure the unendurable: to accept the Allied terms and end the war. He declared his intention to broadcast his decision to the people on the following day. Upon hearing his words, the opposition of the military leaders was immediately withdrawn. However, as word spread through the army, a hard core of fanatical middle-grade officers interpreted the decision as a betrayal and plotted a desperate coup d'état to rescue the emperor from "evil advisers." The vice chiefs of the two services were also irreconcilably opposed to surrender. The vice chief of the naval general staff, Ōnishi, originator of the corps of kamikaze pilots, argued that Japan should be ready to sacrifice 20 million lives in a kamikaze attack to win the war. The coup d'état failed when key generals refused to lend their support. War Minister Anami was sincerely opposed to the surrender, but he would not defy the emperor. General Umezu, chief of staff of the army, also rejected the planned coup. The commanding general of the First Imperial Guard Division, Mori Takeshi, refused to fall in with the plotters, and they murdered him on the spot. At length, the commanding general of the Eastern District Army, Tanaka Seiichi, took steps to quell the rebellion. The plan by the rebels to prevent the imperial broadcast from being made was also foiled.

In the early hours of August 15, General Anami committed seppuku in true samurai fashion, leaving the words, "Believing firmly that our sacred land shall never perish, I—with my death—humbly apologize to the emperor for the great crime."[39] Among other high-ranking officers who committed suicide were General Sugiyama, General Tanaka Seiichi, General Honjō,[40] and Vice Admiral Ōnishi. More than five hundred military and naval personnel committed suicide following the surrender.

On August 15, 1945, the people of Japan heard the voice of their emperor for the first time as he broadcast his decision to terminate the war. On September 2, the instrument of surrender was signed on board the battleship USS *Missouri* in Tokyo Bay with General Umezu representing Japan and General MacArthur representing the Allied powers. Thus ended the costliest venture Japan had ever embarked upon, a dire calamity for Japan as well as for the victims of its aggression. The suffering inflicted upon the victims of Japanese imperialism remains incalculable.[41]

There were some significant, though indirect, consequences of Japanese imperialism. For instance, the triumph of the Communists in China was made possible in part by the Japanese invasion, which weakened the Nationalist government and created political, economic, and social conditions that fostered the spread of communism. It is equally true that the independence of the Southeast Asian nations from European colonial powers was facilitated by the defeat of these powers by the Japanese during the early phase of the war in the Pacific.

Japanese army casualties from the outbreak of the war in the Pacific to Japan's surrender in 1945 included 1.14 million dead (200,000 of whom died in banzai charges), 300,000 wounded, and 4.47 million sick (of whom 40,000 died). The casualties for the navy included 415,000 dead and 1,400 missing. The victims of air raids numbered 393,000 dead and 310,000 injured. Moreover, as many as 500,000 civilians may have perished in the war zone. The death and destruction, brutalities and atrocities, and hardships and agonies resulting from the war proved once again, as has been demonstrated throughout history, that the factor most responsible for the miseries of humankind is the human himself.

Virtually all the major cities of Japan lay in waste. Kyoto, however, was spared by the United States because of its historical and cultural value. The economy was at a virtual standstill; there was an acute shortage of food, housing, and all basic necessities. In the midst of this the people awaited the arrival of the occupation forces with fear and trepidation.

Notes

1. As to why the warnings from intercepted messages were not heeded, the following has been suggested: "It is much easier after the event to sort the relevant from the irrelevant signals. . . . We failed to anticipate Pearl Harbor not for want of the relevant materials, but because of a plethora of irrelevant ones." Roberta Wholstetter, *Pearl Harbor: Warning and Decisions* (Stanford: Stanford University Press, 1962), p. 387.

2. Nearly 80 percent of the crew of the USS *Arizona* was lost; 47 officers and 1,056 men were killed or missing. The total casualties were 2,403 killed and 1,178 wounded. In contrast, the Japanese lost only twenty-nine planes and five midget submarines, and suffered about 100 casualties.

3. Samuel Eliot Morison, *History of the United States Naval Operations in World War II,* 15 vols. (New York: Little, Brown, 1947–1962), vol. 3, p. 132.

4. They damaged or destroyed seventeen B-17s and thirty fighter planes, thus reducing American bomber strength by one-half and fighter strength by one-third.

5. In the course of moving the prisoners of war from southern Bataan sixty-five miles north to San Fernando, the infamous Bataan Death March took place, in which an estimated 5,000 men died because of the brutalities of the Japanese captors. At the trials conducted after the war, General Homma was held responsible for this, and he was later executed as a war criminal.

6. Hayashi Shigeru, *Taiheiyō Sensō* (The Pacific War) (Tokyo: Chūō Kōronsha, 1967), p. 320.

7. At the end of the war the Japanese forces in New Guinea surrendered, and only 13,000 of the original 140,000 men were still alive.

8. American casualties came to 1,000 dead and more than 2,000 wounded, but the entire Japanese marine force of 4,800 men died in the battle.

9. They killed 7,870 Japanese. American losses during this battle were 372 dead or missing. At Eniwetok, which was also captured, the Japanese burial count came to 2,677, compared to the American toll of 195.

10. Of 11,000 men, fewer than 1,000 were alive at the end of the engagement. Some three hundred Japanese aircraft and two destroyers were lost.

11. The Japanese casualties in the Imphal campaign came to 30,000 dead and 42,000 sick and wounded.

12. In the two-day engagement Ozawa had lost three carriers, had seen four more crippled, and suffered 395 carrier planes downed or destroyed on deck. He had but 35 carrier planes left as he escaped to Okinawa. In all, the Japanese lost 476 aircraft, and 445 badly needed aviators. The United States had lost 130 planes and 76 airmen. Operation A was a disastrous failure.

13. American casualties were also high: 3,426 dead and 13,099 wounded. Morison, *History of the United States Naval Operations,* vol. 8, p. 338. For a vivid account of the grisly story of Saipan, see John Toland, *The Rising Sun: The Decline and Fall of the Japanese Empire, 1936–1945* (New York: Random House, 1970), pp. 504–519.

14. The raid left 83,793 dead, 40,918 injured, and 1 million homeless. It also destroyed a quarter of the city.

15. On the average, these cities were 40 percent destroyed. Approximately 2.3 million houses had gone up in smoke by war's end—about 20 percent of the habitations in all of Japan.

16. For example, on Leyte, Japanese soldiers yielded the island inch by inch, and about 80,000 of them died in the battle.

17. American casualties in the Philippines from January to June 1945 came to 8,140 killed, 29,557 wounded, and 157 missing. The Japanese lost through battle, starvation, and disease 250,000 men and 7,297 prisoners of war.

18. The conquest of Iwo Jima's eight square miles cost the United States 6,821 lives and more than 19,000 wounded. Japanese dead numbered 22,500.

19. Antiaircraft emplacements downed 116 American planes, but 528 of Japan's last aircraft were also destroyed.

20. In the gruesome slaughter 110,000 Japanese soldiers and Okinawan militiamen died. It is estimated that some 100,000 Okinawan civilians also perished in the conflict. American casualties included 5,000 navy men killed by kamikaze attacks and an equal number wounded;

the army counted 7,374 dead, 31,807 wounded, and 239 missing. Thirty naval vessels had been sunk, and 368 ships were damaged.

21. It was calculated that if Japan lost 1 million tons of shipping the first year and 800,000 tons in the years following, the 3 million level could be maintained by constructing 600,000 tons annually. The actual toll, however, was much heavier. Japanese shipping losses for the first year were 1.25 million tons, the second year 2.56 million, and the third year 3.484 million.

22. Stores of oil dropped from nearly 49 million tons in 1941 to 13.8 million in 1944 and to 4.9 million in the first half of 1945. Coal stocks similarly diminished from roughly 63.4 million metric tons in 1941 to 51.7 million in 1944 and then down to 11 million in the first half of 1945. Bauxite, essential for the production of aluminum, dropped from a December 1941 supply of 254.7 million metric tons to 176.2 million in June 1944, and then down to 2.6 million in December of that year.

23. In 1942 it had increased by only 2 percent over 1940. During the same period in the United States it had grown by 36 percent.

24. A comparison of the aircraft production figures of Japan with those of other nations during the four-year period between 1941 and 1944 shows what Japan was faced with. In this period it produced a total of 58,822 aircraft: Germany, however, built 92,656; England, 96,400; and the United States, 261,826.

25. By February 1944, there were 3.98 million men in uniform. This represented about 10 percent of the male population and 17 percent of the male working population. The figure for military personnel increased to 5.36 million men at the end of 1944, and when the war ended, there were 7.19 million men in the armed forces.

26. In 1941 the average output in the Japanese steel industry was 54 tons of ingot steel per worker; in 1944 this average fell to 21 tons. In the coal industry, output per employee per year dropped from 164 metric tons in 1941 to 119 in 1944. In contrast, in the United States in 1941 the figure was 1,021 metric tons of coal per worker, and by 1944 this figure rose to 1,430.

27. Japan had to import about 20 percent of its rice supply from Korea, Taiwan, and Southeast Asia. Total rice imports fell to 30 percent of normal in 1944 and 11 percent of normal in 1945. A disastrous drop in domestic rice production occurred in 1945, when bad weather resulted in a yield 27 percent below that of 1944.

28. During the war, food consumption in general was reduced to 1,782 calories per capita per day and 58 grams of protein, compared to the minimum requirement of 2,165 calories and 76 grams. The figures in this section have been taken primarily from Jerome B. Cohen, *Japan's Economy in War and Reconstruction* (Minneapolis: University of Minnesota Press, 1949).

29. Following the Casablanca Conference of January 1943, President Roosevelt announced that the Allied nations had agreed to continue the war against the Axis powers until they surrendered unconditionally. This policy was reiterated in the Cairo Declaration of December 1, 1943.

30. These were: (1) the preservation of the status quo in Outer Mongolia (that is, it was to remain in the Soviet sphere); (2) the restoration of the southern part of Sakhalin Island to Russia; (3) the internationalization of Dairen and the leasing of Port Arthur by China to Russia; (4) Sino-Soviet control of the Chinese Eastern Railroad and the South Manchurian Railroad; and (5) the transference of the Kurile Islands to Russia.

31. The Cairo Declaration proclaimed that "Japan shall be stripped of all the islands in the Pacific which she has seized or occupied since the beginning of the First World War in 1914,

and that all the territories that Japan has stolen from the Chinese, such as Manchuria, Formosa, and the Pescadores, shall be restored to the Republic of China. Japan will also be expelled from all other territories which she has taken by violence and greed."

32. Quoted in Robert J. C. Butow, *Japan's Decision to Surrender* (Stanford: Stanford University Press, 1954), p. 148.

33. Michihiko Hachiya, *Hiroshima Diary*, trans. and ed. Warner Wells (Chapel Hill: University of North Carolina Press, 1955), pp. 14–15.

34. Ibid.

35. John Hersey, *Hiroshima* (New York: Knopf, 1946), p. 49.

36. Ibid., p. 60.

37. Ibid., p. 69. For effects of the atomic bomb, see the Committee for the Compilation of Materials on Damage Caused by the Atomic Bombs in Hiroshima and Nagasaki, *Hiroshima and Nagasaki: The Physical, Medical and Social Effects of the Atomic Bombings*, trans. Eisei Ishikawa and David L. Swain (New York: Basic Books, 1981).

38. Raymond Dennett and Robert R. Turner, eds., *Documents on American Foreign Relations, 1945–1946* (Princeton: Princeton University Press, 1948), vol. 8, pp. 107–108.

39. Quoted in Butow, *Japan's Decision*, pp. 219–220.

40. Honjō (1876–1945) was commander of the Kwantung Army during the Manchurian Incident.

41. According to the estimates of the Nationalist government of China, the number of Chinese soldiers killed and wounded since the start of the China Incident came to about 5.62 million. Chinese civilians killed and injured in the occupied areas was estimated at 350,000, and the victims of air raids at 760,000. Property damage suffered by the Chinese was calculated at 29.42 billion prewar Chinese yüan. At that time, 100 yüan was worth approximately $30.

15

The Postwar Years (I)

Reform and Reconstruction

THE MACARTHUR ERA

The aftermath of war and defeat found Japan in an appalling condition. The country had been devastated by the air raids. Most of its major cities lay in ruin. Tokyo had lost 57 percent of its dwellings and Osaka about 60 percent. In all, eighty-one cities had been damaged by air raids. Nationally about 20 percent of the houses had been destroyed by the air raids, and about 8 million people had become homeless. Three years after the end of the war one in four families still did not have regular dwellings. Those who lost their homes lived in shacks, packing crates, and corrugated iron lean-tos, or slept in railroad station passageways. Makeshift huts remained in the major cities as long as a decade after the war ended. The transportation system, telephones, power plants, and other utilities were on the verge of breaking down, having been subjected to maximum use without replacements during the war. The United States air and naval attacks had destroyed 30 percent of Japan's industrial capacity, 80 percent of its shipping, and 30 percent of its thermal power. At the end of the war industrial production stood at barely 10 percent of the normal prewar level.[1]

Territorially Japan was now back to where it was when Commodore Perry arrived in 1853. It was compelled to relinquish Taiwan, the Pescadores, Korea, and southern Sakhalin. The Kuriles were now occupied by the Soviet Union, and Okinawa was placed under US administration. Millions of soldiers and civilians from the former colonies and the occupied areas of the Asian mainland and Southeast Asia began to return to the already crowded Japanese islands.

The immediate problem, and a matter of life and death for the urban populace, was the food shortage. Bad weather had caused rice production to drop 27 percent below that of 1944, and about 32 percent below the prewar average. Having lost its colonial possessions, Japan could no longer obtain additional food from Korea, Taiwan, or Manchuria.

The fishing industry, which Japan had relied upon as a major source of food, had also deteriorated and was about 40 percent below normal. Official food rations for each person per day came to 1,050 calories. The chief preoccupation of the urban dwellers was to scurry about in search of additional food. They scoured the black markets or went out into the villages to obtain sweet potatoes from the farmers, a quest that frequently ended in failure. If a person obeyed the law and abstained from getting food through the black market he was apt to starve to death.

A judge in a Tokyo court died of malnutrition in November 1947. He left behind a diary in which he had written,

> The food control law is a bad law. But as long as it is the law of the land we must observe it strictly. Regardless of how much agony it causes me I will not buy food in the black market. I have always respected Socrates' spirit when he readily accepted the punishment imposed on him though he knew it was a bad law. . . . I have decided to fight the black market and accept death by starvation. I live each day in the presence of death.[2]

Mass starvation of the Japanese people was avoided, however, by the American occupation authorities, who began transporting food to the country after the spring of 1946, following General Douglas MacArthur's request for emergency shipments of food and medicine. About 800,000 tons of food was shipped to the country in the following year.[3]

The shortage of basic necessities and the issuance of a large amount of currency caused acute inflation. In 1945 the amount of currency in circulation was fourteen times greater than that of 1937, and by 1949 it was six and a half times greater than it had been in 1945. The occupation authorities sought to impose price controls and curtail the flow of currency, but the cost of living rose by approximately 10 percent each month for about two years.[4]

In the throes of a virtually collapsed economy, and under a politically impotent government, a thoroughly bewildered and apprehensive Japanese people awaited the arrival of the occupying forces. To prepare for the unprecedented event, the imperial court appointed Prince Higashikuni prime minister immediately after the termination of the war. On August 28, 1945, the first contingent of the occupying troops arrived at Atsugi. On August 30, General MacArthur, who was appointed the Supreme Commander of the Allied Powers as well as the commander of the American military forces in the Far East, arrived. The new ruler of Japan stepped off his plane, corncob pipe in hand and dressed casually in his work clothes. Thus began the occupation of Japan, which was to last until April 28, 1952.

General MacArthur was acting on behalf of the Allied powers, whose policies were theoretically formulated by the eleven-member Far Eastern Commission. In fact, the US government held the ultimate authority. If, for example, the commission failed to agree on a matter of policy, the United States was empowered to issue "urgent unilateral interim directives." There was also an advisory council in Tokyo—the Allied Council for Japan—consisting of representatives of the United States, the British Commonwealth, the Soviet Union, and China. But it had little real authority over General MacArthur, and it became primarily a forum in which the Soviet Union berated American occupation policies. The strong personality of General MacArthur made the occupation of Japan a one-man show. Still, his forceful leadership, self-assurance, dignified bearing, sense of mission, and astute political acumen won him the respect of the Japanese.

Contrary to the expectations of some Americans who had been struck by the fanaticism of the soldiers of the imperial army, the Japanese people cooperated willingly with the occupation authorities. The defeat and devastation of war swept away the self-confidence and psychological props that had sustained the people for so long. They lacked the will to resist the conquerors, but their defiance came as time passed and the Japanese regained their self-assurance. The initial period was characterized by a remarkable degree of harmony. The emperor's acceptance of defeat and his submission to the Allied authorities of course made it easier for the people to do likewise. The Japanese were conditioned to bow to authority and accept the established order of things. In times of extreme stress some resorted to desperate actions of fanaticism, but under normal circumstances Japanese are a practical people, very rational and sensible, as well as friendly, cooperative, and courteous. Demonstrations against the US military bases would not occur until much later.

Sakaguchi Ango (1906–1955), a postwar writer, commenting on the Japanese people's reaction to the occupation authorities, said, "Of all peoples the Japanese basically muster up the least hatred and maintain it for the shortest time. Yesterday's enemy is today's friend. . . . We want to serve a second master as soon as the first one is out of the way."[5]

Cooperation with the occupying authorities was facilitated by the conquerors. The US military did not display the kind of pomp and ceremony and overbearing haughtiness that had so frequently characterized the rule of the Japanese military over conquered peoples. The friendliness and spontaneous warmth manifested by the occupying troops made the relationship between the two peoples relatively harmonious. The ends pursued by the occupation authorities were not vengeance or exploitation, but rather reforms that would enable Japan to achieve a free and democratic society. Some of the US measures and methods lacked good sense from the Japanese point of view, but no other conquered people in history had been treated more humanely and benefited more at the hands of its conquerors.

General MacArthur's authority as Supreme Commander of the Allied Powers (SCAP) in Japan was prepared by US government officials and approved by President Truman. In theory the occupation authorities were not to function as a military government. SCAP was to exercise supervisory authority, but the task of governing the country was to be left to the Japanese government. In fact, however, there was no question that the real power in Japan resided with SCAP, from whence emanated all important directives ordering the Japanese government to implement them. The policy decisions transmitted to General MacArthur stated: "The authority of the Emperor and the Japanese Government to rule the State is subordinate to you as Supreme Commander for the Allied powers. You will exercise your authority as you deem proper to carry out your mission."[6]

The chief objectives of SCAP were demilitarization and democratization. The US military authorities demobilized the 3.7 million Japanese troops at home and repatriated Japanese forces from abroad. This meant transporting back to Japan approximately 3.3 million troops and 3.2 million civilians. This task was completed largely by the beginning of 1948. Those not repatriated by then were mainly prisoners of war in the Soviet Union. By May 1949 a total of 900,000 people had been repatriated from Soviet-controlled territories. This still left, according to Japanese estimates, 420,000 persons.[7] Disclosures after the collapse of the Soviet Union indicated that as many as 500,000 Japanese made captive after the war had died doing forced labor. In contrast to the Soviet performance, repatriation from China, where the largest contingent of Japanese overseas troops was located and the largest number of people were killed by the Japanese troops, was facilitated by Jiang Jieshi, who hoped to use Japan as allies against the Chinese Communist Party. He told his fellow countrymen to cease regarding the Japanese as enemies and treat them as friends.

Under SCAP's direction military installations and equipment were destroyed, and what remained of the navy vessels, with the exception of those ships needed by the occupation forces to carry out their assignments, were divided among the four principal Allied nations.

War Crime Trials

An essential part of demilitarization was the prosecution and punishment of those who had committed war crimes. Two generals had already been tried and executed by ad hoc military courts established in the Philippines by General MacArthur immediately after the war. They were Generals Yamashita Tomoyuki and Homma Masaharu, who were held responsible for the atrocities committed by the Japanese troops in the Philippines, even though Yamashita was not in the Philippines when the atrocities were committed.

The International Military Tribunal for the Far East was created by the Allied powers for the purpose of trying the political leaders who were responsible for "crimes against peace." Twenty-eight major or Class A war criminals were characterized as a "criminal, militaristic clique" that dominated Japanese politics from January 1, 1928, to September 2, 1945. They were charged with "the planning, preparation, initiation, or waging" of aggressive war. Most of these men were also charged with violations of the laws and customs of war as well as crimes against humanity.

The Tokyo trial, presided over by eleven judges, began on May 3, 1946, and went on until April 1948. The sentences were handed down in November. Seven persons, including Tōjō, were sentenced to death by hanging. Sixteen were given life imprisonment; one was given twenty years; another was given seven years.

On December 22, 1948, those who were sentenced to death were hanged. The seven men were Tōjō and generals Itagaki, Doihara, Matsui Iwane (commanding general of the forces that assaulted Nanjing; 1878–1948), Mutō Akira (chief of military bureau from 1939 to 1942), Kimura Heitarō (vice minister of war from 1941 to 1944, and commanding general of the Japanese forces in Burma; 1888–1948), and Hirota (the only civilian). All those who were executed, except Hirota, composed a short poem before they were hanged. Tōjō's poem reads, "From tomorrow, without offending anyone, I shall rest in peace, beside the Amida Buddha."[8]

Among those who were sentenced to life imprisonment were Kido, Hiranuma, Araki, Koiso, Umezu, and Colonel Hashimoto (charged with the bombing of the British gunboat *Ladybird*). Former foreign ministers Tōgō and Shigemitsu were sentenced to prison for twenty and seven years, respectively.

Eight of the eleven justices fully concurred with the tribunal's decision. Two disagreed on certain aspects. Justice Radhabinod Pal of India (1886–1967) believed that the accused were innocent of all counts: the existence of a conspiracy had not been proven, aggressive war was not a crime in international law, and none of the conventional war crimes charges had been proven.

Matsuoka, Admiral Nagano, and Ōkawa Shūmei were also charged as Class A war criminals, but the first two died and Ōkawa experienced mental difficulties during the trial. Prince Konoe committed suicide when he discovered that he was to be arrested. Tōjō also attempted to commit suicide before his arrest by shooting himself through the heart, but survived. In 1957 the sentences of war criminals of all classes who had been tried in Tokyo and sentenced to imprisonment were commuted. Many had died during incarceration, but some managed to play active political roles after their release.

The question of trying the emperor as a war criminal was raised, but the idea was quashed by American officials who concluded that it would make the occupation forces' task in Japan virtually impossible. In his *Reminiscences* General MacArthur wrote: "I believed that if the Emperor were indicted, and perhaps hanged, as a war criminal, military government would have to be instituted throughout all Japan, and guerrilla warfare would probably break out."[9] Yoshida Shigeru, who served as prime minister from 1946 to 1947 and from 1948 to 1954, wrote in his memoirs, "It was the attitude adopted by General MacArthur towards the Throne, more than any other single factor, that made the Occupation an historical success."[10]

Before the decision to exclude the emperor from the list of war criminals, members of the prosecuting team prepared briefs for his trial. Kido Kōichi was interrogated at length about the emperor's political role by a member of the Military Tribunal's prosecution team. The interviews make clear the emperor was informed of all the decisions for military action made by the army and navy general staff. The decision had already been made not to try the emperor when Kido was interrogated, so the transcripts of his interviews were not used in the war crimes trial.[11]

George Atcheson (1897–1947), political adviser in the diplomatic section of SCAP, reported in a memorandum to the State Department that General MacArthur told him when he met the emperor the latter stated he assumed full responsibility for the war on behalf of the Japanese people. "The Emperor said that he had not intended that the attack on Pearl Harbor take place before receipt by the US Government of the Japanese declaration of war on the United States but Tōjō had tricked him."[12] The emperor's stance contrasts with Tōjō's, who at the war crimes trials "took pains to protect the imperial position and to present his arguments in such a way as not to compromise the person of the Emperor."[13]

Beside Class A war criminals, hundreds of others were charged as war criminals. High-ranking military officers were charged as Class B criminals; that is, they were accused of violating the laws and customs of war and were charged with command responsibility for the troops who had committed atrocities. As noted previously, two generals were tried by the ad hoc military court in the Philippines and executed. The others were tried by the military courts set up in Tokyo and were acquitted. Lesser officers and soldiers were charged as Class C criminals; that is, they were accused of crimes against humanity, such as mistreatment of prisoners of war and other atrocities. They were tried by military commissions under the United States Eighth Army and by Allied military authorities where the crimes were committed. The local war crimes trials were completed by the fall of 1949. It is contended that those who had engaged in bacteriological experiments on the Chinese in Manchuria were not tried in return for turning over the data to US authorities.[14]

In addition to trying and punishing war criminals, the occupation authorities, in accordance with the directives of the US government, sought to remove from positions of responsibility and leadership all those who had been exponents or agents of militarism, aggression, and militant nationalism. This entailed the purging of all high-ranking army and navy officers as well as most of the high government officials and leaders of business and industry, and right-wing nationalists and politicians. SCAP's directive to the Japanese government to proceed with the investigation of those who fell into the stipulated categories was issued in January 1946. Despite the policy of holding government officials responsible, the powerful bureaucracy was left largely intact.[15]

The other objective of SCAP, to free political prisoners detained in the prewar years, was implemented at the outset of the occupation. SCAP immediately issued directives to the Japanese government to release all political prisoners. Thus people who had been imprisoned, such as the Communist leader Tokuda Kyūichi, were released from prison. In addition, scholars who had lost their teaching positions because of their political beliefs were restored to their positions.

Initially SCAP had adopted a policy of having Japan pay reparations in the form of industrial equipment to the nations that had been victimized by its imperialism. This policy, however, was terminated in May 1948, because it conflicted with the policy to stabilize the Japanese economy and help it become self-sufficient. Reparation arrangements were made by Japan with several Asian nations after it had gained its independence.[16]

In addition to the punitive measures that were implemented, the occupation authorities introduced radical changes in the economic, educational, and political realms to foster and strengthen democratic forces in Japan.

Economic Reforms

The US government's policy of democratizing Japan included instituting "democracy" and freedom in the economic sector, which meant breaking up the stranglehold on the economy that the giant business conglomerates *(zaibatsu)* had on the Japanese economy. Included among those purged for militaristic and imperialistic activities were business executives, especially those in the zaibatsu and those who had a part in Japanese expansion overseas.

To encourage the rise of democracy through a wider distribution of income and the ownership of the means of production and trade, the US policy statement of September 6, 1945, directed SCAP "to favor a program for the dissolution of the large industrial and banking combinations which have exercised control of a great part of Japan's trade and industry." The economic democratization policies were basically products of progressive New Deal thinking.

The first step in a three-stage plan for "zaibatsu busting" was to require the chief holding companies of the zaibatsu to sell their stocks to the general public. The sale of shares laid the basis for the emergence of the massive Tokyo stock exchange system. The second step taken was the passage of an antimonopoly law that prohibited institutions and practices such as trusts, cartels, interlocking corporate controls, and restraint of trade agreements. The third step was the most controversial. It involved the enactment of the "Law for the Elimination of Excessive Concentration of Economic Power," designed to break up the zaibatsu.

To implement these policies a commission under SCAP was given the authority to dissolve any company that it regarded as being too big or monopolistic. Initially the commission expected to liquidate about 1,200 companies, but the program aroused considerable opposition among American business and political leaders who complained that the plan was socialistic and as such would retard the economic recovery of Japan. As a result a review board was created in May 1948 to reexamine the program, and eventually the number of companies destined for dissolution was reduced from several hundred to eleven. Nonetheless, eighty-three zaibatsu holding companies were dismantled, and about 5,000 other companies were forced to reorganize by means of the antimonopoly laws. The Mitsui and Mitsubishi organizations, for example, were fragmented into 240 separate firms.

Although zaibatsu control over the Japanese economy was disrupted, the effort to eliminate big business conglomerates turned out to be the least enduring of the occupation reforms because most of the old zaibatsu firms reunited, albeit in a looser form, after SCAP departed. The mergers increased with the rapid economic growth of the late 1950s and 1960s. However, the cartel-busting program did foster free competition and opened the way for individuals and independent companies, like Honda, Toyota, Sony, and Matsushita, to emerge as major players in the Japanese and world economies.

The land reform program was another economic measure designed to bring about a more equitable distribution of wealth. It turned out to be much more effective than zaibatsu busting. In fact, it was perhaps the most successful reform measure implemented by SCAP. At the end of the war, 70 percent of Japanese farmers were tenants or rented some land to augment their own holdings. About 46 percent of the cultivated land was tenanted, but there were no gigantic landowners. Only about 2,000 landlords owned as much as 100 acres; most individuals owned no more than 10 acres.

Under the direction of SCAP the Diet passed the Farm Land Reform Law in October 1946. This law prohibited absentee landlordism. A landlord who lived in the community where he owned land could hold a maximum of 2.5 acres. An active farmer could own a maximum of 7.5 acres for his own use plus an additional 2.5 acres that he did not cultivate. The government purchased the land from the landowners and sold it to former tenants, who were required to repay the government over a thirty-year period at an interest rate of 3.2 percent. The transfer of land was managed by 13,000 locally elected land commissions.

Skyrocketing inflation and the consequent decline in the value of money between the time when the amount of compensation was determined and when the transaction was actually completed resulted in landowners receiving practically no compensation. In some instances the price per acre paid to the landowners was the same as the cost of a carton of cigarettes on the black market. This, of course, made it possible for any tenant, no matter how impoverished, to purchase his share of land. The transfer of land was completed by August 1950.[17]

Another feature of the US policy of strengthening democratic forces and effecting a more equitable distribution of wealth was the attempt to foster an independent trade union movement in Japan. Following SCAP's directives, a number of labor laws were enacted by the Japanese Diet. In December 1945 a trade union law was passed that guaranteed workers, including public service employees and teachers, the right to organize, engage in collective bargaining, and strike. In 1946 legislation was enacted to set up grievance procedures to settle labor disputes, at the same time denying public-safety and administrative employees the right to strike. In 1947 a Labor Standards Law was enacted that set minimum standards for working hours, vacation, safety and sanitation safeguards, sick leaves, accident compensation, and restrictions on the hours and conditions under which women and children could work. The law "significantly exceeded the United States' Fair Labor Standards Act in coverage."[18]

It was thus through SCAP's paternalistic policies that Japanese workers acquired the protection and rights that had been denied them under the old regime. The number of unions and union members mushroomed by virtue of these sanctions.[19]

Educational Reforms

Educational reforms were initiated to remove militaristic and ultra-nationalistic influences from the schools and to inculcate democratic values in the students. SCAP suspended the teaching of Japanese history and geography until new textbooks were written. The teaching of morals was eliminated from the curriculum. In March 1946 an educational mission headed by George D. Stoddard (1897–1981), New York State commissioner of education, submitted a report to SCAP recommending that militaristic or ultranationalistic teachers be purged from the schools, textbooks be revised, and numerous changes made in the curriculum. It also recommended the extension of compulsory education to nine years; decentralization of control; establishment of more institutions of higher learning; and fundamental revision of the basic educational program, which stressed rote learning, to one that encouraged students to think by responding to new situations and by taking the initiative to explore new ideas.

Changes in the educational system were introduced on the basis of the Stoddard report.[20] Control of the public elementary and secondary schools was turned over to locally elected boards of education. Regional boards, which were elected by the people, were established to coordinate the educational program in each prefecture, to certify teachers and administrators, and to approve the textbooks. The control that the Education Ministry formerly exercised was eliminated; it was to provide only technical aid and professional counsel to the boards. It no longer authored public school textbooks, but it retained the practice of certifying them. The ministry issued a curriculum guide that the local school boards turned to for guidance.

To increase the number of institutions of higher education, sixty-eight national universities and ninety-nine other universities were newly established in 1949. Junior colleges came into existence in 1950; by 1952 they numbered 205. The quality of many of these institutions, however, was poor because they formerly had been higher schools, teacher training schools, and technical institutions. Consequently, the prestige of the older institutions was enhanced even further. This led to fierce competition among the young students aspiring to enter the prestigious institutions.

The drastic changes initially created problems during the transition, but the reforms were incorporated into the national school system. There was criticism of the changes by those who defended the traditional system. They complained that the positive aspects of the former system had been ignored and the changes produced lower educational standards; in their view the introduction of the one-track system (eliminating the former technical schools) hindered students who were more likely to benefit from a good technical education than from a liberal arts general education program. They also contended that incorporation of progressive educationist philosophy reduced education merely to instruction in life adjustment. Nevertheless, educators agreed that in general the freer atmosphere in the schools and the emphasis on "independent thought and initiative, and on developing a spirit of inquiry" was beneficial.

Another aspect of the postwar changes was the emergence of a new force in the educational field. This was the Japan Teachers Union, a militant labor union strongly influenced by Marxist political sentiments. It has to the present kept a watchful eye on any trend that might presage a reversion to the former ways of imperial Japan. The militancy of the union leaders was heightened by the government's campaign in 1949 to remove all Communists from the school system. At the college level, another powerful political force emerged in the form of student organizations. The National Student Federation (Zengakuren), which was organized in September 1948, provided forceful leadership in staging political demonstrations to combat whatever it deemed antidemocratic.

Political Reforms

The most significant effort at democratizing Japan occurred in the political realm, which entailed granting civil rights and freedom. In this area the United States set the following objectives: eliminate the power of the emperor, make the executive power of the government responsible to the people or their representatives, establish a legislative body that would be directly responsible to all adult citizens, and develop democratically controlled political parties. The essential undertaking to realize these objectives was the adoption of a new constitution.

The US government had not formulated any plan to revise the Japanese Constitution, so the planning committee on Japanese occupation did not specifically mention constitutional revisions in its directive to SCAP. General MacArthur took the initiative to do so in order to accomplish the goal of democratizing the country. He encouraged the Japanese leaders to work on constitutional revisions. The version presented to SCAP retained much of the Meiji Constitution and ascribed sovereign authority to the emperor. Of course, this conflicted with the SCAP principle that sovereignty resided in the people. General MacArthur rejected the Japanese version and had SCAP officials form a committee to draft the constitution. He instructed them to incorporate three principles: limited monarchy, renunciation of war, and abolition of feudalism. The committee completed a draft that consisted of ninety-two articles.

When the Japanese authorities were presented with the SCAP draft they were disturbed and attempted to modify it by carefully choosing Japanese terms in the translation so as to make it closer in meaning to their version. The new constitution was made public on March 7, 1946, as a creation of the Japanese government, but the public suspected that it was a product of SCAP because the text read like a translation. One distinctive feature of the new constitution was its rendition in standard Japanese rather than the elevated official language, the first official document to be so written.

The draft constitution was then turned over to the Diet for consideration and adoption. After lengthy deliberation about the wordings in the translation, the House of Representatives of the Diet adopted the new constitution on August 21, 1946, by a vote of 429 to eight. Five of the nay votes were cast by Communists who opposed preserving the imperial institution. On October 6, the House of Peers approved the new constitution. It was proclaimed the law of the land on November 3 and went into effect in May 1947.[21]

The new constitution changed the identity and role of the emperor from that of an absolute monarch to "the symbol of the State and unity of the people." Sovereignty was now vested in the people. The cabinet was made directly responsible to the Diet, which was made "the highest organ of state power." The members of the two houses were to be elected directly by the people. The upper house (House of Councilors) was given less power than the lower house (House of Representatives), which could override a negative vote in the upper house by passing a bill a second time with a two-thirds majority.

The new constitution provides comprehensive coverage of the rights of the people. In addition to the rights and liberties provided for in the US Bill of Rights, the Japanese constitution has provisions concerning social welfare. It states that "All people have the right to maintain the minimum standards of wholesome and cultured living. In all spheres of life, the State shall use its endeavors for the promotion and extension of social welfare and security, and of public health." It also guarantees the people's right to an education, the right of labor to organize and engage in collective bargaining, and the equality of husband and wife. The constitution also provides for full legal protection against arbitrary arrest and punishment. In other words, rule of law had finally become a reality in Japan.

To bolster the bill of rights, a law on habeas corpus was enacted in 1948. The judiciary was made independent of the Ministry of Justice, and the Supreme Court was given the responsibility of supervising the lower courts. The concept of judicial review was introduced, and the Supreme Court was made "the court of last resort with power to determine the constitutionality of any law, order, regulation or official act." The jury system was not incorporated into the new judicial system.

A unique feature of the new constitution is Article 9, the "no-war" clause:

> Aspiring sincerely to an international peace based on justice and order, the Japanese people forever renounce war as a sovereign right of the nation and the threat or use of force as means of settling international disputes.
>
> In order to accomplish the aim of the preceding paragraph, land, sea and air forces, as well as other war potential, will never be maintained. The right of belligerency of the State will not be recognized.

Japanese officials inserted the clause "in order to accomplish the aim" to leave open the possibility of arms for self-defense. Yoshida Shigeru was opposed to the idea of limiting the no-war clause only to aggressive war because, he contended, wars can be started in the name of defense. Article 9 later proved to be an embarrassment for the Japanese government and the United States, which, in the course of growing tension with the Communist powers, began to favor rearming Japan. Consequently, a circuitous reinterpretation of the clause condemning war was made to enable Japan to maintain "self-defense" forces.

Changes were also introduced at the local level so as to strengthen the autonomy of local governments and to foster democratic tendencies. The authority that the Ministry of Home Affairs formerly exercised over local governments was removed. The prefectural governors, who formerly were appointed by the central government, are now elected by the prefectural voters. The governors can no longer override the prefectural assemblies, to which they are now responsible. In the town and village governments fewer changes were necessary because they already had a greater degree of autonomy than the prefectural governments. The mayors are now elected directly by the voters rather than by the town or village assemblies, as had formerly been the rule. In addition, the principles and procedures of referendum, initiative, and recall were introduced at the municipal and prefectural levels.

Significant reforms were also introduced in the police system. In 1947 a police reorganization law was enacted to decentralize the police, which formerly was under the authority of the Ministry of Home Affairs and the prefectural governors. Municipalities with a population of more than 5,000 were required to maintain their own police force. A small national police force, under the control of a five-man National Public Safety Commission, was created for less-populated rural areas. In a national emergency the prime minister has the right to assume operational control of both the rural and local police, subject to approval of the Diet within twenty days. Efforts were made to inculcate democratic values among the police to expunge the arrogant, overbearing attitude commonly manifested by the former police force.

Other changes on behalf of democracy included the introduction of universal suffrage in April 1946. Women were given the right to vote, and the voting age was lowered from twenty-five to twenty. On New Year's Day 1946, Emperor Hirohito, with the encouragement of SCAP, officially announced that he was not divine. The emperor also began more and more to come out of his closely guarded palace in an effort to mingle with the people.

SCAP prohibited the teaching of Shinto doctrine in the schools and abolished state control and support of Shinto shrines. In addition, another pillar of imperial authority, the peerage, was eliminated. As a result, 913 families ranging from barons to princes lost their special status and privileges.

The US postsurrender policy also called for instituting freedom of religion, assembly, speech, and the press. Having endured years of censorship, the people and the press began to express their opinions freely and even began criticizing SCAP and US policies. This resulted in SCAP being placed in the awkward position of curbing material that "disturbs public tranquility." Censorship was gradually extended to cover books and movies that were "detrimental to the purpose of occupation."

Social Reforms

In the realm of social reforms the most significant legal changes were introduced in the family system, in particular the status of women. The equal right of the wife with her husband was guaranteed, the wife was given the right to own property independently, and she gained the right to divorce her husband on the same grounds that he could appeal to in divorcing her. Primogeniture was abolished, and daughters were given the right to inherit the same share of the family property as sons. The authority formerly held by the head of the extended family was removed. Family registries were compiled on the basis of the nuclear, conjugal family. A male at the age of eighteen and a female at the age of sixteen could now marry without the consent of the parents. Legal changes, of course, did not bring about an immediate end to the old ways. Women continued to occupy a subordinate position in the family and society, although women gradually began to play an increasingly prominent role in all areas of society.

Among the social reforms initiated later by the Japanese was the antiprostitution law of 1956, which finally removed the many brothels that had occupied fixed quarters of the towns and cities for centuries. Another movement that gained popular support was birth control, which resulted in the legalization of abortion in June 1949.

POLITICAL DEVELOPMENTS
DURING THE OCCUPATION YEARS

The United States did not want to establish its own military government, so it carried out its policies through the Japanese government. The cabinet and the Diet were essentially handmaidens of SCAP until the peace treaty went into effect in April 1952. Higashikuni, who became prime minister at the end of the war, was replaced in October 1945 by Shidehara, who had been an advocate of international cooperation during the 1920s. He dissolved the Diet and the first postwar election under the new provisions of universal suffrage was held in April 1946. With the lifting of the political barriers a host of new and former political parties had emerged, 363 of them, including numerous one-man parties. The former Seiyūkai members formed the Liberal Party, headed by Hatoyama Ichirō. The former Minseitō members formed the Progressive Party, headed by Shidehara. The socialists organized the Japan Socialist Party, and Katayama Tetsu became its head. A Communist party was founded, led by Tokuda Kyūichi, who had just been released from prison after eighteen years of incarceration.

In the election the Liberal Party won the most seats, so Hatoyama expected to become the next prime minister, but he was purged by SCAP for his prewar political activities. The party members then turned to Yoshida Shigeru to head the government. Yoshida had had a distinguished career as a foreign service officer and was incarcerated by Tōjō during the war for being involved in a plan to end the war. The first Yoshida cabinet remained in office for a year. During this period many of the reforms that had been initiated during the Shidehara regime were adopted, such as Diet approval of the new constitution, land reforms, and implementation of the new educational system.

The new constitution was to come into effect in May 1947, so SCAP ordered new elections in April of that year. The election resulted in the Socialist Party gaining the most seats and emerging as the largest party. The head of the Socialist Party, Katayama, formed a coalition with the newly formed Democratic Party, headed by Ashida Hitoshi (1887–1959), and together they formed the cabinet.

Thus the first, and until 1994, the only Socialist government came into existence in May 1947. Like other postwar governments the Katayama cabinet was beset with problems of unemployment, food shortages, inflation, and labor unrest. Unable to keep contending factions in the party together, Katayama resigned in March 1948 and was replaced by Ashida. Ashida's cabinet proved even more ineffective, and he was forced to resign in October when a scandal involving government officials was exposed.

In March 1948 the Liberal Party joined with a faction of the Democratic Party to form the Democratic Liberal Party. As the head of the party, Yoshida got sufficient support to form his second cabinet. Retaining the support of his party members, he was able to remain in office over a six-year period from October 1948 to December 1954, longer than any prime minister before him.

Yoshida dissolved the Diet and held a national election in January 1949. His party won a decisive victory, the first party to win an absolute majority in the 466-member postwar Diet. The Democratic Party and the Socialist Party lost seats, whereas the Communist Party rose from four to thirty-five seats, having gained strong support in the inner-city working-class districts of Tokyo and Osaka. Yoshida's victory in this election is also seen as the ascendancy of the former bureaucrats; sixty-two Diet members were former bureaucrats. This marked the beginning of the triangular power bloc of the Conservative Party members, bureaucrats, and business interests that dominated Japan for the next four and a half decades.

Yoshida formed his third cabinet in February 1950 and concentrated on preserving political stability and advancing the country's economic recovery. He was faced with opposition from the left, the Communists in particular, who accused him of pursuing a "reverse course policy"—that is, seeking to undo many of the reforms introduced by SCAP.

The Communists had focused on gaining support of the workers to gain political ascendancy. They succeeded in gaining leadership in one of the major labor organizations and staged political strikes to challenge established authorities. SCAP's initial move to foster an active labor movement subsided somewhat as the Communists came to dominate the unions involved in state-owned services such as the railroad and telecommunication systems. In February 1947, SCAP intervened to prevent a general strike. The labor movement suffered a further setback when SCAP permitted the Japanese government to restrict the right of employees of state-owned enterprises to strike, and in late 1948, legislation to this effect was enacted. In 1949 the trade union law was revised to ensure democratic control of the unions by members to prevent the takeover of the organizations by Communists.

The Communists came upon a popular cause to challenge the Yoshida government when in 1949 the government adopted a plan to reduce the workforce by 260,000 workers in state-run enterprises. It had set out to implement a policy of retrenchment recommended by Joseph Dodge, a Detroit banker sent by the United States to stabilize the Japanese economy. The government began to effect its plan by dismissing national railroad workers. This led to a number of violent incidents that intensified the confrontation between the government and the labor unions.

In June 1950, Communist leaders were forced to go underground again when SCAP ordered the purge of the Communist Party's central committee members and the editors of the Communist organ, the *Red Flag*. The ostensible reason given by SCAP for the purge was the Communist advocacy of revolution by force, but no doubt it was the growing tensions in the Cold War. The Korean War had just broken out, and SCAP was compelled to adopt a tough anti-Communist policy. It was not just SCAP that was concerned about the Communist ascendancy; members of the Japanese establishment were even more nervous, and they were critical of SCAP's lenient policy toward Communists.

Non-Communist leaders began to come to the fore in the unions, and in 1950 they organized the General Council of Trade Unions (Sōhyō). It soon became the largest federation of unions in the country. But even the non-Communist union leaders began to become increasingly critical of SCAP and the United States, whose policies appeared to be governed by Cold War contingencies. They objected to the tougher labor policies being instituted and resented the close alliance that was developing between SCAP and the conservative parties.

As tension in the Cold War continued to mount, some union leaders tended to become increasingly sympathetic to Communist nations; others favored maintaining a position of "positive neutrality." The leadership of the Sōhyō began to fall to men with leftist or Marxist leanings. In 1953 the federation claimed that "monopoly capital at home and abroad supported by the United States is planning to throw the peoples of the entire world into the crucible of war." This remained more or less the position of Sōhyō and its political arm, the Socialist Party, throughout the 1950s. The union leaders who disapproved of the drift to the left broke away from Sōhyō and formed a separate federation that supported right-wing socialists. In 1962 moderate right-wing labor groups merged and organized the Japanese Confederation of Labor (Dōmei Kaigi), the second largest federation of labor unions.

Yoshida, an ardent anti-Communist, began purging Communists from government posts and government corporations even before the outbreak of the Korean War. The Red purge was also extended to the press and private industry.[22] In July 1952, after the occupation ended, the Yoshida government enacted the Subversive Activities Prevention Law to keep the Communists in check. In 1955, as the Hatoyama government pursued a policy of improving relations with the Soviet Union, Communist leaders began to reappear in the public scene.

The Peace Treaty

One of Yoshida's cardinal objectives was the signing of a peace treaty to end the presence of US occupation forces. US officials also wanted to conclude a peace treaty and end the occupation. The US policy toward Japan had shifted from the objective of keeping Japan from reemerging as a military power to rebuilding its economy and transforming it into an important bastion in the anti-Communist bloc that the United States was forging since the Cold War intensified. Thus, the conclusion of a peace treaty with Japan was essential to strengthen its ties with the United States in the confrontation with Communist powers.

The United States decided to terminate the occupation because SCAP had achieved its major objectives, demilitarization and democratization, and under the capable direction of Yoshida, the country had apparently achieved a significant degree of political, social, and economic stability. General MacArthur was convinced that a prolonged occupation would have adverse effects, and as early as the spring of 1947 he began advocating the conclusion of a peace treaty. Moreover, the international situation had changed radically since the occupation policies were first formulated. The primary concern of US involvement in Asia was no longer to prevent Japan's reemergence as a major power. In the Far East the victory of the Chinese Communists in the fall of 1949 made fears about the revival of Japanese militarism seem to be merely a phobia of the past. MacArthur believed that the "consummation of a just peace for Japan is one way—possibly the most dramatic and dynamic way open at this time—of asserting our leadership and regaining our lost initiative in the course of Asian affairs."[23] Then, after the outbreak of the Korean War, the chief concern of the United States in Japan became the defense of the country from the potential threat of Communist powers.

In the spring of 1950, John Foster Dulles (1888–1959) was assigned the task of preparing the groundwork for the peace treaty. The plan devised by Dulles entailed linking the peace treaty to the conclusion of a bilateral security pact, and provisions for the United States to maintain military bases in Japan. Okinawa was to remain under US occupation with the United States retaining the right to maintain military bases.

A meeting to sign the peace treaty in San Francisco in September 1951 was scheduled, and invitations were sent to fifty-five nations. Forty-eight nations signed the peace treaty. The Soviet Union attended the conference but did not sign the treaty because its wish to amend provisions of the treaty was denied. Neither the Chinese Communist government nor the Taiwan government was invited because the United States and Great Britain failed to agree on which government to invite. Later in 1951, Japan signed a peace treaty with Jiang's Taiwanese regime at the urging of the United States. The issue of the four Kurile Islands occupied by the Soviet Union at the end of the war was not resolved. The question of reparations was not dealt with. Each nation was to negotiate directly with Japan. It was understood that reparations would take the form of industrial assistance rather than monetary compensations.

On the same day that the peace treaty was signed, a mutual security treaty was concluded between Japan and the United States. It provided for continued US military presence in Japan to protect it from external aggressors and internal rebellions supported by external powers. The terms of the security agreement were spelled out in an administrative agreement signed in February 1952.

The conservative parties favored ratification of the peace treaty. The right-wing Socialists favored ratification without Soviet participation but opposed linking it to the security agreement. Left-wing Socialists and Communists opposed signing the treaty without Soviet participation and opposed the security treaty. Yoshida's Liberal Party had a majority in the Diet, so the treaty was ratified in October 1951 and went into effect on April 28, 1952.

Thus ended SCAP as a de facto ruling power in Japan, a presence that brought about a truly revolutionary change in the country. The mandate given SCAP was accomplished: the end to militarism, imperialism, and the building of the foundation for a democratic government and freer society by the introduction of numerous political, social, and economic reforms. Reforms were instituted by a governing authority that accomplished the revolution without bloodshed, a truly remarkable occupation achievement. Even the Japanese are compelled to admit the striking contrast between the US occupation policy, conduct, and record in Japan, and the record of Japanese occupation in China and Southeast Asia during World War II.

General MacArthur, the man most responsible for the transformation of Japan, was gone from the country when the peace treaty was signed, having been relieved of his post in April 1951 because of his disagreement with President Truman regarding the Korean campaign. He was succeeded by General Matthew Ridgway.

Notes

1. In January 1946, industrial production was still severely depressed and had climbed to only 18.3 percent. For the entire year of 1946, it remained at 30.7 percent of the 1934–1936 level.

2. Quoted in Tsurumi Shunsuke et al., eds., *Nihon no Hyakunen* (Hundred Years of Japan), 10 vols. (Tokyo: Chikuma Shobo, 1961–1964), vol. 2, pp. 301–302.

3. Kazuo Kawai, *Japan's American Interlude* (Chicago: University of Chicago Press, 1960), pp. 137–138.

4. The wholesale price index in 1945 was 3.5 times that of 1934–1936, and in December 1949 it was 212.8 times; the consumer price index during the same period rose to 240 times the prewar level. Eventually the yen, which was worth about 4 yen to the dollar before the war, was fixed at 360 yen to the dollar.

5. Donald Keene, *Dawn to the West: Japanese Literature in the Modern Era* (New York: Holt, 1984), pp. 1075–1076.

6. Supreme Commander for the Allied Powers, Government Section, *Political Reorientation of Japan, September 1945 to September 1948: Report,* 2 vols. (Grosse Pointe, Mich.: Scholarly Press, 1968), vol. 2, p. 427.

7. The Soviet Union claimed it had only 105,000 more Japanese prisoners and returned 95,000 by the end of 1949. It is estimated that 55,000 Japanese died in Soviet detention camps.

8. Tsurumi, *Nihon no Hyakunen,* p. 66.

9. Douglas MacArthur, *Reminiscences* (New York: McGraw-Hill, 1964), pp. 282–283.

10. Yoshida Shigeru, *The Yoshida Memoirs* (Cambridge, Mass.: Riverside Press, 1962), p. 51.

11. Daikichi Irokawa, *The Age of Hirohito: In Search of Modern Japan,* trans. M. Hane and J. K. Urda (New York: Free Press, 1995), p. 79ff.

12. Matsuo Takayoshi, *Kokusai Kokka e no Shuppatsu* (Takeoff Toward an International Nation-State) (Tokyo: Shueisha, 1993), p. 20.

13. Robert J. C. Butow, *Tojo and the Coming of the War* (Stanford: Stanford University Press, 1961), p. 495.

14. . Kawai, *Japan's American Interlude*, pp. 22–24; and Fujiwara Akira, *Sekai no Naka no Nihon* (Japan in the World Community) (Tokyo: Shogakukan, 1980), pp. 61–62. Estimates vary, but somewhere between 5,500 to 6,000 persons were charged and tried for war crimes. Over 930 persons were executed, and the vast majority of the rest were sentenced to prison for varying lengths of time.

15. By May 1948 some 220,000 persons, including 180,000 former military officers, were purged. Most of the people purged were forced to remain inactive until they were rehabilitated during 1950 and 1951.

16. By April 1964 Japan had paid $477 million in reparations to six Southeast Asian nations.

17. About 2.8 million acres of rice land and 1.95 million acres of upland had been purchased from 2.34 million landowners and resold to 4.75 million tenants and farmers who possessed less land than the legal maximum. Only 12 percent of all arable land remained under tenancy, and low rents were fixed by law on this land. The percentage of full tenants dropped from 27.7 percent of the farmers in 1941 to about 5 percent in 1950. In addition, 600,000 acres of pastureland were acquired by the government for redistribution.

18. Sheldon Garon, *The State and Labor in Modern Japan* (Berkeley: University of California Press, 1987), p. 236.

19. By 1949 more than 6.5 million out of a total of 15 million industrial workers were enrolled in more than 35,000 unions. A drop in membership occurred when the unions began engaging in controversial political activities, but it began to rise again in the 1950s. In 1969 there were close to 59,000 unions, with a combined membership of more than 11 million workers.

20. The school system was reorganized in accordance with the American 6-3-3-4 (elementary, junior high, senior high, and college) system instead of the former 6-5-3-3 (elementary, middle, higher, and college) system.

21. The inherent linguistic differences between English and Japanese made for ambiguities and resulted in some changes in meaning. Professor Kyoko Inoue, comparing the English version and the Japanese (translated) version, sees differences in illocutionary force. She concludes that in drafting a democratic constitution "the Americans used, to a considerable extent, the language of their own Constitution. This, however, resulted in an inconsistency in the illocutionary force of the Japanese Constitution as drafted in English." Kyoko Inoue, *MacArthur's Japanese Constitution: A Linguistic and Cultural Study of Its Making* (Chicago: University of Chicago Press, 1991), p. 69.

22. Consequently, 22,000 persons were discharged, including 600 in the press and radio, and more than 10,000 in industry.

23. MacArthur, *Reminiscences,* p. 323.

16

The Postwar Years (II)

Political Developments After Independence

THE YOSHIDA YEARS

Freed from the authority of SCAP, the Yoshida government moved to revise some of the reforms that had been introduced, thus giving rise to a trend that the opposition labeled a "reverse course," a tendency some critics see as emerging earlier when SCAP began to adopt its anti-Communist stance. The confrontation between the government and its critics, led by the opposition parties, labor unions, students, and intellectuals, became increasingly acrimonious.

The antagonism of labor unions toward the Yoshida government and the strident opposition of cultural and intellectual leaders to the projected law on the prevention of subversive activities touched off, on May 1, 1952, the first of a series of violent confrontations between the demonstrators and police. The other controversial issue was the government's agreement to permit American military bases to remain in Japan. Any move by the United States to increase its military facilities in Japan touched off massive demonstrations under the leadership of left-wing politicians, labor leaders, students, and intellectuals.

At the same time, a series of confrontations between Yoshida and the opposition parties rocked the Diet. The prime minister sought to enact legislation to modify some of the laws that had been passed during the occupation era. In addition to the antisubversive activities bill, Yoshida sought to introduce restrictive legislation in education. He claimed that he was concerned about

the decline in public morals, the need for curbing excesses arising from a misunderstanding of the meaning of freedom, the neglect into which respect for the nation and its traditions had fallen due to mistaken ideas of progress, the biased political outlook prevalent among university students . . . the need for raising the standards of teachers.[1]

Yoshida's primary object, however, was to curb the influence of communism in the public school system. For this purpose he introduced two bills: one bill prohibited teachers of elementary and junior high schools from engaging in political activities, and the other proscribed introduction of educational material on politics into schools by the teachers' union. There was much opposition to the bills, but with some modifications they were passed by the Diet in May 1954.

Another controversial measure that was sponsored by the prime minister was the centralization of the police. Yoshida contended that fragmentation of the police into local units caused inefficiency and prevented the police force from being used effectively on a national scale. Opponents of this plan feared that Yoshida's move was in reality an effort to return to the prewar system to suppress political dissenters. The bill was nevertheless introduced in the Diet, where it faced fiery protest from opposition party members, who ultimately resorted to physical obstruction to prevent its passage. In June 1954, however, the bill was passed; opponents boycotted the session. The measure provided for the abolition of municipal police and their replacement by prefectural police forces that would be coordinated at the top by the National Public Safety Commission and the national police.

Another aspect of the so-called reverse course that disturbed the leftists, the liberals, and the opponents of militarism was the rebirth, under new appellations, of a military force. Shortly after the outbreak of the Korean War, SCAP issued a directive to the Japanese government calling for the creation of a national reserve police force consisting of 75,000 men. The object was to have this force replace American troops being transferred to Korea. Thus, in August 1950, the National Police Reserve was established. The government justified its creation, contending that it was designed to maintain order within Japanese territory so did not violate the no-war clause of the constitution. Soon after the peace treaty went into effect, the National Police Reserve was increased to 110,000 men. The maritime safety force, which functioned as a coast guard, was also strengthened by a loan of eighteen frigates and fifty landing craft from the United States. To be eligible for further military aid under the US mutual security act in 1954, Yoshida submitted two bills to the Diet to transform the police reserve into a defense force. These were the Defense Agency Establishment Bill and the Self-Defense Force Bill.

The Socialist Party vigorously opposed the bills, asserting that they were the first step in the rearmament of Japan. The Progressive Party supported the bills and managed to get them passed, thus establishing the Defense Agency. It was charged with the task of defending the peace and independence of Japan. The

Ground Self-Defense Force, the Maritime Self-Defense Force, and the Air Self-Defense Force were established under the aegis of the Defense Agency. The apparent violation of Article 9 of the constitution, which expressly prohibits the maintenance of military forces, was dismissed by the creators of the defense forces. They contended that the constitution did not rule out self-defense. Yoshida, insisting that there was a difference between rearmament and the creation of the self-defense forces, remarked that "the idea of rearmament has always seemed to be one verging on idiocy."[2]

Yoshida had guided Japan through the difficult occupation years and had set the nation on the path to recovery as a self-sufficient and independent nation, but he began to encounter opposition from within his party. He was a strong leader but had never been very popular. He was tactless, cocksure, and autocratic. His critics charged him with conducting a "one-man" government. In mid-1951, former politicians who had been purged, including Hatoyama, were depurged. Hatoyama and his supporters expected Yoshida to relinquish his post to Hatoyama.

Faced with opposition from the Hatoyama faction, Yoshida sought to increase his support in the Diet and dissolved it in 1952 and 1953 but failed to gain a majority of supporters. In addition to opposition from the Hatoyama faction in his own party, Yoshida faced constant opposition from the left-wing parties. Opposition to Yoshida intensified as Kishi Nobusuke, who had been released from prison after his incarceration as a war criminal for his prewar and wartime activities, aligned himself with Hatoyama and formed a new party, the Japan Democratic Party, to oppose Yoshida. Faced with mounting opposition from members of his own party as well, Yoshida was forced to resign in December 1954. He then severed ties with the Liberal Party and played the role of an elder statesman until his death in 1967.

AFTER YOSHIDA: THE 1955 SYSTEM

Yoshida was succeeded by Hatoyama as prime minister. The Hatoyama government consisted mainly of prewar politicians, in contrast to Yoshida, who had bureaucrats as his key cabinet members. Hatoyama's Democratic Party lacked a majority in the Diet, so he dissolved the Diet, hoping to strengthen his position. In the February 1955 election his party emerged with 185 seats, still lacking a majority. The Liberal Party gained 112 seats.

The business interests wanted the conservative parties to merge to check the left-wing groups. Pressured by business organizations, they merged and formed the Liberal Democratic Party (LDP). This merger set the basis for the one-party control that dominated the Japanese political stage until 1993. This arrangement is referred to as the 1955 System.

Just prior to the conservative party merger, the two Socialist parties also united, functioning as the major opposition party during the thirty-eight years of Liberal Democratic Party dominance. At this point the conservatives held roughly two-thirds of the Diet seats, and the Socialists one-third. This configuration remained more or less intact until 1993.

Unlike Yoshida, Hatoyama favored revising the constitution, rearming, and pursuing an independent course in foreign policy. Thus, he departed from Yoshida's policy of close cooperation with the United States and set out to normalize relations with the Soviet Union and Communist China. He failed in his effort to revise the constitution and to delete Article 9. To normalize relations with the Soviet Union, Hatoyama initiated talks with the Soviet government. When the two sides failed to agree on the disposition of the southern Kurile Islands under Soviet control, Hatoyama decided that to avert a breakdown in the discussions it would be wise not to press the issue. In October 1956 he journeyed to Moscow and personally concluded an agreement to normalize relations between the two countries. Agreements on commerce and fishing were concluded, and trade between the two countries began to increase slowly.

In December 1956, Hatoyama was forced to resign because of poor health. His successor remained in office for only two months and also left office because of illness. The Liberal Democratic Party then turned to Kishi, who upon his release from prison made a comeback in the political world as an active member of the Liberal Party. He left that party to join Hatoyama's Democratic Party, but when the two conservative parties merged to form the Liberal Democratic Party he became its secretary-general.

Kishi remained in office from February 1957 to September 1960. He believed that the constitution needed revision in order to increase somewhat the emperor's authority and to restrict the Diet's power. He also favored increasing the power of the police and removing Communist elements from the schools. Faced with strong opposition from the Socialists, he dissolved the Diet.[3]

In the realm of foreign affairs Kishi sought to adjust Japan's ties with South Korea and the Southeast Asian countries. His policy toward the Communist powers adhered closely to the US anti-Communist line. Although he wanted Japan's foreign policy to be in tune with US policy, he renegotiated the security treaty with the United States to obtain a greater voice for Japan. The revised treaty provided for continued use of Japanese bases by US forces, but the United States agreed to confer with the Japanese government before dispatching US troops in Japan to combat missions abroad and before bringing nuclear weapons into Japan. A ten-year time limit was set for the treaty, after which either side could cancel it on one year's notice.

Kishi and his supporters hailed the new security agreement as an improvement over the former treaty because it was a pact concluded between equals.

However, the Socialists, labor leaders, Communists, students, intellectuals, and pacifists objected vehemently, contending that the provision stipulating cooperation between the two countries to maintain peace in the Far East was an agreement that drew Japan into a military alliance against the Communist nations, particularly Communist China. They were also upset by the increasing authoritarian domestic policies being pursued by Kishi. A massive campaign was launched to prevent ratification of the treaty.

From late 1959, street demonstrations against the security treaty grew larger and more intense. The opponents of the treaty persuaded the labor unions to strike in protest against the pact and millions of workers went on strike in June. Student demonstrators clashed with the police in front of the Diet building, and one student was killed in the turmoil. Kishi, however, remained resolute in his resolve to have the treaty ratified, and he whipped into line the Conservative Party members who were wavering. The left-wing Socialists were bent on blocking ratification by physical obstruction if necessary. On May 19 and May 20, 1960, the Diet was turned into a virtual combat zone as the supporters and the opponents of the treaty ignored parliamentary protocol and resorted to violence to achieve their objectives. Diet members literally wrestled with one another, and thousands of demonstrators snake-danced outside, voicing angry opposition to the pact. The opponents even sought to block the treaty by preventing the speaker from occupying his chair. Finally, Kishi's faction summoned the police, who removed the opponents and placed the speaker in his chair. Then, although the Socialists boycotted the session, the Liberal Democrats approved the treaty.

In conventional political dealings it is understood that a simple majority in the Diet does not entitle the majority party to ignore the wishes and interests of the opposition party members. According to one scholar, "In this system if you win sixty percent of the vote you are allowed to carry out sixty percent of your program, not one hundred percent."[4] Hence, when Kishi rammed the mutual security pact through over adamant opposition from the other parties, he was charged with behaving undemocratically. A tumultuous uproar ensued, and a movement to unseat him gained force.

Political agitators as well as radical leaders of the National Student Federation organized mass demonstrations against Kishi. There was also widespread public support for the movement "to defend democracy." The demonstrations began taking an increasingly anti-American cast, and on June 10, President Dwight D. Eisenhower's press secretary, James Hagerty (1909–1981), who was in Japan to prepare for the president's visit, became the target of a student demonstration. Hagerty was forced to escape the mob by helicopter. A few days later, after violence erupted between demonstrators and the police, Eisenhower's visit was canceled. The protest movement finally subsided when the treaty went into effect on June 19, 1960. The demonstrators may have failed to prevent the ratification of the mutual security treaty, but they did succeed in bringing about the downfall of Kishi, who resigned as soon as the ratifications were exchanged on June 23.

Kishi was the last of the prewar and wartime political leaders to assume power in postwar Japan. Following Kishi's resignation a political struggle for the premiership among rival factions in the Liberal Democratic Party ensued. Factional strife and intraparty power struggles had come to characterize the LDP ever since the Hatoyama faction challenged Yoshida's leadership. In the power struggle to succeed Kishi, the contest was finally won by Ikeda Hayato (1899–1965), who assumed the premiership in July 1960 and remained in office until November 1964. He had climbed the ranks of the bureaucracy as an official in the Ministry of Finance. Ikeda avoided Kishi's confrontational tactic vis-à-vis the Socialist Party and adopted a conciliatory approach. One concrete result of this approach was his success in settling the miners' strike against the Mitsui-owned Miike mine that had been in effect from January 1960. He got both sides together and settled the dispute soon after he took office.

Ikeda did not push for constitutional revision or rearmament, unlike Hatoyama and Kishi. Rather than focusing on foreign policy as Kishi did, he concentrated on economic expansion and made doubling the national income in ten years the primary objective of his government. The economy had expanded throughout the 1950s, but Ikeda planned to accelerate the growth by liberalizing government controls and instituting greater government investments.

The general economic prosperity wrought by the conservative parties in the 1950s and 1960s secured their grip on the reins of power. The Socialists continued to wallow in their doctrinaire quagmire and failed to make any inroads into the electoral base of the conservatives. In the Diet election in the fall of 1960, the Socialist Party expected the bitterness that split the country over the mutual security treaty to work in its favor, but it did not turn out that way. The LDP won a resounding victory.[5]

Ikeda's income-doubling plan induced even bitter opponents of the mutual security treaty, such as socialists and labor union leaders, to play down political issues and focus on economic growth. Ikeda's initiative in launching Japan on the path of high-speed economic growth resulted in Japan's emergence as a world-class economic power. In this sense Ikeda's assumption of the premiership in 1960 can be regarded as a milestone in postwar Japanese history.

Suffering from cancer of the throat, Ikeda was compelled to resign in November 1964. He was succeeded by Satō Eisaku (1901–1975), Kishi's brother.[6] Satō was destined to remain in office for nearly eight years, the longest continuous tenure of any Japanese prime minister. He, like Ikeda, had risen through the bureaucracy, and was elected to the Diet in 1949. Satō followed Ikeda's policy of expanding Japan's economy but also devoted more attention to foreign affairs. He visited the United States to negotiate the return of Okinawa and the Bonin Islands to Japan, and he set out to adjust relations with South Korea.

In the lower-house Diet election of February 1967, a new party, the Kōmeitō (Clean Government Party), sponsored by the Sōka Gakkai (Value Creation Society), a secular organization linked to the Buddhist Nichiren sect, ran candidates for the Diet for the first time and captured twenty-five seats. The LDP and the Socialist Party lost some seats. The latter continued to lose voter support in succeeding elections, undoubtedly because it continued to adhere to a doctrinaire Marxist stance at a time when the Japanese economy was expanding rapidly and the standard of living was rising. The Communists won only five seats.

In the prefectural and municipal elections the Socialists and Communists were fairly successful. In the April 1967 election for the governor of Tokyo, a liberal intellectual won with the support of the Socialists and the Communists. Urban population growth and increased urban problems enabled "reformists" to win elections for mayor posts in Osaka, Kobe, Kita-Kyushu, and Yokohama.

After successfully negotiating the return of Okinawa, Satō dissolved the Diet in early 1970, hoping to increase LDP seats. In the subsequent election the LDP managed to gain a solid majority with the support of a number of independents.

With a solid majority in the Diet, Satō was able to renew the mutual security treaty with virtually no opposition. He, like other conservative leaders, had followed US leadership to deal with Communist China, but he lost face when the United States suddenly changed its position, and in 1971 President Richard Nixon (1913–1994) visited China to establish more friendly relations with the Communist government. Having remained in office for nearly eight years, Satō's popularity was beginning to decline. He took the occasion of the official return of Okinawa to Japan to resign in July 1972. He was awarded the Nobel Peace Prize for "insuring that Japan would not develop nuclear weapons and for signing a treaty restricting the spread of nuclear technology."[7]

Satō was succeeded by Tanaka Kakuei (1918–1993), an anomaly because he did not rise through the elite ranks like previous prime ministers. He was not a graduate of the University of Tokyo, and he did not come from the ranks of the bureaucracy. Although he had received only an elementary school education, he made a fortune in the construction business. An ambitious man of action, he got ahead politically by making use of his financial resources. He was a shrewd populist politician who mastered the art of "money politics," bribery, pork barreling, and patronage.

As soon as Tanaka became prime minister, he flew to Hawaii and met President Nixon. Then he flew to China to normalize relations with that country. As part of his plan to "reconstruct" the nation, Tanaka increased the budget by 25 percent over the previous year to build up the infrastructure. This resulted in increased inflation, particularly in real estate. Then Tanaka was confronted with the oil crisis of 1973, as OPEC reduced oil production.[8]

Japan was heavily dependent on oil import for its burgeoning industries; it imported 99.7 percent of its oil. The oil crisis caused panic buying and inflation. Tanaka sought to deal with the oil crisis by regulating and reducing oil consumption and reducing government expenditures. But inflation could not be reined in, and by 1974 wholesale prices rose 31 percent over the previous year. He came under increasing criticism for his shady financial dealings, and with declining political support he resigned in November 1974.[9]

Although Tanaka gave up the premiership he remained a power in the party as the leader of the biggest faction. In 1976 the Lockheed bribery scandal exposed top government officials, including Tanaka, who had accepted bribes to have an airline purchase Tristar passenger planes. Tanaka was indicted and sentenced to four years in prison, but he continued to exercise power as the "Shadow Shōgun." While he was appealing the decision he suffered a stroke in 1985.

After Tanaka a series of short-term cabinets followed, but the Liberal Democratic Party continued to dominate the political scene into the 1990s. Although its seats in the Diet fluctuated from election to election it usually managed to maintain a majority of the seats in the all-important lower house. In the 1986 election it won 300 seats, but with scandals and other problems, such as the imposition of a 3 percent consumption tax, the party was expected to suffer heavy losses in the election held in February 1990.[10]

Tanaka's successors were saddled with the problems created by the 1973 oil crisis. The skyrocketing oil prices were dealt with by the adoption of stringent energy conservation measures and by a shift in the industrial sector away from high-energy-cost smokestack industries to high-technology industries. As the nation regained its self-confidence, the LDP regained public support. The succeeding prime ministers continued the policy of cooperating with the United States. At the same time relations with Communist China were normalized with the conclusion of a diplomatic treaty in 1978. No significant domestic measures were enacted in this period. When Nakasone Yasuhiro (b. 1918) assumed the premiership in November 1982, he assumed an upbeat stance indicative of the resurgence of Japan as a major industrial power. He was inclined to be nationalistic and indicated a desire to revise the constitution and strengthen the defense forces, but he failed to accomplish his objectives. Among the significant changes he effected was the privatization of many state-run enterprises, in line with his policy of limiting bureaucratic control.

In November 1987, Nakasone resigned. Several Liberal Democratic Party leaders resumed the premiership and continued the policy of building Japan's economic strength and enhancing its place in the international arena. Prime Minister Kaifu Toshiki (b. 1931) was confronted with a request by the United

States to provide aid in the Persian Gulf War in 1991. He provided only non-military aid but was criticized nonetheless for violating the spirit of the constitution. The party was beset by exposures of bribery scandals, and also by the defection of a number of party members who formed splinter parties. Hoping to bolster LDP support, Prime Minister Miyazawa Kiichi (1919–2007) called for an election in July 1993. But the LDP failed to gain a governing majority for the first time in thirty-eight years. The splinter parties and minority parties turned to Hosokawa Morihiro (b. 1938), who had defected from the LDP and formed the New Party. Hosokawa assumed the premiership in 1993, thus terminating LDP dominance of the political scene that commenced in 1955.

END OF LDP DOMINANCE

Decades of LDP ascendancy had been facilitated in part by the economic growth and prosperity that prevailed from the 1960s onward. Moreover, the protective umbrella provided by the United States in the international arena enabled the government to concentrate on economic expansion, which resulted in general public satisfaction. Furthermore, the linkage among the conservatives, the bureaucracy, and business interests enabled the entrenched interests to fend off challenges from the opposition parties and labor unions, and deflect criticism by the intellectuals and cultural figures.

The LDP's dominance of the political world did not translate into a monopoly of power. Intraparty factionalism kept the LDP from becoming a steamrolling power machine. The presence of major factions made compromises and mutual accommodations necessary. The factions are not divided over ideological or policy matters, although differences in emphasis do exist. The groupings are instead based on personal and regional ties and historical antecedents. The ability to provide financial support and patronage and effectiveness in dealing with people are factors that determine the choice of a given faction leader as prime minister.

The need to gain access to an enormous amount of money for political purposes necessitated maintaining close ties with major financial and industrial concerns, which have succeeded the prewar zaibatsu. These business interests supplied the party with funds to conduct election campaigns successfully. There are several organizations made up of big business interests. The most important is the Keidanren (Federation of Economic Organizations), which includes among its membership more than 700 of the largest industrial, commercial, and financial corporations.

Although the established interests play down the role of the Keidanren and big business in politics, the close linkage between big business and the LDP is undeniable. The Keidanren has a voice in selecting prime ministers and favors party leaders who joined the party from the higher echelons of the bureaucracy. From 1955 to 1993, Japan was ruled by the Liberal Democratic Party, big business, and high-level bureaucrats, and these elements still dominate the political scene. In the mid-1980s, one out of four LDP members were former high-ranking bureaucrats. Between 1955 and 1979, 40 percent of the cabinet members came from the same group. In December 1993, seventy-six of the lower house members of the Diet were former bureaucrats. Party leaders and high-level bureaucrats generally work closely together.

Some analysts contend that top bureaucrats actually run the government, not party leaders or cabinet members. The bureaucrats have the expertise and knowledge to make policy, draft legislation, and administer it after it has been enacted by the Diet. As the cabinet members come and go, they have little control over the bureaucrats, who have "lifetime" employment. The primary job of the cabinet minister is to be the spokesman for the ministry he is heading. His major concerns are patronage and politically sensitive programs. The most powerful bureaucrats are those in the Ministry of Economic Trade and Industry (METI) and the Finance Ministry who chart the general course of the nation's economy. But all the bureaucrats still retain the elitist mentality that the Meiji bureaucrats inherited from the samurai of the Tokugawa era. Most of the high-ranking bureaucrats are graduates of the elitist University of Tokyo and have prestige, status, and authority. The link in the triangle is closed when high-level bureaucrats find jobs in big business firms after retirement[11] and engage in "networking" for their new employers.

Another reason the LDP succeeded in maintaining control of the Diet for so long is the support that it receives from the rural areas. In 1988 about 80 percent of the Diet members came from agricultural constituencies with close ties to the LDP. Although the population per district in the rural communities is much smaller than in the urban districts, the number of seats per district has been the same. Thus, the political influence of the rural districts has greater impact than their population size would warrant. Accordingly, in order to win and retain the support of the rural districts, the LDP has accommodated farmers with price supports on rice and restrictions on imports of farm products. The LDP has also had the support of white-collar workers, junior executives, and small shopkeepers whose interests are protected by government curbs on supermarket chains.

The opposition parties, among which the Japan Socialist Party (renamed the Social Democratic Party) had been the largest, have failed to make significant inroads into the LDP's political turf. The Socialist Party's popular vote has hovered around the 20 percent mark ever since the 1960s. In 1986 the Socialist Party chose a woman, Doi Takako (b. 1928), to head it. In the election for the upper house of the Diet in 1989 the Socialist Party succeeded in doubling its seats in that house, and received 35.1 percent of the votes cast compared to 27.1 received by the LDP. This victory heightened Doi's prestige. However, in the 1990 election for the more important lower house, although the number of Socialist seats rose from 83 to 136, it was insufficient to shake the LDP's control. In this instance it received 24.4 percent of the votes cast compared with 46.1 percent cast for LDP candidates. Then in the local elections in the spring of 1991, the Socialists did poorly despite popular discontent about the 3 percent consumption tax the LDP had instituted. The poor showing of the Socialists was ascribed in part to its staunch pacifist stand during the Persian Gulf War. Taking responsibility for the failure in this election, Doi resigned as chair of the party in June 1991. The party failed to benefit from the 1993 disarray of the LDP and gained only seventy seats as the voters turned to the newly formed "reform" parties.

The other minor parties, the Kōmeitō, the Democratic Socialist Party (a group that split from the Socialist Party), and the Communist Party, have not succeeded in gaining more than 10 percent of the popular vote in successive elections. The Communists managed to gain only a few seats in the Diet in the 1960s. It rose into the double digits in the 1970s and gained 38 seats in 1972, but it dropped to 16 seats in the 1990 election. It regained some popular support and in the 1996 election captured 26 seats in the lower house. In the 1998 upper house election it won 23 of the 252 seats. The Democratic Socialist Party gained only 14 seats in the 1996 lower house election. The Kōmeitō won 25 seats in its first campaign in 1967 and it has managed to gain 50 seats or so in each succeeding elections.

The lengthy entrenchment of the LDP in the seat of power and its mode of operation have caused some observers to conclude that

> The Japanese government is one of the most corrupt in the world. Not so much in the sense of graft and bribery—although there is enough of that too—corrupt in the sense that it is one-sided, biased, unfair, detrimental to the common good. Government works in the interest of big business and the large agricultural organizations, the latter largely to get the votes. The ruling alliance of the bureaucrats, government and big business is what has shaped present-day Japan.[12]

Perhaps this judgment is not far off the mark when we consider major scandals like the Recruit affair of 1989 in which a major real estate firm gave top LDP leaders a chance to purchase its stocks at lower prices before listing them on the stock exchange. The Recruit stock price shot up once Recruit went public, and the politicians were able to accrue huge profits. This affair forced

Prime Minister Takeshita Noboru (1924–2000) to resign and compelled LDP leaders to retreat into the background temporarily. But Nakasone, Takeshita, and others continued to exercise power from behind the scenes, waiting to reemerge on center stage.

The practice of arriving at a consensus among the various factions and interest groups involved before any decision is made makes quick, decisive measures difficult to adopt by the prime minister. Thus, when a crisis like the Gulf War occurs the Japanese government appears to drag its feet. Nakasone remarked regarding this situation, "We need a prime minister who has real power, who is capable of ruling the majority party, who can control the Diet, who can coordinate with the opposition parties."[13]

Following the LDP's loss of political ascendancy and the formation of the Hosokawa government there was hope that a new political order would prevail. However, the Hosokawa regime failed to remain in office very long. But he did accomplish a measure of success in revising the electoral districts to redress the imbalance in electoral representation between the sparsely populated rural districts and the heavily populated urban areas.[14] The effort to redress this imbalance failed to pass the upper house, but a compromise bill provided for the establishment of electoral districts consisting of single-seat districts along with districts with proportional representation along party lines. Hosokawa was forced to resign when financial scandals from his earlier years were exposed.

Hosokawa was succeeded by a couple of coalition cabinets, including one in which the Socialist Party and the LDP coalesced to have a Socialist prime minister, Murayama Tomiichi (b. 1924), for the first time since 1948. Then in January 1996, the LDP managed to regain the premiership under Hashimoto Ryūtarō (1937–2006). He was followed by a succession of nearly faceless faction leaders who seemed almost interchangeable. Indeed, when questioned, most Japanese could not recall the names of most of them, referring to them as "the one with the polka-dot bow ties" or "the one with the sour face." Only when the next scandal ousted one for another did there seem to be any public interest in any of them.

FOREIGN RELATIONS

During the occupation years Japan, of course, could not follow an independent course in formulating its foreign policy. Japan's external relations were determined by SCAP. With the signing of the peace treaty in 1951 and the withdrawal of occupation authorities in 1952 Japan was free to pursue its own course. However, the Japanese government adhered to the policy of following US leadership, in particular relative to Communist powers during the Cold

MODERN JAPAN

War years. US policy toward Japan shifted from focusing on demilitarization to rebuilding it as a link in the anti-Communist chain along the Eastern Pacific rim. The United States began to build up its military bases in Okinawa as its East Asian bastion after China fell to the Communists.

Although the Japanese government under the conservative party leaders cooperated with the US anti-Communist policy, Japanese liberal and leftist opposition began increasingly to raise their voice against US military presence in Japan and Okinawa as well as US nuclear testing. Among the issues that they objected to was the mutual security treaty the United States and Japan signed in 1951. The treaty made Japan part of the Pacific military network, but it also served as a check on Japan so that it would not revert to militarism and pose a threat to other Asian nations.

The treaty clearly linked Japan to the United States in the Cold War. When the content of the treaty was made public, the People's Republic of China and the Soviet Union denounced it. The latter made it known that as long as foreign troops remained in Japan it would not return the four Kurile Islands to Japan. The Cold War tension had intensified at this time because the US U-2 spy plane flying over Russia was shot down in May 1960, and Khrushchev asserted that the Soviet Union would bomb the spy plane bases. This concerned the opponents of the pact because U-2 spy planes were flying out of the Atsugi air base in Japan.

After the mutual security treaty controversy subsided, US-Japanese relations went back on track. Ikeda, who had succeeded Kishi, concentrated on economic developments and did not take an active position on foreign affairs. Ikeda's successor, Satō, was more active in this area. Upon assuming office he made the termination of US control over Okinawa and its reversion to Japan one of his chief objectives. Technically the United States was exercising administrative authority over Okinawa for the United Nations, which had placed it and the Bonin Islands under US trusteeship.[15]

When Satō traveled to the United States in 1965 and conferred with President Lyndon Johnson (1908–1973), he raised the issue of Okinawa. Johnson agreed to give Japan a greater voice in Okinawa affairs but made no specific commitment about returning Okinawa to Japan. When Satō visited the United States again in 1967, an agreement was reached to finalize in two or three years the date for the return of Okinawa to Japan. In 1969, Satō visited President Nixon. The two leaders agreed on 1972 as the date for Okinawa's reversion to Japan, but the agreement entailed permitting American bases to be retained in Okinawa.

Another matter that strained US relations with Japan, at least with radical student groups and left-wing parties, was the Vietnam War. The United States used its bases in Japan for its military operations in Vietnam. Okinawa in particular served as an important military base for the United States. Military procurements were made in Japan for the Vietnam War, and Japan also served as a rest and recreation center for US troops serving in Vietnam. Opponents of the mutual security treaty and the presence of US bases as well as critics of the government for cooperating with the United States in this venture organized and staged anti–Vietnam War rallies and demonstrations. As the Cold War tension subsided, controversies regarding political issues abated.

The major focus of United States–Japan relations from the 1970s on was trade between the two nations. The United States has remained Japan's biggest trading partner since the end of the war.[16] The disparity in export and import percentiles was reflected in the monetary balance in favor of Japan, which grew increasingly larger.[17]

The United States demanded that Japan redress the trade imbalance by removing stringent import restrictions and opening up its market. Moreover, the United States (and other nations) pressured Japan to strengthen the yen in the international currency exchange market by letting the yen go on a floating exchange rate instead of fixing the yen at 360 yen to a dollar. It was assumed that a stronger yen would result in redressing the trade imbalance.[18]

Automobile exports to the United States increased at a phenomenal pace, partly because the oil crisis of 1973 caused Americans to purchase smaller cars, which Japan was ready to supply in place of the gas guzzlers that Detroit continued to produce. As Japanese cars began to flood the US market, a move to limit Japanese car imports rose. To prevent this from occurring, in 1981 the Japanese government imposed a voluntary quota of 1.85 million units on automobile shipments to the United States.[19] Nonetheless Japan's automobile manufacturers' share of the American car market continued to increase because Japanese automakers began to establish factories in the United States to get around the possibility of US import restrictions.[20]

The number of Japanese exports began to slow down with the economic recession that began in Japan in the late 1980s. As the yen got stronger relative to the dollar, automobile exports, especially, began to decline.[21]

Before the 1970s, other Japanese export goods were a source of friction between the two countries. Initially, textiles were the issue. In 1971 Japan agreed to restrict its textile exports to the United States. Then steel and chemical products became important export items for Japan. These were followed by consumer electronics, automobiles, metal working machines, precision machines, and computer chips as major export items.[22]

To redress the imbalance the United States has requested that Japan not only reduce protective tariffs but also revise the web of red tape that was designed to keep out foreign goods. For example, on car imports, rather than granting a blanket approval of a given make and year of automobiles, car-by-car inspection has been imposed. In 1994 only Jeep Cherokee received a blanket certification.

US businesspeople complain that standards are manipulated against foreign products, that foreign investments are discouraged, and the distribution network is virtually a closed system. Business dealings are often conducted through an old-boy network of personal friendships and traditional ties that constitute a "multilayered lattice." An Australian who has lived in Japan for a number of years explains how the system functions in lower-level business transactions:

> In the village outside Tokyo in which I live there are four gas stations, offering gasoline at four different prices. The one I patronize charges three yen a liter more than the one that happens to be closest to my house. Why don't I switch? Because the proprietor is a friend of mine (and how could he not be since we have done business for years?), but even if he wasn't, he would still be entitled by social convention to a cash payment in compensation for the loss of my business from my new supplier, which would have to be long and carefully negotiated between the two men. . . . While theoretically I am free to switch, village opinion is on the side of my staying where I am.[23]

Just as the "closed system" prevails within the country, Japan essentially maintains closure toward the external world, that is, the Japanese government with the support of business interests and politicians have maintained a protectionist policy.

The critics of the Japanese distribution system contend that the manufacturers and wholesale dealers have a stranglehold on the market, stifle competition, and keep foreign competitors out. Under the existing system of marketing, consumer prices for the Japanese buyer remain high.[24] Among the US requests is the elimination of the Big Store Law, which favors small-scale retailers over chain stores and supermarkets. But its elimination will bring about the demise of the millions of "mom and pop" stores and their replacement by huge chains and supermarkets much like in the United States, where since the 1950s the corner grocery store has mostly disappeared.

There was much heated discussion about Japanese restriction against the imports of farm products like beef, citrus fruits, and rice. In 1991 the ban on importation of beef and citrus fruits was finally lifted, though high tariffs remained. For example, the tariff on beef remained at 70 percent. Restrictions on rice in part continued because of the stubborn opposition of the farm bloc. The electoral system is tilted heavily in favor of the rural districts, so the politicians tend to hesitate going against the farmers' interests. Thus the consumers are compelled to pay exorbitant prices for rice. In 1992 an Osaka sushi vendor's plan to make sushi in California and ship it to Japan was blocked until the Finance Ministry relented. Only in 1993, when a poor harvest resulted in rice shortage, did the government allow some American rice to enter the Japanese market. But the imported rice was purchased and distributed by the Food Agency of the Agriculture Ministry. It sold imported rice at the same price as domestic rice, which costs six times more than rice grown by other nations. Of course, it is not unusual to have special-interest groups protect their turf. On a smaller scale the US peanut growers' success in restricting peanut imports is much like the story of the Japanese rice farmers. Despite the dispute over Japanese restrictions on imports of certain farm products, Japan has been the largest importer of American farm products.[25]

The removal of all restrictions on imports from the United States is not expected to redress the trade imbalance, but it would at least remove the perception that Japan does not play fairly. There is no question that the United States had provided a wide-open market for Japan and enabled the Japanese economy to expand phenomenally since the 1960s.

The difficulty of penetrating the Japanese market has not been entirely Japan's fault. US auto manufacturers had complained for years about the barriers imposed on US automakers' entry into the Japanese market. Until the 1990s they consistently sought to market automobiles with left-hand drive. The Japanese drive on the left side of the road, so right-hand drive is essential there. Only in 1993 did one automaker, Chrysler, introduce a right-hand-drive Jeep Cherokee. Then other manufacturers began to follow suit.

However, US-Japanese economic relationship is not as one-sided as it is often perceived. Aside from imports and exports, sales of US companies operating in Japan came to $80 billion a year in goods and services, compared with $14 billion in sales by Japanese companies in the United States in 1990. Japanese investments in highly visible landmarks such as Rockefeller Center in New York in the boom years of the 1970s and 1980s heightened American concern that the United States was being bought up by Japan, Inc., even though in reality Japanese investments were below those by Great Britain and Canada.[26]

Although trade has been the major issue in US-Japanese relations, military cooperation has also been a matter of ongoing concern, and the matter was aggravated further during the 1991 Persian Gulf crisis. The United States wanted Japan to play a more active role in the war against Iraq, but there was strong opposition in Japan to provide direct military assistance because of the antiwar clause in the constitution. Even the Japanese government's decision to send minesweepers to the Persian Gulf was met with opposition, and many Asian nations that had been victims of Japanese aggression in the 1930s and 1940s indicated their concern about Japanese military participation in the Gulf War.

Before the Gulf War US leaders had called on Japan to increase its defense budget to lighten the US burden to provide a military umbrella for Japan. In 1976 the Japanese government imposed a ceiling of 1 percent of the GNP on defense expenditures.[27]

The difficulty in resolving the existing issues, especially in the area of trade and economic reciprocity, has resulted in what the Japanese media describes as "Japan bashing," that is, increasingly shrill criticism of Japan. The report written for the Central Intelligence Agency by participants in a conference at the Rochester Institute of Technology in 1991 described Japan as being nondemocratic and racist, and an "immoral, manipulative and controlling culture."[28]

In US-Japanese negotiations over trade and defense matters, differences in negotiating style have often produced misunderstandings. The Japanese shy away from blunt, explicit statements, whereas Americans prefer to be candid and outspoken.[29] Misunderstandings thus occur that lead US officials or businesspeople to often conclude that the Japanese are being two-faced, opportunistic, or lacking in principle. In this respect, writer Ishihara Shintarō's insistence in his book, *The Japan That Can Say No,* that Japan must learn to say "no" may be a positive suggestion because it will avoid misunderstanding or charges that Japanese are two-faced (for further discussion of Ishihara's book, see chapter 18).[30] In 1970, when President Nixon and Prime Minister Satō discussed the US request to restrict Japanese textile exports to the United States, Nixon thought that Satō had agreed to his request, whereas Satō meant that he would do his best. When Satō did not implement what Nixon thought was an agreement, Nixon felt that he had been double-crossed. In short, for the US official or businessperson substance is important, whereas for the Japanese form or style tends to be of greater significance. James D. Hodgson (b. 1915), the former US ambassador to Japan, concluded that "if you try to accommodate the Japanese in matters of style, they will usually try to accommodate you in matters of substance."[31]

Japan's relations with the Soviet Union had been somewhat strained since the end of the war. With the onset of the Cold War the Soviet Union was virtually frozen out of formulating occupation policies in Japan. With the Communist victory in China in 1949 and the outbreak of the Korean War, the United States concluded a peace treaty with Japan and pursued a policy of building Japan into an important component in the chain of defense against Communist powers in the Pacific.

The Soviet Union refused to sign the peace treaty with Japan, and a number of issues that concerned Japan remained unresolved. As agreed upon at Yalta, the peace treaty provided for the transference of South Sakhalin and the Kuriles to the Soviet Union. Japan held that the four islands of Etorofu, Kunashiri, Shikotan, and Habomai were not part of the Kurile Islands and were historically Japan's Northern Territories. This issue continued to serve as a stumbling block in the effort to normalize relations between the two countries.

Prime Minister Yoshida followed a policy of adhering to the US Cold War line, but, as noted earlier, when Hatoyama became prime minister in late 1954 he set out to normalize relations with the Soviet Union. He failed to reach an agreement on the four Kurile Islands, but the Soviet Union agreed to return the two southernmost islands, Habomai and Shikotan, after a peace treaty between the two nations has been concluded. The fate of the other two islands was to be left to further negotiations. Relations between the countries were resumed, and the Soviet Union consented to the admission of Japan to the United Nations. President Mikhail Gorbachev visited Japan in 1991, hoping to get financial assistance, but the negotiations stalled again over the island question. As a result, a formal peace treaty remained unsigned. Trade between the two countries has been limited.[32]

In its relations with the People's Republic of China, Japan followed US leadership even after Japan regained its sovereignty with the peace treaty in 1951. Neither Chinese Nationalist nor Communist governments were signatories of the peace treaty, but in April 1952 Prime Minister Yoshida signed a peace treaty with the Nationalist government in Taiwan. Both the People's Republic of China and Japan were interested in resuming economic relations, and during 1954–1956 cultural and economic exchange between the two countries began to develop. In late 1962 a commercial agreement was concluded by the two countries. As a result, trade between the two countries began to increase. But political ties were not resumed because Japan was following the US policy of not establishing political relations with the People's Republic. In 1970 and 1971, Japan voted with the United States in the UN to oppose the expulsion of Taiwan and seating delegates of the People's Republic.

As a result, the Japanese leaders were completely caught off guard in the summer of 1971 when President Nixon suddenly announced his plan to visit China and establish US-Chinese relations. Japan followed suit, and in 1972 Prime Minister Tanaka visited China and concluded an agreement with China to normalize relations. China relinquished its reparation claims, and Tanaka expressed regret for the suffering Japan inflicted on the Chinese people. No explicit statement about Japan's relation with Taiwan was mentioned in the agreement, though China seemed to have tacitly accepted Japan's continued relationship with Taiwan. When the agreement to normalize relations between Japan and China was concluded the Taiwan government announced its decision to break off relations with Japan. But economic relations were sustained by the establishment of nongovernment organizations for cultural and economic relationships, and an agreement for nongovernment ties was signed in January 1973.

In 1978 a formal treaty of peace and friendship was signed between the People's Republic and Japan. Since then political relations between the two countries have remained harmonious. In 1987 the Chinese leader Deng Xiaoping visited Japan, and in 1992 Emperor Akihito visited China. China, however, was not fully satisfied with Japan's acknowledgment of the aggression and atrocities committed by Japan in the 1930s and 1940s. For example, when the Education Ministry required a textbook publisher to change the word "aggression" into China and Korea to "advance," the governments of China and South Korea protested vehemently. Also, each time a Japanese prime minister (starting with Nakasone) visited the Yasukuni Shrine, wherein the spirits of Japan's war dead are enshrined, China and the Koreas objected strenuously.

The commercial relationship between the two countries continued to expand after Tanaka's visit to China.[33] Japanese business operations in China continued to increase. For example, as soon as the peace treaty was signed a Japanese firm got an approval to build a steel mill in Shanghai, and a joint venture to drill for oil off the China coast was started. By the mid-1980s more than 300 Japanese companies, such as Sony and Mitsubishi, had offices in Beijing.

Although Japan's formal diplomatic relations with Taiwan were discontinued with the resumption of Japan's relations with the People's Republic of China, cultural and commercial relations continued.[34]

Relations with the Republic of Korea have been delicate because of the bitter memories harbored by the Koreans over the Japanese occupation of their country between 1910 and 1945. The continued discrimination against Korean residents in Japan, moreover, does not help to improve relations between the two nations. Also, recent revelations about the conscription and enslavement of thousands of young Korean women during the war to force them to serve as "comfort women" (euphemism for military sexual slaves) for the Japanese armed forces, and the procrastination of the Japanese authorities to acknowledge such practices and pay indemnities, have continued to sustain the Korean distrust of Japan.

At the end of the war there were over a million Japanese military personnel and civilians in Korea. Of these, the 170,000 troops and 500,000 civilians in South Korea were repatriated to Japan by early 1946. In the north, of 74,000 military personnel, 56,000 were sent by the Soviet authorities to work as slave laborers in Siberia. The rest of the military personnel and 300,000 civilians were sent back to Japan in 1947. About 1,000 technicians were detained in North Korea.

The division of Korea into north and south resulted in Japan having to deal with two Korean governments. The outbreak of the Korean War in 1950 forced Japan to align with the United States in its relationship with the South and North Korean governments. To normalize relationships, bilateral negotiations were conducted between South Korea and Japan in 1952. The negotiations failed to resolve problems stemming from the Japanese colonization of Korea. Japan refused to accede to Korean demands that Japan apologize for its annexation of Korea and pay reparations. Subsequent negotiations failed to resolve issues of reparations and dispute over the coastal boundaries that South Korea had established.

Finally, in 1965, an agreement was arrived at and a treaty was concluded. Instead of paying reparations Japan persuaded the Korean government to accept grants and loans. In return, the Korean government agreed to provide financial compensation to individual Koreans who lodged claims against Japan. Japan agreed to recognize the South Korean government as the only legitimate government of Korea but avoided acknowledging its sovereignty over all of Korea and recognized it only south of the 38th parallel.

Economic relations between Japan and South Korea steadily grew even before the treaty was concluded. By 1995 Japan's exports to South Korea amounted to 7.1 percent of its total exports, and imports came to 5.1 percent of its total imports. The trade surplus with South Korea from 1965 to 1991 amounted to $66.2 billion, causing South Korea to complain like other nations about Japanese market barriers.

Efforts to improve political relations between the two countries continued. When President Roh Tae Woo of South Korea (b. 1932) visited Japan in 1990, the emperor of Japan made a public apology for Japan's past actions against that country. Also, during his visit to Korea, Prime Minister Kaifu apologized for Japan's colonial practices. Japan has not established official relations with the Democratic People's Republic of Korea (North Korea). Informal discussions were conducted, but little progress resulted because of North Korea's demand for war reparations and damages caused after the end of the war by the political division of Korea into north and south.

Early in the twenty-first century a series of problems with North Korea cropped up. A series of famines ravaged North Korea, and that regime tried to use its development of nuclear weapons in order to extort foreign aid from Japan, South Korea, and even the United States. Early in 2005 North Korea "tested" two missiles by firing them into the Japan Sea, understandably causing tremendous consternation in Japan. Moreover, North Korea finally divulged that it had kidnapped a number of Japanese civilians in the 1950s and 1960s in order to help train North Korean spies. The repatriation of those captives to Japan continues to cloud relations between the two countries.[35]

Because of Japan's wartime activities in the Southeast Asian countries, bitterness toward Japan persisted in this region. Japan had forced the people of the occupied countries to labor for its military projects, causing heavy losses of life. The growing economic penetration of Japanese business interests into Southeast Asia in the postwar years was regarded by some people in the region as an economic version of the wartime Japanese political hegemony that was established in the name of the East Asian Co-prosperity Sphere.

After the peace treaty was signed Japanese authorities sought to establish close ties with the newly independent Southeast Asian nations. In 1957, Prime Minister Kishi traveled to Southeast Asia and sought to lay the base for economic cooperation. In the 1960s the Japanese public's attention in Southeast Asia was focused on the Vietnam War, and some public opposition to US war efforts erupted. Following the end of the Vietnam War, Japanese efforts to develop close economic links with the region gained momentum. A number of prime ministers traveled to Southeast Asian nations to pledge friendship and cooperation and to express regrets for Japan's actions during the Pacific war.

To foster commercial relations Japan made extensive capital investments. Exports to this region steadily increased.[36] The percentage of imports from these countries totaled 13.3 percent of its total imports. Traditionally, Japan has relied heavily on crude oil imports from Southeast Asia, but with heavier imports from the Middle East, imports from Southeast Asia dropped somewhat.[37]

Japanese investments in these countries increased steadily.[38] In 1990 about 15 percent of Thai workers in manufacturing plants were employed by Japanese firms. Japanese exports of automobiles and electronic products steadily increased until the general economic recession that hit Southeast Asia and Japan in the late 1990s.

Japanese who conduct business in these countries have often been criticized for their condescending attitude toward the local populace. They have also been criticized for being cliquish, aloof, arrogant, and indifferent to local problems. There have been complaints about "sex tours" (that is, trips to visit Southeast Asian brothels), recruiting of women to serve as "entertainers," and other unsavory activities. Japanese wartime imperialism, it has been charged, has been replaced by economic imperialism, and Japan's indifference to the plight of its fellow Asians was reflected in its virtual lockout of Vietnamese refugees, the so-called boat people. Asians who were victims of Japanese imperialism in the 1930s and 1940s contend that Japan has never acknowledged its past misdeeds, and they remain extremely sensitive to any possibility that Japan might reemerge as a military power.

A Catholic priest who has lived in Japan since 1929 observed, "One thing that bothers me is that I do not think they [the Japanese] show much concern for the welfare of others in their international economic relations. They do not seem to show much responsibility for other people, unless it will bring them a profit."[39]

That Japanese businesspeople occasionally treat persons from economically less-developed societies less fairly than they do Americans and Europeans was demonstrated, perhaps, by the complaints of a Mexican textile manufacturer who had ordered advanced textile machines from a major Japanese trading company but instead was sent used, defective machines that brought about the ruination of his business. His repeated complaints got him nowhere, and he finally took the company to court in 1985.[40] A Philippine writer who spent some time doing research in Japan concluded, "The Japanese will take advantage of those who are weak. It is therefore imperative for us to build strong societies so that we will not be sucked away. We must also continually remind the Japanese of what they did during the war and should not be deluded about their weeping over Hiroshima." He observed that Emperor Hirohito traveled to the United States and Europe "apologizing" for what the Japanese army did in World War II but did not make a similar trip to Southeast Asia.[41]

Japanese leaders have been trying to heed these criticisms, and they have increased Japan's contribution to international aid programs.[42] During the 1980s, when a labor shortage developed in Japan, workers from other Asian nations were allowed to enter Japan and meet the labor need. At the same time the number of illegal immigrants began to increase. The treatment accorded the immigrants was less than fair, and they came to suffer the same kind of indignities that Asian residents in Japan have been subjected to.

Japan's relations with Australia have been cordial, and trade has benefited both countries. In 1976 the two countries signed a treaty of friendship and cooperation. Economic ties between them increased steadily.[43] A large portion of goods imported from Australia consisted of foodstuffs, minerals, and coal. Automobiles and machinery were the major Japanese exports to Australia. Between 1951 and 1990, Japan invested $16 billion in Australia, about 5 percent of its world investments. Interest in the Japanese language and Japanese studies has increased enormously in Australia because of close economic and cultural ties.

The other area of major concern for Japan has been the Middle East Arab states because of its heavy dependence on oil from that region.[44] Thus, Japan's interest in the area's political developments remains high, and it seeks to avoid getting involved in the political conflicts in that region. In the 1973 oil crisis that resulted from the Arab-Israeli conflict Japan called for Israel's withdrawal from occupied territories to get designated as a friendly nation by the Arab nations. It was also reluctant to play an active role in the Persian Gulf War of 1991.

Europe has remained a center of attraction for Japanese tourists as well as for intellectuals who regard it as the quintessence of Western culture, but the trade imbalance has also created acrimonious charges by many European nations. French and general European criticism of Japanese trade practices stems from the imbalance of trade between Japan and the European Economic Community (EEC).[45] In 1991 the prime minister of France, Edith Cresson (b. 1934), remarked that "Japanese are short yellow people who stay up all night thinking of ways to screw the Americans and the Europeans" and that Japan has "an absolute determination to conquer the world."[46] This remark was especially galling to Japanese Francophiles, who want so much to be loved by the cultured French and are so eager to adopt French culture, fashions, and cuisine.

The French market has not been as open to Japanese products as other European markets have been: restrictions on Japanese goods by the French have been more stringent than those imposed by other European nations. As a result the export of Japanese goods to France in 1995 was only 1.4 percent of Japan's total export, and the import was 2.0 percent.[47] Political relations between Japan and Germany have been good, with few acrimonious comments emanating from either side. Whatever strains that exist between the two countries result from the closed nature of the Japanese market. Relations with the United Kingdom have been fairly smooth also, in spite of vestiges of bitterness about World War II, manifested during Emperor Hirohito's visit to England and Europe in 1971 and during the anniversary of Pearl Harbor.

ECONOMIC DEVELOPMENTS

The most urgent task that faced the Japanese leaders at the end of the war was the revival of the economy so that inflation, unemployment, and shortages in all areas could be dealt with. Industrial production was at a virtual standstill at the end of the war, and recovery was slow.[48]

The economy was given a boost by the United States as it adopted the policy of rebuilding the Japanese economy with the outbreak of the Cold War.[49]

After SCAP's control over Japan ended in 1952, the Japanese government began to relax the antimonopoly measures introduced during the occupation. As Korean War procurements began to decrease, business interests began to advocate easing the antimonopoly laws, and in 1953, the laws were made more flexible. Thus, the former financial and industrial conglomerates, the zaibatsu, began to reemerge. These conglomerates are known as *keiretsu* (enterprise groups). Keiretsu consists of a group of firms in different industries that maintain close relationships through cross shareholding, interlocking directorates, intragroup financial commitments, customer-supplier agreements, and personal and historical ties. There are two types of keiretsu: horizontal and vertical. The former, composed of prewar zaibatsu complexes like Mitsubishi, Mitsui, and Sumitomo, has at its core a large bank or trading company, and major industrial firms from all key industries are affiliated with it. The vertical keiretsu has a giant producer at the top, like Toyota, Honda, Nissan, Sony, or Matsushita, and a complex of satellite firms that supply it with the necessary parts for its products. Under this arrangement, Toyota, for instance, can assemble its cars by using parts supplied almost entirely by its subsidiaries. So even though major Japanese automobile manufacturers have established plants in the United States, most of their parts are provided by its subsidiaries in Japan.

The laissez-faire policies initiated by the SCAP began to be modified, and the Ministry of Economic Trade and Industry (METI) began to play a dominant role in guiding the nation's economic growth. What emerged was a "managed economy." The government began to provide subsidies and tax breaks to companies to foster economic growth. Laws were passed to facilitate the growth of machine and electrical machinery industries. It expedited the importation of technology and implemented policies to increase foreign trade.

In the prewar years the textile industry constituted the most important sector of Japan's exports. It was among the first sector of the economy to revive, and by 1950 it came to constitute 48.2 percent of Japan's export value. With the growth of other sectors of industry and the drop in the textile market as developing countries began to develop their own textile industries, it began to decline as Japan's export item.[50]

There was a slight recession after the end of the Korean War because of the reduction in US procurements. But by 1955, food shortage was no longer a concern.[51] Increasingly, durable consumer goods came to be purchased, and electric washing machines, refrigerators, and televisions, referred to as "the three sacred jewels" (modeled after the three sacred jewels of the imperial dynasty: bronze mirror, sword, and curved-bead necklace), came into greater use. Consumer spending increased because of the greater purchasing power gained by farmers, who became more prosperous thanks to the land reform program. Factory workers' wages also increased to enable them to purchase more goods. Consumption expenditures per family grew by 36 percent between 1955 and 1960. During the latter half of the 1950s, industrial production grew by 9.3 percent a year. So the period from 1955 to 1961 is seen as the takeoff point in postwar Japanese economic growth.

During this period business companies in key industries made large capital investments, modernizing plants and equipment. Demilitarization resulted in minimal defense spending, which enabled the government to invest money in public works and social welfare programs. Exports began to increase.[52] Until 1965 the balance of trade remained unfavorable, but with increased production and with the opening of the US market and markets of other countries a significant increase in exports began to transpire in the 1960s.

Truly spectacular growth began in the 1960s under the leadership of Prime Minster Ikeda, who set out to implement his income doubling plan. The groundwork for economic growth had been laid since the early 1950s but Ikeda pursued a policy of lowering interest rates and taxes to stimulate economic activities in the private sector, and he adopted an aggressive policy of capital investments in the infrastructure. Government expenditures on the infrastructure were increased by 40 percent in 1960 over the previous year and were increased 30 percent each year after that during the 1960s. Regional governments also invested in public work projects, and local governments were granted subsidies to develop local projects. Ikeda also got Japan to play a more active role in international trade associations. The yen became a currency in the international currency exchange system. Access to the Japanese market by foreign producers was hindered, however, by complex rules and minute, stringent, item-by-item inspection of imported goods.

All these measures plus the favorable international market enabled Japan to expand its economy at a high speed. In 1964, the last year of the Ikeda government, the GNP (gross national product—that is, the total output of goods and services) grew at the rate of 13.9 percent. Exports continued to rise in the 1960s. A positive balance of trade was achieved in 1965, and, except for a couple of years, the trade surplus began to increase steadily.[53]

By 1965 manufacturing as well as the economy as a whole had risen to nearly four times the level reached before the war, whereas the population had only grown 42 percent, from 69 million to 98 million. The average family in 1965 consumed 75 percent more goods and services than did its counterpart in the mid-1930s.[54] Especially significant growth occurred in the heavy industrial and petrochemical sectors. Advances in the petrochemical industry led to the production of new products such as synthetic rubber, plastic, and synthetic fiber. And the production of electric home appliances, optical instruments, and precision and electronic machinery and instruments became a significant component of the Japanese industry. Cameras, watches, and television sets soon emerged as major export commodities. These products and heavy industrial goods came to replace textiles as major export items in the 1960s. A highly significant development in this period of high-speed economic growth was the increase in auto production.

The emphasis on industrial expansion resulted in a shift in the working population from the primary sector (agriculture, forestry, fisheries) to the secondary (mining, construction, and manufacturing) and tertiary (commercial, financial, government, service) sectors.[55]

The Japanese economy continued to grow at a phenomenal rate in the 1970s, most notably in industrial manufacturing and high technology. Then in October 1973 the Middle East war broke out and OPEC began to raise the price of oil drastically.[56] Faced with this crisis, industrial leaders and government officials in METI formulated plans to reduce energy use in industrial production and concentrated on high-technology industries.

The policy of cutting back the use of oil and "rationalizing" (which meant cutting costs down by reducing the number of workers) business practices led to readjustments that enabled Japan to cope with the oil crisis. Traditional oil-guzzling smokestack industries were cut back. After the oil crisis a shift from heavy industries to the production of high-tech goods like precision machineries and electronic products came about. Production of steel and pig iron dropped substantially from this period into the 1980s.[57] Oil for transportation and heating was reduced as well and allocated to industries that produce export goods. Part of this policy to reduce heavy dependence on oil entailed greater reliance on nuclear energy. After 1983, over 25 percent of Japan's electricity was generated by nuclear plants. The government's plan to continue building additional nuclear plants, however, encountered opposition from people who feared nuclear accidents.

As a result of these measures industrial and high-technology production began to rise and continued to expand. By 1983 industrial production had increased 40 percent over 1974, and it continued to increase throughout the 1980s. The oil crisis had a positive effect on Japanese auto production. Japanese cars were smaller in size compared to US cars and were much more fuel efficient; thus huge gas-guzzling cars were dropped in favor of smaller cars. As a result Japan was able to make significant inroads in the US car market.[58]

As noted earlier, despite the voluntary quota agreed upon, Japanese manufacturers' share of the US auto market continued to increase because they began to establish auto manufacturing plants in the United States. In 1990 slightly more than half of the Japanese cars sold in the United States were produced there. Other manufacturers beside automobile makers began establishing plants in the United States.[59]

It was not only the automobile industry that made Japan a dominant manufacturing nation in the 1980s. The production of crude steel, which was at 4.8 million metric tons in 1950, reached a high of 119.322 tons in 1973. Then it began to level off following the oil crisis of the 1970s to around 100 million tons.[60] Production of electric home appliances, like washing machines, refrigerators, and vacuum cleaners, also began to increase in the 1960s and after. Japan also began to out-produce and challenge the supremacy of other major industrial nations in electronic cameras, radios, quartz watches, television sets, calculators, home videos, video cassette recorders, computers, silicon memory chips, robotics, and genetic engineering.

To save labor and improve productivity, Japan began to use industrial robots. In 1990 about 60 percent of the world's industrial robots in use were in Japan. By 1981 Japan had gained 70 percent of the world market in computer chips, and in mid-1985, the *New York Times* concluded that "Japan has won the computer chip race."[61]

Japan's share in international trade also increased steadily. It was less than 4 percent in 1960, but it rose to about 8 percent during 1980–1990. Japan's overall balance of trade was mostly unfavorable until 1980, when it began to shift steadily in its favor; in 1994 exports over imports came to $120.9 billion.[62] The same situation developed in Japan's trade with the European Community, with the balance of trade in Japan's favor peaking in 1992 and then declining somewhat. A similar balance of trade in Japan's favor prevailed in its trade with the Asian nations.

By the early 1990s Japan's economy had peaked, and it began to experience economic difficulties and entered a period of recession. During the years of high-speed economic growth the GNP grew at a rate of over 10 percent annually, but it had dropped to 0.8 percent in 1992, and even lower subsequently.[63] During the years of high-speed economic growth the banks had overextended themselves by making risky loans, overpriced real estate investments, and corporate investments. Some hyper-inflated property dropped by as much as 90 percent in value. The recessionary trend affected the stock market negatively, and one major stock company, Yamichi Securities, went bankrupt in 1997, as did some major banks.

Japan's supremacy in auto production also came to be challenged by the recovery of the US auto industry. The higher yen made Japanese cars more expensive and contributed to the drop in US Japanese car imports.[64] By 1994 Japan began falling behind in consumer electronics because of the emerging information superhighway and the merging of the computer and consumer-electronics industries. The open, creative software industry of the United States surpassed Japan's tightly knit proprietary computer operating systems by 1994.

Until about 1990, Japan was regarded as having surpassed the United States in the economic realm in terms of efficiency, productivity, and technological innovations, but by 1994 the situation had been reversed.[65]

Reasons for Japan's Economic Growth

Numerous interpretations have been made to explain Japan's success in strengthening and expanding its economy since the end of World War II when its economic state was in shambles. It is interesting to note, in any case, that Japan's economic growth was not a sudden development in the postwar era. Since the early Meiji years the Japanese economy had undergone steady and significant growth.[66]

Perhaps the most significant factor in Japan's economic recovery is the support the United States provided to rebuild Japan's economy. When the United States decided to foster Japan's recovery, it provided financial and technical assistance. Also, the outbreak of the Korean War, as noted earlier, gave the Japanese economy a boost because of the huge "special procurements" by the United States for its military needs.

Undoubtedly the US policy that benefited Japan most significantly was the open market the United States provided for Japan's products. An authority on the Japanese economy writes:

> The American approach to Japan after the war was to declare that Japan was of great strategic importance and very little economic importance. It is for this reason that we allowed Japan to maintain protection of its domestic markets much longer than any European country, to maintain an undervalued currency much longer, why we transferred huge amounts of technology to Japan at bargain basement prices, and also gave Japan virtually unlimited access to the world's largest market, namely, the American market, in a way that we didn't do for anybody else.[67]

In addition to opening its markets to Japanese goods, the United States persuaded other non-Communist nations to open their markets to Japan, and it also sponsored Japan's membership in GATT in 1955. And thanks to the imposition of the no-war clause in the Japanese constitution by SCAP, Japan was relieved of investing huge sums of money in defense forces and was able to invest in rebuilding its economy. In order to take advantage of the markets opened to it, Japan had to make the best use of the technical, social, human, institutional, and intellectual resources available.

Regarding other reasons for Japan's success, different authorities cite the Japanese mastery of management technology (that is, the science of manufacturing goods efficiently); others credit the social systems and mores, the astute planning by government agencies, the close cooperation between government and big business, the dual structure of the economy in which small businesses absorb the negative costs, and the complex web of obstacles that keeps foreign competition out. Some ascribe Japan's success to "cartels, regulations, subsidies, graft, barriers against imports and foreign investors, [and] a rigged capital market."[68] Also cooperation between labor and management, a well-educated, skilled, disciplined, hardworking labor force, the work ethic, and the communitarian spirit can be cited as important qualities that contributed to Japan's success in rebuilding its economy.

The managerial class played a significant role by making long-range plans and continuously adopting and improving modern technology to make its plants more efficient. The fact that most of the country's old plants had been destroyed by the war provided the Japanese business companies with the opportunity to start from scratch. Management moved swiftly to build modern industrial facilities and adopt advanced technological innovations from abroad. Capital investments in new equipment were facilitated by the high rate of savings. Savings are encouraged by the Japanese tax system, which does not tax interest on savings but does not allow tax exemptions on interest payments—the reverse of the situation in the United States.[69]

Serious attention was paid by Japanese manufacturers in perfecting the quality of the goods produced. In the late 1940s, W. Edwards Deming, an American pioneer in the field of quality control, failed to get American manufacturers to adopt his suggestions, but the Japanese turned to him for assistance. He advised them on quality control, and his ideas have been incorporated in the production system. Since 1951 the Deming Prize has been awarded to firms for outstanding achievements in production and quality control. Most major companies organized quality-control teams in the workforce and got them to devise ways to improve efficiency and productivity at the workplace. In a recent survey of twenty-three industrial countries on product quality, Japan ranked first. Investments in research and development have also been stressed by Japanese corporations. Research investments have resulted in greater reliance on automation and higher productivity per worker. Frequently, concepts or instruments conceived or invented in the United States that fail to find industrial firms interested in them in the United States will be adopted by Japanese firms.

The effort to improve productivity and quality has enabled Japanese business firms to adjust constantly to world economic developments. For instance, in the immediate postwar years, textile production constituted an important component of Japan's economy; then, when the industry faced stiff tariff barriers and foreign competition, the Japanese industrialists moved on to consumer electronic products.

Government agencies, especially METI, and the business sector have cooperated closely to chart the course of economic developments. METI does not have absolute control over the economy, however. Analysts who downplay METI's role note that automobile manufacturers ignored its advice to pool their resources to produce a low-cost "people's car." And there are instances in which its policies failed. But in the 1970s it restructured the shipbuilding industry to cope with the surplus capacity in world shipbuilding. The government also assisted nascent industries, such as the auto industry in the postwar years, with high tariffs, and a web of complex rules and regulations that discouraged foreign manufacturers from penetrating the Japanese market. So, despite the fact that METI's influence over the private entrepreneurs, who have been charting their own course as their resources expanded, diminished somewhat, it still remains an important force in charting the course of the Japanese economy. Japan inclines toward managed economy rather than the free-market system of the United States.

Japanese management is also credited with long-term planning and a willingness to accept low levels of profits in the short run. Unlike US executives,

Japanese business leaders are not subjected to constant pressure to increase profits and dividends because they are secure in their positions, given the assurance of lifetime employment. In addition, much of their capital investment is borrowed from banks, which are more concerned with interest payments than with stock dividends. Also, many of the industrial and financial conglomerates are built around banks that constitute the core of the keiretsu. Thus, they are not subjected to constant pressure by stockholders to maximize dividends. Moreover, two-thirds of major companies' shares are not traded on the stock exchange, so these companies are not dependent on daily stock fluctuations. Thus, management can engage in long-term planning and concentrate on maximizing market shares rather than maximizing profits like US management. If some stockholders are inclined to raise troublesome questions at stockholders' meetings, the company in question may well rely on a core of corporate racketeers known as *sōkaiya*—corporate extortionists, linked to the Mafia-like gangster groups, the *yakuza*—to keep them in line.

Most Japanese executives have a strong sense of public service. Although they tend to regard individual property rights as sacred, Japanese businesspeople tend to consider property rights secondary to communal social needs and regard business companies to be public entities that must meet social needs. This difference in attitude is reflected in the compensation received by top executives in the two countries. In 1990 a typical Japanese executive salary was six times that of the average employee, whereas in the United States it was ninety-three times larger in the same period.

In the immediate postwar years conflict between labor and management was prevalent, but with the onset of high-speed economic growth in the 1960s, labor unrest abated. Thus the perception emerged that Japanese management's labor policy is benevolent and paternalistic. This perception sustains a generally harmonious relationship between management and workers and fosters a sense of group cohesion and commonality of interests. The managerial staff, office workers, and laborers in the plant all identify with the company, which is like an extended family organization. In most major companies there was the assurance of lifetime employment, though during the recession of the early 1990s some cracks began to appear in this system. When personnel reduction has to be made, however, the major firms usually do not dismiss the employees outright but send them to work in subsidiary firms, keep them on half-pay, or assist them to start their own businesses.

The workers are well educated, well trained, and governed by a strong work ethic. They are loyal and dedicated to the company, and they have a sense of "belonging" to the company rather than merely working for it. Thus, they take pride in their jobs. They are also willing to sacrifice for the success of their company and to work long hours at an intense pace. The payoffs are fewer labor disputes and higher productivity. In addition, the workers do not resist the increasing trend toward automation because in large companies they are retrained and kept on the payroll.

Working in a modern plant may not be anything like laboring in the textile plants of Meiji Japan, but it is still strenuous work. According to Ronald Dore, a sociologist specializing in Japanese society, a job at Toyota "as a regular worker is indeed rather more like joining the army in America than going to work for General Motors."[70] But the benefits of being a regular worker for a major manufacturing firm are much greater than those extended to temporary workers or workers in smaller companies. In general, regular workers are paid well, have job security, and receive generous bonuses when the company makes high profits.

It is noteworthy that labor unions in Japan are far less militant than those in other countries. Unions consist of enterprise unions or company-based unions rather than groups whose membership cuts across the industry. Thus, Japanese unions identify closely with the company rather than with fellow machinists or welders in other companies, and they avoid making exorbitant demands or staging lengthy strikes that might damage the company.[71] The identity of the union leaders with the company is strengthened further by the fact that many aspire to rise up into the management circle. Younger workers appear not to be as interested in becoming union members. In fact, union membership has been declining since 1970.[72]

There is a strong sense of community and cohesiveness among managerial and office staff members because of close personal contact among the business staff. Elite companies pick graduates of top universities, who are then assured of lifetime employment. They become part of the "family" in a much more tightly knit fashion than is true of factory workers. They give themselves over to the company, leaving almost no time for their own families. Their superiors look after their interests in a paternalistic manner, to the point of watching over their personal lives and assisting them when necessary. After hours, the staff members are expected to go out together and socialize until late at night—yet another necessary part of developing a sense of family or a community of interests. As Jared Taylor (b. 1951), who grew up in Japan, has noted, "Many Japanese have been happy to let the company arrange their weekends, their hobbies, their vacations, their marriages—in short their lives."[73]

Individual ambition must be stifled in favor of group interest as well as the hierarchic order of things. One's status is fixed by seniority in this hierarchy. Even the wives of employees are ranked according to their husbands' status, much like military personnel in Western nations. In short, the paternalistic "total embrace" of the employees by the company and its executives, which would be stifling to an individualistic Western worker, is accepted by Japanese employees because the social tradition has conditioned them to accept a communitarian, holistic lifestyle.

This kind of communalism entails working for consensus in decision making. For instance, lower-echelon staff members are often asked to prepare proposals or working papers that are then passed around for study by the managerial staff. Eventually a consensus is arrived at. Thus the decision becomes a joint one that presumably everyone can support. In addition, the process may also diffuse responsibility such that no one person can be blamed if anything goes wrong. In a crisis situation, however, the chief executive officer takes the responsibility whether he is personally responsible or not. Such was the case in August 1985, when the crash of a Japanese airline plane resulted in the death of over five hundred people. The president of the airline resigned. In the late 1990s, when company bankruptcies and business failures mounted, numerous executive officers took responsibility and resigned. When briberies involving company officials and Finance Ministry officials were exposed, some officials committed suicide.

Lifetime employment, a common practice in large companies but not in smaller firms, has been cited as one of the reasons for the success of Japanese management. Although it ensures the loyalty of employees to the company, it also has its negative side because it entails the retention of "deadwood," who, as they attain seniority, are given meaningless jobs. It also results in a lack of flexibility in personnel utilization and, for the employees, a loss of opportunities to move on to better jobs. Employees are stuck with particular jobs whether they like it or not.

In the early 1990 recession some adjustments in the lifetime employment practice began to occur. "Corporate labor-adjustment" moves became noticeable in the autumn of 1992 when the recession following the collapse of the "bubble economy" of the late 1980s finally hit home.[74] Also, some workers were encouraged to take early retirement. Part-time or temporary workers, often housewives, who work without fringe benefits or privilege of lifetime employment, were released. There have also been some plant closings.[75]

Big business firms cooperate not only with the government but also with each other. The conglomerate complexes, the keiretsu, work as a networking mechanism for in-group cooperation and coordination of business planning and action. Conglomerate members confer with one another and coordinate their efforts in the use of resources, technology, overseas trade, and so on. What prevails is a closed system, a club in which the members derive benefits and privileges and outsiders are closed out. Because Japan as a nation is a closed society (insofar as it does not really admit outsiders readily into the family that is Japan), the society can be seen as consisting of a closed system within a closed system. In the intertwined relationship of business interests, favors are exchanged. In 1991 it was revealed that the top four brokerages expended over $1 billion to compensate big investors for their losses. Taking care of members of the privileged circle means, of course, that the little investors and the public at large get short-changed. This affair also revealed the shady relationship that exists between business and financial circles, and the Japanese Mafia, the yakuza.

The additional factor that makes it difficult for outsiders, foreign firms in particular, to break into the closed system is the personal relationship of an "old-boy network" that involves not only members of the conglomerates favoring each other but a similar personal bond between influential bureaucrats, especially from METI and the Finance Ministry, and top company officials. This bond is cemented by the conglomerate firms providing positions for top bureaucrats after their retirement. Thus personal contacts between the firm and members of the bureaucracy are established to ensure that favorable government decisions are made for their firm.

Normally the subsidiary firms of a vertical keiretsu toe the line and submit to the demands of the company at the top. If an official in the subsidiary firm challenges the top firm, he will find himself removed from his position. This was demonstrated in 1991, when the chairman of a parts supplier to Nissan was removed from his post when he objected to Nissan's interference in his firm's management policies. He then protested publicly against Nissan's action and became the first insider to expose the system that treats the suppliers as docile subordinates.

Not all Japanese manufacturing plants are modern, efficient, gigantic complexes, however. Japan has a dual economy—a two-tier system in which only about 30 percent of the companies are highly productive major corporations using advanced technology, whereas 70 percent are smaller, less efficient companies and family businesses.[76] Although the labor shortage prior to the oil crisis improved the pay both of the temporary workers in the major companies and that of second-tier workers, compared with regular workers in major firms, they continue to receive less pay, lack job security, and do not receive the large bonuses that first-tier workers get. Their working conditions are poorer, and they have lower prestige. In the late 1980s workers in small companies were paid about 70 percent of the wages of workers in the first-tier companies. In plants that employ fewer than thirty workers and in family-run shops, workers earned 50 to 60 percent of the wages paid to major company workers.

Major companies lower production costs by making use of the smaller satellite and subcontracting companies. In the mid-1980s, 70 percent of the production costs of Nissan Motors was absorbed by work done by subcontractors. The latter are at the mercy of the big companies, serving as buffers to cushion their costs and losses. In an economic recession, when it becomes necessary to reduce production costs, the major companies cut to the bone the price they pay the subcontracting firms. As a result, it is the small companies that go bankrupt. In 1981, 17,600 small firms went under. So the concern for the common good applies only to the "core family" and not to people outside the "family" circle. Toyota and Nissan must prosper and survive even if adjunct companies go under. Of course, when times are good and the labor market is in the workers' favor, the workers can shift to better jobs because lifetime employment is not the norm in these jobs. To cope with this situation, small plant owners began to rely more on automation.

To concentrate high-tech production in a handful of elite companies poses the danger of an economic collapse, some analysts assert. For example, in the early 1990s, 50 percent of the close to $100 billion of exports to the United States consisted of goods produced by twenty companies in the electronics and auto industries. So the well-being of the Japanese economy is largely dependent on the success of these twenty companies. Moreover, 13 percent of the 67 million workers are in the electronics and auto industry. The other 87 percent are in secondary and tertiary economic domains in which they are incapable of competing with US manufacturers. They are able to survive by government assistance provided in the form of lower taxes and artificially rigged high prices for their products. In effect, 13 percent of the workers are subsidizing the other 87 percent. The wholesale and retail businesses are incapable of competing with their US counterparts. So when the top twenty companies began to fall behind in international trade, the Japanese economy as a whole began to slow down.[77]

Some analysts believe that the most important reason for the phenomenal growth of the Japanese economy has much less to do with the ingenuity of management than with the work ethic, the same force that propelled the Japanese economic growth from the early years of Meiji. Jared Taylor maintains that "the single most important ingredient in Japan's success is the Japanese attitude toward work. . . . The individual worker brings to his job a set of attitudes and expectations that make him the perfect company man." These attitudes are conformity, group loyalty, and a sense of national uniqueness.[78] A survey of salaried workers in Japan revealed that "work is the most important thing in their life." Peer pressure spurs one to work hard, for goldbrickers are likely to be ostracized. Management, by making the company the most important thing in the workers' lives, effectively uses these traditional qualities. Some observers have contended that the idea of homogeneity used by prewar militarists to emphasize the uniqueness of the Japanese nation is now being employed by big business interests to "convince the Japanese that they must work hard, train, save, do all sorts of things to protect the image of the nation in order to confront the outside world."[79]

Adherence to a rigid work ethic means for office—salaried—workers putting in long hours, and a six- or seven-day workweek. There has been growing concern about overwork resulting in physical breakdown and death, particularly among middle management executives. It was estimated that in 1992 as many as 10,000 Japanese worked themselves to death every year. One middle-level manager who died of overwork used to go to sleep setting three alarm clocks and wearing a wristwatch with an alarm on it to make sure that he would not be late for work. Those who take time off are seen as shirkers and are often passed over for promotion.

It is not only the work ethic that has made the Japanese successful competitors in the international market. It is also their concern for quality and meticulous attention to minute details. These traits are revealed in the way that strawberry growers cover each individual berry with protective tissue paper and the way apple farmers nurture and pamper every single fruit. In short, the spirit of the artisan who strives for perfection seems to survive among the industrial workers. As Frank Gibney (1924–2006), a longtime American resident in Japan, observed, "In the search for quality, the modern Japanese workers perpetuate the same feeling of respect for the craftsman which makes Japan one of the few countries in the world to honor her artisans and skilled performers with the designation of Living National Treasure."[80]

Labor Movement

As noted earlier, SCAP introduced measures such as the trade union law and labor standards law to improve the plight of laborers.

As a result of the liberal labor union policies supported by SCAP, a massive move to organize labor unions commenced. When the war ended there were no labor unions, but less than a year later, in June 1946, there were 12,006 unions, with 3.679 million members. The Sōdōmei (All Japan Federation of Labor Unions), linked to the Socialist Party, was organized in the fall of 1945. Then the Communists organized the Sanbetsu (National Congress of Industrial Unions).

As discussed in the section on political developments, the unions led largely by the Communists combined political activism with the fight for better wages and benefits for labor. Faced with politically motivated strikes and demonstrations, SCAP began to curb radical labor activities such as the move to overthrow the Yoshida government. The Communist-led unions' move to stage a general strike was curbed by SCAP, and it allowed the Yoshida government to restrict workers in state-owned enterprises to strike and also revise the trade union law to prevent dominance of the unions by the Communists. A number of acts of violence followed the government's policy of rationalization—that is, the decision to reduce the number of workers in government-run enterprises cast labor's political activism in a bad light. Public support for the union movement declined, and union membership began to fall.

To curb the unions' political activism, the Yoshida government passed the Subversive Activities Prevention Law in 1952. Opposition to Yoshida's move to get a law passed to prevent general strikes led to massive protest demonstrations on May 1 that year. The strikes undertaken in the coal and electric-power industries led to the enactment of the Strike Regulation Act by the Yoshida government in 1953, outlawing work stoppages in these industries.

In the 1960s, when the economy entered a period of high-speed growth under Ikeda, labor militancy began to abate. Real wages rose by 150 percent in ten years, and unemployment dropped below 1 percent. Workers began to focus on furthering the economic gains of the company where they were employed because its success meant higher wages. As mentioned earlier, for enterprise-based or company unions of Japan, it was to labor's advantage to have a strong, successful company. Thus, the trend toward cooperation rather than confrontation came to characterize labor-management relations.[81]

Agriculture

In 1950, a few years after the war ended, 48.3 percent of the workforce was engaged in agriculture, and in 1960, 26.8 percent was still working on the farm. As a result of the rapid turn toward industrialization, however, in 1994, only 5.2 percent of the workforce was in agriculture. In 1994 agriculture accounted for only 1.6 percent of the gross domestic product, compared with 9 percent in 1960. Even though there were fewer workers on the farms, agricultural production nonetheless increased.

Traditionally rice was the main food in the Japanese diet, although in the feudal years of Tokugawa reign the authorities expropriated as much rice as possible and instructed the peasants to eat millet, barnyard grass, and vegetable leaves. In the pre–World War II years about 59 percent of the total caloric intake came from rice, making it Japan's chief agricultural product. Yet in the prewar years about 20 percent of the rice required by the country had to be imported. But with improved farming methods and greater use of chemical fertilizers, farm production increased.[82] At the same time, the dietary pattern of the people changed, and rice comprised only 28 percent of the food intake by the mid-1980s. As a result, by 1968 Japan began to produce a rice surplus. There also has been tremendous growth in the fishing industry, with the annual haul, excluding whales, increasing from 3.374 million tons in 1950 to 9.978 million tons in 1992. But the fishery haul began to decrease by the 1990s owing to decreased fishery resources, international restrictions, and increased imports. In the postwar years, whaling continued, despite criticism from environmentalists, but it began to decline after 1965.[83]

The agrarian population and number of rural households declined steadily as the urban centers drew more and more people, especially young people, away from the villages.[84] Only 13.7 percent of the nation's land was under cultivation. Over 90 percent of farm households farmed less than three hectares, and about 58 percent farmed less than one hectare (1 hectare equals 2.47 acres). In 1989, one acre of rice land cost about $33,600.

Until the mid-1990s, the price of rice was not determined by the law of supply and demand but was fixed by the government, which purchased the rice from the farmers at a price higher than the world market and sold it to consumers at a lower price. This policy kept the price of rice artificially high for the rice producers.[85] In 1995 the policy of releasing rice in the market became commonplace, although the government continued to purchase up to 1.5 million tons a year. The government stored the surplus. In some years about half the annual rice production was in government warehouses.

Rice producers have been protected from external competition with a near-total ban on rice imports except in years when rice crops dropped because of bad weather. The farm bloc has vigorously opposed any move to relax the restrictions on rice imports, and rice has become symbolic of Japanese barriers against foreign imports. Farm interests seek to create a mystique of rice to keep from opening up the Japanese market. They say rice is "a source of Japanese culture, the Japanese mind, the Japanese way of thinking."

Government price support ensures a farm household income higher than that of the rest of the nation.[86] In 1991 the farm household income was about 3.7 percent more than the average worker household income. The special measures to support the farmers in combination with import restrictions kept food prices high.[87] Despite the surplus in rice, the production of wheat, barley, soybeans, and other farm products do not meet the consumers' demand. In 1990 Japan was only 67 percent self-sufficient in food production. In 1992, 16 percent of Japan's total imports consisted of foodstuff.[88]

THE JAPANESE ECONOMY
IN THE EARLY 1990s: RECESSION

The Japanese economic engine began to slow down in the late 1980s, and in the early 1990s it appeared to enter a period of recession and stagnation. The bubble had burst. "The sun also sets," people said. Japan no longer appeared invincible, and the United States began to regain its former supremacy. One analyst concluded that Japan's economic success up until 1990 depended on "hard work, good management and productive investment" plus adoption of "technological advances already pioneered abroad." Since the mid-1970s, "exports benefited from . . . a low value of the yen and sleepy competitors that underestimated Japanese products." But these advantages were no longer present in 1990. "There aren't many major foreign technological advances left to borrow." The value of the yen has risen, and "US companies have awakened to Japanese competition."[89]

The banks (which form the lynchpin of the keiretsu) had invested heavily in speculative real estate ventures. They found themselves in a bind when the stock market and real estate market began their collapse in 1989. In 1992 it was estimated that Japanese banks had loaned 70 percent of their entire loan portfolio collateralized by real estate property. But real estate value dropped significantly.[90] The boom years when the economy often grew by over 10 percent a year had expired, and the 1990s were down to a growth rate of 1 to 2 percent. Many of the "go-go" companies began to see the bottom line drop into the red.[91] To stimulate the economy, the government lowered interest rates that had hit 6 percent in 1992 to just above 0 percent in 2002. Despite these indications of economic difficulties, some analysts believe that it is premature to pronounce the end of the Japanese economic ascendancy. So long as there is a world market open to Japanese goods and the demand exists, Japanese manufacturers will find ways to supply the market. James Fallows (b. 1959) believes that counting the Japanese out is premature. Since the end of the war, US observers counted the decline of Japan as an economic force a half-dozen times.[92]

Notes

1. Yoshida Shigeru, *The Yoshida Memoirs* (Cambridge, Mass.: Riverside Press, 1962), p. 172.

2. Ibid., p. 191.

3. In the May 1958 election his party lost 10 seats and dropped to 287 seats in the lower house. The Socialists won 166 seats, the Communists 1.

4. Charles E. Gallagher in *The Japan Experience*, ed. Ronald Bell (New York: Weatherhill, 1973), p. 186.

5. They gained 296 seats, compared with the Socialist Party's 145.

6. Sato had been adopted by a political ally of the family, a common tactic to cement alliances between families.

7. *New York Times,* December 17, 1993.

8. The price of oil rose rapidly from three dollars a barrel, ultimately reaching thirty-five dollars a barrel by 1981.

9. One positive accomplishment of Tanaka was to enhance the welfare system. He made medical care for old people free. Hence 1973 is regarded as "Year 1" of the welfare system.

10. The LDP managed to win a majority of the 512 seats by capturing 275 seats, and with the addition of eleven independents in its circle it managed to claim 295 seats.

11. This is called derisively *amakudari,* or "to descend from heaven."

12. Hoshii-Herzen in Bell, *Japan Experience,* p. 75.

13. Ronald Yates in the *Chicago Tribune,* August 18, 1991.

14. For example, in 1992 a district in the Yokohama area had nearly 2 million residents per Diet seat. In the outlying district in Western Honshu there were only slightly over 300,000

residents per seat. Each vote in this district had 6.5 times the weight as the vote in the Yoko-hama district.

15. With the intensification of the Cold War following the outbreak of the Korean War in 1950, the US National Security Council and the military hoped to maintain long-term control over Okinawa and began to strengthen and upgrade the bases there, where 13 percent of the land was utilized for US military bases.

16. In 1970, 30.7 percent of Japan's exports (in terms of dollar value) and 29.4 percent of its imports were to and from the United States. The figure remained in the 20 to 30 percent range to the 1990s. In 1995, exports to the United States came to 27.3 percent and imports from the United States amounted to 22.4 percent.

17. In 1960 the balance of trade favored the United States, amounting to $452 million, but by 1970 it favored Japan by $380 million. Following the oil crisis of 1973–1974 the balance again favored the United States, but since then the trade surplus in Japan's favor increased by leaps and bounds. By 1993 it had risen to $59.3 billion.

18. In December 1971 the finance ministers of ten industrial nations met in the United States and fixed the yen at 306 yen to a dollar. The value of the yen continued to rise. By 1994 it went higher than 100 yen, but the strong yen still failed to correct the trade imbalance.

19. The quota was voluntary and flexible. In 1990 the number of passenger cars sent to the United States was down to 1.719 million compared with 2.383 million in 1986.

20. Thus, by 1993 Japan had gained 30 percent of the US automobile market. Slightly more than half of the Japanese cars sold in the United States were manufactured there. Although the cars were assembled in the United States, most of the parts were imported from the Japanese automakers' subsidiary plants in Japan.

21. In April 1994, for example, auto exports dropped 16.2 percent compared with the same month in 1993.

22. Because of voluntary export restrictions on a number of products as well as an increase in exports and the appreciation of the yen relative to the dollar, the trade surplus with the United States dropped from $59 billion in 1993 to $45.45 billion in 1995.

23. Murray Sayle, "Japan Victorious," *New York Review of Books,* March 28, 1985, p. 36.

24. For example, in the mid-1980s, retail prices were 4.21 times higher than wholesale prices, whereas in the United States they were only twice as high. In the 1980s there were 2.4 million retail outlets and 400,000 different distributors in Japan. In the 1980s small retail stores accounted for 56 percent of retail sales in Japan compared with 3 percent in the United States.

25. In 1990 Japan imported 20.5 percent of US agricultural exports. In that year Japan imported, in terms of tonnage, 27 percent of the US corn exports, 22.6 percent of US soybean exports, 56.5 percent of US beef exports, and 63 percent of US pork exports. In 1995, 66.3 percent of Japan's grain and processed grain products were imported from the United States.

26. But direct investment in the United States by Japan, $18 billion in 1991, was much larger than US direct investment in Japan, which was $1.3 billion that year. The total investments Japan made in the United States between 1951 and 1990 came to $130.5 billion. However, the buyouts and investments that were made during the boom years abated by the 1990s, when the Japanese economy began to fall into a state of recession.

27. In 1992 Japan spent 6.3 percent of its government expenditures on defense, slightly less than 1 percent of the GNP. This amounted to $275 per capita. In the same year the United States devoted 5.0 percent of its GNP, and $1,122 per capita, on defense.

28. *New York Times,* June 20, 23, 1991.

29. A Japanese is likely to say "yes" to mean "I understand your point," not "I agree with you." But "yes" to an American would imply assent. When a Japanese negotiator says, "I'll try to do my best," he really means, "It will be difficult to do what you ask."

30. Shintaro Ishihara, *The Japan That Can Say No,* trans. Frank Baldwin (New York: Simon & Schuster, 1991).

31. Robert C. Christopher, *The Japanese Mind: The Goliath Explained* (New York: Linden Press, 1983), p. 174.

32. In 1990, before the USSR collapsed, 0.9 percent of Japanese exports went to the Soviet Union, and 1.4 percent of its imports came from that country. In 1992, after the breakup of the Soviet Union, 0.3 percent of Japanese exports went to Russia, and 1.0 percent of its imports came from Russia.

33. In 1970, 2.9 percent of Japan's exports went to China, and 1.3 percent of its imports came from that country. By 1995 the figures had risen to 5 percent and 10.7 percent. In 1990 Japan imported 16 percent of China's total exports, and Japanese products constituted 15.1 percent of China's imports. Between 1951 and 1990, Japan invested $2.8 billion in China, about 6 percent of its total investments in all Asian nations.

34. In 1995 Japan's exports to Taiwan came to 6.5 percent of its total exports, and its imports from Taiwan came to 4.3 percent.

35. At least four of those captives were returned to Japan, bringing with them their children, who spoke no Japanese. North Korea refused to give a total account of the deaths of a handful more of the captives.

36. In 1995 its exports to Southeast Asian countries amounted to 2.3 percent to Indonesia, 3.8 percent to Malaysia, 1.6 percent to the Philippines, 5.2 percent to Singapore, and 4.5 percent to Thailand.

37. In 1995, however, 8.1 percent of Japan's oil imports came from Indonesia and 2.2 percent from Malaysia. In 1990 Japan imported 42.5 percent of Indonesia's total exports.

38. Between 1951 and 1990, Japan invested $11.54 billion in Indonesia, $6.555 billion in Singapore, and $4.422 billion in Thailand.

39. Hugo M. Enomiya-LaSalle in Bell, *Japan Experience,* p. 96.

40. *New York Times,* March 11, 1985.

41. *New York Times,* August 6, 1988.

42. The government contributed $458 million to the international ODA (official development assistance) fund in 1970 and by 1995 increased it to $14.484 billion, becoming the world's biggest contributor.

43. In 1995, 1.8 percent of Japan's exports went to Australia and 4.3 percent of its imports came from that country.

44. Middle East nations supplied 71.6 percent of Japan's oil imports in 1995; the United Arab Emirates was the heaviest supplier, with 27.4 percent, followed by Saudi Arabia's 23.1 percent.

45. In 1992 Japan had a favorable balance of trade with the EEC of $31 billion. European nations have been much more willing to adopt stronger retaliatory measures than the United States. Because of such measures Japan's favorable balance of trade dropped slightly to $21.479 billion in 1995.

46. *Newsweek,* June 24, 1991.

47. Among the EEC nations, Japan's trade with Germany is largest, with 4.6 percent of its exports and 4.1 percent of imports being conducted with Germany in 1995. The dollar value in exports that year was $20.3 billion, and the imports value was $13.7 billion. The next biggest trading partner for Japan in 1995 in the EEC was the United Kingdom, with 3.2 percent and 2.1 percent.

48. In 1946 industrial production stood at 30.7 percent of what it had been during 1934–1936. In the few years after 1946 it rose slowly. In 1947 it rose to 37.4 percent; in 1948, 54.6 percent; in 1949, 71.0 percent; and in 1950, 83.6 percent. Statistics in this section are based primarily on 1980s–1990s publications of *Japan Almanac (Asahi Shimbun); Facts and Figures of Japan; Japan: A Pocket Guide* (Tokyo Foreign Press Center); *Nippon: A Chartered Survey of Japan* (Tokyo: Kokuseisha); *Statistical Handbook of Japan* (Bureau of Statistics, Office of the Prime Minister); *Japan Statistical Yearbook* (Tokyo: Japan Statistical Association); *Japan of Today* (Tokyo: Ministry of Foreign Affairs); *Japan, An International Comparison* (Keisai Koho Center); and *Far Eastern Economic Reviews, New York Times, Japan Times Weekly,* and other journals and newspapers.

49. By 1951 the United States had poured more than $2 billion into the Japanese economy. The economy also received a strong boost from US procurements during the Korean War. By the mid-1950s the United States had spent about $4 billion in Japan by purchasing supplies, equipment, services, and recreation facilities for American troops. As a result the Japanese economy began to recover, and between 1953 and 1960 the economy grew at a rate of more than 9 percent each year. By 1965 manufacturing as well as the economy as a whole rose to nearly four times the prewar level while the population grew only from 70 million to 98 million.

50. In 1993 it accounted for only 3 to 4 percent of Japan's total factory output and exports.

51. A rich rice harvest of 12.385 million metric tons was harvested, over 3 million tons more than the prewar 1940 harvest.

52. In 1946 exports amounted to only $103 million, but by 1956, they rose to over $2 billion.

53. Ikeda's successors followed his policy of expanding the economy, and by the end of the 1960s exports had risen to $19.363 billion, $490 million over imports.

54. During the sustained economic growth in the 1960s, Japan's GNP constituted 6 percent of world production. It reached $202 billion in 1970, the third largest in the world, after $1 trillion in the United States and the Soviet Union's $350 billion.

55. In 1950, 48.3 percent of Japan's workers were in the primary sector, 22 percent were in the secondary sector, and 29.6 percent were in the tertiary sector. In 1991 the ratio was 6.7 percent primary, 34.1 percent secondary, and 59.2 percent tertiary.

56. Japan relied on oil imports for 75 percent of its energy requirements—99.5 percent of Japan's oil had to be imported, and 88 percent of the oil import came from the Middle East in 1973. The price of oil increased from $2 a barrel to $11 in 1973. Then it went up to $24 a barrel in 1979 and $34 by 1981.

57. Between 1973 and 1979, the amount of energy required to produce motor vehicles was reduced by 25 percent; during the same years it was reduced by 23 percent in the chemical industry. By 1980 unit energy consumption in the iron and steel industry had been reduced by 27.8 percent since 1975. General dependence on oil for energy needs was reduced from 80.3 percent in 1972 to 61 percent by 1983.

58. In 1950 Japan manufactured only 1,593 passenger cars, but in 1980 it produced 7.038 million passenger cars, and in 1990 it produced 9.948 million. In the 1990s recession, production began to drop somewhat. In 1995 it was down to 7.611 million cars.

59. *Japan Times Weekly,* April 4–10, 1994. Between 1987 and 1992, the number of such companies increased from 774 to 2,070, and the number of American workers employed in these companies rose from 303,000 to 707,000.

60. Merchant ship manufacturing reached a high of nearly 17 million tons, 49.7 percent of world production, in 1975. It began to decline and dropped to 4.04 million tons in 1988, but it recovered to top 9 million tons in 1995.

61. This turned out to be a somewhat premature prediction because by 1993, the United States was beginning to turn the tide. A study conducted by the Japanese government in 1982 predicted that by the year 2000 Japan would have the world's highest per capita GNP. In fact, this was achieved by 1990 with a per capita GNP of $25,840 compared with $21,810 for the United States. But in 1993 the trend was reversed, with the US per capita national income rising to $23,000 whereas it was $19,800 for Japan.

62. Then the surplus began to drop somewhat as the surplus in trade with its major trading partner, the United States, began to decline somewhat. In 1997 the surplus was at $105.3 billion, but it rebounded to $124 billion in 1998.

63. In fact, the downturn in the Japanese economy was presaged by a drastic drop in the Tokyo stock market, which saw the Nikkei average drop from 39,000 yen in 1989 to 22,000 yen, and below 15,000 in the late 1990s.

64. Also in 1993 production of audio and video equipment dropped by 12.7 percent from the previous year, a consecutive double-digit drop. Overall consumer electronics production dropped by 5.9 percent in 1993 from 1992.

65. In 1992 US factory productivity increased 4.3 percent over 1991, whereas Japan's dropped by 5 percent. Japan was behind the United States by 17 percent in labor productivity in 1990. The average American worker produced $49,600 worth of goods and services a year; a Japanese worker produced $38,200. Japan was behind the United States in the use of computers: 9 to 34.5 for every 100 workers.

66. For example, between the First and Second World Wars, Japanese manufacturing output grew 600 percent, compared with only about 66 percent in the United States.

67. *Intersect,* June 1990, p. 9.

68. *Far Eastern Economic Review*, November 2, 1989, p. 46.

69. Per household savings in 1990 averaged $71,016 (compared with $28,125 in the United States). The household savings rate in 1993 came to 14.7 percent, compared with 4.2 percent in the United States.

70. Ronald Dore, introduction to *Japan in the Passing Lane: An Insider's Account of Life in a Japanese Auto Factory,* by Satoshi Kamata, trans. Tatsuru Akimoto (New York: Pantheon, 1982), p. xii.

71. The days lost in labor disputes in Japan in the 1980s came to about 3.7 percent of the days lost in such disputes in the United States.

72. In 1970, 35.4 percent of workers were in unions. By 1995 the percentage had dropped to 23.8 percent.

73. Jared Taylor, *Shadows of the Rising Sun: A Critical View of the "Japanese Miracle"* (New York: Morrow, 1983), p. 305.

74. During 1993, 783 companies, or nearly half of the 1,664 listed on the Tokyo Stock Exchange, eliminated 88,423 jobs. Some companies began to lower the retirement age from sixty to fifty-six.

75. For example, in 1993 Nissan announced its plan to close the Zama plant, affecting 2,500 workers. As a result, the unemployment rate, which was low in the years of economic growth, began to increase. It was 2 percent in 1990 but hit 4.1 percent in 1998.

76. In the mid-1980s, 60 percent of Japanese workers held jobs in plants that employed fewer than 100 workers, and only 13 percent worked in companies employing more than 1,000 workers.

77. Ōmae Kenichi in *Bungei Shunju,* March 1994, p. 124.

78. Taylor, *Shadows of the Rising Sun,* p. 171.

79. Charles F. Gallagher in Bell, *Japan Experience,* p. 183.

80. Frank Gibney, *Miracle by Design: The Real Reasons Behind Japan's Economic Success* (New York: Times Books, 1982), p. 161.

81. Overall, union membership among workers dropped from the high of 35.4 percent in 1970 to 23.8 percent in 1995. Through the 1970s and 1980s, and into the 1990s, labor generally adhered to a policy of cooperation with the business-industrial community and advanced Japan's economic expansion in the world market. Very few serious labor disputes occurred in this period.

82. In 1935 the yield per hectare was 2.71 tons. By 1969 it rose to 4.5 tons, and in 1991, 5.86 tons. In 1935 Japan's total rice production was 8.619 million tons. By 1975 it had risen to 13.170 million tons. Then, with lower rice consumption at just over 10 million tons, production dropped to 10.750 million tons by 1995.

83. With index 100 for 1960, it reached 114 in 1965 and then steadily dropped, hitting index 0.1 in 1994.

84. In 1964 there were 5.667 million farm households, but by 1992 the number was down to 2.888 million. Of these, only 15.6 percent were engaged in full-time farming. The farm household population, which numbered 37.670 million in 1950, was down to 12.857 million by 1995.

85. It was 7 times the price of rice in the world market and 9.4 times the price in the United States in 1995.

86. Disregarding the shift in purchasing value of the yen, the yen income of farm household rose by 16.7 percent from 1960 to 1991. The worker household income rose by 13.4 percent in that period. In 1980 the annual income per farm household was 7.6 percent above the national per household income.

87. In 1992 food comprised 23.6 percent of consumer expenditures, compared with about 19 percent in the United States.

88. The statistics on agriculture are primarily from *Nippon: A Charted Survey,* 1993–1994, and *Japan Almanac,* 1997.

89. Robert Samuelson, "Japan as Number Two," *Newsweek,* December 6, 1993.

90. A square foot of land that cost $375 in 1990 dropped below $200 in 1998. It was estimated that in 1992, banks were saddled with about $300 billion of nonperforming loans in which no interest was being paid. Estimates for bad bank loans rose as high as $650 billion in 1998.

91. Nissan saw its net losses rise to $835 million in fiscal year 1993 that ended in March 1994. The stock market that hit 39,000 in the Nikkei index dropped to below 15,000 in 1998.

92. James Fallows, *More Like Us: Making America Great Again* (Boston: Houghton Mifflin, 1989), p. 13.

17

Social and Educational Developments

SOCIAL DEVELOPMENTS

Population

The population of Japan in 1945 was 72.147 million. By 2006 it had risen to 127.5 million, and it is expected to peak at 130.44 million in 2011. The density per square mile in 1998 was 863, compared to 70-plus in the United States.

The general improvements in Japan's material condition—better diet, medical care, sanitation—resulted in the attainment of the highest life expectancies in the world: 53.96 for women in 1947 and 50.06 for men. By 1998 it had risen to 84 for women and 77 for men. This rise in life expectancy has resulted in an increase in the number of people over age sixty-five. In 1992 about 13 percent of the population was age sixty-five or older. By the year 2000 it rose to 17 percent, and by 2025, it is projected to rise to 25.8 percent. The death rate in Japan in 1947 was 14.6, and in 1998 it was 7.5, an increase from a low of 6.2 in 1980 owing perhaps to the aging of the population.[1]

Because of the low death rate and longer life expectancy the population continued to increase despite the drop in the birth rate.[2] If the current rate of drop in the birth rate continues, it is believed that in thirty years the Japanese population will drop by 20 percent from 1991. The reason for the decline in birth rate is due to more women working and marrying later. Women's age of marriage was 27.2 years in 1994 whereas it was 24.6 in 1970.

Beginning in the late Meiji period women increasingly took jobs outside their home or local communities, but when they married they were expected to leave their jobs and return to housekeeping and childrearing. In 1992 a childcare leave law went into effect. Companies with more than thirty employees are

427

required to allow the mother or father to take a year of leave from work to care for newborn babies. The other reason for the drop in the birth rate compared to the immediate postwar years is the legalization of abortion in 1949. In 1990, doctors performed 456,797 abortions.

General Living Conditions

The phenomenal economic growth naturally resulted in a rise in the standard of living.[3] The household savings of Japan was among the highest in the world. In 1980 it was 17.9 percent, but with the increasing tendency toward greater consumption the percentage dropped to 14.7 percent by 1993. Still, the Japanese saving rate was higher than the 4.2 percent in the United States.[4]

The public's sense of well-being is reflected in their perception of their class standing. In 1990, 89 percent of the people considered themselves to belong to the lower-middle class or the upper-middle class. The highest number of people, 53.1 percent, considered themselves belonging to the middle class. Only 7.2 percent considered themselves being in the lower class, and 0.7 percent the upper class.

This sense of well-being has been reflected in the realm of conspicuous consumption. This can be seen in the phenomenal increase in the number of automobiles and household appliances in use: By 1991, 79.5 percent of the households had a passenger car, 99.3 percent had a color television set, 99.4 percent had a washing machine, 98.8 percent had a refrigerator, and 68.1 percent had an air conditioner. The increase in household income and general economic prosperity has resulted in more money being spent on leisure activities and travel.[5]

A nation's well-being used to be measured in terms of daily caloric food consumption. The caloric intake per person per day in 1934–1938 was 2,020, consisting primarily of cereals and vegetables with little meat. By the 1990s the caloric intake surpassed 2,600, with some increase in fats and oil, which in the 1930s constituted just 3 percent of the diet. By the 1990s it reached over 13 percent. The Japanese consumption of approximately 2,500 to 2,600 calories a day, in combination with a low-meat and low-fat diet, is regarded as having contributed to the increase in life expectancy. The low incidence of heart disease in Japan is seen as a product of this diet. In 1990 there were only 135 deaths per 100,000 persons from heart disease, compared to 302 in the United States. The general increase in protein intake is believed to be responsible for taller youngsters. Between 1960 and 1980, the average height of seventeen-year-old boys increased by 1.7 inches.

Cost of Living

With the growth in the economy, the price of goods skyrocketed. A government survey conducted in November 1991 indicated that consumer prices in

Tokyo were 27 percent higher than in New York. In 1994 gasoline cost $4.25 a gallon.[6] Before the recession of the early 1990s there was a great deal of conspicuous consumption.[7]

In the 1980s Japanese buyers boosted the price of paintings at art auctions abroad. The Mitsukoshi Department Store sold twenty to thirty paintings that each cost more than $1 million every year in the age of high-speed economic growth and conspicuous consumption. At a 1990 auction, bidding for Vincent van Gogh's *Portrait of Doctor Gachet* started at $25 million and was acquired by a Japanese collector for $82.5 million.

For people who are not into acquisition of luxury goods the price of daily necessities remains high because the retail stores are under the control of manufacturers and the wholesale distribution system, and they cannot freely reduce prices at the retail level.[8]

With the economic downturn in the early 1990s, conspicuous consumption and purchases of expensive name-brand goods began to ease off somewhat. The sale of super-expensive imported luxury goods began to decline, and consumers began to buy more domestic products. Also, luxury items began to be discounted in many stores. But discounting in certain areas is strictly controlled.[9]

Social Problems

Despite the rise in the standard of living and increase in conspicuous consumption, Japan remained far behind the other major economic powers in such areas as housing, roads, sewage, sanitation facilities, and so forth. The steady increase in population size has created problems of overcrowding, housing shortages, congestion, pollution, and so on.

The general overcrowding has been aggravated by the concentration of the population in major urban areas. In 1990 close to 60 percent of the population was concentrated in four major metropolitan areas around Tokyo, Osaka, Nagoya, and Kita-Kyushu.[10] The population shift from rural to urban centers meant loss of residents, especially the young, in rural areas. The population in northern Japan and Shikoku Island began to drop as early as 1950.

Urban sprawl has resulted in aesthetically unattractive landscapes. The eastern coastal region from Tokyo all the way to Hiroshima has turned into a continuous urban strip. One British scholar teaching in Japan observed,

> Tokyo is admittedly an urban planner's nightmare. . . . Ignore the skyscrapers of the central districts . . . and downtown Tokyo is a patchwork of bath houses, pachinko [pinball] parlors, stand bars and tenements, in competition with factories, timberyards, offices and school playgrounds for the precious space. Motorways weave overhead to add to the noise and neon. It is rarely

pretty but Tokyo is undeniably alive in contrast to some European and American inner cities.

The uncontrolled urban sprawl into the suburban areas "without the slightest aesthetic pretense," he further remarked, has caused tourist information offices' pictures of Japan largely to disappear.[11]

The concentration of the population in a few urban centers has resulted in serious housing problems. The situation is especially acute in Tokyo prefecture, where in 1992 close to 12 million people were crowded together in cramped houses and apartments. There were 5,444 persons per square kilometer compared to 337 in Hiroshima. Houses and apartments in Tokyo sell or rent for exorbitant prices. Residential area land prices in large cities rose by 200 percent between 1955 and 1990.[12] In metropolitan Tokyo the cost of housing in 1991 was 8.99 times a house owner's annual income, compared to the national average of 5.7 times. (In the United States it was 3.4 times.) The cost of a family-size apartment was over $516,000.[13]

Prior to the downturn in the economy, fueled by real estate speculators, banks, and investors, property prices nationally grew by over 10 percent annually. In 1990 they rose from 13 percent in residential areas to 14 percent in commercial areas. But with the economic downturn in 1991, the inflation in land prices slowed. By 1992 a third of the speculative investments had evaporated.[14]

Despite the heavy concentration of the population in urban areas, the sewage and sanitation systems have not been modernized sufficiently, and there is very little modern plumbing. Only about 9 percent of the homes had flush toilets in the late 1980s; in 1990 just half of the dwellings in the cities were connected to the sewage system. Most homes have no central heating or hot-water systems. Housing is not available in the center of the cities, so people spill over into the outskirts, spending hours every day commuting in overcrowded buses, electric trains, subways, and cars.[15]

Given the cost of land and housing it is not unreasonable that average Japanese people feel financially pinched despite the high average per capita income and high rate of savings per household. Naturally, there are pockets of poverty; many urban dwellers live in cramped, substandard housing with inadequate sanitation facilities.

Environmental Problems

The price of industrialization has been pollution. One of the most widely publicized cases of such pollutions occurred in 1953, when the seawaters off the coast of northwestern Kyushu in Minamata Bay were poisoned with methyl mercury by a chemical plant. The fish contaminated by this mercury were then consumed by the people in the region. Consequently many people were paralyzed or suffered loss of vision, speech defects, and other muscular disorders. A large number of babies were born with symptoms akin to cerebral palsy. The cause of the difficulties was eventually traced to a major chemical industries plant, but neither the plant owners nor the government took any action until the public furor and legal action against the company compelled them to do so. One thousand people died as a result of mercury poisoning, and thousands continued to suffer physical difficulties into the new century.[16]

Other cases of chemical pollution began to surface in different areas of Japan, including PCB (polychlorinated biphenyl) in fish and pollution of the air by smokestack industries and auto emissions. Public opinion was aroused, and demand for pollution control and environmental protection grew in intensity. Finally, in 1970 the government enacted environmental laws to control chemical and industrial pollution and clean up air and water pollution. Strict auto emission standards were established by the Transportation Ministry. The air in Tokyo, which was so polluted that policemen wore masks to cover their noses and mouths, became clean enough to inhale.

The other issue of concern has been the preservation of the natural environment. Urban sprawl has transformed the natural environment into concrete and asphalt jungles. Moreover, the general lack of concern for preserving the natural environment is seen in the conversion of scarce land into golf courses. In 1992 there were 1,700 golf courses in Japan. Their combined area exceeded the landmass of Tokyo, and hundreds more courses were being planned for construction. To keep the courses from reverting to their natural state, vast quantities of herbicides and chemicals are regularly sprayed over the area. The resulting groundwater pollution poses a threat to nearby farmland.

Welfare Programs

Japan's growing population of elderly people has placed an increasingly heavy strain on the national budget. As noted earlier, the percentage of people age sixty-five and over in the coming years is expected to increase significantly. The resulting imbalance between the percentage of young and old people is expected to put a strain on the Japanese social security system. In the next thirty years, the number of pensioners is expected to triple, whereas the working population contributing to the pension fund will continue to shrink. By 2020 every two working persons are expected to be supporting one pensioner. In 1992 the ratio was five to one.[17]

The constitution stipulates that "the State shall use its endeavors for the promotion and extension of social welfare and security, and of public health." Thus the government has instituted comprehensive social security and welfare measures as well as public health and medical care programs. Social welfare benefits cover the elderly, people with physical or mental disabilities, single mothers and their dependents, and those suffering from diseases difficult to cure. The benefits include pensions, stipends, and home-care helpers.[18]

Health and Medicine

The steady improvement in the people's health in the postwar years clearly is the product of advances in medical science, such as the discovery and use of antibiotics, better health care, and better diet. The American occupation authorities contributed greatly to the improvement in medicine and hygiene. SCAP initiated a massive inoculation and vaccination program, and many diseases were reduced or eliminated. Though limited in scope, the Japanese government had instituted a health insurance law as early as 1927. The program was expanded in the postwar years, and in 1961 all Japanese citizens were covered by a health insurance and pension plan.

Health care for the elderly was made comprehensive. For those over age seventy, or over sixty-five with severe handicaps, the national health insurance covers the entire medical cost, whether the affliction is a cold or cancer. Naturally, the cost of national health care has continued to rise at a high rate.[19]

The tradition of family members caring for the elderly and the needy has continued, although the percentage of the elder members living with their children has been declining somewhat. In 1996, 55 percent of those older than sixty-five lived with their children, compared to 80 percent in 1970. Pension payments for retirees have been increasing, but they still remain relatively low.[20]

The problem for retirees becomes acute when they are compelled to retire before age sixty. In 2002 over 95 percent of the firms had retirement ages between fifty-five and sixty. Even though many are required to retire before age sixty the government's social security payments do not start until age sixty. Although privileged executives of the first-tier companies are provided with nominal jobs in the company or with satellite firms, retirees from second-tier companies generally find themselves cut loose without adequate pension or retirement benefits. Thus they have to find postretirement jobs to supplement their limited retirement income. The need to save for life after retirement undoubtedly accounts for the comparatively high household savings.

Social Tensions

Because of overcrowding as well as intense pressure to study hard, work hard, and live up to personal and professional expectations, social tensions, which have always been present, have intensified in recent years. Suicides (albeit traditionally regarded as an acceptable way out of a dilemma) have been increasing—especially among people over sixty-five years of age.[21]

The reason for the higher suicide rate for men may be the traditional early retirement age and the absence of a meaningful life after retirement. The traditional concept of *inkyo,* a secluded existence, a concept with a more negative connotation than the Western concept of retirement, may persist to give old people a sense of being simply a person marking time until death. Many retired people, especially civil servants, "lapse into depression and even commit suicide. These men have spent their working lives in a conservative, authoritarian world where everything is done by the book."[22] After they retire, contrary to their expectations, society does not appreciate them. They are not wanted even as husbands or fathers.

Social Unrest and Crime

The stereotypical image of the docile, conformist Japanese governed by a sense of social harmony is shattered from time to time. The protest movements of the 1960s and 1970s certainly challenged this stereotypical picture.

Incidences of violent crimes are low in Japan compared to many other countries. One can walk alone in the streets of Tokyo late at night without fear of being molested. Firearms are stringently controlled. For example, in 1983 there were only 66 cases in which murders by handguns were committed, compared to 15,000 in the United States.[23]

Yakuza

A darker side of this image of Japan as a land safe from crime and violence is the existence of an active gangster group known as the *yakuza.* An organized crime group that has been in existence since the pre-Meiji years, the yakuza has been involved in gambling, drugs, petty crimes, prostitution, and extortion in the modern era.

Running houses of prostitution was not made illegal until after the end of World War II, that is, not until 1956. But even after it was made illegal, prostitution continued as a business operation by the yakuza. Those who were forced into the business were not only Japanese women but young women from abroad who were lured to Japan and then forced to engage in prostitution. The yakuza do not hesitate to commit acts of violence against those they deem as their foes. In May 1992 the filmmaker Itami Juzō (1933–1997) was attacked and his face, neck, and hand were slashed repeatedly for making a satirical movie on how to fend off yakuza extortion schemes.

The number of gang members peaked at 184,000 in 1963 but began to drop as the police cracked down on them more strenuously.[24] Recently the yakuza gangs have moved up from engaging in petty crimes to extorting huge sums of money from large business firms. In 1990 the National Police Agency reported that one-third of all Japanese corporations give in to threats from the yakuza and pay extortion money. Business corporations have been known to hire yakuza to silence critics at shareholder meetings. These corporate racketeers, known as *sōkaiya*, receive payoffs. In 1997, exposure of the links to the yakuza caused high officials of Nomura Securities, the biggest stock brokerage, and the Dai-Ichi Kangyō Bank, the second biggest bank, to resign in disgrace.[25]

Yakuza gang leaders have established ties with the political establishment. One ultra-right-wing activist contends that "almost all politicians have relations with the yakuza."[26] For example, in 1963, former premier Kishi put up bail for a Yamaguchi-gumi boss convicted of murder. The yakuza gang played a role in helping Prime Minister Takeshita curb public protests against him in 1991, and they have been instrumental in raising campaign funds for their political allies.[27] In 2007 Ito Itcho (1945–2007), the mayor of Nagasaki, was assassinated by a yakuza member, reportedly because of Ito's criticism of a public works bid involving the Yamaguchi-gumi.[28]

Social Discrimination

Japan's insularity of outlook—an outlook that tends to confine itself to narrow national concerns without taking into account the broader international perspective—has often been an object of criticism by the international community. Although some Japanese stress the need to become more international-minded, the society for the most part remains inward-looking and adheres to an ethnocentric outlook, emphasizing the Japanese people's uniqueness and homogeneity. Antonin Raymond (1888–1976), an American architect who lived in Japan for fifty years, concluded, "The Japanese think—no, they know—that they are a chosen people, more so than the Jews. They are chosen to dominate the world; not dominate physically so much as being above every other nation."[29]

The Japanese propensity toward perceiving things in a hierarchical order inclines them to rank Western nations, especially the United States, at the top in terms of political, economic, and social importance, and the underdeveloped nations lower down the scale. Japan's defeat in the war resulted in a shattering of self-confidence and ushered in the age of uncertainty. But its success economically brought about a "recovery of nerve." The desire to be Number One returned.

However, this recovery of nerve has not resulted in a self-confidence that freely opens the nation of Japan to the world. Americans and Europeans living in Japan express irritation and frustration at the fact that regardless of how long they live in Japan and how well they learn the language, they are ultimately not really accepted in the Japanese community. They remain *gaijin* (outsiders). In fact, if a gaijin becomes too well versed in things Japanese (particularly in the language), the Japanese begin to feel ill at ease with that person. Such a person threatens the faith that only the Japanese can truly understand the Japanese mind and soul. According to Jared Taylor, "Their language is vital to their image of themselves and is an essential ingredient in their sense of uniqueness."[30]

The area most difficult for outsiders to penetrate is that of the traditional arts. One young American who apprenticed with a prominent pottery family was at first regarded as a cute bungler: "But when I got good, I was a threat."[31] Ultimately, he was no longer welcome in the studio and was forced out. Gaijin are discriminated against even in institutions that presumably are more internationally minded. One American professor at a Japanese university asserts that "basic attitudes toward foreign instructors have not changed in 100 years." Foreigners are virtually denied permanent appointments, and business firms seldom hire foreigners for management positions.[32]

The belief in the homogeneity of the Japanese people, a myth believed by most Japanese, was also responsible for their unwillingness to accept refugees such as the Vietnamese fleeing their country in the 1970s following the Communist victory. In the mid-1970s, thousands of Vietnamese were fleeing their land on boats, but only a few hundred were admitted reluctantly by the Japanese when other nations admitted thousands. In 1985 the Japanese government finally agreed to accept 10,000 Vietnamese refugees, but the public did not welcome them with open arms. A public opinion poll taken at that time showed that a majority of the Japanese objected to allowing Vietnamese refugees into Japan. They argued in terms of the need to preserve the homogeneity of the Japanese people. One Japanese critic lamented, "The glorification of homogeneity implies an intolerance of that which is alien."[33]

A foreigner cannot easily become a Japanese citizen even if he or she is born in Japan. As one resident in Japan observed, for instance, "I have found that the Japanese do not tend to think that 'all men are brothers' but that 'all Japanese are brothers.'"[34] A strong sense of "we" and "they" pervades the Japanese mentality. Within the society itself outsiders or strangers are treated as "nonpersons." In years when the range of communication was limited, people outside the province, prefecture, or even the village were regarded as "foreigners." For the most part, then, the Japanese are courteous and polite to acquaintances and people in their own circle but not to outsiders. So when a crowd of people fight to get on the train or subway cars, they push, shove, elbow, and jostle, with little consideration for the convenience of others.

Of course, the clannish, parochial outlook of the Japanese is not unique to them. One longtime student of Japan divides the world into two types: clubs and missions. "France and China, for example, are missions: If you conform, if you learn the language and adopt their customs, the people accept you entirely. . . . Britain and Japan, on the other hand, are clubs: You can be accepted and belong to them as corresponding associates, but you are never really a standing member. . . . In fact, for foreigners it is more difficult socially in England than it is in Japan."[35]

Koreans in Japan

The parochial outlook and sense of hierarchy that governs Japanese thinking lead essentially to a racist mentality. Thus non-Japanese are frequently treated in an inhumane fashion. The Korean residents of Japan, for instance, are still treated as "outsiders" despite the fact that most of them have been born in Japan. Many of their forefathers were brought to Japan against their will and were forced to work in mining and construction projects. Many were drafted to work as laborers in the war zones during World War II.

Tens of thousands of Korean women were forced to serve as "comfort women" for the Japanese troops. Some estimates run as high as 100,000. They were kidnapped by the Japanese police or were led to believe that they were being recruited to work in a factory and then were sent to work in government-run brothels. Many were "broken" by beatings, rapes, and other brutal treatment. Initially the Japanese authorities did not acknowledge that such practices prevailed or insisted that they were volunteers in the war effort. In 1992 the Japanese government officials finally acknowledged the practice when scholars studying public documents were able to verify the fact.[36]

Some of the women, who had remained silent because of a sense of shame and disgrace, began in 1990 to demand that the Japanese government compensate them for their enslavement and filed lawsuits. The Japanese government refused to compensate them until August 1993, when Japanese authorities acknowledged that women from at least six Asian countries were forced into sexual slavery by the Japanese army to perform similar services. Some historians estimate that as many as 200,000 young women from China, Southeast Asia, and the South Pacific were forced to serve in brothels from 1932, following the Japanese takeover of Manchuria, to the end of the Pacific War.

In 1995 the government established the Asian Women's Fund, a privately funded "philanthropic organization" to pay survivors. Private Japanese companies were urged to contribute money, and several did. In 2007 it dissolved after it provided 285 women in the Philippines, South Korea, and Taiwan two million yen (US$17,800) each in compensation, helped set up nursing homes for Indonesian former sex slaves, and offered medical assistance to some 80 Dutch former sex slaves.

In 2007 Japanese American congressman Mike Honda (b. 1941) called on the Japanese government to formally acknowledge, apologize, and accept historical responsibility in "this horrible crime while following the recommendations of the international community with respect to the comfort women." When questioned by the press, then prime minister Abe Shinzo (b. 1954) responded, "The fact is, there is no evidence to prove there was coercion." A month later, after a firestorm of criticism in the international media, Abe apologized for his earlier comments and stated that Japan would abide by the words of Yohei Kono (b. 1937), the chief cabinet secretary of the Japanese government, who said in 1993 that Japan "sincerely apologizes and expresses its remorse to all those, irrespective of place of origin, who suffered immeasurable pain and incurable psychological wounds."[37]

During the war, between 1940 and 1945, about 1 million Koreans were brought to Japan to work as virtual slaves; at the end of the war there were close to 2.4 million Koreans in Japan proper. It is estimated that as many as 240,000 Koreans were conscripted to serve in the army or work as civilian laborers on military bases overseas. Many managed to return to Korea, but in the 1990s there were 700,000 Koreans residing in Japan. Of these Koreans who were forced to serve the Japanese forces, 43,000 were sent to Sakhalin Island, which was then under Japanese control. In the 1980s they and their offspring, numbering 60,000 or so, still remained there, unable or unwilling to return to their homeland.[38]

The Koreans in Japan are not accepted as part of the "homogeneous" Japanese nation and continue to suffer discrimination socially, economically, and politically. A Korean born in Japan does not automatically become a Japanese citizen but must adopt a Japanese name and then undergo the process of naturalization. Until 1992, Koreans were required to be fingerprinted even if they were born in Japan.

This did not mean, of course, that the numerous obstacles that beset Koreans and other non-Japanese residents were eliminated. There is virtually no intermarriage between the Japanese and the Koreans, and if a Korean manages to get a job with a business firm by adopting a Japanese name, he is likely to be fired as soon as his identity is revealed. In general, Koreans are paid 30 percent less than Japanese for comparable jobs. Also, non-Japanese are barred from holding government jobs. In 1991, because of a shortage of workers, the Osaka municipal government sought to drop the nationality clause that bars foreign nationals from holding certain municipal jobs. There were about 110,000 Koreans in Osaka, and the aim was to employ them in these jobs. The Osaka city government had to abandon its plan because the Ministry of Home Affairs of the central government, still adhering to rigid bureaucratic rules, objected.[39]

About 100,000 Koreans were living in the two cities of Hiroshima and Nagasaki (many were brought there from their homeland to work as forced laborers) when the atomic bombs were dropped on those cities. About 20,000 Koreans in Hiroshima and 2,000 in Nagasaki were killed in the atomic bombings. In other words, one in seven who died in Hiroshima were Koreans. But the Koreans' request that a monument commemorating the Korean dead be erected in the Peace Park was denied for half a century because officials claimed there was no room. Moreover, until 1978, the Japanese government did not extend the kind of medical care for Korean A-bomb victims that it provided for Japanese victims.

One longtime American resident of Japan noted,

No minority in the world (no minority that I know anything about) is treated more badly by a majority than the Koreans and the Chinese by the Japanese. And it makes the black-white thing in America look like kindergarten in some ways because it is so pervasive and so insidious and it's an absolute blanket condemnation.[40]

In 1999 there were about 137,000 Chinese residents in Japan, who suffered legal and social discrimination similar to what the Koreans endure.

Ainu

An indigenous people who have experienced years of discrimination—since the Yamato era, in fact—are the Ainu. They were eventually driven out of their homeland and compelled to settle in Japan's northernmost major island, Hokkaido. During the Tokugawa period a northern feudal lord extended his authority into Hokkaido and deprived the Ainu of their economic rights, reducing them to semi-slavery status. The Meiji government brought Hokkaido under its administrative control and deprived the Ainu of their land and fishing and hunting rights. Then to "Japanize" the Ainu, the government banned traditional Ainu practices and compelled Ainu children to learn Japanese and forsake their native language. Today the Ainu number about 50,000 people. They have been fighting an uphill battle to gain recognition of their rights, such as fishing rights and use of Ainu language in instruction in their schools. In March 1997 the Ainu were recognized by a Japanese court as an indigenous and minority people. Izutsu Katsunobu (b. 1969) and a group of Japanese scholars at Hokkaido University of Education published the first comprehensive Ainu language dictionary in 2003.

The Okinawans

Another island people who had been regarded as outsiders are the Okinawans, residents of the Ryukyu Islands. Historically China regarded the island as being under its territorial sovereignty and collected tributes from the islanders, but the Ryukyuans considered themselves an independent nation with their own king. In the Tokugawa era the lord of Satsuma (the southern province of Kyushu) conquered the northernmost islands and held them as his feudal domain. The rest of the Ryukyu Islands were ruled by a king as an independent nation. When Western nations approached in the early nineteenth century, the king signed treaties with them. The United States, represented by Commodore Perry, signed a treaty with the Ryukyu nation in 1854.

Following the establishment of the Meiji government, Japanese officials asserted Japan's claim over the Ryukyu Islands. After bickering with China over both nations' territorial claim over the islands, Japan forcibly incorporated the islands under its administrative system as Okinawa prefecture in 1879, despite China's protestation. The people of Okinawa considered themselves to possess their own culture and history, whereas the Japanese tended to regard Okinawans as being on the fringes of "real" Japan. In the nationalistic 1930s, the Japanese government forced the Okinawans to replace their dialect with standard Japanese.

Recent Immigrants

Restrictions on allowing immigrants to enter Japan have been stringent, but recently the labor shortage has led the government to admit more people from Southeast Asia and South Asia into the country to engage in menial and back-breaking work that many Japanese young people are not willing to undertake. In addition, there has been an increase in the number of illegal immigrants. Immigrants are often subjected to a host of abuses and unfair treatment. As noted earlier, many women have been induced by yakuza gangs to come to Japan from other Asian nations with promises of attractive jobs and then are frequently compelled to work as hostesses in bars or as prostitutes.

A recent phenomenon, which is somewhat inexplicable in light of the Japanese bias against interracial marriages, is the importing of young women from Southeast Asia and South Asia to marry young farmers in rural areas because young Japanese women refuse to marry farmers in out-of-the-way villages, preferring to seek their fortune in more glamorous urban centers like Tokyo. If this practice of interracial marriage continues and becomes more widespread, perhaps the narrow ethnocentrism that prevails in Japan might gradually change, and a more cosmopolitan outlook might emerge.

Currently, however, discrimination against "non-Japanese" persists. It is virtually impossible for foreigners to gain Japanese citizenship. Until 1992, non-Japanese were fingerprinted, and in the courts foreigners, especially Asian foreigners, were treated more harshly than Japanese.

The Burakumin

Despite public denial of discrimination by business and political leaders, discrimination against the *burakumin,* who are indigenous Japanese, continues. There may be 2 million to 3 million people who fall in this category. An uphill struggle against discrimination is being carried on by the Buraku Liberation League with only limited resources. In the discrimination against the burakumin, the "we-they" mentality spreads its insidious influence in the job market, social relations, and marital arrangements.

As previously noted, discrimination against the "outcaste" burakumin was firmly entrenched in the Tokugawa era. With the founding of the Meiji government the legal class distinctions were eliminated in 1871, and the outcaste people were in theory accorded legal equality. But they were classified as "new commoners" in the family register so employers and schools could easily identify them as outcastes; in any application for jobs or school admissions the applicant had to submit a copy of his or her family register. Social and economic discrimination continued without any improvement in outcaste status. Job discrimination persisted, even in factory or office jobs, so they remained impoverished. Nonburakumin avoided intermarriage with burakumin, and they were compelled to continue living in ghetto-like districts. In the Taishō period (1912–1926), outcaste members sought to fight for their rights and organized the Suiheisha (the Levelers Association), but they failed to make headway, especially with the upsurge of nationalism and militarism in the 1930s.

After the end of World War II, the practice of identifying outcaste members as "new commoners" was dropped. According to the new constitution, equality was to be accorded to all Japanese, but discrimination persisted. Unofficial estimates indicate that there are as many as 6,000 burakumin districts, with a total population of 3 million. The practice of tracking down the background of job applicants and marriage candidates to ascertain if they are or not members of the buraku community continues. "There are even computer data-banks with lists of burakumin names so people can investigate prospective employees and spouses."[41]

A burakumin educator visiting the United States in 1991 reported, "We face discrimination at work, in school, and in marriage. . . . We are ten times more likely to be on welfare than the general population. We are twice as prone to illness. Half of all burakumin live in public housing. . . . Our children drop out of school at a high rate. As a people we have been vilified, shunned and segregated."[42]

The average buraku family income is only about 60 percent of the national average. Those who are successful in the entertainment or business world conceal their burakumin background. "The only visibly wealthy *buraku* people are gangsters, one of the few professions which does not seem to discriminate. The pre-eminence of *buraku* people within the *yakuza* . . . does little to improve the minority's image."[43]

Those who have sought to "pass" live in constant fear of being exposed. About thirty such people commit suicide every year. Most of them are women rejected by their fiancés after their burakumin status is uncovered.

The Urban Poor

As Japan's economy grew and the nation emerged as a world economic power, the standard of living of the population in general improved and the entire nation seemed to be wallowing in luxury and conspicuous consumption, but pockets of poverty, the homeless, could be found in the major cities. They tend to escape the attention of the media and society at large, but occasionally they come to the surface. In early 1994 a deceased homeless person's diary recording his daily struggle in Tokyo was discovered. His story hit the airwaves, but rather than making sure that such people would be taken care of so that they would not die in the streets, the Tokyo authorities cleared the street where he died to make sure that others would not find refuge there. The tendency to pretend that the homeless, beggars, and vagrants do not exist still seems to prevail in Japan.

Among the "festering sores" are the districts of San'ya in Tokyo and Kamagasaki in Osaka. San'ya in Tokyo is a half-mile-square area. It became the center of the homeless and poor after the war when SCAP designated it as a temporary dwelling zone for those who had lost their homes because of air raids and other ravages of war. Since then the homeless, the unemployed, the down and out, and the poor have found refuge there. Many are aging and are "ravaged by diseases, including tuberculosis and cirrhosis, and mental disorders."[44] Subcontractors come here to hire day workers for construction and public works. In the mid-1990s, every morning as many as 10,000 laborers lined up hoping to be hired for the day.[45]

Many homeless people sleep in underground passages of Tokyo's rail and subway stations. One reporter toured these areas after midnight and found hundreds of homeless people, many sleeping in cardboard boxes. Police come along and sweep away the boxes they sleep in and drive the homeless away, turning them into vagrants. There are also similar homeless people struggling to survive in other major cities.

The Status of Women

The 1946 constitution embodied the principle of equality between the sexes. Article 14 states, "All of the people are equal under the law and there shall be no discrimination in political, economic or social relations, because of race, creed, sex, social status or family origin." Article 24 reads,

> Marriage shall be based only on the mutual consent of both sexes and it shall be maintained through mutual cooperation with the equal rights of husband and wife as a basis. With regard to choice of spouse, property rights, inheritance, choice of domicile, divorce and other matters pertaining to marriage and the family, laws shall be enacted from the standpoint of individual dignity and the essential equality of the sexes.

Although the constitution and reforms introduced by SCAP strengthened the legal rights of women, their social, political, and economic condition improved very slowly.

In terms of jobs that women are most likely to be engaged in, the vast majority are office workers or workers in service industries. Very few are in career-track positions. Very few are in career-administrative tracks. Women comprise a large number of part-time workers or temporary workers.[46]

Discrimination against women is most glaringly evident in the corporate world. According to Jared Taylor, "The male supremacy that lurks in the background on campus is a sacred institution at the office, and women soon learn their place."[47] Indeed, it remained well nigh impossible for women to get on the track that leads to higher executive positions, although by the 1980s some women had managed to gain administrative positions. But most female college graduates are hired as an "O.L." (office lady) and are expected to serve tea to their male office staff colleagues and do errands for them. A woman who became the first bureau chief of the state radio broadcasting system in 1991 recalled that when she started out at the NHK, "My first job of the day was to wash the glasses left by male reporters."[48]

Even well-educated, well-trained women are regarded as temporary workers who will, or are expected to, leave their jobs as soon as they get married. Thus, whereas men are given positions of responsibility, women are assigned clerical support jobs. The emergence of women in administrative or executive positions has occurred at a snail's pace. In the 1980s, when the economy was booming and the need for well-educated, highly trained workers increased, women began to make some gains, and more women college graduates began to be hired by corporations.

In May 1985 the Diet passed the Equal Employment Opportunity Law (enacted in 1986), prohibiting discrimination in the job market on the basis of gender, but women's groups were unhappy that the bill had no provisions to penalize companies that fail to comply with the law. The director of the Federation of Employers' Association decried the bill, saying that it would undermine the lifetime employment system because women will marry and quit their jobs. Others were convinced that the resolutely male-oriented society will pay little heed to the law. In 1999, amendments were passed by the Diet to promote gender equality and strengthen the equal opportunity law, but critics contend that many companies still maintain a "separate track personnel management system."

Together with the economic boom of the 1980s, the 1986 law may have contributed to the employment of more women in managerial track positions. In 1986, 2.6 percent of middle management positions were held by women. By 1993 it had edged up to 3.6 percent. In mid-1999, a survey indicated that 9.3 percent of corporate executives in Japan were women, compared to 44.3 percent in the United States. Japanese banks have been especially slow to entrust key positions to women. In 1993 less than 1 percent of branch bank managers were women. Pay for women has been low compared to male employees.[49]

The economic slowdown of the early 1990s adversely affected the situation when opportunities for women seemed to be on the upswing. A Labor Ministry survey of 1,000 companies in 1993 revealed that more than half the companies indicated plans to cut back on hiring women so they could keep on hiring male students because they generally remain longer with the company and virtually make no demands for child-care leaves.[50] Also with the economic slowdown companies began to lay off part-time workers, most of whom were women. Prior to the law of 1986, many Japanese firms made it clear that they would not consider applications from women college graduates. The director of the Japanese Federation of Employers' Association justified the policy of preventing women from entering the executive track by saying that "generally, women lack loyalty to the groups to which they belong. They are extremely egotistical and individualistic."[51]

Historically a large number of women have been employed in factories. Since the Meiji period young women workers labored in textile mills, silk filatures, and small plants. In 1914, 86 percent of all women workers were laboring in textile mills. Fewer women were employed in heavy industrial plants, but in recent years, as mechanization and computers were introduced in the factories, more women have come to be employed in the industrial labor force. In 1990, 37.9 percent of workers in major industries were women.[52] Taking into account the labor output by housewives working on household affairs and family farms, women easily contribute 50 percent of Japan's labor output. During the period of high-speed economic growth from 1965 to 1975, more women left the family household to take part-time and full-time jobs. The fact that housework became less time-consuming with the widespread use of electrical and mechanical home appliances made it possible for more housewives to take advantage of job opportunities that opened up during the boom years of the 1960s and 1970s. In the 1980s, 90 percent of part-time workers were housewives.[53] Business companies preferred to hire temporary women workers because they could pay them low wages and drop them from the workforce when their labor was not needed. They did not have the encumbrance of life-time employment.

In conducting business negotiations, foreign businessmen are warned not to include women in the negotiating group. As one American who was sent to Japan to do business in the early 1980s remarked, "Would you send a black to do business in South Africa, or a Jew to work in Saudi Arabia? They would actually be better off than a woman in Japan. If a company sends a woman to Tokyo, it is setting her up for failure and frustration."[54] But this may not always be the case. Women negotiators for the office of the United States Trade Representative found that being a woman negotiator often proved to work in their favor because the Japanese negotiators "may be thrown off balance . . . and feel extremely uncomfortable with female negotiators."[55]

The government's record is no better than business firms in providing equal job opportunities for women, even though it has the responsibility for reducing discrimination. There are few women in the upper ranks of the central government. Not until 1989 was a woman, Moriyama Mayumi (b. 1927), appointed to a cabinet position as chief cabinet secretary, equivalent to the U.S. president's chief of staff; she was removed from her post in the cabinet reshuffling in late 1990. At the same time another woman was appointed state minister to serve as director general of the Agency for Science and Technology. In 1991, Moriyama observed, "In the past five or six years, women's rights and the growing role of women in Japan have been the biggest change . . . and will continue to be. . . . But in Japan politics is the last bastion of men, and women now are beginning to enter that world too."[56] In 1993, Prime Minister Hosokawa appointed three women to his cabinet. As noted earlier, in 1989, a woman, Doi Takako, was chosen to head the Social Democratic Party, the first women to head a major political party.

Women have not made many inroads in the Diet either, especially in the more powerful lower house. In the 1946 election, the first since women were granted the franchise, thirty-nine women won seats in the Diet, but the number dropped drastically after that. In most elections the number of seats won by women hovered below ten; only occasionally was it above ten. In 1996, women won 23 of the 500 lower house seats. But by December 2004 the number of women elected to both houses of the Diet had risen again to numbers just below those of 1946. At the local level, women made significant progress. In the April 1999 local elections, women won 1,081 out of 11,552 seats in mayoral and city chamber elections nationwide.[57]

No woman gained the governorship in prefectural elections until the year 2000. That February, a woman won the Osaka governor's election, and that April a woman won the governorship of Kumamoto prefecture. Thus, inroads were being made in this sector of the political arena also.

The situation in the academic community has not been much better. In 1980 there was only one woman professor at the University of Tokyo. Because education for women is often regarded as a superfluous ornament, the best universities still cater predominantly to male students. By 1992 more female high school graduates (40.8 percent) went on to college (whereas 37.0 percent of men did so), but a large percentage of those graduates entered junior college. In the early 1980s only 22 percent of the four-year college students were women, whereas 88 percent of junior college students were women.

Only a small number of women are in professional fields. In 1983, 6.4 percent of scientists, 2.4 percent of engineers, and 9.3 percent of lawyers were women. In 1990 women made up only 6.1 percent of Japan's lawyers and 2.9 percent of certified public accountants. But there are indications that the number of women in the professional fields has been rising. In 1979 there were 14,000 women engineers; in 1990, there were 62,000.[58]

Women's place is in the home, many Japanese men (and many women) would argue. Every woman should stay home and take care of her husband so that he can go out and do a good job. One union leader contended that he fights for higher wages for men so that the wives can stay home and not have to take part-time jobs to supplement the family income.[59] Women have been conditioned to believe that they must marry and become keepers of the house. A typical young woman will go to junior college or technical school and learn to do office work. When she marries she gives up her job and takes on the task of keeping things running smoothly for her husband, taking charge of their home. With this system, economic security, social and familial harmony, and personal stability are all woven together.

Some surveys indicate that most women are content with their role as housewives, although the younger generation tends to be less satisfied. And those who believe that women need not marry and become housewives have been increasing. In a 1990 survey 52 percent said that it was acceptable for women not to marry. Both men and women are marrying at a later age. The belief that women should stop working after they marry is also weakening. In 1990, 60 percent of women left their jobs to get married, but many returned to the workplace after their children grew up.

There are indications that wives are happy to have the husband spend as little time as possible at home, where he would otherwise get underfoot. The wife takes charge of household affairs, the family finances, and the children's upbringing and education. Men spend little time at home; they work until late at night and spend their weekends on the golf course. Some observers contend that the housewives are content because they have full authority at home, but everyone understands that the ultimate authority rests with the husband. If a husband was having an affair with another woman, a marriage counselor would be likely to advise the wife, "For the sake of your baby's happiness you should hold on and try to win back the heart of your husband. Treat him more kindly. Perhaps you could set out the table more beautifully for him and take more care of him."[60] The traditional ideal wife, the *yamato nadeshiko* (small pink flower), has been depicted by a popular film star who has played the role of the perfect wife: "gentle on the surface, supportive of her man to the last." She is the counterpart of women in the samurai age; she "takes care of the home while her man fights hard in the outside world."[61] But such attitudes are changing among contemporary Japanese women, especially the young.

As noted earlier, the constitution provides for equal rights for women, and the 1979 civil code reform increased the wife's share of inheritance from one-third to one-half. Upon marriage the wife is usually registered in the family register under the husband's family name. Employers usually insist that women employees, even professional women, use their husband's family name in their work. Some women have been fighting to use their own family name and are seeking to change the law to retain their maiden surname in the family register.

Given the better education and rising consciousness of younger women, the movement to enhance women's rights has been gaining some force. The current generation is less inclined to be content with egotistical husbands. "Men want servants and slaves," they charge; and even though divorced women are treated as failures with flawed personalities, more women are leaving their husbands. The majority of the divorces were initiated by the wives, unlike in earlier years, indicating their unwillingness to endure their husbands' infidelities like their predecessors. It is also an indication of the growing sense of individualism among women. Under the postwar legal reforms the wife now has gained the right of child custody. In 1990, in 71.4 percent of the divorce cases, the wife got custody. But even today the children of divorced parents remain registered in the husband's family register. The plight of the young wife has become less stressful in many cases, specifically because the former practice whereby three generations lived under one roof is now less common and the nuclear family is more prevalent.[62]

Abortion was made legal in 1949. A 1983 survey indicated that 500,000 abortions, or one for every three births, were performed that year. Two out of three women had at least one abortion. Perhaps the number of abortions remained high because the government did not approve the use of birth control pills until the 1980s. Abortions plus other methods of birth control reduced the birth rate significantly.[63] As a result the government is proposing a program of subsidies for each preschool child. This has led some women's organizations to protest the government's plan because, they say, it is reminiscent of the prewar government's program that honored families with eight children or more.

As the average number of children per family has declined, the burden of child care has lessened. And with modern household appliances at her disposal, the average housewife has more leisure time than her prewar counterpart. Thus, she has more time to devote to the supervision of her children—especially her sons' education. The prewar practice of arranged marriages has also become less common, although a fairly high percentage of marriages are still arranged by parents.

In 2001 a controversy arose when Masako, the Crown Princess (b. 1963), gave birth to a girl. Since all the other children born into the imperial family for over forty years are female, heated arguments sprang up in the Diet when some members suggested a constitutional amendment to allow women into the imperial line of succession. The controversy subsided somewhat when Princess Kiko, the wife of the second son of the emperor, gave birth to a boy in 2006, who then became third in line of succession. All of this controversy was made ironic when several newspaper editorials reminded their readers that Japan had at least eight (ten if one counts the nearly mythical third-century sovereigns Himiko and Iyo) female emperors in its history, all descending from Japan's divine ancestor the Sun Goddess Amaterasu.

EDUCATION

As noted earlier, under SCAP in the immediate postwar years the American authorities sought to decentralize the educational system and weaken the Ministry of Education's near total control over the education system. They set out to foster democracy and academic freedom and provide the students with a chance to develop their personality and individuality.

After the end of the occupation some prewar attitudes began to emerge. Critics of local control contended that educational policy got embroiled in ideological squabbles as the teachers union came to be dominated by Marxist ideologues. Financial exigencies also led local boards to turn to prefecture governments for support, and the latter were closely linked to the central government. As a result the process of centralization gained force, and the Ministry of Education—which has control over the bulk of the finances and authority over the prefecture superintendents of schools—weakened the concept of local control introduced by SCAP. In 1956 elected school boards were replaced by board members appointed by governors and mayors in committees to oversee educational programs in the prefectures.

The ministry regained the authority to determine the nature of the curriculum of the elementary schools and junior and senior high schools. It now provides each local board of education an approved list of textbooks from which the latter can select titles for use in its schools. The ministry accredits all textbooks in the public schools, specifies the subjects to be taught, and regulates the curriculum stringently. It reintroduced morals instruction, Japanese history, geography, and Chinese literary-style texts that had been dropped by SCAP.

The ministry did not accept any input from the teachers in the school system. The thinking of the ministry bureaucrats is seen in the words of one official who asserted, when some teachers expressed an interest in having a say in the formulation of the curriculum, "The curriculum is none of their business."[64]

The teachers, then, do not have any flexibility regarding what they teach or how they teach the subject. All the students are to be taught the same subject at the same rate, regardless of differences in ability or interest. This practice is justified by the authorities by an appeal to the principle of equality. If the teachers group students according to their abilities, the defenders of the system contend, they will get in trouble because parents don't want their children labeled "slow learners."[65]

The return of centralized control over the school system reflects conservative government leaders' reaction to the growing political activism of the teachers union. The union became increasingly militant in opposing the government's foreign policy after the official end of US occupation. It followed the political line of the left-wing Socialist and Communist parties, and the Marxist-leaning Sōhyō (General Council of Trade Unions of Japan), which were critical of the government's adherence to the US Cold War anti-Communist power stance.

In certifying textbooks, ministry officials are disinclined to include controversial subjects and apt to play down Japan's wartime activities. Chinese authorities became upset when the Ministry of Education sought to change the phrase "invasion of China" to "advance into China." The ministry's policy tends to keep schoolchildren ill informed about World War II. A recent newspaper article quoted a high school teacher who said his students were surprised to learn that there had been a war with the United States. The first thing they wanted to know was who won the war.[66]

Professor Ienaga Saburō (1913–2002), whose textbook was rejected for certification, challenged the constitutionality of the government's practice of certification in 1965. The Ministry of Education had asked Ienaga to rewrite portions of his high school history textbooks. For example, he was asked to revise his account of the Nanjing massacre of 1937, that is, the atrocities committed by the Japanese troops, as well as his account of the Japanese army's use of thousands of Chinese individuals for human experiments.[67]

In the 1960s, as the era of high-speed economic growth commenced and people became "economic animals" more interested in personal economic issues, public support for militant political activism tended to abate, and membership in the teachers union also began to drop. In Gifu prefecture, membership in the union dropped from 12,000 in 1959 to 2,000 by 1964.

Nature and Quality of Japanese Education

The belief in the importance of education and the need to concentrate on the learning process from kindergarten years until one entered college remains strongly embedded in the minds of Japanese parents and children. There is no stinting when it comes to education.

Japanese students attend school 5.5 days a week and 240 days a year, compared to 180 days in the United States. In 1992 the government decided to reduce the number of days schoolchildren are required to attend classes on

Saturday (when students attend class a half a day) and decreed that schools should close one Saturday each month. The period of compulsory education was extended to nine years by SCAP, so youngsters now attend three years more than children did in the prewar years. The number of those who continue on to high school has steadily increased.[68] By 1990 the percentage of female students exceeded the percentage of male students continuing on to college (though, as noted earlier, many were enrolled in junior colleges). As economic growth became the goal of the society, more high school graduates began to enroll in technical schools.[69]

Although the number of students going on to institutions of higher learning steadily increased, the phenomenon of young people turning away from school also began to increase. Between 1975 and 1988, the number of Japanese young who refused to go to school had quadrupled.[70] Some observers ascribe this change to a less conformist tendency developing among the young people, whereas others decry this tendency as "a change in personality of youths toward immature, self-centered persons who are languid and unemotional." Others blame excessive emphasis on cramming to pass entrance exams to enter prestigious institutions for the growing dropout rates and misconduct by students.[71]

For many students, the goal of education has not been learning for the sake of learning but entry into elite schools and upward mobility in the social, economic, and political hierarchy. The ambition of some upwardly mobile middle-class parents is to get their children, especially their sons, into the right kindergarten and then into the elite schools until they reach the cream of the elite universities, preferably the University of Tokyo, which virtually guarantees entry into the bureaucracy or elite private companies. To get into the right school from one level to the next requires almost incessant cramming if the entrance examinations are to be passed. Thus students from most middle-class and upper-class families are sent to the *juku* (cram schools) after classes in the regular school are over. The process starts during kindergarten. Jared Taylor, who started his education in a school in Japan, wrote in 1983, "In Japan there are many high-powered kindergartens that have competitive entrance examinations. The rat race starts at age five. Some kindergartens have such a backlog of applicants that only a few children have a chance to even take the exam, much less be admitted. For the very best in preschool education, parents are advised to put in an application for their child as soon as he is born."[72]

In 1992 close to 4.4 million students were enrolled in 50,000 to 60,000 juku.[73] Some parents send pre-kindergarten children to a cram school. One of the most prestigious cram schools is for two- and three-year-olds. The jukus are expensive, so only the wealthy can afford to send their children to them. The job of most mothers in these families is to see to it that their sons prepare night and day so that they will stay on the right track. Indeed, some "education mamas" put their sons through "education hell." It is common for school children to start their day at 6 AM and go on until midnight. A teacher who is critical of the juku system says, "Jukus are raising a generation of kids who can only pass entrance exams. But the most important educational purpose is giving children the ability to live in society. That's being left out."[74]

Because education below the college level is geared toward training students to pass the next series of entrance examinations, memorization of facts and information is vital. Thus, rote memory rather than analysis or creative thinking is emphasized. Mastering what is known rather than creative thinking is what takes place in the schools. Deviation from the standardized course of study prescribed by the Ministry of Education is discouraged. Students are not encouraged to come up with innovative or creative ideas. In fact, they are discouraged from doing so. There is only one right way to solve a given problem. One teacher noted, "There may be thirty-six ways to solve a mathematics problem, but we don't have time to let them see more than one. So we produce children who can solve every problem with one method."[75] Jared Taylor recalled, "My brother, who went to the same school [as I did] and was always good at math, once amused himself by solving test problems in imaginative ways of his own devising. He never did it again. His answers were right, but his methods were wrong, so he lost credit for the problems. The way we arrived at the solution was as important as the right answer."[76]

Benjamin Duke, an American scholar who has studied the Japanese educational system, concludes that "What is absent in far too many Japanese classrooms is the searching and probing for the spark of creativity, innovativeness, and originality. Too few Japanese teachers recognize, stimulate, and reward the creative response, the imaginative thought, the original idea that may deviate from the planned lesson."[77]

Teachers who attempt innovative teachings of their own are likely to get in trouble: for example, two high school social studies teachers in Fukuoka prefecture "who carried on education of their own contrivance in order to cultivate the students' independent and critical thinking were fired by the Education Board."[78] The teacher's job, then, is to teach from approved textbooks and instill in the students information and knowledge that will help them to pass entrance examinations and enable them to get into "name" schools. And the students' job is to listen and learn what they are told. "The teacher conveys knowledge, the students accept knowledge. That's it."[79]

The school system, then, instills in the students the age-old principle of emulating their masters—doing as they are told by their teachers. A student who deviates from the orthodox way of doing things is deviating from the group. This kind of education may produce more expert technicians than creative thinkers. Ezaki Reona (b. 1925), who won the Nobel Prize in physics in 1973, asserted that Japanese society was not conducive to originality. A dozen years before he won the Nobel Prize, Ezaki left Japan for the United States to engage in research at IBM's research center. He observed that in Japan the best college graduates go into manufacturing, the next best into product development, and the rest into research. In the United States it is the other way around. He also said, "Americans are motivated to make the unknown known. The Japanese are highly motivated to make the known work and function better."[80] This undoubtedly accounts for the Japanese success in adopting and improving discoveries and inventions made by other nations.

Some observers believe that the Japanese educational system is designed to serve specific objectives—in particular, the long-range interests of the economy and the nation by developing academically and technically competent blue- and white-collar workers and a stable, orderly, and harmonious society. The object of education from the Meiji era to today has been to produce capable and willing workers for the nation's offices and factories. Benjamin Duke contends that the Japanese workers' attitude is formed in the schools: cooperation with the group (group training starts in the first grade), emphasis on harmony in the group, and loyalty to the group. The stress is on perseverance, endurance, trying hard, and the spirit of *gambare* (doing one's best).[81]

Japanese leaders have slowly come to the conclusion that excessive emphasis on memorization in the school system is not conducive to creative thinking. In 1984 a council on educational reform was appointed by the prime minister. In its report submitted in 1987 it emphasized the need to take into consideration students' individuality and needs, and to foster independent thinking. It called for more flexibility in the curriculum. The council also criticized both the tradition of relating the student's ability with the kind of college he or she attends and the assumption that products of prestigious colleges are, ipso facto, first-rate minds.

The Japanese educational system, some observers believe, is not preparing the students for the high-tech information age. "With its strict emphasis on uniformity and single-minded focus on the preparation of students for standardized testing, the post-war educational system has spawned two generations of diligent, highly literate workers. It has also quashed independent thinking and given graduates few of the analytical skills necessary to excel in knowledge-based industry."[82] The need to produce students prepared to meet the needs of knowledge-intensive technologies is not being met.

There is some evidence, however, that Japan's school system does not inhibit analytical and creative thinking as extensively as some critics believe. In 1970, when a UN-sponsored group administered identical tests to schoolchildren ten and fourteen years of age in nineteen countries, Japanese students received the highest scores in both age groups. Equally important, the tests did not screen for facts and information alone but required understanding and application of the information the students possessed.

Discipline in the Schools

Despite the post–World War II liberalization of the educational system, the age-old practice of enforcing rules rigidly and instituting Spartan discipline among the students still prevails. A host of rules are imposed on the students, ranging from rigid dress codes, to the color of the bicycles the students may ride to school, to strict enforcement of school hours. This occasionally results in tragedy. In 1990 a young girl was crushed to death when a teacher lowered a heavy metal gate as some students were trying to rush into the school compound at the last minute. Administering corporal punishments remains a common practice. Sometimes excessively harsh measures are resorted to, such as beating with a board or kicking students for minor infractions of school regulations.

In 1980 the head of a sailing school designed to rehabilitate autistic children beat an autistic student to death, and in 1982, he committed a similar act of "involuntary manslaughter." The defense lawyers argued that the principal should be acquitted because corporal punishment is indispensable in treating autistic children, and corporal punishment is legal. They contended that the school had de facto authorization to punish the children.[83] In 1991 two students in a private school died of heat and asphyxiation when they were locked in a suffocating hot shed for forty-five hours by the principal for violating the school's no-smoking rule. Numerous cases in which students were physically injured by harsh punishments have been reported. The *Asahi* newspaper reported that in junior high schools in Aichi prefecture, corporal punishment was being practiced almost on a daily basis in the late 1980s. One Japanese critic of Japanese society observed, "The old military spirit of Spartan discipline and rules is alive and well today in sports and in schools."[84]

In addition, there are accounts of some students in Japan who have resorted to beating up teachers. In 1983 there were 2,125 incidents of violence in private and public schools and 929 cases in which students assaulted teachers. The number of public junior and senior high schools where general acts of violence occurred in 1982 came to 1,803. In 1990 the number was 1,685. In January 1993 a lower-class junior high student was killed by bullying students in Yamagata prefecture.[85]

After all the cramming and continuous work before entering college, once the Japanese young person enters, his or her studying virtually comes to a standstill. One student remarked, "We work so hard to get into college, and when we get out, we can expect a life without any vacations . . . so we want a four year moratorium."[86] And the professors don't expect students to study either. Class attendance is not taken, and the professor himself may cut class as often as he pleases. At the end of the class term, students cram by reading the professor's books and lecture notes (taken and sold by enterprising students) and take the final exam.

An American professor who taught several years at major Japanese universities as a visiting professor in the 1980s listed the following characteristics of the Japanese university system: student class attendance of 10 percent to 35 percent is common, except for mandatory-attendance courses, primarily in languages; the rate of class cancellations by professors is 10 percent to 50 percent, with the latter more common in highly rated national universities; 90 percent of the grades are As or Bs (as in some American institutions of higher learning); midterm grades are substituted for final grades if the student misses or cuts the final exam; and widespread cheating occurs on in-class examinations.[87]

An American woman student slaved away to pass the entrance exam to enter Tokyo University to pursue graduate studies. She passed the exam and was admitted. She recalled, "Once I was, my reaction was, 'My God, is this all it is? Is this what people are killing themselves for?' An American graduate school would have given me an education that was ten times better." All she had to do for her class work was just show up, period. She attended a class taught by a famous professor. He turned the class over to a student to speak on any subject he liked. "The famous professor slept through every class. He might as well have been a piece of furniture."[88] If anything, she remarked, undergraduate school at Tokyo University is worse.

The students are aware that what the potential employer looks for is the prestige of the school and participation in extracurricular activities. "Students from top-ranked universities (such as Tokyo, Waseda, and Keio) are granted almost automatic admission to the top levels of the country's legal, governmental, scientific, and business echelons."[89]

Student Activism of the 1950s, 1960s, and early 1970s

Since hitting the books does not take all the students' time, if social or political issues arouse their interest they have all the time and freedom they need to engage in protest demonstrations. And that came to characterize college life for many students, especially students attending colleges and universities in Tokyo in the 1950s and 1960s. Political activism among college students was triggered by the anti-American, antiestablishment activities initiated by Communist and Socialist leaders. The students were influenced most extensively by the Communists. In 1948 the Communist Party organized a national student organization, the Zengakuren (National Federation of Student Self-Government

Associations). All major universities were represented in this organization, and it took the leadership in protesting and demonstrating against the government and what the Communist Party regarded as its pro-American, anti-Communist policies. The Zengakuren played a key role in rallying public opinion against the mutual security treaty. Opposition to the Vietnam War provided members with an issue to arouse anti-American, anticapitalist fervor. Then they turned their rapiers against the "feudalistic" university system.

Japanese universities, the student radicals complained, are run by professors at the top of the hierarchical pyramid as their personal fiefdom. They may mouth liberal ideas, but they behave like autocratic feudal barons who jealously guard their privileged bailiwicks. Student demonstrations started with protests against tuition increases in the mid-1960s in a number of Tokyo universities. All in all, 115 universities were confronted with student protests, demonstrations, and riots in 1968. Massive strikes were staged, barricades were built, and key buildings were occupied. Often professors were given the hotbox treatment and subjected to kangaroo courts run by militant students, who yelled and screamed at them to confess their sins.

After student attacks on the universities abated, student activists turned their attention to other issues. They protested and demonstrated against American actions in the Vietnam War as well as the entry of the US aircraft carrier *Enterprise* into Japanese waters because it had nuclear weapons on board. They also supported the farmers' protestation and obstruction of the construction of the Narita airport. In 1970 the student radicals protested the renewal of the mutual security pact and threw Molotov cocktails at the police. In opposing the construction of the Narita airport, 25,000 people demonstrated and engaged in violent clashes with the police. Firebombs were thrown over arguments concerning the reversion of Okinawa to Japan. A bomb mailed to the home of a Tokyo district police chief resulted in the death of the chief's wife and serious injury to his son. In 1972 three radical Japanese youths joined the Palestine Liberation Organization, went to the Tel Aviv Airport, and fired automatic handguns, indiscriminately killing twenty-six people.

This frenzy of violence and activism peaked in the early 1970s as the era of high-speed economic growth began to turn most students into "economic animals." Most of them eventually settled down to the routine of completing their education and joining the suit-and-tie contingent of the prim and proper business world.

Notes

1. The crude death rate dropped from 14.6 per thousand in 1947 to 6.2 in 1987 and edged up somewhat since then to 6.9 in 1995. The infant mortality rate, which was 124.2 per

thousand live births in 1930–1934, was 13.1 in 1970 and dropped further, to 4 per thousand, in 1996. (In 1997 the infant mortality rate in the United States was 8.6.)

2. In 1947 the birth rate per thousand was 34.3. In 1998 it had dropped to 9.6. The natural increase in population—birth rate minus death rate—dropped from 19.7 per thousand population in 1947 to 2 by 1998. The fertility rate, that is, the average number of children a woman gives birth to in her lifetime, was 1.38 in 1998, less than the 2.1 needed to sustain the existing level of population.

3. The per capita gross domestic product, which was $9,068 in 1980, rose to $23,801 by 1990. With the recession of the 1990s, it dropped to $22,700 in 1996. In 2006 it was up to $28,405. The per capita national income increased from $284 in 1958 to $31,244 in 2006. (It was $27,382 in the United States in 2006.)

4. *Japan Almanac,* 1997, p. 193.

5. Ibid., p. 265. In 1965 the average family spent 17.2 percent of family expenditures on leisure activities. By 1991 the figure had risen to 24.2 percent. In 1995 over 15 million Japanese traveled abroad. About 83 percent of these travelers went abroad on sight-seeing tours.

6. In the mid-1990s, one might pay $13 a pound for an ordinary cut of beef and $100 or more a pound for a top grade of beef. If one wished to bring an extravagant gift on a visit, one might pay $150 for a musk melon, $16 apiece for cherries, $210 for a bottle for Remy Martin XO, $3,800 for a case of six bottles of Romanee Conti, or $400 for a box of matsutake mushrooms.

7. For stepping out on the town a smart man wore his Chester Barrie jacket from London, put on a $22,900 Swiss Corum wristwatch, and slipped on Gianni Rossi shoes that cost $270 a pair. Then he might get into his BMW 7501, which cost $104,000. His wife could join him with an $800 Louis Vuitton bag on her arm.

8. Around 1990, retail prices in Japan on the average were 4.21 times higher than wholesale prices in the United States, where retail prices were only twice as high as wholesale prices.

9. In 1994, an airline ticket agent offered half-price airline tickets because of the sky-high cost of domestic airfares. It cost about $400 for a round trip from Tokyo to Sapporo, a few hundred miles away. The agent was forced to close down his business for discounting the tickets. *Chicago Tribune,* February 6, 1994.

10. The population of the region centering on the Tokyo metropolitan area rose from 13 million in 1950 to over 30 million by 1996. This meant 23.7 percent of the nation's population converged here. Within Tokyo's city limits there were 7.8 million people, raising the population density per square mile to 32,850, compared to 23,705 in New York.

11. Roger Buckley, *Japan Today* (Cambridge: Cambridge University Press, 1985), p. 59.

12. The best residential property in Tokyo cost $69,000 a square yard in 1990. A 3.3-meter-square plot in the suburb of Tokyo that cost 39 cents in 1927 cost $92,000 in 1990, a 236,000 percent increase.

13. Residential land prices in Tokyo in 1990 were estimated to be eighty-nine times higher than those in New York. Commercial space was costlier still. A square yard of commercial space in Tokyo cost $210,000 in 1990. This means a 2,000-square-foot structure would cost $51.1 million.

14. At its peak in 1989, Japan's landmass, the size of California, was valued by the real estate industry at $13.986 trillion, four times the land value of the United States, which has a landmass 24.5 times larger than Japan's.

15. In 1985 about 40 percent of the salaried workers commuting to Tokyo from the outskirts spent from 90 to 120 minutes traveling one way.

16. See Mikiso Hane, *Peasants, Rebels, and Outcastes: The Underside of Modern Japan* (New York: Pantheon, 1982), pp. 262–265.

17. *Japan Report,* December 1992.

18. The major portion of the welfare cost was devoted to the elderly. In 1991 about 60 percent of the budget was given over to the elderly.

19. In 1990 the national medical care expenditure came to 6.0 percent of the national income. But the per capita annual medical cost in Japan in 1992 was $1,171, less than half of the $2,566 of the per capita cost in the United States.

20. In 1991 the employees' pension insurance came to only 41.3 percent of the average wage. A large number of people are covered by the pension plans. In 1994, 69.5 million people, out of the total population of 125.5 million, were on some form of pension program.

21. The total number of suicides in 1998 was 32,863, amounting to 26 suicides per 100,000 persons. The suicide rate of people in their early twenties was 16.8 per 100,000 population but rose to 44.1 for people in their fifties, and for those above sixty-five it was 40. The suicide rate for men was much higher than for women. For men in their fifties the rate was 68.9 per 100,000 persons, and for women it was 19.8. For those over sixty-five the rate was 53.3 for men and 30.7 for women.

22. Noda Masaaki, "Why Are Middle-Aged Men Killing Themselves?" *Japan Echo* 15, 1988, p. 25.

23. *Intersect,* November 1993, pp. 10ff. In 1991 firearms were used in only 74 murders and 22 robberies. In 1995 there were 1,281 cases of homicide (about 1 per 100,000 population), compared to 9.4 per 100,000 population in the United States. The number of robberies committed in 1995 amounted to 1.8 per 100,000 population, compared to about 230 per 100,000 population in the United States. Drug use has traditionally remained low compared to other societies. In 1991 there were 271 arrests for use of narcotics and 126 for opium.

24. In 2006 the police reported that there were 86,300 yakuza belonging to 3,300 different groups, with most affiliated with three major gangs. The biggest syndicate, known as Yamaguchi-gumi, is centered in Kobe with about 21,700 members, and like other gangs controls much of the construction business.

25. *New York Times,* June 11, 1997.

26. *Far Eastern Economic Review,* December 3, 1992, p. 18.

27. On the yakuza see David E. Kaplan and Alec Dubro, *Yakuza: The Explosive Account of Japan's Criminal Underworld* (Reading, Mass.: Addison-Wesley, 1986).

28. *International Herald Tribune,* April 17, 2007.

29. Antonin Raymond in *The Japan Experience,* ed. Ronald Bell (New York: Weatherhill, 1973), p. 166.

30. Jared Taylor, *Shadows of the Rising Sun: A Critical View of the "Japanese Miracle"* (New York: Morrow, 1983), p. 32.

31. Ibid., p. 33.

32. *Intersect,* September 1987, p. 10.

33. Miyachi Sōshichi, "The Dangerous Tide of 'Soap Nationalism,'" *Japan Echo,* spring 1987, p. 53.

34. Hugo M. Ninomiya-LaSalle in Bell, *Japan Experience,* pp. 96–97.

35. Fasco Maraini in ibid., pp. 10–11.

36. An early account of this practice was presented by Kim Il-meon in *Tennō no Guntai to Chōsenjin Ianfu* (The Emperor's Army and Korean Comfort Women) (Tokyo: San'ichi Shobo, 1976).

37. *Japan Times,* June 22, 2007.

38. *Japan Times,* July 6, 1990.

39. In 1997 Kawasaki became the first municipality to hire a Korean national. So far, three prefectures—Osaka, Nara, and Kanagawa—have granted voting rights to permanent foreign residents.

40. Donald Richie in Bell, *Japan Experience,* p. 60.

41. *Chicago Tribune,* May 16, 1992.

42. *Intersect,* May 1991, pp. 25–26.

43. Robert Guest, "A Tale of Two Sisters," *Far Eastern Economic Review,* July 9, 1992, p. 29.

44. *Japan Times,* July 8, 1990.

45. On San'ya, see Edward B. Fowler, *San'ya Blues: Laboring Life in Contemporary Tokyo* (Ithaca, N.Y.: Cornell University Press, 1996).

46. In 1990, 58 percent of office workers, 51.3 percent of service industry employees, and 42 percent of technicians and other specialists were women. In 1993, 70 percent of part-time workers (those who work less than thirty-five hours a week) were women. "Part-timers" are virtually full-time employees minus benefits, security, and competitive wages.

47. Taylor, *Shadows of the Rising Sun*, p. 198.

48. *Chicago Tribune,* May 5, 1991.

49. Salaries for full-time women employees averaged 60.2 percent of men's in 1995. Still, it was up from 56.1 percent in 1985. In the United States, on the average, women's pay was 75 percent of men's.

50. The employment of female college graduates in 1993 dropped by 23.7 percent compared to the previous year, whereas male employment dropped by only 5.1 percent. In 1992, among the top business firms, Mitsubishi hired only 4 women, compared to 213 men. At the spring graduation period of 1994 a Labor Ministry survey indicated a 39.9 percent drop from the previous year in the number of women students who found employment. For male students the decline was 28.8 percent.

51. *New York Times,* February 24, 1985.

52. *Japan Almanac,* 1993, p. 82.

53. Kumazawa Makoto, *Nihon no Rōdōsha-zō* (Tokyo: Chikuma Shobo, 1993), pp. 232, 261–262.

54. Taylor, *Shadows of the Rising Sun*, p. 166.

55. *New York Times,* July 4, 1988.

56. *Chicago Tribune,* June 16, 1991.

57. Many women rose to local and national prominence in the so-called green movements of consumerism and environmentalism.

58. Even in the culinary field women are frequently blocked out. Although men would not be caught dead in the kitchen at home, of the 55,000 sushi makers employed in sushi bars in 1985, only 15 were women.

59. *PHP* (Tokyo: PHP Institute), December 1981, p. 7.

60. *Nichibei Times,* San Francisco, April 20, 1980.

61. Louise de Rosari, "The Perfect Woman," *Far Eastern Economic Review,* February 10, 1994, p. 62.

62. The number of divorces in Japan, though low, has been increasing. In 1970 it was 0.93 per 1,000 population. In 1997 it had risen to 1.78. See *Japan Almanac,* 1997, p. 54; *Japan Times Weekly,* June 22–28, 1998. Divorce among women married for a fairly long time has been on the increase also.

63. *Japan Almanac,* 1997, p. 53.

64. Imamura Taketoshi and Kyōiku, Gyōsei (educational administration), cited by Harry Wray in his study on Japanese education, *Japanese and American Education: Attitudes and Practice* (Westport, Conn.: Bergin and Garvey, 1999).

65. *Intersect,* May 1988, p. 11.

66. *New York Times,* November 3, 1991.

67. The Ienaga case dragged on until 1994, when the Tokyo Higher Court held that the Ministry of Education had the right to certify textbooks, but it had illegally ordered Ienaga to make changes and deletions. Hence, Ienaga won his case. *Japan Times Weekly,* September 8–14, 1997.

68. In 1954 the percentage of junior high school graduates going on to senior high school exceeded 50 percent for the first time. By 1995 the percentage had risen to 95.8 percent.

69. In 1991, 29.6 percent of senior high graduates entered technical colleges.

70. In 1991, 2.1 percent of senior high school students dropped out before graduation. The number of students who dropped out of elementary and junior high schools in 1990 was 3.5 times more than the number in 1978.

71. *Japan Report,* March 1989 (New York: Japan Information Center Consulate General).

72. Taylor, *Shadows of the Rising Sun,* p. 97.

73. This represents 18.6 percent of elementary school children and 52.2 percent of students in middle school.

74. *New York Times,* April 27, 1992.

75. *New York Times,* July 13, 1983.

76. Taylor, *Shadows of the Rising Sun,* p. 95.

77. Benjamin Duke, *The Japanese School: Lessons for Industrial America* (New York: Praeger, 1986), pp. 200–201.

78. Japanese educator Seiichi Endō's letter to the author, May 25, 1991.

79. *New York Times,* July 11, 1983.

80. David Halberstam, "Can We Rise to the Japanese Challenge?" *Parade,* October 9, 1983; *New York Times,* June 30, 1991.

81. Duke, *Japanese School,* pp. 20ff.

82. Jonathan Friedland, "Disconnected," *Far Eastern Economic Review,* June 30, 1994, p. 47.

83. *Japan Times Weekly,* February 10–16, 1992.

84. *New York Times,* August 4, 1991.

85. In 1985 there were about 150,000 cases of students bullying other students in the elementary and junior high schools. The number of such cases dropped to 22,156 in 1990 because of tighter supervision by the teachers.

86. *New York Times,* June 29, 1988.

87. *New York Times,* June 24, 1983.

88. Taylor, *Shadows of the Rising Sun,* p. 98.

89. *Intersect,* May 1988, p. 10.

18

Cultural Developments

The defeat in the war inflicted a crushing blow on the Japanese people's world-view. Since childhood they had been taught the uniqueness, the superiority, the invincibility of Japan; the godlike sanctity of the benevolent, holy emperor living high above the clouds; the importance of self-denial and self-sacrifice for the good of the nation; the honor of dying for the glory of Japan and of the emperor; the social hierarchy and gender discrimination as a natural order of things; the wisdom and superiority of the ruling elite; the almighty power of the military, government officials, and police; and the virtue of being obedient, submissive, and deferential to those above. All of these beliefs and values were shattered by the war. The people were reduced to ground zero of the moral, intellectual, and spiritual life. What counted was to stay alive, find enough food to eat, find a place to live, and to rely on the assistance of family, relatives, and friends. They found that Americans, which they had been led to believe were "foreign devils," were not vicious animals but human beings, many of whom gave chewing gum and chocolate bars to children.

AMERICAN INFLUENCE

Soon the intellectual and cultural vacuum began to be filled with American pop culture, Western liberalism, Marxist ideology, and humanistic impulses that had been crushed underfoot under prewar and wartime militarism. A new age of "civilization and enlightenment" was beginning to dawn. Books and magazines that were banned began to reappear as well as American and Japanese movies, jazz, pop music, strip-tease shows, "pan pan" girls (street walkers), pinball machines, rock music, Coca-Cola, hot dogs, professional sports, American television shows, garish advertisements, Japanized English words, and fashionable apparel. Whatever was in vogue in the United States appeared instantly in Japan.

The cause for the frenzied turn to "pop" culture and things Western, primarily American, can be attributed to the exposure to American ways and culture during the occupation era. At no time in the history of Japan had there been so much direct contact with Americans. A large number of American troops remained in the country for more than two decades. Thousands of businessmen, students, scholars, missionaries, government officials, and professional people have resided in Japan. In the 1980s, annually, close to a quarter-million Americans traveled to Japan. In turn, millions of Japanese traveled to the United States. In 1990, 3.1 million Japanese tourists trekked to the United States. By 2007, that number had increased to over 4.4 million—almost a million to Hawaii alone. Also thousands of Japanese students and scholars came to study in the United States.

The craze for Western things continued without letup. The affluent crowd also favored Western over Japanese products to show their sophistication. High-brow as well as low-brow intellectuals interjected English words into almost every sentence they wrote. If one were to flip through a middle-brow monthly journal, one now finds Japanized English words interspersed throughout. As one Japanese observer remarked, "There reigns a veritable babel of confusion in the Japanese language today as a result of this uncalled-for adoption of English words, to the utter despair of purists and conservatives. . . . To a Western observer this craze for English words may appear to be another instance of Japanese imbecility."[1]

Labels, signs, trademarks, brand names, and control knobs on electric appliances are frequently in English. An advertisement for an apartment may read: "The *manshon* [mansion] is *hai kurasu* [high class] and *gōjasu* [gorgeous]." Remarked an American resident in Japan, "This must be very tiring for the Japanese because very few really understand English. English ultimately loses all meaning and becomes nothing but a decorative pattern."[2]

In high culture, too, the model is Western culture. In art classes students learn to paint and sculpt in the Western style. Music instructors, largely ignoring Japanese music, teach students to play Western musical instruments and learn Western classical music. Suzuki Shinichi (1898–1998) won international renown for his innovative way of teaching children how to play the violin, not the *koto*. The curriculum formulated by the Ministry of Education overlooks Japanese art in favor of Western art, which has become an integral part of the school system. Visiting Western symphony orchestras pack the concert halls, whereas *No* drama is performed before tiny audiences. Western rock-and-roll stars enthrall Japanese youngsters. The people who show a serious interest in Japanese traditional art and culture are by and large Western scholars. As one such scholar has observed, "I feel that the best in Japan and in Japanese culture is indeed being destroyed. . . . I think the strongest aesthetic virtue of the Japanese was always based upon *wabi,* on a frugal spirit. . . . This attitude . . . is changing so rapidly in the new age of affluence. . . . To young people a great deal of their culture is no longer understandable to them."[3] The interest in Western culture, however, has resulted in the emergence of internationally renowned performers such as Seiji Ozawa, conductor of the Boston Symphony, and the violinist Midori.

In the intellectual world, professors and thinkers who had been silenced returned to the podium and the pages of journals and newspapers. Historical figures—for example, the early Meiji Westernizers like Fukuzawa Yukichi, the most prominent proponent of "civilization and enlightenment"—regained popularity in the intellectual community. So did the Taishō era proponent of democracy, Yoshino Sakuzō, and the constitutional scholar, Minobe Tatsukichi, who held the emperor to be simply one among other organs of the state, not above the state. Although Western liberal, Cartesian scholarship was gaining popularity among certain sections of the academe, Marxism captured a strong following among intellectuals. German idealism, which was prominent in the world of philosophical contemplation, retreated from the frontline of the academic world. Some critics of Japanese intellectual circles contend, rightly or wrongly, that Japanese intellectuals tend to follow whatever is in ascendancy in the intellectual world in the West. Ideas are like garnishes on a *sashimi* dish. Western schools of thought are adopted for display.

A prominent intellectual historian, Maruyama Masao (1914–1996), ascribed the importation of diverse ideas without any effort to digest and integrate them into a coherent intellectual system to the fact that Japan lacks an intellectual tradition that serves as a nucleus or a frame of reference to link ideas and thoughts of all ages in relation to one another and permits all intellectual philosophies, even contradictory ones, to find a historical niche relative to it. In the West the Christian mode of thinking has provided the framework to judge and correlate ideas. Such a framework is lacking in Japan, so contradictory and conflicting intellectual systems coexist without any interaction.[4]

Some see a positive side to this because it does not lead to intellectual intolerance and persecution of people for harboring abstract concepts. There has not been in Japan religious persecutions of the kind that prevailed elsewhere, at least not since the two centuries of anti-Christian exclusion (1640–1870). One could argue that prewar suppression of Marxists was political persecution rather than intellectual intolerance. Isaiah BenDasan (1921–1991) compared the postwar revival of interest in Marxism and its popularity among Japanese intellectuals to the popular "fashion model" in the West. When Marxism's popularity began to decline in the West, its appeal among Japanese intellectuals began to fade also.

SURVIVAL OF THE TRADITIONAL OUTLOOK

It is logical to assume that the defeat in the war and the momentous changes in the lives of the people wrought by revolutionary political, social, economic, scientific, and technological developments resulted in fundamental changes in the Japanese society and value system. A steady turning away from traditional values or the seeming lack of any coherent *weltanschauung* characterized postwar Japan. One scholar who returned to Japan after years in the United States remarked,

> The most significant change in the past few years has been the emergence of a kind of social and psychological anarchy in Japan. People don't believe in Japanese politics. There are no heroes in Japan. Before World War II, my generation had the emperor, but today there is nobody for young Japanese to look up to. There is a lack of spiritual force . . . an absence of purpose and meaning. We are professionals without spirits. And we are still a nation of timid, undaring people.[5]

Today, for the first time a generation embracing a wholly new attitude and perspective seems to be emerging. The young are no longer as respectful and deferential to their elders as Japanese youth used to be. Another important barometer of change is the fact that the style of speech in which the hierarchy of age, sex, and status has historically been reflected is beginning to show signs of erosion.

Among the significant conflicts between the traditional and the new value system is the clash between individual versus community interests. In early Japan there were clans *(uji)*, the imperial household, military chieftains, and feudal lords who provided the people with a sense of community and identity. Throughout history there were also family and village ties that endowed individuals with a sense of community. Even after the Meiji Restoration, when Japan entered the industrial age, family bonds continued to remain strong. In addition, the revived emperor system and the unfolding of extremely strong nationalistic sentiments gave the people a resolute sense of purpose and identity. In postwar Japan, for the first time in its history, these institutions have been seriously challenged.

In reaction to the evident rejection of traditional thought and scholarship and the turn toward Western learning and thought in the immediate postwar years, in the 1980s some thinkers began to focus more on things Japanese, and a school of thinking that emphasized what it is to be Japanese, *Nihonjin-ron* (Japanism), emerged. Some observers came to detect a reversion to traditional values among the younger generation also. The core of the Nihonjin-ron thinking is an emphasis on the homogeneity of the Japanese people. Nihonjin-ron advocates seek to pin down the uniqueness of Japanese culture, language, psychology, national character, and so on.

Non-Japanese critics regard all this talk of Japaneseness as a reversion to the prewar nationalistic mode of thinking and that what is regarded as being uniquely Japanese is merely a characteristic common to feudal societies. But the "Japanist" contends that no foreigner can comprehend the essence of Japanism, just as no foreigner can truly master the Japanese language because it is a language beyond mere mouthing of words or explicit expression of reasoned thought. Japanese words lack concrete, precise, and logical meaning or real content, unlike Western languages. Japanese do not communicate by words but do so by the way the language is spoken. What is important are not words but attitude, deportment, intonation, and courtesy. In other words, body language speaks rather than verbal expressions.[6]

Despite the concern that traditional ways and values have been eroded and are vanishing from the Japanese cultural scene, some observers contend that traditional values are reviving. A survey conducted in the late 1980s found respondents indicating that they value "filial piety and repayment of *on*" (social and personal obligations) over "rights" and "freedom." Eighty percent responded favorably to the concept of filial piety, and only 50 percent responded favorably to freedom as a value.

After studying the psychology of postwar Japanese youth in the early 1960s, Robert Jay Lifton (b. 1926) remarked upon "the absence in contemporary Japanese youth of vital and nourishing ties to their own heritage—a break in their sense of connection." The Japanese young people with whom he talked were affected by traditional cultural elements but regarded them as irrelevant and inadequate to meet the demands of the modern world. Half a decade later Lifton interviewed the same young Japanese and found that "they were preoccupied with their cultural and racial heritage—with various aspects of their 'Japaneseness'—to such an extent that I wondered whether [in the essay written in 1961] I had overemphasized the psychological importance of postwar Western influence."[7]

The shift in the attitude of the young people in the 1980s compared to the radical students of the 1950s, 1960s, and early 1970s is seen in their reading habits. In the 1970s the books most widely read by the young generation included Doi Takeo's *Amae* (The Anatomy of Dependence); the novels of Ōe Kensaburō, winner of the 1994 Nobel Prize in literature; Maruyama Masao's *Between War Years and Postwar Years*; and *Age of Uncertainty* by John Kenneth Galbraith (1908–2006). That is, they read books on social and political issues. Among the most popular weekly journals in the 1960s among students was the *Asahi Journal*, which dealt with serious sociopolitical issues from a leftist perspective. But by 1990, its circulation had dropped to about 20 percent of its peak years; the journal was discontinued in 1992. In the 1980s college students spent their leisure time on TV, comic books, and magazines. The most popular weekly publication was a comic magazine for youths that sold 3.3 million copies a week while the *Asahi Journal* was expiring.

RELIGION

Religion might be looked upon as a gauge to measure the values and attitudes prevalent in society, although Japan did not undergo the kind of religious fervor that gripped other societies in the past. But even without that kind of enthusiasm, some critics contend that religious sentiment underlies Japanese society. In fact, the advocates of Japanism contend that Japanism itself is a religion of a sort.

In the postwar period of confusion and chaos, a large number of new "folk" religions, like the dancing "god," came into existence, but none won a large enough following to become a significant force in the society. The only truly vigorous religious movement to emerge has been the Soka Gakkai. It was started in the 1920s by an obscure schoolteacher who maintained that within the amorphous flux of human existence the happiness of people could be enhanced by the adoption of proper values. It was essentially a faith-healing cult that linked itself to the Buddhist Nichiren sect. In the postwar period it was invigorated by a strong, dynamic leadership and became an aggressive, proselytizing religion. It gained supporters among the working-class sector, and its membership rose above 14 million by the end of 1968. The organization formed a political party, the Kōmeitō, to further its ideals through the political medium.

Much of the religious disaffection and sense of anomie in postwar Japan gave rise to other religious movements. In the 1960s many Japanese could be found in virtually every new religious center in the world. Hundreds traveled to such places as Rome, Mecca, Palestine, India, Nepal, and Tibet in search of religious enlightenment. In the 1970s thousands of Japanese joined the Unification Church of the Korean preacher Sun Myung Moon (b. 1920). In the late 1980s and early 1990s many Japanese flocked to the Chinese cult Falun Gong. The nation was shocked in 1995 when the Aum Shinrikyo religious cult released poison gas in a coordinated attack on five trains in the subway system, killing 12 commuters, seriously harming 54, and affecting 980 more. After a nationwide investigation it was discovered that the cult included not just the usual mix of ne'er-do-wells and disaffected crazies but several highly educated college graduates, including scientists, engineers, and civil servants.

For people who are not totally committed to a specific religious faith—and they would constitute a vast majority of the Japanese—there is tolerance and willingness to accept numerous gods and beliefs. People state their religious affiliations if asked, but most people do not have strong commitments to any religious institutions as do Christians, Jews, and Muslims in other societies.

> It seems safe to say that perceptions of religion differ in Japan and the West. Westerners see religion as something objective that must be acquired through education or study. The Japanese, by contrast, think of religion as an internal state. It need not have the clear-cut contours of Christian or Buddhist doctrine; it can be simply a nebulous emotional predisposition lying undetected until the individual is made aware of it.[8]

A late 1980s survey indicates that only about 30 percent of those surveyed said they had personal religious faith. Eighty percent responded that they believed a religious attitude to be important. People may profess affiliation with two or three different religions. In 1990 the total number of people that religious organizations claimed as members came to 217 million, twice the size of the population. The novelist Noma Hiroshi believes that Buddhism is the only religion or philosophy that has captured the spirit of the Japanese masses. He thus contends that the religious thinking of the Japanese is basically Buddhist.

During the occupation years, SCAP officials, nurtured in the credo of separation of church and state, banned state affiliation with Shinto and forbade teaching of Shinto in the schools, but for the Japanese populace in general, folk Shinto remained basically an animistic religion in which spiritual forces are seen to be present in nature as well as in all things in the universe. Unlike other religions, in Shinto there is no absolute distinction among the divine, the natural, and the human. Zen remains popular as a form of spiritual discipline, and its cultural influence remains strong. Christians, as in other countries, take their religion more seriously.

The problems confronting Japan today are not unique. The decline of traditional values and institutions and the search for meaning and purpose continue elsewhere in the industrialized, Westernized societies that have also left their tribal and familial stages far behind. Like other societies, Japan faces such problems as the dislocations and disorientations caused by the exceedingly rapid pace of change that has been brought about by science and technology. They are confronted with problems like air and water pollution, the desecration of nature, the threat of nuclear destruction, the undermining of the sense of mystery and awe by rationalism and science, the abandonment of the sense of unity with nature and the universe that was at the root of Shinto, and the continued inability of people to stop abusing their fellow humans.

LITERATURE

Facts about the war that had been kept from the people became known to them in the postwar years. People were now able to criticize the leaders, even the emperor. Magazines filled with critical, analytical essays dealing with social, economic, political, and cultural issues returned to the bookstores. New left-wing journals gained popular readership among intellectuals and students. The works of popular novelists like Nagai Kafū, Kawabata Yasunari, and Tanizaki Jun'ichirō; philosophers like Nishida Kitarō; and new writers like Dazai Osamu (1909–1948) came to be widely read. Soon popular weekly magazines began to crowd bookstores and newsstands.

Japanese are avid readers of books, newspapers, and magazines. Even if they no longer read as much since the age of television, the number of books, newspapers, and magazines published have continued to increase.[9] Among these magazines are comic books for adults as well as youngsters. They deal with fiction as well as serious issues, including politics, economics, and legal affairs.

The number of books published has remained large and has continued to increase.[10] The size of the publication and circulation of books might be explained by the fact that in contrast to the United States, library facilities are limited. There were 1,804 libraries in Japan in 1992, compared to 8,456 in the United States and 10,936 in Germany.

The large number of books on literature being published indicates the continued popularity of novelists. In the immediate postwar years the works of prominent prewar writers like Tanizaki, Kawabata, and Nagai were reissued and widely read.

During the war years, writers were compelled to produce novels that inspired the people to work for the glory of the state and the emperor. If they could not do so, they were forced to remain silent. Depiction of any "unhealthy," immoral, or unpatriotic ideas and behavior were proscribed by the censors. For example, Tanizaki Jun'ichirō was unable to publish his classical work, *The Makioka Sisters*. The editors of the magazine where it was to be serialized justified their decision not to continue its publication because, they contended, it would not be in the national interest. There was nothing "unpatriotic" in the work. The theme that the traditional and modern way of life had become inseparably intertwined in the characterization of two sisters, one more traditional, the other more modern, was evidently viewed as unacceptable in the rabid anti-Western intellectual world of wartime Japan. When the novel was published in the postwar period, it won instant public acclaim. The novel was translated into English in 1957 and established Tanizaki's reputation in the West. This was followed by numerous translations of his other works.

Among writers who, like Tanizaki, enjoyed a rebirth of their prewar popularity was Kawabata Yasunari, who won the Nobel Prize for literature in 1968. In his acceptance speech he spoke of his appreciation of Japanese culture with its oneness with nature. Although Kawabata was also attuned to Western culture he maintained a lifelong concern about Japanese tradition and culture. He also held an exalted view of the classics of the East, especially the Buddhist scriptures, which he believed "are the supreme works of literature of the world."[11]

Among the established prewar writers unknown to the West until his *Black Rain on Hiroshima* was translated into English is Ibuse Masuji (1898–1993). Even though the novel deals with the city right after the atomic bomb was dropped, John Bester (b. 1927), the translator, notes that Ibuse "avoids all emotional political considerations, all tendency to blame or to moralize." The novel is based on actual records and interviews.[12]

The horrors of the after-effects of the atomic bombing are vividly depicted. "The corpses lay scattered in every conceivable condition—one with only the upper half of the body burned to the bone, one completely skeletonized save for one arm and one leg, another lying face down, consumed from the knees down, yet another with two legs alone cremated—and an unspeakable stench hanging over all." Radiation exposure resulted in "lethargy and heaviness of the limbs. After a few days, the hair would come out without any pain, and the teeth would come loose and eventually fall out. Finally, collapse set in and the patient died."[13]

Besides the return of the prewar writers whose works had been under wraps during the war years, a host of talented younger writers, who commenced working in the 1930s or in the postwar era, began to emerge as new literary personalities. Among those whose works have been translated into English is Dazai Osamu. He started his literary career in the 1930s and was among the writers of the literature of despair that flourished in the postwar era. His early writings were about his driven, intense mental and spiritual anguish. In *The Setting Sun* and *No Longer Human,* the heroes, alienated from society and their fellow men, seek consolation in dissipation that leads ultimately to their destruction. A key personality in *The Setting Sun* writes in his death note, "I cannot think of the slightest reason why I should have to go on living. . . . Just as a man has the right to live, he ought also to have the right to die. . . . Somewhere an element is lacking which would permit me to continue. I am wanting. It has been all I could do to stay alive up to now."[14] Not unlike the heroes of his imagination, Dazai finally succeeded in bringing about his own self-destruction in 1948 by jumping into the Tamagawa Reservoir with a lover.

As might be expected, writers from the left made a strong comeback in the postwar era. Among them was Noma Hiroshi (1915–1991), who had been subjected to oppression by the army because of his political beliefs. In his major work *The Zone of Emptiness* he depicts the brutalities of Japanese army life. The title is derived from the concept that the army post is a "zone of emptiness." Noma explained that the novel was designed "to analyze the responsibilities of the intellectual and revolutionary" elements for Japan's wartime activities. He was drawn to Marxism during his college days, and he continued to support Marxist ideals until the 1960s, when Stalin's brutal policies received public exposure. In his later years Noma turned his attention to the founder of the True Pure Land sect, Shinran, and in 1969 wrote his explication of the *Tan'nishō,* Shinran's teachings transcribed by his disciple. Noma noted that Shinran identified with the masses, spoke to them, and gained a strong following. As was noted earlier, he concluded that Buddhism was the only intellectual force in Japan that captured the mind and spirit of the masses.

Ōoka Shōhei (1909–1988) won renown for novels dealing with his experiences as a soldier during World War II. He served in the Philippines, where he was captured by the Americans and sent to a prisoner of war camp in Leyte. In 1952 he published his masterpiece, *Fires on the Plain,* a vivid depiction of the plight of a soldier who, reduced to insanity and on the verge of starvation, wanders about in Leyte struggling to survive. Ōoka forces the reader to stare directly at the horrors of war and those of life itself as he describes rotting corpses and men reduced to cannibalism. The soldiers abandoned in the Philippine forests kill their fellow soldiers to eat their flesh.

The most talented and versatile of the postwar writers was Mishima Yukio (1925–1970), whom Donald Keene (b. 1922), an authority on Japanese literature, considers "the most gifted and [who] achieved the most of all the writers who appeared after the war."[15] Mishima was well versed in both Western and traditional Japanese literature. He wrote novels, short stories, poems, and Kabuki as well as No plays. He took for his themes the manners and mores of the postwar generation and the sense of despair and emptiness that faced the young, as well as the subject of homosexuality. In *The Temple of the Golden Pavilion* he focuses on the thematic contrasts of love and hate, reality and illusion, selflessness and self-assertion. The plot of the novel concerns the story of a Buddhist acolyte who, in 1950, burned down the Golden Pavilion *(Kinkakuji)* built by Shōgun Ashikaga Yoshimitsu in 1397. The acolyte, who is physically disabled, is obsessed with a sense of his own inadequacy and sees in the perfect beauty of the Golden Pavilion merely another reminder of his own imperfection. He awaits its destruction by American bombers. But the war ends without the anticipated air raid, and the Golden Pavilion still stands. In a desperate act of defiance and self-liberation, the acolyte sets fire to the temple.

In the 1960s Mishima began addressing himself to the problems of student unrest and the apparent lack of mooring in the younger generation. His solu tion to this absence of spiritual anchor has a remarkably traditionalist cast. He wrote: "To the Japanese whatever is new is desirable. Then, when we are so surrounded by new inventions that we are unable to move—every twenty years, that is—we Japanese suddenly begin to feel that old things are much better after all."[16] Mishima retained the prewar Japanese idealization of the emperor system, and he deplored leftist students for their unwillingness to recognize the emperor as the symbolic moral source of loyalty and culture. Increasingly distressed over the disappearance of traditional values among the young, he was profoundly influenced by the teaching of Wang Yang-ming (1472–1528) that one must act on one's convictions. Living up to this dictum, he decided to sacrifice himself "for the old, beautiful tradition of Japan, which is disappearing very quickly day by day."[17] He was determined not to die in an accident or of old age. Death was to be a positive act. In November 1970, after failing to arouse the members of the Self-Defense Force to follow his philosophy, he committed seppuku in classical samurai fashion.

Women writers have traditionally been accorded a prominent place in the Japanese literary world, starting with Lady Murasaki, the creator of the *Tale of Genji*. In the postwar years Japanese women writers gained recognition in the West also as their writings came to be translated into English and other Western languages. Among these writers is Uno Chiyo (1907–1996), who began her career as a writer in the early 1920s. In 1933 she wrote a semiautobiographical novel about thwarted love and passion that earned her renown. After a hiatus she resumed her career in the postwar period. Unlike many of her contemporaries, such as Miyamoto Yuriko (1899–1951) and Sata Ineko (1904–1998), who embraced the Marxist cause, Uno did not concern herself with social issues. Instead, she wrote novels that dealt with the lives of the distinctive personalities whom she had encountered in real life. For example, on one occasion she was impressed by the wood carving of a puppet, sought out the woodcarver in Shikoku, and wrote a novel based on his life. She also wrote of the love life of a second-hand book dealer whom she met on the same trip. The latter story became the basis for her major work, *Ohan* (translated into English as *The Old Woman, the Wife, and the Archer* by Donald Keene). Regarding *Ohan*, Keene remarked, "The author has created an extraordinarily compelling writing style and, disregarding conventions and time and place, invented a kind of novelistic fantasy world in which the words themselves seem to live by their own strength. This is rare in the contemporary novel, which has abjectly surrendered to facts."[18]

Enchi Fumiko (1905–1986) was another woman writer whose career commenced in the prewar years and reached the peak of productivity in the postwar period. The theme that runs through her stories is the fate of women. In her major work, *Onnazaka* (translated into English as *The Waiting Years*),

Enchi depicted the lives of Meiji women who suffered with nobility and resourcefulness the oppression of the paternalistic family system. An old woman in one of her novels remarks, "Buddhism tells us that human beings are expected to live in a world far superior to that inhabited by cows and horses, but now that I think of it, I can count on my fingers the number of pleasurable moments I've had. And how I've had less free time each day than any cow or horse."[19]

A contemporary of Uno was Hayashi Fumiko (1903–1951), who grew up in poverty, moving from place to place with her itinerant peddler parents. Her early novels were based on her life of poverty, and she eventually published over 270 popular novels. In the 1930s and 1940s she traveled to the war zones as a "patriotic" supporter of the war effort. In the postwar years she published one of the most important of her works, *Bangiku* (Late Chrysanthemum), which deals with a geisha and her former lover. Donald Keene observes, "Of the innumerable stories about geishas, written by both women and men, none rings truer than *Late Chrysanthemum*."[20]

Miyamoto Yuriko was born into a well-off family but embraced Marxism after her visit to Russia in 1927, and made it her mission to help bring about a proletarian revolution in Japan. In 1931 she joined the Communist Party, and the following year she married Miyamoto Kenji (1908–2007), who in the postwar years became the secretary-general of the Communist Party in Japan. Miyamoto Yuriko was sent to prison in the late 1930s but was released for poor health. She published two of her most important works in the postwar years. One, *Banshū Heiya* (Banshu Plains), deals with the heroine's visit to Hiroshima after the war. Rather than portray the devastation of the atomic bomb, Miyamoto depicts the suffering inflicted on the Japanese people by the Japanese army and the hardships endured by the war widows. This and her other work "rise above doctrinal classification and stand as the first impressive rejections of the fifteen-year war and all that it involved," Keene opined.[21]

Sata Ineko was another writer of proletarian novels. She endured a life of poverty since childhood and experienced an unhappy marriage that led her to contemplate suicide three times. After she was divorced by her first husband, she married a Marxist and joined the proletarian literary movement. Her early novels were based on her experiences, such as her work in a caramel factory as a young girl and her unhappy marriage with her second husband. Although her stories had a Marxist tinge to them, the authorities continued to allow her to publish, as she, like Hayashi Fumiko, went on tours of the war zone under military sponsorship. These activities led to accusations that she had collaborated with the militarists in the postwar years. Sata justified her travels by saying she just wanted to see what was happening. She sought to regain full acceptance in proletarian circles, played an active role in left-wing women's and literary groups, and in 1955 gained reinstatement into the Communist Party. However, she was expelled once again for criticizing the party's policies and later in life became less enthusiastic about the Soviet Union as Stalin's brutal policies came to light.[22]

Many women writers of the postwar generation are no longer concerned about women who endured traditional social imperatives; instead, they focus on women who chart an independent course. Such a writer is Tsushima Yūko (b. 1949), Dazai Osamu's daughter. Tsushima believes that as the number of single mothers is increasing, they must learn to deal with the world on their own terms. In particular, they must learn to communicate their true feelings. Communication, the basic theme in her novel *Child of Fortune,* reflects the author's concern for the expression of feelings. She once remarked, "Writers wrote about women who didn't speak their feelings, who didn't want to be independent. Ever since I was a little girl, I haven't been satisfied with that kind of heroine. Mine are different."[23] Another theme in Tsushima's works is "the stifling nature of family and blood relationships. The families portrayed in her stories are often disjointed and supply neither warmth nor support."[24]

A number of prominent male writers of the postwar generation have been concerned about alienation and the search for meaning and sense of identity in a world in which all the moorings have been destroyed—a world in which "the center does not hold." Among the most radical of the writers is Ōe Kenzaburō (b. 1935), whose works reflect the lost sense of direction since the end of the war. The values that he was taught to live by as a child were shattered, and "the emptiness and enervation" that resulted led Ōe to write about personalities who seek meaning in "sex and violence and political fanaticism."[25] He has a close affinity with existentialist writers like Jean-Paul Sartre. From the beginning of his writing career he has emphasized "the importance of imagination in perception, diction, imagery, and style." *A Personal Matter,* published in 1964, deals with the protagonist's plan to kill his infant son, born with severe brain damage; in the end, he changes his mind and takes responsibility for his own son's well-being. The story is based in part on Ōe's own experience, for his son was born with serious brain damage. In 1994 Ōe was awarded the Nobel Prize in literature. In awarding the prize to Ōe the Swedish Academy commented on the poetic force of his work in which he "creates an imagined world where life and myth condense to form a disconcerting picture of the human predicament today."[26]

Abe Kōbō (1924–1993), an avant-garde writer who is often compared to Kafka, focuses on people who are alienated and isolated. In *The Woman in the Dunes*, he mingles fantasy with carefully delineated realities. The hero probes his inner consciousness and emerges a whole man.

Perhaps the most important recent writer in Japan is Endō Shūsaku (1923–1996). A Catholic, he often wrote about the struggles of Christian missionaries, who when they came to Japan in the sixteenth and seventeenth centuries were subjected to brutal persecution. In his *Silence,* a story of Jesuits being persecuted for refusing to renounce their faith, the missionaries ask God why he remains silent in the face of all the horrible suffering and pain that the Christian converts are being subjected to. Sebastian Rodrigues, the central figure, hears the Christian peasants moaning as they are being tormented. An apostate missionary tells him that the persecution will not stop unless he steps on the image of Christ. Then he hears Christ tell him to step on the image, and he finally does so. He tells God, "Lord, I resented your silence." The Lord replies, "I was not silent. I suffered beside you." Finally, a Japanese official informs Rodrigues that Christianity will not survive in Japan in its pristine form because "the teaching has slowly been twisted and changed in the swamp called Japan."[27]

An American writer has said, "Endō's art always reminds us that certainties and loyalties are more fluid than we should perhaps like them to be. But in exploring the limits of loyalty he does not forsake it. He remains firmly Catholic in spite of guilt and doubt, and for all his divided feelings about East and West, he remains firmly and mysteriously Japanese. In the end, his most impressive quality as a moralist is his silence."[28]

Despite the creation of superlative works, Japan's literary world seems not to have advanced beyond the search for a new identity following the shattering experience of the Second World War. The earlier conflict between the "traditional" and the "modern" no longer stirs the passions of the writers. Since the war no mainstream genre has surfaced—only trends such as existentialism, nihilism, and the search for meaning and identity by turning inward toward fantasy or, in some instances, to the Buddhist concept of *en* (belief in the interdependence of all things). Commentators reflecting on the literary scene of the early 1980s could only remark that "it has become difficult to grasp the modern age," or that "the novel has entered a difficult period." The search for the "new person" goes on, as symbolized by Ōe's 1983 novel, *Atarashii hito yo mezame yo!* (Wake up, Oh, Young People of the New Age!).[29]

In the 1980s a new generation of writers began to emerge with a point of view that was a departure from earlier writers who founded their literary world on traditional Japanese thought, culture, and language. Among the leading writers of this new school is Murakami Haruki (b. 1949), who disagrees with Tanizaki's opinion that the Japanese language is unique and different, and in some ways superior to Western languages, and that its beauty should be preserved. Murakami asserts that he and his contemporaries are trying to reconstruct the Japanese language, create a new Japanese language, and "break through the barrier of isolation so that we can talk to the rest of the world in our own words." One critic remarks that Murakami's subject matter is different from "the bored esthetes of Yasunari Kawabata, the stiff aristocrats of Junichiro Tanizaki or the tortured young men of Mishima."[30] Another young writer who has gained popularity is Yoshimoto Banana, whose novellas have been translated into English. Her *Kitchen* deals with the orphan heroine's effort to cope with the death of her grandmother who had raised her. It is "a lyrical tale about loss and grief and familial love."[31] The novella starts with the following lines: "The place I like best in this world is the kitchen. No matter where it is, no matter what kind, if it's a kitchen, if it's a place where they make food, it's fine with me." When the heroine is invited to move in with a friend, she explores the kitchen. "Mmm, mmm. It was a good kitchen." Thus she feels a sense of rapport with the young man who has invited her to come and live with him and his "mother," who turns out to be a transvestite.[32]

A new genre of novels emerged with the rise of Japan as an economic superpower. These are the economic novels in which life in the business world is depicted. Some novels look into the inner sanctum of the corporate world, which rather than being the idealized version of harmonious cooperation that governs the business world is "a world of back-stabbing, board-room coups, pressure tactics, cheating and stifling working conditions."[33]

CINEMA

In the postwar era, movies as a popular source of entertainment revived almost instantly. But Japanese movies were more than simply a medium of popular entertainment. An authority on Japanese films comments on the significance of movies in understanding the culture of a nation:

> The Japanese movie continues to show . . . the most perfect reflection of a people in the history of world cinema. . . . If the American film is strongest in action and if the European is strongest in character, then the Japanese film is richest in mood or atmosphere, in presenting people in their own context, characters in their own surroundings. It reflects the oneness with nature which constitutes both the triumph and the escape of the Japanese people. [34]

The sudden international fame gained by Japanese films during the postwar period has made it appear as if the art of the cinema attained instant maturity after the war. This, of course, is not at all the case; the style and technique had been evolving since the 1920s. A number of outstanding directors, such as Mizoguchi Kenji (1898–1956), who produced *Ugetsu*, "the most perfect of all films," and Kurosawa Akira (1910–1998), who made *Rashōmon* and *The Seven*

Samurai, among many other outstanding films, helped to bring about this triumph of cinema as an important art form.

Mizoguchi, possessing the eye of a painter, excelled in presenting superlative pictorial scenes. Kurosawa, perhaps the greatest of the Japanese directors, combined an interest in film aesthetics with a deep concern about social issues. His *Rashōmon,* a study of ambiguity and deception, portrays four contradictory accounts of rape and murder. Kurosawa said the characters have a "sinful need for flattering falsehood" and "cannot survive without lies to make them feel they are better people than they really are."[35] *The Seven Samurai,* which embodies all the strong points of Japanese movies, has been called "the finest Japanese film ever made." Commenting on what he has been trying to do in his films, Kurosawa said, "I keep saying the same thing in different ways. If I look at the pictures I've made, I think they say, 'Why is it that human beings aren't happy?'" He continuously experimented and devised new techniques and approaches, endeavoring to make the style fit the story, the form fit the content. He was a master at producing scenes of striking pictorial beauty. Regarding *Rashōmon,* he remarked, "I wanted to return to the simple pictorial values of the silent picture."[36]

Another movie director active during the same era as Kurosawa was Ōzu Yasujirō (1903–1963), who did not gain a popular following in the United States the way Kurosawa did. But he has had a strong and prolonged following among film connoisseurs. He is considered by some film authorities as the greatest director Japan ever produced and one of the greatest ever to work in the medium for his depiction of "emotional range, character types, and sly humor."[37] His career as a filmmaker started in the late 1920s, but he made widely acclaimed films in the postwar years. His most famous work, *Tokyo Story,* was produced in 1953. What might turn into "soap opera" becomes "high art. Reticence, care, fact and delicacy—those almost archetypal Japanese cultural virtues—combined for sublime aesthetic effects."[38]

After the heyday of the "golden age" of Japanese filmmaking during the 1950s and 1960s, the medium endured a period of lackluster production. One film critic notes, "Cinematic standards began to decline when the economy took off. . . . We have stopped taking an objective look at ourselves. . . . Filmmakers stopped delving into the hearts and minds of the average workers, and the quality of Japanese cinema declined."[39]

Because of the competition from television and videos, movie theater attendance took a nosedive. In 1960 there were 1 billion moviegoers. This dropped to 146 million by 1990. In the 1990s the average family spent a total of eight hours and twelve minutes a day in front of a television set. Quality movies no longer drew large numbers of viewers. More than half of the movies being made in recent years in Japan have been pornographic films. But the old masters have continued to push their creative genius to the limit, struggling to achieve aesthetic perfection while probing into the complexities of human existence. Kurosawa, at the age of seventy-five, produced in 1985 what critics regard as his crowning achievement, *Ran* (Chaos), an adaptation of *King Lear*. According to an American critic, this work ranks with "the greatest epics of Sergei Eisenstein, D. W. Griffith, and Abel Gance."[40]

In the 1980s a younger director, Itami Jūzō, gave Japanese cinema a shot in the arm with his "hip, jazzy, irreverent films" and blithe, satirical comedies. His movies deal with the "collapse of traditional values" since the end of World War II and the Japanese devotion to the acquisition of money. "In his films, the Japanese see themselves not as the stoic, tragic victims of fate, which is the way they are usually portrayed in 'serious' films. Instead, they are the comically fallible, heedless guests at an extraordinary party." Recalling his wartime experience, Itami related,

We were told that the whole nation would fight to death. But within one month of the end of the war, it was suddenly "Banzai democracy! Banzai MacArthur." The US forces were treated as if they were liberators. Praise was directed toward all things American. . . . It taught me something important. . . . All values are relative. There is no such thing as a war between good and evil. Wars are fought between two "goods"; each side believes itself to be justified.[41]

In his *Tampopo,* a comedy with "deadpanned jokes about food and death," a woman sets out to become Tokyo's best noodle maker. A prominent American movie critic observed, "Though Itami's concerns are as deeply rooted in the Japanese culture as the tea ceremony, his methods are as new as the automobiles now being designed for sale in supermarkets."[42] In 1992 he made *Minbō* (The Gentle Art of Japanese Extortion), parodying the yakuza as paper tigers who retreat before determined resistance. This resulted in his being attacked by three yakuza gangsters who cut him with their daggers. This did not deter him from continuing his goal of getting the Japanese to look at themselves from "outside the confines of nationally prevailing cultural values."[43] So he continued to make films as mirrors for the Japanese to see themselves until his untimely death in 1997.

Another sign that Japanese filmmaking was still pulsating was the awarding of the grand prize at the Cannes film festival in 1983 to Imamura Shōhei (1926–2006) for his *Narayamabushi-kō,* a film based on the legend that in the feudal years in some regions old people were abandoned to die alone in the mountains. In 1997 he won the Cannes Prize again for his film *Unagi* (The Eel), about a man who befriends an eel while in prison for stabbing his unfaithful wife to death. Among Imamura's other films is *Karayuki-san,* a film about young girls who were sold abroad to serve as prostitutes in various Asian countries in the prewar years.

In the early 1970s a "New Wave" of Japanese cinema became increasingly as popular as it was controversial. Sexual violence, perversion, and pornography characterized much of this new genre. The leader of the movement was Oshima Nagisa, who had a flurry of controversial films including *Cruel Story of Youth* and *Night and Fog in Japan* (both from the 1960s and banned in several theaters) and *Death by Hanging.* All were criticized for graphic violence and sexual scenes. His later films *In the Realm of the Senses* and *Merry Christmas, Mr. Lawrence* were seldom shown but much discussed among film aficionados.

Another director, Kitano Takeshi, created a series of highly acclaimed films in the 1990s: *Sonatine* (1993), *Kids Return* (1996), and the award-winning (Venice Film Festival, 1997) *Hana-bi.* Miike Takashi carved out an important career with a flurry of some fifty films, including *Audition* (1999), *Dead or Alive* (1999), and *The Bird People of China* (1998). Koreeda Hirokazu, a former documentary director, won considerable acclaim with *Maborosi* (1996) and *After Life* (1999).

By far, however, the most prolific of the new directors is Miyazaki Hayao who directed animated movies in a new genre called "anime," incorporating much of the *manga* style of drawing. These films were not in the Disney or Pixar style of cute comic animals. Miyazaki's *Spirited Away* (2001), *Howl's Moving Castle* (2004), and *Princess Mononoke* (2007) were full-length features with complex stories and dialogue. *Princess Mononoke,* in fact, was nominated for a number of cinema awards—not in the animation category but in competition with live-action films. *Mononoke* was surpassed only by the blockbuster *Titanic* among top-grossing films.

ART AND ARCHITECTURE

In architecture and design, significant creative works have been produced by contemporary Japanese artists. One American architect, a disciple of Frank Lloyd Wright (1867–1959) who spent fifty years in Japan, has asserted that "the Japanese are the best architects in the world today by far."[44]

Tange Kenzō (1913–2005), the first postwar Japanese architect to win international renown, combines aspects of the style of Charles Le Corbusier (1887–1965) with such traditional Japanese characteristics as the post-and-lintel configuration. From his followers emerged a number of outstanding architects. Among them is Isozaki Arata (b. 1931), whose early work includes the striking "Cluster in the Air," consisting of short-term brackets and long-term supports. Among his other architectural projects are the Museum of

Contemporary Art in Los Angeles; Team Disney Building in Orlando, Florida; and the Palau Sant Jordi, the Olympic Hall for the Barcelona Olympics. He too retains elements of the Japanese past in his concepts of space and time. Another leading architect, Maki Fumihiko (b. 1928), combines traditional Japanese elements with modern Western architectural styles. In 1993 he was awarded the Pritzker Architecture Prize, considered architecture's equivalent of a Nobel Prize. The award described him as an architect who "uses light in a masterful way, making it as tangible a part of every design as are the walls and roof. In each building, he searches for a way to make transparency, translucency and opacity exist in total harmony."[45] Another architect who has gained international renown for his concrete construction is Andō Tadao (b. 1941). Andō never went to college, became a professional boxer after graduating high school, and then turned to architecture on his own. He uses mainly unfinished concrete, bringing "astringent sensibility" to his work and paying "meticulous attention to form, structure, space and geometry," making his work appear "reductionist and abstract in the extreme." He fits his architectural structures in with the "spirit of the place," the natural setting.[46] He was awarded the 1995 Pritzker Prize.

Significant creative works have also been produced in other realms of art. Probably the most notable achievements can be seen in the folk arts. For instance, in pottery Hamada Shōji (1894–1978), among others, won international recognition. Wholly without vanity and pretension Hamada lived and worked among village artisans. Considering himself merely a craftsman, not an artist, he did not even sign his work. Hamada studied under the English potter Bernard Leach and was influenced by Korean pottery. Nevertheless, he developed an individual style that is characterized by a rugged strength of shape in concert with somber colors. He created spontaneous and striking designs with the freedom of movement displayed by a master calligrapher. Bernard Leach said of Hamada's work, "His pots articulate like an oak tree, the bones of structure are not concealed, the modulations of form are intuitive, and all his pots stand firm on their feet."[47]

Japanese potters continue to produce innovative ceramics of diverse style ranging from roughly glazed pots to shimmering celadon vases. Also they are "combining sculptural forms with evocative finishes that simulate the look of parched earth, speckled stone, rippled cloth, pitted metal or abstract painting."[48]

There has also been a revival of interest in woodblock printing. A host of artists continue to work in this medium. The most prominent artist in this field is Munakata Shikō (1903–1975). Working very rapidly, he has produced a prodigious number of prints. Munakata was a Zen Buddhist, and much of his work has to do with religious subjects. Carving dynamic and rough-hewn figures, Munakata endows his prints with enormous strength of design, movement of line, and dramatic tension. Another printer who rivaled Munakata as a popular artist was Saitō Kiyoshi (1907–1997). His eye-catching style in depicting snowy landscapes and Buddhist temples and gardens won him a popular following.

Artists in woodblock printing perhaps retained their ties to old Japan more than painters who followed the Western artistic tradition. The latter "found in the West the excitement of novelty and ideas far removed from their own." But the young generation of artists began looking more to Japan's past artistic tradition, the thinking and philosophy prevalent since the fourteenth century. One authority on Japanese art states, "It fits into the Zen tradition . . . artistically that perception reveals itself in evanescence, in short-lived phenomena that expresses the harmony between man and nature."[49]

Folk craft as art is seen in simple everyday things. For example, packaging has developed into an art in Japan. A Japanese graphic designer explains that the highly developed techniques and refined aesthetic sensibilities developed over past centuries. The packagers "were self-conscious craftsmen who endeavored to refine their methods and did so in a spirit of artistry. . . . They were driven by an aesthetic philosophy that said everything could and should be made beautiful." The most distinguishing characteristic is the natural element, which represents the Japanese sense of oneness with nature. An American designer commenting on the Japanese art of packaging remarked, "First one is amazed by the mastery and perfection of all the details: colors and calligraphy, knots and ties, all evolving in some inevitable fashion from the forms or functions contained within and the natural materials used to make them. Finally you stand in awe of the simplicity and clarity of expression."[50]

POPULAR CULTURE

In popular culture, pornography and comic books have become the rage. As one authority on Japanese literature and culture has observed, Japan presents a dichotomy of the puritanical and the sordid: cleanliness and dirtiness exist side by side.[51] In Shinto there is an abhorrence of pollution, but there is also the "muddy goddess of the village, the shamaness who is in touch with the dark mysteries of nature."[52] From this perspective, women are seen as demonic forces that consume men by their passion. Japanese pornographic films and photographs, which are overwhelmingly sadistic, depict brutal abuses of women, thus reflecting, as some believe, a fear of masculine inadequacy. A British woman novelist surmised that Japan's pornographic movies and comic books exhibit "a very real fear and hatred of women, maybe even of the female principle. The recurring themes [are] of bondage and mutilation. . . . Men must be very much afraid of women if they want to load them up with so many chains and cut off their breasts and I don't know what."[53] Traditionally, ghost stories entailed being haunted by terrible hags who come back to avenge the wrong done to them. Thus, the fear of the demonic power of women is not necessarily of recent vintage.

The popularity of comic books (manga) among adults may appear to be a reversion to childhood, but the contents are hardly suitable for children, given the emphasis on "violence, sex and scatology." Comic book sales amount to hundreds of millions of copies each year. One popular weekly comics magazine had a circulation of 6 million in 1991. Their readership includes a wide spectrum of Japanese society, from students and salaried businesspeople to housewives who wish to escape into fantasyland. In the 1970s Paul Theroux came across a comic book left behind by a reader on a train and was appalled when he picked it up and glanced at it. "The comic strips showed decapitations, cannibalism, people bristling with arrows like Saint Sebastian . . . and, in general, mayhem."[54]

Boys' comic books deal with stories about sports, adventure, and science fiction. Girls' comic books contain stories of love and romance. Adult comic books deal with stories about warriors, gamblers, and gigolos, but problems at the workplace and human relationships are treated in a humorous and satirical fashion. A pompous office boss may be lampooned, and the henpecked husband ridiculed. Perhaps the pressure to conform, to preserve harmony, and to abide by social proprieties has prompted people to seek outlets in fantasies of violence and sadism. Some critics have charged that comic books are ruining the minds of Japanese youth, but such cautions have had no effect on their ever-growing popularity. Some enterprising journalists have started a magazine in English, excerpting and translating select strips with the ostensible excuse as a means to help the American reader learn the Japanese language.

Japan is world famous for being a place where the younger generation seems to constantly invent a new craze that captivates the youth of Japan, followed closely a few weeks later by the children in the rest of the world. The "Hello Kitty" phenomenon is familiar to the parents of young girls everywhere. The cartoon cat is emblazoned on virtually every conceivable piece of young girls' paraphernalia: lunch boxes, clothes, note paper, erasers, sun glasses, shoes, jewelry, stuffed toys, bed linen, curtains, watches, and even food. Styled in imitation of the ubiquitous "waving cat" good-luck symbol that graces every retail store, the cartoon logo is a multibillion dollar industry. A similar fad for young boys was the Mighty Morphin Power Rangers cartoon series, which also became a world industry in plastic toy action figures and Halloween costumes.

In the 1980s and 1990s two games became rapidly popular in Japan and then spread to the rest of the world. First was the "virtual pet" electronic gizmo

Tamagotchi. Originally designed for preteens, the electronic game acted like a pet that required its child owner to "feed" and "caress" the hand-held machine like a small animal lest the thing "cry" for attention. Surprisingly the toy became popular among teen girls and even some adults. Very much in the manner of the "pet rock" craze that swept the United States in the 1970s, the toys were more conversation starters than anything else. They also became collectible in the same way that Beanie Babies and Cabbage Patch dolls swept America a decade before. Children and then adults fought over these prized symbols of popular culture.

In the mid-1990s a new craze swept Japan and then the world. The cartoon characters Pokemon (short for "Pocket Monsters") inhabited a netherworld where they said nothing except to shrilly repeat their distinctive names over and over. Embedded in cartoons and video games, each Pokemon character had distinctive abilities in battles with each other. Some social critics commented that they were almost like Shinto kami in that they were powered and limited by their environment (thunder, lightning, fire, water).

BASEBALL AND OTHER SPORTS

Baseball, which had been popular since the later nineteenth century but condemned during the war as a decadent Western sport, made an instant, popular comeback in postwar Japan. The annual high school national baseball championship that had driven the nation into a wild frenzy every August in the prewar years returned, and baseball mania revived. In June 1951 the state broadcasting network, NHK, broadcast a professional ball game for the first time; soon the baseball broadcasts began to rival the high school ball games in popularity. Baseball grew in such popularity that by the 1960s American professionals were lured to play in Japan. In 1964 Murakami Masanori (b. 1944) briefly pitched in the United States, and beginning in 1995 with Nomo Hideo (b. 1968) a deluge of Japanese players defected from Japan to play in the United States.

In September 1951 radio broadcasting rights were extended to private companies, and the government monopoly came to an end. Beginning in February 1953, NHK began regular television broadcasts. In August of that year a private television company began broadcasting. By 1958, there were 1 million TV sets in Japanese homes, and by 2004 there were over 80 million sets.

After Nomo broke the vise-like death grip that Japanese baseball owners had over their players (he "retired" from Japanese baseball before signing with the Los Angeles Dodgers), a legion of top stars jumped to the American major leagues. Before long some twenty of Japan's best were playing in North America. A few, like Suzuki Ichiro, Matsuzaka Daisuke, and Matsui Hideki, became genuine all-stars in the United States. Many Japanese fans feared that the best Japanese players would naturally gravitate to the high salaries and endorsement possibilities abroad and leave the Japanese leagues to be little more than minor league development stations for the American game.

Sumo is a distinctly Japanese sport because many of its arcane customs harken to its ancient Shinto origins. It ceased to be limited to Shinto shrines and became popular in the Tokugawa era, when its hulking wrestlers became cultural idols in the Pleasure Quarters. In the prewar era it took on national dimensions. Beginning in the early 1960s a number of Asian Americans from Hawaii began to drift into sumo. The pioneer was Jesse Takayama, who became immensely popular among Japanese youth. After a decade of wrestling, he retired to form his own "stable" of young Hawaiians, whom he groomed in the arcane traditions. His most popular wrestler was the Samoan Konishiki (born Saleva'a Fuauli Atisano'e), who ballooned up to the improbable weight of 564 pounds. Only his limited mobility prevented him from attaining the ultimate goal of Grand Champion (*yokozuna*) before his knees gave out. He learned enough Japanese to become a sports idol among the young fans, marrying a Japanese actress and opening up a number of successful restaurants. Eventually his stablemate, Akebono (the Hawaiian-born Chad Rowan), managed to become yokozuna, as he pummeled most of his Japanese competitors. His countryman Musashimaru (born Fiamalu Penitani in Samoa) also became yokozuna.

As disturbed as the Japanese were to have two Americans become yokozuna, they were positively shocked when a handful of Mongolians jumped to the top of the sport in late 1990s. Mongolians had for centuries practiced a wrestling style similar to sumo. After World War II some Japanese soldiers who had served in Mongolia during the war helped to bring a number of young wrestlers to Japan. By 2007 two Mongolians rose to the pinnacle of sumo. One, born Dolgorsürengiin Dagvadorj, took the sumo name of Asashōryū Akinori to become yokozuna in 2003. A controversial figure who seemed to thumb his nose at Japanese conventions at every turn, he was very popular with young fans but castigated by the old sumo establishment for his brashness. His younger countryman Hakuho Sho (born Munkhbat Davaajargal) skyrocketed through the ranks to become yokozuna four years later.

A number of East Europeans joined sumo in the early part of the twenty-first century and seemed to be on the cusp of joining the Mongolians as champions. Needless to say, the old conservative ranks of sumo enthusiasts are very worried that no Japanese seems to be able to withstand the flood of foreign wrestlers.

A number of Japanese sports heroes have done very well in several international sports. Long a powerhouse in the Olympic sports of judo and jujitsu, several Japanese have also starred in gymnastics, volleyball, baseball, and soft-ball. Several professional golfers are routinely near the top of the leader boards. Among the some four dozen male professionals is Aoki Isao, who is now the "grand old man" of Japanese golfers, having been inducted into the World Golf Hall of Fame in 2004. Among the women, Okamoto Ayako, Miyazato Ai, Higuchi Hisako, and Ueda Momoko annually are at the top of the Ladies Professional Golf Association.

REVIVAL OF NATIONALISM?

The persistence of ethnocentrism combined with the recovery of self-confidence founded on Japan's phenomenal economic success since the 1960s, some be-lieve, may result in a resurgence of nationalism—not militant nationalism but an inflated sense of "chosen-ness." Indeed, as Jared Taylor has observed, there is a growing sense of self-confidence: "As Japan overtakes the United States in one area after another, the *gaijin* complex [of deferring to Cau-casians] has begun to fade. Those who have long known the Japanese see a new confidence in their foreign and economic policies. . . . Japanese who work in the United States will bow and scrape in the presence of whites but as soon as they are alone . . . they wallow in feelings of superiority."[55] A Japanese reporter who had served overseas and returned to Japan in 1983 after a num-ber of years was surprised at the tone of nationalism in the press: "I realized shortly after I came back that it's intellectually fashionable to criticize the United States."[56]

An indication of this growing willingness to speak up forcefully against US policy was the publication of the book by a former novelist and leading politi-cian who was elected governor of Tokyo in 1999, Ishihara Shintarō (b. 1932), entitled *The Japan That Can Say No*. This struck a certain segment of the US political circle as an abrasive challenge to the United States. Ishihara certainly overestimated Japan's supremacy in the high-tech area, insofar as he assumed that Japan could tip the balance of power between the United States and the Soviet Union one way or the other (for instance, by selling computer chips to the latter), but his advice to Japanese leaders to say "no" when "no" is what they mean rather than pussyfooting politely or continuing the practice of giv-ing ambiguous responses that could be interpreted to mean "yes" could lessen misunderstandings. In his call for Japan to chart an independent course inter-nationally, he writes,

> There is no need for our country to follow the United States slavishly. . . . I
> hardly think that possessing ideals of our own means being overconfident or
> lapsing into an arrogant, dangerous sort of nationalism. . . . We must say "no"

quite firmly when necessary. It is also obvious, however, that we cannot afford suddenly to lose our ties with America. For the sake of the more cooperative and mature relationship that should exist between our two countries, we must say "yes" equally clearly when that is the appropriate response. At times this will require a determination on the part of our political leaders to say "no" to the Japanese people. [57]

Resurfacing Japanese nationalism is not as serious a threat to international peace as some fear, and it is not likely that militant nationalism is on the upsurge. Still, some Japanese leaders seek to purge the stain of guilt from Japanese aggression in the 1930s and 1940s and to instill a sense of national pride in the young generation. The Japanese government does not use the word *haisen* (defeat) but uses *shūsen* (end) of the war instead.

From time to time prominent political leaders play down or deny the aggression and atrocities committed by the Japanese in World War II. As noted previously, the Ministry of Education insisted that the term "aggression" be changed in the textbook written by Ienaga Saburō. In 1986, the minister of education in the Nakasone cabinet said that the Koreans were partly responsible for Japanese colonization of that country. In 1990 Ishihara Shintarō asserted that the Nanjing massacre was a story made up by the Chinese, and in 1994, the justice minister in the Hata cabinet also stated publicly that the Nanjing massacre was a fabrication.[58] In 1990 Motoshima Hitoshi (b. 1922), the mayor of Nagasaki, survived an assassination attempt brought on in part for having suggested that Emperor Hirohito bore substantial responsibility for World War II.

In May 1994 a right-wing nationalist attempted to assassinate former prime minister Hosokawa for asserting that World War II was a war of Japanese aggression and for apologizing for the conduct of the Japanese troops during the war. In August 1994 a cabinet minister in the Murayama cabinet stated in a news conference that Japanese military action in Asia was launched not for conquest, but to liberate Asian countries from Western colonialism. The benefits of Japanese actions are seen in the high literacy rates in East Asia, he asserted.[59] From time to time, prominent government officials pay homage at the Shinto Yasukuni Shrine, where the war dead are enshrined.

There are other indications that a desire to absolve the Japanese of guilt or responsibility for the war and atrocities is increasing. Some movies about the war seek to present Japan's role in a favorable light. A 1982 hit movie, *The Imperial Japanese Empire,* depicted Japan as a victim rather than an assailant at Pearl Harbor, because President Roosevelt was plotting to "get the Japanese to attack us."[60] In the certification of textbooks in 1991, a textbook, referring to the atrocities committed by the Japanese troops in Nanjing in 1938, stated,

"Over 70,000 people were reportedly killed by the Japanese imperial army." Ministry officials suggested that this be changed to: "A large number of Chinese people were killed."[61] The Ministry of Education advised that the national flag be displayed and the national anthem be sung in school ceremonies. And military heroes like Admiral Tōgō who had been purged from history books have been restored in the textbooks.

But concern about the revival of militarism in Japan may be groundless. Writer Mishima Yukio's attempt to arouse nationalistic sentiments failed to move the young men in the Self-Defense Force. There remains a strong sentiment against building up Japan's defense forces. During the Persian Gulf War of 1991, Japan was subjected to strong criticism by the United States for not providing active military support, but Japanese public opinion staunchly opposed Japanese involvement except to make financial contributions for the undertaking. The government's decision to send minesweepers to the Gulf region also aroused the opponents of militarism.

Some members of the Diet, however, began to push for a constitutional amendment to change Article 9, that is, the no-war clause, by taking advantage of US criticism of Japan's failure to support the Gulf War effort militarily. Their contention is that the constitution was imposed on Japan by the United States so that it should be revised to make it conform to Japanese society and culture. The general populace, however, seem disinterested in reviving the military forces. Only 10 percent of adults surveyed in 1991 said they were willing to fight for their country.[62] The Asian nations that were victimized by Japanese militarism in the past are extremely sensitive about any indication that Japan might be planning to strengthen its defense forces. Considerable furor was raised when Japan agreed to contribute auxiliary troops to the American invasion of Iraq in 2003.

In 1985 longtime journalist and authority on Asian affairs, T. H. White (1915–1986), published an article in the *New York Times,* "The Danger from Japan," discussing the economic threat posed by Japan. He regarded Japanese economic expansion into the world market as a move for domination, and he believed that in penetrating the US economy they behaved as if they had "the right to press American livelihood to the wall." He compared Japanese economic activities to its prewar military aggression and warned the Japanese that they "might well remember the course that ran from Pearl Harbor to the deck of the USS *Missouri* in Tokyo Bay just 40 years ago." His article revived "the unpleasant memory of prewar 'yellow peril' rhetoric in the minds of the Japanese."[63]

Most Japanese leaders are aware of the fact that the United States helped Japan's economic recovery after the war, assisted it financially and technologically, and opened up the US market fully to Japanese products to enable electronics, high-tech, and automobile and other industries to grow and prosper. Without the US market Japan would not have been able to develop as one of the world's dominant economic powers. As one observer remarked, "By aligning itself with the United States diplomatically, militarily, and economically over the past four decades, Japan thrived and prospered. . . . Japan got unimpeded access to the US market."[64]

Of course, Japan deserves credit for achieving its economic success by means of the hard work and dedication of the people—in short, through the pursuit of excellence that has historically characterized the country. Roger Buckley remarks,

> Who in 1945 would have prophesied that a nation with a lower per capita income than Malaya would later witness an endless procession of overseas politicians and observers intent on observing Japan's progress? When all the qualifications have been made and the reservations noted, the credit ultimately belongs to the Japanese state and the citizens. Fortune and friends have played their part, but they do not account for more than a portion of the result. Pain and national pride have been the real spur. Contemporary Japan has won its way back and more. [65]

END OF THE SHŌWA REIGN

On January 7, 1989, Emperor Hirohito, now known as Emperor Shōwa, passed away at age eighty-seven, and Prince Akihito became Japan's 125th emperor (counting mythological ones). *Heisei* (attainment of peace) was adopted as the era name. Emperor Shōwa had been on the throne for sixty-two years, the longest reign in Japanese history. Prior to becoming emperor on December 25, 1926, he had served as regent to the ailing Emperor Taishō from November 1921 to the latter's death. Thus, twentieth-century Japan virtually overlaps with Emperor Shōwa's reign.

Hirohito was far from being a charismatic figure or a decisive leader. He had a slightly befuddled look in all of his photographs. The court advisers' efforts to create an aura of mystical majesty never seemed to have been successful. His appearance in prewar days, dressed in military regalia striding atop a white stallion, never made him look like an awesome leader; he remained an unprepossessing figure. And perhaps this was most fitting because he was not meant to be a ruler but a symbol of the nation, just as the SCAP officials defined his position in the postwar constitution. The public was indoctrinated to regard him as a divine figure, the descendant of the Sun Goddess, but his advisers, like Saionji, advised him not to get personally involved in decision making. He was to stick to performing ceremonial duties and endorse decisions made by government and court officials.

Even though SCAP, in accordance with the US government's decision, excluded him from the list of war criminals to be tried at the International Military Tribunal, some Japanese believed that he should be held responsible for the war. Ideologues from the left in particular held firmly to this belief, but even moderates believed that he should have taken responsibility and vacated the throne. Among the latter was Nambara Shigeru (1889–1974), former president of the Imperial University of Tokyo. Others felt that the emperor should have resigned because even though he may not have been legally responsible for the war he was morally responsible. Also his abdication and succession by the crown prince would have symbolized the change in the status of the emperor in the former Meiji constitution to the postwar constitution.[66] Kido Kōichi, his closest adviser at the court as Keeper of the Privy Seal in the war years, also advised the emperor to abdicate. A survey conducted by the *Yomiuri* newspaper in August 1948 indicated that 90.3 percent of the people favored preserving the imperial institution but fewer, 68.5 percent, favored the emperor remaining on the throne. At that time, 83.1 percent of the National Diet members were against the emperor's abdication.[67]

It transpired that the emperor had no intention of abdicating. Evidently, he felt that it was his responsibility to carry on the imperial tradition of lifetime occupancy of the throne that had been established by his grandfather, Emperor Meiji. The idea of renouncing his divine status was not his own but was initiated by SCAP officials under the direction of Colonel Ken Dyke, chief of the Civil Information and Education Section. But the draft of the declaration submitted by SCAP was revised by the emperor to insert the idea that the Japanese political system since the Meiji era had been founded on the Charter Oath of Five Principles proclaimed by Emperor Meiji in 1868. He did so to make the point that Japan has been a democracy since the beginning of the Meiji years, and that democracy and the imperial institution have coexisted.[68]

In 1946 a Communist critic, Masaki Hiroshi (1896–1975), a lawyer who fought for the defense of civil rights, rejected the imperial court's claim that the emperor ended the war, ignoring his own safety to end the suffering of the people. Masaki contended that everything that the emperor did, he did for his own interest; he declared war thinking of his own well-being and he ended the war for the same reason. If he really had been interested in the welfare of the people he would have avoided or ended the war sooner, Masaki argued. The imperial clan had been nothing more than a parasitic entity throughout history.[69] Members of the imperial court, and the emperor himself, propagated the story that the emperor made the difficult decision to end the war for the good of the people. His poem, "Thinking of the people dying endlessly in the air raids, I ended the war, having no thought of my own fate," indicates his true sentiments, they contended.[70]

Both the condemnation and idealization of the emperor system that surfaced in the postwar years continues to the present. Some people favor abolishing the emperor system, whereas others see a mystical ideal in the system. A Marxist thinker contended in 1946 that "the emperor system is nothing more than a form of shamanistic domination made possible by the serf-like existence of the Japanese people." He believed that if the living conditions of the people improved the people will not hold the imperial family in religious awe, and the institution will fade away.[71]

Justification of the imperial institution still persists among those who focus on the mystical aspects of the emperor system that have enabled it to survive over the centuries, and they foresee its survival into the future. They equate the system with non-doctrinaire Shinto, the Japanese language, the national flag— a given, like air. "The emperor doesn't have a position in the secular world. He simply exists, but that very existence is vital, like the air we breathe."[72]

The imperial court set out to transform the image of the emperor from that of a sacred being residing high above the clouds to a being close to the people. Thus, from early 1946, the emperor traveled to out-of-the-way villages, factories, schools, and hospitals and visited those who had suffered from the war. In the first couple of years he covered half of the country by train, sleeping in simple inns. The emperor who was to remain above the political world was worried about the growing number of strikes and "third party elements seeking to further their own interests by taking advantage of the poor conditions in the country." He visited General MacArthur eleven times and discussed the state of affairs with the general. MacArthur told the emperor that the respect and affection that the people had for him was assurance that the people will not turn to destructive, leftist extremism. He encouraged the emperor to continue his travels.[73]

The emperor occasionally gave political advice to SCAP as in 1947 expressing his desire to have the United States continue its occupation of Okinawa for the defense of Japan against the possible threat from the Soviet Union. Hirohito suggested that this be done by a twenty-five to fifty years lease to enable the United States to continue its military occupation of Okinawa.[74] When this information became public in 1979 the Okinawans were understandably upset that the emperor regarded them as mere political pawns, ignoring the huge sacrifices they made during the US invasion of their island.

The policy of creating the image of an emperor close to the people and the image of the imperial family as a social rather than a political elite was enhanced with the marriage of Crown Prince Akihito with a "commoner" in

1959. In 1975 the emperor visited the United States, where his reception was surprisingly cordial with the US public, not manifesting the kind of hostility by English and Europeans when he visited Europe in 1971.

Despite the effort to create the image of an imperial court close to the people, the court was afforded lives as private as possible. Though the staff of the Imperial Household Agency was reduced substantially, from 6,211 to 1,452 by the Socialist government of Katayama in 1947, a large number of attendants committed to preserving the mystic of the imperial family remained at the court. Thus, the people's hope for a more open imperial court was curtailed by the protocol-minded palace guard. When in 1993 Crown Prince Naruhito (b. 1960) married Owada Masako, a Harvard-educated foreign ministry official, some people hoped that she would become involved in public affairs, especially women who hoped she would serve as a role model for Japanese women. But palace guards seemingly succeeded in placing her behind the imperial curtain. The strain of adhering to a narrowly prescribed way of life seems to have caused the current empress, Michiko, to suffer a nervous depression that affected her ability to speak for a short while. Predictably, the court blamed an intrusive press for her discomfort.

In April 1987 Emperor Shōwa became ill with cancer, and after a brief respite he entered a critical stage in September. Upon receiving this news the public went into a period of prayerful waiting until he died on January 7, 1989. Crown Prince Akihito then succeeded him, and the Heisei era began, a new era for the Japanese people. The passing of Emperor Shōwa in a way signifies a final cleansing of the slate because as long as he was on the throne the memory of the onus of war and atrocities committed by the Japanese could not help but remain firmly embedded among peoples of the nations victimized by Japanese militarism and imperialism.

Regardless of Emperor Shōwa's personal role during his reign, there is little question that his reign was as momentous, or even more so, than Emperor Meiji's reign. The Shōwa era saw the years of parliamentary government of the 1920s, the rise of ultranationalism and radical militarism in the 1930s, the invasion of Manchuria and China, the Pacific war, the devastating defeat, the occupation years, and recovery and spectacular growth.

The most spectacular developments unfolded in the economic arena, which saw Japan rise from the ruins to become a major economic force in the world. And despite the problems that accompany rapid industrial and technological changes, the lifestyle of the people, especially among the young generation, and the standard of living have changed dramatically. If, as Marx believed, economic factors determine the nature of all other aspects of life—political, social, cultural, and intellectual—it is likely that the future of Japan will be determined by the course of economic developments.

Given this perception, then, Emperor Shōwa was merely a figurehead, and the successes and failures, the adversities and triumphs, oppressions and freedom, and fortune and misfortune were not of his making. But in the minds of the Japanese people much of these developments emanated from the court. Thus the end of his reign could mean in a sense a cleansing of the stains that the militaristic, imperialistic years had left on the Japanese soul, and the beginning of the chance for a truly new beginning for Japan. Regardless of the actual role he played, as long as Emperor Shōwa was on the throne Japan was still the old semi-feudal land with its legacy of militarism, "fascism," and imperialism.

What then will the new era have in store for Japan in the twenty-first century? Will the reign of the new emperor who has never ridden astride a white horse in military regalia portend a truly liberal, democratic era? Being unstained with even symbolic guilt for the ravages of totalitarianism and war, unlike his predecessor, it is possible that the mind of Japan will be freed from the mystique of the emperor system and the *kokutai* (unique national polity) that lingered in the soul of the generation identified with Emperor Shōwa. Emperor Akihito's formative years were a time when Japanese imperialism and militarism had been crushed and discredited. Democracy, openness, internationalism, and liberalism were ideals that filled the air for forty-five postwar years before he mounted the throne. As a symbol of the nation, perhaps these ideals will be more closely identified with the Heisei era than the Shōwa era.

Notes

1. Ichiro Kawasaki, *Japan Unmasked* (Rutland, Vt.: Charles E. Tuttle, 1969), p. 21.

2. Jared Taylor, *Shadows of the Rising Sun: A Critical View of the "Japanese Miracle"* (New York: Morrow, 1983), p. 229.

3. Donald Richie in *The Japan Experience,* ed. Ronald Bell (New York: Weatherhill, 1973), p. 39.

4. Maruyama Masao, *Nihon no Shisō* (Japanese Thought) (Tokyo: Iwanami Shoten, 1961), pp. 2ff, 128ff.

5. Professor Gen Itasaka quoted in *Chicago Tribune,* June 16, 1991.

6. Isaiah BenDasan, *The Japanese and the Jews,* trans. Richard L. Gage (New York: Weatherhill, 1972), pp. 112–113, 185–188.

7. Robert Jay Lifton, *History and Human Survival: Essays on the Young and Old, Survivors and the Dead, Peace and War, and on Contemporary Psychohistory* (New York: Random House, 1970), pp. 26, 29–30.

8. Hayashi Chikio, "The National Character in Transition," *Japan Echo* 15, 1988, pp. 8–9.

9. In 1991 there were 124 newspapers, with a combined circulation of 72.5 million copies. In 1991 more than 2,300 monthly magazines and 85 weekly magazines were published. The combined total of the number of copies published came to 4.641 billion.

10. In 1995 more than 51,000 new books were published, for a total of 419.9 million copies, a significant increase from the 25,421 titles published in 1968.

11. Donald Keene, *Dawn to the West: Japanese Literature in the Modern Era,* 2 vols. (New York: Holt, 1984), p. 807. In his Nobel lecture Kawabata said, "However alienated one may

be from the world, suicide is not a form of enlightenment. However admirable he may be, the man who commits suicide is far from the realm of the saint." Yet, ironically, he did commit suicide in 1972 by inhaling gas.

12. Ibuse Masuji, *Black Rain*, trans. John Bester (New York: Bantam Books, 1985), introduction, p. 2.

13. Ibid., pp. 14, 108.

14. Osamu Dazai, *The Setting Sun,* trans. Donald Keene (New York: New Directions, 1956), pp. 165–166.

15. Keene, *Dawn to the West*, p. 1216.

16. Yukio Mishima, "Party of One, Japan the Cherished Myths," *Holiday,* October 1961, p. 13.

17. *New Yorker,* December 12, 1970, pp. 40–41.

18. Keene, *Dawn to the West*, p. 1136.

19. Christine Chapman, "Women Writers: Three Portraits," *PHP*, November 1984, p. 40.

20. Keene, *Dawn to the West*, p. 1144.

21. Ibid., p. 1150.

22. Ibid., pp. 115–159.

23. Chapman, "Women Writers," p. 44.

24. Yukiko Tanaka and Elizabeth Hanson, trans. and ed., *This Kind of Woman: Ten Stories by Japanese Women Writers, 1960–1976* (New York: Perigee Books, 1982), p. 226.

25. Translator's note in Kenzaburō Ōe, *A Personal Matter,* trans. John Nathan (New York: Grove, 1968), pp. viii–ix.

26. *New York Times,* October 14, 1994.

27. Shusaku Endo, *Silence,* trans. William Johnston (New York: Taplinger, 1980), pp. 281, 285.

28. A. N. Wilson, "Firmly Catholic and Firmly Japanese," *New York Times Book Review,* July 21, 1985.

29. Masaaki Kawanishi, "A Survey of Japanese Literature in 1983," *Japanese Literature Today,* Japan P.E.N. Club, March 1984, p. 1.

30. *New York Times Book Review,* September 27, 1992, p. 29.

31. Review by Michiko Kakutani, *New York Times,* January 13, 1993.

32. Banana Yoshimoto, *Kitchen,* trans. Megan Backus (New York: Washington Square Press, 1993), pp. 3, 10.

33. *New York Times,* May 17, 1993.

34. Donald Richie, *Japanese Movies* (Tokyo: Japan Travel Bureau, 1961), p. vii.

35. *New York Times,* September 7, 1998.

36. Richie, *Japanese Movies*, p. 161.

37. *New York Times,* April 3, 1994.

38. Michael Wilmington in *Chicago Tribune,* August 14, 1994.

39. Nagasaka Toshihisa in *Japan Echo,* autumn 1991, p. 87.

40. *New York Times,* December 15, 1985.

41. Vincent Canby, "What's So Funny about Japan," *New York Times Magazine,* June 18, 1989, pp. 26ff.

42. Ibid.

43. Nick Bornoff, "The Gentle Art of Savage Satire," *Intersect,* July 1988, p. 29.

44. Raymond in Bell, *Japan Experience*, p. 169.

45. *Chicago Tribune,* April 26, 1993.

46. Peter McGill, "Boxing Ando," *Intersect,* November 1993, pp. 34–40.

47. Bernard Leach, *Hamada, Potter* (Tokyo: Kodansha International, 1975), p. 125.

48. *New York Times,* January 2, 1994.

49. *New York Times,* May 19, 1985.

50. Hideyuki Oka, *How to Wrap Five More Eggs: Traditional Japanese Packaging,* with photographs by Michikazu Sakai (New York: Weatherhill, 1975), pp. 7–13.

51. Edward Seidensticker, *This Country Japan* (Tokyo: Kodansha, 1984), p. 52.

52. Ian Buruma, *Behind the Mask: On Sexual Demons, Sacred Mothers, Transvestites, Gangsters, Drifters and Other Japanese Cultural Heroes* (New York: Pantheon, 1984), p. 36.

53. Angela Carter in Bell, *Japan Experience,* p. 29.

54. Frederick L. Schodt, "Reading the Comics," *Wilson Quarterly,* summer 1985, p. 57.

55. Taylor, *Shadows of the Rising Sun,* p. 58.

56. Yoshihisa Komori in *Intersect,* February 1985, p. 9.

57. *Japan Echo,* spring 1990, p. 35.

58. *Japan Times Weekly,* May 25–29, 1994.

59. *New York Times,* May 21, August 15, 1994.

60. James Bailey, "At the Movies," *Wilson Quarterly,* summer 1985, p. 70.

61. *Japan Times Weekly,* July 8–14, 1991.

62. *Newsweek,* July 6, 1991.

63. Theodore H. White, "The Danger from Japan," *New York Times Magazine,* July 28, 1985, pp. 38ff.

64. Ronald Yates in *Chicago Tribune,* June 18, 1991.

65. Roger Buckley, *Japan Today* (Cambridge: Cambridge University Press, 1990), p. 133.

66. Matsuo Takayoshi, *Kokusai Kokka e no Shuppatsu* (Takeoff Toward an International State) (Tokyo: Shueisha, 1993), p. 117.

67. Ibid., pp. 119, 121.

68. Ibid., pp. 20, 41.

69. Irokawa Daikichi, *Aru Shōwashi* (A Showa History) (Tokyo: Chūō koronsha, 1975), pp. 348–350.

70. Daikichi Irokawa, *The Age of Hirohito: In Search of Modern Japan,* trans. Mikiso Hane and John K. Urda (New York: Free Press, 1995), p. 97.

71. *Japan Echo,* summer 1989, p. 10.

72. Shichihei Yamamoto in ibid., p. 14. Also *Bungei Shūnjū,* July 1993, pp. 116ff.

73. Irokawa, *Age of Hirohito,* p. 106.

74. Ibid.

APPENDIX A

The Internet

Generally speaking, the Internet has been a great boon to historians in general, but especially so for those who study Japan. That being said, it can also be a great hindrance if the scholar is not careful.

The nature of samurai culture draws serious aficionados as well as hundreds of less serious people. Many people who took a series of martial arts courses or who saw the *Karate Kid* on television seem to want to spread the bits of misinformation that they acquired. The Internet is thus replete with hundreds of Web sites offering wildly inaccurate suppositions, rumors, statistics (always suspect anyway), and folklore.

That is not to say that there aren't many sites with good material. Generally, I use Web sources the same way I use other scholarly sources: with great care and cynicism. Using one isolated source is dangerous. Even the same information found in two or more sites can be worse than useless if they are all crackpot sites.

One semester I had an upper-division class jointly write an essay on an incident in ancient Japanese history. The assignment was to write the article using 50 percent historical fact and 50 percent pure invention. After they had done so, we posted the article to one of the Web sites that solicits "user input." The site claims that all items are checked for accuracy before they are posted to the site. The upshot of the exercise was that the Web site posted our misinformation almost verbatim. Two dates were corrected, but otherwise the article was posted with all the innuendo, supposition, and inaccuracy that we had invented.

Fearing retribution from my historian colleagues, we allowed the article to stand for only two days before I wrote a note to the Web site managers pointing out the inaccuracies. The Web managers took nearly two weeks (the original article remained online the entire time) to respond to my note, noting that my correction was precisely how their system works. Such chutzpah! So let the reader beware.

I do not allow students to cite Web sources in their scholarly work unless they download the information complete with Web address, then print a hard copy that they attach to the research paper.

On any given day, commercial search engines such as Google or Ask.com will offer over a hundred sites if one searches using the term "Japanese history." The order in which they are posted has very little to do with reliability of the sites. The order is generally a mix of the most-used and advertisers.

I have classified some Web sites into six general categories, in descending order of reliability: Scholarly Links, Labors of Love, Commercial Ad–Driven, Travel-Based, Samurai Wares, and Special Interest Groups. I will examine them in that order and make some general comments.

Scholarly Links

These are generally links created by legitimate scholars, often working for museums, universities, or research "think tanks." The information is usually reliable, often with source citations embedded in the text. Often they contain hot links, which take the viewer to another site with one or two clicks of the mouse. Here are some of my favorites:

Kansai Institute of Information Systems (KIIS)

http://www.kiis.or.jp/rekishi/kaido-e.html

This is a reliable site run by academics in Japan. One must be careful, however, because translations can give variant spellings of historical names. For instance, Ito Hirobumi sometimes has his named rendered "Hirofumi," which has to do with alternate pronunciation systems. The site says that it "helps promote the Rekishi Kaido (historic route) project by providing a database for historic cultural resources in and around the Kansai region through Web pages Kansai Digital Archives. These pages are expected to encourage cultural activities and the use of advanced information technology, contributing to revitalization of the region."

History of Japan: An Annotated Directory of Internet Resources

http://newton.uor.edu/Departments&Programs/AsianStudiesDept/japan-history.html

This site is very informative, with many links to scholarly articles and bibliographies by well-known scholars. The site, however, is not well-maintained. Many of the links are inoperative. For instance, the "Bibliography of Japanese History to 1912," compiled by Peter Kornicki, University of Cambridge, is now unavailable, presumably because Kornicki ceased to maintain his personal Web site.

Library of Congress: Country Studies

http://lcweb2.loc.gov/frd/cs/jptoc.html

This is an excellent semiofficial site maintained by professionals working for the Library of Congress. Some care is needed, however, since I have been told by friends who work for the Library that some of the material is "farmed out" to consultants. The site contains excellent links complete with extensive bibliographies.

Arts of China Consortium (formerly Chinese and Japanese Art History WWW Virtual Library)

http://www.nyu.edu/gsas/dept/fineart/html/chinese/

This site was constructed with grant money in 2002. A few years later, the money ran out, and the site became a little messy. It is much better now. According to the site's home page, its original raison d'être was "to promote the study and understanding of Chinese art history, archaeology, and visual and material culture, and to support the research and professional activities of its members. ACC is currently in the process of applying for affiliation with the College Art Association and the Association for Asian Studies, where ACC hopes to organize annual thematic panel sessions. To encourage more informal dialogue among members, ACC conducts an e-mail listserv and maintains this website to provide information on graduate programs in Asian art, symposia and conferences, fellowships and grants, positions available, and web links to facilitate research and pedagogy."

The site goes on to say, "We welcome faculty and graduate students in art history and related fields, museum professionals, independent scholars, and serious collectors worldwide to become members of ACC."

H-Japan
http://www.h-net.org/~japan/

This is a very good site maintained by Michigan State University. It is part of a consortium of Listserv discussion sites. It maintains some archived materials, including an excellent links page and book reviews by scholars.

The editors say, "Welcome to H-Japan, a member of H-Net Humanities & Social Sciences Online. H-Japan is an international, nonpartisan electronic discussion group. It provides scholars, graduate students and professionals a free daily forum to discuss Japanese history, culture, religion, and society, including contemporary political, diplomatic, security, and economic issues."

National Museum of Japanese History
http://www.rekihaku.ac.jp/english/index.html

This is one of the best museum sites that contain links to their gallery exhibitions. But like all museums, what appears on the online site is idiosyncratic, depending on curator interest and what the museum wants to emphasize.

Labors of Love

These are sites constructed by interested individuals out of the love they have for Japanese studies. They consist mainly of links to existing sites, but in some cases they are decidedly more.

Teaching (and Learning) about Japan
http://www.csuohio.edu/history/japan/

Professor Makela constructed the site for his own students at his home university. The illustrated lectures grew until they became stand-alone links. I have used his site for class assignments.

A Short Chronology of Japanese American History
http://www.janet.org/janet_history/niiya_chron.html

Adapted from *Japanese American History: An A-to-Z Reference from 1868 to the Present*, the site is edited by Brian Niiya, resource center director at the Japanese Cultural Center of Hawaii.

A Chronology of Japanese History
http://www.shikokuhenrotrail.com/japanhistory.html

A usually reliable site with only a few inaccuracies. It is written and compiled by David Turkington, project coordinator at University of Illinois at Chicago's National Center for Data Mining.

Nixi Cura's personal Web page
http://asnic.utexas.edu/asnic/countries/japan/index.html

Nixi Cura is an editor of H-Japan. Her academic specialty is Chinese art history, but she exhibits a deep understanding of Japan as well. This site contains links to many excellent scholarly Web sites.

Outlines of Japanese History

http://www.stockton.edu/~gilmorew/consorti/1ceasia.htm

The site is of limited use because it was prepared by William J. Gilmore-Lehne, who died in 1999. That caveat aside, the site has some surprisingly sophisticated links to scholarly research, including the Richard Hooker series and the Rekishi Kaido Web pages, managed by the Kansai Institute of Information Systems.

Commercial Ad–Driven Sites

These are sites that rely on advertisements paid by commercial companies. As such, these sites are somewhat unreliable. Many of the short articles on Japanese history are written by pedestrian historians (at best). Sometimes they are written by press agents. They do not always check their facts. Here are just a few, to give examples:

Japan-Guide.com

http://www.japan-guide.com/e/e641.html

Wikipedia

http://en.wikipedia.org/wiki/History_of_Japan

I place this here because while generally it is accurate, it is one of the "user-input" sites. It is probably as accurate as most low-end encyclopedias that do not employ academics as editors. It is fact-based with good links.

Infoplease

http://www.infoplease.com/ipa/A0107666.html

This page is short, like an encyclopedia entry with statistics; there are not many good links.

Travel-Based

These sites are linked to travel agencies. They are intended for folks who are thinking of traveling to Japan and therefore contain bare-bones information about Japan. They are unreliable.

Japan 101

http://www.japan-101.com/history/

This site has minimal information but good pictures.

About.com

http://gojapan.about.com/od/japanhistory/Japan_History_Samurai.htm

This is another great example of a travel-linked site; the history coverage is pedestrian at best.

Samurai Wares

There are dozens of these sites geared toward samurai aficionados. Many of the sites exist purely to sell samurai-esque items (ersatz swords, armor, etc.). Historical accuracy is clearly a matter of random chance.

Samurai Archives

http://www.samurai-archives.com/

A perfect example of a commercial-based page selling samurai whatnots. It contains the subheading "Shop for Samurai Archives Items and Logo Wear." Its history page includes links to "Sengoku Biographic Dictionary," "Famous Generals," and "Daimyo House Codes," but also "Famous Women" (twenty-four samurai-linked women including Empress Jingu and Hojo Masako). Not much historical reasoning or historiographic material, but if you wish to know what banners samurai marched under, this is certainly the place to look.

Reconstructing Japanese History
http://www.reconstructinghistory.com/japanese.php?c=8&d=101&w=3&r=Y/brief history.html.

This site is for wannabes such as reenactors. It provides dressmaker patterns to construct replica clothing and the like.

Special Interest Groups

These sites are decidedly unreliable. They are made for and maintained by people who have axes to grind and hobbyhorses to ride. For instance:

Japanese History for Gay Men
http://www.geocities.co.jp/Berkeley/3508/japanesehistory.html

ABC of Japanese History
http://www.jiyuu-shikan.org/e/index.html

This site is little better than those created by Holocaust deniers. It is an excellent example of attempts by Japanese scholars to refute stories about Japanese atrocities, including original "unretouched" photos of the Rape of Nanjing. I quote directly from the site:

> The Association for Advancement of Unbiased View of History (Jiyuu-Shugi-Shikan Kenkyuu-Kai) is a non-profit group set up in 1995, by Professor Fujioka Nobukatsu of Tokyo University.
>
> What We Believe In:
> - Gathering different viewpoints together, free, active, rational debate, and overcoming taboos and restraints of ideology to pursue historical truths.
> - We are a non-partisan group of volunteers interested in history related to Japan.
> - We are unconnected with any historical movements or study groups based outside Japan.
> - We are opposed to all political ideology and concepts which are against upholding and protecting human dignity and equality.
>
> What We Do:
> - Teachers' seminars and skills-up programs on modern and contemporary history classes
> - Publications; journals on modern history class reform & bestseller books on Japanese history
> - Hosts lectures by historians and specialists on controversial issues of contemporary interest
> - Providing information in Japanese and English through the internet as a basis for stimulating debate and constructive dialogue.

Summary

By far, the best services available on the Internet are those that permit the reader to link to peer-reviewed scholarly work. One such is J-STOR (http://www.jstor.org/), a subscription service that links to many scholarly journals. Most college online library sites have links to J-STOR, but one may subscribe as an individual. The search engine provides dozens of links to research articles in journals such as *Journal of Asian Studies, Monumenta Nipponica,* and the *Journal of Japanese Studies.*

One can use the Internet as a valuable tool. But as with all other research tools, it cannot be assumed to be accurate. One must test all facts, ideas, and opinions through other sources.

APPENDIX B

Chronological Chart

Tokugawa Period (1600–1867)

1825   An edict to drive off foreign vessels is issued.
1833–1836   The Tempō famine
1837   Ōshio Heihachirō leads an insurrection.
1841   Rōjū Mizuno Tadakuni initiates the Tempō Reforms.
1849   The woodblock artist Hokusai dies.
1853   Commodore Perry arrives.
1854   The Treaty of Kanagawa is signed with the United States.
1858   Ii Naosuke is appointed great councilor (tairō); a commercial treaty with the United States is concluded; the woodblock artist Hiroshige dies.
1867   Shōgun Keiki restores political power to the imperial court.

Meiji Period (1868–1912)

1868   A new government is established; Tokyo (formerly Edo) becomes the capital.
1869   Four major daimyō relinquish control over their han to the imperial government.
1871   The han are replaced by prefectures; the postal system is introduced; Tokugawa class distinctions are eliminated; the Iwakura mission is dispatched to the West.
1872   The Tokyo-Yokohama Railroad is opened; the freedom to buy and sell land is granted; compulsory elementary education is instituted.
1873   The Gregorian calendar is adopted (Dec. 3, 1872, of the old lunar calendar is converted to Jan. 1, 1873); universal military conscription and a new land tax are instituted.
1874   A request for the establishment of a national assembly is submitted by Itagaki and others.
1876   The wearing of swords by former samurai is banned.
1877   Saigō Takamori leads Satsuma Rebellion.
1879   The Ryukyu Islands become Okinawa prefecture.
1881   A national assembly is promised by the government.
1884   The peerage is created; the Chichibu Uprising occurs.
1885   The cabinet system is adopted; Itō Hirobumi becomes the first prime minister.

1887	Electric lighting is introduced.
1888	The Privy Council is established.
1889	The Meiji constitution is promulgated.
1890	The first Diet convenes; the Imperial Rescript on Education is issued; telephone service is introduced.
1894	A treaty revision is agreed upon between Japan and England.
1894	First Peace Preservation Law
1894–1895	The Sino-Japanese War
1895	Triple Intervention by Russia, Germany, and France
1898	The Ōkuma-Itagaki cabinet is formed.
1900	Public Order and Police Law
1902	The Anglo-Japanese Alliance is concluded.
1904–1905	The Russo-Japanese War is concluded by Treaty of Portsmouth.
1910	Korea is annexed; Kōtoku Shūsui and others are executed.
1912	Emperor Meiji dies.

Taishō Period (1912–1926)

1914	Japan enters the First World War.
1915	The Twenty-One Demands are presented to China.
1918	The Hara Cabinet is formed.
1921	The Washington Conference on naval arms limitations convenes.
1923	The Great Earthquake
1925	Universal manhood suffrage is enacted; radio broadcasting commences.
1925	Second Peace Preservation Law
1926	Emperor Taishō dies.

Shōwa Period (1926–1989)

1930	London Naval Conference
1931	The Manchurian Incident
1932	Prime Minister Inukai is assassinated; party government ends.
1933	Lytton Report; Japan withdraws from the League of Nations.
1935	Minobe Tatsukichi's Organ Theory is condemned.
1936	Prominent leaders are assassinated by radical militarists; the Anti-Comintern Pact with Germany is concluded.
1937	War with China breaks out.
1940	Japanese troops move into French Indochina; a tripartite alliance with Germany and Italy is concluded.
1941	Japan attacks Pearl Harbor, beginning the Pacific war.
1942	The Battle of Midway (June)
1944	The tide of war shifts; Saipan falls; Prime Minister Tōjō resigns; US bombers carry out massive air raids on Japanese cities.
1945	US troops land in the Philippines and Okinawa; atomic bombs are dropped on Hiroshima and Nagasaki; Russia enters the war; Japan surrenders; Allied occupation under General MacArthur begins.
1946	A new constitution is promulgated.
1948	General Tōjō and others are executed.

1951	The peace treaty is signed in San Francisco.
1951	A United States–Japanese Mutual Security Agreement is signed; television broadcasting begins.
1952	The Allied occupation ends.
1955	The Liberal Democratic Party (LDP) is formed.
1956	Japan is admitted to the United Nations.
1960	A new United States–Japan Mutual Security Agreement is concluded.
1964	Japan hosts the Olympic games in Tokyo.
1965	Ienaga Saburo, a prominent historian, files the first of his three lawsuits against the ministry of education, charging that the process of textbook approval is unconstitutional.
1970	Mishima Yukio commits suicide.
1971	The United States agrees to relinquish control of Okinawa by 1972.
1972	Prime Minister Tanaka visits China and normalizes relations.
1973	Arab oil embargo and energy crisis
1975	Emperor Hirohito visits the United States.
1975	Prime Minister Miki Takeo visits the Yasukuni Shrine as a "private individual" on the thirtieth anniversary of the end of World War II.
1978	Fourteen Class A war criminals (convicted by the International War Tribunal for the Far East), including Tōjō Hideki, are quietly enshrined as "Martyrs of Shōwa" at Yasukuni Shrine.
1979	Prime Minister Ohira Masayoshi visits the Yasukuni Shrine.
1980	Japan produces more automobiles than the United States.
1980	Prime Minister Suzuki Zentaro visits the Yasukuni Shrine.
1981	Prime Minister Suzuki Zentaro visits the Yasukuni Shrine.
1982	Prime Minister Suzuki Zentaro visits the Yasukuni Shrine.
1982	Honda opens first car plant in the United States.
1983	Prime Minister Nakasone Yasuhiro visits the Yasukuni Shrine.
1983	President Reagan visits Japan.
1984	Matsui Yayori publishes short article in *Asahi Shinbun* on subject of "comfort women," the first time any major newspaper addresses the issue.
1985	Prime Minister Nakasone Yasuhiro visits the Yasukuni Shrine.
1986	Equal Employment Opportunity Law comes into effect to protect women's rights.
1987	Privatization of national railways begins.
1987	Okinawan supermarket owner burns Japanese flag in protest of Japan's treatment of Okinawa.
1988	Recruit Scandal: Prime Minister Takeshita resigns for accepting bribes from the Recruit Company.
1988	Supreme Court rules that Nakaya Yasuko cannot prevent government from enshrining the soul of her deceased husband (killed while serving in the Self-Defense Forces) at Yasukuni Shrine.
1989	Emperor Hirohito dies; Crown Prince Akihito is enthroned as Heisei Emperor.

The Heisei Era (1989–)

1990	Nagasaki mayor Motoshima Hitoshi survives assassination attempt for suggesting Hirohito assume blame for World War II atrocities committed in his name.

1991	Japan pledges billions of dollars to support the Gulf War; refuses to send troops, citing Article 9 of the Peace Constitution.
1991	In Diet session, Japanese government denies the involvement of the wartime state and its military in the matter of "comfort women."
1991	Mount Unzendake in southern Japan erupts, leaving 43 people dead and nearly 2,300 homeless.
1992	Historian Yoshimi Yoshiaki publishes documentary evidence proving the Japanese government was actively involved in wartime "comfort women" program.
1992	Mohri Minoru is the first Japanese astronaut in space.
1992	Kanemaru Shin is forced to resign his Diet seat for bribes from the Sagawa Kyubin Company.
1992	Itami Juzo, film director, is attacked and seriously injured by Japanese mobsters upset over his unflattering portrayal of yakuza in a film.
1992	Prime Minister Miyazawa Kiichi officially apologizes to South Korea over the "comfort women" issue.
1992	Prime Minister Miyazawa Kiichi visits the Yasukuni Shrine.
1993	The LDP loses its majority in the Diet lower house for the first time since 1955.
1993	As millions of Japanese watch on television, Crown Prince Naruhito marries commoner Owada Masako in an elaborate Shinto religious ceremony.
1993	American Chad Haaheo Rowan becomes first non-Japanese Sumo Grand Champion (Yokozuna), under name Akebono.
1993	Earthquake measuring a magnitude of 7.8 strikes northern Japan, killing 196 people.
1994	The LDP returns to power.
1994	Ōe Kenzaburo, Japanese novelist, wins the Noble Prize for literature.
1994	Japan fires a rocket to the moon.
1995	Japanese government creates the Asian Women's Fund to receive private contributions to aid "comfort women."
1995	Aum Shinrikyo religious cult under the leadership of Asahara Shoko releases deadly sarin gas in Tokyo subway, killing seven people and injuring hundreds more.
1995	Kansai Earthquake strikes in Kobe, causing $100 billion in property losses and killing over 5,000 people.
1995	On the anniversary of the end of World War II, Prime Minister Murayama makes the first official apology to other Asian countries for Japan's wartime atrocities.
1995	US President Bill Clinton formally apologizes to Japan for rape of young girl by three US Marines in Okinawa.
1996	Tupac Amaru guerillas capture Japanese ambassador in Peru.
1996	Prime Minister Hashimoto Ryutaro visits the Yasukuni Shrine.
1997	Consumption tax is raised from 3 percent to 5 percent over loud public outcry.
1997	Japan signs an international agreement promising to remove remnants of chemical warfare agents left in China after World War II.
1997	In response to historian Ienaga Saburo's third lawsuit alleging government interference in textbook contents, Supreme Court finds partially for Ienaga.
1998	Winter Olympic games are held in and around Nagano.

1998	Prime Minister Obuchi issues an apology to the people of South Korea for thirty-five years of brutal colonial rule.
1999	"Kimigayo" is reinstated as national anthem; Rising Sun reinstated as official national flag.
1999	The Health Ministry approves Viagra (after six months of consideration) but still holds back approval for the birth control pill (which has been in consideration nine years).
1999	Tokaimura nuclear power plant accident exposes at least seventy people to various levels of radiation and ends up taking the lives of two.
2000	Empress Dowager Nagako dies. She was chosen as Hirohito's wife when she was fourteen years old.
2000	Ota Fusae is elected governor of Osaka, becoming the first woman governor in Japan.
2000	A new 2,000-yen bill is released into circulation by the bank of Japan. This is the first release of a new banknote since 1958.
2001	US submarine *Greeneville* sinks Japanese fishing vessel *Ehime Maru* near Honolulu, Hawaii. Nine people on the *Ehime Maru* die as the trawler sinks.
2001	Prime Minister Mori and Russian President Putin sign an accord for return of two Kurile Islands, Etorofu and Kunashiri, to Japan.
2001	First case of Mad Cow Disease in Japan
2001	United States turns over to Japanese authorities an American serviceman accused of rape.
2001	Prime Minister Koizumi makes a surprise visit to Yasukuni Shrine.
2001	Prime Minister Koizumi visits China and South Korea in an attempt to smooth relations between countries.
2001	Japan dispatches two destroyers and a supply ship to the Indian Ocean to support US forces fighting in Afghanistan. This is the first time for Japan to send military ships outside of its own waters since the end of World War II.
2001	Crown Princess Masako gives birth to a daughter, and lineage controversy ensues.
2002	Japan and Korea cohost the 2002 Soccer World Cup.
2002	North Korean leader Kim Jung Il allows five Japanese who had been kidnapped twenty years earlier to return to Japan.
2002	A Tokyo court acknowledges for the first time Japan's use of biological weapons before and during World War II.
2002	Prime Minister Koizumi visits Yasukuni Shrine.
2002	Koizumi is the first prime minister to visit North Korea.
2003	Prime Minister Koizumi visits Yasukuni Shrine.
2004	Prime Minister Koizumi visits Yasukuni Shrine.
2004	Japan dispatches Army Self Defense Forces to Samawah, in southern Iraq. This is the first time troops have been deployed to an active war zone since World War II.
2004	Death sentence for Aum Shinrikyo leader Asahara is confirmed.
2004	Nonradioactive steam leaks from Mihama nuclear power plant, killing four workers and severely burning seven others.
2004	Japan applies for a permanent seat on the UN Security Council.
2005	Prime Minister Koizumi visits Yasukuni Shrine.

2005   Anti-Japanese protest in Beijing

2005   Princess Sayako (age thirty-six), the emperor's only daughter, quits monarchy and marries Yoshiki Kuroda, a forty-year-old urban planner.

2005   Bills finally pass both houses of the Diet to privatize the postal system.

2005   More than a hundred people are killed when a commuter train crashes near Amagasaki.

2006   Prime Minister Koizumi visits Yasukuni Shrine.

2006   North Korea test-fires missiles over Sea of Japan.

2006   Japan agrees to pay $6 billion of the $10 billion cost in transferring 8,000 US marines from Okinawa to Guam.

2006   Crown Prince's younger brother, Akishino, and his wife have a baby boy, the first male heir to the imperial throne born since the mid-1960s. He is named Hisahito and is now the third in line to the throne.

2007   Japan recalls ships that supported fighting in Afghanistan.

2007   Radiation leaks, burst pipes, and fires at Kashiwazaki nuclear power plant follow a 6.8 magnitude earthquake near Niigata.

2007   Nagasaki mayor Ito Itcho is assassinated by yakuza.

2007   Japanese whaling fleet sets sail on a six-month mission described as scientific research.

2007   Asian Women's Fund (founded in 1995) dissolves. It had provided 285 women in the Philippines, South Korea, and Taiwan 2 million yen (US$17,800) each in compensation, helped set up nursing homes for Indonesian former sex slaves, and offered medical assistance to some eighty Dutch former sex slaves.

2008   A US marine accused of raping a young girl in Okinawa surrenders to Japanese jurisdiction (case was later dropped).

2008   Defamation lawsuit against novelist Ōe Kenzaburo over statements that military officers ordered civilians to commit mass suicide in Okinawa during World War II is rejected in Osaka district court.

2008   District Court of Nagoya rules that Japan's 2004 dispatch of air force troops to Iraq breached the country's pacifist constitution.

2008   Former agricultural minister Shimamura Yoshinobu joins 159 other lawmakers to pray at the Yasukuni shrine. Prime Minister Fukuda Yasuo does not attend.

2008   Tokyo prosecutors arrest Tamio Araki, former president of Pacific Consultants International, and three other company executives for allegedly misusing 120 million yen of government funds meant for the disposal of about 400,000 chemical weapons that Japanese troops left behind in China at the end of the war.

2008   Poll by *Yomiuri* newspaper finds 43.1 percent of Japanese supports keeping the 1947 pacifist constitution as is, against 42.5 percent who back revisions.

APPENDIX C
List of Prime Ministers

Prime Minister	Assumed Office	Party
Itō Hirobumi	December 22, 1885	None
Kuroda Kiyotaka	April 30, 1888	None
Yamagata Aritomo	December 24, 1889	None
Matsukata Masayoshi	May 6, 1891	None
Itō Hirobumi	August 8, 1892	None
Matsukata Masayoshi	September 18, 1896	None
Itō Hirobumi	January 12, 1898	None
Ōkuma Shigenobu	June 30, 1898	Kenseito
Yamagata Aritomo	November 8, 1898	None
Itō Hirobumi	October 19, 1900	Rikken Seiyūkai
Katsura Tarō	June 2, 1901	None
Saionji Kimmochi	January 7, 1906	Rikken Seiyūkai
Katsura Tarō	July 14, 1908	None
Saionji Kimmochi	August 30, 1911	Rikken Seiyūkai
Katsura Tarō	December 21, 1912	None
Yamamoto Gonnohyōe	February 20, 1913	Rikken Seiyūkai
Ōkuma Shigenobu	April 16, 1914	Rikken Doshikai
Terauchi Masatake	October 9, 1916	None
Hara Kei	September 29, 1918	Rikken Seiyūkai
Takahashi Korekiyo	November 13, 1921	Rikken Seiyūkai
Katō Tomosaburō	June 12, 1922	National Union
Yamamoto Gonnohyōe	September 2, 1923	National Union
Kiyoura Keigo	January 7, 1924	None
Katō Kōmei	June 11, 1924	Coalition
Wakatsuki Reijirō	January 30, 1926	Kenseito
Tanaka Giichi	April 20, 1927	Rikken Seiyūkai
Hamaguchi Yūkō	July 2, 1929	Rikken Minseito
Wakatsuki Reijirō	April 14, 1931	Rikken Minseito
Inukai Tsuyoshi	December 13, 1931	Rikken Seiyūkai
Saitō Makoto	May 26, 1932	National Union

Okada Keisuke	July 8, 1934	National Union
Hirota Kōki	March 9, 1936	National Union
Hayashi Senjūrō	February 2, 1937	National Union
Konoe Fumimaro	June 4, 1937	National Union
Hiranuma Kiichirō	January 5, 1939	National Union
Abe Nobuyuki	August 30, 1939	National Union
Yonai Mitsumasa	January 16, 1940	National Union
Konoe Fumimaro	July 22, 1940	Taisei Yokusankai
Tōjō Hideki	October 18, 1941	Taisei Yokusankai
Koiso Kuniaki	July 22, 1944	None
Suzuki Kantarō	April 7, 1945	National Union
Prince Higashikuni	August 17, 1945	National Union
Shidehara Kijūrō	October 9, 1945	National Union
Yoshida Shigeru	May 22, 1946	Liberal
Katayama Tetsu	May 24, 1947	Socialist
Ashida Hitoshi	March 10, 1948	Democratic
Yoshida Shigeru	October 15, 1948	Liberal
Hatoyama Ichirō	December 10, 1954	Democratic
Ishibashi Tanzan	December 23, 1956	Liberal Democratic
Kishi Nobusuke	February 25, 1957	Liberal Democratic
Ikeda Hayato	July 19, 1960	Liberal Democratic
Satō Eisaku	November 9, 1964	Liberal Democratic
Tanaka Kakuei	July 7, 1972	Liberal Democratic
Miki Takeo	December 9, 1974	Liberal Democratic
Fukuda Takeo	December 24, 1976	Liberal Democratic
Ōhira Masayoshi	December 7, 1978	Liberal Democratic
Suzuki Zenkō	June 17, 1980	Liberal Democratic
Nakasone Yasuhiro	November 27, 1982	Liberal Democratic
Takeshita Noboru	November 6, 1987	Liberal Democratic
Uno Sousuke	June 3, 1989	Liberal Democratic
Kaifu Toshiki	August 9, 1989	Liberal Democratic
Miyazawa Kiichi	November 6, 1991	Liberal Democratic
Hosokawa Morihiro	July 29, 1993	Japan New
Hata Tsutomu	April 28, 1994	Renewal
Murayama Tomiichi	June 29, 1994	Socialist
Hashimoto Ryūtarō	January 11, 1996	Liberal Democratic
Obuchi Keizō	July 30, 1998	Liberal Democratic
Mori Yoshirō	April 5, 2000	Liberal Democratic
Koizumi Junichirō	April 26, 2001	Liberal Democratic
Abe Shinzō	September 26, 2006	Liberal Democratic
Fukuda Yasuo	September 26, 2007	Liberal Democratic
Aso Taro	September 22, 2008	Liberal Democratic

Selected Bibliography

Historical and Biographical Dictionaries and Encyclopedias

Allinson, Gary D. *The Columbia Guide to Modern Japanese History.* New York: Columbia University Press, 1999.

Bowring, Richard J., and Peter F. Kornicki, eds. *Cambridge Encyclopedia of Japan.* Cambridge: Cambridge University Press, 1993.

Campbell, Alan, David S. Noble, et al., eds. *Japan: An Illustrated Encyclopedia.* 2 vols. Tokyo: Kodansha, 1993.

Goedertier, Joseph M. *Dictionary of Japanese History.* New York: Weatherhill, 1968.

Hisamatsu, Senichi. *Biographical Dictionary of Japanese Literature.* Tokyo: Kodansha, 1976.

Huffman, James L., ed. *Modern Japan: An Encyclopedia of History, Culture, and Nationalism.* New York: Garland, 1998.

Hunter, Janet. *Concise Dictionary of Modern Japanese History.* Berkeley: University of California Press, 1984.

Itasaka, Gen, ed. *Japan Encyclopedia.* 9 vols. Tokyo: Kodansha, 1978.

Iwao, Seiichi. *Biographical Dictionary of Japanese History.* Tokyo: Kodansha, 1978.

O'Neil, P. G. *Japanese Names.* Tokyo: Weatherhill, 1972.

Roberts, Laurance P. A. *Dictionary of Japanese Artists.* Tokyo: Weatherhill, 1976.

Schilling, Mark. *The Encyclopedia of Japanese Pop Culture.* New York: Weatherhill, 1997.

Geographical Works

Cressey, George B. *Asia's Land and Peoples.* New York: McGraw-Hill, 1963.

Dempster, Prue. *Japan Advances: A Geographical Study.* New York: Barnes & Noble, 1968.

Ishida, Ryujiro. *Geography of Japan.* Tokyo: Kokusai Bunka Shinkokai, 1969.

Trewartha, Glenn T. *Japan: A Physical, Cultural, and Regional Geography.* Madison: University of Wisconsin Press, 1965.

General Histories on Premodern Japan

Hall, John W. *Japan: From Prehistory to Modern Times.* New York: Delacorte, 1970.

Hall, John W., and Richard K. Beardsley, eds. *Twelve Doors to Japan.* New York: McGraw-Hill, 1965.

Hall, John W., et al., eds. *The Cambridge History of Japan.* 6 vols. New York: Cambridge University Press, 1989–1999.

Hane, Mikiso. *Premodern Japan: A Historical Survey.* Boulder, Colo.: Westview Press, 1991.

Inoue, Mitsusada. *Introduction to Japanese History: Before the Meiji Restoration.* Tokyo: Kokusai Bunka Shinkokai, 1968.

Kaempfer, Engelbert. *History of Japan.* 3 vols. Translated by J. G. S. Schenchzer. Glasgow: MacLehose, 1906.

Murdoch, James. *A History of Japan.* 3 vols., each with two parts. 1903, 1926. Reprint, New York: Ungar, 1964.

Reischauer, Edwin O. *Japan: The Story of a Nation.* New York: McGraw-Hill, 1990.

Reischauer, Edwin O., and Albert M. Craig. *Japan: Tradition and Transformation.* Boston: Houghton Mifflin, 1978.

Sansom, Sir George B. *A History of Japan.* 3 vols. Stanford: Stanford University Press, 1963.

———. *Japan: A Short Cultural History.* New York: Appleton, 1943.

Tiedemann, Arthur E., ed. *Introduction to Japanese Civilization.* New York: Columbia University Press, 1974.

Totman, Conrad. *Japan Before Perry.* Berkeley: University of California Press, 1981.

Transactions of the Asiatic Society of Japan. Tokyo: Asiatic Society of Japan, 1872–1998.

Early Years to 1185

Aoki, Michiko Y. *Records of Wind and Earth: A Translation of Fudoki with Introduction and Commentaries.* Ann Arbor: Center for Japanese Studies, University of Michigan, 1997.

Borgen, Robert. *Sugawara No Michizane and the Early Heian Court.* Cambridge, Mass.: Harvard University Press, 1986.

Brown, Delmer M., ed. *Ancient Japan. Vol. 1 of Cambridge History of Japan.* New York: Cambridge University Press, 1993.

Campbell, Joseph. *The Masks of God: Oriental Mythology.* New York: Viking, 1952.

Carter, Steven D. *Regent Redux: A Life of the Statesman-Scholar Ichijō Kaneyoshi.* Ann Arbor: Center for Japanese Studies, University of Michigan, 1996.

Chamberlain, Basil H., trans. *Kojiki* (Records of Ancient Matters). London: Routledge & Kegan Paul, 1932.

Farris, William W. *Heavenly Warriors: The Evolution of Japan's Military, 500–1300.* Cambridge, Mass.: Harvard University Press, 1992.

———. *Population, Disease, and Land in Early Japan, 645–900.* Cambridge, Mass.: Harvard University Press, 1985.

Hayashi, Chikio, and Kuroda Yasumasa. *Japanese Culture in Comparative Perspective.* Westport, Conn.: Praeger Press, 1997.

Hurst, Cameron. *Insei: Abdicated Sovereigns in the Politics of Late Heian Japan, 1086–1185.* New York: Columbia University Press, 1976.

Kidder, Edward. *Japan Before Buddhism.* New York: Praeger, 1959.

Komatsu, Isao. *The Japanese People: Origins of the People and the Language.* Tokyo: Kokusai Bunka Shinkokai, 1962.

Morris, Ivan I. *The World of the Shining Prince: Court Life in Ancient Japan.* New York: Knopf, 1964.

Philippi, Donald L., trans. *Kojiki.* Princeton: Princeton University Press, 1968.

Sadler, A. L., trans. "Heike Monogatari" (The Tale of the Heike). *Transactions of the Asiatic Society of Japan,* 1:46, pt. 2, 1918, and 1:49, pt. 1, 1921.

Sansom, Sir George B. *History of Japan to 1334*. Stanford: Stanford University Press, 1958.

Shively, Donald H., and William H. McCullough, eds. *Heian Japan*. Vol. 2 of *The Cambridge History of Japan*. New York: Cambridge University Press, 1999.

Tsunoda, Ryusaku, trans., and L. Carrington Goodrich, ed. *Japan in the Chinese Dynastic Histories: Later Han Through Ming Dynasties*. South Pasadena, Calif.: Perkins, 1931.

Young, John. *The Location of Yamatai*. Baltimore, Md.: Johns Hopkins University Press, 1957.

The Ascendancy of the Military Houses, from 1185 to 1600

Asakawa, Kanichi, ed. *The Documents of Iriki, Illustrative of the Development of the Feudal Institution in Japan*. Tokyo: Japan Society for the Promotion of Science, 1955.

Berry, Mary Elizabeth. *The Culture of Civil War in Kyoto*. Berkeley: University of California Press, 1997.

———. *Hideyoshi*. Cambridge, Mass.: Harvard University Press, 1982.

Boxer, Charles R. *The Christian Century in Japan, 1549–1650*. Berkeley: University of California Press, 1951.

Brown, Delmer M. *The Future and the Past: A Translation and Study of the Gukansho*. Berkeley: University of California Press, 1979.

Butler, Lee. *Emperor and Aristocracy in Japan, 1467–1680: Resilience and Renewal*. Cambridge, Mass.: Harvard University Asia Center, 2002.

Conlan, Thomas. *State of War: The Violent Order of Fourteenth-Century Japan*. Ann Arbor: Center for Japanese Studies, University of Michigan, 2003.

Cooper, Michael S. J., ed. *They Came to Japan: An Anthology of European Reports on Japan, 1543–1640*. Berkeley: University of California Press, 1965.

Dening, Walter. *The Life of Toyotomi Hideyoshi (1536–1598)*. Tokyo: Hokuseido, 1955.

Dilworth, David A., Valdo H. Viglielmo, and Agustin Jacinto Zavala. *Sourcebook for Modern Japanese Philosophy: Selected Documents*. Westport, Conn.: Greenwood Press, 1999.

Duus, Peter. *Feudalism in Japan*. New York: Knopf, 1969.

Elison, George, and Bardwell Smith, eds. *Warlords, Artisans, and Commoners: Japan in the Sixteenth Century*. Honolulu: University of Hawaii Press, 1981.

Friday, Karl. *Samurai, Warfare, and the State in Early Medieval Japan*. New York: Routledge, 2004.

Gay, Suzanne. *The Moneylenders of Late Medieval Kyoto*. Honolulu: University of Hawaii Press, 2001.

Hall, John W., and Takeshi Toyoda. *Japan in the Muromachi Age*. Berkeley: University of California Press, 1977.

Hall, John W., et al., eds. *Japan Before Tokugawa Consolidation and Economic Growth*. Princeton: Princeton University Press, 1981.

Jansen, Marius, ed. *Warrior Rule in Japan*. Cambridge: Cambridge University Press, 1995.

Kang, Etsuko Hae-jin. *Diplomacy and Ideology in Japanese-Korean Relations: From the 15th to the 18th Century*. New York: St. Martin's, 1997.

Keene, Donald, ed. *Yoshimasa and the Silver Pavilion: The Creation of the Soul of Japan*. New York: Columbia University Press, 2003.

Kitabatake, Chikafusa. *A Chronicle of Gods and Sovereigns*. Translated by H. Paul Varley. New York: Columbia University Press, 1980.

Mass, Jeffrey P. *The Development of Kamakura Rule, 1180–1250: A History with Documents*. Stanford: Stanford University Press, 1979.

_____. *The Kamakura Bakufu: A Study in Documents*. Stanford: Stanford University Press, 1976.

_____. *Warrior Government in Early Medieval Japan: A Study of the Kamakura Bakufu, Shugo and Jitō*. New Haven: Yale University Press, 1975.

Mass, Jeffrey P., ed. *Court and Bakufu in Japan: Essays in Kamakura History*. New Haven: Yale University Press, 1982.

_____. *The Origins of Japan's Medieval World: Courtiers, Clerics, Warriors, and Peasants in the Fourteenth Century*. Stanford: Stanford University Press, 1997.

Mass, Jeffrey P., and William B. Hauser, eds. *The Bakufu in Japanese History*. Stanford: Stanford University Press, 1985.

McCullough, Helen, trans. *Okagami: The Great Mirror*. Princeton: Princeton University Press, 1980.

_____. *The Taiheiki: A Chronicle of Medieval Japan*. New York: Columbia University Press, 1959.

_____. *The Tale of Heike*. Stanford: Stanford University Press, 1988.

_____. *Yoshitsune: A Fifteenth-Century Japanese Chronicle*. Stanford: Stanford University Press, 1966.

Rodrigues, Joao S. J. *This Island of Japan: Joao Rodrigues' Account of 16th Century Japan*. Translated by Michael Cooper. Tokyo: Kodansha, 1973.

Sansom, Sir George B. *A History of Japan, 1334–1615*. Stanford: Stanford University Press, 1960.

Shinoda, Minoru. *The Founding of the Kamakura Shogunate, 1180–1185*. New York: Columbia University Press, 1960.

Souyri, Pierre François, and Käthe Roth. *The World Turned Upside Down: Medieval Japanese Society*. New York: Columbia University Press, 2001.

Thornton, S. A. *Charisma and Community Formation in Medieval Japan: The Case of the Yugyō-Ha (1300–1700)*. Ithaca, N.Y.: Cornell University Press, 1999.

Varley, H. Paul. *Imperial Restoration in Medieval Japan*. New York: Columbia University Press, 1971.

_____. *The Onin War: History of Its Origins and Background, with a Selective Translation of the Chronicles of Onin*. New York: Columbia University Press, 1967.

Yamamura, Kozo, ed. *Medieval Japan*. Vol. 3 of *The Cambridge History of Japan*. New York: Cambridge University Press, 1990.

The Tokugawa Period: Political, Social, and Economic Affairs

Arnesen, Peter J. *The Medieval Japanese Daimyo*. New Haven: Yale University Press, 1979.

Bix, Herbert. *Peasant Protest in Japan, 1590–1884*. New Haven: Yale University Press, 1986.

Bolitho, Harold. *Treasures Among Men: The Fudai Daimyo in Tokugawa Japan*. New Haven: Yale University Press, 1974.

Borton, Hugh. "Peasant Uprisings in Japan of the Tokugawa Period." *Transactions of the Asiatic Society of Japan*, 2:16, 1938.

Hall, John W. *Tanuma Okitsugu, 1719–1788, Forerunner of Modern Japan*. Cambridge, Mass.: Harvard University Press, 1955.

Hall, John W., ed. *Early Modern Japan*. Vol. 4 of *The Cambridge History of Japan*. New York: Cambridge University Press, 1991.

Hall, John W., and Marius Jansen, eds. *Studies in the Institutional History of Early Modern Japan*. Princeton: Princeton University Press, 1968.

Hanley, Susan B. *Everyday Things in Premodern Japan: The Hidden Legacy of Material Culture.* Berkeley: University of California Press, 1997.

Hanley, Susan B., and Kozo Yamamura. *Economic and Democratic Change in Pre-Industrial Japan, 1600–1868.* Princeton: Princeton University Press, 1977.

Hesselink, Reinier H. *Prisoners from Nambu: Reality and Make-Believe in Seventeenth-Century Japanese Diplomacy.* Honolulu: University of Hawaii Press, 2002.

Jannetta, Ann B. *Epidemics and Mortality in Early Modern Japan.* Princeton: Princeton University Press, 1987.

Kalland, Arne. *Fishing Villages in Tokugawa Japan.* Honolulu: University of Hawaii Press, 1995.

Katsu, Kokichi. *Musui's Story: The Autobiography of a Tokugawa Samurai.* Translated by Teruko Craig. Tucson: University of Arizona Press, 1988.

Nakane, Chie, and Shintaro Oishi, eds. *Tokugawa Japan.* Tokyo: University of Tokyo Press, 1990.

Ooms, Herman. *Charismatic Bureaucrat: A Political Biography of Matsudaira Sadanobu.* Chicago: University of Chicago Press, 1975.

_____. *Tokugawa Village Practice: Class, Status, Power, Law.* Berkeley: University of California Press, 1996.

Perrin, Noel. *Giving Up the Gun: Japan's Reversion to the Sword, 1543–1879.* Boulder, Colo.: Shambhala, 1980.

Roberts, John C. *Mitsui Empire: Three Centuries of Japanese Business.* New York: Weatherhill, 1973.

Sadler, A. L. *The Maker of Modern Japan: The Life of Tokugawa Ieyasu.* London: Allen and Unwin, 1937.

Sansom, Sir George B. *A History of Japan, 1615–1867.* Stanford: Stanford University Press, 1963.

Sheldon, C. D. *The Rise of the Merchant Class in Tokugawa Japan.* Locust Valley, N.Y.: Augustin, 1958.

Smith, Neil Skene, ed. "Materials on Japanese Social and Economic History: Tokugawa Japan." *Transactions of the Asiatic Society of Japan,* 2:14, 1937.

Smith, Thomas C. *The Agrarian Origins of Modern Japan.* Stanford: Stanford University Press, 1959.

_____. *Nakahara: Family Farming and Population in a Japanese Village, 1717–1830.* Stanford: Stanford University Press, 1977.

_____. *Native Sources of Japanese Industrialization.* Berkeley: University of California Press, 1988.

Toby, Ronald P. *State and Diplomacy in Early Modern Japan.* Princeton: Princeton University Press, 1984.

Totman, Conrad D. *Early Modern Japan.* Berkeley: University of California Press, 1993.

_____. *Politics in the Tokugawa Bakufu, 1600–1843.* Cambridge, Mass.: Harvard University Press, 1967.

_____. *Tokugawa Ieyasu.* South San Francisco: Heian, 1982.

Vlastos, Stephen. *Peasant Protests and Uprisings in Tokugawa Japan.* Berkeley: University of California Press, 1986.

Walthall, Anne, ed. and trans. *Peasant Uprisings in Japan: A Critical Anthology of Peasant Histories.* Chicago: University of Chicago Press, 1991.

_____. *Social Protest and Popular Culture in Eighteenth Century Japan.* Tucson: University of Arizona Press, 1968.

Webb, Herschel. *The Japanese Imperial Institution in the Tokugawa Period.* New York: Columbia University Press, 1968.

Wigmore, John H. *Law and Justice in Tokugawa Japan.* 2 vols. Tokyo: University of Tokyo Press, 1969.

Tokugawa Period: Intellectual Developments

Ackroyd, Joyce, trans. *Told Round a Brushwood Fire: The Autobiography of Arai Hakuseki.* Tucson: University of Arizona Press, 1989.

Arai, Hakuseki. *Lessons from History.* Translated by Joyce Ackroyd. St. Lucia, Queensland: University of Queensland, 1982.

Bolitho, Harold. *Bereavement and Consolation: Testimonies from Tokugawa Japan.* New Haven: Yale University Press, 2003.

Brownlee, John S. *Japanese Historians and the National Myth, 1600–1945: The Age of the Gods and Emperor Jimmu.* Vancouver: University of British Columbia Press, 1997.

Dardess, John W. *Confucianism and Autocracy.* Berkeley: University of California Press, 1983.

Dore, Ronald P. *Education in Tokugawa Japan.* Berkeley: University of California Press, 1965.

Earl, David M. *Emperor and Nation in Japan: Political Thinkers of the Tokugawa Period.* Seattle: University of Washington Press, 1964.

Elison, George. *Deus Destroyed: The Image of Christianity in Early Modern Japan.* Cambridge, Mass.: Harvard University Press, 1973.

Harootunian, H. D. *Things Seen and Unseen: Discourse and Ideology in Tokugawa Nativism.* Chicago: University of Chicago Press, 1988.

Keene, Donald. *The Japanese Discovery of Europe, 1720–1830.* Stanford: Stanford University Press, 1969.

Koschmann, J. Victor. *The Mito Ideology: Discourse, Reform, and Insurrection in Late Tokugawa Japan.* Berkeley: University of California Press, 1987.

Maruyama, Masao. *Studies in the Intellectual History of Tokugawa Japan.* Translated by Mikiso Hane. Tokyo: University of Tokyo Press, 1974.

Matsumoto, Shigeru. *Motoori Norinaga, 1730–1801.* Cambridge, Mass.: Harvard University Press, 1970.

Najita, Tetsuo. *Visions of Virtue in Tokugawa Japan: The Kaitokudō Merchant Academy of Osaka.* Chicago: University of Chicago Press, 1987.

Najita, Tetsuo, ed. *Tokugawa Political Writings.* New York: Cambridge University Press, 1998.

Najita, Tetsuo, and Erwin Scheiner, eds. *Japanese Thought in the Tokugawa Period, 1600–1868: Methods and Metaphor.* Chicago: University of Chicago Press, 1978.

Nakai, Kate Wildman. *Shogunal Politics: Arai Hakuseki and the Premises of Tokugawa Rule.* Cambridge, Mass.: Harvard University Press, 1988.

Ng, Wai-Ming. *The I Ching in Tokugawa Thought and Culture.* Honolulu: University of Hawaii Press, 2000.

Norman, E. H. "Ando Shoeki and the Anatomy of Japanese Feudalism." *Transactions of the Asiatic Society of Japan,* 3:2, 1949.

Nosco, Peter, ed. *Confucianism and Tokugawa Culture.* Princeton: Princeton University Press, 1984.

Ogyu, Sorai. *The Political Writings of Ogyu Sorai.* Translated by J. R. McEwan. London: Cambridge University Press, 1962.

Ooms, Herman. *Tokugawa Ideology: Early Constructs, 1570–1680*. Princeton: Princeton University Press, 1985.

Passin, Herbert. *Society and Education in Japan*. New York: Bureau of Publications, Teachers' College and East Asian Institute, Columbia University, 1965.

Platt, Brian. *Burning and Building: Schooling and State Formation in Japan, 1750–1890*. Cambridge, Mass.: Harvard University Asia Center, 2004.

Sansom, Sir George B. *The Western World and Japan*. New York: Knopf, 1980.

Takemura, Eiji. *The Perception of Work in Tokugawa Japan: A Study of Ishida Baigan and Ninomiya Sontoku*. Lanham, Md.: University Press of America, 1998.

Vande Walle, W. F., and Kazuhiko Kasaya. *Dodonæus in Japan: Translation and the Scientific Mind in the Tokugawa Period*. Leuven: Leuven University Press, 2001.

Wakabayashi, Bob Tadashi. *Anti-Foreignism and Western Learning in Early-Modern Japan*. Cambridge, Mass.: Harvard University Press, 1992.

_____. *Japanese Loyalism Reconstrued: Yamagata Daini's Ryushi Shinron of 1759*. Honolulu: University of Hawaii Press, 1995.

Yamamoto, Tsunetomo. *Hagakure: The Book of the Samurai*. Trans. by William S. Wilson. Tokyo: Kodansha, 1978.

Tokugawa Period: Cultural Developments

Hur, Nam-Lin. *Prayer and Play in Late Tokugawa Japan: Asakusa Sensōji and Edo Society*. Cambridge, Mass.: Harvard University Asia Center, 2000.

Ihara, Saikaku. *Five Women Who Loved Love*. Translated by William T. de Bary. Rutland, Vt.: Tuttle, 1956.

_____. *The Life of an Amorous Woman and Other Writings*. Translated by Ivan Morris. Norfolk, Conn.: Laughlin, 1963.

Kita, Sandy. *The Last Tosa: Iwasa Katsumochi Matabei, Bridge to Ukiyo-E*. Honolulu: University of Hawaii Press, 1999.

Nenzi, Laura. *Excursions in Identity: Travel and the Intersection of Place, Gender, and Status an Edo Japan:* Honolulu: University of Hawaii Press, 2008.

Nishiyama, Matsunosuke. *Edo Culture: Daily Life and Diversions in Urban Japan, 1600–1868*. Translated by Gerald Groemer. Honolulu: University of Hawaii Press,1997.

Perez, Louis G. *Everyday Things in Early Modern Japan*. Westport, Conn.: Greenwood Press, 2001.

Tanizaki Junichiro. *Secret History of the Lord of Musashi and Arrowroot*. Translated by Anthony H. Chambers. New York: Knopf, 1982.

Vaporis, Constantine Nomikos. *Breaking Barriers: Travel and the State in Early Modern Japan*. Cambridge, Mass.: Harvard University Asia Center, 1995.

Yonemoto, Marcia. *Mapping Early Modern Japan: Space, Place, and Culture in the Tokugawa Period (1603–1868)*. Berkeley: University of California Press, 2003.

The Last Years of Tokugawa Rule

Alcock, Sir Rutherford. *The Capital of the Tycoon: A Narrative of Three Years' Residence in Japan*. 2 vols. New York: Harper, 1863.

Beasley, W. G., ed. and trans. *Select Documents on Japanese Foreign Policy, 1853–1868*. London: Oxford University Press, 1955.

Black, John R. *Young Japan: Yokohama and Yedo, 1858–1879.* 2 vols. London: Oxford University Press, 1969.

Burns, Susan. *Before the Nation: Kokugaku and the Imagining of Community in Early Modern Japan.* Durham, N.C.: Duke University Press, 2003.

Craig, Albert M. *Chōshū in the Meiji Restoration.* Cambridge, Mass.: Harvard University Press, 1961.

Frederik, L. Schodt. *Native American in the Land of the Shōgun: Ranald Macdonald and the Opening of Japan.* Berkeley: Stone Bridge Press, 2003.

Harootunian, H. D. *Toward Restoration: The Growth of Political Consciousness in Tokugawa Japan.* Berkeley: University of California Press, 1970.

Jansen, Marius B. *Sakamoto Ryōma and the Meiji Restoration.* Princeton: Princeton University Press, 1961.

Roberts, Luke S. *Mercantilism in a Japanese Domain: The Merchant Origins of Economic Nationalism in Eighteenth-Century Tosa.* Cambridge: Cambridge University Press, 1998.

Satow, Sir Ernest M. *A Diplomat in Japan.* London: Seeley Service, 1921.

Totman, Conrad. *The Collapse of the Tokugawa Bakufu, 1862–1868.* Honolulu: University Press of Hawaii, 1980.

Walworth, Arthur. *Black Ships Off Japan: The Story of Commodore Perry's Expedition.* New York: Knopf, 1948.

Yamamura, Kozo. *A Study of Samurai Income and Entrepreneurship.* Cambridge, Mass.: Harvard University Press, 1974.

General Histories of Modern Japan

Beasley, W. G. *The Japanese Experience: A Short History of Japan.* Berkeley: University of California Press, 1999.

_____. *The Modern History of Japan.* New York: Praeger, 1963.

Beckmann, George M. *The Modernization of China and Japan.* New York: Harper & Row, 1962.

Borton, Hugh. *Japan's Modern Century.* New York: Ronald, 1970.

Brownlee, John S. *Japanese Historians and the National Myths, 1600–1945.* Vancouver: University of British Columbia Press, 1997.

Duus, Peter, ed. *The Rise of Modern Japan.* Boston: Houghton Mifflin, 1976.

_____. *The Twentieth Century.* Vol. 6 of *The Cambridge History of Japan.* New York: Cambridge University Press, 1989.

Eisenstadt, S. N. *Japanese Civilization: A Comparative View.* Chicago: University of Chicago Press, 1997.

Fairbank, John K., Edwin O. Reischauer, and Albert M. Craig. *A History of East Asian Civilization: The Modern Transformation.* Boston: Houghton Mifflin, 1965.

Jansen, Marius B., ed. *The Nineteenth Century.* Vol. 5 of *The Cambridge History of Japan.* New York: Cambridge University Press, 1989.

Michael, Franz H., and George E. Taylor. *The Far East in the Modern World.* New York: Holt, Rinehart & Winston, 1964.

Najita, Tetsuo. *Japan.* Englewood Cliffs, N.J.: Prentice-Hall, 1974.

Perez, Louis G. *The History of Japan.* Westport, Conn.: Greenwood Press, 1998.

Pyle, Kenneth B. *The Making of Modern Japan.* Boston: Heath, 1978.

Storry, Richard. *A History of Modern Japan.* Baltimore: Penguin, 1965.

Yanaga, Chitoshi. *Japan Since Perry.* New York: McGraw-Hill, 1949.

Special Aspects of Modern History and Culture

Andrew, Dudley, and Carole Cavanaugh. *Sanshō Dayū*. London: British Film Institute, 1999.

Ashton, Dore. *The Delicate Thread: Teshigahara's Life in Art*. London: Kodansha International, 1997.

Asquith, Pamela J., and Arne Kalland, eds. *Japanese Images of Nature: Cultural Perspectives*. Richmond, U.K.: RoutledgeCurzon, 1997.

Beasley, W. G., and E. G. Pulleyblank, eds. *Historians of China and Japan*. London: Oxford University Press, 1961.

Benedict, Ruth. *The Chrysanthemum and the Sword: Patterns of Japanese Culture*. Boston: Houghton Mifflin, 1946.

Borton, Hugh, ed. *Japan*. Ithaca, N.Y.: Cornell University Press, 1951.

Brownless, John S. *Political Thought in Japanese Historical Writing*. Waterloo, Ontario: Wilfrid Laurier University Press, 1991.

Chamberlain, Basil H. *Things Japanese*. London: Routledge & Kegan Paul, 1939.

Coleman, Jon T. *The Lost Wolves of Japan*. Seattle: University of Washington Press, 2005.

Craig, Albert M., and Donald H. Shively. *Personality in Japanese History*. Berkeley: University of California Press, 1971.

Fitzhugh, William, and Chisato Dubreuil. *Ainu: Spirit of a Northern People*. Seattle: University of Washington Press, 1999.

Hall, John Whitney. *Government and Local Power in Japan*. New York: McGraw-Hill, 1965.

Hanes, Jeffrey E. *The City as Subject: Seki Hajime and the Reinvention of Modern Osaka*. Berkeley: University of California Press, 2002.

Hasegawa, Nyozekan. *The Japanese Character: A Cultural Profile*. Translated by John Bester. Tokyo: Kodansha International, 1965.

Hearn, Lafcadio. *Japan: An Attempt at Interpretation*. New York: Macmillan, 1913.

Hibbett, Howard. *The Chrysanthemum and the Fish: Japanese Humor Since the Age of the Shōguns*. Tokyo: Kodansha Press, 2002.

Hickman, Money L., et al. *Japan's Golden Age: Momoyama*. New Haven: Yale University Press, 1996.

Hirakawa, Sukehiro, ed. *Rediscovering Lafcadio Hearn: Japanese Legends Life and Culture*. Folkestone, U.K.: Global Books, 1997.

Hurst, G. Cameron III. *Armed Martial Arts of Japan*. New Haven: Yale University Press, 1998.

Johnston, William. *The Modern Epidemic: A History of Tuberculosis in Japan*. Cambridge, Mass.: Harvard University Asia Center, 1995.

Kendrick, Douglas Moore. *Jomon of Japan: The World's Oldest Pottery*. New York: Columbia University Press, 1995.

Kidder, J. Edward, Jr. *The Lucky Seventh: Early Horyu-Ji and Its Time*. Tokyo: International Christian University Press, 1999.

Klompmakers, Inge. *Of Brigands and Bravery: Kuniyoshi's Heroes of the Suikoden*. Leiden, Netherlands: Hotei Press, 1998.

Knight, John. *Waiting for the Wolves in Japan: An Anthropological Study of People-Wildlife Relations*. Oxford: Oxford University Press, 2003.

Koschmann, Victor J., ed. *Authority and Individual in Japan: Citizen Protests in Historical Perspective*. Tokyo: University of Tokyo Press, 1978.

Martin, Peter. *The Chrysanthemum Throne: A History of the Emperors of Japan*. Honolulu: University of Hawaii Press, 1997.

McClain, James L., and Wakita Osamu. *Osaka: The Merchants' Capital of Early Modern Japan.* Ithaca, N.Y.: Cornell University Press, 1999.

McNally, Mark. *Proving the Way: Conflict and Practice in the History of Japanese Nativism.* Cambridge, Mass.: Harvard University Asia Center, 2005.

Morris, Ivan. *The Nobility of Failure: Tragic Heroes in the History of Japan.* New York: Holt, 1975.

Morris-Suzuki, Tessa. *The Technological Transformation of Japan: from the Seventeenth to the Twenty-First Century.* Cambridge: Cambridge University Press, 1994.

Nakamura, Hajime. *Ways of Thinking of Eastern People: India, China, Tibet, Japan.* Honolulu: East-West Center Press, 1964.

Nitobe, Inazo. *Bushido: The Soul of Japan: An Exposition of Japanese Thought.* 10th revised and enlarged edition. New York: Putnam, 1905.

Okakura, Kakuzō. *The Book of Tea.* Rutland, Vt.: Tuttle, 1956.

Orr, James J. *The Victim as Hero: Ideologies of Peace and National Identity in Postwar Japan.* Honolulu: University of Hawaii Press, 2001.

Packard, Jerrold M. *Sons of Heaven.* New York: Macmillan, 1987.

Pflugfelder, Gregory M. *Cartographies of Desire: Male-Male Sexuality in Japanese Discourse, 1600–1950.* Berkeley: University of California Press, 2000.

Piggott, Joan R. *The Emergence of Japanese Kingship.* Stanford: Stanford University Press, 1997.

Pincus, Leslie. *Authenticating Culture in Imperial Japan: Kuki Shūzō and the Rise of National Aesthetics.* Berkeley: University of California Press, 1996.

Pratt, Edward E. *Japan's Protoindustrial Elite: The Economic Foundations of the Gōnō.* Cambridge, Mass.: Harvard University Asia Center, 1999.

Silberman, Bernard S., ed. *Japanese Character and Culture: A Book of Selected Readings.* Tucson: University of Arizona Press, 1962.

Singleton, John. *Learning in Likely Places: Varieties of Apprenticeship in Japan.* Cambridge: Cambridge University Press, 1998.

Smith, Robert J., and Richard K. Beardsley. *Japanese Culture: Its Development and Characteristics.* Chicago: Aldine, 1962.

Sugimoto, Masayoshi, and David L. Swain. *Science and Culture in Traditional Japan.* Cambridge, Mass.: MIT Press, 1978.

Sugimoto, Yoshio. *An Introduction to Japanese Society.* Cambridge: Cambridge University Press, 1997.

Sumiya, Mikio, and Koji Taira. *An Outline of Japanese Economic History: 1602–1940.* Tokyo: University of Tokyo Press, 1979.

Takekoshi, Yosaburo. *Economic Aspects of the History of the Civilization of Japan.* 3 vols. 1930. Reprint, New York: Paragon, 1967.

Tsunoda, Ryusaku, et al., eds. *Sources of Japanese Tradition.* New York: Columbia University Press, 1958.

Walker, Brett L. *The Conquest of Ainu Lands: Ecology and Culture in Japanese Expansion, 1590–1800.* Berkeley: University of California Press, 2000.

Wigen, Karen. *The Making of a Japanese Periphery, 1750–1920.* Berkeley: University of California Press, 1995.

Modern History: Cultural, Social, and Political Topics

Aoki, Michiko Y., and Margaret B. Dardess, eds. *As the Japanese See It.* Honolulu: University Press of Hawaii, 1981.

Atkins, E. Taylor. *Blue Nippon: Authenticating Jazz in Japan*. Durham, N.C.: Duke University Press, 2001.

Austin, Lewis. *Japan: The Paradox of Progress*. New Haven: Yale University Press, 1976.

Barshay, Andrew E. *State and Intellectual in Imperial Japan*. Berkeley: University of California Press, 1988.

Bartholomew, James R. *The Formation of Science of Japan*. New Haven: Yale University Press, 1989.

Bayley, David H. *Forces of Order: Police Behavior in Japan and the United States*. Berkeley: University of California Press, 1975.

Beasley, W. C. *Japan Encounters the Barbarians: Japanese Travelers in America and Europe*. New Haven: Yale University Press, 1995.

Beasley, W. C., ed. *Modern Japan: Aspects of History, Literature, and Society*. Berkeley: University of California Press, 1975.

Beckmann, George M., and Okubo Genji. *The Japanese Communist Party, 1922–1945*. Stanford: Stanford University Press, 1969.

Befu, Harumi. *Japan: An Anthropological Interpretation*. New York: Harper & Row, 1971.

BenDasan, Isaiah. *The Japanese and the Jews*. Translated by Richard L. Gage. New York: Weatherhill, 1972.

Bernstein, Gail Lee. *Isami's House: Three Centuries of a Japanese Family*. Berkeley: University of California Press, 2005.

Berry, Mary Elizabeth, *Japan in Print: Information and Nation in the Early Modern Period*. Berkeley: University of California Press, 2007.

Botsman, Daniel V. *Punishment and Power in the Making of Modern Japan*. Princeton: Princeton University Press, 2005.

Brown, Delmer M. *Nationalism in Japan*. Berkeley: University of California Press, 1955.

Carter, Steven D. *Householders: The Reizei Family in Japanese History*. Cambridge, Mass.: Harvard University Asia Center, 2007.

Clancey, Gregory. *Earthquake Nation: The Cultural Politics of Japanese Seismicity, 1868–1930*. Berkeley: University of California Press, 2006.

Conroy, Hilary, et al., eds. *Japan in Transition*. Rutherford, N.J.: Fairleigh Dickinson University Press, 1984.

Coulmas, Floria. *Population Decline and Ageing in Japan: The Social Consequences*. New York: Routledge, 2007.

Craig, Albert M. *Japan: A Comparative View*. Princeton: Princeton University Press, 1979.

Craig, Timothy J. *Japan Pop! Inside the World of Japanese Popular Culture*. New York: M. E. Sharpe, 2000.

Dalby, Liza Crihfield. *Geisha*. Berkeley: University of California Press, 1983.

Davidann, Jon Thares. *A World of Crisis and Progress: The American YMCA in Japan, 1890–1930*. Bethlehem, Pa.: Lehigh University Press, 1998.

Davis, Darrell William. *Picturing Japaneseness: Monumental Style, National Identity, Japanese Film*. New York: Columbia University Press, 1996.

Davis, Winston. *The Moral and Political Naturalism of Baron Katō Hiroyuki*. Berkeley: University of California Press, 1996.

DeVos, George, and Hiroshi Wagatsuma. *Japan's Invisible Race: Caste in Culture and Personality*. Berkeley: University of California Press, 1966.

Doak, Kevin Michael. *The Dreams of Difference: The Japan Romantic School and the Crisis of Modernity*. Berkeley: University of California Press, 1994.

Doi, Takeo. *Amae: The Anatomy of Dependence*. Tokyo: Kodansha, 1974.

Dore, Ronald P., ed. *Aspects of Social Change in Modern Japan.* Princeton: Princeton University Press, 1967.

Edgerton, Robert B. *Warriors of the Rising Sun: A History of the Japanese Military.* New York: Norton, 1997.

Fogel, Joshua A. *The Literature of Travel in the Japanese Rediscovery of China, 1862–1945.* Stanford: Stanford University Press, 1996.

Fuess, Harold. *Divorce in Japan: Family, Gender, and the State, 1600–2000.* Stanford: Stanford University Press, 2004.

Fujitani, T. *Splendid Monarchy: Power and Pageantry in Modern Japan.* Berkeley: University of California Press, 1996.

Fukutake, Tadashi. *Japanese Social Structure: Its Evolution in the Modern Century.* Tokyo: University of Tokyo Press, 1982.

_____. *Rural Society in Japan.* Tokyo: University of Tokyo Press, 1980.

Garon, Sheldon. *Molding Japanese Minds: The State in Everyday Life.* Princeton: Princeton University Press, 1997.

_____. *The State and Labor in Modern Japan.* Berkeley: University of California Press, 1987.

Giffard, Sydney. *Japan Among the Powers, 1890–1990.* New Haven: Yale University Press, 1994.

Gordon, Andrew. *Labor and Imperial Democracy in Prewar Japan.* Berkeley: University of California Press, 1991.

Hane, Mikiso. *Peasants, Rebels, and Outcastes: The Underside of Modern Japan.* New York: Pantheon, 1982.

Henderson, Dan F. *Conciliation and Japanese Law.* 2 vols. Seattle: University of Washington Press, 1965.

Hogan, Michael J. *Hiroshima in History and Memory.* Cambridge: Cambridge University Press, 1996.

Howes, John F. *Nitobe Inazo: Japan's Bridge Across the Pacific.* Boulder, Colo.: Westview Press, 1995.

Howland, Douglas R. *Translating the West: Language and Political Reason in Nineteenth-Century Japan.* Honolulu: University of Hawaii Press, 2001.

Iriye, Akira, ed. *The Chinese and the Japanese: Essays in Political and Cultural Interactions.* Princeton: Princeton University Press, 1980.

Ishida, Takeshi. *Japanese Society.* New York: Random House, 1971.

Jansen, Marius B., ed. *Changing Japanese Attitudes toward Modernization.* Princeton: Princeton University Press, 1965.

Kaigo, Tokiomi. *Japanese Education: Its Past and Present.* Tokyo: Kokusai Bunka Shinkokai, 1968.

Kaplan, David E., and Alec Dubro. *Yakuza: The Explosive Account of Japan's Criminal Underworld.* Reading, Mass.: Addison-Wesley, 1986.

Kasza, Gregory J. *The State and the Mass Media in Japan, 1918–1945.* Berkeley: University of California Press, 1988.

Kayano, Shigeru. *Our Land Was a Forest: An Ainu Memoir.* Translated by Kyoko Selden and Lili Selden. Boulder, Colo.: Westview Press, 1994.

Keenleyside, Hugh L., and A. F. Thomas. *The History of Japanese Education and Present Educational System.* Tokyo: Hokuseido Press, 1937.

Kelly, William W. *Deference and Defiance in Nineteenth-Century Japan.* Princeton: Princeton University Press, 1985.

Kersten, Rikki. *Democracy in Postwar Japan: Maruyama Masao and the Search for Autonomy.* London: Routledge, 1995.

Koschmann, J. Victor, ed. *Authority and the Individual in Japan.* Tokyo: University of Tokyo Press, 1978.

Krauss, Ellis, Thomas Rohlen, and Patricia Steinhoff, eds. *Conflict in Japan.* Honolulu: University Press of Hawaii, 1984.

Large, S. Stephen. *Shōwa Japan: Political, Economic, and Social History, 1926–1989.* New York: Routledge, 1998.

Lebra, Takie Sugiyama. *Japanese Patterns of Behavior.* Honolulu: University Press of Hawaii, 1976.

Lederer, Emil, and Emy Lederer-Seidler. *Japan in Transition.* New Haven: Yale University Press, 1938.

Leheny, David. *The Rules of Play: National Identity and the Shaping of Japanese Leisure.* Ithaca, N.Y.: Cornell University Press, 2003.

Leng, Thang Leng. *Generations in Touch: Linking the Old and Young in a Tokyo Neighborhood.* Ithaca, N.Y.: Cornell University Press, 2001.

Lesbirel, S. Hayden. *NIMBY Politics in Japan: Energy Siting and the Management of Environmental Conflict.* Ithaca, N.Y.: Cornell University Press, 1998.

Lewis, Michael. *Becoming Apart: National Power and Local Politics in Toyama, 1868–1945.* Cambridge, Mass.: Harvard University Asia Center, 2000.

———. *Rioters and Citizens: Mass Protest in Imperial Japan.* Berkeley: University of California Press, 1990.

Lifton, Robert Jay, et al. *Six Lives, Six Deaths: Portraits from Modern Japan.* New Haven: Yale University Press, 1979.

Lippit, Seiji M. *Topographies of Japanese Modernism.* New York: Columbia University Press, 2002.

Livingston, Jon, et al., eds. *The Japanese Reader.* 2 vols. New York: Pantheon, 1973.

Long, Susan Orpett, ed. *Caring for the Elderly in Japan and the US: Practices and Policies.* Routledge Advances in Asia-Pacific Studies 3. New York: Routledge, 2000.

———. *Lives in Motion: Composing Circles of Self and Community in Japan.* Ithaca, N.Y.: East Asia Program, Cornell University Press, 1999.

Maeda, Ai. *Text and the City: Essays on Japanese Modernity.* Edited by James A. Fujii. Durham, N.C.: Duke University Press, 2004.

Mainichi Newspaper. *Japan and the Japanese.* Tokyo: Japan Publications, 1974.

Maraini, Fosco. *Japan: Patterns of Continuity.* Tokyo: Kodansha, 1971.

———. *Meeting with Japan.* Translated by Eric Mosbacher. New York: Viking, 1959.

Martinez, D. P. *The Worlds of Japanese Popular Culture: Gender, Shifting Boundaries, and Global Cultures.* Cambridge: Cambridge University Press, 1998.

McCreery, John. *Japanese Consumer Behavior: From Worker Bees to Wary Shoppers.* Honolulu: University of Hawaii Press, 2000.

McVeigh, Brian J. *Nationalisms of Japan: Managing and Mystifying Identity.* Lanham, Md.: Rowman & Littlefield, 2004.

Mehl, Margaret. *History and the State in Nineteenth-Century Japan.* New York: St. Martin's Press, 1998.

Minear, Richard H., ed. *Through Japanese Eyes.* New York: Praeger, 1974.

Minichiello, Sharon A. *Japan's Competing Modernities: Issues in Culture and Democracy, 1900–1930.* Honolulu: University of Hawaii Press, 1998.

Mitchell, Richard H. *Censorship in Imperial Japan*. Princeton: Princeton University Press, 1983.

_____. *The Korean Minority in Japan*. Berkeley: University of California Press, 1967.

_____. *Political Bribery in Japan*. Honolulu: University of Hawaii Press, 1996.

Mori, Hiromi. *Immigration Policy and Foreign Workers in Japan*. New York: St. Martin's Press, 1997.

Morris-Suzuki, Tessa. *Re-Inventing Japan: Time, Space, Nation*. New York: M. E. Sharpe, 1999.

Mosk, Carl. *Making Health Work: Human Growth in Modern Japan*. Berkeley: University of California Press, 1996.

Muramatsu, Michio. *Local Power in the Japanese State*. Berkeley: University of California Press, 1997.

Murphy, Joseph A. *Metaphorical Circuit: Negotiations Between Literature and Science in Twentieth-Century Japan*. Ithaca, N.Y.: Cornell University East Asia Program, 2004.

Nagashima, Yōichi. *Objective Description of the Self: A Study of Iwano Hōmei's Literary Theory*. Aarhus, Denmark: Aarhus University Press, 1997.

Najita, Tetsuo, and J. Victor Koschmann. *Conflict in Modern Japanese History*. Princeton: Princeton University Press, 1982.

Nakane, Chie. *Japanese Society*. Berkeley: University of California Press, 1970.

Neary, Ian. *Political Protest and Social Control in Pre-war Japan: The Origins of Buraku Liberation*. Atlantic Highlands, N.J.: Humanities Press, 1989.

Nolte, Sharon. *Liberalism in Modern Japan*. Berkeley: University of California Press, 1986.

Norbeck, Edward. *Changing Japan*. New York: Holt, 1965.

Ohnuki-Tierney, Emiko. *Illness and Culture in Contemporary Japan: An Anthropological View*. Cambridge: Cambridge University Press, 1984.

_____. *The Monkey as Mirror*. Princeton: Princeton University Press, 1987.

Oka, Yoshitake, Andrew Fraser, and Patricia Murray. *Five Political Leaders of Modern Japan*. Tokyo: University of Tokyo Press, 1985.

Olsen, Dale. *The Chrysanthemum and the Song: Music, Memory, and Identity in the South American Japanese Diaspora*. Gainesville: University Press of Florida, 2004.

Pharr, Susan J., and Ellis S. Krauss. *Media and Politics in Japan*. Honolulu: University of Hawaii Press, 1996.

Piovesana, Gino K. *Recent Japanese Philosophical Thought, 1862–1962*. Tokyo: Enderle, 1963.

Plath, David W. *Long Engagement: Maturity in Modern Japan*. Stanford: Stanford University Press, 1980.

Reischauer, Edwin O. *The Japanese*. Cambridge, Mass.: Harvard University Press, 1977.

Reynolds, Jonathan M. *Maekawa Kunio and the Emergence of Japanese Modernism*. Berkeley: University of California Press, 2001.

Richardson, Bradley M. *Political Culture in Japan*. Berkeley: University of California Press, 1974.

Roden, Donald T. *Schooldays in Imperial Japan: A Study in the Culture of a Student Elite*. Berkeley: University of California Press, 1980.

Rohlen, Thomas P. *For Harmony and Strength: Japanese White-Collar Organization in Anthropological Perspective*. Berkeley: University of California Press, 1974.

Rohlen, Thomas P., and Christopher Björk, eds. *Education and Training in Japan*. 3 vols. New York: Routledge, 2001.

Ruoff, Jeffrey, and Kenneth Ruoff. *The Emperor's Naked Army Marches On: Yukiyukite Shingun*. Wiltshire, U.K.: Flicks Books, 1998.

_____. *The People's Emperor: Democracy and the Japanese Monarchy, 1945–1995*. Cambridge, Mass.: Harvard University Asia Center, 2001.

Saga, Junichi. *Confessions of a Yakuza*. Tokyo: Kodansha, 1991.

Satsuki Kawano. *Ritual Practice in Modern Japan: Ordering Place, People, and Action*. Honolulu: University of Hawaii Press, 2005.

Scalapino, Robert A. *Democracy and the Party Movement in Prewar Japan*. Berkeley: University of California Press, 1953.

_____. *The Japanese Communist Movement, 1920–1966*. Berkeley: University of California Press, 1967.

Scheiner, Irwin. *Modern Japan: An Interpretive Anthology*. New York: Macmillan, 1974.

Schwantes, Robert. *Japanese and Americans: A Century of Cultural Relations*. New York: Harper & Row, 1955.

Seidensticker, Edward. *Low City, High City: Tokyo, 1867–1923*. New York: Knopf, 1983.

_____. *Tokyo Rising: The City Since the Great Earthquake*. Rutland, Vt.: Tuttle, 1991.

Selden, Mark, and Alvin Y. So, eds. *War and State Terrorism: The United States, Japan, and the Asia-Pacific in the Long Twentieth Century*. Lanham, Md.: Rowman & Littlefield, 2004.

Seymour, Christopher. *Yakuza Diary*. New York: Atlantic Monthly Press, 1996.

Shively, Donald H., ed. *Tradition and Modernization in Japanese Culture*. Princeton: Princeton University Press, 1971.

Singer, Kurt. *Mirror, Sword, and Jewel: The Geometry of Japanese Life*. Tokyo: Kodansha, 1981.

Skrzpczak, Edmund, ed. *Japan's Modern Century*. Rutland, Vt.: Tuttle, 1969.

Smethurst, Richard A. *A Social Basis for Prewar Japanese Militarism*. Berkeley: University of California Press, 1974.

Smith, Robert J. *Japanese Society*. Cambridge: Cambridge University Press, 1983.

Spaulding, Robert M., Jr. *Imperial Japan's Higher Civil Service Examination*. Princeton: Princeton University Press, 1967.

Steiner, Kurt. *Local Government in Japan*. Stanford: Stanford University Press, 1965.

Streeck, Wolfgang, and Kozo Yamamura. *The Origins of Nonliberal Capitalism: Germany and Japan in Comparison*. Ithaca, N.Y.: Cornell University Press, 2001.

Sugimoto, Yoshio. *An Introduction to Japanese Society*. Cambridge: Cambridge University Press, 1997.

Tanaka, Stefan. *New Times in Modern Japan*. Princeton: Princeton University Press, 2004.

Tanji, Miyume. *Myth, Protest and Struggle in Okinawa*. New York: Routledge, 2006.

Tsurumi, E. Patricia. *Japanese Colonial Education in Taiwan, 1895–1945*. Cambridge, Mass.: Harvard University Press, 1977.

Tsuzuki, Chushichi. *The Pursuit of Power in Modern Japan*. New York: Oxford University Press, 2000.

Uno, Kathleen S. *Passages to Modernity: Motherhood, Childhood, and Social Reform in Early Twentieth-Century Japan*. Honolulu: University of Hawaii Press, 1999.

Vlastos, Stephen, ed. *Mirror of Modernity: Invented Traditions of Modern Japan*. Berkeley: University of California, 1998.

Wakabayashi, Tadashi, ed. *Modern Japanese Thought*. New York: Cambridge University Press, 1997.

Wan, Ming. *Japan Between Asia and the West: Economic Power and Strategic Balance*. New York: M. E. Sharpe, 2000.

Ward, R. E., ed. *Political Development in Modern Japan*. Princeton: Princeton University Press, 1968.

Ward, R. E., and D. A. Rustow, eds. *Political Modernization in Japan and Turkey.* Princeton: Princeton University Press, 1964.

Waswo, Ann. *The Japanese Landlord.* Berkeley: University of California Press, 1977.

_____. *Modern Japanese Society, 1868–1994.* Oxford: Oxford University Press, 1996.

Waswo, Ann, and Yoshiaki Nishida, eds. *Farmers and Village Life in Twentieth-Century Japan.* London: RoutledgeCurzon, 2003.

Weiner, Michael, ed. *Japan's Minorities: The Illusion of Homogeneity.* London: Routledge, 1997.

_____. *The Origins of the Korean Community in Japan, 1910–1923.* Atlantic Highlands, N.J.: Humanities Press, 1989.

Wray, Harry, and Hilary Conroy, eds. *Japan Examined.* Honolulu: University Press of Hawaii, 1983.

Yano, Christine R. *Tears of Longing: Nostalgia and the Nation in Japanese Popular Song.* Cambridge, Mass.: Harvard University Asia Center, 2002.

Modern History: International Relations

Auslin, Michael R. *Negotiating with Imperialism: The Unequal Treaties and the Culture of Japanese Diplomacy.* Cambridge, Mass.: Harvard University Press, 2004.

Beasley, W. G. *Japanese Imperialism, 1894–1945.* New York: Oxford University Press, 1987.

Burkman, Thomas W. *Japan and the League of Nations: Empire and World Order, 1914–1938.* Honolulu: University of Hawaii Press, 2007.

Dingman, Roger. *Ghost of War: The Sinking of the* Awa Maru *and Japanese-American Relations, 1945–1995.* Annapolis, Md.: Naval Institute Press, 1997.

Drifte, Reinhard. *Japan's Security Relations with China Since 1989: From Balancing to Bandwagoning?* London: RoutledgeCurzon, 2003.

Dudden, Alexis. *Japan's Colonization of Korea: Discourse and Power.* Honolulu: University of Hawaii Press, 2004.

Duus, Peter. *The Abacus and the Sword: The Japanese Penetration of Korea, 1895–1910.* Berkeley: University of California Press, 1995.

Duus, Peter, Ramon H. Myers, and Mark R. Peattie, eds. *The Japanese Informal Empire in China, 1895–1937.* Princeton: Princeton University Press, 1989.

Hellmann, Donald. *Japanese Foreign Policy and Domestic Politics.* Berkeley: University of California Press, 1969.

Ikle, Frank. *German-Japanese Relations, 1936–1940.* New York: Bookman, 1956.

Iriye, Akira. *Across the Pacific: An Inner History of American–East Asian Relations.* New York: Harcourt Brace, 1967.

_____. *After Imperialism: The Search for a New Order in the Far East, 1921–1931.* Cambridge, Mass.: Harvard University Press, 1965.

_____. *Japan and the Wider World: From the Mid-Nineteenth Century to the Present.* London: Longman, 1997.

_____. *Pacific Estrangement: Japanese and American Expansion, 1897–1911.* Cambridge, Mass.: Harvard University Press, 1972.

Iriye, Akira, and Robert A. Wampler. *Partnership: The United States and Japan, 1951–2001.* New York: Kodansha International, 2001.

Jansen, Marius B. *Japan and China: From War to Peace, 1894–1972.* Chicago: Rand McNally, 1975.

_____. *The Japanese and Sun Yat-sen.* Cambridge, Mass.: Harvard University Press, 1954.

Johnson, Sheila K. *American Attitudes toward Japan, 1941–1975.* Stanford: Stanford University Press, 1975.

Ka, Chih-Ming. *Japanese Colonialism in Taiwan: Land Tenure, Development, and Dependency, 1895–1945.* Boulder, Colo.: Westview Press, 1995.

Kennedy, Malcolm D. *The Estrangement of Great Britain and Japan, 1917–1935.* Berkeley: University of California Press, 1969.

MacNair, H. F., and D. E. Lach. *Modern Far Eastern Relations.* New York: Van Nostrand, 1950.

Mayo, Marlene, ed. *The Emergence of Imperial Japan: Self-Defense or Calculated Aggression?* Lexington, Mass.: Heath, 1970.

Morley, James W. *The Japanese Thrust into Siberia, 1918.* New York: Columbia University Press, 1957.

Morley, James W., ed. *Japan's Foreign Policy, 1868–1941: A Research Guide.* New York: Columbia University Press, 1974.

Myers, Ramon H., and Mark R. Peattie. *The Japanese Colonial Empire, 1895–1945.* Princeton: Princeton University Press, 1984.

Neu, Charles E. *The Troubled Encounter: The United States and Japan.* New York: Wiley, 1975.

Neumann, William L. *America Encounters Japan: From Perry to MacArthur.* Baltimore, Md.: Johns Hopkins University Press, 1963.

Nish, Ian, ed. *Anglo-Japanese Alienation, 1919–1952.* Cambridge: Cambridge University Press, 1982.

Peattie, Mark R. *Japanese Foreign Policy, 1869–1942.* London: Routledge & Kegan, 1977.

————. *Nan'yo: The Rise and Fall of the Japanese in Micronesia, 1885–1945.* Honolulu: Center for Pacific Islands Studies, 1988.

Perez, Louis G. *Japan Comes of Age: Mutsu Munemitsu and the Revision of the Unequal Treaties.* Madison, N.J.: Fairleigh Dickinson University Press, 1999.

————. *Mutsu Munemitsu and Identity Formation of the Individual and the State in Modern Japan.* Lewiston, N.Y.: Edwin Mellen Press, 2001.

Plutschow, Herbert. *Phillip Franz Von Siebold and the Opening of Japan: A Re-Evaluation.* Honolulu: University of Hawaii Press, 2007.

Rimer, J. Thomas. *A Hidden Fire: Russian and Japanese Cultural Encounter, 1868–1926.* Stanford: Stanford University Press, 1995.

Soeya, Yoshihide. *Japan's Economic Diplomacy with China, 1945–1978.* Oxford: Oxford University Press, 1999.

Storry, Richard. *Japan and the Decline of the West in Asia, 1894–1943.* New York: St. Martin's, 1979.

Takeuchi, Tatsuji. *War and Diplomacy in the Japanese Empire.* Garden City, N.Y.: Doubleday, 1935.

Thomson, J. C., P. W. Stanley, and J. C. Perry. *The American Experience in East Asia.* New York: Harper & Row, 1981.

White, John Albert. *The Diplomacy of the Russo-Japanese War.* Princeton: Princeton University Press, 1964.

Wigen, Karen. *The Making of a Japanese Periphery, 1750–1920.* Berkeley: University of California Press, 1991.

Modern History: Economic Developments

Allen, G. C. *A Short Economic History of Modern Japan, 1867–1937.* New York: Macmillan, 1946.

Caves, Richard E., and Masu Uekusa. *Industrial Organization in Japan.* Washington, D.C.: Brookings Institution, 1976.

Colignon, Richard A., and Chikako Usui. *Amakudari: The Hidden Fabric of Japan's Economy.* Ithaca, N.Y.: Cornell University Press, 2003.

Doane, Donna L. *Cooperation, Technology, and Japanese Development: Indigenous Knowledge, the Power of Networks, and the State.* Boulder, Colo.: Westview Press, 1998.

Francks, Penelope. *Technology and Agricultural Development in Pre-war Japan.* New Haven: Yale University Press, 1984.

Gao, Bai. *Economic Ideology and Japanese Industrial Policy: Developmentalism from 1931 to 1965.* Cambridge: Cambridge University Press, 1997.

Halliday, Jon. *A Political History of Japanese Capitalism.* New York: Pantheon, 1975.

Hirschmeier, Johannes, and Tsunehiko Yui. *The Development of Japanese Business, 1600–1973.* Cambridge, Mass.: Harvard University Press, 1975.

Hoshi, Takeo, and Anil Kashyap. *Corporate Financing and Governance in Japan: The Road to the Future.* Cambridge, Mass.: MIT Press, 2001.

Howe, Christopher. *The Origins of Japanese Trade Supremacy.* Chicago: University of Chicago Press, 1996.

Howell, David L. *Capitalism from Within: Economy, Society, and the State in a Japanese Fishery.* Berkeley: University of California Press, 1995.

Klein, Lawrence, and Kazushi Ohkawa. *Economic Growth: The Japanese Experience Since the Meiji Era.* Homewood, Ill.: R. D. Irwin, 1968.

Lockwood, William W. *The Economic Development of Japan: Growth and Structural Change, 1863–1938.* Princeton: Princeton University Press, 1954.

Lockwood, William W., ed. *The State and Economic Enterprise in Japan.* Princeton: Princeton University Press, 1965.

Marsh, Robert, and Hiroshi Mannari. *Modernization and the Japanese Factory.* Princeton: Princeton University Press, 1976.

Marshall, Byron. *Capitalism and Nationalism in Prewar Japan: The Ideology of the Business Elite, 1868–1941.* Stanford: Stanford University Press, 1967.

Morley, James, ed. *The Dilemma of Growth in Prewar Japan.* Princeton: Princeton University Press, 1971.

Ogura, Shinji. *Banking, the State, and Industrial Promotion in Developing Japan, 1900–1973.* New York: Palgrave, 2002.

Ohkawa, Kazushi, and Henry Rosovsky. *Japanese Economic Growth.* Stanford: Stanford University Press, 1973.

Patrick, Hugh, ed. *Japanese Industrialization and Its Social Consequences.* Berkeley: University of California Press, 1976.

Patrick, Hugh, and Henry Rosovsky, eds. *Asia's New Giant: How the Japanese Economy Works.* Washington, D.C.: Brookings Institution, 1976.

Smith, Thomas C. *Native Sources of Japanese Industrialization, 1750–1920.* Berkeley: University of California Press, 1988.

Smitka, Michael, ed. *Japanese Economic History: 1600–1960.* 7 vols. Hamden, Conn.: Garland Publishing, 1998.

Sumiya, Mikio, and Koji Taira. *An Outline of Japanese Economic History, 1603–1940.* Tokyo: University of Tokyo Press, 1979.

Taira, Koji. *Economic Development and the Labor Market in Japan.* New York: Columbia University Press, 1970.

Takahashi, Masao. *Modern Japanese Economy Since 1868.* Tokyo: Kokusai Bunka Shinkokai, 1967.

Tanimoto, Masayuki. *The Role of Tradition in Japan's Industrialization: Another Path to Industrialization.* Cambridge: Oxford University Press, 2006.

Yamamura, Kozo, ed. *The Economic Emergence of Modern Japan.* Cambridge: Cambridge University Press, 1997.

Yamamura, Kozo, et al., eds. *The Changing International Context.* Vol. 2 of *Political Economy of Japan,* eds. Takashi Inoguchi and Daniel I. Okimoto. Stanford: Stanford University Press, 1987–1988.

_____. *Cultural and Social Dynamics.* Vol. 3 of *Political Economy of Japan,* eds. Shumpei Kumon and Henry Rosovsky. Stanford: Stanford University Press, 1987–1988.

_____. *The Domestic Transformation.* Vol. 1 of *Political Economy of Japan,* eds. Kozo Yamamura and Yasukichi Yasuba. Stanford: Stanford University Press, 1987–1988.

_____. *A Vision of a New Liberalism? Critical Essays on Murakami's Anticlassical Analysis.* Stanford: Stanford University Press, 1997.

Vanoverbeke, Dimitri. *Rural Economic Development in Japan: from the Nineteenth Century to the Pacific War.* New York: Routledge, 2006.

Modern History: The Condition of Women

Arai, Paula Kane Robinson. *Women Living Zen.* Oxford: Oxford University Press, 1999.

Bernstein, Gail. *Haruko's World: A Japanese Farm Woman and Her Community.* Stanford: Stanford University Press, 1983.

Bernstein, Gail, ed. *Recreating Japanese Women, 1600–1945.* Berkeley: University of California Press, 1990.

Birnbaum, Phyllis. *Modern Girls, Shining Stars, the Skies of Tokyo: Five Japanese Women.* New York: Columbia University Press, 1999.

Brinton, Mary C. *Women and the Economic Miracle: Gender and Work in Postwar Japan.* Berkeley: University of California Press, 1993.

Broadbent, Kaye. *Women's Employment in Japan: The Experience of Part-Time Workers.* London: RoutledgeCurzon, 2003.

Buckley, Sandra. *Broken Silence: Voices of Japanese Feminism.* Berkeley: University of California Press, 1997.

Condon, Jane. *Japanese Women in the Eighties: Half a Step Behind.* New York: Dodd Mead, 1985.

Cook, Alice, and Hiroko Hayashi. *Women in Japan: Discrimination, Resistance, and Reform.* Ithaca, N.Y.: Cornell University Press, 1980.

Faison, Elyssa. *Managing Women: Disciplining Labor in Modern Japan.* Berkeley: University of California Press, 2007.

Frühstück, Sabine. *Colonizing Sex: Sexology and Social Control in Modern Japan.* Berkeley: University of California Press, 2003.

Fujimura-Fanselow, Kumiko, and Atsuko Kameda, eds. *Japanese Women: New Feminist Perspectives on the Past, Present, and Future.* New York: City University Press, 1995.

Hane, Mikiso, ed. and trans. *Reflections on the Way to the Gallows: Rebel Women in Prewar Japan.* Berkeley: University of California Press, 1988.

Henshall, Kenneth G. *Dimensions of Japanese Society: Gender, Margins, and Mainstream.* New York: St. Martin's Press, 1999.

Hopper, Helen M. *A New Woman of Japan: A Political Biography of Kato Shidzue.* Boulder, Colo.: Westview Press, 1997.

Imamura, Anne E., ed. *Re-Imaging Japanese Women.* Berkeley: University of California Press, 1995.

Ishimoto, Shidzue. *Facing Two Ways: The Story of My Life.* New York: Farrar & Rinehart, 1935.

Iwao, Sumiko. *The Japanese Women: Traditional Image and Changing Reality.* New York: Free Press, 1992.

Izuhara, Misa. *Family Change and Housing in Post-War Japanese Society: The Experiences of Older Women.* Burlington, Vt.: Ashgate, 2000.

Johnston, William. *Geisha, Harlot, Strangler, Star: A Woman, Sex, and Morality in Modern Japan.* New York: Columbia University Press, 2004.

Kaneko, Fumiko. *The Prison Memoirs of a Japanese Woman.* Translated by Jean Inglis. Armonk, N.Y.: M. E. Sharpe, 1991.

Kano, Ayako. *Acting Like a Woman in Modern Japan: Theater, Gender, and Nationalism.* New York: Palgrave Macmillan, 2001.

Keyso, Ruth Ann. *Women of Okinawa: Nine Voices from a Garrison Island.* Ithaca, N.Y.: Cornell University Press, 2000.

Kim, Jackie J. *Hidden Treasures: Lives of First-Generation Korean Women in Japan.* Lanham, Md.: Rowman & Littlefield, 2005.

Leblanc, Robin. *Bicycle Citizens: The Political World of the Japanese Housewife.* Berkeley: University of California Press, 1999.

Lebra, Joyce, et al. *Women in Changing Japan.* Boulder, Colo.: Westview Press, 1976.

Lebra, Takie Sugiyama. *Japanese Women: Constraint and Fulfillment.* Honolulu: University Press of Hawaii, 1984.

Mackie, Vera C. *Creating Socialist Women in Japan: Gender, Labour, and Activism, 1900–1937.* New York: Cambridge University Press, 1997.

_____. *Fighting Women: A History of Feminism in Modern Japan.* New York: Columbia University Press, 1997.

Marran, Christine L. *Poison Woman: Figuring Female Transgression in Modern Japanese Culture.* Minneapolis: University of Minnesota Press, 2007.

McClellan, Edwin. *Woman in the Crested Kimono.* New Haven: Yale University Press, 1985.

Molony, Barbara, and Kathleen Uno, eds. *Gendering Modern Japanese History.* Cambridge, Mass.: Harvard University Press, 2008.

Morley, John David. *Pictures from the Water Trade.* New York: Harper & Row, 1985.

Morley, Patricia. *The Mountain Is Moving: Japanese Women's Lives.* New York: New York University Press, 1999.

Mouer, Ross. *Gender and Human Rights Politics in Japan: Global Norms and Domestic Networks.* Stanford: Stanford University Press, 2004.

Mulhern, Chieko Irie, ed. *Heroic Women with Grace: Legendary Women in Japan.* Armonk, N.Y.: M. E. Sharpe, 1991.

Murase, Miriam. *Cooperation over Conflict: The Women's Movement and the State in Postwar Japan.* New York: Routledge, 2006.

Ogasawara, Yuko. *Office Ladies and Salaried Men: Power, Gender, and Work in Japanese Companies.* Berkeley: University of California Press, 1998.

Pharr, Susan. *Political Women in Japan.* Berkeley: University of California Press, 1981.

Raddeker, Hélène Bowen. *Treacherous Women of Imperial Japan: Patriarchal Fictions, Patricidal Fantasies.* London: Routledge, 1997.

Robins-Mowry, Dorothy. *The Hidden Sun: Women of Modern Japan.* Boulder, Colo.: West-view Press, 1983.

Rokkum, Arne. *Goddesses, Priestesses, and Sisters: Mind, Gender, and Power in the Monarchic Tradition of the Ryukyus.* Oslo: Scandinavian University Press, 1998.

Rose, Barbara. *Tsuda Umeko and Women's Education in Japan.* New Haven: Yale University Press, 1992.

Sato, Barbara. *The New Japanese Woman: Modernity, Media, and Women in Interwar Japan.* Durham, N.C.: Duke University Press, 2003.

Sievers, Sharon. *Flowers in Salt: The Beginnings of Feminist Consciousness in Modern Japan.* Stanford: Stanford University Press, 1983.

Smith, R. J., and E. L. Wiswell. *Women of Suye-Mura.* Chicago: University of Chicago Press, 1982.

Sugimoto, Etsu. *A Daughter of the Samurai.* Garden City, N.Y.: Doubleday, 1928.

Tamanoi, Mariko Asano. *Under the Shadow of Nationalism: Politics and Poetics of Rural Japanese Women.* Honolulu: University of Hawaii Press, 1998.

Tanaka, Yuki. *Japan's Comfort Women: Sexual Slavery and Prostitution During World War II and the US Occupation.* New York: Routledge, 2001.

Tomida, Hiroko. *Hiratsuka Raichō and Early Japanese Feminism.* Leiden, Netherlands: Brill, 2004.

Tomida, Hiroko, and Gordon Daniels, eds. *Japanese Women: Emerging from Subservience, 1868–1945.* New York: Global Oriental, 2005.

Trager, James. *Letters from Sachiko: A Japanese Women's View of Life in the Land of Economic Miracle.* New York: Atheneum, 1982.

Tsurumi, Patricia E. *Factory Girls: Women in the Thread Mills of Meiji Japan.* Princeton: Princeton University Press, 1990.

Ueno, Chizuko. *Nationalism and Gender.* Trans. by Beverley Yamamoto. Melbourne: Trans Pacific Press, 2004.

Walthall, Anne. *The Weak Body of a Useless Woman: Matsuo Taseko and the Meiji Restoration.* Chicago: University of Chicago Press, 1999.

Women's Division of Soka Gakkai, ed. *Women Against War.* Tokyo: Kodansha International, 1986.

Yamazaki, Tomoko. *Sandakan Brothel No. 8: An Episode of Lower-class Japanese Women.* Translated by Karen Colligan-Taylor. Armonk, N.Y.: M. E. Sharpe, 1999.

_____. *The Story of Yamada Waka: From Prostitute to Feminist Pioneer.* Tokyo: Kodansha International, 1985.

The Meiji Period

Akita, George. *Foundations of Constitutional Government in Modern Japan, 1868–1900.* Cambridge, Mass.: Harvard University Press, 1967.

Baelz, Erwin O. E. Von. *Awakening Japan: The Diary of a German Doctor.* Translated by Eden and Cedar Paul. New York: Viking, 1932.

Baxter, James C. *The Meiji Unification Through the Lens of Ishikawa Prefecture.* Cambridge, Mass.: Harvard University Asia Center, 1994.

Beasley, W. G. *The Meiji Restoration.* Stanford: Stanford University Press, 1972.

Beauchamp, Edward R. *An American Teacher in Early Meiji Japan.* Honolulu: University Press of Hawaii, 1976.

Beauchamp, Edward, and Akira Iriye, eds. *Foreign Employees in Nineteenth-Century Japan.* Boulder, Colo.: Westview Press, 1990.

Beckmann, George M. *The Making of the Meiji Constitution: The Oligarchs and the Constitutional Development of Japan, 1868–1891.* Lawrence: University of Kansas, 1957.

Blacker, Carmen. *The Japanese Enlightenment: A Study of the Writings of Fukuzawa Yukichi.* New York: Cambridge University Press, 1964.

Bowen, Roger W. *Rebellion and Democracy in Meiji Japan.* Berkeley: University of California Press, 1980.

Bowring, Richard J. *Mori Ogai and the Modernization of Japanese Culture.* Cambridge: Cambridge University Press, 1979.

Braisted, William, and Yuji Kikuchi, trans. *Meiroku Zasshi: Journal of the Japanese Enlightenment.* Cambridge, Mass.: Harvard University Press, 1973.

Burks, Ardath W. *The Modernizers: Overseas Students, Foreign Employees, and Meiji Japan.* Boulder, Colo.: Westview Press, 1985.

Chisolm, Lawrence W. *Fenollosa: The Far East and American Culture.* New Haven, Conn.: Yale University Press, 1963.

Conroy, Francis Hilary. *The Japanese Seizure of Korea, 1868–1910.* Philadelphia: University of Pennsylvania Press, 1960.

Cortazzi, Hugh. *Dr. Willis in Japan, 1862–1877.* London: Althone Press, 1985.

———. *Victorians in Japan: In and Around the Treaty Ports.* London: Althone Press, 1987.

Dower, John W., ed. *Origins of Modern Japanese State: Selected Writings of E. H. Norman.* New York: Pantheon, 1975.

Duus, Peter, ed. *The Abacus and the Sword: The Japanese Penetration of Korea, 1895–1910.* Berkeley: University of California Press, 1995.

———. *The Japanese Discovery of America: A Brief History with Documents.* Boston: Bedford Books, 1997.

Ericson, Steven J. *The Sound of the Whistle: Railroads and the State in Meiji Japan.* Cambridge, Mass.: Harvard University Asia Center, 1996.

Finn, Dallas. *Meiji Revisited: The Sites of Victorian Japan.* New York: Weatherhill, 1995.

Fraser, Andrew, R. H. P. Mason, and Philip Mitchell. *Japan's Early Parliaments, 1890–1905.* New York: Routledge, 1995.

Fujitanai, T. *Splendid Monarchy: Power and Pageantry in Modern Japan.* Berkeley: University of California Press, 1996.

Fukuzawa, Yukichi. *Autobiography.* Translated by Eiichi Kiyooka. New York: Columbia University Press, 1966.

Gluck, Carol. *Japan's Modern Myths: Ideology in the Late Meiji Period.* Princeton: Princeton University Press, 1985.

Hackett, Roger F. *Yamagata Aritomo in the Rise of Modern Japan, 1838–1922.* Cambridge, Mass.: Harvard University Press, 1971.

Hall, Ivan Parker. *Mori Arinori.* Cambridge, Mass.: Harvard University Press, 1973.

Hanashiro, Roy. *Thomas William Kinder and the Japanese Imperial Mint, 1868–1875.* Leiden, Netherlands: Brill, 1999.

Hardacre, Helen, and Adam L. Kern, eds. *New Directions in the Study of Meiji Japan.* Leiden, Netherlands: Brill, 1997.

Havens, Thomas. *Nishi Amane and Modern Japanese Thought.* Princeton: Princeton University Press, 1969.

Hirschmeier, Johannes. *Origins of Entrepreneurship in Meiji Japan.* Cambridge, Mass.: Harvard University Press, 1964.

Huber, Thomas M. *The Revolutionary Origins of Modern Japan.* Stanford: Stanford University Press, 1981.

Huffman, James. *Creating a Public: People and Press in Meiji Japan.* Honolulu: University Press of Hawaii, 1997.

_____. *Politics of the Japanese Press: The Life of Fukuchi Gen'ichiro.* Honolulu: University Press of Hawaii, 1980.

_____. *A Yankee in Meiji Japan: The Crusading Journalist Edward H. House.* Lanham, Md.: Rowman & Littlefield, 2003.

Ike, Nobutaka. *The Beginnings of Political Democracy in Japan.* Baltimore, Md.: Johns Hopkins University Press, 1950.

Irokawa, Daikichi. *The Culture of the Meiji Period.* Translated and edited by Marius B. Jansen. Princeton: Princeton University Press, 1985.

Iwata, Masakazu. *Okubo Toshimichi: The Bismarck of Japan.* Berkeley: University of California Press, 1964.

Kaikoku, Hyakunen Kinen Bunka, ed. *Japanese Culture in the Meiji Era.* 10 vols. Tokyo: Obunsha, 1955–1958.

Keene, Donald. *Emperor of Japan: Meiji and His World, 1852–1912.* New York: Columbia University Press, 2002.

Kido, Takayoshi. *The Diary of Kido Takayoshi.* 2 vols. Translated by Sidney Brown and Akiko Hirota. Tokyo: University of Tokyo Press, 1983–1986.

Kinmonth, Earl H. *The Self-Made Man in Meiji Japanese Thought.* Berkeley: University of California Press, 1981.

Kornicki, Peter. *Meiji Japan: Political, Economic, and Social History, 1868–1912.* New York: Routledge, 1998.

Kublin, Hyman. *An Asian Revolutionary: The Life of Katayma Sen.* Princeton: Princeton University Press, 1964.

Minear, Richard H. *Japanese Tradition and Western Law.* Cambridge, Mass.: Harvard University Press, 1970.

Mutsu, Munemitsu. *Kenkenroku: A Diplomatic Record of the Sino-Japanese War, 1894–1895.* Translated by Gordon Mark Berger. Princeton: Princeton University Press, 1983.

Nakamura, James I. *Agricultural Production and the Economic Development of Japan, 1873–1922.* Princeton: Princeton University Press, 1966.

Nitobe, Inazo, et al. *Western Influences in Modern Japan.* Chicago: University of Chicago Press, 1931.

Norman, E. H. *Japan's Emergence as a Modern State.* New York: Institute of Pacific Relations, 1940.

Notehelfer, Fred. *Kōtoku Shūsui: Portrait of a Japanese Radical.* Cambridge: Cambridge University Press, 1971.

Notehelfer, P. G. *American Samurai: Captain L. L. Janes and Japan.* Princeton: Princeton University Press, 1985.

Okakura, Kakuzo. *The Awakening of Japan.* New York: Century, 1904.

Okamoto, Shumpei. *The Japanese Oligarchy and the Russo-Japanese War.* New York: Columbia University Press, 1971.

Okuma, Shigenobu, comp. *Fifty Years of New Japan.* 2 vols. New York: Dutton, 1909.

Perez, Louis G. *Japan Comes of Age: Mutsu Munemitsu and the Revision of the Unequal Treaties.* Madison, N.J.: Fairleigh Dickinson University Press, 1999.

Pierson, John D. *Tokutomi Sohō, 1863–1957: A Journalist for Modern Japan.* Princeton: Princeton University Press, 1980.

Pittau, Joseph. *Political Thought in Early Meiji Japan, 1868–1889.* Cambridge, Mass.: Harvard University Press, 1967.

Pyle, Kenneth B. *The New Generation in Meiji Japan.* Stanford: Stanford University Press, 1969.

Ravina, Mark. *The Last Samurai: The Life and Battles of Saigō Takamori.* Hoboken, N.J.: John Wiley & Sons, 2004.

Redesdale, A. G. *Mitford's Japan: The Memoirs and Recollections, 1866–1906.* Ed. Hugh Cortazzi. London: Athlone Press, 1985.

Rosenstone, Robert A. *Mirror in the Shrine: American Encounters with Meiji Japan.* Cambridge, Mass.: Harvard University Press, 1988.

Rubin, Jay. *Injurious to Public Health: Writers and the Meiji State.* Seattle: University of Washington Press, 1984.

Scheiner, Irwin. *Christian Converts and Social Protest in Meiji Japan.* Berkeley: University of California Press, 1970.

Siemes, Johannes. *Hermann Roesler and the Making of the Meiji State.* Tokyo and Rutland, Vt.: Sophia University and Tuttle, 1968.

Sims, Richard. *French Policy towards Ahe Bakufu and Meiji Japan, 1854–1895.* Surrey, U.K.: Japan Library and Curzon Press, 1998.

Smith, Thomas C. *Political Change and Industrial Development in Japan: Government Enterprise, 1868–1880.* Stanford: Stanford University Press, 1955.

Tamaki, Norio. *Yukichi Fukuzawa, 1835–1901: The Spirit of Enterprise in Modern Japan.* New York: Palgrave, 2001.

Umegaki, Michio. *After the Restoration: The Beginning of Japan's Modern State.* New York: New York University Press, 1988.

Walder, David. *The Short Victorious War: The Russo-Japanese Conflict, 1904–1905.* New York: Harper & Row, 1973.

Walthall, Anne. *The Weak Body of a Useless Woman: Matsuo Taseko and the Meiji Restoration.* Chicago: University of Chicago Press, 1999.

Warner, Dennis, and Peggy Warner. *The Tide of Sunrise: The Russo-Japanese War.* New York: Charterhouse, 1974.

Westwood, J. N. *Russia Against Japan, 1904–1905.* Albany, N.Y.: SUNY Press, 1986.

The Taisho Period

Arima, Tatsuo. *The Failure of Freedom: A Portrait of Modern Japanese Intellectuals.* Cambridge, Mass.: Harvard University Press, 1969.

Bernstein, Gail. *Japanese Marxist: A Portrait of Kawakami Hajime.* Cambridge, Mass.: Harvard University Press, 1978.

Dickinson, Frederick R. *War and National Reinvention: Japan in the Great War, 1914–1919.* Cambridge, Mass.: Harvard University Asia Center, 1999.

Duus, Peter. *Party Rivalry and Political Change in Taisho Japan.* Cambridge, Mass.: Harvard University Press, 1968.

Havens, Thomas. *Farm and Nation in Modern Japan.* Princeton: Princeton University Press, 1974.

Large, Stephen S. *Organized Workers and Socialist Politics in Interwar Japan.* New York: Cambridge University Press, 1981.

———. *The Rise of Labor in Japan: The Yuaikai, 1912–1919.* Tokyo: Sophia University Press, 1972.

Najita, Tetsuo. *Hara Kei in the Politics of Compromise, 1905–1915*. Cambridge, Mass.: Harvard University Press, 1967.

Nishida, Kitaro. *A Study of Good*. Translated by V. H. Viglielmo. Tokyo: Japanese Government Printing Bureau, 1960.

Silberman, Bernard S., and H. D. Harootunian, eds. *Japan in Crisis: Essays in Taishō Democracy*. Princeton: Princeton University Press, 1974.

Smith, Henry. *Japan's First Student Radicals*. Cambridge, Mass.: Harvard University Press, 1972.

Smith, Kerry. *A Time of Crisis: Japan, the Great Depression, and Rural Revitalization*. Cambridge, Mass.: Harvard University Asia Center, 2001.

Stanley, Thomas. *Ōsugi Sakae: Anarchist in Taishō Japan*. Cambridge, Mass.: Harvard University Press, 1982.

Tipton, Elise K., and John Clark. *Being Modern in Japan: Culture and Society from the 1910s to the 1930s*. Honolulu: University of Hawaii Press, 2000.

The Military Ascendancy and the Road to World War II

Alen, G. C. *Appointment in Japan*. London: Althone Press, 1983.

Ballard, J. G. *Empire in the Sun*. New York: Simon & Schuster, 1984.

Barnhart, Michael A. *Japan Prepares for Total War: The Search for Economic Security, 1919–1941*. Ithaca, N.Y.: Cornell University Press, 1987.

Behr, Edward. *Hirohito: Behind the Myth*. New York: Villard Books, 1989.

Berger, Gordon M. *Parties Out of Power in Japan, 1931–1941*. Princeton: Princeton University Press, 1977.

Borg, Dorothy. *The United States and the Far Eastern Crisis of 1933–38*. Cambridge, Mass.: Harvard University Press, 1964.

Boyle, John Hunter. *China and Japan at War*. Stanford: Stanford University Press, 1972.

Byas, Hugh. *Government by Assassination*. New York: Knopf, 1942.

Chang, Iris. *The Rape of Nanking*. New York: Basic Books, 1997.

Ching, Leo T.S. *Becoming "Japanese": Colonial Taiwan and the Politics of Identity Formation*. Berkeley: University of California Press, 2001.

Coffey, Thomas. *Imperial Tragedy*. Cleveland: World Publishing, 1970.

Coox, Alvin D. *Nomonhan: Japan Against Russia, 1939*. Stanford: Stanford University Press, 1985.

Coox, Alvin D., and Hilary Conroy. *China and Japan: Search for Balance Since World War I*. Santa Barbara, Calif.: ABC-Clio, 1978.

Crowley, James B. *Japan's Quest for Autonomy: National Security and Foreign Policy, 1930–1938*. Princeton: Princeton University Press, 1966.

Dorn, Frank. *The Sino-Japanese War, 1937–1941*. New York: Macmillan, 1974.

Dower, John W. *Empire and Aftermath: Yoshida Shigeru and the Japanese Experience, 1878–1954*. Cambridge, Mass.: Harvard University Press, 1979.

Drea, Edward J. *In the Service of the Emperor: Essays on the Imperial Japanese Army*. Lincoln: University of Nebraska Press, 1998.

Evans, David C., and Mark R. Peattie. *Kaigun: Strategy, Tactics, and Technology in the Imperial Japanese Navy, 1887–1941*. Annapolis, Md.: Naval Institute Press, 1997.

Feis, Herbert. *The Road to Pearl Harbor*. Princeton: Princeton University Press, 1950.

Fletcher, William Miles. *The Search for a New Order: Intellectuals and Fascism in Prewar Japan*. Chapel Hill: University of North Carolina Press, 1982.

Fogel, Joshua A. *The Nanjing Massacre in History and Historiography*. Berkeley: University of California Press, 2000.

Grew, Joseph C. L. *Ten Years in Japan*. New York: Simon & Schuster, 1944.

Hane, Mikiso, ed. and trans. *Emperor Hirohito and His Chief Aide de Camp: The Honjo Diary, 1933–1936*. Tokyo: University of Tokyo Press, 1982.

Honda, Katsuichi. *The Nanjing Massacre: A Japanese Journalist Confronts Japan's National Shame*. Translated by Karen Sandness. Armonk, N.Y.: M. E. Sharpe, 1999.

Iriye, Akira. *Pearl Harbor and the Coming of the Pacific War*. Boston: Bedford/St. Martin's, 2000.

Japanese Ministry of Education. *Kokutai no Hongi* (Cardinal Principles of the National Entity of Japan). Translated by John O. Gauntlett. Edited by Robert K. Hall. Cambridge, Mass.: Harvard University Press, 1949.

Kutakov, Leonid N. *The Japanese Foreign Policy on the Eve of the Pacific War—A Soviet View*. Tallahassee, Fla.: Diplomat Press, 1972.

Large, Stephen S. *Emperor Hirohito and Shōwa Japan: A Political Biography*. London: Routledge, 1992.

Lee, Bradford A. *Britain and the Sino-Japanese War, 1937–1939*. Stanford: Stanford University Press, 1973.

Li, Lincoln. *Japanese Army in North China: July, 1937–December, 1941*. London: Oxford University Press, 1975.

Lu, David J. *From the Marco Polo Bridge to Pearl Harbor: Japan's Entry into World War II*. Washington, D.C.: Public Affairs, 1961.

Maruyama, Masao. *Thought and Behaviour in Modern Japanese Politics*. Edited by Ivan Morris. London: Oxford University Press, 1963.

Matsusaka, Yoshihisa Tak. *The Making of Japanese Manchuria, 1904–1932*. Cambridge, Mass.: Harvard University Asia Center, 2001.

Maxon, Yale C. *Control of Japanese Foreign Policy*. Berkeley: University of California Press, 1957.

Mayer-Oakes, Thomas Francis, trans. *Fragile Victory: Prince Saionji and the 1930 London Treaty Issue from the Memoirs of Baron Harada Kumao* (the so-called Saionji-Harada Memoirs). Detroit: Wayne State University Press, 1968.

Meskill, Johanna. *Hitler and Japan: The Hollow Alliance*. New York: Atherton, 1966.

Miller, Frank O. *Minobe Tatsukichi, Interpreter of Constitutionalism in Japan*. Berkeley: University of California Press, 1965.

Minichiello, Sharon. *Retreat from Reform: Patterns of Political Behavior in Interwar Japan*. Honolulu: University Press of Hawaii, 1984.

Mitchell, Richard H. *Thought Control in Prewar Japan*. Ithaca, N.Y.: Cornell University Press, 1976.

Montgomery, Michael. *Imperial Japan: The Yen to Dominate*. New York: St. Martin's, 1988.

Morley, James William, ed. *China Quagmire: Japan's Expansion on the Asian Continent, 1933–1941: Selected Translations from Taiheiyō Sensō e no michi, kaisen gaikō shi*. New York: Columbia University Press, 1983.

_____. *Deterrent Diplomacy: Japan, Germany, and USSR, 1935–1940: Selected Translations from Taiheiyō Sensō e no michi, kaisen gaikō shi*. New York: Columbia University Press, 1976.

_____. *The Fateful Choice: Japan's Advance into Southeast Asia, 1939–1941: Selected Translations from Taiheiyō Sensō e no michi, kaisen gaikō shi*. New York: Columbia University Press, 1980.

_____. *The Final Confrontation: Japan's Negotiations with the United States, 1941.* New York: Columbia University Press, 1994.

_____. *Japan Erupts: The London Naval Conference and the Manchurian Incident, 1928–1932: Selected Translations from Taiheiyō Sensō e no michi, kaisen gaikō shi.* New York: Columbia University Press, 1984.

Morris, Ivan. *Nationalism and the Right Wing in Japan.* London: Oxford University Press, 1960.

Oates, Leslie Russell. *Populist Nationalism in Prewar Japan: A Biography of Nakano Seigo.* London: Allen & Unwin, 1985.

Ogata, Sadako N. *Defiance in Manchuria: The Making of Japanese Foreign Policy, 1931–1932.* Berkeley: University of California Press, 1964.

Oka, Yoshitake. *Konoe Fumimaro.* Translated by Shumpei Okamoto and Patricia Murray. Tokyo: University of Tokyo Press, 1983.

Peattie, Mark R. *Ishiwara Kanji and Japan's Confrontation with the West.* Princeton: Princeton University Press, 1975.

_____. *Sunburst: The Rise of Japanese Naval Air Power, 1909–1941.* Annapolis, Md.: Naval Institute Press, 2001.

Pelz, Stephen E. *Race to Pearl Harbor.* Cambridge, Mass.: Harvard University Press, 1974.

Ramseyer, J. Mark, and Frances M. Rosenbluth. *The Politics of Oligarchy: Institutional Choice in Imperial Japan.* Cambridge: Cambridge University Press, 1995.

Schencking, J. Charles. *Making Waves: Politics, Propaganda, and the Emergence of the Imperial Japanese Navy, 1868–1922.* Stanford: Stanford University Press, 2005.

Schroeder, Paul W. *The Axis Alliance and Japanese American Relations, 1941.* Ithaca, N.Y.: Cornell University Press, 1958.

Shillony, Ben-Ami. *Revolt in Japan: The Young Officers and the February 26, 1936, Incident.* Princeton: Princeton University Press, 1973.

Silverberg, Miriam. *Changing Song: The Marxist Manifestos of Nakano Shigeharu.* Princeton: Princeton University Press, 1990.

Storry, Richard. *The Double Patriots: A Study of Japanese Nationalism.* Boston: Houghton Mifflin, 1957.

Thorne, Christopher G. *The Limits of Foreign Policy: The West, the League, and Far Eastern Crisis of 1931–1933.* New York: Putnam, 1972.

Titus, David Anson. *Palace and Politics in Prewar Japan.* New York: Columbia University Press, 1974.

Togo, Shigenori. *The Cause of Japan.* Translated and edited by Fumihiko Togo and Ben B. Blakeney. New York: Simon & Schuster, 1956.

Totten, George O. *The Social Democratic Movement in Prewar Japan.* New Haven: Yale University Press, 1966.

Wetzler, Peter. *Hirohito and War: Imperial Tradition and Military Decision Making in Prewar Japan.* Honolulu: University of Hawaii Press, 1998.

Wilson, Dick. *When Tigers Fight: The Story of the Sino-Japanese War, 1937–1945.* New York: Viking, 1982.

Wilson, George M. *Radical Nationalist in Japan: Kita Ikki, 1883–1937.* Cambridge, Mass.: Harvard University Press, 1969.

Yoshihashi, Takehiko. *Conspiracy in Manchuria: The Rise of the Japanese Military.* New Haven: Yale University Press, 1963.

Young, Louise. *Japan's Total Empire: Manchuria and the Culture of Wartime Imperialism.* Berkeley: University of California Press, 1998.

The Pacific War

Allen, Louis. *The End of the War in Asia.* London: Hart-Davis, 1976.

Barker, Robert. *Hiroshima Maidens: A Story of Courage, Compassion, and Survival.* New York: Viking, 1985.

Borg, Dorothy, and Shumpei Okamoto, eds. *Pearl Harbor as History.* New York: Columbia University Press, 1973.

Boyer, Paul. *By the Bombs' Early Light: American Thought and Culture at the Dawn of the Atomic Age.* New York: Pantheon, 1985.

Brook. Timothy. *Collaboration: Japanese Agents and Local Elites in Wartime China.* Cambridge, Mass.: Harvard University Press, 2005.

Butow, Robert J. C. *Japan's Decision to Surrender.* Stanford: Stanford University Press, 1954.

_____. *Tojo and the Coming of the War.* Princeton: Princeton University Press, 1961.

Carlile, Lonny E. *Divisions of Labor: Globality, Ideology, and War in the Shaping of the Japanese Labor Movement.* Honolulu: University of Hawaii Press, 2005.

Collier, Basil. *The War in the Far East, 1941–1945: A Military History.* New York: Morrow, 1969.

Conroy, Hilary, and Harry Wray, eds. *Pearl Harbor Reexamined: Prologue to the Pacific War.* Honolulu: University Press of Hawaii, 1989.

Costello, John. *The Pacific War.* New York: Rawson Wade, 1981.

Craig, William. *The Fall of Japan.* New York: Dial, 1967.

Dower, John W. *War Without Mercy: Race and Power in the Pacific War.* New York: Pantheon, 1986.

Earhart, David C. *Certain Victory: Images of World War II in the Japanese Media.* New York: M. E. Sharpe, 2008.

Feis, Herbert. *Japan Subdued: The Atomic Bomb and the End of the War in the Pacific.* Princeton: Princeton University Press, 1961.

Fiset, Louis. *Imprisoned Apart: The World War II Correspondence of an Issei Couple.* Seattle: University of Washington Press, 1997.

Friend, Theodore. *The Blue-Eyed Enemy: Japan Against the West in Java and Luzon, 1942–1945.* Princeton: Princeton University Press, 1988.

Gallicchio, Marc, ed. *The Unpredictability of the Past: Memories of the Asia-Pacific War in US–East Asian Relations.* Durham, N.C.: Duke University Press, 2007.

Gibney, Frank, ed. *Sensō: The Japanese Remember the Pacific War: Letters to the Editor of Asahi Shimbun.* Translated by Beth Cary. New York: M. E. Sharpe, 1995.

Gin, Ooi Keat. *Japanese Empire in the Tropics: Selected Documents and Reports of the Japanese Period in Sarawak, Northwest Borneo, 1941–1945.* Athens: Ohio University Center for International Studies, 1998.

Hachiya, Michihiko. *Hiroshima Diary.* Translated and edited by Warner Wells. Chapel Hill: University of North Carolina Press, 1955.

Havens, Thomas R. H. *Valley of Darkness: The Japanese People and World War II.* New York: Norton, 1978.

Hersey, John. *Hiroshima.* New York: Knopf, 1946.

Howarth, Stephen. *The Fighting Ships of the Rising Sun.* New York: Atheneum, 1983.

Ienaga, Saburo. *The Pacific War: World War II and the Japanese, 1931–1945.* Translated by Frank Baldwin. New York: Pantheon, 1978.

Ike, Nobutaka, ed. *Japan's Decision for War: Records of the 1941 Policy Conferences.* Stanford: Stanford University Press, 1967.

Iriye, Akira. *The Origins of the Second World War in Asia and the Pacific.* London: Longman, 1987.

_____. *Power and Culture: The Japanese-American War, 1941–1945.* Cambridge, Mass.: Harvard University Press, 1981.

Ito, Masanori. *The End of the Imperial Japanese Navy.* Translated by Andrew Y. Kuroda and Roger Pineau. New York: Norton, 1962.

Jones, Francis C. *Japan's New Order in East Asia: Its Rise and Fall, 1937–1945.* London: Oxford University Press, 1954.

Kanda, Mikio, ed. *Widows of Hiroshima: The Life Stories of Nineteen Peasant Wives.* New York: St. Martin's, 1989.

Kratoska, Paul H. *The Japanese Occupation of Malaya (1941–1945): A Social and Economic History.* Honolulu: University of Hawaii Press, 1998.

Layton, Edwin T. *And I Was There: Pearl Harbor and Midway.* New York: Morrow, 1985.

Lebra, Joyce. *Japanese Trained Armies in Southeast Asia.* New York: Columbia University Press, 1977.

Lensen, George A. *The Strange Alliance: Soviet-Japanese Relations During the Second World War, 1941–1945.* Tallahassee, Fla.: Diplomat Press, 1972.

Levine, Hillel. *In Search of Sugihara: The Elusive Japanese Diplomat Who Risked His Life to Rescue 10,000 Jews from the Holocaust.* New York: Free Press, 1996.

Lewin, Ronald. *The American Magic: Codes, Ciphers, and the Defeat of Japan.* New York: Farrar, Strauss & Giroux, 1982.

Lifton, Robert Jay. *Death in Life: Survivors of Hiroshima.* New York: Random House, 1967.

Lord, Walter. *Incredible Victory (The Battle of Midway).* New York: Harper & Row, 1967.

Lundstrum, John B. *The First Team: Pacific Air Combat from Pearl Harbor to Midway.* Annapolis, Md.: Naval Institute Press, 1984.

Manchester, William. *American Caesar: Douglas MacArthur.* Boston: Little, Brown, 1978.

Minear, Richard H., ed. and trans. *Hiroshima: Three Witnesses.* Princeton: Princeton University Press, 1990.

Morison, Samuel Eliot. *History of the United States Naval Operations in World War II.* 15 vols. Boston: Little, Brown, 1947–1962.

Nagai, Takashi. *The Bells of Nagasaki.* Translated by William Johnston. Tokyo: Kodansha, 1974.

Okihiro, Gary. *Storied Lives: Japanese-American Students and World War II.* Seattle: University of Washington Press, 1999.

Pacific War Research Society. *Japan's Longest Day.* Palo Alto, Calif.: Kodansha International, 1968.

Prange, Gordon W. *At Dawn We Slept.* New York: McGraw-Hill, 1981.

_____. *Miracle at Midway.* New York: McGraw-Hill, 1982.

_____. *Pearl Harbor: The Verdict of History.* New York: McGraw-Hill, 1985.

_____. *Target Tokyo: The Story of the Sorge Spy Ring.* New York: McGraw-Hill, 1984.

Rosenberg, Emily S. *A Date Which Will Live: Pearl Harbor in American Memory.* Durham, N.C.: Duke University Press, 2003.

Sakamoto, Pamela Rotner. *Japanese Diplomats and Jewish Refugees.* Westport, Conn.: Praeger Press, 1998.

Shillony, Ben-Ami. *Politics and Culture in Wartime Japan.* London: Oxford University Press, 1981.

Shiroyama, Saburo. *War Criminal: The Life and Death of Hirota Koki.* Translated by John Bester. Tokyo: Kodansha, 1977.

Sigal, Leon V. *Fighting to the Finish: The Politics of War Termination in the United States and Japan, 1945.* Ithaca, N.Y.: Cornell University Press, 1988.

Spector, John H. *Eagle Against the Sun.* New York: Free Press, 1985.

Spurr, Russell. *A Glorious Way to Die: The Kamikaze Mission of the Battleship Yamato.* New York: Harper & Row, 1981.

Stahl, David C. *The Burdens of Survival: Ōoka Shōhei's Writings on the Pacific War.* Honolulu: University of Hawaii Press, 2003.

Stephen, John J. *Hawaii Under the Rising Sun: Japan's Plan for Conquest After Pearl Harbor.* Honolulu: University Press of Hawaii, 1983.

Tanaka, Yuki. *Hidden Horrors: Japanese War Crimes in World War II.* Boulder, Colo.: Westview Press, 1996.

Thorne, Christopher G. *Allies of a Kind: The United States, Britain, and the War Against Japan, 1941–1945.* London: Oxford University Press, 1978.

_____. *The Issue of War: States, Societies, and the Far Eastern Conflict of 1941–1945.* London: Oxford University Press, 1985.

Toland, John. *Infamy: Pearl Harbor and Its Aftermath.* New York: Doubleday, 1982.

_____. *The Rising Sun: The Decline and Fall of the Japanese Empire, 1936–1945.* New York: Random House, 1970.

Trefousse, Hans L. *Pearl Harbor: The Continuing Controversy.* Melbourne, Fla.: Krieger, 1982.

Tsurumi, Shunsuke. *An Intellectual History of Wartime Japan, 1931–1945.* New York: Routledge & Kegan, 1986.

Wetzler, Peter. *Hirohito and War: Imperial Tradition and Military Decision-Making in Prewar Japan.* Honolulu: University Press of Hawaii, 1998.

Williams, Peter, and David Wallace. *Unit 731: Japan's Secret Biological Warfare in World War II.* New York: Free Press, 1989.

Wohlstetter, Roberta. *Pearl Harbor: Warning and Decision.* Stanford: Stanford University Press, 1962.

Wyden, Peter. *Day One: Before Hiroshima and After.* New York: Simon & Schuster, 1984.

Yahara, Hiromichi. *The Battle for Okinawa.* Translated and edited by Roger Pineau and Uehara Masatoshi. New York: John Wiley & Sons, 1995.

Yamazaki, Tomoko. *Sandakan Brothel No. 8: An Episode in the History of Lower-Class Japanese Women.* Translated by Karen Colligan-Taylor. New York: M. E. Sharpe, 1999.

Young, Louise. *Japan's Total Empire: Manchuria and the Culture of Wartime Imperialism.* Berkeley: University of California Press, 1998.

The Postwar Period

Allinson, Gary D. *Japan's Postwar History.* Ithaca, N.Y.: Cornell University Press, 1997.

_____. *Suburban Tokyo.* Berkeley: University of California Press, 1979.

Beardsley, Richard K., et al. *Village Japan.* Chicago: University of Chicago Press, 1959.

Brackman, Arnold. *The Other Nuremberg: The Untold Story of the Tokyo War Crimes Trials.* New York: Morrow, 1987.

Brines, Russell. *MacArthur's Japan.* Philadelphia: Lippincott, 1948.

Buckley, Roger. *Occupation Diplomacy: Britain, the United States, and Japan, 1945–1952.* Cambridge: Cambridge University Press, 1982.

Caprio, Mark, and Sugita Yoneyuki, eds. *Democracy in Occupied Japan: The U.S. Occupation and Japanese Politics and Society.* New York: Routledge, 2007.

Cohen, Jerome B. *Japan's Economy in War and Reconstruction.* Minneapolis: University of Minnesota Press, 1949.

Cohen, Theodore. *Remaking Japan.* New York: Free Press, 1987.

Colbert, Evelyn S. *The Left Wing in Japanese Politics.* New York: Institute of Pacific Relations, 1952.

Dore, Ronald P. *City Life in Japan: A Study of a Tokyo Ward.* Berkeley: University of California Press, 1958.

————. *Land Reform in Japan.* London: Oxford University Press, 1959.

Dower, John. *Embracing Defeat: Japan in the Wake of World War II.* New York: Norton, 1999.

Duke, Benjamin C. *Japan's Militant Teachers: A History of the Left-Wing Teachers' Movement.* Honolulu: University Press of Hawaii, 1973.

Farley, Miriam S. *Aspects of Japan's Labor Problems.* New York: Day, 1950.

Fearey, Robert A. *The Occupation of Japan: Second Phase, 1948–1950.* New York: Macmillan, 1950.

Feis, Herbert. *Contest over Japan.* New York: Norton, 1967.

Field, Norma. *From My Grandmother's Bedside: Sketches of Postwar Tokyo.* Berkeley: University of California Press, 1997.

Finn, Richard B. *Winners in Peace: MacArthur, Yoshida, and Postwar Japan.* Berkeley: University of California Press, 1992.

Gibbs, Michael H. *Struggle and Purpose in Postwar Japanese Unionism.* Berkeley: University of California Press, 2000.

Gordon, Andrew. *The Wages of Affluence: Labor and Management in Postwar Japan.* Cambridge, Mass.: Harvard University Asia Center, 1998.

Gordon, Andrew, ed. *Postwar Japan as History.* Berkeley: University of California Press, 1993.

Gordon, Beate Sirota. *The Only Woman in the Room.* London: Kodansha International, 1998.

Hadley, Eleanor H. *Antitrust in Japan.* Princeton: Princeton University Press, 1970.

Halloran, Richard. *Japan: Images and Realities.* New York: Knopf, 1969.

Hane, Mikiso. *Eastern Phoenix: Japan Since 1945.* Boulder, Colo.: Westview Press, 1995.

Harries, Meirion, and Susie Harries. *Sheathing the Sword: The Demilitarization of Japan.* London: Hamish Hamilton, 1987.

Havens, Thomas R. H. *Artists and Patrons in Postwar Japan: Dance, Music, Theatre, and the Visual Arts, 1955–1980.* Princeton: Princeton University Press, 1982.

Helleger, Dale. *We, the Japanese People: World War II and the Origins of the Japanese Constitution.* Stanford: Stanford University Press, 2001.

Hosoya, Chihiro, et al., eds. *The Tokyo War Crimes Trial.* Tokyo: Kodansha International, 1986.

Igarashi, Yoshikuni. *Bodies of Memory: Narratives of War in Postwar Japanese Culture, 1945–1970.* Princeton: Princeton University Press, 2000.

Inoue, Kyoko. *MacArthur's Japanese Constitution: A Linguistic and Cultural Study of Its Making.* Chicago: University of Chicago Press, 1991.

Irokawa, Daikichi. *The Age of Hirohito: In Search of Modern Japan.* Translated by Mikiso Hane and John K. Urda. New York: Free Press, 1995.

Kawai, Kazuo. *Japan's American Interlude.* Chicago: University of Chicago Press, 1960.

Kawasaki, Ichiro. *Japan Unmasked.* Rutland, Vt.: Charles E. Tuttle, 1969.

Kersten, Rikki. *Democracy in Postwar Japan: Maruyama Masao and the Search for Autonomy.* London: Routledge, 1996.

Kiyota, Minoru. *Beyond Loyalty: The Story of a Kibei.* Translated by Linda Klepinger Keenan. Honolulu: University of Hawaii Press, 1997.

Kohno, Masaru. *Japan's Postwar Party Politics.* Princeton: Princeton University Press, 1997.

Koschmann, J. Victor. *Revolution and Subjectivity in Postwar Japan.* Chicago: University of Chicago, 1996.

Koseki, Shoichi. *The Birth of Japan's Postwar Constitution.* Translated and edited by Ray A. Moore. Boulder, Colo.: Westview Press, 1997.

MacArthur, Douglas. *Reminiscences.* New York: McGraw-Hill, 1964.

Martin, Edwin M. *The Allied Occupation of Japan.* New York: Institute of Pacific Relations, 1948.

Matsuda, Takeshi. *Soft Power and Its Perils: U.S. Cultural Policy in Early Postwar Japan and Permanent Dependency.* Stanford: Stanford University Press, 2007.

Minear, Richard H. *Victor's Justice: The Tokyo War Crimes Trial.* Princeton: Princeton University Press, 1971.

Moore, Ray A. and Donald L. Robinson. *Partners for Democracy: Crafting the New Japanese State Under MacArthur.* New York: Oxford University Press, 2002.

Nakamura, Masanori. *The Japanese Monarchy, 1931–1991: Ambassador Grew and the Making of the "Symbolic Emperor System."* Translated by Herbert P. Bix et al. Armonk, N.Y.: M. E. Sharpe, 1997.

Nakamura, Takafusa. *A History of Shōwa Japan, 1926–1989.* Berkeley: University of California Press, 1998.

Nishi, Toshio. *Unconditional Democracy: Education and Politics in Occupied Japan, 1945–1952.* Stanford: Hoover Institution Press, 1982.

O'Brien, David M., and Yasuo Ohkoshi. *To Dream of Dreams: Religious Freedom and Constitutional Politics in Postwar Japan.* Honolulu: University of Hawaii Press, 1996.

Orr, James J. *Victim As Hero: Ideologies of Peace and National Identity in Postwar Japan.* Honolulu: University of Hawaii Press, 2001.

Passin, Herbert, ed. *The United States and Japan.* Englewood Cliffs, N.J.: Prentice-Hall, 1966.

Pritchard, R. John, and Sonia M. Zaide, eds. *The Tokyo War Crimes Trial.* 22 vols. New York: Garland, 1981.

Sams, Crawford F. *"Medic": The Mission of an American Military Doctor in Occupied Japan and Wartorn Korea.* Armonk, N.Y.: M. E. Sharpe, 1998.

Sandler, Mark, ed. *The Confusion Era: Art and Culture in Japan During the Allied Occupation, 1945–1952.* Seattle: University of Washington Press, 1998.

Sasaki-Uemura, Wesley. *Organizing the Spontaneous: Citizen Protest in Postwar Japan.* Honolulu: University of Hawaii Press, 2001.

Scalapino, Robert A., and Junnosuke Masumi. *Parties and Politics in Contemporary Japan.* Berkeley: University of California Press, 1962.

Schaller, Michael. *The American Occupation of Japan.* London: Oxford University Press, 1985.

_____. *Douglas MacArthur, Far Eastern General.* London: Oxford University Press, 1989.

Schlesinger, Jacob M. *Shadow Shōguns: The Rise and Fall of Japan's Postwar Political Machine.* New York: Simon & Schuster, 1997.

Sebald, William. *With MacArthur in Japan.* New York: Norton, 1965.

Seraphim, Franziska. *War Memory and Social Politics in Japan, 1945–2005.* Cambridge, Mass.: Harvard University Press, 2008.

Slaymaker, Doug. *Confluences: Postwar Japan and France.* Ann Arbor: Center for Japanese Studies, University of Michigan, 2002.

Smith, Robert J. *Kurusu: A Japanese Village, 1951–1975.* Stanford: Stanford University Press, 1978.

Supreme Commander for the Allied Powers, Government Section. *Political Reorientation of Japan, September 1945 to September 1948: Report.* 2 vols. Grosse Pointe, Mich.: Scholarly Press, 1968.

Takeda, Kyoko. *The Dual Image of the Japanese Emperor.* New York: New York University Press, 1989.

Takemae, Eiji, et al. *Inside GHQ: The Allied Occupation of Japan and Its Legacy.* New York: Continuum, 2002.

Trefalt, Beatrice. *Japanese Army Stragglers and Memories of the War in Japan, 1950–1975.* New York: Taylor & Francis, 2007.

Tsurumi, Kazuko. *Social Change and the Individual: Japan Before and After Defeat in World War II.* Princeton: Princeton University Press, 1970.

Tsurumi, Shunsuke. *A Cultural History of Postwar Japan, 1945–1980.* New York: Columbia University Press, 1994.

Unger, J. Marshall. *Literacy and Script Reform in Occupation Japan.* New York: Oxford University Press, 1996.

Upham, Frank K. *Law and Social Change in Postwar Japan.* Cambridge, Mass.: Harvard University Press, 1987.

Weinstein, Martin E. *Japan's Postwar Defense Policy, 1947–1968.* New York: Columbia University Press, 1971.

Yamamoto, Mari. *Grassroots Pacifism in Post-War Japan: The Rebirth of a Nation.* Sheffield Centre for Japanese Studies. London: RoutledgeCurzon, 2004.

Yamamura, Kozo. *Economic Policy in Postwar Japan.* Berkeley: University of California Press, 1967.

Yanaga, Chitoshi. *Big Business in Japanese Politics.* New Haven: Yale University Press, 1968.

Yoshida, Shigeru. *The Yoshida Memoirs.* Translated by Kenichi Yoshida. Boston: Houghton Mifflin, 1962.

Japan Today

Aoyagi, Hiroshi. *Islands of Eight Million Smiles: Idol Performance and Symbolic Production in Contemporary Japan.* Cambridge, Mass.: Harvard University Asia Center, 2005.

Apter, David E., and Nagayo Sawa. *Against the State: Politics and Social Protest in Japan.* Cambridge, Mass.: Harvard University Press, 1984.

Bachnik, Jane M., ed. *Roadblocks on the Information Highway: The IT Revolution in Japanese Education.* Lanham, Md.: Lexington Books, 2003.

Baerwald, Hans H. *Japan's Parliament: An Introduction.* Cambridge: Cambridge University Press, 1974.

Barshay, Andrew E. *The Social Sciences in Modern Japan: The Marxian and Modernist Traditions.* Berkeley: University of California Press, 2004.

Befu, Harumi. *Hegemony of Homogeneity: An Anthropological Analysis of "Nihonjinron."* Melbourne: Trans Pacific Press, 2001.

Bell, Ronald, ed. *The Japan Experience.* New York: Weatherhill, 1973.

Benjamin, Gail R. *Japanese Lessons: A Year in a Japanese School Through the Eyes of an American Anthropologist.* New York: New York University Press, 1997.

Bestor, Theodore C. *Tsukiji: The Fish Market at the Center of the World.* Berkeley: University of California Press, 2004.

Bix, Herbert P. *Hirohito and the Making of Modern Japan.* New York: HarperCollins, 2000.

Boronoff, Michael. *Pink Samurai: Love, Marriage, and Sex in Contemporary Japan.* New York: Pocket Books, 1991.

Broadbent, Jeffrey. *Environmental Politics in Japan: Networks of Power and Protest.* Cambridge: Cambridge University Press, 1998.

Buckley, Roger. *Japan Today.* Cambridge: Cambridge University Press, 1990.

Burks, Adrath. *Japan: A Postindustrial Power.* Boulder, Colo.: Westview Press, 1981.

Buruma, Ian. *Behind the Mask: On Sexual Demons, Sacred Mothers, Transvestites, Gangsters, Drifters and Other Japanese Cultural Heroes.* New York: Pantheon, 1984.

Campbell, John C. *How Politics Change: The Japanese Government and the Aging Society.* Princeton: Princeton University Press, 1992.

Campbell, John Creighton, and Naoki Ikegami. *The Art of Balance in Health Policy.* Cambridge: Cambridge University Press, 1998.

Christensen, Ray. *Ending the LDP Hegemony: Party Cooperation in Japan.* Honolulu: University of Hawaii Press, 2000.

Christopher, Robert C. *The Japanese Mind: The Goliath Explained.* New York: Linden Press, 1983.

_____. *Second to None: American Companies in Japan.* New York: Crown, 1986.

Clammer, John. *Contemporary Urban Japan: A Sociology of Consumption.* Malden, Mass.: Blackwell Publishers, 1997.

Clark, Rodney. *The Japanese Company.* New Haven: Yale University Press, 1979.

Cole, Robert C. *Japanese Blue Collar.* Berkeley: University of California Press, 1971.

Cummings, William A. *Education and Equality in Japan.* Princeton: Princeton University Press, 1980.

Curtis, Gerald L. *The Japanese Way of Politics.* New York: Columbia University Press, 1988.

_____. *The Logic of Japanese Politics: Leaders, Institutions, and the Limits of Change.* New York: Columbia University Press, 1999.

Cutts, Robert L. *An Empire of Schools: Japan's Universities and the Molding of a National Power Elite.* New York: M. E. Sharpe, 1997.

Dale, Peter N. *The Myth of Japanese Uniqueness.* New York: St. Martin's, 1986.

Denison, Edward F., and William K. Chung. *How Japan's Economy Grew So Fast.* Washington, D.C.: Brookings Institution, 1976.

DeVos, George, and William Witherall. *Japan's Minorities: Burakumin, Koreans, Ainus, and Okinawans.* Claremont, N.Y.: Minority Rights Group, 1983.

Dore, Ronald. *British Factory—Japanese Factory.* Berkeley: University of California Press, 1973.

_____. *Shinohata: A Portrait of a Japanese Village.* London: Allen Lane, 1978.

_____. *Taking Japan Seriously.* Stanford: Stanford University Press, 1987.

Duke, Benjamin. *The Japanese School: Lessons for Industrial America.* New York: Praeger, 1986.

Eades, J. S., Tom Gill, and Harumi Befu. *Globalization and Social Change in Contemporary Japan.* Melbourne: Trans Pacific Press, 2000.

Feldman, Eric A. *The Ritual of Rights in Japan: Law, Society, and Health Policy.* Cambridge: Cambridge University Press, 2000.

Field, Norma. *From My Grandmother's Bedside: Sketches of Postwar Tokyo.* Berkeley: University of California Press, 1997.

_____. *In the Realm of the Dying Emperor.* New York: Pantheon, 1991.

Fowler, Edward. *San'ya Blues: Laboring Life in Contemporary Tokyo.* Ithaca, N.Y.: Cornell University Press, 1996.

Freeman, Laurie Anne. *Closing the Shop: Information Cartels and Japan's Mass Media*. Princeton: Princeton University Press, 2000.

Fukuoka, Yasunori. *Lives of Young Koreans in Japan*. Melbourne: Trans Pacific Press, 2000.

George, Timothy S. *Minamata: Pollution and the Struggle for Democracy in Postwar Japan*. Cambridge, Mass.: Harvard University Asia Center, 2001.

Goldstein-Gidoni, Ofra. *Packaged Japaneseness: Weddings, Business, and Brides*. Honolulu: University of Hawaii Press, 1997.

Goodman, Roger. *Children of the Japanese State: The Changing Role of Child Protection Institutions in Contemporary Japan*. Oxford: Oxford University Press, 2000.

Goodman, Roger, and Ian Neary, eds. *Case Studies on Human Rights in Japan*. Richmond, Surrey, U.K.: Japan Library of Curzon Press, 1996.

Grossberg, Kenneth A., ed. *Japan Today*. Philadelphia: Institute for the Study of Human Issues, 1981.

Hardacre, Helen. *Marketing the Menacing Fetus in Japan*. Berkeley: University of California Press, 1997.

Harootunian, Harry. *History's Disquiet: Modernity, Cultural Practice, and the Question of Everyday Life*. New York: Columbia University Press, 2000.

Hashimoto, Akiko. *The Gift of Generations: Japanese and American Perspectives on Aging and the Social Contract*. Cambridge: Cambridge University Press, 1996.

Hatch, Walter, and Kozo Yamamura. *Asia in Japan's Embrace: Building a Regional Production Alliance*. Cambridge: Cambridge University Press, 1996.

Hein, Laura, and Mark Selden, eds. *Censoring History: Citizenship and Memory in Japan, Germany, and the United States*. New York: M. E. Sharpe, 2000.

_____. *Islands of Discontent: Okinawan Responses to Japanese and American Power*. Lanham, Md.: Rowman and Littlefield, 2003.

_____. *Living with the Bomb: American and Japanese Cultural Conflicts in the Nuclear Age*. New York: M. E. Sharpe, 1997.

Hendry, Joy. *An Anthropologist in Japan: Glimpses of Life in the Field*. New York: Routledge, 1999.

Herbert, Wolfgang. *Foreign Workers and Law Enforcement in Japan*. New York: Kegan Paul International, 1997.

Hirschmeier, Johannes, et al. *Politics and Economics in Contemporary Japan*. Tokyo: Kodansha, 1979.

Holloway, Susan D. *Contested Childhood: Diversity and Change in Japanese Preschools*. New York: Routledge, 2000.

Hook, Glenn D. *Militarization and Demilitarization in Contemporary Japan*. London: Routledge, 1996.

Ienaga, Saburō, and Richard H. Minear. *Japan's Past, Japan's Future: One Historian's Odyssey*. Lanham, Md.: Rowman & Littlefield, 2001.

Ito, Satoru, Ryuta Yanase, and Francis Conlan. *Coming Out in Japan: The Story of Satoru and Ryuta*. Melbourne: Trans Pacific Press, 2001.

Iwasawa, Yuji. *International Law, Human Rights, and Japanese Law*. Oxford: Clarendon Press, 1998.

Jannetta, Ann. *The Vaccinators: Smallpox, Medical Knowledge, and the 'Opening' of Japan*. Stanford: Stanford University Press, 2007.

Johnson, Chalmers. *MITI and the Japanese Miracle: The Growth of Industrial Policy, 1925–1975*. Stanford: Stanford University Press, 1985.

_____. *Okinawa: Cold War Island*. Cardiff, Calif.: Japan Policy Research Institute, 1999.

Johnson, David T. *The Japanese Way of Justice: Prosecuting Crime in Japan*. Oxford: Oxford University Press, 2002.

Johnson, Sheila K. *The Japanese through American Eyes*. Stanford: Stanford University Press, 1988.

Jolivet, Muriel. *Japan: The Childless Society?* New York: Routledge, 1997.

Karan, P. P., and Kristin Stapleton, eds. *The Japanese City*. Lexington: University Press of Kentucky, 1997.

Katzenstein, Peter J. *Cultural Norms and National Security: Police and Military in Postwar Japan*. Ithaca, N.Y.: Cornell University Press, 1997.

Kawano, Satsuki. *Final Days: Japanese Culture and Choice at the End of Life*. Honolulu: University of Hawaii Press, 2005.

Kim, Hyung-Ki, et al., eds. *The Japanese Civil Service and Economic Development: Catalysts of Change*. Oxford: Clarendon Press, 1995.

Kimura, Hiroshi. *The Kurillian Knot: A History of Japanese-Russian Border Negotiations*. Stanford: Stanford University Press, 2008.

Koh, B. C. *Japan's Administrative Elite*. Berkeley: University of California Press, 1989.

Komai, Hiroshi. *Foreign Migrants in Contemporary Japan*. Translated by Wilkinson Jens. Melbourne: Trans Pacific Press, 2001.

Lee, Changsoo, and George DeVos. *Koreans in Japan: Ethnic Conflict and Accommodation*. Berkeley: University of California Press, 1982.

Lee, Yong Wook. *The Japanese Challenge to the American Neoliberal World Order: Identity, Meaning, and Foreign Policy*. Stanford: Stanford University Press, 2008.

Levine, Solomon B., and Hiroshi Kawada. *Human Resources in Japanese Industrial Development*. Princeton: Princeton University Press, 1980.

Maynard, Senko K. *Japanese Communication: Language and Thought in Context*. Honolulu: University of Hawaii Press, 1997.

McCargo, Duncan. *Contemporary Japan*. New York: St. Martin's Press, 2000.

McLelland, Mark. *Queer Japan from the Pacific War to the Internet Age*. Lanham, Md.: Rowman & Littlefield, 2005.

Miyoshi, Masao, and H. D. Harootunian, eds. *Japan in the World*. Durham, N.C.: Duke University Press, 1993.

Mizoguchi, Koji. *Archaeology, Society, and Identity in Modern Japan*. New York: Cambridge University Press, 2006.

Moeran, Brian. *Okubo Diary: Portrait of a Japanese Valley*. Stanford: Stanford University Press, 1985.

Murakami, H., and J. Hirschmeier. *Politics and Economics in Contemporary Japan*. Tokyo: Kodansha, 1983.

Neary, Ian. *The State and Politics in Japan*. Cambridge: Polity Press, 2002.

Parker, L. Craig, Jr. *The Japanese Police System Today: A Comparative Study*. New York: M. E. Sharpe, 2001.

Partner, Simon. *Toshié: A Story of Village Life in Twentieth-Century Japan*. Berkeley: University of California Press, 2004.

Peng-Er, Lam. *Green Politics in Japan*. London: Routledge, 1999.

Pharr, Susan J. *Losing Face: Status Politics in Japan*. Berkeley: University of California, 1990.

Plath, David, ed. *Work and Life Course in Japan*. Albany, N.Y.: SUNY Press, 1983.

Roesgaard, Marie H. *Moving Mountains: Japanese Educational Reform*. Aarhus, Denmark: Aarhus University Press, 1998.

Ryang, Sonia. *Japan and National Anthropology: A Critique*. New York: Routledge, 2004.

_____. *North Koreans in Japan Today: Language, Ideology, and Identity*. Boulder, Colo.: Westview Press, 1997.

Sakamoto, Takayuki. *Building Policy Legitimacy in Japan: Political Behavior Beyond Rational Choice*. New York: St. Martin's Press, 1999.

Samuels, Richard J. *Securing Japan: Tokyo's Grand Strategy and the Future of East Asia*. Ithaca, N.Y.: Cornell University Press, 2007.

Schoppa, Leonard J. *Race for the Exits: The Unraveling of Japan's System of Social Protection*. Ithaca, N.Y.: Cornell University Press, 2008.

Seidensticker, Edward. *This Country Japan*. Tokyo: Kodansha, 1984.

Smith, Patricia. *Japan: A Reinterpretation*. New York: Pantheon, 1997.

Sumii, Sue. *The River with No Bridge*. Translated by Susan Wilkinson. Rutland, Vt.: Tuttle, 1990.

Suzuki, Hikaru. *The Price of Death: The Funeral Industry in Contemporary Japan*. Stanford: Stanford University Press, 2001.

Takeda, Kiyoko. *The Dual Image of the Japanese Emperor*. New York: New York University Press, 1989.

Thayer, Nathaniel B. *How the Conservatives Rule Japan*. Princeton: Princeton University Press, 1969.

Thurston, Donald R. *Teachers and Politics in Japan*. New York: Columbia University Press, 1973.

Traphagan, John W. *Taming Oblivion: Aging Bodies and the Fear of Senility in Japan*. Albany: State University of New York, 2000.

Treat, John Whittier. *Great Mirrors Shattered: Homosexuality, Orientalism, and Japan*. Oxford and New York: Oxford University Press, 1999.

Tsurumi, Patricia, ed. *The Other Japan: Postwar Realities*. Armonk, N.Y.: M. E. Sharpe, 1988.

Vogel, Ezra F. *Japan as Number One*. Cambridge, Mass.: Harvard University Press, 1979.

_____. *Japan's New Middle Class: The Salary Man and His Family in a Tokyo Suburb*. Berkeley: University of California Press, 1963.

Wada, Junichiro. *The Japanese Election System*. London: Routledge, 1996.

Wender, Melissa. *Lamentation as History: Narratives by Koreans in Japan, 1965–2000*. Stanford: Stanford University Press, 2005.

White, Merry. *The Japanese Educational Challenge*. New York: Free Press, 1986.

_____. *The Japanese Overseas: Can They Go Home Again?* New York: Free Press, 1988.

_____. *Perfectly Japanese: Making Families in an Era of Upheaval*. Berkeley: University of California Press, 2002.

Whittaker, D. Hugh. *Small Firms in the Japanese Economy*. Cambridge: Cambridge University Press, 1997.

Wilson, Sandra, ed. *Nation and Nationalism in Japan*. London: RoutledgeCurzon, 2002.

Wray, Harry. *Japanese and American Education: Attitudes and Practice*. Westport, Conn.: Bergin & Garvey, 1999.

Yamazaki, Masakazu. *Individualism and the Japanese: An Alternative Approach to Cultural Comparison*. Tokyo: Japan Echo, 1994.

Yoder, Robert Stuart. *Youth Deviance in Japan: Class Reproduction of Non-Conformity*. Melbourne: Trans Pacific Press, 2004.

Yoneyama, Shoko. *The Japanese High School: Silence and Resistance*. New York: Routledge, 1999.

Literature: Premodern

Arntzen, Sonja. *The Kagero Diary.* Ann Arbor: Center for Japanese Studies, University of Michigan, 1997.

Aston, W. G. *A History of Japanese Literature.* New York: Appleton, 1899.

Aston, W. G., trans. *Nihongi (Chronicles of Japan from the Earliest Time to A.D. 697).* 1924. Reprint, New York: Paragon, 1956.

Bargen, Doris G. *A Woman's Weapon: Spirit Possession in the Tale of Genji.* Honolulu: University of Hawaii Press, 1997.

Blyth, Reginald H. *Haiku.* 4 vols. Tokyo: Hokuseido Press, 1950–1952.

Brazell, Karen, trans. *The Confessions of Lady Nijo.* Stanford: Stanford University Press, 1973.

Brower, Robert H., and Earl R. Miner. *Japanese Court Poetry.* Stanford: Stanford University Press, 1961.

Dalby, Liza. *The Tale of Murasaki: A Novel.* New York: Doubleday, 2000.

D'Etcheverry, Charo B. *Love After* The Tale of Genji: *Rewriting the World of the Shining Prince.* Cambridge, Mass.: Harvard University Asia Center, 2007.

Ebersole, Gary L. *Ritual Poetry and Politics of Death in Early Japan.* Princeton: Princeton University Press, 1989.

Field, Norma. *The Splendor of Longing in* The Tale of Genji. Princeton: Princeton University Press, 1987.

Graham, Masako Nakagawa. *The Yang Kuei-Fei Legend in Japanese Literature.* Lewiston, N.Y.: Edwin Mellen Press, 1998.

Henderson, Harold G. *An Introduction to Haiku.* Garden City, N.Y.: Doubleday, 1958.

Hibbett, Howard. *The Floating World in Japanese Fiction.* New York: Grove, 1960.

Hijiya-Kirschmereit, Irmela. *Rituals of Self-Revelation: Shishōsetsu as Literary Genre and Socio-Cultural Phenomenon.* Cambridge, Mass.: Harvard University Asia Center, 1996.

Huey, Robert N. *The Making of Shinkokinshū.* Cambridge, Mass.: Harvard University Asia Center, 2002.

Kawashima, Terry. *Writing Margins: The Textual Construction of Gender in Heian and Kamakura Japan.* Cambridge, Mass.: Harvard University Asia Center, 2001.

Keene, Donald. *Japanese Literature: An Introduction to Western Readers.* New York: Grove, 1955.

_____. *Living Japan.* Garden City, N.Y.: Doubleday, 1959.

_____. *The Pleasures of Japanese Literature.* New York: Columbia University Press, 1988.

Keene, Donald, ed. *Anthology of Japanese Literature from the Earliest Era to the Mid-Nineteenth Century.* New York: Grove, 1955.

Keene, Donald, trans. *Essays in Idleness: The Tsurezuregusa of Kenkō.* New York: Columbia University Press, 1967.

Kornicki, Peter. *The Book in Japan: A Cultural History from the Beginnings to the Nineteenth Century.* Leiden, Netherlands: Brill, 1998.

Marra, Michael F., trans. and ed. *Kuki Shūzō: A Philosopher's Poetry and Poetics.* Honolulu: University of Hawaii Press, 2004.

McCullough, Helen C., trans. *Tales of Ise: Lyrical Episodes from Tenth-Century Japan.* Stanford: Stanford University Press, 1968.

Miner, Earl. *An Introduction to Japanese Court Poetry.* Stanford: Stanford University Press, 1968.

Murasaki, Shikibu. *The Tale of Genji.* Translated by Edward G. Seidensticker. New York: Knopf, 1978.

_____. *The Tale of Genji.* Translated by Arthur Waley. New York: Random House, 1960.

Nippon Gakujutsu Shinkokai, pub. *Manyōshū: One Thousand Court Poems*. New York: Columbia University Press, 1965.

Sarra, Edith. *Fictions of Femininity: Literary Inventions of Gender in Japanese Court Women's Memoirs*. Stanford: Stanford University Press, 1999.

Sei, Shonagon. *The Pillow Books of Sei Shonagon*. Translated and edited by Ivan Morris. 2 vols. New York: Columbia University Press, 1967.

Seidensticker, Edward G., trans. *The Gossamer Years: A Diary by a Noblewoman of Heian Japan*. Rutland, Vt.: Tuttle, 1964.

Shirane, Haruo. *Traces of Dreams: Landscape, Cultural Memory, and the Poetry of Bashō*. Stanford: Stanford University Press, 1998.

Thomas, Roger K. *The Ways of Shikishima: Waka Theory and Practice in Early Modern Japan*. New York: University Press of America, 2008.

Ueda, Makoto. *Light Verse from the Floating World: An Anthology of Premodern Japanese Senryu*. New York: Columbia University Press, 1999.

_____. *Literary and Art Theories in Japan*. Cleveland: Case Western Reserve, 1967.

Yoda, Tomiko. *Gender and National Literature: Heian Texts in the Constructions of Japanese Modernity*. Durham, N.C.: Duke University Press, 2004.

Literature: Modern

Akita, George. *Evaluating Evidence: A Populist Approach to Reading Sources on Modern Japan*. Honolulu: University of Hawaii Press, 2008.

Aston, W. G. *A History of Japanese Literature*. New York: Appleton, 1899.

Bardsley, Jan. *The Bluestockings of Japan: New Woman Essays and Fiction from Seitō, 1911–1916*. Ann Arbor: Center for Japanese Studies, University of Michigan, 2007.

Beichman, Janine. *Embracing the Firebird: Yosano Akiko and the Birth of the Female Voice in Modern Japanese Poetry*. Honolulu: University of Hawaii Press, 2002.

Bourdaghs, K. Michael. *The Dawn that Never Comes: Shimazaki Tōson and Japanese Nationalism*. New York: Columbia University Press, 2003.

Brodey, Inger Sigrun, and Sammy I. Tsunematsu. *Rediscovering Natsume Sōseki: Celebrating the Centenary of Sōseki's Arrival in England 1900–1902: With the First English Translation of "Travels in Manchuria and Korea."* Folkestone: Global Oriental, 2000.

Cohn, Joel R. *Studies in the Comic Spirit in Modern Japanese Fiction*. Cambridge, Mass.: Harvard University Asia Center, 1998.

Copeland, Rebecca. *Lost Leaves: Women Writers of Meiji Japan*. Honolulu: University of Hawaii Press, 2000.

Copeland, Rebecca L., and Esperanza Ramirez-Christensen. *The Father-Daughter Plot: Japanese Literary Women and the Law of the Father*. Honolulu: University of Hawaii Press, 2001.

Cornyetz, Nina. *Dangerous Women, Deadly Words: Phallic Fantasy and Modernity in Three Japanese Writers*. Stanford: Stanford University Press, 1999.

Danly, Robert Lyons. *In the Shade of Spring Leaves: The Life and Writings of Higuchi Ichiyo*. New Haven: Yale University Press, 1981.

Dodd, Steven. *Writing Home: Representations of the Native Place in Modern Japanese Literature*. Cambridge: Harvard University Asia Center, 2005.

Ericson, Joan E. *Be a Woman: Hayashi Fumiko and Modern Japanese Women's Literature*. Honolulu: University of Hawaii Press, 1997.

Fessler, Susanna. *Wandering Heart: The Work and Method of Hayashi Fumiko*. Albany: State University of New York Press, 1998.

Flores, Linda M. *The Body in Postwar Japanese Fiction.* New York: RoutledgeCurzon, 2004.

Gabriel, Philip. *Mad Wives and Island Dreams: Shimao Toshio and the Margins of Japanese Literature.* Honolulu: University of Hawaii Press, 1999.

_____. *Spirit Matters: The Transcendent in Modern Japanese Literature.* Honolulu: Hawaii University Press, 2006.

Hibbett, Howard, ed. *Contemporary Japanese Literature.* New York: Knopf, 1977.

Hirata, Hosea. *Discourses of Seduction—History, Evil, Desire, and Modern Japanese Literature.* Cambridge, Mass.: Harvard University Press, 2005.

Inouye, Charles Shirō. *The Similitude of Blossoms: A Critical Biography of Izumi Kyōka (1873–1939), Japanese Novelist and Playwright.* Cambridge, Mass.: Harvard University Asia Center, 1998.

Ishikawa, Jun. *The Legend of Gold and Other Stories.* Translated by William J. Tyler. Honolulu: University of Hawaii Press, 1998.

Kamei, Hideo. *Transformations of Sensibility: The Phenomenology of Meiji Literature.* Translation edited by Michael Bourdaghs. Ann Arbor: Michigan Monograph Series in Japanese, 2001.

Kamens, Edward. *Utamakura, Allusion, and Intertextuality in Traditional Japanese Poetry.* New Haven: Yale University Press, 1997.

Keene, Donald. *Dawn to the West: Japanese Literature in the Modern Era.* 2 vols. New York: Holt, 1984.

_____. *Landscapes and Portraits: Appreciations of Japanese Culture.* Tokyo: Kodansha International, 1971.

Kimball, Arthur G. *Crisis in Identity and Contemporary Japanese Novels.* Rutland, Vt.: Tuttle, 1973.

_____. *Five Modern Japanese Novelists.* New York: Columbia University Press, 2003.

_____. *Mishima on Stage: The Black Lizard and Other Plays.* Ann Arbor: Center for Japanese Studies, University of Michigan, 2007.

_____. *The Pleasure of Japanese Literature.* New York: Columbia University Press, 1988.

Kinsella, Sharon. *Adult Manga: Culture and Power in Contemporary Japanese Society.* Honolulu: University of Hawaii Press, 2000.

Kuribayashi, Tomoko, and Mizuho Terasawa. *The Outsider Within: Ten Essays on Modern Japanese Women Writers.* Lanham, Md.: University Press of America, 2002.

Lyons, Phyllis. *The Saga of Dazai Osamu.* Stanford: Stanford University Press, 1985.

MacWilliams, Mark W., ed. *Japanese Visual Culture: Explorations in the World of Manga and Anime.* New York: M. E. Sharpe, 2008.

McClellan, Edwin. *Two Japanese Novelists: Sōseki and Tōson.* Berkeley: University of California Press, 1969.

Mertz, John Pierre. *Novel Japan: Spaces of Nationhood in Early Meiji Narrative, 1870–1888.* Ann Arbor: Center for Japanese Studies, University of Michigan, 2003.

Miller, Stephen D., ed. *Partings at Dawn: An Anthology of Japanese Gay Literature.* San Francisco: Gay Sunshine Press, 1996.

Miyoshi, Masao. *Accomplices of Silence: The Modern Japanese Novel.* Berkeley: University of California Press, 1974.

Nakamura, Mitsuo. *Contemporary Japanese Fiction, 1926–1968.* Tokyo: Kokusai Bunka Shinkokai, 1969.

_____. *Modern Japanese Fiction, 1868–1926.* Tokyo: Kokusai Bunka Shinkokai, 1968.

Napier, Susan J. *Anime from Akira to Princess Mononoke: Experiencing Contemporary Japanese Animation.* New York: Palgrave, 2000.

_____. *The Fantastic in Modern Japanese Literature: The Subversion of Modernity.* London and New York: Routledge, 1996.

Nara, Hiroshi. *The Structure of Detachment: The Aesthetic Vision of Kuki Shūzō.* Honolulu: University of Hawaii Press, 2004.

Nathan, John. *Mishima: A Biography.* New York: Little, Brown, 1974.

Rabson, Steve. *Righteous Cause or Tragic Folly: Changing Views of War in Japanese Poetry.* Ann Arbor: Center for Japanese Studies, University of Michigan, 1998.

Reichert, Jim. *In the Company of Men: Representations of Male-Male Sexuality in Meiji Literature.* Stanford: Stanford University Press, 2006.

Rimer, J. Thomas. *Mori Ōgai.* Boston, Mass.: Twayne, 1975.

Rosenfeld, David M. *Unhappy Soldier: Hino Ashihei and Japanese World War II Literature.* Lanham, Md.: Lexington Books, 2002.

Rowley, G. G. *Yosano Akiko and the Tale of Genji.* Ann Arbor: Center for Japanese Studies, University of Michigan, 2000.

Ryan, Marleigh C. *The Development of Realism in the Fiction of Tsubouchi Shoyo.* Seattle: University of Washington Press, 1975.

_____. *Japan's First Modern Novel: Ukigumo of Futabatei Shimei.* New York: Columbia University Press, 1967.

Sato, Hiroaki. *Breeze Through Bamboo: Kanshi of Ema Saikō.* New York: Columbia University Press, 1998.

Sato, Hiroaki, trans. *Japanese Women Poets: An Anthology.* New York: M. E. Sharpe, 2007.

Schalow, Paul Gordon, and Janet Walker, eds. *The Woman's Hand: Gender and Theory in Japanese Women's Writing.* Stanford: Stanford University Press, 1996.

Seidensticker, Edward G. *Kafū the Scribbler.* Stanford: Stanford University Press, 1965.

Shirane, Haruo, ed. *Early Modern Japanese Literature: An Anthology, 1600–1900.* New York: Columbia University Press, 2002.

Shirane, Haruo, and Tomi Suzuki, eds. *Inventing the Classics: Modernity, National Identity, and Japanese Literature.* Stanford: Stanford University Press, 2001.

Silver, Mark. *Purloined Letters: Cultural Borrowing and Japanese Crime Literature, 1868–1937.* Honolulu: University of Hawaii Press, 2008.

Snyder, Stephen. *Fictions of Desire: Narrative Form in the Novels of Nagai Kafū.* Honolulu: University of Hawaii Press, 2000.

Solt, John. *Shredding the Tapestry of Meaning: The Poetry and Poetics of Kitasono Katue (1902–1978).* Cambridge, Mass.: Harvard University Asia Center, 1999.

Starrs, Roy. *An Artless Art: The Zen Aesthetic of Shiga Naoya: A Critical Study with Selected Translations.* Surrey: Japan Library, 1999.

_____. *Soundings in Time: The Fictive Art of Kawabata Yasunari.* Richmond, Surrey: Japan Library, 1998.

Strecher, Matthew Carl. *Dances with Sheep: The Quest for Identity in the Fiction of Murakami Haruki.* Ann Arbor: Center for Japanese Studies, University of Michigan, 2002.

Suter, Rebecca. *The Japanization of Modernity: Murakami Haruki Between Japan and the United States.* Cambridge, Mass.: Harvard University Asia Center, 2008.

Tachibana, Reiko. *Narrative as Counter-Memory: A Half-Century of Postwar Writing in Germany and Japan.* Albany: State University of New York Press, 1998.

Tomasi, Massimiliano. *Rhetoric in Modern Japan: Western Influences on the Development of Narrative and Oratorical Style.* Honolulu: University of Hawaii Press, 2004.

Tyler, William J., ed. *Modanizumu: Modernist Fiction from Japan, 1913–1938.* Honolulu: University of Hawaii Press, 2008.

Ueda, Atsuko. *Concealment of Politics, Politics of Concealment: The Production of "Literature" in Meiji Japan*. Stanford: Stanford University Press, 2007.

Ueda, Makoto. *Modern Japanese Poets and the Nature of Literature*. Stanford: Stanford University Press, 1983.

————. *Modern Japanese Writers and the Nature of Literature*. Stanford: Stanford University Press, 1976.

Ueda, Makoto, ed. and trans. *Modern Japanese Tanka: An Anthology*. New York: Columbia University Press, 1996.

Washburn, Dennis. *The Dilemma of the Modern in Japanese Fiction*. New Haven: Yale University Press, 1995.

Washburn, Dennis, and Alan Tansman, eds. *Studies in Modern Japanese Literature: Essays and Translations in Honor of Edwin McClellan*. Ann Arbor: Center for Japanese Studies, University of Michigan, 1997.

Wilson, Michiko Niikuni. *Gender Is Fair Game: (Re)Thinking the (Fe)Male in the Works of Oba Minako*. New York: M. E. Sharpe, 1999.

Yiu, Angela. *Chaos and Order in the Works of Natsume Sōseki*. Honolulu: University of Hawaii Press, 1998.

Zebroski, Claire. *Japanese Women Writers in English Translation: An Annotated Bibliography*. New York: Garland, 1989.

Zwicker, Jonathan E. *Practices of the Sentimental Imagination: Melodrama, the Novel, and the Social Imaginary in Nineteenth-Century Japan*. Cambridge, Mass.: Harvard University Asia Center, 2006.

Theater Arts

Ando, Tsuruo. *Performing Arts of Japan: Bunraku, the Puppet Theatre*. New York: Walker/Weatherhill, 1970.

Asai, Susan M. *Nōmai Dance Drama: A Surviving Spirit of Medieval Japan*. Westport, Conn.: Greenwood Press, 1999.

Bowers, Faubion. *Japanese Theatre*. New York: Hill & Wang, 1959.

Brandon, James R. *Nō and Kyōgen in the Contemporary World*. Honolulu: University of Hawaii Press, 1997.

Brazell, Karen. *Traditional Japanese Theater: An Anthology of Plays*. New York: Columbia University Press, 1998.

Chikamatsu, Monzaemon. *The Major Plays of Chikamatsu*. Translated by Donald Keene. New York: Columbia University Press, 1961.

Coaldrake, A. Kimi. *Women's Gidayū and the Japanese Theatre Tradition*. New York: Routledge, 1997.

Ernst, Earle. *The Kabuki Theatre*. New York: Oxford University Press, 1956.

Keene, Donald, ed. *Twenty Plays of the Nō Theatre*. New York: Columbia University Press, 1970.

Kominz, Laurence R. *Avatars of Vengeance: Japanese Drama and the Soga Literary Tradition*. Ann Arbor: Center for Japanese Studies, University of Michigan, 1996.

————. *The Stars Who Created Kabuki: Their Lives, Loves, and Legacy*. London and New York: Kodansha International, 1997.

Kominz, Laurence R., ed. *Mishima on Stage: The Black Lizard and Other Plays*. Ann Arbor: Center for Japanese Studies, University of Michigan, 2007.

Kondo, Dorinne. *About Face: Performing Race in Fashion and Theater.* London and New York: Routledge, 1997.

Kyōka, Izumi, and M. Cody Poulton. *Spirits of Another Sort: The Plays of Izumi Kyōka.* Ann Arbor: Center for Japanese Studies, University of Michigan, 2000.

Law, Jane Marie. *Puppets of Nostalgia: The Life, Death, and Rebirth of the Japanese Awaji Ningyo Tradition.* Princeton: Princeton University Press, 1997.

Nakamura, Yasuo. *Noh, the Classical Theater.* Translated by Don Kenny. New York: Walker/Weatherhill, 1971.

Ortolani, Benito. *The Japanese Theater, from Shamanistic Ritual to Contemporary Pluralism.* Princeton: Princeton University Press, 1995.

Rath, Eric C. *Revealed Identity: The Noh Plays of Komparu Zenchiku.* Ann Arbor: Center for Japanese Studies, University of Michigan, 2006.

Scott-Stokes, Henry. *The Life and Death of Yukio Mishima.* New York: Ballantine, 1985.

Senda, Akihiko. *The Voyage of Contemporary Japanese Theatre.* Translated by J. Thomas Rimer. Honolulu: University of Hawaii Press, 1998.

Thornbury, Barbara E. *The Folk Performing Arts: Traditional Culture in Contemporary Japan.* Albany: State University of New York Press, 1997.

Waley, Arthur. *The Nō Plays of Japan.* London: Allen & Unwin, 1911.

Japanese Film

Anderson, Joseph L., and Donald Ritchie. *The Japanese Film: Art and Industry.* Princeton: Princeton University Press, 1982.

Baskett, Michael. *The Attractive Empire: Transnational Film Culture in Imperial Japan.* Honolulu: University of Hawaii Press, 2008.

Broderick, Mick, ed. *Hibakusha Cinema: Hiroshima, Nagasaki and the Nuclear Image in Japanese Film.* London and New York: Kegan Paul International, 1996.

Cazdyn, Eric. *The Flash of Capital: Film and Geopolitics in Japan.* Durham, N.C.: Duke University Press, 2002.

Desser, David, ed. *Ozu's Tokyo Story.* Cambridge: Cambridge University Press, 1997.

Field, Simon, and Tony Rayns, eds. *Branded to Thrill: The Delirious Cinema of Suzuki Seijun.* London: Institute of Contemporary Arts, 1994.

High, Peter B. *The Imperial Screen: Japanese Film Culture in the Fifteen Years' War, 1931–1945. Wisconsin Studies in Film.* Madison: University of Wisconsin Press, 2003.

Hutchinson, Rachael. *Shadows on the Screen: Tanizaki Jun'ichiro on Cinema and "Oriental" Aesthetics.* Ann Arbor: Center for Japanese Studies, University of Michigan, 2005.

Iles, Timothy. *Reading a Japanese Film: Cinema in Context.* Honolulu: University of Hawaii Press, 2006.

McDonald, Keiko I. *From Book to Screen: Modern Japanese Literature on Film.* New York: M. E. Sharpe, 2000.

———. *Japanese Classical Theater in Films.* New York: Associated University Presses, 1994.

Richie, Donald. *The Films of Akira Kurosawa.* Berkeley: University of California Press, 1996.

———. *Japanese Movies.* Tokyo: Japan Travel Bureau, 1961.

Richie, Donald, and Joseph I. Anderson. *The Japanese Film: Art and Industry.* Princeton: Princeton University Press, 1982.

Senda, Akihiko. *The Voyage of Contemporary Japanese Theatre.* Translated by J. Thomas Rimer. Honolulu: University of Hawaii Press, 1998.

Wada-Marciano, Mitsuyo. *Nippon Modern: Japanese Cinema of the 1920s and 1930s.* Honolulu: University of Hawaii Press, 2008.

Washburn, Dennis, and Carole Cavanaugh. *Word and Image in Japanese Cinema.* Cambridge: Cambridge University Press, 2001.

Yoshimoto, Mitsuhiro. *Kurosawa: Film Studies and Japanese Cinema.* Durham, N.C.: Duke University Press, 2000.

Modern Japanese Fiction Translated into English

Abe, Kōbō. *The Box Man.* Translated by E. Dale Saunders. New York: Putnam Perigee, 1981.

_____. *Friends.* Translated by Donald Keene. New York: Grove, 1969.

_____. *Secret Rendezvous.* Translated by Juliet W. Carpenter. New York: Knopf, 1979.

_____. *Women in the Dunes.* Translated by E. Dale Saunders. New York: Knopf, 1964.

Akutagawa, Ryunosuke. *Japanese Short Stories.* Translated by Takashi Kojima. New York: Liveright, 1961.

_____. *Rashōmon and Other Stories.* Translated by Takashi Kojima. New York: Liveright, 1952.

Arishima, Takeo. *A Certain Woman.* Translated by Kenneth Strong. Tokyo: Tokyo University Press, 1978.

Ariyoshi, Sawako. *The Doctor's Wife.* Translated by Wakako Hironaka and Ann Siller Kostant. Tokyo: Kodansha, 1978.

_____. *The River Ki.* Translated by Mildred Tahara. Tokyo: Kodansha, 1982.

_____. *The Twilight Years.* Translated by Mildred Tahara. Tokyo: Kodansha, 1984.

Biernbaum, Phyllis, trans. *Rabbits, Crabs, Etc.: Stories by Japanese Women Writers.* Honolulu: University Press of Hawaii, 1989.

Dazai, Osamu. *No Longer Human.* Translated by Donald Keene. New York: New Directions, 1958.

_____. *The Setting Sun.* Translated by Donald Keene. New York: New Directions, 1956.

Enchi, Fumiko. *Mask.* Translated by Juliet Winters Carpenter. New York: Random House, 1983.

_____. *The Waiting Years.* Translated by John Bester. Tokyo: Kodansha, 1981.

Endō, Shūsaku. *The Samurai.* Translated by Van C. Gessel. New York: Harper & Row, 1980.

_____. *Silence.* Translated by William Johnston. New York: Taplinger, 1980.

_____. *Stained Glass Elegies.* Translated by Van C. Gessel. New York: Dodd, Mead, & Co, 1984.

_____. *Wonderful Fool.* Translated by Francis Mathy. New York: Harper & Row, 1974.

Furui, Yoshikichi. *Child of Darkness: Yōko and Other Stories.* Translation and commentary by Donna George Storey. Ann Arbor: Center for Japanese Studies, University of Michigan, 1997.

Hayashi, Fumiko. *I Saw a Pale Horse and Selected Poems from Diary of a Vagabond.* Translated by Janice Brown. Ithaca, N.Y.: Cornell University Press, 1997.

Honda, Katsuichi. *Harukor: an Ainu Woman's Tale.* Translated by Kyoko Selden. Berkeley: University of California Press, 2000.

Ibuse, Masuji. *Black Rain.* Translated by John Bester. New York: Bantam Books, 1985.

Katō, Shūichi. *A Sheep's Song: a Writer's Reminiscences of Japan and the World.* Translated and annotations by Chia-Ning Chang. Berkeley: University of California Press, 1999.

Kawabata, Yasunari. *The Dancing Girl of Izu and Other Stories.* Translated by Martin Holman. Boulder, Colo.: Westview Press, 1998.

_____. *The Old Capital.* Translated by J. Martin Hofman. Berkeley, Calif.: North Point Press, 1987.

_____. *Snow Country.* Translated by Edward G. Seidensticker. New York: Knopf, 1956.

_____. *The Sound of the Mountain.* Translated by Edward G. Seidensticker. New York: Berkeley Publishing, 1970.

_____. *Thousand Cranes.* Translated by Edward G. Seidensticker. New York: Knopf, 1958.

Keene, Donald, ed. and trans. *Modern Japanese Literature from 1868 to the Present Day.* New York: Grove, 1956.

_____. *The Old Woman, the Wife, and the Archer: Three Modern Japanese Short Novels.* New York: Viking, 1961.

Lippit, Noriko M., and Kyoko Seldon, ed. and trans. *Japanese Women Writers: Twentieth Century Short Stories.* Armonk, N.Y.: M. E. Sharpe, 1991.

_____ *Stories by Contemporary Japanese Women Writers.* Armonk, N.Y.: M. E. Sharpe, 1982.

Mishima, Yukio. *After the Banquet.* Translated by Donald Keene. New York: Knopf, 1963.

_____. *Confessions of a Mask.* Translated by Meredith Weatherby. New York: New Directions, 1958.

_____. *Five Modern Nō Plays.* Translated by Donald Keene. New York: Knopf, 1957.

_____. *The Sound of Waves.* Translated by Meredith Weatherby. New York: Knopf, 1956.

_____. *Sun and Steel.* Translated by John Bester. Tokyo: Kodansha, 1970.

_____. *The Temple of the Golden Pavilion.* Translated by Ivan Morris. New York: Knopf, 1959.

Mori, Ōgai. *The Wild Geese.* Translated by Kingo Ochiai and Sanford Goldstein. Rutland, Vt.: Tuttle, 1959.

Morris, Ivan, ed. *Modern Japanese Stories: An Anthology.* Rutland, Vt.: Tuttle, 1962.

Murakami, Haruki. *Dance, Dance, Dance.* Translated by Alfred Birnbaum. Tokyo: Kodansha, 1994.

_____. *The Elephant Vanishes.* Translated by Alfred Birnbaum. New York: Knopf, 1993.

_____. *The Hard-Boiled Wonderland and the End of the World.* Translated by Alfred Birnbaum. Tokyo: Kodansha, 1991.

_____. *A Wild Sheep.* Translated by Alfred Birnbaum. Tokyo: Kodansha, 1989.

_____. *The Wind-Up Bird Chronicle.* Translated by Jay Rubin. New York: Knopf, 1997.

Nakano, Makiko. Translated and Edited by Kazuko Smith. *Makiko's Diary: A Merchant Wife in 1910 Kyoto.* Stanford: Stanford University Press, 1995.

Natsume, Sōseki. *Grass on the Wayside.* Translated by Edwin McClellan. Chicago: University of Chicago Press, 1969.

_____. *Kokoro.* Translated by Edwin McClellan. Chicago: Regnery, 1967.

_____. *Light and Darkness.* Translated by V. H. Viglielmo. Honolulu: University of Hawaii Press, 1970.

_____. *Wayfarer.* Translated by Beong-cheon Yu. Detroit: Wayne State University Press, 1967.

Noma, Hiroshi. *Zone of Emptiness.* Translated by Bernard Frechtman. Cleveland, Ohio: World, 1956.

Ōe, Kenzaburo. *A Personal Matter.* Translated by John Nathan. New York: Grove, 1968.

_____. *The Pinch Runner Memorandum.* Translated by Michiko N. Wilson and Michael K. Wilson. Armonk, N.Y.: M. E. Sharpe, 1994.

_____. *The Silent Cry.* Translated by John Bester. Tokyo: Kodansha, 1981.

_____. *Teach Us to Outgrow Our Madness.* Translated by John Nathan. New York: Grove, 1977.

Ooka, Shohei. *Fires on the Plain*. Translated by Ivan Morris. New York: Knopf, 1957.

Osaragi, Jiro. *Homecoming*. Translated by Brewster Horowitz. New York: Knopf, 1955.

Shimazaki, Tōson. *Broken Commandment*. Translated by Kenneth Strong. Tokyo: University of Tokyo Press, 1974.

Tanaka, Yukiko, and Elizabeth Hanson, eds and trans. *This Kind of Woman: Ten Stories by Japanese Women Writers, 1960–1976*. Stanford: Stanford University Press, 1982.

Tanizaki, Junichiro. *The Key*. Translated by Howard Hibbett. New York: Knopf, 1971.

_____. *The Makioka Sisters*. Translated by Edward G. Seidensticker. New York: Knopf, 1957.

_____. *Seven Japanese Tales*. Translated by Howard Hibbett. New York: Knopf, 1963.

_____. *Some Prefer Nettles*. Translated by Edward G. Seidensticker. New York: Knopf, 1955.

Tsushima, Yuko. *Child of Fortune*. Translated by Geraldine Harcourt. Tokyo: Kodansha, 1983.

_____. *The Shooting Gallery*. Translated by Geraldine Harcourt. New York: Pantheon, 1988.

Ueda, Makoto, ed. *The Mother of Dreams and Other Short Stories: Portrayals of Women in Modern Japanese Fiction*. Tokyo: Kodansha, 1986.

Yamasaki, Toyoko. *Bonchi*. Translated by Harue Summersgill and Travis Summersgill. Honolulu: University Press of Hawaii, 1982.

Yoshimoto, Banana. *Amrita*. Translated by Ann Sherif. New York: Grove, 1988.

_____. *Kitchen*. Translated by Megan Backus. New York: Washington Square Press, 1993.

_____. *Lizard*. Translated by Ann Sherif. New York: Grove, 1994.

_____. *N.P.* Translated by Ann Sherif. New York: Grove, 1993.

Fine Arts

Akiyama, Terukazu. *Treasures of Asia: Japanese Painting*. Cleveland, Ohio: World, 1961.

Binyon, Lawrence. *Painting in the Far East*. New York: Dover, 1959.

Boger, H. Batterson. *The Traditional Arts of Japan*. Garden City, N.Y.: Doubleday, 1964.

Brandt, Kim. *Kingdom of Beauty: Mingei and the Politics of Folk Art in Imperial Japan*. Durham, N.C.: Duke University Press, 2007.

Brown, Kendall H. *The Politics of Reclusion: Painting and Power in Momoyama Japan*. Honolulu: University of Hawaii Press, 1997.

Conant, Ellen P., ed. *Challenging Past and Present: The Metamorphosis of Nineteenth-Century Japanese Art*. Honolulu: University of Hawaii Press, 2006.

Conant, Ellen P., et al. *Nihonga, Transcending the Past: Japanese-Style Painting 1868–1968*. New York: Weatherhill, 1995.

Cox, Rupert A. *The Zen Arts: An Anthropological Study of the Culture of Aesthetic Form in Japan*. London: Routledge, 2003.

Davis, Julie Nelson. *Utamaro and the Spectacle of Beauty*. Honolulu: University of Hawaii Press, 2008.

Fowler, Sherry D. *Murōji: Rearranging Art and History at a Japanese Buddhist Temple*. Honolulu: University of Hawaii Press, 2005.

Graham, Patricia J. *Faith and Power in Japanese Buddhist Art, 1600–2005*. Honolulu: University of Hawaii Press, 2008.

_____. *Tea of the Sages: The Art of Sencha*. Honolulu: University of Hawaii Press, 1998.

Hillier, J. *Masters of the Colour Print*. London: Phaidon, 1954.

Hisamatsu, Shinichi. *Zen and the Fine Arts*. Tokyo: Kodansha, 1971.

Hockley, Allen. *The Prints of Isoda Koryūsai: Floating World Culture and Its Consumers in Eighteenth-Century Japan.* Seattle: University of Washington Press, 2003.

Kirby, John B. *From Castle to Teahouse: Japanese Architecture in the Momoyama Period:* Rutland, Vt.: Tuttle, 1962.

Kuitert, Wybe. *Themes in the History of Japanese Garden Art.* Honolulu: University of Hawaii Press, 2002.

Lee, Sherman E. *A History of Far Eastern Art.* Englewood Cliffs, N.J.: Prentice-Hall, 1964.

Lloyd, Fran, ed. *Consuming Bodies: Sex and Contemporary Japanese Art.* London: Reaktion Books, 2003.

Meech, Julia. *Frank Lloyd Wright and the Art of Japan: The Architect's Other Passion.* New York: Harry Abrams, 2001.

Michener, James. *The Floating World: The Story of Japanese Prints.* New York: Random House, 1954.

Munsterberg, Hugo. *The Arts of Japan: An Illustrated History.* Rutland, Vt.: Tuttle, 1957.

_____. *The Folk Arts of Japan.* Rutland, Vt.: Tuttle, 1958.

_____. *Zen and Oriental Art.* Rutland, Vt.: Tuttle, 1965.

Ohnuki-Tierney, Emiko. *Kamikaze, Cherry Blossoms, and Nationalisms: The Militarization of Aesthetics in Japanese History.* Chicago: University of Chicago Press, 2002.

Paine, Robert T., and Alexander C. Soper. *The Art and Architecture of Japan.* Baltimore, Md.: Penguin, 1955.

Parker, Joseph. *Zen Buddhist Landscape Arts of Early Muromachi Japan (1336–1573).* Albany: State University of New York Press, 1999.

Put, Max. *Plunder and Pleasure: Japanese Art in the West, 1860–1930.* Leiden: Hotei Press, 2000.

Stevens, Carolyn. *Japanese Popular Music: Culture, Authenticity and Power.* New York: Routledge, 2007.

Swann, Peter C. *The Art of Japan, from the Jōmon to the Tokugawa Period.* New York: Grove, 1966.

Takeuchi, Melinda, ed. *The Artist As Professional in Japan.* Stanford: Stanford University Press, 2004.

Tokyo National Museum. *Pageant of Japanese Art.* 6 vols. Tokyo: Toto Bunka, 1952–1954.

Warner, Langdon. *The Enduring Art of Japan.* New York: Grove, 1952.

Watsky, Andrew M. *Chikubushima: Deploying the Sacred Arts in Momoyama Japan.* Seattle: University of Washington Press, 2004.

Weisenfeld, Gennifer. *Mavo: Japanese Artists and the Avant-Garde, 1905–1931.* Berkeley: University of California Press, 2002.

Weston, Victoria. *Japanese Painting and National Identity: Okakura Tensbin and His Circle.* Ann Arbor: Center for Japanese Studies, University of Michigan, 2004.

Yashiro, Yukio. *Art Treasures of Japan.* 2 vols. Tokyo: Kokusai Bunka Shinkokai, 1960.

Yiengpruksawan, Mimi Hall. *Hiraizumi: Buddhist Art and Regional Politics in Twelfth-Century Japan.* Cambridge, Mass.: Harvard University Asia Center, 1998.

Religion

Abe, Ryūichi. *The Weaving of Mantra: Kūkai and the Construction of Esoteric Buddhist Discourse.* New York: Columbia University Press, 1999.

Abe, Ryūichi, and Peter Haskel. *Great Fool: Zen Master Ryōkan—Poems, Letters, and Other Writings.* Honolulu: University of Hawaii Press, 1996.

Addiss, Stephen, et al. *Old Taoist: The Life, Art, and Poetry of Kodōjin.* New York: Columbia University Press, 2000.

Aizan, Yamaji. *Essays on the Modern Japanese Church: Christianity in Meiji Japan.* Translated by Graham Squires. Ann Arbor: Center for Japanese Studies, University of Michigan, 1999.

Amstutz, Galen. *Interpreting Amida: History and Orientalism in the Study of Pure Land Buddhism.* Albany: State University of New York Press, 1997.

Anesaki, Masaharu. *History of Japanese Religion.* Rutland, Vt.: Tuttle, 1963.

_____. *Religious Life of the Japanese People.* Tokyo: Kokusai Bunka Shinkokai, 1961.

Baroni, Helen J. *Obaku Zen: the Emergence of the Third Sect of Zen in Tokugawa Japan.* Honolulu: University of Hawaii Press, 2002.

Barrett, William, ed. *Zen Buddhism: Selected Writings of D. T. Suzuki.* Garden City, N.Y.: Doubleday, 1956.

Bellah, Robert N. *Tokugawa Religion: The Values of Pre-Industrial Japan.* Glencoe, Ill.: Free Press, 1957.

Blacker, Carmen. *The Catalpa Bow: A Study of Shamanistic Practices in Japan.* London: Allen & Unwin, 1975.

Bunce, William K. *Religions in Japan: Buddhism, Shinto, Christianity.* Rutland, Vt.: Tuttle, 1955.

Carter, Steven D. *Unforgotten Dreams: Poems by the Zen Monk Shōtetsu.* New York: Columbia University Press, 1997.

Collcut, Martin. *Five Mountains: The Rinzai Monastic Institution in Medieval Japan.* Cambridge, Mass.: Harvard University Press, 1981.

Covell. Stephen G. *Japanese Temple Buddhism: Worldliness in a Religion of Renunciation.* Honolulu: University of Hawaii Press, 2005.

Davidson, Keir. *A Zen Life in Nature: Muso Soseki in His Gardens.* Ann Arbor: Center for Japanese Studies, University of Michigan, 2007.

Dobbins, James. *Letters of the Nun Eshinni: Images of Pure Land Buddhism in Medieval Japan.* Honolulu: University of Hawaii Press, 2004.

Dumoulin, Heinrich. *History of Zen Buddhism.* New York: Random House, 1963.

Earhart, H. Bryan. *Japanese Religion: Unity and Diversity.* Rutherford, N.J.: Fairleigh Dickinson University Press, 1974.

_____. *Religion in the Japanese Experience.* Rutherford, N.J.: Fairleigh Dickinson University Press, 1974.

Faure, Bernard. *Visions of Power: Imagining Medieval Japanese Buddhism.* Translated by Phyllis Brooks. Princeton: Princeton University Press, 1996.

Graham, Patricia J. *Faith and Power in Japanese Buddhist Art, 1600–2005.* Honolulu: University of Hawaii Press, 2008.

Hardacre, Helen. *Religion and Society in Nineteenth-Century Japan: A Study of the Southern Kanto Region, Using Late Edo and Early Meiji Gazetteers.* Ann Arbor: Center for Japanese Studies, University of Michigan, 2002.

_____. *Shinto and the State, 1869–1988.* Princeton: Princeton University Press, 1989.

Herrigal, Eugene. *Zen.* New York: McGraw-Hill, 1964.

Holtom, Daniel C. *The National Faith of Japan: A Study in Modern Shinto.* New York: Dutton, 1938.

Hur, Nam-lin. *Death and Social Order in Tokugawa Japan: Buddhism, Anti-Christianity, and the Danka System.* Cambridge, Mass.: Harvard University Asia Center, 2007.

Jaffe, Richard M. *Neither Monk Nor Layman: Clerical Marriage in Modern Japanese Buddhism.* Princeton: Princeton University Press, 2001.

Kaminishi, Ikumi. *Explaining Pictures: Buddhist Propaganda and Etoki Storytelling in Japan.* Honolulu: University of Hawaii Press, 2006.

Kapleau, Philip. *The Three Pillars of Zen.* New York: Harper & Row, 1966.

Kasulis, Thomas P. *Shinto: The Way Home.* Honolulu: University of Hawaii Press, 2004.

Kisala, Robert J., and Mark R. Mullins. *Religion and Social Crisis in Japan: Understanding Japanese Society Through the Aum Affair.* New York: Palgrave Macmillan, 2001.

Kitagawa, Joseph M. *Religion in Japanese History.* New York: Columbia University Press, 1966.

Miyake, Hitoshi, and H. Byron Earhart. *Shugendō: Essays on the Structure of Japanese Folk Religion.* Ann Arbor: Center for Japanese Studies, University of Michigan, 2001.

Mullins, Mark R. *Christianity Made in Japan: A Study of Indigenous Movements.* Honolulu: University of Hawaii Press, 1998.

Nelson, John K. *Enduring Identities: The Guise of Shinto in Contemporary Japan.* Honolulu: University of Hawaii Press, 2000.

Pandey, Rajyashree. *Writing and Renunciation in Medieval Japan: The Works of the Poet-Priest Kamo No Chōmei.* Ann Arbor: Center for Japanese Studies, University of Michigan, 1998.

Pereira, Ronan Alves, and Matsuoka Hideaki, eds. *Japanese Religions in and Beyond the Japanese Diaspora.* Berkeley and Los Angeles: University of California Press, 2007.

Pickens, Stuart. *Shinto: Japan's Spiritual Roots.* Tokyo: Kodansha, 1980.

Ramirez-Christensen, Esperanza. *Emptiness and Temporality: Buddhism and Medieval Japanese Poetics.* Stanford: Stanford University Press, 2008.

_____. *Murmured Conversations: A Treatise on Poetry and Buddhism by the Poet-Monk Shinkei.* Stanford: Stanford University Press, 2008.

Reader, Ian. *Making Pilgrimages: Meaning and Practice in Shikoku.* Honolulu: University of Hawaii Press, 2005.

_____. *A Poisonous Cocktail? Aum Shinrikyō's Path to Violence.* Copenhagen: Nias Books, 1996.

Reader, Ian, and George J. Tanabe Jr. *Practically Religious: Worldly Benefits and the Common Religion of Japan.* Honolulu: University of Hawaii Press, 1998.

Ruch, Barbara, ed. *Engendering Faith: Women and Buddhism in Premodern Japan.* Ann Arbor: Center for Japanese Studies, University of Michigan, 2002.

Ruppert, Brian D. *The Jewel in the Ashes: Buddha Relics and Power in Early Medieval Japan.* Cambridge, Mass.: Harvard University Asia Center, 2000.

Saunders, Ernest Dale. *Buddhism in Japan: With an Outline of Its Origins in India.* Philadelphia: University of Pennsylvania Press, 1964.

Sawada, Janine. *Practical Pursuits: Religion, Politics, and Personal Cultivation in Nineteenth-Century Japan.* Honolulu: University of Hawaii Press, 2004.

Sawada, Mitziko. *Tokyo Life, New York Dreams: Urban Japanese Visions of America 1890–1924.* Berkeley: University of California Press, 1996.

Schattschneider, Ellen. *Immortal Wishes: Labor and Transcendence on a Japanese Sacred Mountain.* Durham, N.C.: Duke University Press, 2003.

Shinran. *The Collected Works of Shinran.* Translated and edited by Dennis Hirota et al. Kyoto: Jodo Shinshu Hongwanji-Ha, 1997.

Smith, Richard J. *Ancestor Worship in Contemporary Japan.* Stanford: Stanford University Press, 1974.

Smyers, Karen A. *The Fox and the Jewel: Shared and Private Meanings in Contemporary Japanese Inari Worship.* Honolulu: University of Hawaii Press, 1999.

Stalker, Nancy K. *Prophet Motive: Deguchi Onisaburo, Oomoto, and the Rise of New Religion.* Honolulu: University of Hawaii Press, 2007.

Statler, Oliver. *Japanese Pilgrimage.* New York: Morrow, 1983.

Susumu Shimazono. *From Salvation to Spirituality: Popular Religious Movements in Modern Japan.* Melbourne: Trans Pacific Press, 2004.

Suzuki, Daisetsu T. *Essays in Zen Buddhism.* New York: Harper & Row, 1949.

_____. *An Introduction to Zen Buddhism.* New York: Grove, 1964.

_____. *Zen and Japanese Culture.* New York: Pantheon, 1959.

Tamaru, Noriyoshi, and David Reid, eds. *Religion in Japanese Culture: Where Living Traditions Meet a Changing World.* London: Kodansha International, 1996.

Ten Grotenhuis, Elizabeth. *Japanese Mandalas: Representations of Sacred Geography.* Honolulu: University of Hawaii Press, 1999.

Terasaki, Etsuko. *Figures of Desire: Wordplay, Spirit Possession, Fantasy, Madness, and Mourning in Japanese Noh Plays.* Ann Arbor: Center for Japanese Studies, University of Michigan, 2002.

Tsang, Carol. *War and Faith: Ikko Ikki in Late Muromachi Japan.* Cambridge, Mass.: Harvard University Asia Center, 2007.

Watanabe, Shoko. *Japanese Buddhism: A Critical Appraisal.* Tokyo: Kokusai Bunka Shinkokai, 1968.

Wheeler, Post, ed. and trans. *The Sacred Scriptures of the Japanese.* New York: Abelard-Schuman, 1952.

White, James W. *The Sokagakkai and Mass Society.* Stanford: Stanford University Press, 1970.

Index